An Inexplicable Deformity Volume I

By

Anant Kumar Tripati LLM, Merit

An Inexplicable Deformity Volume 1
Cruel and Unusual Punishment

Published by:
SureShot Books Publishing LLC
P.O. Box 924
Nyack, New York 10960
www.sureshotbooks.com

Libarary of Congress Cataloging-in-Publication Data

An Inexplicable Deformity.

This book has been published and made available as an e-book.

FOREWARD

This book has been painstakingly researched and written in hopes of enabling the basic humane treatment for all those incarcerated in the United States today and in the future.

THE AUTHOR

ANANT KUMAR TRIPATI LLM, Merit (2014)
UNIVERSITY OF LONDON
UNIVERSITY COLLEGE LONDON
QUEEN MARY UNIVERSITY OF LONDON

Mr. Tripati has specializations in Public International Law (2014), Public Law (2014), and European Law (2013).

TABLE OF CONTENTS

CITES AND AUTHORITIES

CITES AND AUTHORITIES

INTRODUCTION

In 1776 Thomas Jefferson in the Declaration of Independence proposed a philosophy of human rights "all men are created equal, that they are endowed by their Creator with certain inalienable Rights that among them are Life, Liberty and the pursuit of Happiness" which is "the most quoted statement of human rights in recorded history." Joseph J. Ellis, (198) (1996) American Sphinx: The Character Of Thomas Jefferson "The American Declaration Of Independence was the first civic document that set a modern definition of human rights, Carol Devine, Carol Hansen, Ralph Wilde, Hilary Poole (1999) Human Rights: The Essential Reference, pp 26-29.

Though the United States benefits from globalization it refuses to as a matter of practice follow human rights treaties it ratifies. "Among mainstream politicians and commentators of Western Europe, it is a truism that the criminal justice system of the United States is an inexplicable deformity" Cruel And Unusual Punishment, U.S. Sentencing Practices In A Global Context, Center For Law And Global Justice. University Of San Francisco School Of Law, Page 17 (May 2012). In theory the United States guarantees human rights it in practice violates rights with impunity Michael Ignatieff, American Exceptionalism and Human Rights (2005).

By declaring that the International Covenant On Civil And Political Rights (ICCPR) is not self-executing the United States has failed to provide a remedy for its violations within its jurisdiction Sosa v Alvarez-Machin, 542 U.S. 692, 735 (2004) When ratifying ICCPR Congress stated " the United States understands that this Covenant shall be implemented by the federal government to the extent it exercises legislative and judicial jurisdiction over the matters contained therein and otherwise by state and local governments." 138 Cong. Rec. S4781 (daily edition April 2, 1992) No state or local government has provided for a remedy for ICCPR violations and the federal judicial branch has declined to provide for a remedy stating that ICCPR is not self executing.

According to constitutional scholars as human rights treaties create a duty to refrain from acting in a particular manner or confer specific rights; they are automatically self executing and require no implementing legislation. They state it is a violation of separation of powers to declare them not self executing. F. Martin, International Human Rights and Humanitarian Law, Cambridge University Press, 200, p 221 and following. The five declarations and understandings used by the United States in ratifying ICCPR is incompatible with the Supremacy Clause Louis Henkin, U.S. Ratification Of Human Rights Treaties: The Ghost Of Senator Bricker, 89 Am J. Int'l. Law. 341 (1995) As the reservations are incompatible with the object and purpose of ICCPR they as a matter of international law are void Vienna Convention On The Law Of Treaties Article 19 115 U.N.T.S. 331.

The terms of a treaty are given their ordinary meaning in the context of the treaty and interpreted in a way so as to best fulfill the purposes of the treaty United States v Stuart, 489 U.S. 353, 365-66 (1989) Kolovrat v Oregon, 366 U.S. 187, 193-94 (1962) "The ultimate question remains what was intended when the language actually employed...was chosen, imperfect as that language may be Great West Life Ass. V U.S., 678 F.2d. 180, 188 (Ct. Cl. 1982). The United States has refused to interpret ICCPR as to fulfill its purposes. In Belilos v Switzerland, A 1328 (1988); 1 EHRR 466 Para 55 the Court stated a reservation is invalid if it is "coached in terms that are too vague or broad for it to be possible to determine their exact meaning and scope." The reservations by the United States are invalid as they are vague and broad at the same time. Courts in the United States refuse to implement ICCR as provided by the terms of the treaty.

As is shown in this these human rights violations by States are not "isolated incidents" but reflect a "history of widespread abuse" Brown v Crawford, 906 F.2d 667, 671 (11th Cir. 1990) for which state authorities have given "tacit authorization" Fruit v Norris, 905 F.2d 1147, 1151 (8th Cir. 1990). These violations are the result of "custom or usage" which is "so permanent and well settled" as to have "the force of law" Monnell v New York City Dept. Of Social Services. 436 U.S. 658, 690-91 (1978)

They are deeply embedded in the state system. Knight v Carlson, 478 F.Sup. 53, 59 (E.D.Ca. 1979) Though "It is a well established principle that courts will not permit themselves to become agents for the commission of recognized wrongs. If a (litigant) may use the judicial process to delay, diminish, or even defeat a valid claim, then the court has in effect become a partner in the abuse. The essential policy question is whether there is any adversarial conduct which will not be tolerated by the courts. The court should not, by default, acquiesce in conduct which is designed to perpetrate…injustice. If such conduct goes unchecked, public confidence in the law and the legal profession will be undermined." Van Patten & Willard, The Limits Of Advocacy: A Proposal For The Tort Of Malicious Defense In Civil Litigation 35 Hastings L.J. 891, 927 (1984)(emphasis added footnote deleted) courts and legislators refuse to take corrective action.

The Prison Litigation Reform Act (PLRA) and its counterpart the Antiterrorism And Effective Death Penalty Act Of 1996 (AEDPA) violate Art 2.3(a) ICCPR for they require exhaustion of ineffective administrative and judicial remedies Eugene Novikov, Comment Stacking The Deck: Futility And The Exhaustion Provision Of the Prison Litigation Reform Act, 156 U. Pa .L .Rev. 817 (2008) Mark Tushnet & Larry Yackle, Symbolic Statutes And Real Laws: The Pathologies Of The Substances Of The Antiterrorism And Effective Death Penalty Act and the PLRA, 47 Duke L.L. 1 (1997). In Ross v Blake, (2016) No. 15-379 Justice Kagan stated "as Booth made clear an administrative procedure is unavailable when (despite what regulation or guidance materials may promise) it operates as a simple dead end…with officers unable or consistently unwilling to provide any relief to aggrieved inmates …The procedure is not then "capable of use for the pertinent purpose…In Booth's words "some redress for a wrong is presupposed by the statute's requirement of an "available remedy…if administrative officials have apparent authority, but decline to exercise it." In the United States as discussed infra, administrative remedies are unavailable and not withstanding this unavailability, courts require their exhaustion, in violation of Art. 2.3(a) ICCPR.

It is the norm for state prisons to violate Art. 10.1 ICCPR "all persons deprived of their liberty shall be treated with humanity and with respect for the inherent dignity of the human person" and neither the courts nor the legislative or executive branches do anything to correct this as shown infra. Addo & Grief, 20 E.L.R. 178 (1995)

In short PLRA renders all remedies for prisoners ineffective within the meaning of Art. 2.3(a) ICCPR. Because of Congressional restrictions prisoners, notwithstanding the fact that they are being subjected to human rights abuses in state prisons, do not have the same access to the courts as non-prisoners, and the limited access they have are futile, under a heightened standard. During litigation prison authorities are allowed to conceal evidence of misconduct and do not have to provide the same disclosure that non prisoners are given Rule 26(a)(1)(B)(iv) Federal Rules of Civil Procedure. As such prisoners' accesses to courts violate Art. 14.1 ICCPR. Frowein and Perkert, Europaische Menschenrechts Konvention: EMRK-Kommentar; (2nd ed. 1996)

Because of PLRA prisoners are increasingly tortured, subjected to cruel, inhumane, degrading treatment and punishment in violation of Art. 7 ICCPR; Green, The European Court Of Human Rights, (2006) prisoners are not treated with humanity as required by Art. 10.1 ICCPR; their rights to freedom of thought, conscience, religion as required by Art. 18.1 and 27 ICCPR is violated; retaliation for petitioning the courts and government is the norm in violation of Art. 25.a ICCPR. In short PLRA encourages ICCPR and human rights violations Malcolm M. Feley & Van Swearingen, The Prison Conditions Cases and The Bureaucratization Of American Corrections: Influences, Impacts and Implications; 24 Pace L. Rev. 433 (2004) describes the increase in prison litigation due to prison authorities that violation human rights How Prisoners' Rights Lawyers Are Preserving the Role Of the Courts, 69 U. Miami L. Rev.

Professor Tim Farer in the Rise Of The Inter-American Human Rights Regime : No Longer A Unicorn Not Yet An Ox, Human Rights Quarterly 19 (1997) 510-546 states "the stolid, efficient application of energy and the consequently consistent production of effective decisions, all within the context of an orderly, stable, and prosperous community, "at 510 resulted in "Western Europe's human rights institutions, the European Commission on Human Rights and the European Court of Human Rights, also charged governments with violations of human rights. But the violations almost invariably involved actions undertaken openly along the thinly marked border between the legitimate exercise of public authority on behalf of the community and the irreconcilable claims of individual liberty. The various European governments employing challenged acts no doubt regarded them as useful, but hardly as essential, means to the preservation of order or the execution of any other public function." At 510 the states in the United States are doing exactly what Farer discusses but the courts due to PLRA are unable to afford relief.

Art. 9.4 ICCPR is similar to Art. 5(4) ECHR which provides "Anyone who is deprived of his liberty by arrest or detention shall be entitled to take proceedings before a court, in order that that court may decide without delay on the lawfulness of the detention and order him released if the detention is not lawful." This provision applies even if the detention is by order of a court De Wilde, Odoms and Versyp v Belgium A 12 (1971); 1 EHRR 373 Para 76 PC. The review must be adversarial with "equality of arms Nikolva v Bulgaria 199-II; 31 EHRR 64 Para 58 GC. However in these states as is shown overzealous prosecutors use the grand jury process to detain persons and courts hence lack the authority to review the evidence that form the charges. After trial review of the basis of the charges is denied.

Art. 14.3 ICCPR provides "in determination of any criminal charge against him, everyone shall be entitled to the following minimum guarantees, in full equality; (e) To examine, or have examined, the witnesses against him and to obtain the attendance and examination of witnesses on his behalf under the same conditions as witnesses against him;" Art. 14.1 ICCPR reads "All persons shall be equal before the courts and tribunals." Art. 14.2 ICCPR "Everyone charged with a criminal offence shall have the right to be presumed innocent until proven guilty according to law." Art. 14.5 ICCPR "Everyone convicted of a crime shall have the right to his conviction and sentence being reviewed by a higher tribunal according to law." Art. 15.1 ICCPR reads "If, subsequent to the commission of the offense, provision is made by law for the imposition of the lighter penalty, the offender shall benefit thereby." While in theory the United States affords these protections, in practice, as discussed, these protections are not afforded.

Outrageously harsh sentences is the norm with ameliorative laws not being retroactive In With The New, Out with The Old: Expanding The Scope Of Retroactive Amelioration, 37 Am. J.Cr.Law 1, 5 (2009) Consecutive sentences that exceed the penalty for the charged crimes is routine Carl-Friedrich Struckenberg "A Cure For Concursus Delictorium In International Criminal Law" 16 Cr. Law Forum 36 (2005)

Penalties disproportionate with the seriousness of the crime are normal due to mandatory minimums Michael Tonry, The Mostly Intended Effects of Mandatory Penalties: Two Centuries of Consistent Findings, 35 Cr. Law Just. 65 (2009) this is so though in Thompson v Oklahoma, 487 U.S. 815, 830 (1988) the court stated "we have previously recognized the relevance of the views of the international community."

When penalties are reduced they are not applied retroactively because courts presume the legislative process that reduced the penalties was "motivated by a desire of vengeance, a conclusion not permitted in view of modern theories of penology" In Re Estrada, 65 Cal. 2d 740. 745 (1965) Though when ratifying ICCPR the United States was aware Article 10.3 ICCPR "the penitentiary system shall comprise treatment of prisoners, the essential aim of which shall be their reformation and social rehabilitation" it does not comply with this because compliance burdens corporate profits. The Institute on Money in State Politics, Policy-Lockdown: Prison Interests Court Political Players (2006)As a matter of routine practice to increase corporate profits prison systems provide inmates with food that causes diseases such as diabetes, sell tobacco products because of tax revenue etc. They delay and deny medical care to increase corporate profits. They fail to take into consideration the fact that when released these prisoners will burden the public for their medical care. They promulgate policies and regulations that only take into account the prison budget not the effect on the state, which is bad public policy. Martha Elena Mendenez, Human Rights Advocate Prison Privatization and Prison Labor: The Human Rights Implications 6 (2012)

Because of lack of Congressional action private corporations and prison officials are not held accountable. Brian Gran & William Henry, Holding Private Prisons Accountable: A Socio-Legal Analysis Of "Contracting Out" Prisons, 34 Social Justice 73 (2007-08). This is what has allowed entities such as Corizon and Wexford to delay/deny healthcare for profit Alexander Volokh, Privatization and the Law and Economics of Political Advocacy, 66 Stan. L. Rev. 1197 (2008).

In his paper "How Legislative Bans on Foreign and International Law Obstruct the Practice and Regulation of American" David L. Nersessian, J.D., Ph.D. Arizona State Law Journal *44 Ariz. St. L.J. 1647 states in pertinent part: "* The world is globalizing. As long-standing economic, social, cultural, geographic, financial, and communication barriers fall, these various dimensions of modern life become increasingly connected in even more complex, and often unpredictable, ways. Lawyers play a key role in both facilitating and regulating transnational dealings, even as the underlying legal structures themselves experience significant change.

Since 2010 alone, thirty-three states have introduced "blocking" initiatives that prohibit state court judges from referencing international, foreign, and/or religious law. At least ninety-three distinct measures have been introduced, with multiple types filed in some jurisdictions. Blocking measures even have become law in five states.

The specific texts vary considerably, but many include departures from ordinary usages of legal terminology. Legislative prohibitions on "foreign law" typically encompass both public and private international law as well as domestic law from foreign nations. Arizona's initiative, for example, provides that "unless the context otherwise requires, "foreign law' means any law, rule or legal code or system other than the constitution, laws and ratified treaties of the United States and the territories of the United States, or the constitution and laws of this state." Iowa's bill covers any law enacted by a jurisdiction or a governmental or quasi-governmental body other than the federal government or a state of the United States ... [including] a religious law, legal code, accord, or ruling ... by an international organization, tribunal, or formal or informal administrative body.

Blocking measures often are styled as responses to amorphous foreign or international "threats" described in ambiguous "findings" and vague statements about citizens' rights and public policy. Their genuine necessity is highly suspect, however. They have been critiqued as a solution in need of a problem, and the primary motivation for many provisions appears to be political posturing by state legislators.

Whatever the true motivations, it is important to note that this is hardly the first time that states have legislated hostility to foreign law. The practice dates back to the nation's founding. It also is not confined to the states. Congressional efforts aimed at state and federal judges failed in 2004 but expressed remarkably similar sentiments about "threats" from foreign law. History continues to repeat itself even today in both legislative and political settings.

Full blocking initiatives are outright bans on foreign law, regardless of circumstance or context. The court looks no further than the source of the legal tenet in question. If it comes from "foreign law," it must be disregarded. Oklahoma's law, which is a constitutional amendment adopted through a ballot initiative known as State Question 755 ("SQ 755"), is a good illustration:

The Courts ... shall uphold and adhere to the law as provided in the United States Constitution, the Oklahoma Constitution, the United States Code, federal regulations promulgated pursuant thereto, established common law, the Oklahoma statutes and rules promulgated pursuant thereto, and if necessary the law of another state of the United States provided the law of the other state does not include Sharia Law, in making judicial decisions. The courts shall not look to the legal precepts of other nations or cultures. Specifically, the courts shall not consider international law or Sharia Law. The provisions of this subsection shall apply to all cases before the respective courts including, but not limited to, cases of first impression.

Rights-based initiatives consider the application of foreign rules and prohibit usages that interfere with the state or federal rights of citizens. A court must consider not only the source of the law, but also whether it works a rights infringement in practice. Arizona's rights-based measure became law in April 2011:

A court, arbitrator, administrative agency or other adjudicative, mediation or enforcement authority shall not enforce a foreign law if doing so would violate a right guaranteed by the Constitution of this state or of the United States or conflict with the laws of the United States or of this state.

Reciprocity-based initiatives block foreign laws that do not provide the same rights protection as American state or federal law. As with rights-based measures, the court must consider the rule's source and whether rights are infringed in practice. But it also must consider operational equivalency and the extent to which the foreign jurisdiction as a system would protect rights guaranteed under state or federal law. A Kansas initiative provides that: Any court, arbitration, tribunal or administrative agency ruling or decision shall violate the public policy of this state and be void and unenforceable if the court, arbitration, tribunal or administrative agency bases its rulings or decisions in the matter at issue in whole or in part on any foreign law, legal code or system that would not grant the parties affected by the ruling or decision the same fundamental liberties, rights and privileges granted under the United States and Kansas constitutions.

The three categories may amount to distinctions without a difference. All are framed in the imperative ("shall" / "shall not"), which means that their prohibitions are absolute. Rights-based and reciprocity-based measures both seek to ensure identical treatment for American citizens. It is unlikely that this standard can be met in practice because foreign law rarely provides the same protections as those available in the United States.

These wholesale bans on foreign and international law create serious legal complications for the states that adopt them. While the benefits are dubious, the costs are substantial, including a direct impact on commercial matters. While foreign forum selection and choice of law clauses in private contracts normally are enforceable, blocking provisions seek to eviscerate contractual clauses selecting foreign law on public policy grounds. They also create substantial uncertainty over the enforceability of international commercial arbitration awards. Indeed, they could prevent the adjudication of any legal dispute where the validity of a foreign law or legal determination is at issue (e.g., in family law cases involving foreign marriages and adoption, in commercial disputes or state tax cases where the ownership of foreign property is in question, etc.).

Blocking measures also create serious problems of constitutional federalism as it relates to foreign affairs. To the extent that they reject international law, for example, blocking measures likely violate state obligations under the Supremacy Clause to respect this dimension of federal law. The absolute nullification of all foreign law also implicates international comity, which is the harmony arising out of respect demonstrated by judicial officers in one jurisdiction for legal determinations in another, particularly on matters involving the foreign state's own laws. This in turn could impact federal interests in preserving good relations with foreign nations, in terms of either the Executive's broad foreign relations power, or congressional authority under the Foreign Commerce Clause.

Blocking measures create constitutional problems domestically as well. To the extent that they prohibit the enforcement of judgments from other American states or federal courts that are grounded in foreign law, they violate the Full Faith and Credit and Due Process Clauses of the federal Constitution. Where initiatives specifically focus on prohibiting Sharia law, this direct targeting of Muslims for divergent treatment gives rise to a variety of constitutional claims as well as questions of federal anti-discrimination law.

Apart from these general issues, as discussed below, blocking measures have a particularly negative impact on American lawyers, who now will have little certainty about the source or scope of their ethical obligations while practicing abroad. They also interfere directly with judicial regulation of the admission, ethical conduct, and discipline of lawyers. These negative outcomes are particularly ironic because consideration of how blocking measures could impact the American legal profession appears to have played no role whatsoever in the legislative process.

Blocking measures also have negative implications for the American federalist system. The ethical duties of state and federal practitioners are not automatically coextensive, even in the same jurisdiction. Although federal courts normally adopt the ethical rules of the states where they sit, they nevertheless retain inherent authority to sanction parties and lawyers before them. They also may impose different ethical obligations on lawyers admitted to a particular court's federal bar. Breaches of state rules on legal practice can form the basis of federal crimes. While federal government lawyers must abide by state ethics rules, they also are subject to additional public integrity requirements (e.g., restrictions on financial holdings). Even when state and federal rules mirror one another, there is no guarantee that federal courts (or courts in other states, for that matter) will interpret this identical language in the same way.

While federal courts accommodate state interests whenever possible, federal law will prevail in the event of a conflict. This includes conflicts with international rules that are incorporated into federal law, which preempt inconsistent state laws dealing with the same subject matter. Blocking measures that infringe upon these federal interests in foreign affairs thus would be unconstitutional.

Defenders of blocking initiatives might suggest that there is no such intrusion on the federal province. Many blocking measures instruct state courts to respect and apply federal law. Where federal law and international law overlap, presumably the exception would include any "federalized" foreign law, such that there might be no genuine conflict in such cases. That said, it remains an open question whether blocking provisions are meant to apply to federal courts sitting in diversity and applying state law. And the fact is that some state initiatives aim directly at federal judges as well. A proposal in Iowa subjects federal judges to criminal penalties, civil lawsuits, and bar discipline if they "violate" the rights of an Iowan citizen through the application of foreign law. A Montana proposal even authorizes its state legislature to nullify federal law entirely. At the very least, blocking measures create a quandary for federal judges applying state law in case where the relevant rule of decision would involve foreign law. This could arise, for example, in discipline cases arising out of overseas conduct where the federal court normally applies ethics rules from the state where it sits to a member of its federal bar. It also could become an issue in malpractice cases where a lawyer resolves a question of foreign law incorrectly, or in determining whether the crime/fraud exception to the attorney-client privilege applies to foreign or international crimes.

It is unlikely that a federal court would respect state rules that purport to exclude wide swaths of substantive federal law (treaties, federal statutes incorporating international rules by reference, and customary international law as federal common law). Federal courts independently supervise their own bar members, and it is unlikely that they will choose to limit the materials they may deem relevant to that task. As with reciprocal discipline, the serious potential for anomalous results created by the blocking initiatives (e.g., different disciplinary outcomes for identical conduct in state versus federal courts) is readily apparent (and best avoided).

Table of State Blocking Measures on International and Foreign Law (as of July 22. 2012) . States with International Law / Foreign Law Blocking Measures: 33[]'] (93 proposals)

AL, AK, AZ, AR, FL, GA, ID, IN, IA, KS, KY, LA, ME, MI, MN, MS, MT, MO, NB, NH, NJ, NM, NC, OK, PA, SC, SD, TN, TX, UT, VA, WV, WY

CUSTOMARY INTERNATIONAL LAW

There is no judicial remedy available to citizens of the United States for human rights violations, however, aliens have available remedies for violations of customary international law, in federal courts. As such those who are victims of state authorities and are foreign citizens may bring claims for violations of customary international law in federal courts.

The ATS grants to the district courts "original jurisdiction of any civil action by an alien for a tort only, committed in violation of the law of nations or a treaty of the United States." 28 U.S.C. § 1350. The scope of the ATS is limited to suits "by an alien." 28 U.S.C. § 1350; see In re Estate of Marcos Human Rights Litig., 978 F.2d 493, 499 (9th Cir. 1992) ("[The ATS] requires a claim by an alien . . . ."). The ATS admits no cause of action by non-aliens. See Yousuf v. Samantar, 552 F.3d 371, 375 n.1 (4th Cir. 2009) ("To the extent that any of the claims under the ATS are being asserted by plaintiffs who are American citizens, federal subject-matter jurisdiction may be lacking.").

A "self-executing" treaty has "automatic domestic effect as federal law upon ratification. Conversely, a 'non-self-executing' treaty does not by itself give rise to domestically enforceable federal law." Medellin v. Texas, 552 U.S. 491, 128 S. Ct. 1346, 1356 n.2, 170 L. Ed. 2d 190 (2008). While "[t]he interpretation of a treaty . . . begins with its text," Medellin, 552 U.S. at 506, it does not end there. Because the purpose of treaty interpretation is to "give the specific words of the treaty a meaning consistent with the shared expectations of the contracting parties," Air France v. Saks, 470 U.S. 392, 399, 105 S. Ct. 1338, 84 L. Ed. 2d 289 (1985), courts -- including the United States Supreme Court -- look to the executive branch's interpretation of the issue, the views of other contracting states, and the treaty's negotiation and drafting history in order to ensure that their interpretation of the text is not contradicted by other evidence of intent. See Abbott v. Abbott, 560 U.S. 1, 15-20, 130 S. Ct. 1983, 176 L. Ed. 2d 789 (2010) (examining these factors following its textual analysis); Medellin, 552 U.S. at 508-13 (same); see also Vo, 447 F.3d at 1246 n.13 (consulting a letter of submittal from the Secretary of State).

ICCPR confers individual rights and is self executing as a matter of both human rights and international law. "For any treaty to be susceptible to judicial enforcement it must both confer individual rights and be self-executing." Cornejo v. County of San Diego, 504 F.3d 853, 856 (9th Cir. 2007). A treaty is self-executing when it is automatically enforceable in domestic courts without implementing legislation. See Medellin v. Texas, 552 U.S. 491, 504-05, 128 S. Ct. 1346, 170 L. Ed. 2d 190 & n.2 (2008); Khan v. Holder, 584 F.3d 773, 783 (9th Cir. 2009). According to the courts in the United States the ICCPR fails to satisfy either requirement because it was ratified "on the express understanding that it was not self-executing and so did not itself create obligations enforceable in the federal courts." Sosa v. Alvarez-Machain, 542 U.S. 692, 735, 124 S. Ct. 2739, 159 L. Ed. 2d 718 (2004) However this position is contrary to the intent of the treaty because the treaty specifically provides for a remedy to those who have their rights violated. The Universal Declaration of Human Rights, suffers from the same problem as a source of justiciable rights. See Sosa, 542 U.S. at 734-35.

Princz v. Federal Republic of Germany, 26 F.3d 1166, 1174 n.1, 307 U.S. App. D.C. 102 (D.C. Cir. 1994) ("While it is true that 'international law is part of our law,' it is also our law that a federal court is not competent to hear a claim arising under international law absent a statute granting such jurisdiction." (Citation omitted)); see also Sosa, 542 U.S. at 720 ("'[O]ffences against this law of nations are principally incident to whole states or nations,' and not individuals seeking relief in court." (Quoting Blackstone, 4 Commentaries 68) (Alteration omitted)). The Alien Tort Statute ("ATS"), 28 U.S.C. § 1350, is the only possible vehicle for a claim for violation of customary international law. See Sosa, 542 U.S. at 731 n.19 (resisting the implication "that every grant of jurisdiction to a federal court carries with it an opportunity to develop common law" and distinguishing the ATS's unique invitation to entertain "common law claims derived from the law of nations" from the strictures of § 1331 federal-question jurisdiction). If any plaintiff could bring any claim alleging a violation of the law of nations under federal-question jurisdiction, there would be no need for statutes such as the ATS and the Torture Victim Protection Act, 28 U.S.C. § 1350, note, which recognize or create limited causes of action for particular classes of plaintiffs (aliens) or particular violations (torture).

Courts determine the content of international law by reference "to the customs and usages of civilized nations, and, as evidence of these, to the works of jurists and commentators". Siderman de Blake v. Republic of Argentina, 965 F.2d 699, 715 (9th Cir. 1992) (quoting The Paquete Habana, 175 U.S. 677, 700, 44 L. Ed. 320, 20 S. Ct. 290 (1900)). Cruel, inhuman, and degrading treatment is prohibited by Article 5 of the Universal Declaration of Human Rights, G.A. Res. 217A(III), U.N. GAOR, 3d Sess., Supp. No. 1, U.N. Doc. A/810 (1948); by Article 7 of the International Covenant on Civil and Political Rights, Dec. 19, 1966, 999 U.N.T.S. 171, 175; by Article 16 of the Convention Against Torture and Other Cruel, Inhuman or Degrading Treatment or Punishment, Dec. 10, 1984, 23 I.L.M. 1027, 1031 (1984), as modified, 24 I.L.M. 535 (9185); by Article 5(2) of the American Convention on Human Rights, Nov. 22, 1969, 9 I.L.M. 673, 676; by Article 3 of the European Convention for the Protection of Human Rights and Fundamental Freedoms, Nov. 4, 1950, 213 U.N.T.S. 222, 224; and by Article 5 of the African Charter on Human and Peoples' Rights, June 27, 1981, 21 I.L.M. 58, 60. These documents consistently link such treatment to torture, which this court has held is prohibited not only by a specific, universal, and obligatory norm but by one that reaches the level of jus cogens. Siderman de Blake, 965 F.2d at 714-717. Indeed, the international conventions or declarations banning such treatment indicate that "torture constitutes an aggravated and deliberate form of cruel inhuman or degrading treatment or punishment."

Although enacted in 1789 as part of the first Judiciary Act, the ATCA received little attention until 1980, when the Second Circuit, in a comprehensive analysis of the statute, held that the ATCA provided subject matter jurisdiction over an action brought by Paraguayan citizens for torture -- a violation of the law of nations -- committed in Paraguay. See Filartiga v. Pena-Irala (Filartiga I), 630 F.2d 876 (2d Cir. 1980). In 1975, Judge Friendly remarked that the statute had been invoked so rarely since its inception that it existed as "a kind of legal Lohengrin; although it has been with us since the first Judiciary Act . . . no one seems to know whence it came." IIT v. Vencap, Ltd., 519 F.2d 1001, 1015 (2d Cir. 1975) (noting the paucity of cases under the Act and holding that no jurisdiction existed under the Act for fraud and securities claims against foreign corporations).

Since the Filartiga I decision, the ATCA has been invoked in a variety of actions alleging human rights violations. See, e.g., Abebe-Jira v. Negewo, 72 F.3d 844 (11th Cir. 1996) (affirming judgment under ATCA against former Ethiopian official for torture and cruel, inhuman, and degrading treatment); Kadic v. Karadzic, 70 F.3d 232 (2d Cir. 1995) (concluding that alleged war crimes, genocide, torture, and other atrocities committed by a Bosnian Serb leader were actionable under the ATCA); Tel-Oren v. Libyan Arab Republic, 233 U.S. App. D.C. 384, 726 F.2d 774 (D.C. Cir. 1984) (dismissing for lack of subject matter jurisdiction claims brought against the Palestine Liberation Organization, the Libyan government, and other entities for terrorist activities allegedly in violation of the law of nations); Xuncax v. Gramajo, 886 F. Supp. 162 (D. Mass. 1995) (deeming torture, summary execution, "disappearance," and arbitrary detention by Guatemalan military to be actionable violations under the ATCA).

Trajano v. Marcos (In re Estate of Marcos Human Rights Litig.) ("Marcos I"), 978 F.2d 493 (9th Cir. 1992), a wrongful death action against former Philippine President Ferdinand Marcos and his daughter for the torture and murder of a Philippine citizen, recognized that "it would be unthinkable to conclude other than that acts of official torture violate customary international law," and concluded that the plaintiff, an alien, had properly invoked the subject matter jurisdiction of the federal courts under the ATCA. Id. at 499 (citation and internal quotation marks omitted). Referencing an April 1787 letter from James Madison to Edmond Randolph, the court concluded that "there is ample indication that the 'Arising Under' Clause was meant to extend the judicial power of the federal courts . . . to 'all cases which concern foreigners.'" Id. at 502. Because the "Arising Under" Clause gave Congress the power to enact the ATCA, it held that exercising jurisdiction over the claims would not run afoul of Article III of the Constitution. Id. at 502-03.

When the Marcos litigation returned to court in Hilao v. Estate of Marcos (In re Estate of Marcos, Human Rights Litig.) ("Marcos II"), 25 F.3d 1467 (9th Cir. 1994), the court further delineated the contours of the ATCA. It resolved that the Act not only provides federal courts with subject matter jurisdiction, but also creates a cause of action for an alleged violation of the law of nations: "Section 1350 does not require that the action 'arise under' the law of nations, but only mandates a 'violation of the law of nations' in order to create a cause of action." Id. at 1475 (quoting Tel-Oren, 726 F.2d at 779 (Edwards, J., concurring)). In other words, "nothing more than a violation of the law of nations is required to invoke section 1350." Id. (citation omitted).

Of course, not every violation of international law constitutes an actionable claim under the ATCA. In Marcos II, the court was careful to limit actionable violations to those international norms that are "specific, universal, and obligatory." Id. at 1475. This formulation, which lays the foundation for the judicial approach to international norms, is in keeping with the narrow scope of ATCA jurisdiction and the general practice of limiting judicial review to those areas of international law that have achieved sufficient consensus to merit application by a domestic tribunal. See Banco Nacional de Cuba v. Sabbatino, 376 U.S. 398, 428, 11 L. Ed. 2d 804, 84 S. Ct. 923 (1964) ("The greater the degree of codification or consensus concerning a particular area of international law, the more appropriate it is for the judiciary to render decisions regarding it . . . ."); cf. United States v. Smith, 18 U.S. (5 Wheat.) 153, 162, 5 L. Ed. 57 (1820) (finding piracy "universally treated . . . as an offence against the law of nations" and "sufficiently and constitutionally defined" by commentators to be punishable by Congress).

The term jus cogens refers to a category of "peremptory norms" that are "'accepted and recognized by the international community of states as a whole as . . . norms from which no derogation is permitted.'" Siderman de Blake v. Republic of Argentina, 965 F.2d 699, 714 (9th Cir. 1992) (quoting Vienna Convention on the Law of Treaties, art. 53, May 23, 1969, 1155 U.N.T.S. 332, 8 I.L.M. 679). Customary international law, a direct descendent of the "law of nations," is a related, but distinct, concept. Id. It refers more generally to those established norms of contemporary international law that are "ascertained . . . 'by consulting the works of jurists, writing professedly on public law; or by the general usage and practice of nations; or by judicial decisions recognizing and enforcing that law.' " Id. at 714-15 (quoting Smith, 18 U.S. at 160-61).

Courts have explained the difference between these two concepts as follows:

While jus cogens and customary international law are related, they differ in one important respect. Customary international law, like international law defined by treaties and other international agreements, rests on the consent of states. A state that persistently objects to a norm of customary international law that other states accept is not bound by that norm . . . .

In contrast, jus cogens embraces customary laws considered binding on all nations and is derived from values taken to be fundamental by the international community, rather than from the fortuitous or self-interested choices of nations. Whereas customary international law derives solely from the consent of states, the fundamental and universal norms constituting jus cogens transcend such consent . . . .

Because jus cogens norms do not depend solely on the consent of states for their binding force, they enjoy the highest status within international law.

Id. at 715 (internal quotation marks and citations omitted).

The commentators embrace this distinction. See 1 M. Cherif Bassiouni, International Criminal Law 40 (2d ed. 1999) ("[A] jus cogens norm holds the highest hierarchical position among all other norms and principles. As a consequence of that standing, jus cogens norms are deemed to be 'peremptory' and 'non-derogable.'"); Ian Brownlie, Principles of Public International Law 515 (5th ed. 1998) ("The major distinguishing feature of [jus cogens] rules is their relative indelibility.").

Given the non-derogable nature of jus cogens norms, it comes as no surprise that courts have found that a jus cogens violation is sufficient to satisfy the "specific, universal, and obligatory" standard. See Marcos II, 25 F.3d at 1475. But the fact that a violation of this subcategory of international norms is sufficient to warrant an actionable claim under the ATCA does not render it necessary. Indeed, our recent cases lay out the components of an actionable violation without reference to jus cogens. See Papa v. United States, 281 F.3d 1004, 1013 (9th Cir. 2002) (remanding case to district court to apply the "applicable standard," which requires plaintiffs to allege "specific, universal, and obligatory" norms as part of their claim); Martinez v. City of Los Angeles, 141 F.3d 1373, 1383-84 (9th Cir. 1998) (recognizing, without a discussion of jus cogens, that arbitrary detention meets the standard for a cognizable ATCA claim).

The notion of jus cogens norms was not part of the legal landscape when Congress enacted the ATCA in 1789. See Brownlie, supra, at 516 (explaining the modern evolution of jus cogens). Thus, to restrict actionable violations of international law to only those claims that fall within the categorical universe known as jus cogens would deviate from both the history and text of the ATCA.

Although a strict categorical approach may have surface appeal for its apparent ease of application, it is far from certain which norms would qualify for jus cogens status. The development of an elite category of human rights norms is of relatively recent origin in international law, and "although the concept of jus cogens is now accepted, its content is not agreed." Restatement (Third) of the Foreign Relations Law of the United States § 102 n.6 (1987) ("Restatement on Foreign Relations"). As one respected commentator put it, "more authority exists for the category of jus cogens than exists for its particular content. . . ." Brownlie, supra, at 516-17; see also Theodor Meron, On a Hierarchy of International Human Rights, 80 A.J.I.L. 1, 14-15 (1986) (explaining the difficulties of strict categorization in defining peremptory norms).

It is the Supreme Court's directive that the law of nations "may be ascertained by consulting the work of jurists, writing professedly on public law; or by the general usage and practice of nations; or by judicial decisions recognising and enforcing that law." Smith, 18 U.S. at 160-61; see also The Paquete Habana, 175 U.S. 677, 700, 44 L. Ed. 320, 20 S. Ct. 290 (1900) ("Where there is no treaty, and no controlling executive or legislative act or judicial decision, resort must be had to the customs and usages of civilized nations; and, as evidence of these, to the works of jurists and commentators . . . ."). Evidence of the law of nations may also be garnered from international agreements and United Nations declarations. See Siderman, 965 F.2d at 716-17; Filartiga I, 630 F.2d at 883-84.

Article 38 of the Statute of the International Court of Justice serves as a convenient summary of the sources of international law, although courts recognize that defining "the 'sources' of international law is a subject of much continuing scholarship." United States v. Yousef, Nos. 98-1041, 98-1197, 98-1355, 99-1544, 99-1554, 327 F.3d 56, 2003 U.S. App. LEXIS 6437, at *71 (2d Cir. Apr. 4, 2003). Article 38 provides, in part:

1. The Court, whose function is to decide in accordance with international law such disputes as are submitted to it, shall apply:

a. international conventions, whether general or particular, establishing rules expressly recognized by the contesting states;

b. international custom, as evidence of a general practice accepted as law;

c. the general principles of law recognized by civilized nations;

d. subject to the provisions of

Article 59, judicial decisions and the teachings of the most highly qualified publicists of the various nations, as subsidiary means for the determination of rules of law.

Statute of the International Court of Justice, June 26, 1945, art. 38, 59 Stat. 1055, U.S.T.S. 993.

Article 59 states: "The decision of the Court has no binding force except between the parties and in respect of that particular case."

Courts have recognized that the Universal Declaration, although not binding on states, constitutes "a powerful and authoritative statement of the customary international law of human rights." Siderman, 965 F.2d at 719. One threshold question in any ATCA case is whether the alleged tort is a violation of the law of nations. Courts have recognized that torture, murder, and slavery are jus cogens violations and, thus, violations of the law of nations. See United States v. Matta-Ballesteros, 71 F.3d 754, 764 n.5 (9th Cir. 1995). Rape can be a form of torture. See Farmer v. Brennan, 511 U.S. 825, 852, 854, 128 L. Ed. 2d 811, 114 S. Ct. 1970 (1994) (Blackmun, J., concurring) (describing brutal prison rape as "the equivalent of" and "nothing less than torture"); Kadic v. Karadzic, 70 F.3d 232, 242 (2d Cir. 1995) (describing allegations of "murder, rape, forced impregnation, and other forms of torture" (emphasis added)); In re Extradition of Suarez-Mason, 694 F. Supp. 676, 682 (N.D. Cal. 1988) (stating that "shock sessions were interspersed with rapes and other forms of torture" (emphasis added)); see also generally Evelyn Mary Aswad, Torture by Means of Rape, 84 Geo. L.J. 1913 (1996). Moreover, forced labor is so widely condemned that it has achieved the status of a jus cogens violation. See, e.g., Universal Declaration of Human Rights, G.A. Res. 217(A) III (1948) (banning forced labor); Agreement for the Prosecution and Punishment of the Major War Criminals of the European Axis, and Charter of the International Military Tribunal, Aug. 8, 1945, art. 6, 82 U.N.T.S. 280 (making forced labor a war crime). Accordingly, all torts alleged in the present case are jus cogens violations and, thereby, violations of the law of nations.

Jus cogens norms are norms of international law that are binding on nations even if they do not agree to them. See Siderman de Blake v. Republic of Argentina, 965 F.2d 699, 714-15 (9th Cir. 1992). Courts stress that although a jus cogens violation is, by definition, "a violation of 'specific, universal, and obligatory' international norms" that is actionable under the ATCA, any "violation of 'specific, universal, and obligatory' international norms" -- jus cogens or not -- is actionable under the ATCA. Papa, 281 F.3d at 1013 (quoting Marcos II, 25 F.3d at 1475). Thus, a jus cogens violation is sufficient, but not necessary, to state a claim under the ATCA

VINDICTIVE PUBLIC ACTION

"Vindictive" is defined as " having a bitterly vengeful character" or "characterized by an intent to cause unpleasantness, damage, or pain" Webster's Third New International Dictionary (unabridged 1966).

One presumes the legislature and public officials do not act vindictively. However the following articles show that acting with vindictive intent the legislature refuses to enact legislation to bar contracts to entities that violate human rights and public officials continue awarding these contracts.

Fair Care for All: Humane Treatment, Just Reform

The Fair Care for All Campaign is a priority for the ACLU of Arizona. We seek to end Arizona's reliance on incarceration by advocating for more humane and cost-efficient alternatives together with fair and equitable criminal justice reforms.

Arizona's prisons are over-crowded, understaffed, and unsafe. Incarcerating more people in these unconstitutional conditions comes with a hefty price to taxpayers and does nothing to

increase public safety. Arizona needs prison reform. And that reform must address the inadequate medical and mental health care, unsafe conditions, overuse of solitary confinement, and increasing reliance on privatization.

UNCONSTITUTIONAL AND INHUMANE CONDITIONS IN ARIZONA PRISONS

The failure of Arizona prison officials to provide basic medical care has resulted in people suffering serious injury and even death. In March of 2012, a legal team led by the ACLU and the Prison Law Office filed a lawsuit against the Arizona Department of Corrections (ADC) demanding an end to solitary confinement and improvements to the provision of medical and mental health care for people in Arizona prisons. The deficiencies are systemic; ADC's policies and practices put the health and safety of everyone in their custody at risk. In March 2013, Judge Neil Wake ruled that the case can move forward as a class-action lawsuit.

SOLITARY CONFINEMENT

Solitary confinement is fundamentally inhumane, does nothing to make our communities safer, and wastes taxpayer dollars. Yet three thousand people are held in isolation in Arizona prisons each year. The overuse of solitary confinement is a national epidemic that is making our prisons more dangerous for prisoners, staff, and communities. We need to reduce the number of people held in isolation in Arizona's prisons. Take Action: Stop the abuse of solitary!

PRIVATIZING PRISONS

More and more prisons and prison services in Arizona are run by private, for-profit corporations. Keeping more people locked up longer means greater profits, but not greater safety. Cutting corners on medical and mental health care, security officers, and rehabilitation programs make prisons more dangerous for inmates, staff, and communities. Contracts with for-profit companies do not change the state's obligation to protect people in prison from cruel and unusual punishment or to ensure that contractors comply with the Constitution.

STORIES FROM ARIZONA PRISONS

These are the real stories of people who were incarcerated in Arizona and subjected to constitutional and human rights abuses including grossly inadequate medical care and inhumane conditions in solitary confinement. They are sharing their stories to highlight the need for greater accountability in the Arizona prison system.

ADMINISTRATIVE PROCESSES AND REMEIDIES ARIZONA PRISONS

802.05 FORMAL GRIEVANCE PROCESS (FOR MEDICAL IN ARIZONA)

1.1 An inmate may file a Formal Grievance should he/she be unable to resolve their complaint informally. The inmate has five workdays from receipt of the response from the Contract Director of Nursing to submit a Formal Grievance to the unit CO IV Grievance Coordinator, using the Inmate Grievance form. Upon receipt of any Medical Grievance, the unit CO IV Grievance Coordinator shall immediately forward the Formal Grievance form to the Contract Facility Health Administrator. Within 15 workdays of receipt, the Contract Facility Health Administrator shall:

1.1.1 Investigate the complaint.

1.1.2 Prepare a written response to the inmate's Formal Grievance. The written response to the inmate shall include:

1.1.2.1 A summarization of the inmate's complaint.

1.1.2.2 A description of what action was taken to investigate the complaint to include the date and content if a personal meeting with the inmate was conducted.

1.1.2.3 A summary of findings.

1.1.2.4 The decision and supporting rationale in reaching the decision.

1.1.2.4.1 The decision from the facility level shall either be "Resolved" or "Not Resolved."

1.1.3 Maintain a copy of the inmate's Formal Grievance and return the completed grievance in a sealed envelope to the unit CO IV Grievance Coordinator clearly marked with the inmate's name, Arizona Department of Corrections (ADC) number, housing unit location, and the Grievance number.

1.1.3.1 The unit CO IV Grievance Coordinator shall utilize the Grievance number on the envelope to close out their tracking log and forward the completed Formal Grievance to the inmate in the sealed envelope.

1.1.4 Email copies of the Grievance, Response, and supporting documentation to the ADC Contract Compliance Monitor or designee.

1.2 The decision

The prison authorities have given the unfettered discretion to Corizon to deny inmates treatment for their serious medical needs. They do not which to hear from inmates complaints that Corizon is denying them treatment for their serious medical needs. They have done this inspite of the statutory duty that Arizona is responsible for the treatment of inmate medical needs.

EXHAUSTION OF INEFFECTIVE ADMINISTRATIVE REMEDIES

In plain language Article 2.3(a) ICCPR requires all administrative and judicial remedies be effective, but, due to PLRA and AEDPA these are ineffective in the United States. Prison systems such as the Arizona system bleed inmates and their families for money. They receive kickbacks from vendors who supply food, commissary, phone and other services. Friends and family members desiring to visit inmates must pay a $25 application fees. Foreign nationals though held in custody are not allowed to participate in any programs though they must pay for these programs. Non-Christians are prevented from practicing their religions. These actions constitute torture, cruel, inhuman treatment and punishment under ICCPR.

These decisions show due to PLRA and AEDPA inmates are denied their rights under Articles 7, 10.1, 10.3, 18.6, 26, 27 ICCPR which federal courts due to Congressional legislation have no authority to prevent. State court judges with authority refuse to prevent these violations for fear they may be removed from office.

If administrative remedies are effective the need to seek judicial review shall not be there and both the state as well as the prisoner would save substantial resources It appears the authorities feel threatened in resolving issues through the administrative remedy process mandating judicial intervention.

PLRA's exhaustion provisions are noble, but prison authorities, such as Arizona, do not wish to take action to prevent future violations. Arizona has recently amended Department Order 802 which reads in part:

FOR PROFIT HEALTH CARE PROVIDERS

The following information provided is taken directly from corporate media.

BEECKEN PETTY O'KEEFE & COMPANY

Beecken Petty O'Keefe & Company is a major investor in Corizon and it states" they are "one of the longest-tenured, pure play healthcare private equity firms in the United States, BPOC has structured, managed and realized investments on behalf of institutional and individual investors for nearly two decades. Founded in 1996, BPOC ranks among the country's oldest private equity management firms in the United States that specialize exclusively in healthcare. The firm and its investment professionals provide a powerful combination of financial and operational experience and expertise. Our industry knowledge combined with a long-term historical perspective has resulted in successful investments across regulatory, economic and financial market cycles. BPOC's goal is to deliver superior performance, form enduring partnerships and provide unparalleled investment leadership."

They "seek to partner with healthcare companies poised for strong, transformational growth. We assume an active role as collaborative partners from the very onset of our investment and have been praised for our sense of fair dealing and teamwork." Beecken states "we look for companies whose management teams are creative and inventive and that require capital for growth and significant value creation. We support management with our deep experience, but when additional expertise is needed, we may also augment our skills with our healthcare relationships forged over decades of involvement in the industry.

"Whether you're an investor, a company or an executive, we'd like to hear from you."

They boast that "we seek to partner with healthcare companies poised for strong, transformational growth.

"We assume an active role as collaborative partners from the very onset of our investment and have been praised for our sense of fair dealing and teamwork."

And

".. look for companies whose management teams are creative and inventive and that require capital for growth and significant value creation. We support management with our deep experience, but when additional expertise is needed, we may also augment our skills with our healthcare relationships forged over decades of involvement in the industry."

WEXFORD HEALTH

Wexford Health Sources, the nation's leading innovative correctional health care company, provides clients with experienced management and technologically advanced services, combined with programs that control costs while ensuring quality.

For the past two decades, Wexford Health has consistently delivered proven staffing expertise and a full range of medical, behavioral health, pharmacy, utilization management, provider contracting, claims processing, and quality management services.

QUALITY CARE

Our Quality Management Program ensures patients receive appropriate care and helps our clients maintain accreditation and legal compliance. Wexford Health has a 100% success rate for our clients who choose to pursue industry accreditation.

Our dedicated internal Quality Management and Contract Compliance Team includes certified clinical auditors, licensed nurses, and other industry experts. Through easy-to-use manuals, ongoing educational initiatives, and innovative programs like our Preceptor training and Quality Scorecard, this Team monitors contract compliance and quality of care and assists our clients to prepare for - and achieve - desired health care certifications.

EXPERIENCED MANAGEMENT TEAM

Wexford Health's leaders are industry experts, with years of experience managing both the clinical and financial aspects of correctional health care programs.

Wexford Health's management team includes not only experienced corrections and health care professionals, but also expert's clinical programs, human resources, and finance.

Because our management team includes board-certified physicians, executives from major health insurance companies, and former officials from some of the largest correctional systems in the nation, Wexford Health can offer clients the perfect blend of consulting skills to ensure that every aspect of the health care program is functioning at its peak operational and cost-efficiency level.

PROVEN STAFFING EXPERTISE

Our dedicated human resources professionals and creative recruitment and retention programs make Wexford Health the industry leader in correctional health care staffing.

Wexford Health has consistently demonstrated our ability to recruit and retain qualified health care professionals to meet the ever-changing needs of each of our contracted facilities 0 in sparsely populated rural areas, as well as in complex urban facilities.

We use a wide variety of techniques - including social media, a Speaker's Bureau, our Employment Hotline, and our innovative Shadow-A-Nurse/Provider programs - to provide both the quantity and quality of health care staff our clients require.

We are willing to go the extra mile, financially as well as operationally, to create and implement unique staffing programs specifically tailored for each of our contracted facilities.

TECHNOLOGICALLY ADVANCED SERVICES

Wexford Health specializes in implementing the newest technology that is affordable, easy to implement, and user-friendly.

Wexford Health uses its considerable technology expertise to successfully implement systems and programs at each of our contracted facilities. We understand that for technology to be successful, people have to be willing to use it. That's why we don't just install information systems at our facilities. We take the time to make sure users are comfortable and understand the program. Our investment of time and resources up front ensures that the technology pays off for our clients - financially and operationally - in the long run.

With our comprehensive data warehouse that facilitates reporting and analysis; our proven telemedicine program; successful Electronic Medical Record (EMR) implementations; state-of-the-art application tracking (iCMS) and human resources (Kronos®) information management systems; and comprehensive, fully integrated WexCare medical management software, Wexford Health is the industry leader in providing technology solutions that save our clients time and money.

COST CONTROL

Wexford Health's innovative programs cut costs - not corners.

Wexford Health does not sacrifice quality in order to save money. Instead, we develop programs that cut costs without having any negative impact on care or customer service.

Our national presence and Preferred Provider Network discounts create economies of scale and cost savings that we pass on to our clients.

Our utilization management program ensures that patients receive the right care, in the right facility, for the right length of time. Our state-of-the-art claims processing system adds even more savings by preventing fraud and overpayment. Together, these programs have saved our clients literally millions of dollars.

Telemedicine also generates substantial savings for clients. Based on the latest 50,000+ sessions we have conducted, a telemedicine encounter saves in excess of $700 in transportation, security, and meal costs.

To revolutionize health services, exceeding the ever-changing expectations of our clients

CORE VALUES

"R.A.I.S.E. the Standard"

Responsive & innovative partner: Wexford Health listens to client needs and is quick to take action, offering new and alternative solutions that address the unique requirements of our clients and our industry.

Adaptability & efficiency: Wexford Health is nimble and flexible, offering our clients dynamic, cost-effective solutions in response to ever-changing conditions and expectations.

Integrity & ethics: Ethical conduct is part of the foundation of Wexford Health's culture. We are committed to moral and principled business practices that drive our decision-making process.

Superior service: We provide uncompromised, consistent service that exceeds expectations and defines excellence, raising the standard for our industry.

Engaged and empowered workforce: Wexford Health's management team sets goals; allocates resources; delegates authority; and gives employees the trust they need to do their jobs better and faster. This result in a highly developed, motivated, and dedicated team trained and committed to providing nothing less than superior service.

MISSION STATEMENT

Wexford Health Sources' mission is to be a responsive, adaptable, and ethical partner.

We strive to provide innovative solutions that meet patients' needs and exceed clients' expectations.

Our culture fosters an empowered, engaged workforce that provides unparalleled customer service and delivers quality, cost-effective results.

CORIZON HEALTH

Corizon Health states as follows:

As the leading provider of correctional healthcare services in the United States, Corizon Health is uniquely positioned to meet the needs of both our clients and our patients. With the Corizon Health Vision, Mission and Values as our guide, we provide quality service to our patients, successful partnerships with our clients and an engaging work environment for our employees.

Corizon Health Vision

Corizon Health will lead the industry by providing quality healthcare and inmate reentry services that ultimately improve the communities where we live and work.

Corizon Health Mission

Corizon Health will exceed our correctional healthcare clients' expectations by partnering with them to deliver safe, effective and efficient services using clinical best practices and evidence-based medicine.

Our Values

CorizonSMART

Safety.

We put safety first in all that we do.

Motivation; We take pride in achieving excellence. We always strive to do better.

Accountability; We honor our commitments. We do the right thing regardless of the situation. Respect.; We treat every individual with dignity and compassion. We encourage the growth, development and well-being of all employees.

Teamwork; We value our team diversity. Our differences, backgrounds and experiences make us better.

CHOOSING CORIZON HEALTH

"10 REASONS"

Ten Reasons to Choose Corizon Health as Your Correctional Healthcare Partner

There are nurses…and then there are Corizon nurses.

We have the right leaders with exceptional track records.

We don't just practice healthcare in a correctional setting. We practice the specialty of correctional healthcare.

We have an unmatched Clinical Services Department supporting the field to deliver care precisely and affordably.

We have created one of the largest and best correctional pharmacies in the nation.

From county jails to statewide prison systems, we deliver for every client partner.

We're not just the biggest. We're the best. Clinically-focused. Patient-centered. Evidence-based.

We're more than a vendor. We're your partner.

Our client partners love working with us. You will, too.

Our number one focus is patient health and safety.

BENEFITS OF OUR SERVICES

As the leading provider of correctional healthcare services in the United States, Corizon Health is uniquely positioned to meet the needs of both our clients and our patients. With the Corizon Health Vision, Mission and Values as our guide, we provide quality service to our patients, successful partnerships with our clients and an engaging work environment for our employees.

Corizon Health Vision

Corizon Health will lead the industry by providing quality healthcare and inmate reentry services that ultimately improve the communities where we live and work.

Corizon Health Mission

Corizon Health will exceed our correctional healthcare clients' expectations by partnering with them to deliver safe, effective and efficient services using clinical best practices and evidence-based medicine.

Our Values: CorizonSMART

Safety: We put safety first in all that we do.

Motivation: We take pride in achieving excellence. We always strive to do better. Accountability. We honor our commitments. We do the right thing regardless of the situation.

Respect. We treat every individual with dignity and compassion. We encourage the growth, development and well-being of all employees.

Teamwork. We value our team diversity. Our differences, backgrounds and experiences make us better.

STAFFING MODEL

We recognize that a collaborative effort between the medical and behavioral healthcare providers is a key component of our delivery system and enhances the outcomes of our patients. Because of the high rates of mental illness and the previously unmet medical needs of the inmate population prior to incarceration, it is paramount to embrace a delivery system of this type. For example, in order for the special needs of individuals with chronic diseases such as HIV/AIDS, Hepatitis C, and cancer to be managed optimally, all disciplines must work diligently together. This integration of care by both the medical and behavioral health providers is a hallmark of Corizon Health's healthcare delivery system, whether we are the provider of comprehensive services or solely the medical or behavioral health provider.

PARTNER LOCATIONS

Corizon Health provides quality healthcare services to our clients at 429 facilities serving over 320,000 patients in 25 states. With its corporate headquarters in Brentwood, Tenn. Corizon Health is the leading provider of correctional healthcare services in the United States.

ACCREDITATIONS AND INDUSTRY PARTNERS

Corizon Health's expertise in facilities accreditation can help you meet and exceed the standards of local, state and national agencies. We have extensive experience working with the National Commission on Correctional Health Care (NCCHC), the American Correctional Association (ACA), the National Sheriffs Association,(NSA) the American Jail Association,(AJA) the National Patient Safety Foundation(NPSF) and multiple local and state organizations.

Whether or not a facility where we provide healthcare is accredited, awareness and compliance are part of our employee orientation, training and continuing education. NCCHC and ACA standards are the basis for our policy and procedures, as well as the foundation of our clinical and operational programs. Because of this, Corizon Health has a 100% success rate in obtaining and maintaining accreditation in every facility of ours in which accreditation is required.

A CULTURE OF PATIENT SAFETY

Corizon Health's company culture includes an emphasis on open communication and transparency, teamwork and accountability. These same goals provide the foundation for our corporate commitment to a culture of patient safety.

Corizon Health recognizes excellence in patient safety as a journey, rather than a destination. We are always striving to enhance the quality of the healthcare we deliver, ever mindful of safety, efficacy and cost-effectiveness.

Corizon Health has partnered with the National Patient Safety Foundation (NPSF) with the core mission of "improving the safety of care provided to patients." We are the first correctional healthcare provider to be a member of the "Stand Up For Patient Safety" organization and the only provider to have a Chief Quality Officer. Corizon Health is committed to:

Promoting a culture of patient safety

Enhancing teamwork and communication across the continuum of care at all levels of the organization

Seeking new resources to build organizational awareness for patient safety, employee engagement and accountability

Complementing current Corizon CE training with the NPSF Professional Learning Series

Facilitating Company-wide organizational learning and process improvements

Participating in NPSF Annual Patient Safety Awareness Week

Corizon Health has endorsed the NPSF report Free from Harm: Accelerating Patient Safety Improvement Fifteen Years after To Err is Human. As an endorsement organization we support and participate in the report's strategic recommendations for advancing progress in patient safety. Corizon Health is striving to achieve a meaningful, proactive, total systems approach, balanced with Corizon SMART values, as a roadmap to advance patient safety moving forward.

To learn more about the National Patient Safety Foundation, visit www.NPSF.org.

NEWS ON FOR PROFIT HEALTH ORGANIZATIONS

8.3 MILLION FOR JAIL DEATH -- LARGEST WRONGFUL DEATH CIVIL RIGHTS SETTLEMENT IN CALIFORNIA STATE HISTORY - HADDAD & SHERWIN.WEBLOC

The United States District Court for the Northern District of California, to correct fundamental failures that led to Mr. Harrison's unnecessary death. Corizon agreed to implement major changes in how it staffs jails throughout the entire state as a part of this settlement. The lawsuit revealed that Corizon allows uncredentialed Licensed Vocational Nurses to do the intake medical assessments only Registered Nurses are allowed to do under California law. When Mr. Harrison was arrested and taken to jail, he told the Corizon LVN that he drinks every day, his last drink was that day, and he has a history of alcohol withdrawal. The LVN decided not to provide Mr. Harrison with life-saving alcohol withdrawal protocols, and she sent him to the general jail population with no medical follow-up. Three days later, Mr. Harrison went into severe alcohol withdrawal -- Delirium Tremens – was having hallucinations, and was Tased and beaten to death by deputies. One of the family's attorneys, Michael Haddad, said, "After jail deputies beat and Tased their father to death, Martin Harrison's children beat them in court to win the largest wrongful death settlement in a civil rights case in California history." Haddad also said, "It was very important for us to stop Corizon from endangering jail inmates by staffing California jails with unqualified nurses." Haddad's partner, Julia Sherwin, said, "This settlement is going to change the business of correctional medicine around the country. If California inmates are entitled to have Registered Nurses -- and not unqualified LVN's -- do the work of RN's then so are inmates in Arizona, Florida, Alabama, New York, Michigan, and every other state where Corizon has contracts." Sherwin also said, "Corizon failed Martin Harrison. His legacy is to make sure Corizon does not fail other people who suffer from serious health conditions like alcohol dependence. Martin's family was committed to making sure his death was not in vain, and they succeeded completely." After four years of litigation, Haddad & Sherwin were joined at trial by co-counsel, Rick Friedman, of Friedman - Rubin, from Bremerton, Washington.

Arek Sarkissian writes

A company that provides health care services for state prisons throughout North Florida has replaced two of its top-level managers in Florida as it fights to save its nearly $1.2 billion relationship with the Florida Department of Corrections.

In mid-June, St. Louis-based Corizon Health Care appointed its southeast chief executive officer, JM Courtney, as interim replacement for John Dallas, who was relieved of his role as vice president overseeing the DOC contract.

Corizon also brought in Dr. Renee Fallhowe as chief clinical officer for its southeast region, which includes health wards within prisons that stretch from the Panhandle to Port St. Lucie.

The new leaders were brought in after Corizon was fined $67,500 by the DOC in May for failing a series of performance audits conducted over the past year. The problems ranged from improperly filing paperwork to distributing psychotropic drugs to inmates without evaluations.

The poor audits prompted DOC Secretary Julie Jones to begin looking for possible new vendors for the $229-million-a-year contract, well before the five-year contract is due to expire in 2018. The DOC said Jones plans to release an Invitation to Negotiate in December.

"We have high expectations for our vendors, and it doesn't matter whether you're a food vendor or a health care vendor," said McKinley Lewis, DOC spokesman. "Secretary Jones has made it abundantly clear these expectations need to be met."

Corizon spokesman Stuart Ramsay said the company has remedied the problems found by the DOC audits.

"Some of the improvements and changes that we have undertaken have been achieved quickly; others can take more than a year to fully take effect," he said.

Ramsay said the company looks forward to the negotiations with DOC.

"We are pleased to see Secretary Jones doing exactly what she promised to do when she took over leadership of the DOC — making whatever changes are necessary to ensure the best outcomes for the state, its taxpayers, and its inmate population," he said.

Audits reveal problems

The audits carried out in Corizon-managed facilities began in April 2014 — six months after its five-year contract began in October 2013 — which gave the company time to settle in.

The first round of reviews found a variety of problems, from improper paperwork to mistreatment of infection. The contract requires Corizon to maintain an industry standard for the way medical staff at the Lake Butler Reception and Medical Center — DOC's only prison hospital — treats an inmate's infection, but it failed during a review performed in August 2014, according to one audit.

During the same review period, Corizon's medical staff at the hospital received a grade of zero for failing to place inmates with physical and mental impairments in settings that would "adequately provide for their health care needs."

An audit of the Columbia Correctional Institution, just outside Lake City, noted a general failure to provide the DOC with information required under the contract. Other infractions found during the review, which covered January 2014 to March 2014, included inmates without psychiatric evaluations who were given psychotropic drugs. Also, the prison failed to pass along autopsy reports on deceased inmates to the agency's mortality review coordinator, the report states.

An audit at the Lowell Correctional Institution in Marion County conducted from January 2014 to April 2014 also found a failure of medical staff to provide the prisons bureau with autopsy reports.

In another review conducted at the Union Correctional Institution in Raiford from January 2014 to July 2014, nursing staff failed to document patient visits, medical records were mismanaged and most inmates were not given periodic screenings.

The poor performance reviews continued into 2015. For instance, a follow-up review performed at the Lake Butler Reception and Medical Center from March 17-19 noted that physicians were only performing rounds 15 percent of the time they were scheduled to do so.

However, the prison hospital audit also noted improvement. Most inmates were no longer waiting more than three months for dental appointments, and wound treatments that previously received a zero grade received a 93 percent grade, a report shows.

ALLEGHENY COUNTY ENDS ITS CONTRACT WITH CORIZON HEALTH PITTSBURGH POST-GAZETTE BY MOLLY BORN

As Allegheny County moves closer to the end of its contract with Corizon Health, the controller's office will perform a second audit of the county's contract with the embattled jail health care provider.

Controller Chelsa Wagner made the announcement at the jail oversight board meeting Thursday, nearly two weeks after county officials announced they will not renew the contract with the Tennessee-based firm that expires at the end of August. The agreement included three one-year options that could have moved it into 2018.

"I think we need to memorialize exactly where we are as Corizon is leaving," said the board's chairman, Common Pleas Judge Joseph Williams III, who requested the audit.

Fieldwork for the audit, set to begin Wednesday, will follow the same process as one last year that found continuing problems with the medical care at the jail. An entrance conference with Corizon is scheduled for June 17.

Corizon oversaw an inmate mortality rate here that was double national norms for jails last year. Four inmates have died this year.

County Executive Rich Fitzgerald announced May 22 that the county will bring the jail infirmary operation in-house, but he has yet to name what Judge Williams' called Thursday the "medical giants and universities" set to be involved. In May, the judge said Carnegie Mellon University, the University of Pittsburgh, UPMC and Allegheny Health Network "have agreed that they'll partner in different ways to help us get on track as to where we ought to be with respect to health care" at the jail.

Judge Williams told reporters after the meeting that he wasn't sure how much the new system would cost but was certain it would include more doctors and more psychiatrists and some current staff. The county paid Corizon $11.5 million for its first year running the infirmary.

Also during the meeting, Bret Grote, legal director for the Abolitionist Law Center and other advocates from the Allegheny County Jail Health Justice Project, called for the resignation or firing of jail Warden Orlando Harper. Austin Davis, executive assistant to Mr. Fitzgerald, said the warden has the "full support of our administration."

County Councilman John DeFazio said a public hearing on jail health issues is forthcoming.

AUDIT OF ALLEGHENY COUNTY JAIL HEALTH PROVIDER SAYS MONEY BEING WASTED BY AARON AUPPERLEE

The Allegheny County Jail's medical care provider has "ripped off" taxpayers and put the health of inmates and employees at risk, county Controller Chelsa Wagner said Monday.

The controller's office released a scathing audit of Corizon Health Inc., saying the company failed to comply with a $12 million-a-year contract it signed last year.

Warden Orlando Harper and Corizon fired back, disputing Wagner's claims of unsafe staffing levels, poor clinical and mental health care, unfair labor practices and inmates released without plans for followup care. They called the audit premature and questioned its fairness.

Wagner called their responses "evasive" and said a review in October, more than a year into the contract, showed no progress.

"Corizon Health strongly disagrees with the conclusions in the controller's audit report. The findings are not based in medicine, nor are they balanced, complete or accurate," Corizon spokeswoman Susan Morgenstern said in a statement. "The audit was scheduled at the beginning of the contract, during the 90-day transition period. Typically, there are challenges related to the start-up of any jail health care operation, as issues are being identified and resolved."

Morgenstern said Corizon has provided nursing staffing levels above contract requirements, improved record-keeping, implemented disease management and infection control tools, enhanced clinical services and reduced emergency room visits and hospital stays.

She said it is seeking accreditation and is working with the jail and other service providers to prepare inmates for release.

Harper considered the audit premature. He called it unfair and "not representative of the transition progress which has been made" in a letter sent to Wagner on Dec. 10.

"There's an issue of inmate health. There's an issue of employee health, and then there's an issue of the taxpayers' money," Wagner said. "It's very clear that the taxpayers are being ripped off. We're paying them for services that they are not providing."

Wagner started her audit of Corizon in February, citing reports of substandard care, and examined the first six months of the contract. Corizon, a Tennessee-based health care giant, began offering care at the jail Sept. 1, 2013. It won a five-year contract that could cost the county more than $62.55 million.

The jail has 2,700 inmates.

Marion Damick, the Allegheny County representative for the Pennsylvania Prison Society, said overall conditions at the jail have improved, but problems remain with medical care. Frequent leadership changes have hampered progress. Inmates complain that the medical staff are slow to give medication. Those complaints, however, have grown less over the last few months, Damick said.

"So based on that, you would think that things have gotten better," she said.

Wagner called for the county to penalize Corizon $20,000 for losing the jail's National Commission on Correctional Health Care accreditation, an accreditation required by the contract. Corizon blamed the loss of accreditation on the previous health care provider and said it is working toward re-accreditation.

Allegheny Correctional Health Services Inc. provided health care services to the jail for more than a decade. Six companies bid for the contract when the county asked for proposals early in 2013.

The American Civil Liberties Union urged the county to develop a plan in the next 30 days to address "the widespread and, at the time, life-threatening deficiencies" in jail health care.

NEW HEALTH CARE PROVIDER PICKED FOR OREGON JAIL AFTER AUDIT CRITICIZES CORIZON BY MARK WILSON- PRISON LEGAL NEWS

A Birmingham, Alabama health care company has taken over medical care at the Washington County jail in Hillsboro, Oregon in the wake of a scathing audit that led county officials to terminate a contract with Corizon Health two years early. The audit found that a lack of county oversight of the Corizon contract resulted in inadequate prisoner medical care and cost the county hundreds of thousands of dollars.

Birmingham-based NaphCare, Inc. assumed control over health care at the jail on June 1, 2015 under a contract to provide services to the approximately 570 prisoners at the facility.

"We are eager to embark on this partnership with NaphCare. They are an organization that shares our commitment to value-driven service while providing progressive medical care within our jail," Sheriff Pat Garrett said in a statement.

In addition to selecting a new provider for jail health services, county officials stripped the Washington County Department of Health and Human Services of its responsibility for overseeing the contract, instead appointing the county Finance Department to do so.

A 34-page report issued by County Auditor John Hutzler in November 2014 deliberately avoided directly evaluating the quality of prisoner healthcare at the jail, instead pointing out inadequacies based on what the audit found in the county's monitoring of the Corizon contract.

"Evaluating the quality of care provided to inmates was beyond the scope of this audit, and we express no opinion on the quality of care provided," the report stated. However, it added, "We did review the processes implemented by the contract administrator to monitor quality of care and concluded they did not provide the County with reasonable assurance that quality care was being provided."

News reports published in The Oregonian described lawsuits against the Washington County jail, including one filed by former prisoner Alexander Heap, 34, alleging medical negligence. Heap filed suit in federal court in March 2014 against the county, Corizon and several jail medical workers and guards, claiming he was mistreated during his approximately three-month incarceration at the facility.

His complaint alleged the jail had a defective health care policy, and that jail staff and Corizon were negligent and intentionally inflicted emotional distress by denying and delaying medical treatment.

"This is not unusual behavior at Washington County jail," the complaint said. "The jail does not give inmates or pretrial detainees medical attention when it is needed, instead ignoring inmates' medical issues." Heap settled his lawsuit with Corizon in February 2015. See: Heap v. Wortham, U.S.D.C. (D. Ore.), Case No. 3:14-cv-00105-ST.

In another lawsuit filed in May 2014, former prisoner Marco Antonio Jiminez Ramos claimed he was forced to take the wrong medications while he was held at the Washington County jail over a five-week period starting in mid-March 2013, which caused a myriad of additional health problems. His lawsuit accused jail officials of violating his Fourth, Eighth and Fourteenth Amendment rights.

"Defendants' unlawful acts and omissions caused plaintiff extensive damages, including vomiting blood, defecating blood, loss of appetite, extreme panic attacks, pain and suffering, humiliation, mental and psychiatric problems, anxiety, nervousness, fear, trauma, emotional distress, paranoia, depression, nightmares, and related serious medical needs," the complaint stated. Ramos settled his suit in December 2014. See: Ramos v. Washington County, U.S.D.C. (D. Ore.), Case No. 3:14-cv-00778-BR.

Instead of citing health care inadequacies directly, Hutzler's audit focused on staffing violations that created inadequate conditions at the jail, using a budgetary analysis to make the point. The audit found that Corizon and jail officials had violated the terms of their contract by failing to properly monitor prisoner health care.

"The contract ... required that all jail healthcare services be reviewed and evaluated for quality of care through established and regularly performed audits," the report stated. "We found no evidence that these audits had been performed. Although [Corizon] represented that it had a quality assurance program, it did not report the results of its quality assurance audits to the MAC (Medical Audit Committee) or the contract administrator."

Further, Hutzler cited the contract administrator – an individual he later refused to name – for failing to ensure that Corizon kept an adequate number of qualified employees on duty at the jail during all shifts. As a result, the administrator "did not require the contractor to report staffing in sufficient detail to determine whether staffing specifications were met or whether the staffing actually provided was adequate to ensure quality of care."

Consequently, the audit continued, Corizon was paid for health care services it did not provide. "We estimate the value of the minimum specified staffing that the county didn't receive between July 1, 2008, and June 30, 2012, to be at least $350,000," Hutzler wrote. The county was forced to pay additional costs for outside medical care when Corizon staffers were not on duty.

"Failing to enforce minimum staffing requirements may also have increased other County costs for jail healthcare," the audit stated. When the Medical Director's hours dropped more than five hours below what was required by the contract, "the average number of referrals to external physicians was 42% higher, and the average number of deputy transports for medical care was 48% higher," according to the report. "Deputy transports, and additional hospitalizations, ER visits, external referrals and pharmaceutical expenses resulted in additional costs to the County beyond the contract fee."

The audit further found that the contract with Corizon created cost overruns because it was not administered in accordance with the county's guidelines and best practices, it contained certain terms that did not adequately protect the county's interests, and the county didn't forecast and include sufficient funds in the jail's budget to cover all costs.

Corizon was entitled to a four-year extension of its $8 million two-year contract, but the audit led county officials to cut the extension in half until competitive bids could be sought to improve medical care at the jail.

One condition of Washington County's new contract with NaphCare is that the company is subject to accuracy checks from a third-party auditor who will examine hospital billings. The contract also tightens budgetary controls and health service requirements, and includes specific staffing criteria for day and night shifts at the jail. Such contractual provisions are a good idea considering that NaphCare, a for-profit company, has the same business model as Corizon and thus the same financial incentives to skimp on staffing and medical care for prisoners.

MORE JURISDICTIONS DON'T RENEW CORIZON CONTRACTS – INCLUDING BIG LOSS IN NEW YORK CITY BY GREG DOBER - PRISON LEGAL NEWS OCTOBER, 2015

Recent news for for-profit prison and jail healthcare provider Corizon with respect to contract renewals has not been good. In June 2015, it was announced that two of the company's clients, the New York City jail system – including Rikers Island – and the Allegheny County Jail in Pennsylvania, would not be renewing their contracts with Corizon to provide medical services to prisoners. In both cases, the contracts were not renewed due to issues related to the company's performance.

The jails are at opposite ends of the size spectrum, with Rikers holding approximately 11,000 prisoners and the Allegheny County Jail housing approximately 2,000. Yet Corizon was unable to effectively manage either facility, resulting in the loss of the contracts. Both New York City and Allegheny County chose not to have the contract rebid to any of the other large private medical care providers, such as Centurion, Naphcare or Wexford Health Sources.

Additionally, according to an April 2015 news report, "since 2012, Corizon has lost statewide contracts covering 84,000 inmates in Maine, Maryland, Minnesota and Pennsylvania." [See: *PLN*, March 2014, p.1]. Corizon also lost its contract to provide medical care in Tennessee prisons, while the District of Columbia recently decided not to contract with the company for its jail system and the Florida Department of Corrections is rebidding Corizon's medical care contract following reports of an increasing number of prisoner deaths.

New York City and Rikers Island

On June 10, 2015, New York City Mayor Bill de Blasio announced he would not renew Corizon's contract to provide healthcare at Rikers Island and other city jails; the $126.6 million contract is set to expire on December 31, 2015. According to *DNAinfo New York*, the company's contracts are actually worth over $400 million. Corizon was awarded a $126.6 million contract for management of medical services in the city's jail system. The city also awarded Correctional Medical Associates of NY (CMA of NY) a $270 million contract to provide health care to jail prisoners, and awarded Correctional Dental Associates of NY (CDA of NY) $8.98 million to provide dental care. CMA of NY has the same corporate address as Brentwood, Tennessee-based Corizon, and prior to 2012, CDA of NY was registered as PHS Dental Services, Inc. PHS, or Prison Health Services, was a predecessor to Corizon. [See: *PLN*, July 2015, p.1].

Corizon (and previously PHS) had provided health care at New York City jails since 2001. According to media reports, Corizon is allegedly responsible for over a dozen prisoner deaths due to inadequate treatment. The most recent contract, which was renewed in 2012, was awarded despite poor performance by the company in prior years. Incredibly, New York City officials agreed to indemnify Corizon from lawsuits to induce the firm to renew its contract. The *New York Times* noted that Corey Johnson, a city councilman who held hearings on health care at Rikers in March 2015, said Corizon had been a "failure" and the city's decision to indemnify the company was "unconscionable."

Corizon and government officials often note that health care for prisoners is adequate so long as it meets a basic standard of care. At Rikers, even the basic standard was not always met by Corizon. For example, a 20-year-old prisoner who complained of chest pains and difficulty breathing for several days received no treatment for his condition. The prisoner died of a ruptured aorta. In another case, a 32-year-old prisoner complaining of stomach pain and blood in his stools was not given medical care. Only after other prisoners protested did he receive treatment. However, it came too late and the prisoner died from a bacterial infection.

The worst case of medical neglect at Rikers may be that of Bradley Ballard. Ballard, a diabetic prisoner with severe schizophrenia, was placed in a segregation cell on a mental observation ward on September 4, 2013 for dancing by himself and folding a T-shirt into the shape of a phallic symbol and waving it at a female guard. Little did Ballard realize that such simple, non-violent acts would result in his death at the jail.

Ballard died a week later on September 11, 2013 after he was deprived of insulin and locked in his cell without food or running water, including a working toilet, for several days. The *New York Times* noted that a warden, an assistant deputy warden, guards, doctors, mental health clinicians, nurses and other jail employees made at least 57 visits to Ballard's cell as he slowly deteriorated. Despite his worsening condition, staff did nothing to assist him despite the abhorrent stench of urine and feces emitting from his cell.

Though guards, doctors and other employees were visibly repulsed by the smell, none would help Ballard. When medical personnel finally arrived to remove Ballard from his cell, they handed two prisoner workers a blanket and gloves and instructed them to go in and get him. The prisoners, covering their faces due to the stench, said later that Ballard tried to move but was unable to stand or walk. After he was placed on a gurney and wheeled into the hallway, the medical staff saw that he had tied a rubber band tightly around his genitals, where it had remained unnoticed until the flesh began rotting.

In a subsequent lawsuit filed by Ballard's family, the complaint noted, "Mr. Ballard was clearly on the brink of death, yet he lay neglected on the gurney," and medical staff "held back, unwilling even to touch his body. For an inexcusable period, they continued to stand idly by and do nothing." The complaint also stated that "On June 3, 2014 following an autopsy ... the Medical Examiner declared Mr. Ballard's death a homicide." See: *Griffin v. City of New York,* U.S.D.C. (S.D. NY), Case No. 1:14-cv-07329-NRB.

In June 2015, the New York City Department of Investigations (DOI) released the findings of its review of Corizon's performance. The report focused on mental health clinicians and aides employed by Corizon, and noted alarming gaps in the company's hiring procedures, including criminal background checks. For example, a Corizon records clerk was arrested when he was caught smuggling a straightedge razor into Rikers; investigators from the DOI ran his prints and found he had done a 13-year stint in prison for kidnapping. Another applicant listed as many as 13 prior criminal convictions, but was hired without a detailed explanation regarding the circumstances of the convictions. Other findings by the DOI included failures to adequately check professional licenses, applicant references and prior employment history. The report criticized Corizon for hiring employees who had few qualifications or did not meet minimum qualifications for mental health aide positions. It also faulted the city's Department of Corrections for requiring the company to obtain fingerprint cards from job applicants but failing to process hundreds of the cards over several years.

Corizon's CEO said he "would have preferred to stay in New York," adding, "If at all possible, one day we'd love to get back."

After Corizon's contract expires at the end of the year, medical care for prisoners in New York City's jail system will be provided by the city's public Health and Hospitals Corporation.

Allegheny County Jail

Following eleven deaths within an 18-month period at the Allegheny County Jail in Pittsburgh, Pennsylvania, county executive Rich Fitzgerald announced that the jail's contract with Corizon would not be renewed after expiring at the end of August 2015.

In September 2013, Corizon was awarded a two-year, $23 million contract to provide health care services to prisoners at the Allegheny County Jail. However, problems with the company's performance began almost immediately. A prisoner jumped from a tier at the jail in October 2013 and was severely injured; he was not transported to the hospital until the following day. Within hours of his transfer, he died at the hospital from injuries sustained in the fall. Early on in the contract there were problems related to the proper and timely distribution of medication to prisoners, lack of adequate recordkeeping procedures, and staffing cuts that resulted in fewer registered nurses, physicians and mental health care personnel.

In 2014 the jail recorded seven medical-related deaths, a rate well above the national average for a facility of its size. The inadequate care provided by Corizon resulted in health care workers organizing with the United Steel Workers of America (USW). That process became mired in litigation against Corizon when, in February 2014, a Catholic nun who worked as a registered nurse at the jail was allegedly fired for union organizing activities. Sister Barbara Finch was dismissed after she openly expressed concerns at a meeting regarding patient safety and care. The USW filed an unfair labor complaint against Corizon over Finch's dismissal, and a settlement was eventually reached that allowed her to retain her job. [See: *PLN*, March 2014, p.1].

During the first five months of 2015, four more prisoners died due to health care-related issues. The first was Frank Smart, Jr., 39. Despite telling staff that he needed his seizure medications, Smart was told he would have to wait a few days. He died within 48 hours of his arrival at the jail; according to a medical examiner's report, his death was caused by a seizure disorder and being "physically restrained in [a] prone position." One of Smart's nine children, Tiara Smart, filed a wrongful death suit against Corizon and the county in Common Pleas Court in July 2015.

Allegheny County Controller Chelsa Wagner conducted an audit of Corizon's contract. The audit, released in December 2014, cited 14 areas in which the company allegedly failed to perform contractually-required services, ranging from failure to maintain emergency equipment and inadequate staffing to long delays in providing prisoners with physical exams and medication. [See: *PLN*, March 2015, p.30].

Apparently fed up with the many problems related to Corizon's performance, Allegheny County decided not to renew its contract with the company. As of September 1, 2015, the Allegheny Health Network began providing medical care at the jail.

El Paso and Santa Barbara Counties

At the El Paso County Jail in Texas, Corizon had held the contract for health care services since 2009. However, county officials began negotiations with the University of Texas Health System and the Emergence Health Network of El Paso to provide prisoner medical and mental health services at the facility. Corizon's contract expired and the company was granted a six-month extension until December 31, 2015 to continue to provide medical care for prisoners. The expired contract was worth approximately $8 million per year.

In Santa Barbara County, California, the county's contract with Corizon expired on June 30, 2015. Although jail officials wanted to renew the contract, county commissioners granted only a 4-month extension, putting the $9.8 million annual contract on hold. At issue was deaths of prisoners at the facility, complaints of understaffing and medication shortages.

One of the prisoners who died, Raymond Herrera, 52, was serving 10 days in jail for probation violations. According to a news report, he started having convulsions in his cell in June 2015, then passed out, hit his face against a railing and had another seizure. He was "eventually" taken to a hospital, where he died due to a ruptured spleen caused by cirrhosis of the liver. A local group, Families ACT!, claimed that substandard care by Corizon employees was a contributing factor in Herrera's death.

Conclusion

In a June 2015 interview with The Marshall Project, Corizon CEO Dr. Woodrow Myers noted that losing contracts is part of the business. When asked about contract losses at Rikers Island and in Maine, Minnesota, Pennsylvania and Maryland, Myers replied, "It's a lumpy business, you win some, you lose some."

That attitude may well describe the outcome of the smaller contracts in Allegheny, El Paso and Santa Barbara counties, but for a company that has had its rating repeatedly downgraded by Moody's, a research and risk assessment agency, the loss of the $400 million Rikers Island contract may be more problematic. In Moody's last downgrade of Corizon's bond rating in August 2014, the agency stated, "The rating action reflects the company's continued operating performance weakness and the further deterioration of credit metrics beyond Moody's previous expectations, attributable to recent contract losses, margin declines from competitive pricing pressure on renewed contracts, and delays in the realization of earnings from certain start-up contracts."

Thus, while sometimes "losing some," the loss of the lucrative Rikers contract may become a larger issue for the ratings agency – and a bigger problem for Corizon – than Dr. Myers is willing to acknowledge.

CIVIL LAWSUIT AGAINST CORIZON HEALTH PROVIDER - BY DAVID KLUGH, ANCHOR CHATHAM CO., GA (WTOC)

Another civil lawsuit against the contractor hired to handle all the healthcare needs of inmates at the Chatham County Jail has been filed in Savannah.

This time it involves a non-violent inmate who claims negligence on the part of Corizon Health nurses at the jail, leaving him with permanent injuries.

That inmate says Corizon withheld medication over a period of months that may have saved the company a few hundred dollars, but cost him his eyesight.

Eddie Robinson is a truck driver by trade. Well, he was until he lost sight in his right eye last year. In January, he was brought to the Chatham County Jail on charges of violating his probation for a non-violent crime.

With him came a trucker's medical examination showing that Robinson had 20/20 vision. He only maintained that vision with the help of prednisolone, an eye drop he got a prescription for from Corizon as soon as he arrived at the jail. That's when Robinson's problems began.

"Unfortunately in the first 25 days that he was in the jail, he should have received 100 administrations of his eye drops, four times a day. He got six," says Robinson's attorney, Will Claiborne. "By the time the month of January was over, he was effectively blind in his eye."

Jail records in fact show, the administration rate for Robinson. For the entire month of January, he was prescribed drops four times a day, every day. The record shows he got those 4 drops, just six times.

"I've got a record that says I have to have it four times a day and they said they don't care what the outside doctor says. It's what their boss says," says Robinson.

I also got a hold of an inmate request form Robinson filled out in May, once the sight was gone and the pain had become too much to bare. In it, Robinson complains about not getting his medication and says, "Try the cornea surgery or remove the eye to relieve the burning and the pain. PLEASE."

"The whole time, like I was telling them, I was having headaches. It was like someone was hitting me with a sledgehammer constantly. Because it was that, I had migraines. And they started giving me something for migraines."

"In this country if you get arrested for a crime we don't punish you by cutting off your hand," says Claiborne. "We don't punish you by putting out your eye. We provide constitutionally sufficient healthcare so that individuals don't get further harmed while they're in jail."

Prednisolone is cheap, a few dollars a month. But where Robinson and his attorney believe Corizon really saved money came once the staff finally allowed Robinson to get an outside opinion on his medical issue.

The suit claims doctors at The Georgia Eye Institute determined Robinson needed a cornea transplant, quote, "as soon as possible." He says Corizon saw that as a non-emergency and schedule that transplant surgery several months out, after Robinson was out of jail, and that he says saved the company perhaps tens of thousands of dollars.

"Every penny that they save is a penny that they pocket," insists Claiborne. "And if they can save pennies on eye drops or dimes on pills, unfortunately that appears to be what they do and they don't seem to be concerned about the consequences to real people."

While Corizon Health won't comment on a pending lawsuits, the company's director of External Relations told me:

"It is important to emphasize that a lawsuit is not necessarily indicative of quality of care or any wrongdoing. By their very nature, lawsuits are one-sided documents but we unfortunately are limited by patient privacy laws and the existence of this litigation from providing information that would give you and your viewers important facts about this case. We intend to vigorously defend our care in responding to this legal action."

Thursday, Robinson has had his cornea transplant. While it has relieved the burning and pain of his medical condition, he says it does not relieve the financial stress he now faces having lost his ability to drive a truck for a living.

"Those people in Chatham County that's got family in jail need to constantly check on them as far as their medication," Robinson warns. "Because they're not giving it the way they're supposed to and they really don't give a dern about it."

It helps to know how the contract works when the county hires a company to handle the healthcare for inmates at the jail. In this case, the county pays Corizon $5 million a year. Corizon in turn, pays for all medical care, medicine, surgeries and dental care for those who come to the jail. Whatever Corizon doesn't spend by the end of the year, it gets to keep.

On the surface, it may seem like a system that invites problems like Eddie Robinson's. Corizon might argue it also invites undue criticism that it's putting profits above patients when it insists it is providing quality care to these inmates every day.

CORIZON NEEDS A CHECKUP: PROBLEMS WITH PRIVATIZED CORRECTIONAL HEALTHCARE BY GREG DOBER PUBLISHED - PRISON LEGAL NEWS MARCH, 2014

Corizon, the nation's largest for-profit medical services provider for prisons, jails and other detention facilities, was formed in June 2011 through the merger of Prison Health Services (PHS) and Correctional Medical Services(CMS).

In April 2013, the debt-rating agency Moody's downgraded Corizon's nearly $360 million worth of debt to a rating of B2 – an indication the company's debt is highly speculative and a high credit risk. According to Moody's, the rating downgrade was due to an "expectation of earnings volatility following recent contract losses, margin declines from competitive pricing pressure on new and renewed contracts, and Moody's belief that Valitás [Corizon's parent corporation] will be unable to restore metrics to levels commensurate with the prior B1 rating over the near to intermediate term."

Valitás Health Services is majority owned by Beecken Petty O'Keefe & Company, a Chicago-based private equity management firm. Beecken's other holdings are primarily in the healthcare industry.

On September 23, 2013, Moody's again downgraded Corizon's debt rating and changed the company's rating outlook from "stable" to "negative." The following month Corizon announced that it had replaced CEO

Rich Hallworth with Woodrow A. Myers, Jr., the former chief medical officer at WellPoint Health. Hallworth, who had been appointed Corizon's CEO in 2011, previously served as the president and CEO of PHS. At the same time that Hallworth was replaced, Corizon president Stuart Campbell also stepped down.

Prison Medical Care for Profit

According to Corizon's website, the company provides healthcare services at over 530 correctional facilities serving approximately 378,000 prisoners in 28 states. In addition, Corizon employs around 14,000 staff members and contractors. The company's corporate headquarters is located in Brentwood, Tennessee and its operational headquarters is in St. Louis, Missouri.

The 2011 merger that created Corizon involved Valitás Health Services, the parent company of CMS, and America Service Group, the parent company of PHS. The Nashville Business Journal reported the deal was valued at $250 million.

"Corizon's vision is firmly centered around service – to our clients, our patients and our employees," Campbell said at the time. "To that we add the insight of unparalleled experience assisting our client partners, and caring professionals serving the unique healthcare needs of [incarcerated] patients."

Corizon has around $1.5 billion in annual revenue and contracts to provide medical services for the prison systems in 13 states. The company also contracts with numerous cities and counties to provide healthcare to prisoners held in local jails; some of Corizon's larger municipal clients include Atlanta, Philadelphia and New York City (including the Rikers Island jail). Additionally, the company has its own in-house pharmacy division, PharmaCorr, Inc.

The prison healthcare market has flourished as state Departments of Corrections and local governments seek ways to save money and reduce exposure to litigation. [See: PLN, May 2012, p.22]. Only a few major companies dominate the industry. Corizon's competitors include Wexford Health Sources, Armor Correctional Health Services, NaphCare, Correct Care Solutions and Centurion Managed Care – the latter being a joint venture of MHM Services and Centene Corporation. Around 20 states outsource all or some of the medical services in their prison systems.

As Corizon is privately held, there is little transparency with respect to its internal operations and financial information, including costs of litigation when prisoners (or their surviving family members) sue the company, often alleging inadequate medical care.

For example, when Corizon was questioned by the news media in Florida during a contract renewal, the company initially tried to prevent the release of its litigation history, claiming it was a "trade secret."

In 2012, Corizon agreed to settle a lawsuit filed against PHS – one of its predecessor companies – by Prison Legal News, seeking records related to the resolution of legal claims against the firm in Vermont. Based on the records produced pursuant to that settlement, PHS paid out almost $1.8 million in just six cases involving Vermont prisoners from 2007 to 2011. [See: PLN, Dec. 2012, p.16].

Companies like Corizon provide healthcare in prisons and jails under the HMO model, with an emphasis on cutting costs – except that prisoners have no other options to obtain medical treatment except through the contractor.

Arizona Department of Corrections

A former Corizon nurse had her license suspended and is currently under investigation by the Arizona State Board of Nursing for incompetence. In January 2014, nurse Patricia Talboy was accused of contaminating vials of insulin at three units at the ASPC-Lewis prison, potentially exposing two dozen prisoners to HIV or hepatitis.

Talboy reportedly used a needle to stick prisoners' fingers to check their blood sugar levels. She then used the same needle to draw insulin from vials of the medication utilized for multiple prisoners, possibly contaminating the insulin in the vials. After placing the vials back into inventory, other staff members may have unknowingly used them to dispense insulin.

"Every indication is that the incident is the result of the failure by one individual nurse to follow specific, standard and well-established nursing protocols when dispensing injected insulin to 24 inmates," Arizona Department of Corrections (ADC) director Charles L. Ryan said in a January 9, 2014 statement.

Talboy's failure to follow procedures was discovered after a prisoner told a different nurse about the issue. Corizon reportedly delayed three days before publicly reporting the incident; in a press release, the company admitted that one of its nurses had been involved in "improper procedures for injections." Talboy received her nursing license in August 2012 and became an RN in June 2013; as a rookie nurse, Corizon likely paid her less than more experienced nurses.

Following the insulin-related incident, the company was ordered to develop a comprehensive plan that includes "supplemental training and competency testing procedures for blood glucose testing and administration of insulin," as well as "nurse-peer reporting education to ensure professional accountability" and "patient awareness education on injection protocols."

Granted, Corizon isn't alone with respect to such incidents. In August 2012, a nurse employed by the ADC's previous medical services contractor, Wexford Health Sources, contaminated the insulin supply at ASPC-Lewis through improper injection protocols, potentially exposing 112 prisoners to hepatitis C. [See: PLN, July 2013, p.1].

Corizon has a three-year, approximately $370 million contract to provide medical care in Arizona state prisons, which began in March 2013. The contract award generated controversy because former ADC director Terry Stewart was hired by Corizon as a consultant; current director Charles Ryan had previously worked under Stewart, raising a potential conflict of interest. Ryan denied any improprieties.

According to a report by the American Friends Service Committee released in October 2013, titled "Death Yards: Continuing Problems with Arizona's Correctional Health Care," medical services in Arizona prisons did not improve after Corizon replaced Wexford as the ADC's healthcare contractor. "Correspondence from prisoners; analysis of medical records, autopsy reports, and investigations; and interviews with anonymous prison staff and outside experts indicate that, if anything, things have gotten worse," the report stated.

Florida Department of Corrections

In 2013, the Florida Department of Corrections (FDOC) awarded Corizon a five-year, $1.2 billion contract to provide medical services to state prisoners in north and central Florida. Wexford Health Sources was contracted to provide similar services in the southern region of the state for $240 million. [See: PLN, June 2013, p.24]. The wholesale privatization of healthcare in Florida's prison system followed a 2011 legislative decision to disband the state's Correctional Medical Authority, which had oversight over prison medical care. [See: PLN, May 2012, p.30].

The contracts were part of the Republican administration's initiative to expand privatization of government services, including prison management and healthcare, in spite of previous setbacks. In 2006, PHS withdrew two months into an almost $800 million contract to provide medical care to Florida prisoners; at that time, the company said the contract was not cost-effective and claimed it would lose money.

The 2013 contract awards to Corizon and Wexford followed a two-year legal fight. In 2011, AFSCME Florida and the Federation of Physicians and Dentists/Alliance of Healthcare and Professional Employees filed suit challenging the prison healthcare contracts, in an effort to protect the jobs of nearly 2,600 state workers.

On June 21, 2013 the First District Court of Appeals approved the privatization of medical care in FDOC facilities, overturning a ruling by the Leon County Circuit Court. The appellate court noted in its decision that "The LBC [Legislative Budget Committee] simply moved funds from different line items within the Department's Health Services' program, providing additional funds for contracts that the Department otherwise had the authority to enter." See: Crews v. Florida Public Employers Council 79, 113 So.3d 1063 (Fla. Dist. Ct. App. 1st Dist. 2013).

Under the terms of the FDOC's contract with Corizon, the company must provide medical care to Florida state prisoners for 7% less than it cost the FDOC in 2010. When entering into the contract, state officials apparently had few concerns about the numerous lawsuits previously filed against Corizon, and no hard feelings toward the company's predecessor, PHS, when it terminated its 2006 contract to provide medical services to Florida prisoners because it wasn't profitable.

"Most people feel, as long as they achieve their 7 percent savings who cares how they treat inmates?" noted Michael Hallett, a professor of criminology at the University of North Florida.

Florida Counties

In a September 6, 2012 unpublished ruling, the Eleventh Circuit Court of Appeals affirmed a $1.2 million Florida jury verdict that found Corizon – when it was operating as PHS – had a policy or custom of refusing to send prisoners to hospitals. The Court of Appeals held it was reasonable for jurors to conclude that PHS had delayed medical treatment in order to save money. See: Fields v. Corizon Health, 490 Fed.Appx. 174 (11th Cir. 2012).

The jury verdict resulted from a suit filed against Corizon by former prisoner Brett A. Fields, Jr. In July 2007, Fields was being held in the Lee County, Florida jail on two misdemeanor convictions. After notifying PHS staff for several weeks that an infection was not improving, even with antibiotics that had been prescribed, Fields was diagnosed with MRSA. PHS did not send him to a hospital despite escalating symptoms, including uncontrolled twitching, partial paralysis and his intestines protruding from his rectum. A subsequent MRI scan revealed that Fields had a severe spinal compression; he was left partly paralyzed due to inadequate medical care.

The Eleventh Circuit wrote that PHS "enforced its restrictive policy against sending prisoners to the hospital," and noted that a PHS nurse who treated Fields at the jail "testified that, at monthly nurses' meetings, medical supervisors 'yelled a lot about nurses sending inmates to hospitals.'" Further, PHS "instructed nurses to be sure that the inmate had an emergency because it cost money to send inmates to the hospital."

At trial, the jury found that PHS had a custom or policy of deliberate indifference that violated Fields' constitutional right to be free from cruel and unusual punishment. The jurors concluded that Fields had a serious medical need, PHS was deliberately indifferent to that serious medical need, and the company's actions proximately caused Fields' injuries. The jury awarded him $700,000 in compensatory damages and $500,000 in punitive damages. [See: PLN, March 2013, p.54; Aug. 2011, p.24].

More recently, the estate of a 21-year-old prisoner who died at a jail in Manatee County, Florida filed a lawsuit in October 2013 against the Manatee County Sheriff's Office and Corizon, the jail's healthcare provider. The complaint accuses the defendants of deliberate indifference to the serious medical needs of Jovon Frazier and violating his rights under the Eighth Amendment.

In February 2009, Frazier was incarcerated at the Manatee County Jail; at the time of his medical intake screening, staff employed by Corizon, then operating as PHS, noted that his health was unremarkable. Frazier submitted a medical request form in July 2009, complaining of severe pain in his left shoulder and arm, and a PHS nurse gave him Tylenol.

Throughout August and September 2009, Frazier submitted five more medical requests seeking treatment for his arm and shoulder. "It really hurts! HELP!" he wrote in one of the requests. PHS employees saw him and recorded his vital signs. Despite the repeated complaints, Frazier was never referred to a doctor or physician assistant; on September 9, 2009 his treatment was documented as routine but he was placed on the "MD's list."

An X-ray was taken on September 17, 2009 to rule out a shoulder fracture. The X-ray was negative for a fracture, and Frazier was not referred to a doctor. He submitted two more medical requests that month and five requests in October 2009 seeking treatment for his increasingly painful condition. The complaint alleges that in total, Frazier submitted 13 medical request forms related to pain over a period of three months; he was seen by a nurse each time but not examined by a physician.

On October 29, 2009, Frazier received an X-ray to determine if he had a tendon injury. An MRI was recommended and he was transported to a hospital where an MRI scan revealed a large soft tissue mass on his shoulder. A doctor at the hospital, concerned that the mass was cancerous, recommended additional tests.

After being diagnosed with osteosarcoma, a form of bone cancer, Frazier was returned to the jail and subsequently treated at the Moffitt Cancer Center, where he received chemotherapy, medication and surgery. Despite this aggressive treatment the cancer progressed and Frazier's left arm was amputated. The cancer continued to spread, however, and he was diagnosed with lung cancer in June 2011. He died within three months of that diagnosis, on September 18, 2011.

In a letter to the attorney representing Frazier's estate, Florida oncologist Howard R. Abel wrote that the lack of treatment provided by Corizon at the Manatee County Jail constituted "gross negligence and a reckless disregard to Mr. Frazier's right to timely and professionally appropriate medical care."

The lawsuit filed by Frazier's estate claims that Corizon was aware of his serious medical condition but failed to provide adequate treatment. In addition, the complaint contends the company has a widespread custom, policy and practice of discouraging medical staff from referring prisoners to outside medical practitioners and from providing expensive medical tests and procedures. Finally, the lawsuit states that "Corizon implemented these widespread customs, policies and practices for financial reasons and in deliberate indifference to [the] serious medical needs of Frazier and other inmates incarcerated at Manatee County Jail."

On January 10, 2014, U.S. District Court Judge James Moody denied Corizon's motion to dismiss the case. The company had argued that the allegations in the lawsuit failed to assert sufficient facts to establish deliberate indifference, amounted only to medical negligence and were insufficient to establish gross negligence, and failed "to adequately allege a policy or custom that violated Frazier's rights." Judge Moody disagreed, finding the claims set forth in the complaint were "sufficient to establish a constitutional violation."

The Manatee County Sheriff's Office had better luck with its motion to dismiss. The Sheriff argued the complaint did not establish facts indicating that the jail had a similar practice – like Corizon – of providing deliberately indifferent medical care to prisoners. The court agreed and dismissed the claims against the Sheriff's Office; the claims against Corizon remain pending. See: Jenkins v. Manatee County Sheriff, U.S.D.C. (M.D. Fla.),

Case No. 8:13-cv-02796-JSM-TGW.

Idaho Department of Corrections

In February 2013, the Idaho Department of Corrections (IDOC) announced it had reached a one-year extended agreement with Corizon to provide medical care in the state's prison system. However, the Idaho Business Review reported that the extension also resulted in a rate increase. Then-Corizon president Stuart Campbell informed the IDOC Board of Correction that the company wouldn't sign an extension for less money, stating the current contract had become too costly. During the preceding three years of the contract the IDOC had incurred approximately 20% in cumulative rate increases.

Both sides agreed that the contract would run through December 2013 and the IDOC would pay an additional $250,000. It seems odd that Idaho was willing to continue contracting with the company, though, as the relationship between the IDOC and Corizon has been a rocky one.

The quality of medical care at the Idaho State Correctional Institution (ISCI) in Boise has been an ongoing issue for nearly three decades. The prison was the focus of a class-action lawsuit filed on behalf of prisoners alleging a variety of problems, including inadequate healthcare. The lawsuit was known as the Balla litigation after plaintiff Walter Balla.

In July 2011, after new complaints were filed regarding medical care at ISCI, U.S District Court Judge B. Lynn Winmill appointed a special master, Dr. Marc F. Stern, to assess the situation at the facility. The court wanted Stern to confirm whether ISCI was in compliance with the temporary agreements established in the Balla case, and to investigate and report on "the constitutionality of healthcare" at the facility.

Dr. Stern, a former health services director for the Washington Department of Corrections who also had previously worked for CMS, one of Corizon's predecessor companies, issued a scathing report in February 2012.

With the aid of psychiatrist Dr. Amanda Ruiz, Stern and his team reviewed ISCI over a six-day period and met with dozens of prisoners, administrators and Corizon employees.

Stern stated in the report's executive summary: "I found serious problems with the delivery of medical and mental health care. Many of these problems have either resulted or risk resulting in serious harm to prisoners at ISCI. In multiple ways, these conditions violate the rights of prisoners at ISCI to be protected from cruel and unusual punishment. Since many of these problems are frequent, pervasive, long-standing, and authorities are or should have been aware of them, it is my opinion that authorities are deliberately indifferent to the serious health care needs of their charges."

The report found that prisoners who were terminally ill or in long-term care were sometimes left in soiled linens, given inadequate pain medication and went for long periods without food or water. The findings regarding sick call noted instances in which prisoners' requests either resulted in no care, delayed care or treatment that was deemed dangerous. Emergency care situations had insufficient oversight, delays or no response; inadequately trained medical staff operated independently during emergencies without oversight from an RN or physician. The report also found problems with the pharmacy and medication distribution at ISCI.

In one case, a prisoner with a "history of heart disease was inexplicably dropped from the rolls of the heart disease Chronic Care Clinic." As a result, medical staff stopped conducting regular check-ups and assessments related to the prisoner's heart condition. A few years later the prisoner went in for a routine visit, complaining of occasional chest pain. No evaluation or treatment was ordered and the prisoner died four days later due to a heart attack. In another case, Corizon staff failed to notify a prisoner for seven months that an X-ray indicated he might have cancer.

Dr. Stern's report not only reviewed processes but also staff competency and adequacy. The report cited allegations that a dialysis nurse at ISCI overtly did not like prisoners, and routinely "failed to provide food and water to patients during dialysis, prematurely aborted dialysis sessions or simply did not provide them [dialysis] at all and failed to provide ordered medications resulting in patients becoming anemic." Stern concluded that prison officials were aware of this issue and the danger it presented to prisoners, but "unduly delayed taking action."

The mental health care provided by Corizon at ISCI was found to be deficient by Dr. Ruiz, who conducted the psychiatric portion of the court-ordered review. The report noted that the facility had 1) inadequate "screening of and evaluating prisoners to identify those in need of mental health care," 2) "significant deficiencies in the treatment program at ISCI" which was "violative of patients' constitutional right to health care," 3) an "insufficient number of psychiatric practitioners at ISCI," 4) incomplete or inaccurate treatment records, 5) problems with psychotropic medications, which were prescribed with no face-to-face visits or follow-up visits with prisoners and 6) inadequate suicide prevention training.

The report concluded: "The state of guiding documents, the inmate grievance system, death reviews and a mental health CQI [continuous quality improvement] system at ISCI is poor. While not in and of themselves unconstitutional, it is important for the court to be aware of this and its possible contribution to other unconstitutional events."

In March 2012, shortly after Dr. Stern's report was released over the objection of state officials, Corizon disagreed with its findings. The company retained the National Commission on Correctional Health Care (NCCHC) to review the report. Corizon described the review as an "independent assessment," even though it was paying NCCHC accreditation fees.

The NCCHC review consisted of a three-person team assessing the facility over a two-day period in April 2012. Unlike Stern's assessment of medical and mental health care, the NCCHC team did not interview prisoners or include a psychiatrist. Regardless, the agency concluded that "The basic structure of health services delivery at ISCI meets NCCHC's standards."

Corizon stated in a press release that Dr. Stern's report was "incomplete, misleading and erroneous," and then-CEO Rich Hallworth appeared in a video defending the company. The NCCHC had previously accredited Corizon's healthcare services at ISCI, thus in essence the NCCHC's review was self-validating the organization's prior accreditation findings. Also, according to NCCHC's website, two Corizon officials sit on the agency's health professionals certification board of trustees.

Corizon's criticism of Dr. Stern's report is just one example where the company has objected to an independent, third-party assessment of its medical services. The Balla case settled in May 2012 after 30 years of litigation. [See: PLN, Feb. 2013, p.40].

Indiana Department of Corrections

Following a competitive bidding process, Corizon was selected to continue providing medical care to Indiana state prisoners under a three-year contract effective January 1, 2014. The contract has a cap of $293 million, based on a per diem fee of $9.41 per prisoner.

Three weeks later, a lawsuit filed in federal court named Corizon and the Indiana Department of Correction as defendants in connection with the wrongful death of prisoner Rachel Wood. Wood, 26, a first-time drug offender, died in April 2012; the suit, filed on behalf of her family, claims she was transferred from prison to prison and denied care for her serious medical conditions, which included lupus and a blood clotting disorder.

"Notwithstanding the duty of the prison medical staff to provide adequate medical care to Rachel and to treat her very serious life threatening conditions, prison medical staff willfully and callously disregarded her condition, and allowed Rachel to deteriorate and die," the complaint stated.

"That is just the attitude of these guys, is saving money rather than providing health care," said Michael K. Sutherlin, the attorney representing Wood's family.

Prison officials reportedly moved Wood among several different prisons and hospitals, and at one point lost track of her and claimed she had escaped even though she was still incarcerated.

"She died a horrible death and she died alone," stated her father, Claude Wood. The lawsuit remains pending. See: Williams v. Indiana DOC, Marion County Superior Court (IN), Case No. 49D05-1401-CT-001478.

Maine Department of Corrections

In an October 2013 Bangor Daily News article, Steve Lewicki, coordinator of the Maine Prisoner Advocacy Coalition, discussed the state of healthcare in Maine's prison system. "Complaints by prisoners are less," he said, noting that while medical services provided to prisoners are better than in the past, there are still concerns. This relative improvement coincided with the end of the state's contract with Corizon. The contract, valued at approximately $19.5 million, was awarded to another company in 2012.

A year earlier, the Maine legislature's Office of Program Evaluation and Government Accountability (OPEGA) completed a review of medical services in state prisons. The agency contracted with an independent consultant, MGT of America, to conduct most of the fieldwork, and the review included services provided under Corizon's predecessor company, CMS.

The OPEGA report, issued in November 2011, cited various deficiencies in medical care at Maine prisons – including medications not always being properly administered and recorded by CMS staff. Although the company was notified of the problem, no corrective action was taken. CMS employees did not follow policies related to medical intake and medical records; OPEGA reported that 38% of prisoners' medical files had inadequate or inaccurate documentation regarding annual physical assessments, and that files were not complete or consistently maintained. The report found 11% of sick calls reviewed were either not resolved timely or had no documented resolution. OPEGA also criticized CMS for inadequate staff training.

At a January 2012 legislative committee hearing, state Senator Roger Katz asked Corizon regional vice president Larry Amberger, "My question to you is in light of this history, why should the state seriously be considering any proposal your company might make to get this contract back again?"

In response, Amberger criticized the methodology used by MGT during the assessment and said he believed Corizon provided quality medical care. Questioning and challenging the findings of an independent reviewer is the same tactic the company used in Idaho. Regardless, Corizon's contract to provide medical care to Maine state prisoners is now a part of history.

Louisville, Kentucky

While some jurisdictions, like Maine, have chosen not to renew their contracts with Corizon due to performance-related problems, in 2013 the Metro Department of Corrections in Louisville, Kentucky (LMC) offered the company a chance to rebid for its $5.5 million contract to provide medical care at the LMC jail. This time, however, it was Corizon that said "no thanks."

The rebid offer was made even though seven healthcare-related prisoner deaths occurred in a seven-month period in 2012 during Corizon's prior contract, which expired in February 2013. Nevertheless, LMC and Corizon agreed to extend the contract through July 30, 2013 on a month-to-month basis pending a formal rebid.

After the expiration of the month-to-month contract extension, Corizon notified LMC that it was no longer interested in providing services to the corrections department and would not seek to rebid the contract. LMC director Mark Bolton told the Courier Journal he was "surprised" by the company's decision. What seems more surprising is that LMC wanted to continue contracting with Corizon to provide medical services in spite of the number of prisoner deaths.

In April 2012, Savannah Sparks, 27, a heroin addict and mother of three, was arrested and held on shoplifting charges at the LMC jail. While withdrawing from heroin she vomited, sweat profusely, could not sit up, could not eat or drink, and defecated and urinated on herself. Six days later she was dead. According to the medical examiner, her death was due to "complications of chronic substance abuse with withdrawal."

A subsequent wrongful death suit alleged that Corizon and LMC employees were negligent in failing to provide treatment for Sparks' opiate addiction and withdrawal. Corizon settled the suit under confidential terms. See: May v. Corizon, Jefferson County Circuit Court (KY), Case No. 13-CI-001848.

Four months after Sparks' death, on August 8, 2012, another LMC prisoner, Samantha George, died. A lawsuit filed in Jefferson County Circuit Court claimed that George was moved from the Bullitt County Jail to the LMC facility on a charge of buying a stolen computer. According to the complaint, she told a Corizon nurse that she was a severe diabetic, needed insulin, and was feverish and in pain from a MRSA infection.

The nurse notified an on-call Corizon physician, who was not located at the facility and thus could not examine George in person, to decide if she should be taken to an emergency room. The doctor recommended monitoring George and indicated he would see her the next day. George's condition rapidly deteriorated while she was monitored by staff at the jail; she was found unresponsive a few hours after being admitted to the facility and pronounced dead a short time later.

An autopsy concluded that George died due to complications from a severe form of diabetes compounded by heart disease. According to the lawsuit, the Corizon doctor never saw George; among other defendants, the suit named Corizon and LMC director Mark Bolton as defendants. The case was removed to federal court, then remanded to the county circuit court in October 2013. See: George v. Corizon, U.S.D.C. (W.D. Ky.), Case No. 3:13-cv-00822-JHM-JDM.

A few weeks after George's death, Kenneth Cross was booked into the LMC jail on a warrant for drug possession. According to a subsequent lawsuit, upon Cross' arrival at the jail a nurse documented that he had slurred speech and fell asleep numerous times during the medical interview. Several hours later he was found unconscious, then died shortly thereafter due to a drug overdose. The lawsuit filed by Cross' estate alleged that employees at the LMC jail were deficient in recognizing and treating prisoners' substance abuse problems and that the facility was inadequately staffed for such medical care.

After the deaths of Sparks, George, Cross and four other prisoners in 2012, LMC director Bolton said he believed Corizon took too long to evaluate and treat prisoners at the jail. According to the Courier-Journal, Bolton sent an email to his staff in December 2012 regarding the prisoners' deaths, stating, "Mistakes were made by Corizon personnel and their corporation has acknowledged such missteps." He further indicated that Corizon employees – not LMC staff members – were responsible for the care of the prisoners who died. Six Corizon employees at the LMC jail resigned in December 2012 during an internal investigation; they were not identified.

Bolton's criticism was too little, too late to prevent the deaths of the seven LMC prisoners, though the jail has since made improvements to its medical services, including a full-time detox nurse and new protocols for prisoners experiencing withdrawal. One could speculate that LMC's critique of Corizon might be a litigation tactic, to deflect responsibility. The fact remains that seven deaths occurred under Corizon's watch and, notwithstanding those deaths, LMC was willing to renew its contract with the company.

In January 2014, the Louisville Metro Police's Public Integrity Unit concluded investigations into three of the deaths at the jail, and criticized both Corizon and LMC. The Commonwealth Attorney's Office found that Sparks' and George's deaths were preventable; however, no criminal charges were filed. Dr. William Smock, a forensic examiner who served as a consultant during the investigations, stated with respect to George's death: "There is compelling evidence of a significant deviation from the standard of care and medical negligence on the part of the medical providers."

"I'm glad to see that the government's investigation matches exactly what our investigation showed, which is that her death and others like hers is easily preventable," said Chad McCoy, the attorney representing George's estate.

Minnesota Department of Corrections

After providing medical care to Minnesota state prisoners for 15 years, Corizon was not selected when the contract was rebid in 2013 – despite having submitted the lowest bid. Instead, competitor Centurion Managed Care was to begin providing healthcare services in Minnesota's prison system effective January 1, 2014 under a two-year, $67.5 million contract.

Corrections Commissioner Tom Roy said the contract with Centurion was expected to "deliver significant savings to taxpayers while improving the quality of care for offenders."

According to the Star-Tribune, nine prisoners died and another 21 suffered serious or critical injuries in Minnesota correctional facilities due to delay or denial of medical care under the state's previous contract, which had been held by Corizon or its predecessor, CMS, since 1998.

That contract was for a fixed annual flat fee of $28 million. A flat fee contract provides an incentive for the contractor to tightly control costs, as a reduction in expenses results in an increase in profit. The Star-Tribune found that many of the staffing arrangements negotiated in the contract played a role in the deaths and injuries. For example, the contract allowed Corizon physicians to leave at 4:00pm daily and did not require them to work weekends. During off-hours there was only one doctor on call to serve the state's entire prison system, and many of the off-hour consultations were done telephonically without the benefit of the prisoner's medical chart. Under the contract, Corizon was not required to staff most facilities overnight.

The Minnesota Department of Corrections was held liable for nearly $1.8 million in wrongful death and medical negligence cases during the period when the state contracted with Corizon or CMS.

In October 2012, a jury in Washington County awarded Minnesota prisoner Stanley Riley more than $1 million after finding a Corizon contract physician, Stephen J. Craane, was negligent in providing medical treatment. The Star-Tribune reported that Riley suffered from what turned out to be cancer and had written a series of pleading notes to prison officials. One read, "I assure you that I am not a malingerer. I only want to be healthy again."

In May 2013, the state paid $400,000 to settle a lawsuit over the death of a 27-year-old prisoner at MCF-Rush City. Xavius Scullark-Johnson, a schizophrenic, suffered at least seven seizures in his cell on June 28, 2010. Nurses and guards didn't provide him with medical care for nearly eight hours. According to documents obtained by the Star-Tribune, Scullark-Johnson was found "soaked in urine on the floor of his cell" and was "coiled in a fetal position and in an altered state of consciousness that suggested he had suffered a seizure." An ambulance was called several hours later but a nurse at the prison turned it away, apparently due to protocols to cut costs. Corizon settled the lawsuit for an undisclosed sum in June 2013. See: Scullark v. Garin, U.S.D.C. (D. Minn.), Case No. 0:12-cv-01505-RHK-FLN.

Philadelphia, Pennsylvania

In Philadelphia, Mayor Michael A. Nutter has been accused of being too loyal to his campaign contributors, including Corizon. The company donated $1,000 to Nutter's 2012 campaign committee several months before the city renewed Corizon's contract to provide medical care to 9,000 prisoners in Philadelphia's prison system. Further, PHS donated $5,000 to Nutter's mayoral campaign in 2008.

The contract renewal would have been routine except for the fact that Corizon's performance in Philadelphia has been far from stellar. In July 2012 the company agreed to pay the city $1.85 million following an investigation that found Corizon was using a minority-owned subcontractor that did no work, which was a sham to meet the city's requirements for contracting with minority-owned businesses.

The renewed year-to-year Corizon contract, worth $42 million, began in March 2013. Nutter's administration was accused of using the year-to-year arrangement to avoid having the contract scrutinized by the city council; the city's Home Rule Charter requires all contracts of more than one year to be reviewed by the council. Further infuriating opponents of the contract, Corizon was not the lowest bidder. Correctional Medical Care (CMC), a competitor, submitted a bid that would have cost the city $3.5 million less per year than Corizon. Philadelphia Prison Commissioner Louis Giorla defended the city's decision to award the contract to Corizon at a council hearing; however, he declined to answer questions as to why the administration considered Corizon's level of care to be superior to that provided by CMC.

Three union contracts with Corizon covering 270 of the company's workers in Philadelphia's prison system expired on November 26, 2013. Corizon demanded benefit cuts, including changes in employee healthcare programs, to offset wage increases promised under the company's contract with the city. A strike was averted in December 2013 when the mayor's office intervened and both sides reached a settlement. The Philadelphia Daily News reported that the new union contracts provide wage increases but also include a less-generous health insurance plan for Corizon employees.

Since 1995, Corizon and its predecessor, PHS, have received $196 million in city contracts. The company's contract was terminated for several months in 2002 as a result of complaints that a diabetic prisoner had died after failing to receive insulin. The city renewed the contract anyway, citing affordability and pledging increased oversight. The city's law department estimates that Philadelphia has paid over $1 million to settle lawsuits involving claims of deficient prison healthcare; the largest settlement to date is $300,000, paid to a prisoner who did not receive eye surgery and is now partially blind.

Based upon the number of lawsuits filed against Corizon alleging inadequate medical care, its use of a sham subcontractor and the company's treatment of its own employees, it appears that maintaining the status quo – not best practices – may be the controlling factor in Philadelphia's continued relationship with Corizon.

Allegheny County, Pennsylvania

On September 30, 2013, a prisoner jumped from the top tier of a pod at the Allegheny County Jail. Following an investigation, authorities refused to make public their findings and declined to disclose the prisoner's injuries, citing medical privacy laws. The prisoner, Milan Karan, 38, was not transported to the hospital until the following day.

A spokesperson for Corizon, which provides medical care at the 2,500-bed jail, defended the nearly 24-hour delay by noting the prisoner "was under observation" before being sent to a hospital.

In December 2013, the Pittsburgh Post-Gazette reported that Corizon was having difficulty staffing the Allegheny County Jail. When the newspaper requested a comment from Corizon vice president Lee Harrington,

Harrington claimed he had no knowledge of staffing problems – despite having previously received emails from the facility's warden about that exact issue.

The staffing problems resulted in prisoners not receiving their medication in a timely manner. In emails obtained by the Post-Gazette, Warden Orlando Harper wrote to Harrington in October 2013, noting, "We are continuing to experience issues pertaining to the following: 1. Staffing, 2. Medication distribution." Also, on November 17, 2013, Deputy Warden Monica Long sent an email to Corizon and jail staff. "I was just informed by the Captain on shift, the majority of the jail has not received medication AT ALL," she stated, adding, "Staffing is at a crisis."

That crisis had been ongoing since Corizon assumed the medical services contract at the facility on September 1, 2013. Before the $62.55 million, five-year contract was awarded, Corizon vice president Mary Silva wrote in an email that it was imperative the jail have "adequate staffing on ALL shifts." That promise was made despite Corizon laying off many of the former employees of Allegheny Correctional Health Services, the jail's previous healthcare provider.

Allegheny Correctional had provided four full-time and one part-time physician during its contract tenure. Corizon reduced the number of doctors to one full-time and one part-time physician. Allegheny Correctional also employed three psychiatrists and one psychologist. Corizon's contract requires that it provide one full-time psychiatrist and a part-time psychologist.

In January 2014, the United Steelworkers union (USW) filed a petition with the National Labor Relations Board to unionize Corizon employees at the Allegheny County Jail, including nurse practitioners, RNs, physician assistants and psychiatric nurses. USW representative Randa Ruge indicated that the Corizon workers had approached the union for representation due to intolerable working conditions.

"Our folks [Corizon employees] are in danger of losing their licenses to practice by some of the things that the company has them doing," she said. Ruge told the Post-Gazette that the jail had run out of insulin for more than a week and Corizon supervisors had "countermanded doctors' orders.

Several weeks after the USW filed the labor petition, a Catholic nun who worked as an RN at the jail was fired by Corizon, allegedly for union organizing activities. Sister Barbara Finch was dismissed after she openly expressed concerns about staffing, patient care and safety at the facility. The USW filed an unfair labor complaint against Corizon regarding Finch's dismissal, claiming she was terminated in retaliation for her union activities.

"This is a clear case of intimidation and union-busting at its worst," said USW President Leo W. Gerard. "Sister Barbara has been an outspoken advocate of change for these courageous workers and their patients, and this kind of illegal and unjust action, unfortunately, is par for the course with Corizon."

On February 14, 2014, Corizon employees at the Allegheny County Jail voted overwhelmingly to unionize. "The next step is getting to the bargaining table and getting Corizon to bargain in good faith and get some changes made in the health system at the jail," said Ruge.

The previous week, Allegheny County Controller Chelsa Wagner stated she had "grave and serious concerns" about medical care at the facility, including issues related to staffing and treatment for prisoners with certain mental health conditions. "I regard the current situation as intolerable and outrageous, and I fully expect necessary changes to be urgently implemented," she wrote in a letter to Corizon.

Polk County, Iowa

On August 29, 2013, Ieasha Lenise Meyers, incarcerated at the jail in Polk County, Iowa on a probation violation, gave birth on a mattress on the floor of her cell. Her cellmates assisted with the delivery. Earlier, when Meyers, 25, had complained of contractions, a Corizon nurse called an offsite medical supervisor and was told to monitor the contractions and check for water breaking.

Despite Meyers having been twice sent to a hospital earlier the same day, and pleading that she was about to give birth, the nurse did rounds in other parts of the jail. Guards reportedly did not check on Meyers as required, even though the birth could be seen on a nearby security monitor. Only after the baby was born was medical care provided. Sheriff Bill McCarthy defended the actions of jail staff.

Corizon Employee Misconduct

Like most private contractors that provide prison-related services, Corizon tends to cut costs in terms of staffing and operational expenses. As noted above, this includes paying lower wages, providing fewer or inferior benefits and hiring less qualified workers who can be paid less. Sometimes, however, these practices result in employees more like to engage in misconduct.

At the Pendleton Correctional Facility in Indiana, a Corizon nurse was arrested and charged with sexual misconduct, a Class C felony. The Herald Bulletin reported that in April 2013, when Colette Ficklin was working as a contract nurse for Corizon, she convinced a prisoner to fake chest pains so they could be alone in an exam room. A guard told internal affairs officers that she witnessed Ficklin and the prisoner engaging in sex acts in the prison's infirmary. [See: PLN, Sept. 2013, p.17].

In March 2013 at the Indiana State Prison in Michigan City, a Corizon practical nurse was charged with drug trafficking and possession with intent to distribute. Phyllis Ungerank, 41, was arrested and booked into the LaPort County Jail after attempting to smuggle marijuana into the facility. [See: PLN, July 2012, p.50].

A Corizon nurse at the Volusia County Branch Jail in Daytona Beach, Florida was fired after officials learned she was having sex with and giving money to a prisoner. Valerie Konieczny was terminated on December 18, 2012 when the jail was contacted by the brother of prisoner Randy Joe Schimp, who had written in a letter that a nurse was having sex with him and depositing money into his jail account. Investigators determined that Konieczny was the nurse who had sex with Schimp at both the Volusia County facility and another branch jail in 2011.

In New Mexico, Corizon physician Mark Walden was accused of fondling prisoners' genitals and performing prostrate exams that were "excessive and inappropriate in terms of length and method." At times, Walden reportedly did not wear gloves during the prostate exams. He was accused of sexually abusing 25 or more male prisoners while employed as a doctor at two privately-operated facilities, the Guadalupe County Correctional Facility in Santa Rosa and Northeast New Mexico Detention Facility in Clayton.

Lawsuits were filed against Walden, Corizon and private prison operator GEO Group, and Walden's medical license was suspended in December 2013. The suits claim that Corizon allowed Dr. Walden to work at the Clayton prison "despite knowing of the risk of sexual abuse and having the ability to know that [he] was repeatedly sexually abusing patients" at the Santa Rosa facility. [See: PLN, Sept. 2013, p.47].

CORIZON HEALTH SERVICES MAKES BAD PRISON HEALTHCARE EVEN WORSE FOR FLORIDA INMATE

On July 16, 2015 Florida inmate Oberist Saunders filed a federal lawsuit against the state's Department of Correction (FDOC), Corizon Health Services and several staff members the Tomoka Correctional Institute (TCI) in Daytona Beach.

Saunder's suit comes a few months after FDOC Secretary Julie Jones announced her department's intention to rebid nearly $1.4 billion in inmate medical contracts, the majority of which are held by Corizon. Florida prisons have been home to some of the most horrific stories of inmate abuse and medical neglect, including the story of Darren Rainey — a mentally ill man who was killed after guards locked him in a scalding hot shower. He was allegedly being punished for defecating in his cell. Other inmates were made to clean his skin off the shower floor the next morning.

Rainey's story is extreme, but the same basic disregard for inmates' mental and physical health is pervasive across the state's prisons. The following story described in Saunders' complaint covers years of alleged neglect for obvious medical needs that began before the prison privatized its healthcare, and got much worse after it did.

Before Corizon: Filth and negligence

Oberist Saunders arrived at Tomoka in February 2010, already suffering from nerve damage and other severe and chronic health conditions affecting his neck, back, shoulder. He notified medical staff on intake and was eventually given an MRI that confirmed "significant damages" to his right shoulder. Medical records also showed that he had an ongoing digestive disorder aggravated by eating certain foods.

In June of 2011, Saunders was brought to an orthopedic specialist who determined he needed urgent surgery on his shoulder to install a metal plate. In July, he underwent the surgery.

The Jacksonville Memorial Hospital, where Saunders most likely should have spent his recovery, had an entire floor secured for inmates. It is undoubtedly a superior location for him to recuperate than the hot, dirty prison from which he had been driven two hours shackled in the back of a van. It was the surgeon's decision whether or not he would stay and recover there instead of prison. But barely out of his anesthetic daze, Saunders was taken to the van after surgery and brought back to Tomoka. He was not given antibiotics or any other medication to prevent infection.

Back at the prison, Saunders was not brought to the relatively sterile, air-conditioned infirmary on the premises to recover from surgery. Instead was placed back into his normal housing unit. The following day, he went to the medical unit for an evaluation with one of the prison's doctors, Dr. Galbadon. He told the doctor of his concerns with the environment in which he was healing: his housing unit was not well ventilated and was extremely dirty. He was worried about contracting an infection and requested antibiotics. The doctor refused.

That night, he began to experience intense pain in his shoulder. He was given a pass to visit medical the next day, but before he could get there, a different doctor name Dr. Torres sent word via a nurse that Saunders was getting "the only medication that will be given" to him.

For the next several days, Saunders tried in vain to get a doctor to examine his shoulder. His wound was routinely dressed by nurses in a high-traffic "triage station" — a 10×12 foot room that served multiple purposes and was not sterilized for dressing.

Nine days after surgery, a doctor finally examined the incision and found it was not completely healed and draining fluid. "It needs another four days to heal," he told Saunders. A couple days later, re-examining the wound, Torres said, "this thing is infected, he needs to be on antibiotics." The doctor then removed the sutures, "which left a large hole at one end where fluid was draining." He did not clean the wound but did prescribe antbiotics, smeared some ointment over the hole as well. Saunders was told he was not given antibiotics sooner because "the surgeon had not ordered it."

Saunders had developed a staph infection, and it was getting worse. The infection had opened canal under the incision that left his bone exposed. Dr. Torres examined the wound again few days later and said, "What am I supposed to do, the surgeon needs to fix that, he caused it." This time, without cleaning the wound, he smeared ointment on it and re-bandaged it with the same dirty, fluid-covered bandage Saunders had been wearing. The infection subsided after four weeks on antibiotics.

In November 2011, he visited the surgeon again, who decided the plate he had put into Saunders shoulder was infected and would need to be removed. That surgery took place a month later, and this time he was kept in the hospital to recover properly.

In February 2012, a Tomoka physician named Dr. Mesa believed Saunders' digestive issues might be Irritable Bowel Syndrome and prescribed him Bentyl. Four months later, a separate doctor, Dr. Monserrate, came to the same conclusion and, in addition to Bentyl, put Saunders on a special low-residue diet.

Saunders was also seen by a neurologist on two separate occasions, and was diagnosed with carpal tunnel in both wrists. He gave Saunders a brace for his right wrist during his first visit, but gave him a medical pass for the brace for his left wrist, which he would have to collect from the prison.

It was at this point that Saunders started dealing with TCI's Dr. Calderon. After waiting two weeks to give him his anti-inflammatory medication and then denying him his left brace, Dr. Calderon stated, "When you see a specialist, they offer recommendations, it is up to your treating physician to determine if the recommendation meets FDOC policies and procedures. Your chart was reviewed and brace was not ordered."

This doctor would end up being a match made in heaven for Corizon Health Services, which would soon take control of the prison's healthcare.

After Corizon: Criteria, quotas, and punishment

By the end of 2013, Corizon Health Services had signed a lucrative deal to provide medical services to Florida inmates. According to Saunders' suit, Corizon's first order of business was to downsize the medical workforce in its prisons. TCI went from having 3-4 physicians to only one — and that physician was Dr. Calderon. He became both the site physician and medical director, and had a small number of nurses working for him. He was now an employee of Corizon.

Before Corizon, healthcare at the prison had not exactly been sterling, but Saunders had been able to get at least some care from the various physicians that had worked for TCI, including important medical passes that permitted him to have a lower bunk, restricted his lifting of heavy objects and afforded him a "bed-wedge" — a pillow commonly used for patients who have undergone shoulder surgery.

When his passes expired under Corizon's watch, these items were confiscated and he was denied further access to them. Saunders met with the jail's medical administrator, who noted on several occasions his severe pain and recommended treatment and medical passes. Dr. Calderon rejected the requests. The administrator asked him to reconsider the dietary pass at least, but he rejected that, too.

A month later, Saunders and the administrator requested he at least get an increase of his stomach medication if he was going to not be on a special diet. That request was rejected by Dr. Calderon as well. All requests were rejected without subjecting Saunders to another medical screening.

Saunders disputed his treatment by Dr. Calderon by filing several medical grievances — all of which, unfortunately, had to be approved by Dr. Calderon himself. When he tried to schedule an appointment to discuss his lower back pain, a nurse told him it was Corizon's policy that "inmates are required to come to sick call three times before being scheduled to see a physician." This criteria is seemingly in direct conflict with contractual agreements between Corizon and the Florida DOC to provide treatment based on "sound medical judgement," not some bizarre quota system.

In March 2014, without a medical pass for a lower bunk, Saunders injured himself trying to get into bed. His bunk did not have ladders. When he discussed this with Dr. Calderon, he was shown Corizon's lower-bunk medical pass policy and told he did not meet the criteria. He was denied the pass.

Around this same time, Saunders attempted to get his Bentyl prescription renewed that had been provided by Dr. Monserrate before Corizon took over. Dr. Calderon said a test would have to be done, but never ordered it. When Saunders responded by filing a grievance, Dr. Calderon said that the inmate "did not meet the criteria for a low residue diet or Bentyl."

Similar obstacles presented themselves as Saunders attempted to get Dr. Calderon to x-ray of his back and shoulder. Dr. Calderon insisted on using a "small portable low-sensitivity scanner" which can be less accurate than and was not revealing the obvious issues that Saunders was experiencing — some of which could be identified without an x-ray machine, through the popping and grinding sounds made by moving his shoulder. Dr. Calderon wouldn't face him during the exam, standing with his back to Saunders for most of the time.

When Saunders persisted in his demands for adequate care and attention, Dr. Calderon told him "I don't have time for this, you don't like it then go write some more grievances or call your attorney, I don't care."

When Saunders pushed back and said he would not stop, Dr. Calderon "stormed out of the room, flipping off the light on his way out, leaving [Saunders] sitting there by himself."

In the hallway, Saunders encountered Dr. Calderon again, who blocked his path, pointed a finger in his face and said "You should get a [disciplinary report]" — a statement which Saunders interpreted as a threat should he continue pursuing treatment.

For months, Saunders continued filing grievances and Dr. Calderon kept denying them. In October 2014, Saunders visited with the health services administrator again, who "acknowledged [his] valid points and responded she would consult with Dr. Calderon on the issues." When he asked the administrator a few days later how that went, she said "I spoke to him and pointed out your valid points but he did not want to hear it. I cannot make him do anything."

In January 2015, desperate for some kind of recourse, Saunders wrote a grievance directly to Corizon's corporate headquarters. The following month, he received a response that no action would be taken and that he would not hear from Corizon again.

Saunders' story as told through his lawsuit provides a valuable glimpse at how the healthcare environment can change when an inmate's medical needs are contracted out to a for-profit entity. What was already a situation rife with neglect and disregard for the patient becomes exacerbated by the need to maximize profits by cutting staff and denying treatments based on criteria and policies that fly in the face of basic medical ethics.

Saunders is still in prison and has not received adequate treatment for his many ailments, according to the suit.

CORIZON ABANDONS KENTUCKY JAIL CONTRACT IN WAKE OF DEATH AND LAWSUITS BY DAVID REUTTER COURIER-JOURNAL.COM

In the wake of seven prisoner deaths and subsequent lawsuits, prison healthcare provider Corizon has decided to not seek renewal of its contract at Kentucky's Metro Corrections in Louisville.

For much of the last two decades, Corizon has been Metro Corrections' provider of prisoner healthcare. Its decision to walk away from its $5.5 million annual contract comes on the heels of the deaths of seven sick prisoners in the last year.

Three lawsuits have been filed in recent months, contending Corizon staff ignored or dismissed prisoners' complaints and doctors were slow to review the prisoners' conditions or to send them to a hospital.

A lawsuit filed in August on behalf of the family of Samantha George alleges that when she was taken to Metro Corrections on a charge of buying a stolen computer, she informed a nurse that she was a severe diabetic, needed insulin, and was feverish and in pain from a MRSA infection. She was so ill she was unable to keep water down.

The nurse contacted Corizon's on-call doctor to suggest George be sent to a hospital. To avoid that expense, the doctor said he would see George the next day. He never followed up on the matter.

George's mother, Theresa, called Metro Corrections to advise them of the serious of her daughter's condition, which required insulin hourly. "They said 'I'm looking at her right now and she's fine,'" said Theresa George. "Four hours later, she was dead.

Samantha George was found unresponsive in her cell on August 8, 2012, and was pronounced dead after being taken to a local hospital. It was concluded that she died of complications from a severe form of diabetes, compounded by heart disease.

Weeks after George's death, prisoner Kenneth Cross died at Metro Corrections. He was arrested after a traffic stop that occurred while a friend was taking him to a hospital for an overdose. The arresting officers believed Cross was faking the overdose, so they took him to Metro Corrections on a warrant for a drug possession charge.

The booking nurse noted Cross had "slurred speech" and fell asleep "several times during his interview." He was placed in a cell, where he was found unconscious hours later. A short time later he was pronounced dead; a medical examiner noted the cause of death as a drug overdose.

"Nodding off... clearly should raise a red flag in the case of someone who was arrested for drug possession," said Cross family attorney Gregory Belzley. "Either hospitalize him or put him under very careful observation in which he was not allowed to go to sleep."

The Cross case is similar to the April 2012 death of Savannah Sparks, 27, She died from opiate abuse and withdrawal only six days after entering Metro Corrections.

A December 2012 email from Metro Corrections Director Mark Belton advised his staff, "Mistakes were made by Corizon personnel and their corporation has acknowledged such mistakes." Six Corizon employees resigned amid an investigation into the deaths. With Corizon being out of its contract, a new contract will be selected amongst six proposed bidders.

MEDICAL BATTLE BEHIND BARS: BIG PRISON HEALTHCARE FIRM CORIZON STRUGGLES TO WIN CONTRACTS BY DAVID ROYSE

When Martin Harrison was brought to an Alameda County jail near Oakland, Calif., in 2010 on an outstanding DUI warrant, he received a health screening from a licensed vocational nurse who worked for Corizon, a private company that provided healthcare for the county correctional system. Harrison, 50, was in severe alcohol withdrawal and hallucinating, and his family says the nurse should have recognized he was in crisis.

"Any RN would have understood the gravity of the situation," said the family's lawyer, Michael Haddad.

But Harrison wasn't referred for treatment. A short time later, still hallucinating, he got into a fight with jail guards and was beaten. Two days later, he died.

Corizon, the licensed vocational nurse's employer, is the nation's largest for-profit provider of correctional health services. In February, Corizon and Alameda County together paid an $8.3 million settlement to Harrison's family. It was the largest civil-rights wrongful-death settlement in California history.

That was only the latest high-profile setback for Brentwood, Tenn.-based Corizon, which has lost five contracts with state prison systems over the past three years and is fighting to hold on to others. In New York City, some officials want to end Corizon's contract in city jails because of quality-of-care concerns.

MH TAKEAWAYS Moody's issued a negative outlook on Corizon in August, citing recent contract losses.

The firm also is under pressure in Florida, where the head of the state prison system said she plans to rebid its healthcare contracts, including one with Corizon. In Washington, D.C., members of the District Council, citing litigation and complaints about Corizon services elsewhere, oppose the mayor's push to approve a Corizon contract to serve the city's inmates.

There have been numerous allegations of quality problems with Corizon's care raised in lawsuits and news reports around the country, including charges of long waits for care and prisoners dying after not being properly diagnosed with cancer and other diseases. Corizon staff reportedly gave a 19-year-old Florida inmate Tylenol for severe pain for months before outside doctors found bone cancer that later killed him. In New York City, an inmate allegedly was told to throw his severed finger away because it couldn't be reattached, though it later was.

Last August, Moody's Investors Service downgraded Corizon's parent company Valitas. In issuing its negative outlook, Moody's cited, in part, "operating headwinds due to recent contract losses." Moody's said, "We expect the company to continue to face near-term earnings pressure following recent contract losses and certain underperforming state department of corrections contracts." It noted, however, that Corizon remains the correctional healthcare sector leader, and said that with new contracts, it expected earnings improvements over the next couple years.

Dr. Woodrow Myers, who replaced Rich Hallworth as Corizon's CEO in a management shake-up in October 2013, downplayed the lawsuits and complaints about his company's services. "Every one of my patients has a lawyer," Myers said. And most suits are dismissed, he added. "There's a huge number of lawsuits, but they're not specific to Corizon. They are specific to this industry."

States spend $8 billion a year on prison healthcare, according to the Pew Charitable Trusts. Local governments spend additional millions for care in jails. According to a 2014 report by the Reason Foundation, only 14 states operate their own prison healthcare, while 36 contract for at least part of it and 24 have contracted out all prison healthcare services. There are no data on how many local jails use private medical vendors.

Privately held Corizon became the largest correctional healthcare provider in 2011 when Valitas Health Services, parent of the former Correctional Medical Services, acquired America Service Group, creating a company serving more than 400 facilities.

Valitas is majority-owned by Chicago-based private-equity management firm Beecken Petty O'Keefe and Co.

Corizon had $1.4 billion in revenue for the fiscal year ended June 2014 and now cares for 345,000 inmates in 27 states. Competitors include Nashville-based Correct Care, which cares for about 250,000 people in 37 states, and Pittsburgh-based Wexford Health, which cares for 112,000 inmates in 13 states. Other providers include St. Louis-based Centurion Managed Care, a joint venture between Centene Corp. and MHM Services, and several other smaller for-profit and not-for-profit providers.

Many of Corizon's contracts are holdovers from its predecessor companies. Since the merger, it has won new contracts, including taking over Arizona's state prison contract from Wexford and winning part of Florida's business after a long court fight there over whether prison healthcare could be privatized.

But since 2012, Corizon has lost statewide contracts covering 84,000 inmates in Maine, Maryland, Minnesota and Pennsylvania.

In Maine, a state audit said: "Some prisoners did not receive standard medical services, such as physicals, dental services or sick call response within the timeframe required." In Maryland, Corizon appears to have been underbid by Wexford in 2012. In Corizon's home state of Tennessee, it provides behavioral healthcare to prisoners. But in January, it lost the medical-care contract to Centurion, even though Corizon had a lower bid.

The contracts Corizon lost in the five states will be worth more than $1.2 billion over the next five years.

Corizon also has notched some wins. In February, Alabama renewed its contract, even though the state has been sued by the Southern Poverty Law Center over what the civil-rights group says is inadequate prison healthcare. Corizon isn't named as a defendant. But the company is joining with mental healthcare contractor MHM Correctional Services in paying for the state's defense under the terms of its contract.

Last year, Corizon won a three-year $1.1 billion contract to provide care at Missouri's state prisons, and it got an extension of its contract for Indiana's prisons, while adding some large new local jail contracts.

But those gains have been overshadowed by its difficulties in keeping old contracts and winning new ones. New York City's deputy health commissioner recently said the city was "examining potential new strategies" after complaints about quality of care at Rikers Island led city commissioners to question the contract with Corizon.

Julie Jones, Florida's secretary of corrections, acknowledged to state lawmakers this year that Corizon and Wexford, which split care responsibilities in the state's prisons, have done an inadequate job.

Florida Republican state Sen. Greg Evers, chairman of the state Senate Criminal Justice Committee, recently told the Tampa Bay Times he was concerned that deaths in Florida prisons had gone up 10% since healthcare was privatized two years ago. Florida Democratic state Sen. Jeff Clemens called media reports about the companies' recent care record "disturbing to my sense of humanity."

Corizon is responsible for the care of 74,000 Florida inmates, while Wexford has a contract covering 15,000 in the state. Jones recently said she will move to rebid the contracts, worth $229 million a year for Corizon and $48 million through the end of 2017 for Wexford.

Corizon also faces a battle to serve jail inmates in the District of Columbia, where it won a bidding process but still needs approval from the District Council. The contract would pay Corizon $66 million over three years to take over from Unity Health Care, a not-for-profit that also runs health clinics for low-income patients in the District.

The bad press about lawsuits around the country and quality-of-care questions may derail Corizon's D.C. contract effort. "There's a pretty strong bloc of us here who don't want to see it happen," said council member David Grosso, citing questions about Corizon's care in New York City. "Why should the District of Columbia repeat the mistakes that other places have made?"

Corizon changed leadership in October 2013, with Myers, who previously had served on the board at Valitas and worked as chief medical officer at managed-care company WellPoint, taking over from Hallworth. Stuart Campbell stepped down as president and was replaced last year by Scott Bowers, who previously worked at UnitedHealthcare. While the company declined to comment on the reasons for the leadership changes, they came shortly after an earlier 2013 downgrading of Valitas by Moody's and after the loss of the Maine, Maryland, Pennsylvania and Tennessee state correctional contracts.

Corizon officials and some outside observers say many problems the company faces are inherent in caring for inmates, many of whom have substance abuse, mental health and other chronic health problems. Prisoners also can be hostile to authority, said Dr. Sylvia McQueen, Corizon's vice president of clinical services. And Corizon's doctors and nurses have to accommodate themselves to institutional security priorities.

"Some (inmates) just don't want to be bothered" with interacting with healthcare providers, said McQueen, whose first exposure to the correctional system came when her father was jailed while she was growing up in Washington, D.C.

Myers said that's why it makes sense for correctional agencies to bring in Corizon, which through its predecessor companies has decades of experience and can use its size to save money and improve care. It can, for example, use data it collects about treatments that work in one location to create best practices in others.

While some local officials have cited the number of lawsuits filed against the company—there have been more than 1,300 in five years—as a reason for concern, Corizon officials say litigation isn't a good indicator of quality of care behind bars.

PRIVATE PRISON HEALTH CARE IN DOUBT AS CORIZON CONTRACT COLLAPSES POSTED BY MARY ELLEN, NOV. 30, 2015

After two years of complaints about healthcare in Florida's prisons, the private company that has been responsible for the largest share of inmate care — Corizon Health — decided not to renew its $1.1 billion contract with the state Monday, leaving the future of care for 74,000 inmates in limbo when the company pulls out in six months.

The decision by the Tennessee-based company to exercise its right to terminate the contract that was scheduled to expire in 2018 came as the Florida Department of Corrections was attempting to renegotiate the agreement amid reports of inmate maltreatment, chronic understaffing and rising numbers of unnatural inmate deaths.

"We appreciate the contracts for inmate health services permit very little of the flexibility that Secretary Jones would like in order to address issues such as staffing, mental health care, and electronic health records," Corizon Chief Executive Officer Karey Witty said in a statement. "We have tried to address the department's concerns but have found the terms of the current contract too constraining. At this point, we believe the best way to move forward is to focus our efforts on a successful transition to a new provider."

In February, Department of Corrections Secretary Julie Jones was ordered to renegotiate the contract by Sen. Greg Evers, R-Baker, chairman of the Senate Criminal Justice Committee, after a series of reports in the Miami Herald and other news organizations showed suspicious inmate deaths were covered up or never reviewed, staffing was inadequate, and inmate grievances and complaints of harmful medical care were dismissed or ignored.

Audits conducted by the state's Correctional Medical Authority also found problems with inadequate medical care, nursing and staffing shortages, and hundreds of pending lawsuits against the state and the health care companies claiming inadequate medical care.

Last year, 346 inmates died in Florida prisons — 176 of them listed with no immediate cause of death. It was the highest number on record, even though the number of inmates in Florida prisons has declined.

The decision is a blow to the effort by several legislators and Gov. Rick Scott to privatize medical care in Florida prisons. After trying and failing to pass legislation to authorize the state to contract out its prison health care to companies who contributed heavily to Republican campaigns, a provision was quietly inserted into the 2011 budget during the governor's first term.

The language was challenged in court but ultimately was upheld and the contracts were allowed.

Under the deal first signed in 2013, Corizon Health is being paid $229 million a year until June 30, 2018 to provide healthcare to 74,000 inmates at 111 of Florida's prisons, work camps and work release centers in North and Central Florida. Wexford Health Services is being paid $48 million a year until Dec. 20, 2017, to provide health services to about 15,000 inmates at nine prisons in South Florida.

The contract requires that both companies provide medical care to inmates for 7 percent less than it cost the state in 2010, but both companies sought and received increases in the terms of their original agreement

In 2014, former FDC Secretary Michael Crews agreed to raise the annual contract with Corizon and Wexford by $3.2 million. Subsequent audits revealed that even after the increased payments, Corizon failed to meet it contract obligations regarding staffing and medical care.

Evers asked the agency to renegotiate the contracts with both private prison providers to demand higher standards of care and hold them accountable for deaths and injuries. Jones also criticized the contracts as too lenient for the vendors and issued an invitation to rebid the contract on Feb. 23. The department did not explain what will be next for the prison system, but said in a statement that updates would be forthcoming."In the coming months, Secretary Jones will work closely with the Department's Office of Health Services to ensure that the appropriate staff and resources are available at our facilities to continue seamless delivery of appropriate medical care to our inmate population," the statement said.Evers said he was not prepared to comment on the decision but said he considered it a "good sign" that Jones was following through on directions to hold the company accountable for providing the level of care they agreed to when they signed the contract with the state. "This is good news," said Rep. Carlos Trujillo, R-Miami, who chairs the House Criminal Justice subcommittee that oversees prisons. He had been supportive of the effort to renegotiate the contract because "the health care outcomes were some of the worst in any sort of managed care.""It's a huge contract. People don't' walk away from this easily," Trujillo said. "It further goes to show that the secretary is holding people accountable. Regardless of their reason for leaving, she's forcing people to come to the table and push for the outcomes."Trujillo said that the options include providing a "hybrid" system that would rely on private health care services in areas of the state where that is most efficient and return to in-house medical staffing in other parts of the state.

The New Mexican - Haywood and Justin Horwath

The Central New Mexico Correctional Facility in Los Lunas is among the state facilities where complaints and lawsuits about care have called into question the services of Corizon Medical Services and oversight by the State of New Mexico. Luis Sánchez Saturno/The New Mexican

On the morning of Feb. 20, 2014, a guard at the Guadalupe County Correctional Facility in Santa Rosa found Danny Tavasci lying face down and motionless in his bunk in solitary confinement. Empty blister packs of medication lay scattered around him.

Tavasci was a 54-year-old former highway worker whose life took a drastic turn in 2008 when he shot his son in the hip and the leg during an argument. A judge sentenced him to 17 years. By the time the guard found him that morning, his body had been ravaged by ailments including diabetes and high blood pressure. He also had been diagnosed with a major depressive disorder. His prison cell was a virtual drugstore — hundreds of pills, 26 different kinds of medications — despite his disciplinary history of abusing them.

A coroner later found 23 potassium chloride tablets, which are used to treat high blood pressure, in Tavasci's throat and stomach, and ruled his death a suicide.

Danny Tavasci

Why Tavasci was allowed to keep so many pills with him despite his mental health history is just one of several questions raised in a federal lawsuit filed by his widow. The court case is one of more than 150 filed by over 200 plaintiffs against Corizon Health since the nation's largest for-profit provider of inmate health care won a contract with New Mexico's prison system in 2007. The brunt of the claims has come since the state awarded the company a four-year, $156 million contract renewal in 2012.

Taken together, the lawsuits, often hand-scribbled by inmates representing themselves, depict agonizing details of medical care they say was often delayed and negligent, and of retaliation by prison staff when they complained.

One inmate said he waited 20 days for X-rays after his hand was crushed in a door; another said he was denied a referral to a specialist for a basketball-sized abdominal protrusion. A woman said she waited years for breast cancer treatment until the cancer had reached a critical stage.

The claims bear striking similarities to lawsuits filed across the country against Corizon, which, more than any other company, has capitalized on the wave of privatized health care that has swept prison systems trying to cut costs. Critics say those cuts too often come at the expense of inmates who, because of their crimes, have little power to demand better medical care.

The Brentwood, Tenn.-based company has lost contracts with correctional departments in at least four states since 2012. Last year, New York City ended its relationship with Corizon at Rikers Island after years of complaints. In September, a Florida oversight board found delays in treatment and other problems at a women's prison to be "life-threatening."

But in New Mexico, Corizon has been allowed to operate largely unregulated, despite red flags raised by the lawsuits, a six-month investigation by The New Mexican has found. State lawmakers have paid little attention to the quality of inmate health care. The New Mexico Corrections Department has conducted only a fraction of the medical audits it was supposed to have done. And any record of settlements in claims over medical care, which might help determine the merit of the allegations, has been kept secret through a contract agreement that allows the company to handle litigation against it, even when the state is a co-defendant.

A review by the newspaper of thousands of pages of state records and court documents and interviews with current and former Corizon and Corrections Department employees shows a department seemingly removed from the details of inmate care. Among The New Mexican's findings:

• Despite a Corrections Department policy requiring contracts to be audited quarterly at every facility where services are provided, department officials sometimes went years without auditing Corizon, known as Correctional Medical Services before a 2011 merger. Of about 160 audits that should have been done between 2012 and 2015, the department could only produce records of 20.

• Employee warnings to the department about short staffing, substandard care and a lack of auditing went unheeded.

• Despite those concerns, the number of people assigned to monitor Corizon's performance shrank from four medical professionals to one lawyer. The department says it intends to add three nurses to the team, but those positions have been vacant since they were created last May.

• When the department finally did begin paying close attention to Corizon's medical staffing in May 2015, after years of accepting Corizon invoices with little scrutiny, the contract monitor found staff shortages month after month, and the department fined the company $1 million. It was the only time the company had been fined since its contract was renewed in 2012, according to records and interviews.

The sporadic and often haphazard oversight came despite glaring signs of trouble. These included an internal memo in 2010 that warned of dire medical conditions at the women's prison in Grants, as well as repeated findings by the State Auditor's Office that the department needed to do a better job of ensuring Corizon delivered what it promised.

In one particularly troubling sign, a Corizon doctor accused of sexually abusing inmates in Santa Rosa in 2011 was simply transferred 170 miles north to another facility, where he was accused of molesting dozens more until inmates complained to police and he was finally fired.

Now, as Corizon's contract with New Mexico is set to expire in May, it is again competing with other companies to provide care for the state's inmate population.

Corrections officials acknowledge failings in monitoring the contract. Department Secretary Gregg Marcantel said the newly structured contract will include tougher oversight provisions, though he declined to provide details because he said the state has an active request for proposals for the new contract.

"We pay a lot for those medical services contracts, and as a result of that, I expect something," he said. "Whoever wins that contract is going to be faced with some performance measures that look very much different than the performance measures look like in any other state and have looked in the history of this state."

The Corrections Department oversees 11 prisons scattered across the state with about 7,000 inmates, including more than 700 women. Corizon has the medical contract for all but one of those facilities.

Martha Harbin, a Corizon spokeswoman, defended the company's performance. As evidence, she said, the American Correctional Association, a private accrediting organization that sets standards for prisons, has given the state prison system a "100 percent" in the medical portion of triennial audits of the prison system since Corizon has had the contract.

"This is the result of the commitment and dedication of our front-line health care staff who work hard every day to offer the best possible quality of care, to one of the most vulnerable patient populations, in one of the most challenging environments imaginable," she said.

But some of those excellent scores issued by ACA came as employees with the department were raising concerns over care.

Marc Stern, a correctional health care consultant and former health services director for the Washington state Department of Corrections, said passing an ACA audit is a "necessary but not sufficient" measure of a prison system's health care. ACA audits can determine whether a correctional system has certain standards in place, he said, but they do not test whether officials follow those policies.

"Because you passed, it does not mean that health care is automatically or necessarily safe," said Stern, who is now the medical monitor in a consent decree between Florida's Miami-Dade County and the U.S. Justice Department over issues in the prison system there.

Like many states, New Mexico does not have an independent monitoring system for prison health care, though groups like the American Bar Association and the American Civil Liberties Union have called for such oversight for years.

Harbin, who said Corizon could not comment on pending litigation, downplayed the significance of the volume of lawsuits.

Martha Harbin

"It's important to emphasize that the existence of a lawsuit is not necessarily indicative of quality of care or any wrongdoing," she said. "Malpractice suits are a fact of life for most doctors in America today, and that is particularly true in the correctional health care industry, where our patient population is highly litigious."

But in fact, inmates face significant legal hurdles before they can file a lawsuit. The federal Prison Litigation Reform Act of 1996 and a similar state law were designed to weed out frivolous lawsuits by making prisoners exhaust all levels of administrative grievance processes before filing a court action. By 2006, federal lawsuits nationwide had fallen 60 percent from the time the act passed, according to a report by Human Rights Watch.

In New Mexico, however, the number of inmates filing medical-related lawsuits has shot up under Corizon. Between 2004 and 2007, 53 inmates filed lawsuits against the previous provider, Wexford Health Sources, which the state fired in 2007 amid concerns over inmate care and staffing shortages. By comparison, 138 inmates filed suits against Corizon between 2012 and 2015. Three more have filed suits so far in 2016.

Matthew Coyte, a civil rights attorney who frequently represents prisoners, including some who have sued and won settlements against Corizon, said he doesn't know if the number of complaints against Corizon is abnormal.

"All I can comment on," he said, "is that the cases that come through my office are horrific, terrible, an embarrassment. The amount of money we spend on medical care versus the care the prisoners receive is an absolute embarrassment, and the taxpayers should be ashamed."

A flood of cases

New Mexico plaintiffs filing lawsuits against prison healthcare providers by year.

The number of prisoners filing lawsuits against Corizon Health has soared since it won a contract renewal in 2012 to provide medical services to 10 state prison facilities in New Mexico. The company has held the contract since 2007, when it was known as Correctional Medical Services before a 2011 merger. Wexford Health Sources held the contract from 2004 to 2007 before it was terminated amid concerns over inmate care and staffing shortages. Lawsuits continued to come in against Wexford in the three years after it lost the contract, suggesting that Corizon could expect more after its contract expires in May. The company is among bidders for the new contract. Hover over the colored segments for more information.

Many of the lawsuits center on the now infamous story of Dr. Mark E. Walden. On Sept. 29, 2011, a 30-year-old inmate at the Guadalupe County Correctional Facility filed a complaint with the prison accusing Walden of fondling his genital and anal areas. He also said the doctor gave him repeated prostate exams when he had only gone into the infirmary for a pain in his side. Each time, the inmate asked the doctor if the genital touching was necessary and was told "yes," the inmate said.

The prison responded by placing the inmate in solitary confinement, according to the report by the Corrections Department's Office of Special Investigations and Internal Affairs. Corizon officials say the complaint was unsubstantiated, and they transferred Walden five months later to the Northeast New Mexico Detention Facility in Clayton so he could be closer to home. Complaints began to stack up there until Corizon fired Walden in July 2012 after an inmate complained to Clayton police.

Lawyers for inmates say the Corrections Department and Corizon should have had ample evidence of alleged sexual abuse by Walden before transferring him from Guadalupe, where inmates referred to him as "Dr. Fingers." Walden, for example, performed two times as many rectal exams as his colleagues — including one for an inmate who came in for a broken wrist and another for a patient with an eye injury, the New Mexico Medical Board later found.

At least 77 inmates have joined in lawsuits involving Walden, many claiming sexual abuse but several also questioning Walden's medical competency, which the Medical Board, in suspending his license, determined was insufficient. One of the lawsuits claims an inmate at Santa Rosa was threatened by Walden. According to the complaint, Walden told the inmate that "he had gotten another inmate sent to segregation for attempting to report Walden's conduct."

"Had they put a stop to it at that time, a lot of our other clients wouldn't have been abused," said Katie Curry, a partner at the Albuquerque law firm McGinn, Carpenter, Montoya and Love, which represented 30 inmates who settled with Corizon under confidential terms in one of the first lawsuits against Walden.

Walden, 58, who received his medical degree from the University of Michigan, has denied the allegations in court records and has not been criminally charged. He declined to comment for this story.

Delays in care

While dozens of inmates have filed claims involving Walden, those account for only 20 percent of the lawsuits filed against Corizon since 2012. The vast majority of the other lawsuits involve claims of delayed or negligent care.

Handwritten court filings include painstakingly documented grievances, which prisoners say often go nowhere or are "lost," requiring them to start the process over numerous times.

Andrew Joey Delgado, an inmate serving 18 years for killing a person while driving drunk, crushed his hand and wrist in a cell door on May 3, 2014. A review of his grievance complaints and the prison staff's answers to them show it took nine days for him to be seen by the medical staff, another two weeks to get X-rays and another 26 days after that to have his hand splinted. Though he was still in pain, Corizon staff repeatedly rejected his pleas to see an outside doctor, the records show.

By the time he was sent to an orthopedist at the University of New Mexico Hospital more than six months later, his lawsuit says, he was told there was little they could do and he would likely live with pain and reduced function in the hand for the rest of his life. The suit, filed in August, remains open.

Angelina Gutierrez, 49, had already been diagnosed with breast cancer when she was remanded to the women's prison in Grants in March 2012 for violating her probation on a drug conviction. In a federal lawsuit, she says she told Corizon staff of her condition during an initial medical screening and that she would need additional treatment. She says in the suit that doctors found masses in both of her breasts, yet the staff waited more than a year to order a mammogram.

"I was in pain. I knew something bad was happening." —Angelina Gutierrez, former inmate

Even after those tests found reason for concern, she said in an interview, the prison doctors and nurses continued to put off treatment. At one point, they blamed lost paperwork, even as her right breast turned purple and swelled to twice its size.

"I was in pain," said Gutierrez, of Alamogordo, who is now out of prison. "I knew something bad was happening."

By the time Gutierrez began receiving treatment at UNM Hospital in December 2013, more than 18 months after reporting to prison, she had Stage 3 cancer, according to a federal lawsuit she filed in July. The case is currently in settlement negotiations, court records show. Gutierrez's lawyer, Matthew L. Garcia, declined to share her medical records.

Adam Baker, a Santa Fe civil rights lawyer who has represented prisoners but does not have any current cases against Corizon, said the lawsuits reflect "an inherent conflict" between the profit motive of private health care providers and an inmate's need for care.

"That, in my opinion, is why you see these problems coming up over and over again," he said. "In the most egregious cases, I see a reluctance to take an inmate outside of the facility for specialized care. An inmate may need an MRI or to see an orthopedic specialist … and there is a grave reluctance as a system to provide that level of care because it's so expensive. It's very difficult for an inmate to be seen outside the facility even if there is a need."

Carl Takei, a staff attorney with the ACLU's National Prison Project, said prison health care ideally would not be carried out by private contractors.

"Some states rely on universities to provide prison medical care," he said. "Those systems have their own problems, but it's something where you are taking the profit motive out of it, and the interest of an academic institution is probably more aligned with the interests of their patients."

Harbin said Corizon follows "established guidelines just the way your insurance company or doctor has to based on your insurance. We do the referrals where the evidence and clinical guidelines indicate they are necessary."

In the case of Tavasci, the former highway worker who died from the toxic effects of elevated potassium levels in his blood, the lawsuit contends multiple failures on the part of medical staff at the prison, including an allegation that Corizon staff did not alert emergency responders that Tavasci had overdosed, wasting precious time in the emergency room as doctors tried to revive him. The lawsuit also contends Corizon staff failed to complete a mental health evaluation before placing Tavasci in solitary, as required by prison policy.

"He had a documented history of depression, and clearly he was suicidal," said his family's lawyer, Frances C. Carpenter. "And they let him keep his medications on his person."

A history of problems

Corizon was formed in June 2011 through a merger of Correctional Medical Services and Prison Health Services, two companies that had faced criticism from state and local governments over the quality of care they provided to inmates.

That concern has continued under the company's new name. Today, Corizon operates in 518 facilities across the country, serving more than 332,000 inmates in 26 states, according to its website.

CMS took over the New Mexico contract in 2007 after the state fired Wexford. When the state awarded the newly created Corizon a contract renewal in 2012, the company's performance at an Idaho prison had already received a scathing review from Stern, the correctional health care expert and a former CMS employee, who had been appointed by a federal judge to review that prison's medical care. Stern found "multiple problems, including nursing mistakes that likely resulted in the deaths of some inmates; overcrowding at the pharmacy site where some inmates pick up their daily medications; and terminal inmates sometimes being denied meals and left lying in soiled linens," The Associated Press reported at the time.

But in New Mexico, corrections officials gave CMS glowing reviews in press accounts at the time. In fact, there was ample cause for concern, records and interviews show.

The number of inmate lawsuits filed against CMS in the first four years of its contract was on par with the number against Wexford. Corrections Department medical staff were raising concerns internally about CMS' care. The department itself had clawed back nearly $1 million in payments from the company for staffing shortages, including $230,000 for physician absences, according to staff reconciliation invoices obtained by The New Mexican.

And the number of inmate deaths in the first two full years of CMS' tenure, mostly from health-related causes, far exceeded the national average. In 2008, for example, 31 inmates died, an average of about 490 deaths per 100,000 inmates, compared to the national average of 260 per 100,000 that year.

Nonetheless, Corizon won the contract renewal. Department officials promised that Corizon's new four-year agreement, worth $156 million, would save taxpayers money and provide more accountability than the old one. If the company fell below 90 percent of required staffing levels, for example, it could face penalties of $200 an hour.

But Corizon's new contract contained less specific penalty clauses than the previous one, which had a list of fees associated with failure to deliver care. Those included a $1,000 fine if a physician failed to respond to a page within 20 minutes, a $1,500 fine for failure to conduct chronic care clinics and a $2,500 fine for failing to provide the appropriate level of access to care.

NYC SPLITS WITH FOR-PROFIT PRISON PROVIDER AFTER AUDIT DANI KASS LAW 360

New York City Mayor Bill de Blasio announced Wednesday he won't be renewing the city's contract with for-profit jail health care provider Corizon Health Inc., following a damning report released by the city's Department of Investigation.

Inmate care at Rikers Island and throughout the New York City jail system will be handled by Health and Hospitals Corp. after Corizon's contract ends in December. The decision came after a report showed Corizon allowed employees with criminal backgrounds to work in the jail, among other failures.

"We have an essential responsibility to provide every individual in our city's care with high-quality health services — and our inmates are no different," de Blasio said in a statement. "This transfer to HHC will give our administration direct control and oversight of our inmates' health services — furthering our goal of improving the quality and continuity of health care for every inmate in city custody."

The city also won't renew its contract with Damian Family Care Center Inc. when it expires in August 2016.

The transfer most likely won't lead to any budget reductions, according to a statement from the city. Corizon's $154 million and Damian's $8 million contracts will be budgeted to HCC.

"Although we understand the administration's decision to move forward with a different model, we are disappointed at the prospect of ending our relationship" Corizon said in a statement. "We remain extremely proud of our employees on Rikers Island and throughout the criminal justice system, and we are committed to cooperating with the city to ensure a seamless transition that puts our patients first."

The DOI's report found Corizon failed at properly screening its employees and treating mentally ill inmates, something that contributed to the death of two inmates.

The investigation came after the DOI arrested three Corizon employees from September through May. One was a nurse who is accused of taking bribes to smuggle tobacco and alcohol into Rikers, another was accused of smuggling contraband into the jail, and the third was accused of smuggling a straight edge razor into the jail, according to the DOI. That third employee had several felony convictions, including one for kidnapping for which he served 13 years.

In almost half of the employee files, the DOI found no proof any background investigation had been conducted or that professional licenses were verified or monitored. The company also hired employees who did have a criminal history, including one with a second-degree murder conviction, according to the report.

The DOC and DOMHM both failed to oversee the hirings and supervise Corizon, the report found.

Corizon employees also took an inmate off court-ordered suicide watch without consulting a supervisor or psychiatrist, according to the report. That inmate died days later.

"Later that day, DOC generated a new mental health referral for the inmate because he was 'being depressed,'" the report states. "Despite the referral, [correctional officers] in the inmate's housing area sent the inmate back to his cell; no mental health employee conducted a follow-up assessment with the inmate, who was found the next morning hanging in his cell."

Employees failed to watch inmates take medication once giving them out, violating policies calling for mouth checks, the report states. The DOC and Corizon had both thought it was the other's responsibility.

"Going forward, stringent reforms must be established, and DOC has already begun to implement critical changes," DOI Commissioner Mark G. Peters said in a statement.

The investigation didn't conduct an investigation into the quality of medical care, as they were not qualified to do so, the agency said.

Last August, Corizon was fined $71,000 by the Occupational Safety and Health Administration for not protecting its workers at Rikers from workplace assault and violence. The company failed to properly handle an increase in violence against its staff members, including the circulation of a hit list made by inmates against Corizon workers.

CRIME & LAW BY PAT BEALL - PALM BEACH POST STAFF

Ten weeks before Corizon Health abruptly canceled its $1.2 billion contract to treat Florida prison inmates, yet another account of lethal care by the Tennessee-based company landed on Florida Department of Corrections Secretary Julie Jones' desk.

At Florida Women's Reception Center in Ocala, inspectors found, a woman with diabetes went almost three months without insulin. One inmate with a golf ball-sized lump behind her ear was referred for an MRI and a surgical consult. She got neither.

A doctor's "urgent" request for thyroid surgery for an inmate with a history of thyroid cancer languished for eight months. Another inmate with a brain aneurysm waited two months before seeing a specialist.

Psychiatric care was similarly disturbing. Inmates at risk of self-harm can be held only in certain types of isolation cells for 72 hours. But one woman spent four days in a cell, another spent five days and yet another spent six.

In four cases cited by inspectors, it appeared mentally disturbed inmates were inexplicably taken off their prescribed psychiatric medication.

Anthony Carvajal was a prison inmate whose bone cancer was treated with over-the-counter painkillers and Tums. He has been given weeks

The inspection team requested emergency action by DOC for what they believed could be life-threatening lapses in care.

DOC responded within 72 hours, insisting on more staff, more training, more state oversight, more specialist appointments.

The problems mirrored findings of a 2014 Palm Beach Post investigation that documented soaring fatalities and substandard care after Corizon and Wexford Health Source were awarded control of the state medical system. While inmates are not entitled to excellent care, the U.S. Supreme Court has ruled that they are entitled to adequate care.

Corizon's decision Monday to pull out in six months forces the state to find a health care provider for about 150 prisons and other facilities long before a new contractor can be selected, perhaps not until mid-2017."We have tried to address the department's concerns but have found the terms of the current contract too constraining," Corizon Health CEO Karey Witty said in a prepared statement. "At this point, we believe the best way to move forward is to focus our efforts on a successful transition to a new provider."

Partly because Corizon cares for the vast majority of state inmates, it has been at the center of criticism over care in the newly privatized health system, which quickly delivered lethal consequences.

Prison inmate mortality rates hit a 10-year high within 100 days of privatization, The Post found. Referrals to hospitals and specialists plummeted.

Information on inmate deathswasn't regularly turned over to the state, and medical exams showing whether inmates were injured by guards sometimes were missing.

Post investigation: Prison health

Corizon also was involved in some of the most dramatic incidences of medical neglect uncovered by The Post. Three prisoners dying of cancer were misdiagnosed by Corizon staff, even after, in one case, bulging tumors visibly riddled the inmate's body. All were given Tylenol and ibuprofen for their spreading cancers. Two of the inmates died and a third was given early release for health reasons.

Corizon pledged reform. But problems continued. In February, just 18 months after for-profit firms took full control of prison health care and four months after The Post investigation, Jones scrapped the five-year contracts.

Corizon's contract requires six-month notice, meaning it will provide care through May

Missing records

At the Florida Women's Center, Corizon is responsible for almost 1,000 inmates, many with histories of serious illness.

Corizon spokeswoman Martha Harbin described it as "one of the more challenging locations in which to provide care." It is the central point of entry for all women entering the state prison system, she said. And its population more than doubled just as Corizon assumed responsibility for health and psychiatric care.

In a routine September inspection, the Correctional Medical Authority faulted the company for a myriad of shortcomings. The state watchdog panel, which is independent of DOC, reported inadequate treatment of chronic and serious illnesses, failures to get inmates to off-site surgeons and specialists, and critically, missing or incomplete medical records.

Such records are not just paperwork. For instance, inspectors found medical files where there was no record of an inmate's vital signs, such as pulse and blood pressure. Some medical files didn't include a diagnosis.

Records of whether medicines were given didn't exist, raising the question of whether they were administered. In fact, large numbers of prescriptions had not been filled because the prescription wasn't correctly filled out. Inspectors found a gap of a month or more in paperwork that would have proved psychiatric medicine was being dispensed.

Further, records that would have confirmed medical staff saw four patients on weekends and holidays were missing, as did records to show that medical staffers checked in on certain ill inmates.

In two instances, records weren't just missing, they were suspect. A patient's vital signs in one file were identical for every day for more than a month. In another, vital signs taken twice weekly for several weeks never changed — except to record a massive, and unexplained change in weight from 143 to 250 pounds.

Inmates could wait weeks, or even months, before abnormal test results were looked at by medical staff — and even longer for treatment.

An inmate with lesions in her brain and a history of cancers had an abnormal cancer screen in May, did not get diagnostic testing until August and was not referred to an outside cancer specialist until September. All the while, she was telling medical staff of symptoms indicating a spreading cancer.

An inmate with a large mass in her abdomen was prescribed multiple tests by a surgeon in January, but delays in getting prison medical staff to review the test results meant she was not operated on for another five months.

"We were aware of challenges at the site prior to the Correctional Medical Authority audit and were taking steps, such as adding staff, to resolve them," Corizon spokeswoman Harbin said.

Post-audit, she said, 78 Corizon employees were brought to the prison to discuss medical needs with all 895 inmates. Response from DOC has been positive, said Harbin: "We look forward to CMA's re-inspection."

Governor's push

Despite failures of care, DOC is still embracing privatization, making good on a high-profile campaign promise by Gov. Rick Scott to privatize prison medical care.

The sheer size of Florida's prison population makes that a challenge.

Not only does Florida have the third-largest state prison system in the country, it also houses the fastest-growing number of elderly inmates of any state prison system — a population of inmates in need of increasingly complex, and expensive, medical care.

"We are very aware of scale," said DOC spokesman McKinley Lewis. Part of contracting with new firms, he said, will be "making sure they are aware just how big this project is."

DOC is considering splitting up new contracts into smaller, more manageable units. For instance, one company might handle dental care and another might handle medical care.

Corizon still could be one of those companies. Lewis said the decision to cancel the current contract does not disqualify them from rebidding.

The company hasn't decided yet whether it will do so when invitations to negotiate are issued by DOC, probably later this month.

Both Corizon and Jones say for now, the emphasis will be on maintaining care as the company transfers responsibility for health care to DOC. "Above all," Witty said, "Corizon Health will continue to provide high quality care to Florida's inmates."

Three cancers

Fatal cancers of three inmates were misdiagnosed by Corizon and treated with over-the-counter painkillers:

Donna Pickelsimer, 56. Placed in solitary confinement after telling nurses from Corizon that she was in so much pain she wanted to cut off her arm, Pickelsimer's visible, spreading tumors were treated with Tylenol, ibuprofen and warm compresses. She died in June 2014.

Anthony Carvajal, 44. In work-release, Carvajal's spine fractured in several places, the result of a spreading cancer. Corizon medical staff diagnosed a pulled muscle and given ibuprofen. He was given an early release granted to certain dying prisoners.

Tammie White, 45. White died in January 2015, shortly after prison medical staff from Corizon treated her using Tylenol with codeine and ibuprofen. By then, untreated cancer had spread through her lungs, bones and brain.

What The Post reported

In Dying for Care, an award-winning investigation published in September and October 2014, The Post detailed rising death tolls and incidents of neglect in state prisons after private companies took over the health care of inmates.

prison over medical care

AN ARIZONA PRISON IS ACCUSED OF FAILING TO PROVIDE BASIC MEDICAL CARE TO AN INMATE INJURED IN A PRISON JOB ACCIDENT - FLORENCE, ARIZONA

Eric Carlson, who is serving time for aggravated DUI, filed a legal claim for $1.5 million this week against the Arizona Department of Corrections and medical provider, Corizon Health Services.

His wrist was crushed in April 19 while he was working at his prison job in a recycling center, according to the claim.

"He went down in pain screaming because he had broken the bones in his hand," Carlson's lawyer, Scott Zwillinger, said.

Instead of a trip to the emergency room that day, Carlson was returned to Florence prison complex.

The inmate's wife, Elfi Blair Carlson, is outraged about the medical treatment he received.

"I saw him on Saturday [April 23] for visitation," said Blair Carlson. "His hand was swollen like three times the size, bruised and black."

According to Carlson's legal claim, he was treated with "callous and deliberate indifference." Prison documents show he didn't see a medical provider until 6 days after his injury, although he did have x-rays in the prison clinic showing broken bones. The claim also says he received insufficient pain medication and a makeshift splint.

"Instead of getting what anybody would get going to a school nurses office, at the hospital every emergency room, he receives a piece of cardboard," Zwillinger said.

Zwillinger said the piece of cardboard was fished out of a trash can. He also said the prison clinic had regular medical splints on hand, which Carlson did not receive until he made additional complaints.

"Because it [wrist] was not set properly, because it wasn't taken care of right away like it should've been, the bones in his hands died," said Zwillinger. "He's going to be permanently impaired in his right hand, and he's right-handed."

Corizon told ABC15 it's a "one of the greatest misconceptions" that the company has anything to gain from withholding care.

"What makes the most clinical and business sense is responding early to prevent injuries or illnesses from escalating into conditions requiring more expensive interventions and potentially generating claims against our company," A Corizon spokeswoman said in an email. The full statement is at the bottom of this story.

After more complaints, Carlson had surgery to remove three bones last week, more than two months after his original injury.

In a direct response to Carlson's grievances, a DOC official wrote the allegations were unsubstantiated and "all actions taken have been appropriate with your care."

Carlson is due for release in 2017. Before his sentence, he worked in construction and landscaping.

"I don't know what we're going to do," Blair Carlson said.

"Simply because he went to prison, made mistakes in his life, doesn't mean he's not entitled to have basic medical care," said Zwillinger.

"There they are not animals, they are human beings," said Blair Carlson.

Full statement from Corizon:

Although we cannot comment on this specific case due to patient privacy laws and the notice of claim, we can tell you that one of the greatest misconceptions about our company – and indeed our entire industry – is that we profit by withholding care. On the contrary, what makes the most clinical and business sense is responding early to prevent injuries or illnesses from escalating into conditions requiring more expensive interventions and potentially generating claims against our company. Corizon Health doctors and nurses work on a daily basis in one of the most challenging environments to deliver care to Arizona's 34,000 inmates, many of whom suffer from chronic disease, substance abuse, mental illness, and a lack of preventive care at much higher rates than the general public. Our clinicians interact with a constantly changing patient population hundreds of thousands of time every year ranging from routine physicals to emergency responses and are equipped with the supplies, tools and resources they need to properly do their job. No clinician is compensated based upon financial performance. As with any event that results in a grievance or a bad clinical outcome, doctors and nurses from elsewhere in the company conduct a thorough chart review and inquiry and we take action based on the outcome of that investigation.

AUDIT OF JAIL'S HEALTH CARE CONTRACT SPARKS CHANGES BY KENDRA HOGUE

Washington County is ratcheting down costs and imposing stricter rules on health care contracting at its jail after a recent audit revealed staffing shortages from its medical contractor and a lack of oversight from the county.

A new request for proposals for jail health care services was issued Nov. 25 by the Washington County Administrator's Office. Bids are due Jan. 16 for inmate care beginning July 1.

The current provider, Corizon Health Services, lost its contract two years earlier than usual.

On Nov. 24, the county's auditor, John Hutzler, released a final audit of jail health care services that showed Corizon had not provided adequate staffing for inmate care.

"We estimate the value of the minimum specified staffing that the county didn't receive between July 1, 2008, and June 30, 2012, to be at least $350,000," read an excerpt of Hutzler's audit.

"After we raised concerns about Corizon staffing in an interim report last year, the county extended Corizon's contract for only two years rather than the four, which the contract would have allowed," Hutzler explained. "That extension will expire June 30, 2015."

On Monday, Dec. 1, Washington County Sheriff Pat Garrett and county administrators sent a letter to Hutzler that defended Corizon, "providing context" for Hutzler's interpretations of Corizon's short-staffing and wasted funds.

In the current contract, the rebuttal letter pointed out, "deference was given to the vendor to adjust and react to staffing anomalies based on their professional judgment. It is important to note that this figure ($350,000) does not represent payment for services not rendered. The auditor's analysis of the staffing deviations accounting for 'understaffing' in any shift, per-position, per-day, did not account for the 'overstaffing' in other positions, shifts and days. Based on our analysis, the medical vendor exceeded the total hours in the staffing plan by more than 2,500."

Corizon is eligible to bid again, under significantly changed terms. The new contract should leave little doubt about expectations, checks and balances, and the ramifications of falling short.

Corizon is not the only game in town.

"There are several providers of jail-and prison-based health care operating in the U.S.," said Philip Bransford, communications officer for Washington County.

Whoever wins the contract will be subject to new accuracy checks from a third-party auditor who will check hospital billings.

More than a dozen changes have been made to the document, including tightened performance and service requirements, new budget controls and clearly spelled-out minimum staffing requirements by position, day and shift.

Rapidly rising costs

The audit makes clear that Washington County also was at fault for the contract confusion at the jail. Among its findings:

• The jail's health care contract was not administered in accordance with the county's guidelines and best practices;

• Certain terms of the contract did not adequately protect county interests; and

• The county didn't forecast and include sufficient funds in the jail's budget to cover its costs from 2007 to 2010.

The county has been outsourcing the jail's health care services since it opened in 1998.

The jail can accommodate 572 inmates and is one of the largest jails in the state, with the capacity to book, lodge and release more than 18,000 new arrivals each year. It's not a prison, so inmates typically spend less than a year in the facility.

Prior to 1998, Washington County's inmate medical care was handled at the old county jail, on Lincoln Street by the county's Department of Health and Human Services.

County officials suggested an audit be scheduled for 2012 after noting "significant increases in jail health care costs and significant overruns of the jail health care budgets from 2007 through 2010."

Washington County Jail's health care services costs increased substantially from $1.2 million in 1999 to nearly $4 million in 2013, with dramatic leaps of approximately $500,000 to $1 million each time the contract was rebid.

The county had opened health care bids three times since 1998, awarding the contract to the same vendor each time — Prison Health Services. Prison Health Services merged with Corizon Health Services in 2011.

The jail's health care contract was administered by the county's Department of Health and Human Services until an interim audit released last year blamed the department for failure to monitor Corizon's performance. The responsibility has since been reassigned to the county's Department of Support Services, Finance Division.

Other suggestions from the earlier audit already have been implemented, including adding dedicated staff resources from the county and forming an "operations team" to ensure quality, timely, efficient delivery of inmate health services.

In the written response to Hutzler's audit, county administrator Robert Davis, assistant administrator Don Bohn and Sheriff Garrett wrote:

"The county and sheriff's office are keenly aware of the constitutional, statutory and moral obligation to provide quality and timely health service to all persons in our custody ... as well as the additional goal of providing these services in an efficient and cost-effective manner."

The County Administrator's Office and Sheriff's Office agreed with all of Hutzler's suggestions except one, which stated that the jail may not assess fees to inmates for its mandatory intake health screening.

Garrett disagreed, noting that the current $10 fee "is supported by state and federal law, complies with the national Commission on Corrections Health Care Standards, and helps control jail costs," recouping about $70,000 per year.

THE MARSHALL PROJECT 156 WEST 56TH STREET, SUITE 701, NEW YORK, NY 10019 POSTED ON TUESDAY, JUNE 16, 2015

Corizon Health Inc. is the largest provider of correctional health care in the country. All told, it is responsible for the care of 345,000 jail and prison inmates. The privately held company rode a wave of prison privatization, but has come under fire for putting profits ahead of quality care. Most recently, Corizon lost a contract to manage the care of prisoners at New York City's Rikers Island, which we reported is part of a larger trend of cities choosing to go with local providers. Maura Ewing spoke with Corizon CEO Dr. Woodrow Myers about his take on Corizon's recent setbacks, the pros and cons of privatization, the company's penchant for secrecy, and the challenges of correctional health care. **Corizon has had some serious setbacks lately. You just lost the contract for Rikers. Since 2012, you lost contracts in Maine, Maryland, Minnesota, and Pennsylvania. You're getting flak in Florida. How do you explain the company's turn of fortune?**

You're right. There have been some losses. There have also been a number of gains as well. There are a total of 40 that have come in since 2012. We're the largest entity in the nation that does this kind of work, we're very responsive, we have to respond to RFPs [requests for proposals] that state and city governments put up. We have 114 contracts now in 27 states. It's a lumpy business, you win some, you lose some. We trade some with our competitors, we take some away from our competitors.

You spent a year, in 1990-91, as health commissioner for Mayor Dinkins of New York. Is Rikers fairly typical of big urban jails, or does it present unusual challenges?

With respect to Corizon in New York, the way that the contract was structured was particularly challenging because we technically reported — and we still do — to the Department of Health and Mental Hygiene, and they had the primary relationship with Health and Hospitals Corporation ([anno-selector i=1]HHC[/anno-selector]), and they had the primary relationship with the Department of Corrections (DOC) and all the other entities that touched on what we did. So there are currently many layers in New York that aren't present in our other contracts.

For-profit companies, not-for-profit companies, we all have similar challenges in that we have to find a way to provide services to a very difficult population in the glare of the public spotlight.

Do you sense that privatization in the field of incarceration — prisons and prison services — is on the rise, or is it suffering some kind of backlash? Do you sense that the momentum has shifted one way or the other since you became CEO in October 2013? What's the advantage of having these facilities run and serviced by for-profit companies?

The total number of patients in jails and prisons being taken care of by private companies today is as high as it's ever been, as states and cities figure out that healthcare provision is hard work. There are lots of rules, lots of regulations, lots of changes that are being made to protect patients. The costs are very difficult to manage if you don't do this kind of work every day, which is why we have about 350,000 patients nationwide.

Is it a very tough business for us? Absolutely it is. Is it probably going to get tougher before it gets easier. Do we succeed 100 percent every day? No, we do not. The hundreds of thousands of visits that we have, we succeed far more often than most folks know. When those failures do occur, we try to make sure that we learn from them. That's the same thing that happens every day in every single clinic or hospital across the country. Some people want to portray us as an industry whose goal it is to provide as little care as possible and make as much money as possible. That's simply not true. Our vision is that we'll provide quality health care and reentry services that will improve the health and safety of our patients, reduce recidivism, and better the communities where we all live and work.

Corizon is simultaneously being accused by critics of cutting corners on health care, and by business analysts for not making enough money (Moody's bond rating for Corizon was recently downgraded). What's got to give?

You've nailed it. Our job is to walk the line. Our job is to provide all the care that a patient needs and only the care that a patient needs. Our job is to use the funds that are provided in the most efficient way possible. And we get hit from both sides. We get hit not just from some of the ratings agencies and the advocates that you cited, but from the everyday citizen that ask the question, Why can't inmates get whatever care they need? And let's get them completely serviced up in whatever elective procedures they want because now they're your responsibility and you should just give them whatever they or their families can possibly imagine. Then you've got folks on the other side saying, Why are you giving them anything at all? These are people who have committed very bad crimes and done very bad things, why should they get their disease treated, and I can't get mine treated? Why should my tax dollars pay for their care and they're not paying for my care? We get it from all sides. But that's the business that we're in, so we've got to be tough.

One of the complaints about for-profit providers generally, especially those that are privately held like Corizon, is a lack of transparency. When Corizon was questioned by the news media in Florida during a contract renewal, the company initially tried to prevent the release of litigation history, claiming it was a "trade secret."

There have been more than 1,300 lawsuits against Corizon in the past five years.

Private companies are not under the same obligation to release documents as are public companies. True fact, legally correct, and it's different in every environment. If you're a federal contractor, it's different than if you're a state contractor, it's different if you're a county contractor, it's different if you're in New York vs. Florida vs. wherever you are. So, number one, we follow the law whatever that law is in whatever jurisdiction we're in.

Secondly, we don't provide information that in a competitive business environment can be used by our competitors, that can be used to figure out what innovations we are offering, how we're pricing, what our costs are etc., etc., because the more information they have on us, the easier it is to compete against us. We don't want to make that easy for them at all. The Ford Motor Company doesn't go around and show its plans for a Taurus to GM. GM doesn't show its plan for its new Chevy Volt upgrade to Ford. It's that kind of a business issue that we face in our business as well.

How would litigation history be useful to your competitors?

Litigation is a very complicated area, but the bottom line is that the vast majority of lawsuits are unfounded — are either dismissed or settled. That is because in the United States of America, it is very easy to sue people and to make allegations in statements, especially when it comes to health care, because the laws allow the individual making the accusation to say whatever the heck they want and the laws prevent us from telling what we believe to be the truth because of issues concerning privacy. So if you say that your dad was mistreated in my care and I didn't, as a doctor or the nurse, do the requested test or procedure, folks like yourself will write that down dutifully and come to me and ask the question: is it true or not? I always have to say to you by law I cannot comment on that because of the HIPAA privacy rules, that's the way it works in the United States today. It clearly puts us in an awkward position because we actually know the answers to the questions. That's why it looks as if we are hiding stuff when we're not legally able to give an answer proving we did what we thought was right.

Every single one of my patients has a lawyer, and most of them haven't been paid. They're hungrily looking for any opportunity that they can to find a way to take advantage — in my opinion — to take advantage of our legal system. So we are a frequent target for accusations of something happening in the facility that may or may not have been related to us or that we may or may not have been involved in. But remember that these guys come — and some women, but mostly men — having not had health care in many cases for a long period of time.

A HEALTH CARE PROVIDER THAT SERVES STATE PRISONS ACROSS FLORIDA RECEIVED A $22,500 FINE AFTER THE STATE PRISONS BUREAU FOUND THAT THE FIRM HAS NOT YET MET ITS END OF A $229 MILLION CONTRACT.

By Arek Sarkissian-(As reported in theThe Gainesville Sun)

Corizon Health was issued a fine by the Florida Department of Corrections after a follow-up audit determined the St. Louis-based company failed to correct deficiencies in care that were found in an initial audit last year.

In 2013, Corizon took over health care services for DOC facilities across two-thirds of the state through a $229 million annual contract that expires in June 2018.

Corizon Health officials said their company was faced with difficult challenges when it took over in-house health services provided by DOC. Company officials say Corizon has made a smooth transition despite bumps along the way.

"There were many improvements made in programs and services during the first year of our contract, and our overall scores have improved significantly," Corizon spokeswoman Susan Morgenstern said.

DOC spokesman McKinley Lewis said the request for "liquidated damages" was the result of an auditing process designed to make sure the company met standards upheld by its contract with DOC.

"Anything short of timely, effective and appropriate health care will not be tolerated," Lewis said.

The correctional institutions where subsequent violations were found included Apalachee east and west, Baker, Liberty, Columbia, Hernando, Polk and Sumter.

The lackluster performance that DOC alleged against Corizon was first revealed in September after former DOC Secretary Mike Crews wrote the company a letter that raised concerns over the quality of medical care, nursing, mental health and administration.

Copies of corrective action plans show the audits revealed failures by Corizon employees to properly maintain records, or provide regular mental health counseling, or meet recently enacted federal standards.

For instance, an audit performed at the Avon Park Correctional Institution showed that for the first quarter of 2014, the facility struggled to adhere to the standards of the federal Prison Rape Elimination Act. Another audit conducted at the Columbia Correctional Institution over the first quarter of 2014 found that Corizon failed to send autopsy results to the DOC mortality review coordinator.

In 2012, Corizon and Pittsburgh-based Wexford Health Sources were awarded contracts by the Legislature to privatize health care services for the state prison system, the third largest in the country. Corizon's coverage spans the state north of Orlando and Wexford manages health services for the remaining facilities in the southern region. The move saw staunch opposition from collective bargaining units, but after a court battle, its method of funding from the state spending plan was augmented by the Legislative Budget Commission.

By September 2013, Corizon began its transition into providing services for DOC facilities by requiring members of the state-paid work force to reapply for jobs under comparable salaries but much costlier benefit plans.

Shortly after both contracts went into effect, DOC embarked on routine audits to confirm that both companies were performing as promised. Last week, recently appointed DOC chief Julie Jones told the Senate Committee on Criminal Justice there was plenty of room for growth.

"The standard of health care with our current providers is not at the level that's covered by their contracts," Jones said. "We're working very diligently with those two vendors that the standard of care is up to the level that's required in those contracts."

Corizon is up for another round of audits and has the opportunity to meet or exceed the standards set by its DOC contract. Morgenstern said the second round of audits that yielded the fine also noted several improvements.

"We know that there is still work to be done and we will work in partnership with the DOC to continue making improvements," Morgenstern said.

KLAS HERALD / TIMES TALLAHASSEE BUREAU

BY Mary Ellen

After two years of complaints about healthcare in Florida's prisons, the private company that has been responsible for the largest share of inmate care — Corizon Health — decided not to renew its $1.1 billion contract with the state Monday, leaving the future of care for 74,000 inmates in limbo when the company pulls out in six months.

The decision by the Tennessee-based company to exercise its right to terminate the contract that was scheduled to expire in 2018 came as the Florida Department of Corrections was attempting to renegotiate the agreement amid reports of inmate maltreatment, chronic understaffing and rising numbers of unnatural inmate deaths.

"We appreciate the contracts for inmate health services permit very little of the flexibility that Secretary [Julie] Jones would like in order to address issues such as staffing, mental health care, and electronic health records," Corizon Chief Executive Officer Karey Witty said in a statement. "We have tried to address the department's concerns but have found the terms of the current contract too constraining. At this point, we believe the best way to move forward is to focus our efforts on a successful transition to a new provider."

In February, Department of Corrections Secretary Julie Jones was ordered to renegotiate the contract by Sen. Greg Evers, R-Baker, chairman of the Senate Criminal Justice Committee, after a series of reports in the Miami Herald and other news organizations showed suspicious inmate deaths were covered up or never reviewed, staffing was inadequate, and inmate grievances and complaints of harmful medical care were dismissed or ignored.

Audits conducted by the state's Correctional Medical Authority found problems with inadequate medical care, nursing and staffing shortages, and hundreds of pending lawsuits against the state and the healthcare companies claiming inadequate care.

Last year, 346 inmates died in Florida prisons — 176 of them listed with no immediate cause of death. It was the highest number on record, even though the number of inmates in Florida prisons has declined.

The decision is a blow to the effort by several legislators and Gov. Rick Scott to privatize medical care in Florida prisons. After failing to pass legislation to authorize the state to outsource its prison healthcare to companies that contributed heavily to Republican campaigns, a provision allowing the privatization effort was quietly inserted into the 2011 budget, during the governor's first term.

A union-led lawsuit challenged the language in court but it was upheld and the contracts were allowed.

Under the deal first signed in 2013, Corizon Health is being paid $229 million a year until June 30, 2018, to provide healthcare to 74,000 inmates at 111 of Florida's prisons, work camps and work-release centers in North and Central Florida. Wexford Health Services is being paid $48 million a year until Dec. 20, 2017, to provide health services to about 15,000 inmates at nine prisons in South Florida.

The contract requires that both companies provide medical care to inmates for 7 percent less than it cost the state in 2010, but both companies sought and received increases in the terms of their original agreement.

In 2014, former FDC Secretary Michael Crews agreed to raise the annual contract with Corizon and Wexford by $3.2 million. Subsequent audits revealed that even after the increased payments, Corizon failed to meet its contract obligations regarding staffing and medical care.

Evers asked the agency to renegotiate the contracts with both private prison providers to demand higher standards of care and hold them accountable for deaths and injuries. Jones also criticized the contracts as too lenient for the vendors and issued an invitation to rebid the contract on Feb. 23.

The department did not explain what will be next for the prison system, but said in a statement that updates would be forthcoming.

"In the coming months, Secretary Jones will work closely with the Department's Office of Health Services to ensure that the appropriate staff and resources are available at our facilities to continue seamless delivery of appropriate medical care to our inmate population," the statement said.

Evers said he was not prepared to comment on the decision but said he considered it a "good sign" that Jones was following through on directions to hold the company accountable for providing the level of care they agreed to when they signed the contract with the state.

"This is good news," said Rep. Carlos Trujillo, R-Miami, who chairs the House Criminal Justice subcommittee that oversees prisons. He had been supportive of the effort to renegotiate the contract because "the healthcare outcomes were some of the worst in any sort of managed care."

"It's a huge contract. People don't walk away from this easily," Trujillo said. "It further goes to show that the secretary is holding people accountable. Regardless of their reason for leaving, she's forcing people to come to the table and push for the outcomes."

Trujillo said that the options include providing a "hybrid" system that would rely on private healthcare services in areas of the state where that is most efficient and return to in-house medical staffing in other parts of the state.

THE HEALTH CARE INDUSTRY IN RESPONSE

A LETTER TO D.C. COUNCIL CHAIRMAN PHIL MENDELSON

Corizon Health issued a letter to D.C. City Council Chairman Phil Mendelson in response to several questions he raised regarding Corizon Health's testimony during the March 12 Office of Contracting and Procurement oversight hearing.

Re: Corizon Health Testimony

Dear Chairman Mendelson:

Thank you again for giving me and my Corizon Health colleagues the opportunity to appear before your March 12 Office of Contracting and Procurement oversight hearing. This letter is intended to respond to several questions you raised and, in doing so, provide additional material for the hearing record.

Litigation: As part of my response to your question about litigation, I testified that the ratio of lawsuits to our average daily patient population is substantially lower than Unity Health's. Please let me offer some additional background:

Mr. Chairman, it **is** important to note that Unity has applied for and enjoys the status of a "deemed Federal health center" (please see the attached HRSA public record). As a result, Unity is in many cases protected from malpractice and other professional liability lawsuits filed under the Federal Tort Claims Act. Corizon Health has no such protection. Accordingly, any comparison of lawsuits filed is "apples to oranges" and likely in Unity's favor. Furthermore, inmates and returning citizens who are legitimately harmed and seek legal redress, may well not have the same recourse under the incumbent contract as they would under the awarded agreement. With that stated, the following ratios illustrate our case for Corizon Health having fewer lawsuits per inmate served than Unity:

1. Unity states it has been subject to eleven lawsuits in caring for an average of 2,500 inmates annually over the past five years. That equates to one lawsuit for every 1,136 inmates served.
2. Corizon Health, on the other hand, has served on average 400,000 inmates annually over the past five years and has had 1,364 lawsuits. That equates to one lawsuit for every 1,466 inmates served.

Having provided correctional healthcare services for more than 30 years, our company has gained unique knowledge and experience allowing for the administration of the most effective risk-management available. During the period of June 1, 2009 to May 31, 2014, our company provided literally millions of patient care encounters – yet during this same period, we have only been subjected to 1,364 lawsuits.

Of these 1,364 lawsuits, 942 (69%) are now closed while 422 (31%) remain open. Of the closed lawsuits, fully 821 (87%) were dismissed by the courts, administratively closed or resulted in a judgment in favor of Corizon Health. Furthermore, it serves as compelling evidence of our strong, effective professional liability risk-management program that Corizon Health has elected to settle only approximately 117 (12%) of the closed lawsuits after careful evaluation of the costs associated with continued litigation. Consistent with the highly litigious nature of the correctional healthcare industry, it is important to note that 1,049 (77%) of the healthcare-related lawsuits filed against Corizon Health over the past five years were initiated by pro se inmates. Further, of the 315 represented healthcare-related lawsuits filed against Corizon Health, only 123 (39%) remain open at this time.

As you may be aware, a very detailed five-year combined litigation history for Corizon Health, Inc. and its related company Corizon, LLC. (collectively "Corizon") was provided on a proprietary basis as part of our RFP response, and for consideration in the ultimate award decision.

Partnerships with Certified Business Enterprises, Community Clinics and Other Service Providers: You asked my colleague, Michael Miller, about our relationships with D.C. community clinics able to provide outside clinical, counseling and other pertinent re-entry services.

Partnership has been the foundation of the successful relationships Corizon Health builds with our clients. In our RFP submission, we committed to have our healthcare team work closely and collaboratively with the community providers of the Community-Oriented Correctional Healthcare System (COCHS), including with University Legal Services (ULS), the United States Parole Commission (USPC) and Addiction Prevention and Recovery Administration (APRA), to maintain effectual relationships befitting the inmate population. Corizon will cooperate with ULS in assisting inmates in connecting with Department of Behavioral Health's Core Service Agencies and other providers in the community as part of our discharge planning process.

Corizon Health has contracted with multiple CBE healthcare providers to grant them more than 40 percent of the dollar amount of the primary contract, exceeding the requirement set forth in the RFP. More specifically, we have committed to deliver more than $30 million in CBE revenue to D.C.-based MBI Health Services, LLC, our partner who will provide critical nurse staffing and behavioral health services. MBI has a proven track record of providing quality healthcare services, as well as mentoring, training, job placement, recovery group activity and outreach services to returning citizens. Another local CBE, Business 2IT Solutions, will provide us with technology support.

We have also partnered with George Washington University Medical Faculty Associates to implement cost-effective 24/7 telemedicine services, and have formal letters of partnership intent signed by Family and Medical Counseling Service, Inc. and Mary's Center. Beyond that, as part of our planning and preparation for being awarded the contract, we have contacted an array of other local healthcare centers with requests for partnership to ensure we establish a broad community network.

Corizon Health advocates the philosophy that release-planning efforts begin during the intake process and continue through the continuum of incarceration. Cognizant of this, we will continue the practice of incorporating discharge planning into the intake process, clinical assessing and planning treatment for all patients entering and leaving the DOC system.

The fundamental goals of our discharge planning process committed to the DOC are:

1 To help reduce recidivism;
2 To help increase public health and safety;
3 To assist the inmate patient in acquiring life skills they need to succeed in the community;
4 To increase the inmate patient's awareness of the symptoms of their illness;
5 To increase the inmate patient's awareness of how to care for their illness post release;
6 To increase the inmate's knowledge of the community resources available; and
7 To direct the inmate patient on where to go and how to access the care they need when released.

Mr. Chairman, I sincerely hope these responses address your questions to your satisfaction. Let me reiterate that we at Corizon Health have put our faith in the District's procurement process, and hope you and your colleagues on the Council will do the same.

Sincerely,
Woodrow Augustus Myers, Jr., MD
Chief Executive Officer
Download and share this letter here.

About Corizon Health Corizon Health is the nation's leader in correctional healthcare, providing quality healthcare services to 50 clients at 431 facilities across the country serving over 321,000 inmates in 25 states. With its corporate headquarters in Brentwood, Tenn. Corizon Health is the leading provider of correctional healthcare services in the United States. For more information, please visit www.corizonhealth.com.

MONITARY RETALIATION BY INDUSTRY ON THOSE WHO FILE SUIT

SHIRLEY JENKINS, as Personal Representative for the Estate of Jovon Frazier, deceased, Plaintiff, v. CORIZON HEALTH, INC., Defendant. United States District Court, M.D. Florida, Tampa Division. Case No. 8:13-cv-2796-T-30TGW. May 20, 2016.

THIS CAUSE comes before the Court upon Defendant Corizon Health, Inc.'s Motion for Attorneys' Fees and Costs (Dkt. 110) and Plaintiff's Response in Opposition (Dkt. 116). The Court, having reviewed the motion, response, and being otherwise advised in the premises, concludes that the motion should be denied.

DISCUSSION

Plaintiff Shirley Jenkins, as Personal Representative for the Estate of Jovon Frazier, deceased, brought this section 1983 case against Defendant Corizon Health, Inc., alleging Corizon was deliberately indifferent to Frazier's serious medical needs because Corizon should have referred Frazier to an outside healthcare provider sooner. Specifically, Plaintiff alleged that, by the time Corizon referred Frazier to outside care, it was too late to avoid amputation of his left arm and his subsequent death due to osteosarcoma. And that it was Corizon's custom, policy, and practice to discourage diagnostic testing and outside care for financial reasons.

On March 24, 2016, the Court granted Corizon's dispositive motion for summary judgment (Dkt. 108) and on March 25, 2016, final judgment was entered in its favor (Dkt. 109).

Corizon now argues that it is entitled to attorneys' fees and costs because Plaintiff's section 1983 claim was frivolous, unreasonable, or without foundation. In response, Plaintiff argues that a failure to prevail on the claim does not render the claim frivolous or groundless, and that the Court carefully considered Plaintiff's claim prior to rendering judgment in Corizon's favor. Upon careful consideration of the parties' arguments, the Court declines to award attorneys' fees to Corizon.

In *Sullivan v. School Board of Pinellas County,* 773 F.2d 1182 (11th Cir. 1985), the Eleventh Circuit stated that "a district court may in its discretion award attorneys' fees to a prevailing defendant in a . . . section 1983 action upon a finding that the plaintiff's lawsuit was frivolous, unreasonable, or without foundation." *Id.* at 1188 (internal quotations omitted). "In determining whether a suit is frivolous, 'a district court must focus on the question whether the case is so lacking in arguable merit as to be groundless or without foundation rather than whether the claim was ultimately successful.'" *Id.* at 1189 (quoting *Jones v. Texas Tech University,* 656 F.2d 1137, 1145 (5th Cir. 1981)); *see also Christianburg Garment Co. v. EEOC,* 434 U.S. 412, 421 (1978);*Hughes v. Rowe,* 449 U.S. 5, 14 (1980).

The Supreme Court in *Christianburg* cautioned, as follows:

[i]n applying these criteria, it is important that a district court resist the understandable temptation to engage in post hoc reasoning by concluding that, because a plaintiff did not ultimately prevail, his action must have been unreasonable or without foundation. This kind of hindsight logic could discourage all but the most airtight claims . . . Even when the law or the facts appear questionable or unfavorable at the outset, a party may have an entirely reasonable ground for bringing suit. 434 U.S. at 421-22.

Notably, even if a defendant prevails on summary judgment in a section 1983 suit for damages, an award of attorneys' fees is not appropriate if the case was difficult, or if the "plaintiff's claims [were] meritorious enough to receive careful attention and review." *Busby v. City of Orlando,* 931 F.2d 764, 787 (11th Cir. 1991); *see also Walker v. Nationsbank of Fla. N.A.,* 53 F.3d 1548, 1559 (11th Cir. 1995). In *Hughes,* the Supreme Court noted:

Even those allegations that were properly dismissed for failure to state a claim deserved and received the careful consideration of both the District Court and the Court of Appeals. Allegations that, upon careful examination, prove legally insufficient to require a trial are not, for that reason alone, groundless or without foundation as required by Christianburg.

449 U.S. at 15-16 (internal quotations omitted).

In this case, the Court denied Corizon's motion to dismiss and the parties engaged in discovery. Ultimately, Plaintiff's claim against Corizon failed because the Court determined on summary judgment that Plaintiff could not establish, as a matter of law, that Corizon had a policy or custom in place that was the moving force behind a constitutional violation. Admittedly, the Court stated in its Order that there was not "even a scintilla of evidence establishing, or even suggesting" a policy or custom. But this does not necessarily render Plaintiff's claim baseless. The history of this case reveals that Plaintiff's complaint was sufficiently "meritorious enough to receive careful attention and review." *Busby,* 931 F.2d at 787. Accordingly, Corizon's motion for attorneys' fees is denied.

Corizon also moves for costs in the amount of $13,520.56. Although Corizon is clearly entitled to costs under 28 U.S.C. § 1920, Corizon neglected to file a Bill of Costs and its motion does not otherwise explain the requested costs in any way (other than to attach Exhibit B, which is an itemization of the costs without any supporting documentation), or state that the costs were necessarily obtained for use in this case. Accordingly, the request for costs is denied without prejudice to Corizon to renew its request by filing an appropriate Bill of Costs. The Bill of Costs shall attach documentation in support of the requested costs.

It is therefore ORDERED AND ADJUDGED that:

1. Defendant Corizon Health, Inc.'s Motion for Attorneys' Fees and Costs (Dkt. 110) is denied to the extent stated herein.2. Defendant shall file a Bill of Costs within fourteen (14) days of this Order.The Bill of Costs shall attach documentation in support of the requested costs.3. Any objection to the Bill of Costs shall be filed within fourteen (14) days from the filing of the Bill of Costs.

IMPROPRIETIES IN ARIZONA PRISON CONTRACTS

Even though Wexford has had a checkered history, Arizona awarded it the healthcare contract and the following communications indicate both Arizona and Wexford acting with deliberate indifference and Arizona changing providers to coverup the indifference.

The following is the corrisponence found between Wexford Health Sources and Arizona Department of Corrections.

Arizona Department of Corrections

1601 WEST JEFFERSON

PHOENIX, ARIZONA 85007

(602) 542-5497

www.azcorrections.gov

JANICE K. BREWER GOVERNOR

CHARLES L. RYAN DIRECTOR

Electronic Mail and Certified Mail - Return Receipt Requested

September 28, 2012

Karen Mullenix

Wexford Health Sources

1850 N. Central Avenue, Suite 1050

Phoenix, Arizona 85004

Re: Contract No. 120075DC

Dear Ms. Mullenix:

As a follow-up to Director Ryan's communication to Mr. Hale, the response to Arizona Department of Correction's (ADC) demand for Right to Assurance in accordance with section 8.1 of the Uniform Terms and Conditions shall be delivered by October 1, 2012.

Wexford's response to the Notice of Referral to Take Action shall be delivered no later than October 9, 2012.

Additionally, Wexford shall respond to the Cure Notice no later than October 22, 2012. In granting this extension, it is ADC's expectation that Wexford will begin corrective action on all identified deficiencies immediately, irrespective of the extended response dates.

In furtherance of the Department's commitment to this contract and consistent with Director Ryan's offer to Wexford on Monday, September 24, 2012,1 will make myself, and other ADC Health Service Monitoring staff, available to you to provide any necessary explanation of identified deficiencies and/or clarification of ADC's compliance expectations. We trust that this exchange will be of value as Wexford completes corrective action plans.

Sincerely,

Joe Profiri
Contract Beds Operations Director
Arizona Department of Corrections

Arizona Department of Corrections
1601 WEST JEFFERSON

PHOENIX, ARIZONA 85007
(602) 542-5497
www.azscorrections.gov
JANICE K. BREWER GOVERNOR
CHARLES L. RYAN DIRECTOR
Hand Delivered. Electronic Mail, and
Certified Mail - Return Receipt Requested

September 21, 2012

Karen Mullenix
Wexford Health Sources
1850 N. Central Avenue, Suite 1050
Phoenix, Arizona 85004

Re: Notice of Referral to Take Action - Contract No. 120075DC

Dear Ms. Mullenix:

The purpose of this letter is notify you of a potential monetary sanction of ten thousand dollars ($10,000.00) to be imposed for non-compliance with the terms and conditions of the above referenced contract between Wexford Health Sources ("Wexford") and the Arizona Department of Corrections ("Department").

The action is being made in accordance with the contract's Special Terms and Conditions, Section 2.19 Contract Monitoring General Requirements, paragraph 2.19.6 which states:

2.19.6 If non-compliance issues are identified or discovered, during a quarterly audit required under Section 2.20 or any other monitoring activity, whose gravity or severity cannot be mitigated by the Contractor's ability to bring its performance back into compliance at a future date, the Department Contract Monitor shall notify the Contractor's Arizona CEO and Area Manager in writing that the matter shall be referred to the Chief Procurement Officer to take action against die Contractor, including but not limited to monetary sanctions, suspension, refusal to renew, or termination of the Contract.

This matter is being referred to the Chief Procurement Officer for immediate adverse action for, but not limited to, the following reason(s):

An act of indifference that disregards a known and excessive risk to an inmate's health or safety or violates an inmate's civil rights.

Failure to substantially meet an essential standard of the National Commission on Correctional Health Care ("NCCHC"), to the extent that the Contractor's ability to bring its performance back into compliance at a future date does not mitigate the gravity or severity of the non-compliance.

Substantial failure to provide medically necessary services that the Contractor is required to provide under the terms of a Contract resulting from this Request for Proposal to the extent that the Contractor's ability to bring its performance back into compliance at a future date does not mitigate the gravity or severity of the non-compliance.

Non-compliance identified or discovered, during a monitoring activity, whose gravity or severity cannot be mitigated by the Contractor's ability to bring its performance back into compliance at a future date.

Failure to provide accurate and timely information to the Department or NCCHC.

Failure to comply with any other NCCHC standards not identified in the contract.

The circumstances are as follows:

On August 27, 2012, between approximately 0600 and 0630 hours, while conducting diabetic insulin line in the medical unit at ASPC - Lewis - Morey Unit, Licensed Practical Nurse (LPN) N. Nwaohia contaminated a vial of insulin being used on the line. This contamination occurred when LPN Nwaohia drew insulin with a syringe for a Hepatitis-C positive inmate from a vial of "Regular" insulin and injected this insulin into the inmate. Utilizing the same syringe, she then drew a second dose of insulin from a vial of "Lantus" insulin and injected the secondary dose into the same inmate. LPN Nwaohia's actions contaminated the multi-dose "Lantus" vial. This vial was then utilized to provide insulin to other insulin dependent inmates.

Despite Wexford Nurse Lindsay Stephen becoming aware of this information on August 27, 2012, she did not file a report on the event until September 4, 2012. Rather, on August 27, 2012, she disposed of the insulin vials thought to have been involved in the contamination event and said nothing of the possible contamination event or her actions in destroying the insulin vials.

In speaking with Wexford Site Manager Sumi Erno on September 7, 2012, she reports contacting Wexford Regional leadership on August 28, 2012, specifically, Linda Maschner to report the incident to her. Ms. Erno. reported being directed by Ms. Maschner to begin identifying IDDM inmates so baseline testing of them for Hepatitis-C could commence. As a precaution, baseline testing was also conducted for HIV. (The index inmate, although known to be positive for Hepatitis-C, was subsequently tested for both Hepatitis-C and

HIV.) Pending receipt of those test results, plans were implemented to test all inmates potentially exposed through this event for both Hepatitis-C and HIV. Test results for the index inmate later confirmed him as positive for Hepatitis-C and negative for HIV.

In identifying these inmates, Ms. Erno initially reported on August 28, 2012, as having 105 inmates at Lewis that receive insulin. This number later changed to 103, based on a spreadsheet created by Wexford medical personnel at the Lewis Complex listing inmates receiving insulin at Lewis. In review of this list duplication of some inmates was noted, thus the 103 number derived from this list was determined questionable.

Additionally, the Department received a report from Wexford generated from the online reporting system of their subcontracted Pharmacy (Diamond Pharmacy Service) on September 5, 2012, which reflected 91 inmates receiving insulin at Lewis. In an email coinciding with the provision of this report, Wexford Director Karen Mullenix, stipulates the report was generated by Wexford's Site Manager at Lewis (Sumi Erno) and that she (Mullenix) has concern with the information Ms. Erno has provided thus far.

Due to the continued fluctuation of information from Wexford regarding the number of potentially impacted inmates and the clear lack of systems in place to readily identify insulin dependent inmates/chronic care inmates, ADC deployed the following resources to ASPC-Lewis to support Wexford and ensure all possible data sources were culled to determine a true number of potentially affected inmates:

On September 5, 2012 ADC deployed an Audit Nurse Supervisor and an Audit Nurse

On September 6, 2012, ADC deployed an Audit Nurse Supervisor, two Audit Nurses, a Pharmacy Monitor, Contract Monitor, and administrative support

On September 7, 2012, ADC deployed an Operations Director, an Audit Nurse Supervisor, Contract Monitor and administrative support

On September 6 and 7,2012, ADC Health Service personnel and Wexford's Site Manager Sumi Erno and Director of Nursing Nicole Armenia reviewed inmate Medical files/charts, Medical Administration Records and Diamond Pharmacy's ORP system; conducting comparative review of each to arrive at a comprehensive accounting of the total number of inmates thought to be on insulin. Upon conclusion of the review on September 6, 2012, the total number of inmates was determined to be 111.

On September 7,2012, one additional insulin dependent inmate was identified who had not been previously identified increasing the total number to 112. This inmate was housed in the Inpatient Clinic which maintains its own/separate supply of insulin; thus this inmate would reportedly not have been affected by the cross contamination incident.

Of the 112 identified inmates, eight inmates were determined to not have received insulin on September 27, 2012, as they were being treated with medication that did not require injection. Additionally, seven inmates were determined to have been "no shows" for insulin line on August 27,2012. Two showed for insulin line, but refused their insulin medication.

Based on this data, it was determined that 94 inmates were at risk from the contamination of the "Lantus" insulin vial.

Despite information to indicate that some inmates may not have been exposure candidates, such as the aforementioned that didn't show up for insulin line or refused insulin and/or where known carriers of Hepatitis C prior to the exposure event in conjunction with threat of HIV having been eliminated through HIV testing of inmate involved in the initial contamination event, it was determined during a teleconference with Jim Reinhart and Dan Conn on September 7,2012 that all 112 identified inmates would be baseline tested. This was prudent, based on the noted lack of records management, specifically the inability to readily identify chronic care insulin dependent inmates and the inability to locate Medication Administration Records for five inmates appearing on the list.

Baseline testing occurred at ASPC - Lewis as follows:

August 29, 2012 - .... 1 Blood Draw

August 30,2012 - .... 40 Blood Draws

August 31, 2012- .... 23 Blood Draws

September 5,2012 - .... 4 Blood Draws

September 6,2012 - .... 10 Blood Draws

September 7,2012 -... 29 Blood Draws

Total: 107 Blood Draws

Three inmates appearing on the list were transferred to Kingman before their blood could be drawn at Lewis and ADC made arrangements to have ASP - Kingman Medical complete blood draws on these inmates which were completed by September 10, 2012. ADC also made arrangement for these inmates to be provided information regarding the contamination event necessitating the testing through Kingman medical personnel.

One inmate at Lewis refused to have his blood drawn and one other inmate was released prior to testing. Nicole Armenta, Wexford Director of Nursing at Lewis reported she had telephoned the released inmate's home and left a message for the inmate to contact her to arrange testing. As of September 11, 2012 there had been no known direct contact via Wexford with this inmate. On September, 11, 2012, ADC initiated contact with this released inmate through the Community Correction Bureau. The offender's assigned Community Corrections Officer conducted a site visit at the offender's home, during which the offender telephoned the ADC Contract Monitor at Lewis in the presence of his Community Corrections Officer. The offender informed the Monitor that he had not taken any insulin on August 27, 2012 prior to being released. The offender was offered testing in accordance with the exposure protocol, which he declined and signed a Refusal to Submit to Treatment form 1101-4 on September 17, 2012, which was countersigned by his assigned Community Corrections Officer as a witness. Upon completion of the aforementioned testing, 110 of the potentially affected inmates completed baseline testing, and accounting for the two refusals, all 112 identified inmates have either been tested or offered testing.

The aforementioned significant issues require corrective action. In accordance with the contract's Special Terms and Conditions, Section 2.19 Contract Monitoring General Requirements, paragraph 2.19.7, you have ten (10) calendar days to appeal in writing disputing a finding of non-compliance that results in either a cure notice or a decision to refer the matter to the Chief Procurement Officer for action.

Sincerely,

Joe Profiri
Contract Beds Operations Director
Arizona Department of Corrections

_____

Arizona Department of Corrections
1601 WEST JEFFERSON
PHOENIX, ARIZONA 85007
(602) 542-5497
www.azcorrections.gov

JANICE K. BREWER GOVERNOR
CHARLES L, RYAN DIRECTOR
Hand Delivered, Electronic Mail, and
Certified Mail - Return Receipt Requested

September 21, 2012
Karen Mullenix, Director
Wexford Health Sources
1850 N. Central Avenue, Suite 1050
Phoenix, Arizona 85004

Re: Written Cure Notification - Contract No. 120075DC

Dear Ms. Mullenix:

The purpose of this letter is notify you of details of non-compliance, required corrective actions, and timeline for action to the above referenced contract between Wexford Health Sources ("Wexford") and the Arizona Department of Corrections ("ADC ").

The action is being made in accordance with the contract's Special Terms and Conditions, Section 2.19 Contract Monitoring General Requirements, paragraph 2.19.5, which states:

If non-compliance issues, other than those identified in Subsection 2.19.6, are identified during a quarterly audit required under Section 2.20, or any other monitoring activity, the Department Monitoring Staff shall provide a written cure notice to the Contractor's Arizona CEO and Area Manager regarding the details of the non-compliance, the required corrective action, and the period of time allowed to bring performance back into compliance with Contract requirements.

If, at the end of the specified time period, the Contractor has complied with the cure notice requirements, the Department shall take no further action.

(2.19.5.1)

If, however, the Contractor has not complied with the cure notice requirements, the Department Contract Monitor shall notify the Contractor's Arizona CEO and Area Manager in writing that the matter shall be referred to the Chief Procurement Officer to take action against the Contractor, including but not limited to monetary sanctions, suspension, refusal to renew, or termination of the Contract. (2.19.5.2)

Several events detailing significant issues of non-compliance are described below:

August 17, 2012, ASPC-Perryville/Lumley Unit

On August 17, 2012, Wexford nursing personnel were distributing medication on Lumley Unit - Yard 24 to include "watch swallow" medications. In accordance with "watch swallow" protocols, certain medications in powder form require administration to be completed via "floating" the medication in a small cup of water, which the patient drinks. During this distribution of medication, Wexford nurses depleted their stock of cups prior to completing medication distribution to the inmate population. Wexford nurses tailed to stop the medication line and retrieve additional plastic cups, as would have been appropriate. Rather than refilling the supply of cups, a Wexford nurse placed the powdered "watch swallow" medication in an inmate's hand, directing the inmate to lick the powdered medication from her own hand.

This improper administration of medication instigated disorderly behavior by the affected inmate, requiring a security response. The nurses' disregard for proper protocol in administering this inmate's medication and their disrespect for the inmate are significant non-compliance issues that require corrective action.

August 22, 2012, Medication Expiration Report (Statewide)

During the month of August 2012, ADC conducted random reviews of prescriptions, utilizing the Medication Expiration Report published by Wexford for July 1 - August 11, 2012. In completing this review, ADC learned that a significant number of inmates may not have been receiving their medications as prescribed due to expired prescription(s) and inappropriate renewals or refills. Approximately 8,358 prescriptions required review and potential renewal to ensure inmates received their required medications.

Wexford's lack of communication to its field supervisors regarding the necessary process for reviewing the Medication Expiration Report for renewal of medication, together with Wexford's delayed response and lack of urgency to correct the identified problem, contributed to this significant non-compliance issue. Specifically, during a meeting on August 22, 2012, between ADC's Monitoring Bureau leadership and Wexford Regional and Corporate personnel, it was apparent, based on statements from Wexford's Corporate Pharmacist, Denise Mervis, Pharm.D., that Wexford was aware of the expired medication issue, but had not taken adequate, if any, action to correct it. In this meeting, Dr. Mervis referred to the expired medication renewals as a critical issue.

When asked on August 22, 2012 what actions Wexford had undertaken to correct this problem, Wexford leadership advised that they intended to conduct an initial review of the July 1, 2012 - August 11, 2012 Medication Expiration Report beginning August 27, 2012. Wexford's decision to wait five days to begin reviewing the Medication Expiration Report was an inadequate response to a significant issue of grave concern to ADC. As a result of Wexford's delayed response, ADC deployed State resources on August 23, 2012 to ADC prison complexes statewide to review various data sources in an effort to identify inmates in need of medication renewal and to ensure that renewal actually occurred. Multiple ADC prison complexes also enhanced security vigilance by increasing the rate of security checks to 30-minute intervals on all inmates to ensure the well-being of the inmate population.

August 23, 2012, ASPC-Florence/Central Unit

On August 23, 2012, an inmate was found hanging from a sheet in his housing location. ADC staff removed the sheet, placed the inmate on a gurney, and arranged for air transport to an outside hospital. The inmate (MH-3) was last seen by an ADC psychiatrist provider on May 1, 2012. At that time, the provider prescribed lithium carbonate, a "watch swallow" medication used as a mood stabilizer, for 180 days. Medication Administration Records (MARs) showed this inmate received his medication in May, June, and July. On July 18, 2012, during a psychiatric follow-up, the inmate reported that the lithium carbonate had been helpful in stabilizing his mood. During ADC's investigation of this incident, ADC determined that this inmate had not received his psychotropic medication for the first 23 days of August 2012, as evidenced by the feet that no MAR had been generated. Failing to deliver psychotropic medication as prescribed is a significant, non-compliance issue.

August 27, 2012, ASPC-Lewis/Morey Unit

On August 27, 2012, between approximately 0600 and 0630 hours, while conducting diabetic insulin line in the medical unit at ASPC - Lewis - Morey Unit, Licensed Practical Nurse (LPN) N. Nwaohia contaminated a vial of insulin being used on the line. This contamination occurred when LPN Nwaohia drew insulin with a syringe for a Hepatitis-C positive inmate from a vial of "Regular" insulin and injected this insulin into the inmate. Utilizing the same syringe, she then drew a second dose of insulin from a vial of "Lantus" insulin and injected the secondary dose into the same inmate. LPN Nwaohia's actions contaminated the multi-dose "Lantus" vial. This vial was then utilized to provide insulin to other insulin dependent, inmates.

Despite Wexford's Nurse Lindsay Stephen becoming aware of this information on August 27, 2012, Ms. Stephen did not file an Incident Report on the event, in accordance with ADC policy, until September 4,2012. Rather, on August 27,2012, she disposed of the insulin vials thought to have been involved in the contamination event and failed to notify Wexford management or appropriate ADC staff of the contamination event or her actions in destroying the insulin vials.

Wexford Site Manager Sumi Erno reported contacting Wexford Regional Manager Linda Maschner on August 28, 2012, to report the incident to her. Ms, Erno reported being directed by Ms. Maschner to begin identifying Insulin Dependent Diabetes Mellitus (IDDM) inmates so that baseline testing for Hepatitis-C could commence. As a precaution, baseline testing was also conducted for HIV. (The index inmate, although known to be positive for Hepatitis-C, was subsequently tested for both Hepatitis-C and HIV.) Pending receipt of those test results, plans were implemented to test all inmates potentially exposed through this event for both Hepatitis-C and HIV. Test results for the index inmate later confirmed him as positive for Hepatitis-C and negative for HIV.

Also, on August 28, 2012, upon direction of Wexford Management, Wexford RN Supervisor Sienkiewicz contacted AB Staffing, the subcontracted employer of LPN Nwaohia. Ms. Sienkiewicz reportedly advised AB Staffing that LPN Nwaohia would be prohibited from performing nursing services in support of Wexford contracts in the state. Wexford requested that AB Staffing file a complaint with the Arizona State Board of Nursing regarding LPN Nwaohia's actions. One week later, on September 4, 2012, while following up at ADC's request, Wexford learned that no complaint regarding LPN Nwaohia had been received by the Board. Wexford Regional Manager Maschner then formally submitted the complaint on the afternoon of September 4, 2012.[1]

In identifying IDDM inmates, Ms. Erno initially reported on August 28, 2012, as having 105 inmates at Lewis that receive insulin. This number later changed to 103, following review of a spreadsheet created by Wexford medical personnel at the Lewis Complex listing inmates receiving insulin at Lewis. In review of this list, duplication of some inmates was noted, thus the 103 number derived from this list was determined questionable.

Additionally, the Department received a report from Wexford generated from the online reporting system of their subcontracted Pharmacy (Diamond Pharmacy Service) on September 5, 2012, which reflected 91 inmates receiving insulin at Lewis. In an email coinciding with the provision of this report, Wexford Director Karen Mullenix, stipulated that the report was generated by Wexford's Site Manager at Lewis (Sumi Emo) and that she (Mullenix) had concerns with the validity of the information Ms. Erno had provided thus far.

On September 5, 2012, during a meeting with inmates at ASPC-Lewis, an additional 9 inmates not previously identified by Wexford were added to the list of those potentially exposed.

Due to the continued fluctuation of information from Wexford and the lack of systems in place to readily identify insulin dependent/chronic care inmates, ADC deployed additional compliance monitoring staff to ASPC-Lewis on September 5, 6, & 7. Wexford did not deploy additional resources to the site until September 6, 2012. It was not until Friday, September 7, 2012, that the total population of insulin dependent inmates and the subset of potentially exposed inmates were identified with certainty. Further, baseline testing of this population was not completed until September 10, 2012, despite Wexford's earlier reporting that this had been completed on September 4,2012.

The failure to follow established nursing protocols, poor record keeping, mismanagement of documentation, inadequate and inaccurate communication, lack of timely managerial or administrative support, and failure to ensure that corrective action had been completed represent serious issues of non-compliance.

September 13, 2012, ASPC-Perryville/Santa Rosa Unit

On September 13, 2012, at approximately 1715 hours, Wexford Director Karen Mullenix notified ADC of a possible case of pertussis (whooping cough) at ASPC-Perryville. Wexford management did not know the name(s) or number(s) of inmate(s) affected, or the unit(s) identified with the reported case. Wexford's notification of the reported pertussis case was inadequate and inconsistent. Further, without sufficient factual detail of the incident, Wexford reported no action plan to address the situation.

Ms. Mullenix further reported that Wexford's Dr. Palmer spoke to both the County and State Health Departments about the case. She also reported that Dr. Bell (Regional Medical Manager) was called about this issue two days prior, September 11, 2012, and although he was aware of the potential diagnosis, that information had not been communicated to either Ms. Mullenix or the ADC Site Monitors. ADC Audit Nurse Mendoza contacted Wexford facility personnel and determined that an inmate tested positive for pertussis on August 13, 2012, approximately 30 days prior to Wexford's notification to ADC. ADC Audit Nurse Mendoza also confirmed the inmate's name, number and location.

In a phone conversation later that evening with Site Manager Deb Cherry and Richard Pratt, ADC Interim Assistant Director, Health Services Monitoring Bureau, it was reported that Dr. Palmer had seen the inmate who tested positive for pertussis approximately 10 days prior to Wexford's notification to ADC. Ms. Cherry also advised she was aware of this issue up to 10 days prior and failed to advise either Ms. Mullenix or ADC Site Monitors at that time. During ADC's investigation, Ms. Cherry speculated that the patient may have unknowingly contracted the disease through inmate visitation in the past few weeks, as the inmate was later contacted by her visitor to advise she or her child had been diagnosed with pertussis. Ms. Cherry also reported that Dr. Palmer contacted the County Health Department regarding the case and that she ordered 25 test kits from the Maricopa County Health Department to test any additional suspected cases of pertussis. That, in fact, was not the case. Ms. Cherry sent an "undeliverable" e-mail to the County's website, requesting the test kits.

A known case of a reportable infectious disease went unreported to ADC staff and Wexford State Level Management for 30 days, indicating a lack of urgency, a lack of awareness of the situation's potential seriousness, a breakdown of communication between field personnel and management, or all of the above. Further, Wexford's failure to independently engage in developing a plan by which to identify/confirm current and future suspected cases of pertussis is a significant non-compliance issue.

Required CURE actions

The aforementioned significant events have necessitated ADC to substantially supplement Wexford with personnel resources, operational modifications, and specific direction that should not be expected and are not required under this contract. ADC expects Wexford to effect sustained, systemic operational improvements in the management and delivery of health care services to ADC inmates. ADC is not contractually obligated to deploy its resources to manage Wexford's day-to-day, as well as crisis operations.

The following non-compliance issues, as identified here and/or in previously provided monitoring reports, require corrective action:

STAFFING: Inadequate staffing levels in multiple program areas at multiple locations

1.Inadequate support from corporate staff to field staff during normal and crisis operations

2. Staffing levels creating inappropriate scheduling gaps in on-site medical coverage, including In-Patient Component

3.Staffing levels forcing existing staff to work excessive hours, creating fatigue risks

MEDICATION/DOCUMENTATION: Incorrect, incomplete, inconsistent medication administration or documentation of care provided.

4.Quantitative decrease in routine institutional care: backlog of prescription medication expiration review

5. Incorrect or incomplete pharmacy prescriptions (medication not matching chart order, wrong dosage)

6. Inappropriate discontinuation/change of medication

7.Inconsistent non-formulary medication approval process

8.Inconsistent or contradictory medication refill and/or return procedures

9.Inadequate pharmacy reports

10. Inconsistent documentation of Medication Administration Records (MARs)

11. Inconsistent provision of release, transfer, and/or renewal medications

12.Inability to readily identify specific groups of inmates or chronic conditions based upon medications prescribed (e.g., diabetics)

SENSE OF URGENCY RESPONSE, and COMMUNICATION: ADC deployment of resources to intervene in healthcare operations as a result of corporate inaction

13. Inadequate/untimely communication between field staff, corporate staff, and ADC

14.Lack of responsiveness and/or lack of awareness of incident urgency and reporting requirements

15. Quantitative decrease in routine institutional care: backlog of chart reviews

16.Quantitative decrease in routine institutional care: backlog of provider line appointments

17.Quantitative decrease in routine institutional care: untimely handling of Health Needs Requests

18.Quantitative decrease in routine institutional care: backlog/cancellation of outside specialty consultations

19.Unresponsive approach to ADC inquiries on patient information

20.Unresponsive approach to inmate grievance process

ADC expects Wexford to provide a proposed corrective action plan for all of the identified deficiencies by October 1, 2012. Although Wexford is afforded 7, 30, 60, or 90 days to complete corrective action* it is ADC's expectation that Wexford will begin corrective action on all identified deficiencies immediately. Corrective action must be ongoing throughout the 90-day cure period, and Wexford must regularly demonstrate to ADC Contract Monitors that corrective action is ongoing and being completed throughout the 90-day cure period.

This letter shall also serve as a demand for Right to Assurance in accordance with section 8.1 of the Uniform Terms and Conditions, that it is Wexford's intent to perform and comply with all provisions of the contract. Accordingly, Wexford has ten (10) calendar days from the date of this letter to respond to the demand for assurance.

In accordance with the contract's Special Terms and Conditions, Section 2.19 Contract Monitoring General Requirements, paragraph 2.19.7, Wexford has ten (10) calendar days from the date of this letter to submit a written appeal of this Cure Notice.

Wexford's failure to provide written assurance of its intent to perform and comply with all contractual provisions within ten (10) calendar days, or its failure to cure all deficiencies noted herein within ninety (90) calendar days from the date of this letter may, at the State's option, be the basis for terminating the contract under the Uniform Terms and Conditions or other rights and remedies available by law or provided by the contract.

Sincerely,

Joe Profiri
Contract Beds Operations Director
Arizona Department of Corrections
Enclosures: Cure Matrix Monitoring Report
Cure Matrix Monitoring Summary Report

_____

Arizona Department of Corrections
1601 WEST JEFFERSON
PHOBNIX, AR1ZONA85007
(602) 542-5407
www.azcorrections.gov

JANICE K. BREWER GOVERNOR
CHARLES L. RYAN DIRECTOR
Electronic Mail and Certified Mail - Return Receipt Requested

September 28, 2012

Karen Mullenix
Wexford Health Sources
1850 N. Central Avenue, Suite 1050
Phoenix, Arizona 85004

Re: Contract No. 120075DC

Dew Ms. Mullenix:

As a follow-up to Director Ryan's communication to Mr. Hale, the response to Arizona Department of Correction's (ADC) demand for Right to Assurance in accordance with section 8.1 of the Uniform Terms and Conditions shall be delivered by October 1, 2012.

Wexford's response to the Notice of Referral to Take Action shall be delivered no later than October 9, 2012.

Additionally, Wexford shall respond to the Cure Notice no later than October 22, 2012. In granting this extension, it is ADC's expectation that Wexford will begin corrective action on all identified deficiencies immediately, irrespective of the extended response dates.

In furtherance of the Department's commitment to this contract and consistent with Director Ryan's offer to Wexford on Monday, September 24, 2012, I will make myself, and other ADC Health Service Monitoring staff, available to you to provide any necessary explanation of identified deficiencies and/or Clarification of ADC's compliance expectations. We trust that this exchange will be of value as Wexford completes corrective action plans.

Sincerely,

Joe Profiri
Contract Beds Operations Director
Arizona Department of Corrections
HOOD, JEFF

Subject:Dan Conn <dconn@wexfordhealth.com>

Sent: Wednesday, September 26, 2012 3:24 PM

To: RYAN, CHARLES; HOOD, JEFF

Cc: Mark Hale; Dan Conn

From: RE: Follow-up to our meeting on September 24, 2012

Director Ryan:

We were surprised by your e-mail last evening as we thought we clearly told you in our Monday meeting that Wexford could not respond substantively to a press inquiry regarding the two "notice" letters until we in fact responded to those letters, We explained that any Wexford response to press inquiries until then would be along the lines of: "Wexford is reviewing the letters from the ADC and will respond to all of the issues raised in those letters. Wexford's response will be provided at that time."

As we discussed in our meeting on Monday we too want to collaborate to ensure success of Arizona's inmate health care program. We are attempting to help reform a system after stepping into the contract only a few months ago after several decades of problems. We would have thought that the ADC's expressed desire to collaborate towards this goal would have caused the Department to address the issues raised in the letters in a different manner; it sent the letters without any collaboration, Wexford understands we are obligated to provide the ADC with a complete response to each of the issues raised in the letters and fully explain Wexford's assessment of those issues. We are a company rooted in ethical behavior and the improvement to health care. So that we may have the opportunity to do this in a collaborative manner and with the benefit of additional input from the ADC, as explained more fully below, Wexford requests a three week extension to respond to the letters so that our response is due on October 22, 2012.

Regarding a response to a press inquiry, as noted above, our current thinking would be to state that we are still in the process of reviewing the letters and preparing a response. We would also state at a minimum that our initial reaction to the letters is as follows:

Regarding the Notice of Referral to Take Action letter: Wexford is in the process of reviewing the letter and preparing a response. We understand and appreciate that a terrible mistake was made by a temporary agency nurse. Wexford's goal is to limit the use of temporary agency nurses. This is a daunting task as prior to July 1, agency nurses were used extensively by ADC. While Wexford may not have reported the incident to some people's satisfaction, in no way did Wexford attempt to conceal the matter in any way. Instead we worked to identify the extent of the problem and to ensure that appropriate action was taken to test and then treat any patients who may have been impacted. The investigation into the matter was hampered in many ways. In no way did any of Wexford's actions constitute an act of indifference. With regard to the sanction included in the letter, we are reviewing our contract with the ADC to determine whether any sanction is appropriate under all of the circumstances and our contract. Our goal is to reduce the number of such incidents that have long-plagued this system.

Regarding the Written Cure Notification letter: Wexford is in the process of reviewing the letter and preparing a response. Wexford acknowledges that there are many problems with the system of delivering health care in the ADC. In fact Wexford has discussed with ADC that in our assessment, understanding that we provide correctional health care in 4 various states throughout the country, the health care system in ADC was extremely poor. Most of these problems existed prior to Wexford taking over the program less than 90 days ago and were not known to Wexford during the procurement process. Wexford inherited most of the problems identified in the letter and was brought in by the state to act as a change agent and to provide the appropriate level of health care services. Resolving the problems Wexford inherited will take time and cooperation between Wexford and the ADC. Both the ADC and Wexford have stated that we will cooperate in bringing the health care system into compliance with appropriate levels of care.

To assist us both in dealing with media matters we have retained the services of Rose, Moser, Allyn Public Relations firm, with Jason Rose as our point of contact. He will work in conjunction with Larry Pike.

With regard to other points raised in your e-mail we provide the following information. Wexford reiterates its desire to be successful in providing constitutionally-mandated Inmate Health Care in accordance with our contract. We understand and believe in the fact that the ADC has an obligation to hold us accountable. In holding Wexford accountable, the ADC must recognize that the system that was in place less than 90 days ago was extremely weak. In addition, the ADC's decision (not to disclose to Wexford why it bid on the contract), to hire 34 monitors, many of whom were the first and second level of management personnel at each facility, has created a void in both leadership and institutional knowledge that Wexford is working hard to fill. The fact that these monitors are the people that allowed the system to get to its current state and now these same people are monitoring the performance at these sites and pointing out deficiencies to which they contributed is problematic at best, In addition these monitors are still learning their roles and have interfered with Wexford's efforts to provide appropriate health care services to inmates.

As we've discussed with ADC the decision to issue these letters, as well as the most recent disturbances in your facilities will make retention and recruitment much more difficult. Another important point to note is that we have inherited a culture of complacency with many staff possessing a negative attitude and lack of dedication towards their job. We have discussed this concern with ADC and plan to correct it however, it takes time.

We raise these issues to reiterate the challenge we both have in improving the delivery of health care in the ADC. The type of cooperation you have stated the ADC will provide is an absolute necessity if the state's privatization effort is going to succeed.

As a reminder, Wexford, in conjunction with the ADC, has made great strides toward accomplishing the following tasks.

Assessing existing staffing complements at the prison complexes, adding multiple new clinical positions where appropriate, to enhance the breadth of services we can make available to ADC inmates

Moving all prison health care staff from a manual paper timekeeping system to a state-of-the-art electronic biometric system, to ensure that scheduling, hours worked, and payroll are monitored and reported accurately

Wexford is no stranger to Arizona. For the past decade, the company has provided services to the Yavapai County jail facilities. Its programs there include utilization of an electronic medical record and implementation of the award winning 'Restoration to Competency' program, which has now been adopted by more than half of the counties in Arizona. These programs have been proven to save county taxpayers money, Wexford is excited to now expand its scope of services in Arizona to bring the same responsiveness and creativity to the state, its prison population, and its taxpayers.

ADC was aware prior to sending the two letters that Wexford was working on a plan to address all of the issues raised in the letters. Wexford had intended to implement our plan even before we received the ADC letters, The issues raised in the letters will take some time to resolve. We told you in our meeting on Monday that many of the time frames outlined in the letters are not reasonable, and at your invitation, we intend to work with your staff to develop reasonable time frames. In order for this process to be meaningful, our respective personnel should work together to identify what needs to be done and the time required for implementation.

Wexford would like to meet with the Department on this point as soon as possible to discuss the details of each of the issues identified in the letter and to determine the work and time required to fully address the "cure" issues. We think this dialogue and resolution process may take at least two weeks to identify and then document the appropriate steps that Wexford will take to address and implement solutions to issues cited in the Cure Letter. Suggested reforms are occurring on other fronts simultaneously.

In addition to addressing these issues, and consistent with your statement that the Department wants to partner with Wexford, Wexford would also like to explore with you a mechanism to address and resolve a number of concerns that directly affect the issues raised in the two letters. These concerns include, among other things, (1) the appropriate role of the Department's monitors and the manner in which they interface with Wexford staff, and (2) the condition of the State's inmate health services program as of the date Wexford assumed responsibility for the program, given that Wexford inherited many of the issues identified in the Cure Letter, Wexford prefers to partner with the Department and work through and resolve these issues and those raised by the Department. As such, Wexford requests a meeting to discuss these issues and how they interface with the issues raised in the two letters. The brief extension requested will enable Wexford and the Department to work together to begin to resolve these concerns as well.

Wexford very much wants to succeed on its contract with Arizona and to satisfy the Department's concerns, and can best do that if the actions of the Department do not frustrate or interfere with Wexford's work under the contract. It is simply not reasonable to expect that Wexford can cure in 3 months an inherited sub-standard system. We would be happy to discuss the request for a brief extension with you so please let us know if you have any questions about our request. We are early in this contract and the points raised in the Cure Letter deserve a full and frank discussion to facilitate the prompt resolution of all of these matters.

In light of the short time remaining before our response is due, please let us know the Department's position at your earliest opportunity.

Mark W. Hale
President & CEO
mhale@wexfordhealth.com

From: RYAN, CHARLES [mailto:CRYAN@azcorrections.gov]
Sent: Tuesday, September 25, 2012 7:53 PM
To: Mark Hale; Dan Conn
Subject: Follow-up to our meeting on September 24, 2012
Importance: High

Mr. Hale and Mr. Conn:

As we did not hear from you today, I wanted to take the opportunity to follow up to our conversation of yesterday afternoon.

As we have clearly communicated, the Legislature and the Governor, as a public policy decision, have mandated the privatization of Inmate Health Care, and the Arizona Department of Corrections is fully committed to the success of this privatization venture.

As the vendor selected for award of this contract, we reiterate our support and desire for Wexford Health Sources to be successful in providing constitutionally-mandated Inmate Health Care in accordance with the terms of our contract. While we strongly desire to collaborate with you to help ensure your success, it is also important that you recognize that we will continue to hold Wexford Health accountable to the terms of the Contract, and for the provision of appropriate care for the inmate population.

As briefly mentioned during our call with Mr. Conn on Friday, and again during our conversation with you both yesterday, it is only a matter of time before interested parties external to Wexford Health or ADC become aware of the information contained in our recent correspondence to you. In light of that anticipated development, and with a sincere desire to avoid independent and uncoordinated responses to external inquiries, we reiterate our desire to collaborate with you regarding the release of appropriate information and/or response to anticipated requests for information, and await your reply.

Charles L. Ryan
Director
cryan@azcorrections.gov
Jeff Hood
Deputy Director
jhood@azcorrections.gov

AMENDMENT TO CONTRACT NO. ADC 120075DC

PARTIES:

This Amendment to Contract No. ADC 120075DC is entered into this 30th day of January, 2013 ("Effective Date"), by and between Wexford Health Sources. Inc . a Florida corporation ("Wexford Health") and the State of Arizona acting through Its Department of Corrections ("Department" or "ADC"). Wexford Health and the Department are collectively referred to herein as the "Parties."

RECITALS

The ADC and Wexford Health entered into Contract No. ADC 120075DC (the "Contract") on or about April 2.2012.

Various disputes have arisen between the Parties. On or about November 16, 2012, Wexford Health requested that ADC agree to a mutual termination of the Contract. As a result of this request. ADC and Wexford Health have agreed to terminate the Contract as of the Termination Date defined below and the Parties enter into this Amendment in order to effect that agreed-upon Contract termination. On or about December 3,2012, the parties agreed upon a statement to describe their situation, and the same is attached as Attachment 1, and folly incorporated by this reference. In reliance upon the general agreement described in Attachment I, ADC has sought a new contractor and is prepared to award a contract to Corizon. Inc., contingent upon the signing of this Amendment to Contract, that provides that Corizon, Inc. will begin performance on March 4,2013, following a transition period of at least thirty days.

Wexford Health has agreed to continue to perform under the Contract and to work with ADC to transition existing services through the Termination Date described below, on which date all of Wexford Health's obligations under the Contract will end except as set forth in this Amendment.

The Parties, having reached a settlement of their respective disputes, desire to (i) amend the Contract as set forth in this Amendment in order to conclude their relationship in a mutually convenient and satisfactory manner, and (il) fully resolve all existing claims and disputes between them relating to, arising out of, or in connection with the Contract.

COVENANTS:

In consideration of mutual promises and covenants set forth in this Amendment and for good and valuable consideration, the receipt and sufficiency of which are hereby mutually acknowledged by the Parties, Wexford Health and the ADC agree as follows:

Incorporation of Recitals the Recitals set forth above are true, correct and not

Subject to dispute, and are incorporated as Covenants by this reference. Termination of Agreement. Paragraph 1.4.1 of the Contract is amended to provide at follow*: The term of any resultant Contract shall commence on the date of award and shall continue until March 3,2013." As a result of this Amendment, the Parties agree that the Contract will be mutually terminated effective as of 11:39 PM on Mach 3.2013 (the "Termination I"). ADC shall have no right to extend the Contract beyond the 'termination Date for any reason whatsoever and paragraph 2.5.1, the second sentence of paragraph 2.5 .4, paragraph 2.5.42 and any other provision of the Contract that contemplates or permits an extension of the lam of the Contract beyond the Termination Date are hereby deleted

Transition. Beginning on the Effective Date and continuing until the Tam mat ion Date, Wexford Health shall assist the Department with a transition as provided in section 2.5.4 of the Contract as amended by this Amendment. Wexford Health's obligation to assist the Department in the transition shall continue until the Termination Date as provided by section 2.3.4 of the Contract as amended by this Amendment, but not beyond the Termination Date except as specifically provided by this Amendment Paragraphs 2.5.42,2.5.4 JJ, 2.S.4.3.5, 2.5.4.5, and 2.5.6, of the Contract are deleted. Wexford Health also agrees to make its best efforts to continue to deliver to ADC through the lamination Date those reports in complete or substantially complete form that are referenced on Attachment 2. The Parties agree that Wexford Health will satisfy all Contract requirements to provide financial statements by supplying the information described on Attachment 3 in the times set forth on that attachment All financial statements and information submitted by Wexford Health to the ADC arc confidential and proprietary information, and ADC agrees that such financial statements and information will not be disclosed to any person or entity not a Patty to this Amendment, except as provided by law. Notwithstanding the foregoing ADC shall provide at least five days prior notice to Wexford Health (and longer if reasonably possible, or shorter, if so directed by a court) of ADC's intention to disclose such documents during which time Wexford Health may seek to prevent the release of such documents.. From and after the Termination Date, Wexford Health shall have no Anther obligation whatsoever under the Contract except as set forth in this Amendment.

ADC shall pay Wexford Health all sums due and owing to Wexford Health under the Contract through the Termination Date as soon as conveniently possible but in no event later than fifteen days after receipt of Wexford Health's final invoice without setoff for any claim or other matter arising before or after the Effective Dale, except for the set-offs permitted in this paragraph. The Parties have agreed that ADC may set off the agreed sum of 5145,000, representing a compromise of the amounts that the Parties alleged Wexford Health was obligated to pay ADC under Contract section 2.6.13. In addition, if ADC asserts a claim against Wexford Health on or before the Termination Date for matters occurring after the Effective Date in an amount less than Wexford's final invoice, ADC may withhold from Wexford's final payment an amount equal to 100 percent of ADC's claim. If the • mount of any claim asserted by ADC against Wexford Health as provided herein is greater than the final payment due to Wexford Health from ADC, Wexford Health either shall (a) direct ADC to withhold the entire amount of the final payment and within three business days of Wexford's receipt of ADC* s claim deliver good funds to ADC in an amount equal to (lie difference between ADC's claim and Wexford's final invoice, or (b) direct ADC to make the final payment to Wexford in which case ADC may continue to hold the bond referenced in paragraph 11 of this Amendment pending the outcome of ADC's claim. ADC may hold any funds held under this paragraph until the final adjudication of its claim as provided herein. ADC shall pay Wexford Health any sum withheld hereunder and determined not to be owed to ADC by Wexford Health within fifteen days after either ADC determines such sum is not owed to it by Wexford Health or a final order making such determination is entered in the adjudication initiated by ADC.

Indemnity of ADC bv Wexford Health. The termination of the Contract and the release set forth below shall not afToct the obligations of Wexford Health to (1) indemnify, defend, save and hold harmless the State of Arizona, its depart moots (including without limitation the Department), agencies, boards, commissions, universities and its officers, officials, agents and employees (the "ADC Indemnities") in all the circumstances set forth in the Contract, including without limitation section 1.29.1 and section 2.5.5; and (2) maintain in effect (without any lapsing until the date permitted by the Contract) the insurance coverage's required by the Contract. These obligations of the Contract are expressly continued (without any lapsing until the date or dates permitted by the Contract) by this Amendment. Notwithstanding the foregoing, the Panics agree that no indemnity obligation in the Contract requires Wexford Health to indemnify, defend, save and hold harmless the ADC Indemnities from or against any claim, demand or liability asserted by Corizon, Inc., or any of its affiliates, officers, officials, associates, employees, attorneys, agents, licensees, trustees, insurers, divisions, partnerships, co-ventures, other affiliated entities and any other person or entity acting in any manner for or on behalf of Corizon, Inc. ("Corizon"). Corizon is not a third party beneficiary of this Amendment or the Contract and has no rights under the Contract or any Amendment to the Contract.

Furniture and Equipment. Paragraphs 2.6.12.2,2.6.12.3, 2.6.12.4. and 2.6.12.5 of the Contract ate hereby deleted.

Special Provision for Patients Hospitalized at Transition Date. 11к parties acknowledge that there may be patients admitted to a hospital and in an inpatient status on the Termination Date. Costs related to such patients will be apportioned as set forth in this paragraph unless the parties make a specific arrangement for a particular patient or patients. If the billing for a patient is done based upon a per admission "Diagnosis-Related Group" billing method, then Wexford Health will be responsible for 100% of the cost of the inpatient admission. If the billing is done on a per diem or some form of fee for service basis, then Wexford Health will be responsible for the cost of the admission up to the Termination Date, and Corizon Inc. will be responsible for all costs beginning after the Termination Date.

Release by ADC. Except for the obligations created or continued by this Amendment, ADC and the State of Arizona, for themselves and on behalf of their respective successors, assigns, affiliates, officers, officials, associates, employees, attorneys, agents, licensees, trustees, insurers, divisions, partnerships, co-ventures, other affiliated entities and any other person or entity acting in any manner for or on behalf of ADC (the "ADC Releasors") unconditionally release and forever discharge Wexford Health and its respective predecessors, successors, assigns, affiliates, officers, directors, members, partners, associates, employees, attorneys, agents, sureties (including but not limited to the surety on the bond Wexford Health provided to ADC, Fidelity and Deposit Company of Maryland), licensees, trustees, insurers, shareholders, parents, subsidiaries, divisions, partnerships, co-ventures, other affiliated business entities and any other person or entity acting in any manner for or on behalf of Wexford Health (the "Wexford Released Parties") from any and all claims, liabilities, expenses, losses, demands.

obligations, actions, liens or suits of whatsoever kind and nature that arc either known or unknown, asserted or un-asserted as of the Effective Date of this Amendment arising out of either the Contract, the procurement process for the Contract, or services rendered under the Contract. In addition to the foregoing, the ADC Releasors unconditionally release and forever discharge the Wexford Released Parties from any and all claims, liabilities, expenses, losses, demands, obligations, actions, liens or suits of whatsoever kind and nature that may arise or accrue after the Effective Date and before the Termination Date arising out of either the Contract, the procurement process for the Contract, or services rendered under the Contract, except for claims, liabilities, expenses, losses, demands, obligations, actions, liens or it's that arise out of or result from a material breach of this Amendment

Release by Wexford Health. Except for the obligations created or continued by this Amendment. Wexford Health, individually and on behalf of its respective predecessors, successors, assigns, affiliates officers, directors, members, partners, associates, employees, attorneys, agents, licensees, trustees, insurers, shareholders. parents, subsidiaries, divisions, partnerships, co-ventures, other affiliated business entities and any other person or entity acting in any manner for or on behalf of Wexford Health (the "Wexford Releasors") unconditionally releases and forever discharges ADC and the state of Arizona and their respective predecessors, successors, assigns, affiliates, officers, officials, directors, partners, associates, employees, attorneys, agents, licensees, trustees, insurers, partnerships, co-ventures, other affiliated entities and any other person or entity acting in any manner for or on behalf of ADC (the ADC' Released Parties) from any and all claims, liabilities, expenses, losses, demands, obligations, actions, liens or suits of whatsoever kind and nature that arc cither known or unknown, asserted, un-asserted, as of the Effective Date of this Amendment arising out of either the Contract, the procurement process for the Contract, or services rendered under the Contract. In addition to the ongoing. the Wexford Releasors unconditionally release and forever discharge the ADC Released Parties from any and all claim*, liabilities, expenses, losses, demands, obligations, actions, liens or suits of whatsoever kind and nature that may arise or accrue after the Effective >ate and before the Termination Date arising out of other the Contract, the procurement process or the Contract, or service* rendered under the Contract, except for claims, liabilities, expenses, demands, obligations, actions, lien* or suits that arise out of the result from a material attached of this Amendment.

Provision Concerning Certain Issues The Parties wish to clarify their agreement concerning two specific letters ADC sent to Wexford Health: the September 21. 2012. "Notice >f Referral to Take Action" and the September 21, 2012 "Written Cure Notification." At the request of Wexford Health, the same are hereby withdrawn and neither party has further obligations to respond to or take additional action with regard to the letter* Nothing in this revision shall be deemed any limitation on the Parties' respective duties, obligations and abilities under die Contract as amended by this Amendment, including without limitation the revisions of paragraph 5 above

Release of Bond. Unless ADC asserts a claim against Wexford Health which exceeds the amount of the final payment due to Wexford Health on or be I ore the Term nation late, the performance bond posted by Wexford Health pursuant to section 1-35 of the Contract tall be released, exonerated and discharged on the Termination Date, and ADC shall have no rights under or claims against the bond whatsoever. The bond also shall be released, exonerated and discharged on the Termination Date, and ADC shall have no rights under or claims against the bond whatsoever.

If on or before Ac Termination Date ADC asserts a written claim against Wexford Health which exceeds the final payment to Wexford Health and Wexford Health delivers good funds to ADC in an amount equal to the difference between ADC's claim and Wexford's final invoice as permitted by paragraph 4 above ADC shall return the bond or bonds posted by Wexford Health to Wexford Health within 5 days after the Termination Date unless ADC has asserted a written claim against Wexford Health which exceeds the final invoke amount payable to Wexford Health and Wexford Health does not deliver good funds to ADC in an amount equal to the difference between ADCs claim and Wexford's final invoice within three business days of Wexford Health's receipt of ADCs data as provided *in paragraph 4* of this Amendment Paragraphs 1.35 4.2.5.4.5 and any other provision of the Contract inconsistent with this paragraph 11 are hereby deleted

Attorneys' Pees The parties agree to bear their own coats and attorneys' fees incurred in the negotiation of this Amendment. In case of any proceedings to enforce this Amendment, the ability of any party to recover costs and attorney's fees shall be governed by the laws of the State of Arizona.

Integration Clause This Amendment constitutes the full and complete understanding of the Parties with respect to the subject matters addressed in this Amendment The Contract as amended by this Amendment supersedes aay and all prior or contemporaneous oral agreements or understandings between the Parties and is the final agreement of the Parties with respect to the subject matters addressed in this Amendment

Authorized Execution. Each party executing this Amendment warrants that be or die has read this Amendment, has obtained the advice of legal counsel with respect to the terms of the Amendment and the Contract; and is legally empowered and authorized to execute this Amendment on behalf of the party for which he or die acts, and each party represents that it is empowered to execute this Amendment.

Counterparts. This Amendment may be executed in any number of counterparts, all counterparts are deemed to constitute one and the same Instrument and each counterpart is deemed to be an original of that instrument. This Amendment may be executed and delivered by facsimile or electronic signature

16.Further Actions the Parties shall take all actions reasonably necessary to carry out the provisions and purposes of this Amendment.

17. Interpretation. In case any court or administrative tribunal b called upon to interpret this Amendment, the Parties agree that the Amendment should be interpreted according to its principal purposes, which are to (I) create an agreed, early termination of the Contract and to provide that Wexford Health has no obligation whatsoever to ADC after the Termination Data except as specifically provided in this Amendment; (2) allow an orderly transition to a new private contractor without interruption of the health care services which are the subject matter of the Contract and during which period the Parties will cooperate with each other and the new vendor, (3) maintain Wexford Health's responsibilities to indemnify the ADC Indemnities under the circumstances required by the Amendment and to maintain insurance coverage related to under contract through the Termination Date as described in paragraph *4* above; *(5)* to resolve end release all disputes and claim the parties nay haw against each other relating to the Contract except as otherwise specifically reserved in this Amendment; and (6) to minimize disputes between the parties, including any disputes arising after the Effective Date and before the Termination Date and to provide that any dispute remaining to be resolved under this Amendment or the Contract shall be resolved under the procedures provided by the Arizona procurement Code and procurement rules. In addition to foregoing, the Parties agree that this Amendment stall supersede any conflicting provision *h* the Conti set and that this Amendment shall be prefer rad and control to the extent any provision of this Amendment contradicts any provision of the Contract

18.Severability. If any provision of this Amendment is held to be illegal, invalid or unenforceable for any reason, such provision shall be fully severable from this Amendment and the retaining provisions shell be fully enforceable and effective notwithstanding the severance of the offending clause.

19.No Oral Modification. This Amendment shall not be modified or amended except by a written instrument signed by the Parties.

20. Governing Law. The validity, construction, interpretation and administration of this Amendment shall be governed by the laws of the State of Arizona, including without limitation the Arizona Procurement Code and procurement rules described In The Contract

WEXFORD HEALTH SOURCES INC., a Florida Corporation.

Wexford Health Sources Incorporated

Date ____4/30/13_____   By _____

                                 Its ___President + CEO___

THE STATE OF ARIZONA ACTING BY
AND THROUGH ITS DEPARTMENT OF
CORRECTIONS

Date __1/30/2013_____   By _____

                                 Its _CHIEF PROCUREMENT OFFICER_

Wexford Health

S O U R C E S   I N C O R P O R A T E D

WEXFORD HEALTH SOURCE INCORPORATED

Tuesday, October 9. 3012

Mr. Joe Profiri
Contract Beds Operations Director
Arizona Department of Corrections
1601West Jefferson
Phoenix, Arizona 85007

Dear Mr. Profiri

Wexford Health Source Inc. ("Wexford Health") is in receipt of the Arson* Department of Correct ton*¨ (*ADC* or "Department") September 21, 2012 Notice of Referral to take action ("Notice") to an incident that took place at ASPC-Lewis on August 27, 2012 and a variety of follow on activities alleged omissions. Without sufficient specificity and with no apparent basis under the contract, the letter outline six bulleted reasons why the ADC proposes to refer the described circumstances to the Chief Procurement Officer for immediate adverse action Wexford Health hereby appeals, disputes and requests a hearing to challenge any finding of non-compliance that would result in either a cure notice , a decision to impose sanctions against Wexford Health, or referral of any of the matter* described in the Notice to the Chief Procurement Officer for action. Watford Health's detailed response to the bullet point* la art forth below, but Wexford Health specifically object* to the vagueness of the notice, which Hn-.it* Wexford Health's ability to respond to the allegations.

Wexford Health acknowledge* that one of our subcontracted nurse* potentially contaminated a vial of insulin as described in your letter. This was an isolated incident caused by an individual who foiled to follow basic infection control protocols that are a rudimentary part of any nurse's formal education Her action* were not due either to any lack of established Wexford Health policies and procedures or any direction or omission by the company Wexford Health could not have predicted or anticipated her inability or unwillingness to comply with basic 101 protocols taught as part of every clinician la formal health education.

ADC security officers learned of the incident and reported the Incident to Wexford Health and the ADC at approximately the same time. Upon learning of the incident Wexford Health took appropriate action on several fronts, including destroying the potentially contaminated vial* of medication; identifying potentially exposed inmate*, arranging for appropriate testing for these inmates; contacting the ADC notifying the staffing agency that we would not permit the curse In question to work under any Wexford Health contracts, and working with appropriate county and state boards and agencies to investigate the incident. Under the circumstance*, neither the incident nor Wexford Health* action* and performance following the Incident warrants a referral to the Chief Procurement Officer to take action against Wexford Health

In response to the stated reason* for referral contained tr. the Notice. Wexford Health responds m more detail aa follows

In the first bullet, the ADC asserts that Wexford Health committed an "act of indifference" that "disregards known and excessive risk to an Inmates health or safety or violates an inmate's civil rights." We dispute that the Lewis incident Involved an "act of indifference. Needless to say, Wexford Health did not direct the Incident or have any advance knowledge that the incident would occur And in no way did Wexford Health deliberately Ignore the situation once it did occur. The incident was limited to a single act, committed by one subcontracted employee, who chose to disregard standard protocols upon receiving the Initial report of the potentially contaminated Insulin. Wexford Health took immediate steps to destroy the potentially contaminated insulin vial# in order to protect our patients; to identity any and all *at risk" inmates, and to implement a thorough Hepatitis C and HIV testing process for potentially exposed inmates. Wexford Health's Immediate response to limit the impact of the incident by taking specific action on a number of fronts believe the notion that the incident involved an act of indifference. You should know that Wexford Health's ability to conduct a thorough investigation was impeded by an ADC security officer'* failure to file a report with the Department as required by established ADC policy; and by the unwillingness of ADC personnel to cooperate with Wexford Health. On the day following the incident (August 28, 2012), former Complex Manager Sumi Erno initiated a formal investigation of the incident. As part of her investigation, Ms Rrno received copies of Incident Reports ("IR's") written by ADC Security Officers, in particular, one IR described the actions of the sub-contracted nurse. The ADC later determined that the Security Officer who signed and submitted this IR had not actually witnessed the events he described in his report. Rather, he had beer, told about the incident by a second Security Officer (the one who had actually spoken to the subcontracted nurse about the incident). Unfortunately, this second officer did not follow ADC policy and never submitted his own IR about the incident. The uncertainty associated with the identity of the officer who actually witnessed the incident, combined with discrepancies in the dates and times in the IRs, impeded Wexford Health's ability to conduct a timely, accurate, and thorough investigation.

When asked to clarity their original statement*, the Security Officers involved with the incident refused to be re-interviewed by Wexford Health*» investigative team (Mr. Jim Reinhart and Mr. Glenn Thomas) Their refusal to speak and cooperate with Wexford Health further Impeded our ability to property investigate the incident and to subsequently provide the ADC with a timely and accurate description of the event* of August 27, 2012. Wexford Health would like to know if the ADC directed the security officers not to speak with Wexford Health about the Incident We also point out that while the IR inaccuracies were noted by the ADC during a meeting with Deputy Director Jeff Hood, Joe Profiri, Jennifer Bowser, and Karen Mullenix, the Department has never provided Wexford Health with revised or amended reports.

The fact that we began our investigation within 24 hour* of the incident and started appropriate clinical testing within 72 hour* dearly negates any accusation that Wexford Health was Indifferent* to the Lewis incident

The second bullet charges that Wexford Health (ailed to meet tn essential standard of the National Commission on Correctional Health Care ("NCCHC"). As the ADC neither references the specific standard it relies upon to accuse Wexford Health of nor compliance nor states which of the many acts complained about constitute a failure to meet the unnamed standard, we are unable to respond at this time. Once the ADC provide* Wexford Health with store detail on this point, including a reference to the specific NCCHC standard relied upon, we will respond to this section of the Notice.

The third bullet alleges Wexford Health failed to provide medically necessary services required by the contract. Wexford Health is unable to identify any language in the Notice which specifically describes how we failed to comply with the requirements of our contract with ADC.
In fact, the Notice affirms Wexford Health provided services as contracted and took extra precautionary measures by testing potentially exposed patients Once the ADC provides us with more detail on this point, including a description of the medically necessary services we allegedly failed to provide. Wexford Health will respond to this section of the Notice.

The fourth bullet to similar to that it accuses Wexford Health of *non-compliance identified or discovered during a monitoring activity" Again, we are unable to identify language in the Notice which specifically describe the alleged non-compliance that to the subject of this item. Once the ADC provides us with more on the point, including a description of the non-compliance ADC allege*. Wexford Health will respond to this section of the Notice.

The fifth bullet alleges that Wexford Health foiled to provide accurate and timely information to the Department or to NCCHC. We are unaware of any requirement to report any of the matter* alleged to the Notice to the NCCHC and request more information on the allegation. Under the circumstances in this case we believe Wexford Heath also does not behave our contract required a separate report to the Department regarding the Incident Heel/ because, as explained above. ADC security officers discovered the incident and reported It to Wexford Health and the ADC at approximately the same time. And as discussed above, our ability to report additional Information regarding the events of August 27 was negatively Impacted by the discrepancies in the dates and times in the IRs, and by the ADC Security Officer*⁻ refusal to participate to our ongoing Investigation

In addition, as described below, other factors beyond Wexford Health's control created obstacle* to our providing accurate and timely Information; ADC Itself bears some responsibility for Interfering with Wexford Health ability to provide information to the Department. Similar to the ADC's practice before we commenced performance on July 1, Wexford Health provides insulin to multi-dose visit, on a "stock" rather than a "patient-specific" bases In order to accurately record and track insulin used in a 'stock' pharmacy model, several Information systems must be maintained and used concurrently, including the Diamond Pharmacy reporting system; Inmate Medication Administration Records (MARs), and the ADCIs Inmate Health System IMS)

During the course of our ASPC-Lewis Investigation, we discovered that the Complex has a longstanding common practice which pre-dates July 1,3012, in which staff prepare for provider lines/clinics by removing the scheduled patients' MARs from the approved storage location (the MAR Binder] and placing them, with the individual patients' charts. This is not accepted clinical practice, and conflicts with standard Wexford Health protocol our investigation revealed that despite these facts, the practice of removing MARs from the approved storage location is ongoing. And is a contributing factor as to why our team could not locate the MAR for one insulin dependent diabetes (IDDM) patient Wexford Health's team's Inability to locate the MAR for that patient negatively Impacted our ability to accurately confirm In a timely fashion whether the IDDM patient had received insulin on the morning in question. This in turn interfered with our ability to provide information to the ADC. As noted at the end of this document. Wexford Health has Implemented a training process to correct the unacceptable established practices we have discovered at the prison complexes since we took over responsibility for inmate health care, Including the practice of removing MARs from their proper location.

Wexford Health also discovered that throughout the months preceding our contract start of July 1. 2012, the prison complexes were not consistently maintaining patient chronic care data in the IH8. The lack of updated, accurate information further Impeded Wexford Health to compile a complete and accurate fist of IDDM patients; and necessitated our dependence on MARs and patient charts to gather the Information necessary to identify IDDM patients to the aftermath of the August 27 Incident. Again, this interfered with our ability to gather and then to provide information to the ADC about the incident.

Notwithstanding the problems Wexford Health encountered as we investigated the incident, we did report to the ADC that Wexford Health had reported the subcontracted nurse responsible for the incident to the nursing Board. In addition, Wexford Health provided the ADC with a detailed report of its investigation on September 19.9012. At no time did Wexford Health withhold information from, or misrepresent information to, the Department or otherwise Ceil to cooperate fully with the Department

The sixth and last bullet charges that Wexford Health failed to comply with 'other MCCHC standards not Identified in the contract* since the Notice does not identify the standards, or how Wexford Health violated these standards, we are unable to respond at this time. Once the ADC provide* Wexford Health with more detail on the point, we will respond to this section of the Notice of Referral.

In summary, Wexford Health does not believe that the Notice of Referral supports the ADC* allegations of indifference, non-compliance, failure to meet NCCHC standards, failure to provide contracted medically necessary service*, and failure to provide accurate and timely information. The ADC should not refer this matter to the Chief Procurement Officer and no sanction should be sought (or imposed shold ADC refer this matter to the Chief Procurement Officer).

Wexford Health strives to deliver appropriate patient care and la diligently working with the ADC to identify and resolve Issues related to the provision of inmate health service*. A* one example of our commitment, we recognize the need for ongoing staff training and reserved Wednesday, October 3. 2012 for a "Train the Trainer" session for our nursing staff. All Wexford Health Directors of Nursing and RN Supervisors attended this all-day training event, which addressed issues discussed in this letter, e-g. not removing MARs from the MAR binder, entry of patient Information into the IH8 system; etc. In addition, the training session covered additional sub-optimal) staff practices — pre-dating Wexford Health's assumption of responsibility on July 1 but unfortunately still occurring. Wexford Health has identified opportunities for greater efficiencies and improved quality of care under our contract, and we are training our staff to implement these findings.

This response and nothing in this letter is intended to waive any right, remedy, or claim of Wexford Health under its contract with the state. Wexford Health expressly reserves all of its rights, remedies, and claims under its contract and applicable law.

Please let me know If you have arty questions about this letter or require additional information Sincerely,

Karen Mullenix
Director of Operations
Office: 480-696-7541

AMERCAN CIVIL LIBERTIES UNION (ACLU) LAWSUIT

ACLU Lawsuit Charges Arizona Prison Officials with Failing to Provide Adequate Health Care, Inhumane Use of Solitary Confinement

Prisoners in the custody of the Arizona Department of Corrections receive such grossly inadequate medical, mental health and dental care that they are in grave danger of suffering serious and preventable injury, amputation, disfigurement and even death, according to a federal class-action lawsuit filed today by a legal team led by the American Civil Liberties Union and the Prison Law Office.

The lawsuit also charges that thousands of prisoners are routinely subjected to solitary confinement in windowless cells behind solid steel doors, in conditions of extreme social isolation and sensory deprivation, leading to serious physical and psychological harm. Some prisoners in solitary receive no outdoor exercise for months or years on end, and some receive only two meals a day.

"The prison conditions in Arizona are among the worst I've ever seen," said Donald Specter, executive director of the Berkeley, Calif.-based Prison Law Office. "Prisoners have a constitutional right to receive adequate health care, and it is unconscionable for them to be left to suffer and die in the face of neglect and deliberate indifference."

Specter was the lead counsel in *Brown v. Plata*, a similar case from California in which the Supreme Court last year reaffirmed that prisoners have a constitutional right to adequate health care.

"Courts have consistently ruled that solitary confinement of people with mental illness is unconstitutional because it aggravates their illness and prevents them from getting proper treatment," said David Fathi, director of the ACLU National Prison Project. "Even for those with no prior history of mental illness, solitary confinement can inflict extraordinary suffering and lead to catastrophic psychiatric deterioration."

Critically ill prisoners have begged prison officials for medical treatment, according to the lawsuit, only to be told to "be patient," that "it's all in your head," or that they should "pray" to be cured. Arizona prison officials have repeatedly been warned by their own medical staff of the inadequacy of the care, echoing complaints from prisoner advocates and families that prisoners face a substantial risk of serious harm and death. Yet, they have failed to ensure that minimally adequate health care is provided as required by the Constitution.

In one particularly tragic case, a prisoner at the state prison complex in Tucson died last year of untreated lung cancer that spread to his liver, lymph nodes and other major organs before prison officials even bothered to send him to a hospital. The prisoner, Ferdinand Dix, filed repeated health needs requests and presented numerous symptoms associated with lung cancer. His liver was infested with tumors and swelled to four times its normal size, pressing on other internal organs and impeding his ability to eat. Prison medical staff responded by telling him to drink energy shakes. He died in February 2011, days after finally being sent to a hospital but only after his abdomen was distended to the size of that of a full-term pregnant woman. A photograph of Dix shortly before his death appears in the lawsuit.

Jackie Thomas, one of the lawsuit's named plaintiffs who is housed in solitary confinement at the state prison complex in Eyman, has suffered significant deterioration in his physical and mental health as a result of being held in isolation, where he has become suicidal and repeatedly harmed himself in other ways. Prison staff have failed to treat his mental illness, improperly starting and stopping psychotropic medications and repeatedly using ineffective medications that carry severe side effects. Last November, Thomas overdosed on medication but did not receive any medical care.

"Faced with such gross indifference on the part of prison officials to the needs of prisoners with mental illness in their care, it was essential we get involved," said Jennifer Alewelt, staff attorney with the Arizona Center for Disability Law, one of the plaintiffs in the lawsuit. "Prisoners with mental illness can be particularly vulnerable, and we must do everything we can to ensure their mental health needs are met while incarcerated."

Filed in the U.S. District Court for the District of Arizona against Charles Ryan, director of the Arizona Department of Corrections, and Richard Pratt, the department's interim director of the division of health services, the lawsuit asks, among other things, that constitutionally adequate health care be made available to prisoners, that medications be distributed to patients in a timely manner, and that prisoners not be held in isolation in conditions of social isolation and sensory deprivation that put them at risk of harm. The lawsuit does not seek monetary damages.

"Arizona has used the absence of transparency to callously ignore the basic needs of persons entrusted to its care, at times with deadly results," said Daniel Pochoda, legal director of the ACLU of Arizona. "Absent court intervention the health and well-being of thousands of prisoners will continue to be sacrificed to economic expediency."

According to the U.S. Bureau of Justice Statistics, Arizona has the sixth-highest incarceration rate in the nation.

ARIZONA CLASS ACTION LAW SUIT SETTLEMENT

SETTLEMENT IN PARSONS V RYAN CLASS-ACTION SUIT ON BEHALF OF THE MORE THAN 33,000 PRISONERS IN ARIZONA'S STATE PRISONS

More than a year after the Parsons Settlement agreement with the Arizona Department of Corrections went into effect, it was clear that the ADC had not complied with its terms. ADC's own documents showed them to be chronically out of compliance with key health care performance measures, and experts identified numerous cases in which ADC's failure to provide minimally adequate medical and mental health care had resulted in needless suffering, aggravation of illness, and avoidable death. On April 11, 2016, the ACLU and our co-counsel filed a motion asking the court to order ADC to take immediate steps to comply with its obligations under the settlement agreement.

On February 18, 2015, a federal court approved a settlement in a class-action suit on behalf of the more than 33,000 prisoners in Arizona's state prisons. The agreement was reached by the Arizona Department of Corrections and the ACLU, the ACLU of Arizona, the Prison Law Office, and co-counsel. Under the settlement, the Arizona Department of Corrections must fix a broken health care system plagued by long-term and systemic problems that caused numerous deaths and preventable injuries. The settlement will also allow prisoners in solitary confinement who have serious mental illnesses to have more mental health treatment and time outside their cells, and will make other critical reforms in prison conditions.

The settlement in Parsons v. Ryan requires the Arizona Department of Corrections (ADC) to meet more than 100 health care performance measures, covering issues such as monitoring of prisoners with diabetes, hypertension, and other chronic conditions; care for pregnant prisoners; and dental care.

The settlement also requires ADC to overhaul the rules for prisoners with serious mental illnesses in solitary confinement. Instead of spending all but six hours a week in their cells, such prisoners will now have a minimum of 19 hours a week outside the cell, and this time must include mental health treatment and other programming. ADC must also restrict guards' use of pepper spray on these prisoners, using it only as a last resort when necessary to prevent serious injury or escape.

The settlement provides for ongoing monitoring and oversight by the prisoners' lawyers to make sure the state is complying with its terms.

The groups filed the federal lawsuit in 2012, challenging years of inattention to the health needs of state prisoners and improper and excessive use of solitary confinement, resulting in serious harm and unnecessary deaths. Judge Neil V. Wake of the U.S. District Court in Phoenix certified the case as a class action in March 2013, and the U.S. Court of Appeals for the Ninth Circuit affirmed that ruling in June 2014. Last month, the groups filed reports by nationally recognized experts in corrections and in medical, mental health, and dental care, showing system-wide problems with the prisons' health care and excessive use of solitary confinement.

PARSONS STIPULATION

ADOC entered into the following stipulation about healthcare. However past history has shown that it does not follow orders by courts and have done exactly just that.

Plaintiffs and Defendants (collectively, "the Parties") hereby stipulate as follows:

I. INTRODUCTION AND PROCEDURAL PROVISIONS

1. Plaintiffs are prisoners in the custody of the Arizona Department of Corrections ("ADC"), an agency of the State of Arizona, who are incarcerated at one of the state facilities located in the State of Arizona, and the Arizona Center for Disability Law ("ACDL").

2. Defendants are Charles Ryan, Director of ADC, and Richard Pratt, Interim Division Director, Division of Health Services of ADC. Both Defendants are sued in their official capacities.

3. The Court has certified this case as a class action. The class is defined as "All prisoners who are now, or will in the future be, subjected to the medical, mental health, and dental care policies and practices of the ADC." The subclass is defined as

"All prisoners who are now, or will in the future be, subjected by the ADC to isolation, defined as confinement in a cell for 22 hours or more each day or confinement in the following housing units: Eyman–SMU 1; Eyman–Browning Unit; Florence–Central Unit; Florence–Kasson Unit; or Perryville–Lumley Special Management Area."

4. The purpose of this Stipulation to settle the above captioned case. This Stipulation governs or applies to the 10 ADC complexes: Douglas, Eyman, Florence, Lewis, Perryville, Phoenix, Safford, Tucson, Winslow and Yuma. This Stipulation does not apply to occurrences or incidents that happen to class members while they do not reside at one of the 10 ADC complexes.

5. Defendants deny all the allegations in the Complaint filed in this case. This Stipulation does not constitute and shall not be construed or interpreted as an admission of any wrongdoing or liability by any party.

6. Attached to this Stipulation as Exhibit A is a list of definitions of terms used herein and in the performance measures used to evaluate compliance with the Stipulation.

II. SUBSTANTIVE PROVISIONS

A. Health Care.

7. Defendants shall request that the Arizona Legislature approve a budget to allow ADC and its contracted health services vendor to modify the health services contract to increase staffing of medical and mental health positions. This provision shall not be construed as an agreement by Plaintiffs that this budgetary request is sufficient to comply with the terms of this Stipulation.

8. Defendants shall comply with the health care performance measures set forth in Exhibit B. Clinicians who exhibit a pattern and practice of substantially departing from the standard of care shall be subject to corrective action.

9. Measurement and reporting of performance measures: Compliance with the performance measures set forth in Exhibit B shall be measured and reported monthly at each of ADC's ten (10) complexes as follows.

a. The performance measures analyzed to determine ADC substantial

compliance with the health care provisions of this Stipulation shall be governed by ADC's MGAR format. Current MGAR performance compliance thresholds used to measure contract compliance by the contracted vendor shall be modified pursuant to a contract amendment to reflect the compliance measures and definitions set forth in Exhibit B.

b. The parties shall agree on a protocol to be used for each performance measure, attached as Exhibit C. If the parties cannot agree on a protocol, the matter shall be submitted for mediation or resolution by the District Court.

10. The measurement and reporting process for performance measures, as described in Paragraph 9, will determine (1) whether ADC has complied with particular performance measures at particular complexes, (2) whether the health care provisions of this Stipulation may terminate as to particular performance measures at particular complexes, as set forth in the following sub-paragraphs.

a. Determining substantial compliance with a particular performance measure at a particular facility: Compliance with a particular performance measure identified in Exhibit B at a particular complex shall be defined as follows:

i. For the first twelve months after the effective date of this Stipulation, meeting or exceeding a seventy-five percent (75%) threshold for the particular performance measure that applies to a specific complex, determined under the procedures set forth in Paragraph 9;

ii. For the second twelve months after the effective date of this Stipulation, meeting or exceeding an eighty percent (80%) threshold for the particular performance measure that applies to a specific complex, determined under the procedures set forth in Paragraph 9;

iii. After the first twenty four months after the effective date of this Stipulation, meeting or exceeding an eighty-five percent (85%) threshold for the particular performance measure that applies to a specific complex, determined under the procedures set forth in Paragraph 9.

b. Termination of the duty to measure and report on a particular performance measure: ADC's duty to measure and report on a particular performance measure, as described in Paragraph 9, terminates if:

i. The particular performance measure that applies to a specific complex is in compliance, as defined in sub-paragraph A of this Paragraph, for eighteen months out of a twenty-four month

period; and

ii. The particular performance measure has not been out of compliance, as defined in sub-paragraph A of this Paragraph, for three or more consecutive months within the past 18- month period.

c. The duty to measure and report on any performance measure for a given complex shall continue for the life of this Stipulation unless terminated pursuant to sub-paragraph B of this Paragraph.

11. Defendants or their contracted vendor(s) will approve or deny all requests for specialty health care services using InterQual or another equivalent industry standard utilization management program. Any override of the recommendation must be documented in the prisoner's health care chart, including the reason for the override.

12. Defendants or their contracted vendor(s) will ensure that:

a. All prisoners will be offered an annual influenza vaccination.

b. All prisoners with chronic diseases will be offered the required immunizations as established by the Centers for Disease Control.

c. All prisoners ages 50 to 75 will be offered annual colorectal cancer screening.

d. All female prisoners age 50 and older will be offered a baseline mammogram screening at age 50, then every 24 months thereafter unless more frequent screening is clinically indicated.

13. Defendants or their contracted vendor(s) will implement a training program taught by Dr. Brian Hanstad, or another dentist if Dr. Hanstad is unavailable, to train dental assistants at ADC facilities about how to triage HNRs into routine or urgent care lines as appropriate and to train dentists to evaluate the accuracy and skill of dental assistants under their supervision.

14. For prisoners who are not fluent in English, language interpretation for healthcare encounters shall be provided by a qualified health care practitioner who is proficient in the prisoner's language, or by a language line interpretation service.

15. If a prisoner who is taking psychotropic medication suffers a heat intolerance reaction, all reasonably available steps will be taken to prevent heat injury or illness. If all other steps have failed to abate the heat intolerance reaction, the prisoner will be transferred to a housing area where the cell temperature does not exceed 85 degrees Fahrenheit.

16. Psychological autopsies shall be provided to the monitoring bureau within thirty (30) days of the prisoner's death and shall be finalized by the monitoring bureau within fourteen (14) days of receipt. When a toxicology report is required, the

psychological autopsy shall be provided to the monitoring bureau within thirty (30) days of receipt of the medical examiner's report. Psychological autopsies and mortality reviews shall identify and refer deficiencies to appropriate managers and supervisors including the CQI committee. If deficiencies are identified, corrective action will be taken.

B. Maximum Custody Prisoners.

17. Defendants shall request that the Arizona Legislature approve a budget to allow ADC to implement DI 326 for all eligible prisoners. This provision shall not be construed as an agreement by Plaintiffs that this budget request is sufficient to comply with the terms of this Stipulation.

18. Defendants shall comply with the maximum custody performance measures set forth in Exhibit D.

19. Measurement and reporting of performance measures: Compliance with the performance measures set forth in Exhibit D shall be measured and reported monthly as follows.

a. The performance measures analyzed to determine ADC substantial compliance with the Maximum Custody provisions of this Stipulation shall be governed by the protocol used for each performance measure attached as Exhibit E. If the parties cannot agree on a protocol, the matter shall be submitted for mediation or resolution by the District Court.

20. The measurement and reporting process for performance measures, as described in Paragraph 19, will determine (1) whether ADC has complied with particular performance measures at particular units, (2) whether the Maximum Custody provisions of this Stipulation may terminate as to particular performance measures at particular units, as set forth in the following sub-paragraphs.

a. Determining substantial compliance with a particular performance measure at a particular unit: Compliance with a particular performance measure identified in Exhibit D at a particular unit shall be defined as follows:

i. For the first twelve months after the effective date of this Stipulation, meeting or exceeding a seventy-five percent (75%) threshold for the particular performance measure that applies to a specific unit, determined under the procedures set forth in Paragraph 19;

ii. For the second twelve months after the effective date of this Stipulation, meeting or exceeding an eighty percent (80%) threshold for the particular performance measure that applies to a specific unit, determined under the procedures set forth in Paragraph 19;

iii. After the first twenty four months after the effective date of this Stipulation, meeting or exceeding an eighty-five percent (85%) threshold for the particular performance measure that applies to a specific unit, determined under the procedures set forth in Paragraph 19.

b. Termination of the duty to measure and report on a particular performance measure: ADC's duty to measure and report on a particular performance measure, as described in Paragraph 19, terminates if:

i. The particular performance measure that applies to a specific unit is in compliance, as defined in sub-paragraph A of this Paragraph, for eighteen months out of a twenty-four month period; and

ii. The particular performance measure has not been out of compliance, as defined in sub-paragraph A of this Paragraph, for three or more consecutive months within the past eighteen month period.

c. The duty to measure and report on any performance measure for a given unit shall continue for the life of this Stipulation unless terminated pursuant to sub-paragraph B of this Paragraph.

21. Seriously Mentally Ill (SMI) prisoners are defined as those prisoners who have been determined to be seriously mentally ill according to the criteria set forth in the ADC SMI Determination Form (Form 1103-13, 12/19/12), which is attached hereto as Exhibit F and is incorporated by reference as if fully set forth herein. For purposes of this Stipulation, "intellectual disabilities," as defined by the current version of the Diagnostic and Statistical Manual of Mental Disorders (DSM), shall be added to the list of qualifying diagnoses on Form 1103.13. This definition shall govern this Stipulation notwithstanding any future modification of Form 1103.13 or ADC's definition of "Seriously Mentally Ill." All prisoners determined to be SMI in the community shall also be designated as SMI by ADC.

22. ADC maximum custody prisoners housed at Eyman-Browning, Eyman- SMU I, Florence Central, Florence-Kasson, and Perryville-Lumley Special Management Area (Yard 30) units, shall be offered out of cell time, incentives, programs and property consistent with DI 326 and the Step Program Matrix, but in no event shall be offered less than 6 hours per week of out-of-cell exercise. Defendants shall implement DI 326 and the Step Program Matrix for all eligible prisoners and shall maintain them in their current form for the duration of this Stipulation. In the event that Defendants intend to modify DI 326 and the Step Program Matrix they shall provide Plaintiffs' counsel with thirty (30) days' notice. In the event that the parties do not agree on the

proposed modifications, the dispute shall be submitted to Magistrate Judge David Duncan who shall determine whether the modifications effectuate the intent of the relevant provisions of the Stipulation.

23. Prisoners who are MH3 or higher shall not be housed in Florence Central- CB5 or CB7 unless the cell fronts are substantially modified to increase visibility.

24. All prisoners eligible for participation in DI 326 shall be offered at least 7.5 hours of out-of-cell time per week. All prisoners at Step II shall be offered at least 8.5 hours of out-of-cell time per week, and all prisoners at Step III shall be offered at least 9.5 hours of out-of-cell time per week. The out of cell time set forth in this paragraph is inclusive of the six hours of exercise time referenced in Paragraph 22. Defendants shall ensure that prisoners at Step II and Step III of DI 326 are participating in least one hour of out-of-cell group programming per week.

25. In addition to the out of cell time, incentives, programs and property offered pursuant to DI 326 and the Step Program Matrix for prisoners housed at maximum custody units specified in ¶ 24 above, ADC maximum custody prisoners designated as SMI pursuant to ¶ 21 above, shall be offered an additional ten hours of unstructured of out of cell time per week; an additional one hour of out-of-cell mental health programming per week; one hour of additional out of cell pyschoeducational programming per week; and one hour of additional out of cell programming per week. Time spent out of cell for

exercise, showers, medical care, classification hearings or visiting shall not count toward the additional ten hours of out of cell time per week specified in this Paragraph. All prisoners received in maximum custody will receive an evaluation for program placement within 72 hours of their transfer into maximum custody, including to properly identify all SMI prisoners.

26. If out of cell time offered pursuant to ¶¶ 24 or 25 above is limited or cancelled for legitimate operational or safety and security reasons such as an unexpected staffing shortage, inclement weather or facility emergency lockdown, Defendants shall make every reasonable effort to ensure that amount of out of cell time shall be made up for those prisoners who missed out of cell time. The out of cell time provided pursuant to paragraph 24 above, may be limited or canceled for an individual prisoner if the Warden,or his/her designee if the Warden is not available, certifies in writing that allowing that prisoner such out of cell time would pose a significant security risk. Such certification shall expire after thirty (30) days unless renewed in writing by the Warden or his/her designee.

27. Defendants shall maintain the following restrictions on the use of pepper spray and other chemical agents on any maximum custody prisoner classified as SMI, and in the following housing areas: Florence-CB-1 and CB-4; Florence-Kasson (Wings 1 and 2); Eyman-SMU I (BMU); Perryville-Lumley SMA; and Phoenix (Baker, Flamenco, and MTU).

a. Chemical agents shall be used only in case of imminent threat. An imminent threat is any situation or circumstance that jeopardizes the safety of persons or compromises the security of the institution, requiring immediate action to stop the threat. Some examples include, but are not limited to: an attempt to escape, on-going physical harm or active physical resistance. A decision to use chemical agents shall be based on more than passive resistance to placement in restraints or refusal to follow orders. If the inmate has not responded to staff for an extended period of time, and it appears that the inmate does not present an imminent physical threat, additional consideration and evaluation should occur before the use of chemical agents is authorized.

b. All controlled uses of force shall be preceded by a cool down period to allow the inmate an opportunity to comply with custody staff orders. The cool down period shall include clinical intervention (attempts to verbally counsel and persuade the inmate to voluntarily exit the area) by a mental health clinician, if the incident occurs on a weekday between 8:00 a.m. and 4:00 p.m. At all other times, a qualified health care professional (other than a LPN) shall provide such clinical intervention. This cool down period may include similar attempts by custody staff.

c. If it is determined the inmate does not have the ability to understand orders, chemical agents shall not be used without authorization from the Warden, or if the Warden is unavailable, the administrative duty officer.

d. If it is determined an inmate has the ability to understand orders but has difficulty complying due to mental health issues, or when a mental health clinician believes the inmate's mental health issues are such that the controlled use of force could lead to a substantial risk of decompensation, a mental health clinician shall propose reasonable strategies to employ in an effort to gain compliance, if the incident occurs on a weekday between 8:00 a.m. and 4:00 p.m. At all other times, a qualified health care professional (other than a LPN) shall propose such reasonable strategies.

e. The cool down period may also include use of other available resources/options such as dialogue via religious leaders, correctional counselors, correctional officers and other custody and non-custody staff that have established rapport with the inmate.

28. All maximum custody prisoners shall receive meals equivalent in caloric and nutritional content to the meals received by other ADC prisoners.

III. MONITORING AND ENFORCEMENT

29. Plaintiffs' counsel and their experts shall have reasonable access to the institutions, staff, contractors, prisoners and documents necessary to properly evaluate whether Defendants are complying with the performance measures and other provisions of this Stipulation. The parties shall cooperate so that plaintiffs' counsel has reasonable access to information reasonably necessary to perform their responsibilities required by this Stipulation without unduly burdening defendants. If the parties fail to agree, either party may submit the dispute for binding resolution by Magistrate Judge David Duncan. Defendants shall also provide, on a monthly basis during the pendency of the Stipulation, copies of a maximum of ten (10) individual Class Members' health care records, and a maximum of five (5) individual Subclass Members' health care and institutional records, such records to be selected by Plaintiffs' counsel. The health care records shall include: treatment for a twelve (12) month period of time from the date the records are copied. Upon request, Defendants shall provide the health care records for the twelve months before those originally produced. In addition, Defendants shall provide to Plaintiffs on a monthly basis a copy of all health care records of Class Members who died during their confinement at any state operated facility (whether death takes place at the facility or at a medical facility following transfer), and all mortality reviews and psychological autopsies for such prisoners. The records provided shall include treatment for a twelve (12) month period prior to the death of the prisoner. Upon request, Defendants shall provide the health care records for the twelve months before those originally produced. The parties will meet and confer about the limit on the records that Plaintiffs can request once the ADC electronic medical records system is fully implemented.

30. In the event that counsel for Plaintiffs alleges that Defendants have failed to substantially comply in some significant respect with this Stipulation, Plaintiffs' counsel shall provide Defendants with a written statement describing the alleged non-compliance ("Notice of Substantial Non-Compliance"). Defendants shall provide a written statement responding to the Notice of Substantial Non-Compliance within thirty (30) calendar days from receipt of the Notice of Substantial Non-Compliance and, within thirty (30) calendar days of receipt of Defendants' written response, counsel for the parties shall meet and confer in a good faith effort to resolve their dispute informally.

31. In the event that a Notice of Substantial Non-Compliance pursuant to ¶ 30 of this Stipulation cannot be resolved informally, counsel for the parties shall request that Magistrate Judge John Buttrick mediate the dispute. In the event that Magistrate Judge Buttrick is no longer available to mediate disputes in this case, the parties shall jointly request the assignment of another Magistrate Judge, or if the parties are unable to agree, the District Judge shall appoint a Magistrate Judge. If the dispute has not been resolved through mediation in conformity with this Stipulation within sixty (60) calendar days, either party may file a motion to enforce the Stipulation in the District Court.

32. Plaintiffs' counsel and their experts shall have the opportunity to conduct no more than twenty (20) tour days per year of ADC prison complexes. A "tour day" is any day on which one or more of plaintiffs' counsel and experts are present at a given complex. A tour day shall last no more than eight hours. No complex will be

toured more than once per quarter. Tours shall be scheduled with at least two weeks' advance notice to defendants. Defendants shall make reasonable efforts to make available for brief interview ADC employees and any employees of any contractor that have direct or indirect duties related to the requirements of this Stipulation. The interviews shall not unreasonably interfere with the performance of their duties. Plaintiffs' counsel and their experts shall be able to have confidential, out-of-cell interviews with prisoners during these tours. Plaintiffs' counsel and their experts shall be able to review health and other records of class members, and records of mental health and other programming, during the tours. Plaintiffs' counsel and their experts shall be able to review any documents that form the basis of the MGAR reports and be able to interview the ADC monitors who prepared those reports.

33. With the agreement of both parties, Plaintiffs may conduct confidential interviews with prisoners, and interviews of ADC employees or employees of ADC's contractors, by telephone.

34. Defendants shall notify the Ninth Circuit Court of Appeals of the settlement of this case and of their intention to withdraw the petition for rehearing en banc in case number 13-16396, upon final approval of the Stipulation by the District Court. Defendants agree not to file a petition for writ of certiorari with the United States Supreme Court seeking review of the Ninth Circuit's judgment in case number 13-16396.

IV. RESERVATION OF JURISDICTION

35. The parties consent to the reservation and exercise of jurisdiction by the District Court over all disputes between and among the parties arising out of this Stipulation. The parties agree that this Stipulation shall not be construed as a consent decree.

36. Based upon the entire record, the parties stipulate and jointly request that the Court find that this Stipulation satisfies the requirements of 18 U.S.C. § 3626(a)(1)(A) in that it is narrowly drawn, extends no further than necessary to correct the violation of the Federal right, and is the least intrusive means necessary to correct the violation of the Federal right of the Plaintiffs. In the event the Court finds that Defendants have not complied with the Stipulation, it shall in the first instance require Defendants to submit a plan approved by the Court to remedy the deficiencies identified by the Court. In the event the Court subsequently determines that the Defendants' plan did not remedy the deficiencies, the Court shall retain the power to enforce this Stipulation through all remedies provided by law, except that the Court shall not have the authority to order Defendants to construct a new prison or to hire a

specific number or type of staff unless Defendants propose to do so as part of a plan to remedy a failure to comply with any provision of this Stipulation. In determining the subsequent remedies the Court shall consider whether to require Defendants to submit a revised plan.

V. TERMINATION OF THE AGREEMENT.

37. To allow time for the remedial measures set forth in this Stipulation to be fully implemented, the parties shall not move to terminate this Stipulation for a period of four years from the date of its approval by the Court. Defendants shall not move to decertify the class for the duration of this Stipulation.

VI. MISCELLANEOUS PROVISIONS

38. Information produced pursuant to this Stipulation shall be governed by the Amended Protective Order (Doc. 454).

39. This Stipulation constitutes the entire agreement among the parties as to all claims raised by Plaintiffs in this action, and supersedes all prior agreements, representations, statements, promises, and understandings, whether oral or written, express or implied, with respect to this Stipulation. Each Party represents, warranties and covenants that it has the full legal authority necessary to enter into this Stipulation and to perform the duties and obligations arising under this Stipulation.

40. This is an integrated agreement and may not be altered or modified, except by a writing signed by all representatives of all parties at the time of modification.

41. This Stipulation shall be binding on all successors, assignees, employees, agents, and all others working for or on behalf of Defendants and Plaintiffs.

PARTIAL PERFORMANCE MEASURES

ADOC agreed to the following performance measures as a part of the settlement and as is shown below, it is following these in the breach. This is because the Arizona Attorny General's saff in bad faith encourage breach of these stipulations and oders. It is not following these.

EXHIBIT A

For purposes of the performance measures, the following definitions will be used:

TERM DEFINITION

Active labor & delivery Contractions lasting 45-60 seconds and being 3 to 4 minutes apart ASPC Arizona State Prison Complex. ASPC- Safford includes Ft Grant. ASPC-Florence includes Globe. ASPC-Winslow includes Apache.

ATP Alternate Treatment Plan Chronic Disease Chronic diseases include the following:

diabetes

HIV/AIDs

cancer

hypertension

Respiratory disease (for example, COPD / asthma / cystic fibrosis)

Seizure Disorder

heart disease

sickle cell disease

Hepatitis C

Tuberculosis

Neurological disorders (Parkinson's, multiple sclerosis, myasthenia gravis, etc.)

Cocci (Valley Fever)

End-Stage Liver Disease

Hyperlipidemia

Renal Diseases

Blood Diseases (including those on anticoagulants (or long term >six months))

Rheumatological Diseases (including lupus, rheumatoid arthritis)

Hyperthyroidism

Crohn's Disease

Contracted Vendor For purposes of this agreement, contracted vendor refers directly to Corizon Health and its subcontractors, or any successor contractor/subcontractor.

CQI Continuous Quality Improvement

Diagnostic Service Lab draws and specimen collections, X-rays, vision testing, and hearing testing

DOT Direct-observation therapy (watch-swallow) (medications)

Effective date of the Stipulation The date on which the Court grants final approval to the Stipulation.

Encounter Interaction between a patient and a qualified healthcare provider that involves a treatment and/or exchange of confidential information.

Healthcare staff Includes QHCPs as well as administrative and support staff (e.g. health record administrators, lab techs, nursing and medical assistants and clerical workers).

HNR Health Needs Request

HSCMB ADC's Health Services Compliance Monitoring Bureau

IPC Inpatient Component / Infirmary beds

IR Incident Report

KOP Keep-on-person (medications)

Licensed Healthcare staff who hold an active and unrestricted license in the State of Arizona in the relevant professional discipline.

MAR Medication Administration Record

Medical Provider Physician, Dentist, Nurse Practitioner, Physician's Assistant-C.

Any health care practitioner who has been duly empowered by the State of Arizona to write prescriptions.

Mental Health Clinician Psychologist, Psychology Associate

Mental Health Provider Psychiatrist, Psychiatry Nurse Practitioner

Mental Health Staff Includes QHCP's who have received instruction and supervision in identifying and interacting with individuals in

need of mental health services.

MH-1 (Mental Health 1)

Inmates who have no history of mental health issue or treatment

MH-2 (Mental Health 2)

Inmates who do not currently have mental health needs and are not currently in treatment but have had treatment in the past

MH-3 (Mental Health 3)

Inmates with Mental Health needs, who require current outpatient treatment. Inmates meeting this criterion will be divided into four (4) categories. These categories may change during each interaction with the inmate as their condition warrants.

MH-3A (Mental Health 3A)

Inmates in acute distress who may require substantial intervention in order to remain stable. Inmates classified as SMI in ADC and/or the community will remain a Category MH-3A (or MH-4 or MH-5 if in specialized mental health program).

MH-3B (Mental Health 3B)

Inmates who may need regular intervention but are generally stable and participate with psychiatric and psychological interventions.

MH-3C (Mental Health 3C)

Inmates who need infrequent intervention and have adequate coping skills to manage their mental illness effectively and independently. These inmates participate in psychiatric interventions only.

MH-3D (Mental Health 3D)

Inmates who have been recently taken off of psychotropic medications and require follow up to ensure stability over time.

MH-4 (Mental Health 4)

Inmates who are admitted to a specialized mental health program as identified in the Mental Health Technical Manual outside of inpatient treatment areas.

MH-5 (Mental Health 5)

Inmates with mental health needs who are admitted to an inpatient psychiatric treatment program (Baker Ward and Flamenco).

Prenatal screening tests GA/Preg, RPR, HIV, HEP, B & C, CBC, CMP (standardized lab panel), Urine, Rubella, ABO RH & Antibody

Psychology Associate A mental health clinician who has a master's or doctoral-level degree in a mental health discipline, but is not a licensed psychologist.

Qualified Health Care Professional (QHCP) Physicians, Physician Assistants, Dentists, nurses, nurse practitioners, dentists, mental health professionals, and others, who by virtue of their education, credentials/license, and experience are permitted by law to evaluate and care for patients.

Regular Business Hours Monday through Friday, 0800 am -1600 pm or similar 8-hour time frame; excluding weekends and holidays.

"Seeing a provider"/ seen/ "seen by"

Interaction between a patient and a Medical Provider, Mental Health Provider or Mental Health Clinician that involves a treatment and/or exchange of information in a confidential setting. With respect to Mental Health staff, means an encounter that takes place in a confidential setting outside the prisoner's cell, unless the prisoner refuses to exit his or her cell for the encounter

SMI According to a licensed mental health clinician or provider, possessing a qualifying mental health diagnosis as indicated on the SMI Determination Form (#1103.13) as well as a severe functional impairment directly relating to the mental illness.

All inmates determined to be SMI in the community shall also be designated as SMI in ADC. All inmates designated SMI (as defined in MHTM Chapter 2, Section 2.0) will be designated a MH-3A, MH-4, or MH-5 based on their current program placement.

SNO Special Needs Order

Specialized Medical Housing

Infirmary beds (IPC)

EXHIBIT B

HEALTH CARE OUTCOME MEASURES

Staffing 1 Each ASPC will maintain, at a minimum, one RN onsite 24/7, 7 days/week.

Staffing 2 Each ASPC will maintain, at a minimum, one Medical Provider (not to include a dentist) onsite during regular business hour and on-call at all other times.

Staffing 3 Dental staffing will be maintained at current contract levels –30 dentists.

Staffing 4 Infirmary staffing will be maintained with a minimum staffing level of 2 RNs on duty in the infirmary at all times at Tucson & Florence infirmaries and a minimum of one RN on duty in the infirmary at all times at Perryville and Lewis infirmaries

Medical Records 5 will be accurate, chronologically maintained, and scanned or filed in the patient's chart within two business days, with all documents filed in their designated location.

Medical Records 6 Provider orders will be noted daily with time, date, and name of person taking the orders off.

Medical Records 7 Medical record entries will be legible, and complete with time, name stamp and signature present.

Medical Records 8 Nursing protocols/NETS will be utilized by nurses for sick call.

Medical Records 9 SOAPE format will be utilized in the medical record for encounters.

Medical Records 10 Each patient's medical record will include an up-to-date Master Problem list.

Pharmacy 11 Newly prescribed provider-ordered formulary medications will be provided to the inmate within 2 business days after prescribed, or on the same day, if prescribed STAT.

Pharmacy 12 Medical record will contain documentation of refusals or "no shows."

Pharmacy 13 Chronic care and psychotropic medication renewals will be completed in a manner such that there is no interruption or lapse in medication.

Pharmacy 14 Any refill for a chronic care or psychotropic medication that is requested by a prisoner between three and seven business days prior to the prescription running out will be completed in a manner such that there is no interruption or lapse in medication.

Pharmacy 15 Inmates who refuse prescribed medication (or no show) will be counseled by a QHCP after three consecutive refusals.

Pharmacy 16 Perpetual inventory medication logs will be maintained on each yard.

Pharmacy 17 The Medication Administration Record (MAR) will reflect dose, frequency, start date and nurse's signature.

Pharmacy 18 Daily delivery manifests will be kept in binders located in medication rooms on each yard/complex and will be reviewed and initialed daily by an LPN or RN.

Pharmacy 19 Perpetual inventory medications will be signed off on the Inmate's individual MAR.

Pharmacy 20 Medical AIMs entries are accurately completed within 3 business days from the entry in the medical record.

Pharmacy 21 Inmates who are paroled or released from ASPCs will receive a 30-day supply of all medications currently prescribed by the ADC contracted vendor.

Pharmacy 22 Non-formulary requests are reviewed and approved, disapproved, or designated for an alternate treatment plan (ATP) within two business days of the prescriber's order.

Equipment 23 Automated External Defibrillators (AEDs) will be maintained and readily accessible to Health Care Staff. Equipment 24 Emergency medical response bags are checked daily, inventoried monthly, and contain all required essential items.

Emergency Response 25 A first responder trained in Basic Life Support responds and adequately provides care within three minutes of an emergency.

Quality Improvement 26 Responses to health care grievances will be completed within 15 working days of receipt (by health care staff) of the grievance.

Quality Improvement 27 Each ASPC facility will conduct monthly CQI meetings, in accordance with NCCHC Standard P-A-06

Quality Improvement 28 Every medical provider will undergo peer reviews annually with reviews and recommended actions documented.

Quality Improvement 29 Each ASPC facility Director of Nursing or designee will conduct and document annual clinical performance reviews of

nursing staff as recommended by NCCHC standard P-C-02.

Quality Improvement 30 The initial mortality review of an inmate's death will be completed within 10 working days of death.

Quality Improvement 31 Mortality reviews will identify and refer deficiencies to appropriate managers and supervisors, including CQI committee, and corrective action will be taken.

Quality Improvement 32 A final independent clinical mortality review will be completed by the Health Services Contract Monitoring Bureau for all mortalities within 10 business days of receipt of the medical examiner's findings.

Intake facility 33 All inmates will receive a health screening by an LPN or RN within one day of arrival at the intake facility.

Intake facility 34 A physical examination including a history will be completed by a Medical Provider (not a dentist) by the end of the second full day of an intake inmate's arrival at the intake facility.

Intersystem Transfers 35 All inmate medications (KOP and DOT) will be transferred with and provided to the inmate or otherwise provided at the receiving prison without interruption.

Access to care 36 A LPN or RN will screen HNRs within 24 hours of receipt.

Access to care 37 Sick call inmates will be seen by an RN within 24 hours after an HNR is received (or immediately if identified with an emergent need, or on the same day if identified as having an urgent need).

Access to care 38 Vital signs, to include weight, will be checked and documented in the medical record each time an inmate is seen during sick call.

Access to care 39 Routine provider referrals will be addressed by a Medical Provider and referrals requiring a scheduled provider appointments will be seen within fourteen calendar days of the referral.

Access to care 40 Urgent provider referrals are seen by a Medical Provider within 24 hours of the referral.

Access to care 41 Emergent provider referrals are seen immediately by a Medical Provider.

Access to care

42 A follow-up sick call encounter will occur within the time frame specified by the Medical or Mental Health Provider.

Access to care 43 Inmates returning from an inpatient hospital stay or ER transport will be returned to the medical unit and be assessed

by a RN or LPN on duty there.

Access to care 44 Inmates returning from an inpatient hospital stay or ER transport with discharge recommendations from the hospital shall have the hospital's treatment recommendations reviewed and acted upon by a medical provider within 24 hours.

Diagnostic Services 45 On-site diagnostic services will be provided the same day if ordered STAT or urgent, or within 14 calendar days if routine

Diagnostic Services 46 A Medical Provider will review the diagnostic report, including pathology reports, and act upon reports with abnormal values within five calendar days of receiving the report at the prison.

Diagnostic Services 47 A Medical Provider will communicate the results of the diagnostic study to the inmate upon request and within seven calendar days of the date of the request.

Specialty care 48 Documentation, including the reason(s) for the denial, of Utilization Management denials of requests for specialty services will be sent to the requesting Provider in writing within fourteen calendar days, and placed in the patient's medical record.

Specialty care 49 Patients for whom a provider's request for specialty services is denied are told of the denial by a Medical Provider at the patient's next scheduled appointment, no more than 30 days after the denial, and the Provider documents in the patient's medical record the Provider's follow-up to the denial.

Specialty care 50 Urgent specialty consultations and urgent specialty diagnostic services will be scheduled and completed within 30 calendar days of the consultation being requested by the provider.

Specialty care 51 Routine specialty consultations will be scheduled and completed within 60 calendar days of the consultation being requested by the provider.

Specialty care 52 Specialty consultation reports will be reviewed and acted on by a Provider within seven calendar days of receiving the report.

Chronic care 53 Treatment plans will be developed and documented in the medical record by a provider within 30 calendar days of identification that the inmate has a chronic disease.

Chronic care 54 Chronic disease inmates will be seen by the provider as specified in the inmate's treatment plan, no less than every 180 days unless the provider documents a reason why a longer time frame can be in place.

Chronic care 55 Disease management guidelines will be implemented for chronic diseases.

Chronic care 56 Inmates with a chronic disease will be provided education about their condition/disease which will be documented in the medical record.

THE MOTION TO ENFORCE

The State Of Arizona Department Of Corrections has a well-documented history in all matters, of entering into agreements and not complying with them. They consistently violate rights of prisoners with impunity and this is another instance. The motion to enforce provides in pertinent part as follows:

The Parsons Stipulation requires ADC to comply with a set of 103 health care performance measures. [Doc. 1185 ¶ 8] These performance measures were designed to determine whether ADC was providing essential health care services to the plaintiff class. To fulfill the terms of the Stipulation, ADC must meet or exceed a 75% compliance score on each measure at each prison complex for the first year, 80% for the second year, and 85% thereafter. [*Id.* at 20]

After a full year of auditing compliance with these performance measures, evidence from ADC's own audits reveals a dismal failure to meet the terms of the Stipulation. Review of Defendants' own compliance data for many of the key performance measures related to patient care show that defendants have consistently delivered failing scores.

Defendant health care audits, though skewed in defendants' favor due to methodology errors for some performance measures, amply document defendants' failure to implement critical systemic changes to the medical and mental health care delivery systems.

Month after month, particularly at the larger institutions which house 80% of the prisoners, the audits reveal that patients are exposed to a substantial risk of serious harm because Defendants fail to provide timely medical and mental health appointments, fail to provide timely medications, fail to deliver ordered care and fail to adequately monitor mentally ill patients, including those on suicide watch. For critical performance measures, defendants have consistently failed to reach the 75% compliance benchmark for the Stipulation's first year and, without dramatic changes, have no hope of attaining the 80% benchmark currently required for compliance in year two. As a direct result of these well-documented systemic deficiencies, patients needlessly suffer serious injury, illness and, in some cases, death. Two examples illustrate the all too frequent result of ADC's grossly inadequate health care system. A 26 years old inmate hanged himself at Eyman-Browning Unit .He was diagnosed with bipolar disorder and was treated with Lithium, until the medication was discontinued due to side effects. Mental health staff did not consider any other medication to treat his illness, and did not perform an adequate suicide risk assessment, despite his history of suicide attempts and several other suicide risk factors.

On April 28, 2015, he submitted a Health Needs Request (HNR) saying "I want to get back on my lithium as soon as possible; I'm having serious mental issues." He was scheduled to be seen by mental health staff, but the appointment never happened. After his suicide, the ADC psychological autopsy noted that he had not been seen by mental health staff as required by policy. The ADC Mortality Review Committee concluded that he did not receive adequate mental health care; that his death was preventable; and that a "delay in access to care" was a contributing cause of his death. In the months prior to Mr. Suicide, Defendants failed to comply with Performance Measures 87 (a prisoner with Mr. classification must be seen by a mental health clinician no less than every 30 days) and 98 (mental health HNRs must be responded to within specific timeframes). [Declaration of Pablo Stewart, M.D., Exhibit A [Expert Report of Pablo Stewart, M.D.] ("Stewart Rep.") ¶¶ 50-58, filed concurrently herewith], a Yuma prisoner, died on at age 59, after low-level Nursing staff repeatedly ignored his desperate pleas for help, and did not seek the assistance of a medical doctor, even after open weeping lesions on Mr. Body were swarmed by flies. [Declaration of Todd R. Wilcox ("Wilcox Decl.") ¶¶ 41-43, filed concurrently herewith] Mr. had end-stage liver disease with complications including massive fluid retention, groin wounds, and sepsis. On March 6, 2015, he submitted an HNR stating "my legs were bleeding with open weeping wounds sticking to my prescription socks. I am in severe pain. I cannot wear my socks nor get them on. I am in pain." The nursing response to this sick call request indicates that it is a "duplicate from 3/3/15." However, there was no request dated 3/3/15 in his medical record. Mr. filed another HNR on March 17, 2015 for shortness of breath and painful abdomen. He was told he would see a nurse at an unspecified time, which apparently did not occur. Four days later, he filed an HNR for worsening fluid retention and shortness of breath. Again, he was told "duplicate same as 3/17, you are on nurse line." Mr. Condition deteriorated and his fluid retention worsened to the point that his skin split open and became infected. By March 31, 2015, Mr. Situation deteriorated to the point that he was being swarmed by flies, which he reported to nursing staff in a HNR. Instead of investigating why a patient with split skin oozing pus and serum had a swarm of flies on the injury, the nurse the next day instead decided that Mr. did not need to be seen. More than a week later, on April 9, 2015, he finally was sent to the hospital, where he died. The ADC Mortality Review determined there were multiple triage mistakes made by nurses that impeded and delayed care for Mr. Plaintiffs' experts, Drs. Wilcox and Stewart, agree that compliance with the performance measures required by the Stipulation is not possible with the existing staff.

[Stewart Rep. ¶¶ 17-25, 114; Wilcox Decl. ¶¶ 9-12, 29-35, 140] There are too many vacancies for existing positions, and there are too few allocated positions. Thus, as the two examples above show and ADC's own audits described below confirm, critical lapses of care occur too often, with harmful or fatal results.

PROCEDURAL HISTORY

In October 2014 the parties reached a settlement agreement, the "Stipulation," in the constitutional class action filed by fourteen Arizona Department of Corrections ("ADC") prisoners and the Arizona Center for Disability Law ("Plaintiffs"). The Court found the Stipulation to be "fair, adequate, and reasonable," and it went into effect on February 17, 2015. [Doc. 1458 at 1] Under the Stipulation, Defendants agreed to comply with 103 healthcare measures throughout ADC prison facilities and to allow Plaintiffs' counsel to monitor their implementation of these measures. [Doc. 1185 ¶¶ 8, 29] Class certification was granted, and the plaintiff class consists of approximately 36,000 prisoners at ADC's ten state prisons. *See Parsons v. Ryan*, 289 F.R.D. 513 (D.Ariz. 2013), *aff'd*, 754 F.3d 657 (9th Cir. 2014), *reh'g en banc denied*, 784 F.3d 571 (9th Cir. 2015); ADC contracts the provision of medical, mental health, and dental services to Corizon Health Service, Inc. ("Corizon").

Corizon is not a defendant in this matter because the duty to provide constitutionally adequate health care and constitutionally suitable conditions of confinement is a duty ADC cannot delegate. ADC is the responsible party regardless of who it hires to provide care. [*See* Doc. 175 at 9-10]

STATEMENT OF FACTS

Review of Defendants' own compliance data for many of the critical performance measures related to patient care show that Defendants have consistently delivered failing scores.

DEFENDANTS' AUDITS DOCUMENT A BROKEN SYSTEM

A. Access to Medical Care

1. Sick call

Patients in a prison facility must have an effective method for making their medical needs known to the medical staff. ADC prisoners seeking a medical appointment must submit a written health needs request form ("HNR"). Because these forms provide such a crucial link between medical staff and prisoners, Defendants' response time in triaging HNRs and then providing access to appropriate care is an essential monitoring parameter. Under the Stipulation and the CGAR audit, patients who submit sick call slips must be seen the same day for urgent needs; otherwise, they must be seen by nurses for sick call ("nurse line") within 24 hours of the triage. Based upon the nurse's assessment, the patient may or may not be referred and scheduled to see a primary care provider. Failure to adhere to these timelines places patients at serious risk of substantial harm. Dr. Wilcox, who reviewed the CGAR audit results in addition to medical records, concluded that Defendants' "sick call system remains profoundly deficient." [Wilcox Decl. ¶ 39] According to the CGAR reports, for the eleven month period of February through December 2015, *none* of the six largest ADC prisons achieved an average score of 75% or higher, and at Yuma, on average, just four in ten patients were seen timely during that period. As illustrated in the chart below, for the month of December, two large prisons, Eyman and Lewis, scored under 50%. [Wilcox Decl. ¶ 16] If the nurse determines the patient requires the attention of a primary care provider on a routine basis, the patient must be scheduled and seen by the provider within 14 days of the nurse appointment.9 Defendants' scores on this performance measure are likewise dismal. The CGAR results for the months of February through December demonstrate widespread non-compliance with the 14-day benchmark, particularly at the five largest men's prisons and at Perryville, the women's prison.10 At three of the five largest men's prisons, during the eleven months from February through December 2015, the average compliance rate for Measure 39 was below 75%, with Tucson scoring 50%. Perryville Scored at 48%. [Wilcox Decl. ¶ 46] The data underlying the CGAR reports document that patients who should be seen within two weeks may wait six weeks or more to see the provider. For example:

In November, some patients at Perryville were waiting six weeks to see a provider;

At Tucson's Winchester Unit, six of ten patients referred to the provider in October were not seen by the time of the November 26, 2015 audit; at Catalina Unit, five of ten patients referred in October were not seen by the time of the audit, and an additional patient had been seen but not in relation to the referral; at Santa Rita Unit, five of ten patients referred in October were not seen timely, and three were not seen at all;

At Florence, three of four East Unit patients referred in October were not seen as of the time of November 30, 2015 audit; at Kasson Unit, six of eight patients were not seen timely, and three were not seen at all;

At Eyman, six of six Browning Unit patients, three of six Meadows Unit patients, and three of five Cook Unit patients referred in October had not been seen at time of audit on November 30, 2015;

Tucson complex-wide compliance rate of 60% in December 2015; eleven patients not seen by the time of the January 30, 2016 audit, including one three month delay;

Yuma complex-wide compliance rate of 68% in December;

At Eyman, six of six Browning patients, three of six Meadows patients, and three of five Cook patients referred in October not seen at time of January 30, 2016 audit;

Douglas patient referred to provider on December 3, 2015 not seen as of time of January 29, 2016 audit;

Florence complex-wide compliance rate of 74% in December 2015; at North Unit, three of six patients referred in December not been seen at time of audit on January 28, 2016; and three of five South Unit patients referred in December not

Seen at time of audit;

Phoenix complex-wide compliance rate of 72% for December 2015; multiple prisoners referred to the provider in early to mid-December still had not been seen at time of audit on January 29, 2016. [Wilcox Decl. ¶ 47]

2. Chronic Care

Patients suffering from chronic illness require regular and coordinated health care. "Regularly scheduled appointments allow providers to track the progress of patients with chronic illnesses and ensure appropriate levels of treatment." [Wilcox Decl. ¶ 49] Failure to monitor chronic illness risks the condition or disease getting out of control, ultimately harming the patient.

Performance Measure 5411 requires Defendants to see chronic care patients at medically appropriate intervals. The CGAR reports show widespread and continued noncompliance with this measure. From February through December 2015, five of the largest men's facilities and Perryville Complex all averaged below 75% compliance, with Tucson and Florence barely over 50% compliance. [Wilcox Decl. ¶ 50] What these percentages do not reveal is that some of the delays in chronic care appointments lasted over a year, with one lasting two years. Patients with active cancer diagnoses have had gaps of 2 to 6 months between chronic care appointments. [Wilcox Decl. ¶ 51] The CGAR reports described numerous problems, including, but not limited

To:

At Tucson's Santa Rita Unit, one patient had a two year lapse between chronic care appointments, and at least two lapsed for over a year; on Cimarron Unit, patient with diabetes lapsed for over a year; on Manzanita Unit, patient with active cancer, ordered to be seen monthly, not seen for four months;

Perryville complex-wide compliance rate of 64% for December 2015; at Lumley Unit, a woman with "active cancer . . . with plans for radiation therapy" for thyroid cancer not seen for eight months, and another Lumley patient with rheumatoid arthritis not seen for a chronic care appointment for 19 months after her diagnosis; patient at Santa Rosa Unit with blood disorders and anemia not seen for 14 months;

Douglas complex-wide compliance rate of 45% for December 2015;

Four of ten files reviewed at Florence North Unit showed delayed appointments, including 8-month gap in appointments for patient with thyroid disorder and hypertension; at Central, patients with 9 and 14 month gaps between appointments; another patient with seizure disorder, Hepatitis C, and asthma with no chronic care appointment between early March and mid-

December 2015;

At Yuma's La Paz Unit, two patients with seizure conditions seen late;

Patients at Winslow complex seen six weeks and three months later than medically needed and previously ordered by the provider.[Wilcox Decl. ¶ 51]

These are profound lapses in treatment that imminently endanger the lives of some of the system's most vulnerable patients.

3. Inpatient Care

Many of ADC's sickest patients are housed in the prison infirmaries, where the ADC medical providers are required to see them every 72 hours. The average audit results for two of the three men's prisons with infirmary units over eleven months in 2015 show shockingly poor compliance for this critical measure—32% for Tucson and 19% for Florence. [Wilcox Decl. ¶ 67]

4. Medication Administration

For a prison health care system to achieve a successful system of medication administration it must be able to (1) provide prescribed medications to prisoners in a "timely, consistent manner"; (2) ensure prescribed medications are "renewed regularly and without interruption"; and (3) ensure that prisoners transferred between complexes experience no gaps in medication administration. [Wilcox Decl. ¶¶ 126-127]

Defendants' medication system fails to meet any of these thresholds and "practically guarantees that patients will have gaps in receiving their medications." [*Id.* ¶ 127] The audits show Defendants routinely fail to provide patients with new prescriptions timely, in compliance with Performance Measure 11.13 the average scores over three months off February through December, 2015 were below 75% at six of the ten

Prisons, including at all five of the largest men's prisons. The following chart highlights in yellow each month in 2015 where the prison's compliance level was less than 75.

B. Access to Mental Health Care

1. Inadequate access to care

The Health Needs Request form (HNR) is the primary means by which ADC prisoner's access non-routine mental health services. To ensure that prisoners are able to have their mental health needs addressed in a timely fashion, defendants must monitor responses to HNRs, based upon the category of need. The Mental Health Technical Manual sets forth 5 specific timeframes for different categories of HNRs (e.g. Emergency, Urgent Medication, etc.).17

Defendants have unilaterally decided to monitor only one of these five categories:

Those raising "routine non-medication issues." This presents a risk of serious harm, since without monitoring, there is no way to know if emergency or urgent HNRs are being responded to in a timely fashion, or indeed at all. But even with this critical monitoring defect, Defendants are still noncompliant with this measure, with Eyman and Florence each showing nine consecutive months of noncompliance, and Lewis, Phoenix, Tucson, and 'Winslow each showing two or more consecutive fronts of non compliance.

2. Inadequate monitoring of psychotropic medications. Patients taking psychotropic medication, or who have recently discontinued such medication, must be monitored by a psychiatrist. Performance Measure 8l requires that "MH-34 prisoners who are prescribed psychotropic medications shall be seen a minimum of every 90 days by a mental health provider."rs Dr. Stewart, Plaintifß' psychiatric expert, found that "ADC is persistently noncompliant with PM 81 at multiple prisons." Both Lewis and Tucson, two of Defendants' largest complexes, reported consecutive months of non-compliance with this measure.

II. DEFENDANTS' BROKEN HEALTH CARE SYSTEM HARMS PATIENTS

AND PLACES ALL PRISONERS AT SUBSTANTIAL RISK OF HARM

A. Systemic Failures Result in Treatment Delays and Denials Causing Suffering and Death Defendants' own audits establish that their health care delivery systems fail to Provide reliable access to care. This failure has directly harmed many class members and has placed every prisoner at serious risk of substantial harm. Often denying and/or delaying access to medically necessary care has immediate, catastrophic, and permanent Results that can result in preventable, irreversible injury or death. [*See* Wilcox Decl. ¶¶ 13-17, 41-44, 51, 53-66, 68-70, 78-79, 81-94, 98-116, 119, 121-124, 133; Stewart Rep. ¶¶ 50-71, 73-84, 85-112] While much of this case rests on metrics and audits, behind those numbers are human beings who have suffered immeasurable harm and pain, and

Many of whom have died, as a result of Defendants' abject failures. Perhaps most illustrative of ADC's systemic failures and dangerous care is the case of, who mercifully was released from ASPC-Tucson in March 2016,

And is no longer dependent on Defendants for medical care. Mr. was diagnosed with testicular cancer in August 2015. [Wilcox Decl. ¶ 88] At every juncture, Defendants failed to provide Mr. with timely and appropriate care. His CT scan, ordered on an urgent basis, was performed weeks late on 9/23/15. [*Id.*] Mr. underwent surgery in late October 2015, and that is where his care essentially ended. [*Id.*] The follow-up CT

scan was not performed until November 24, 2015 and the consult notes attached to the CT were missing the pages that discussed the diagnosis and plan.29 [*Id.* ¶¶ 88-89] As such, Mr. received no care for biopsy-proven, CT-proven, surgical pathology-proven cancer. [*Id.* ¶ 89] Mr. is a young man with a highly treatable form of testicular cancer, but the appropriate treatment has to be done and it has to be done in a timely fashion.

Unfortunately, nothing about Mr. care has been timely, only recommended treatment has been accomplished, and there is no evidence that he was ever on anybody's radar within ADC because the last date he had a provider encounter was 10/30/2015—the date of his surgery. [*Id.* ¶ 90] He was never seen by a provider after returning to the facility prior to his release. [*Id.*]

Mr. Case is particularly troubling, for two reasons. First, Dr. Wilcox identified him to defendants in a face-to-face meeting in December 2015 as a patient in need of immediate attention for a potentially life-threatening illness, yet according to the medical record, he received virtually no attention in the ensuing three months. [*Id.* ¶ 91]

Second, Mr. Case is alarmingly similar to two other cases Dr. Wilcox reviewed at ASPC-Tucson, both involving young men with testicular cancer who experienced inexcusable delays in care. [*Id.* ¶¶ 13-15], died at age 42, on. After he underwent an orchiectomy (removal of his testicle), he should have immediately been placed under the care of an oncologist. In fact, he did not see an oncologist for five months, and when he did, he had widespread disease. [*Id.* ¶ 15] The ADC Mortality Review Committee concluded Mr. Death was preventable, and Dr. Wilcox agreed. [*Id.*] Similarly, thirty year old, experienced extreme delays in care for his testicular cancer, resulting in metastasis. Although he is still alive, he has been diagnosed as terminal, with less than a year to live. [*Id.* ¶ 14]

The suffering experienced prior to death by, a Yuma prisoner described above at pages 2-3, illustrates the suffering inflicted when patients cannot access basic nursing care.30 Despite Mr. serious conditions of end stage liver disease with fluid retention, groin wounds, and sepsis, the nursing staff repeatedly failed to respond to his desperate Health Needs Requests in March and April 2015, including at one point when he reported that his skin split open due to swelling, was infected, and swarmed with flies. [Wilcox Decl. ¶¶ 41-42] Shockingly, the nurse declined to see him. [*Id.* ¶ 42] More than a week after reporting the swarm of flies, he was finally transferred to the hospital, where he died. Dr. Wilcox agreed with the Mortality Review Committee's conclusion that multiple triage mistakes by nursing staff impeded and delayed Mr. Care, and concluded that the abysmal care hastened his death. [*Id.* ¶ 43] Patients in Defendants' infirmary units are particularly vulnerable and likely to suffer harm if not promptly seen. , died four days after arriving at ASPC-Tucson, without ever seeing a medical provider. [Wilcox Decl. ¶ 68] Mr. had a daily heroin habit and was placed in the infirmary to go through opiate withdrawal. Although seen by several nurses, who documented that he was experiencing serious withdrawal and was at risk of dehydration due to excessive vomiting, he was apparently never seen a medical provider,31 and was not prescribed IV medications for vomiting. [*Id.* ¶¶ 68, 78] Staff failed to monitor his condition, failed to order appropriate labs, and failed to refer him to a higher level of care. Consequently, Mr. died unnecessarily on, four days after his arrival at prison, at age 44. The Mortality Review Committee report correctly classified this as a preventable death. [*Id.* ¶ 68] A lack of timely access to provider's results in delayed or denied care, and places patients at substantial risk of harm. , died of leukemia at the age of 32 after Defendants failed to provide timely diagnostic care for almost a year. [*Id.* ¶ 103] She died four months after her diagnosis, and while Ms. may ultimately have succumbed to her illness, Dr. Wilcox determined without reservation that she experienced "repeated and inexcusable delays" in receiving a diagnosis and treatment for her leukemia, and that "these serious lapses resulted in hastening her death." [*Id.*] likewise suffered delays in care when she complained of radiating pain in her leg, abdominal pain, and the inability to urinate. Four days later, when her symptoms worsened and she could no longer use her legs, medical staff decided not to send her to a hospital but rather to the prison's medical clinic. While at the clinic,

Temperature registered at 91.9 degrees, a classic symptom of sepsis requiring emergency assessment. While she was eventually taken to the hospital, she died the next day from a staph infection, spinal meningitis, and pneumonia. Had her condition been properly triaged, she likely would have survived. Wilcox Decl. TT 53-54], experienced treatment delays at ASPC-Eyman in part because his very abnormal lab results apparently not reviewed by his provider for weeks. Mr. ultimately died, at the age of 43, with an infection of his heart. Had he been timely diagnosed, Dr. Wilcox opines he would not have died. Significant barriers remain in the provision of specially care for patients in Defendants' care. Essential coordination between Defendants' medical staff and outside specialists continues to fall well below the standard of care, with critical diagnostic results left ignored and unprocessed for extended periods of time.

DECLARATION OF TODD R. WILCOX

Dr. Todd Wilcox submitted his declaration and it reflects a seriously flawed system. Again the State Of Arizona Department Of Corrections with the approval of the Arizona legislature and the designated staff of the Arizona Attorney General's Office, have made it a practice to inflict torture on inmates.

I. Introduction and background

2. This report assesses Arizona's prison medical care one year after the Court approved the parties' Stipulation settling this action. Under the Stipulation, defendants agreed to comply with 103 health care-related performance measures, to request that the Arizona Legislature approve a budget to allow ADC and its contracted health services vendor to modify the health services contract to increase health care staffing, and to implement additional policies and training programs.

3. Through my three-day visit to Arizona State Prison Complex-Tucson on December 2-4, 2015, and my review of patient records, including death records, I have found that ADC prisoners continue to suffer serious harm, and in some cases preventable death, because defendants fail to provide necessary and timely health care on a systemwide basis. Tragically, this situation should come as a surprise to no one. The audits that Defendants have compiled every month since the Stipulation was entered document a system where patients lack reliable access to nurse triage, physicians, specialists, and/or necessary medication. The system is obviously broken, and human suffering is the unavoidable result.

B. Information sources

5. I undertook an extensive investigation of current conditions to develop my opinions expressed in this report. I reviewed the CGAR monitoring reports for the months of February through December 2015, as well as summary charts reflecting CGAR results, well over 100 partial and full healthcare records of Arizona prisoners, and miscellaneous logs and minutes while at ASPC-Tucson. I reviewed staffing reports, lists of prisoners awaiting specialty referrals and meetings minutes of health care staff. I also interviewed staff and approximately two dozen prisoners at the Tucson prison complex. The documents I reviewed are listed in Appendix C.

C. Methodology

6. To prepare this report, I reviewed documents regarding the statewide health care system, prison-specific audits and patient records, as set forth more fully below. I also conducted a prison site visit for three days in December, 2015, at ASPC-Tucson. I chose this prison because it is one of the largest in the state and is one of only two men's prisons with an inpatient/infirmary unit, and because it was one of the five prisons I had visited in 2013, when preparing my initial report.

7. I reviewed all records for people who died in ADC custody during 2015 that were produced to me by 1/19/16. I reviewed patient healthcare records while visiting ASPC- Tucson and also reviewed records provided to me by plaintiffs' counsel. As was true for my previous reports, I did not review a random sample of records during my ASPC-Tucson site visit; instead, I chose to look at files of the same types of prisoners I reviewed for previous reports, including files for patients with diabetes, hypertension, HIV, kidney failure, hepatitis, infections and cancer. I also looked through lab reports, diagnostic test logs, and Health Needs Requests on site to identify patients who had objective findings that were concerning and then I asked for their charts to be pulled for my review. If I found areas of concern in the health care record, I frequently would request that the patient be pulled for me to interview to confirm my findings. I also interviewed patients I identified while on tours of the

various housing units and then would review their charts afterward to gain additional information about their condition and the care plan. As I explained in previous reports, I focus my review on those patients with conditions requiring them to use the health care system.

8. Although my role when touring ASPC-Tucson was to gather information, I felt obligated to report cases to prison officials and their attorneys when I discovered patients who were in imminent risk of harm. I reported such problems for twelve prisoners, many of whom are discussed in some detail in this report.

II. Opinions

9. When I reviewed Arizona's prison medical care system in 2013 and 2014, I found that it was significantly below community standards and placed patients at serious risk of harm. Wilcox Reports, Doc. 1104-1 and 1138-1. Based upon my recent return visit at Tucson prison complex and my review of documents, my opinion has not changed. Prisoners in ADC custody continue to suffer an unreasonable risk of harm because the health care delivery system of their contractor, Corizon Health, Inc., is woefully deficient, and ADC officials do not acknowledge the gravity and impact of these deficiencies.

Many of the deficiencies are rooted in staffing shortages, particularly for primary care providers,2 and are exacerbated by the adoption of a poorly organized and highly inefficient electronic medical record-keeping system that impedes rather than facilitates health care delivery. What is particularly apparent is that, lacking a sufficient number of providers and medical managers, the system is incapable of self-correction, even when gross systemic problems are identified. Consequently, the auditing reports document the same failure to comply with critical performance measures, month after month; class counsel continue to raise serious systemic issues when advocating for individuals with serious unmet medical needs; and patients suffer preventable deaths that are poorly reviewed.

13. Review of three similar cancer cases at one prison, ASPC-Tucson, vividly illustrates a system in disrepair. I discussed the case of in my Second Supplemental Report, served on defendants in September, 2014. Doc. 1138-1 at 165. He experienced unconscionable delays in screening and treatment for testicular cancer, a condition which, if treated timely is almost always curable. The 5-year survival rate of testicular cancer is approximately 95%. Siegel RL, Miller KD, Jemal A., Cancer statistics, 2015. CA Cancer J. Clin. 2015; 65:5. Declaration of Corene Kendrick, filed herewith, Ex. 4,3 PLTF-PARSONS-036248-36272. 14. Mr. 's complaints of testicular pain in mid-June, 2013 were essentially ignored, and despite a urology recommendation for a radical orchiectomy(removal of the testicle) in September, 2013, the surgery was not provided until 3/24/14. Ex. 60 at ADC418740, ADC418712, 418718, 418740. I noted previously that this delay has exposed Mr. to an unreasonable risk of harm. Doc. 1138-1 at 165. I interviewed Mr. recently while at Tucson complex on 12/4/15, and reviewed his current medical record. Tragically, but predictably, the cancer has spread to his lungs and has been deemed inoperable and untreatable. Sadly, Mr. who is 30 years old, has now been diagnosed as terminal, and has less than a year to live. He will die of a treatable and curable disease. In a healthy medical care system, I would expect that the identification of a case with the inexcusable and dangerous health care delays identified in Mr. 's case would trigger a review of the case history and remedial measures to ensure that the deficiencies in Mr. 's case do not recur for future patients.

15. Sadly, Mr. 's case was not an isolated aberration. In addition to his case, I found two other cases of testicular cancer in young men who suffered unconscionable delays in care. , died of testicular cancer on less than a month shy of his 43rd birthday. Mr. sought care for an enlarged testicle in June, 2014. He underwent an orchiectomy (removal of his testicle) in September, 2014, just days after my report was submitted. He should have seen an oncologist immediately after this procedure, but he did not. Indeed, I found no documentation from the hospital following the orchiectomy, and it appears he received virtually no medical attention for the three months following the surgery. He was not seen by an oncologist until five months after the surgery, on 2/12/15. On 10/20/15 he underwent surgery to remove lymph nodes and the surgeons found that he had widespread cancer in major blood vessels. He ultimately died of shock resulting from a severe postoperative bleed. The ADC's Mortality Review Committee concluded, correctly, that Mr. 's death was preventable. Ex. 69 at ADCM228197-199.

16. Twenty-seven year old may be the next victim. Counsel for plaintiffs found Mr. by speaking to random prisoners at cell front while walking through a housing unit, and brought his complaints to my attention. I interviewed him and reviewed his health records, which confirmed his allegations of inadequate care. He started complaining of testicular pain in July 2015. He was initially scheduled to have an orchiectomy on 9/30/15. However, because nobody within the Arizona Department of Corrections or Corizon communicated appropriately, he was fed breakfast that morning and thus his surgery had to be cancelled. It took the system an additional month to get him scheduled for his necessary care, and he had an orchiectomy on 10/30/15.

17. Because of the urgency of his condition, the surgeon ordered a postoperative appointment two weeks later to review pathology, post-operative imaging and to refer him to an oncologist. As of 12/4/15 when I interviewed him, he had not seen an oncologist to consider chemotherapy and radiation. During my prison visit, I notified ADC officials and their attorneys of Mr. 's critical needs. Since visiting Tucson, I reviewed more recent documents from his medical file dated through 2/10/16. Despite the alarm that I raised to ADC staff during the tour of Mr. 's critical need for immediate health care, he still has not received chemotherapy or seen an oncologist, as discussed in more detail in Part II.D.3 below. If provided proper care, Mr. 's condition is curable and he would be able to survive this occurrence of cancer. Given the unconscionable delays and incompetence that appear to be standard in these three cases, I fear he will not.

A. Death Reviews

18. I reviewed medical records and corresponding mortality reviews, when available, for 72 ADC prisoners who died and for whom defendants produced medical records through January, 2016. In most cases, the records I received covered roughly the year leading up to the patient's death. From the 72, I identified 57 files that contained sufficient records to evaluate the quality of care, for patients who died of natural causes. Of these cases, I conclude that 21 prisoners (37%) received grossly deficient care. Tragically, in 11 cases, it is likely that the patient would have lived had he or she received timely adequate care. Ten other cases had significant deficits in care, including delays in diagnosis and delays in obtaining definitive care. Even where the deaths were not preventable, the deficient care resulted in patients enduring unnecessary pain and suffering and resulted in a significant shortening of lifespan.

19. As detailed below, a substantial proportion of the problematic deaths involved health care delivery system failures, including limited access to care based on an insufficient number of qualified providers and nurses; unreliable chronic care programs; failure to provide timely access to specialty care and, when patients do see a specialist, failure to timely follow-up to implement the specialist's recommendations; and failure to effectively track and monitor lab and diagnostic test results. While one or two of these types of deaths in a large system could be considered aberrant, the number and quality of the problematic cases in ADC in 2015 reveal a system that is fundamentally dysfunctional and dangerous. As discussed below, this finding is entirely consistent with the state's own CGAR monitoring scores.

C. Timely access to care

37. As I explained in earlier reports, access to care, *i.e.*, the task of getting patients to see nurses and providers is a basic building block in the structure of a functional health care system. Arizona failed at this fundamental task two years ago when I first evaluated the system, and it fails today. Having interviewed ASPC-Tucson patients and reviewed an extensive number of medical records from Tucson and other facilities, I found a shocking number of delays in access to care and complete denials of care in Arizona's prisons. These delays and denials harm some patients and place all patients at an unreasonable risk of serious harm.

1. Sick Call/HNR System

38. Pursuant to Arizona's policies, prisoners in need of medical care must file written HNR forms, which are required to be triaged within four hours of the time they are stamped as received. Ex. 5 at ADC010827. As I explained in my first report, ADC's policies and Performance Measure # 37 require that patients who submit sick call slips be seen the same day for urgent needs, and immediately if emergent; otherwise, they are to be seen by nurses for sick call ("nurse line") within 24 hours of the triage (or up to 72 hours if it is a weekend and clinically

appropriate). *Id.* If higher level attention is warranted, patients must be seen by providers within fourteen days after that ("provider line"), as monitored on the CGARs as Performance Measure # 39.

39. Two years ago, my review of healthcare records, documents, and depositions and my interviews with patients demonstrated to me that Arizona's sick call process was deficient on a system-wide basis, and that prisoners with serious conditions, including extremely fragile patients with chronic conditions, simply could not get seen by the appropriate medical personnel on a consistent basis. Regrettably, based on my review of the CGAR results, death records and my site visit to Tucson, I have concluded that the sick call system remains profoundly deficient.

40. Defendants' CGAR reports document an ongoing and persistent failure to provide timely sick call triage for patients who submit sick call slips. For the eleven month period of February through December 2015, none of the six largest ADC prisons achieved an average score of 75% or higher, and at Yuma, on average, just four in tenpatients were seen timely during that period. For the month of December, two large prisons, ASPC-Eyman and ASPC-Lewis scored under 50%. Ex. 1 at PLTF-PARSONS-36223.

41. The failure to respond timely to patients' health care requests can have devastating consequences. The case of a Yuma prisoner, is illustrative. He was a 59-year-old male who had been diagnosed with end-stage liver disease. The patient clearly had severe end-stage liver disease with significant complications of that disease including massive fluid retention, groin wounds, and sepsis. Despite Mr. 's serious condition, the nursing staff repeatedly failed to respond to his desperate Health Needs Requests. For example, on 3/6/15, he submitted an HNR that indicated "my legs were bleeding with open weeping wounds sticking to my prescription socks. I am in severe pain. I cannot wear my socks nor get them on. I am in pain." Ex. 46 at ADCM039111. The nursing response to this sick call request indicates that it is a "duplicate from 3/3/15." However, there is no health needs request dated 3/3/15 in his medical record. There is a triage note entered by a licensed practical nurse that urgently referred him to the nurse line at an unspecified time in the future. Ex. 46 at ADCM039213.

42. Mr. filed another HNR on 3/17/15 for shortness of breath and painful abdomen. This was scheduled for a nurse line appointment at an unspecified time that apparently did not occur. Ex. 46 at ADCM039103. He filed a subsequent HNR on 3/21/15 for worsening fluid retention and shortness of breath. Again, the HNR was essentially screened out with the notation "duplicate same as 3/17, you are on nurse line." Mr. 's condition deteriorated and his fluid retention worsened to the point that his skin split open and became infected. By 3/31/15 Mr. 's situation deteriorated to the point that he was being swarmed by flies, which he reported in a HNR. The next day, 4/1/15, instead of investigating why this might be the case in a patient with split skin that oozes serum, the nurse instead decided that this problem did not need to be seen. Ex. 46 at ADCM039197. The flies were attracted to his massively infected wounds and proved to be a harbinger of his death. He was ultimately transferred to the hospital more than a week later, on 4/9/15 where he died on .

43. The ADC Mortality Review determined there were multiple triage mistakes made by Corizon nurses that impeded and delayed care for Mr. Ex. 47 at ADCM044568. I agree with their finding but I add the conclusion that this case falls well below the standard of care, and that the poor care hastened his death. ADCM044566.

44. I interviewed at ASPC-Tucson, a patient with polymyositis (a chronic inflammatory disease causing muscle weakness) and interstitial lung disease. He likewise has had inexcusable delays in nursing and medical care that, while not fatal yet, have caused him serious harm and certainly place him at risk for deterioration and death. On 4/6/15, he submitted a sick call for shortness of breath, severe cough, temp elevated at 99.0, but was not seen by nursing. Six days later, he submitted an emergency HNR for heavy coughing, vomiting, sweating, and breathing. Still, he was not seen by nursing. Finally, on 4/20/15, Mr. presented in person to the medical clinic with a fever, rapid pulse and respirations and a low level of blood oxygen. At that point, he had developed sepsis, and was immediately transferred to an offsite hospital, where he almost died. Had his symptoms been addressed two weeks earlier he would almost certainly have avoided hospitalization. Mr. is immunocompromised because of the medications he has to take to treat his polymyositis. Staff should be on extra high alert if he develops any signs or symptoms of infection, and should evaluate him promptly. Instead, his serious symptoms were virtually ignored for days.

45. As was true two years ago, ADC prisoners still frequently do not see a provider within fourteen days of sick call with a nurse. This is not surprising – Corizon has not increased its medical provider staff, and there are simply not enough providers to treat the number of prisoners in the ADC facilities and the process for seeing patients has become increasingly inefficient with the introduction of the electronic health record.

53. In a system where there are simply not enough providers and medical staff to handle the patient load, critical errors are likely to occur. At Perryville, for example, I found two tragic cases where staff simply failed to recognize that their patients were suffering life-threatening conditions requiring emergency care. who had a history of deep vein thrombosis (blood clots), pulmonary embolus (blockages in her lungs), abscesses and osteomyelitis (bone infection). On 9/6/15, she complained of radiating pain down her leg, abdominal pain and the inability to urinate. Although she was able to void after receiving IV fluids that day, she was unable to urinate the following day. The standard of care in this situation requires an immediate and full assessment to determine whether the patient is in renal failure or has a different condition interfering with urination. Instead, on 9/8/15, Ms. was given Flomax, a drug that was inappropriate, and Toradol, a drug that was actually contraindicated and potentially dangerous.

54. The next day, she complained of chest pain and the inability to move her legs. Instead of sending her offsite for emergency care, which was clearly warranted, Ms. was taken to the prison's central medical clinic, where her temperature was recorded as 91.9 degrees Fahrenheit, which is a critical vital sign abnormality suggestive of sepsis and requiring emergency assessment. She was eventually taken to the hospital, where she died the following day of a staph infection, spinal meningitis and pneumonia. Ex. 68 at ADCM228194. Had she been sent to the hospital emergently on 9/6/15, her infections would have been treated sooner and she very likely would have survived. The Mortality Review Committee's report indicates that her presentation was confusing and concludes that her care met community care standards. Ex. 68 at ADCM228195-96. For the reasons explained above, I strongly disagree.

55. Another woman, clearly should have been sent offsite for emergency care when she fell from her bed early in the morning on and staff found her with bloody fecal matter on her legs and body, a racing pulse and alarmingly low blood pressure. The on-call nurse practitioner ordered Ms. Be taken to Perryville's central medical complex, where she was provided an IV, but her blood pressure continued to drop. Her blood pressure fell dramatically at the complex, and she clearly required emergency care. Instead, despite her life-threatening blood pressure readings, Ms. was returned to her housing unit by nursing staff after receiving her IV fluids. Ex. 26 at ADCM228173. Shockingly, the practitioner did not document an abdominal exam or any explanation for the fecal matter on her body. In the late afternoon that same day, custody staff called another ICS (ADC code for emergency incident) when they noticed Ms. had vomited blood. *Id.* Although her blood pressure again was dangerously low, the staff did not call for an emergency transport for almost 40 minutes. She died shortly thereafter. The ADC Mortality Review Committee classified this death as preventable, and I agree. Ex. 26 at ADCM228171. The emergency response and decision making were beneath the standard of care and the delay in definitive care proved fatal.

56. , a patient at ASPC-Lewis with a history of Type 2 diabetes, should have been sent to a hospital on when he reported left sided chest pain with radiation into his neck, left arm and left shoulder blade. He also was sweating heavily and short of breath. He also had very low blood pressure and a racing pulse. Ex. 57 at ADCM196768. Seen together, these are signs of serious cardiac pain. Rather than send him to a hospital emergency room for lab tests, the nurse treating him had labs drawn at the prison and waited hours for the results, a treatment decision clearly beyond the nurse's scope of practice. When they were reported as abnormal, Mr. was taken to the hospital in the mid-afternoon, where he died the following day. Although his record is limited, it is very likely that the delay in providing him with definitive care and nursing staff's decision to delay his emergency transport hastened his death.

57. The MRC report recognized the delay, and recommended an in-service training on assessment, evaluation and treatment of chest pain. Ex. 57 at ADCM196770. While I agree that training in this case is certainly warranted, the care in this case is so grossly substandard that it warrants an investigation to determine whether employee discipline is appropriate.

58. illustrates the tragic consequences of poor access to the appropriate level of health care and the disorganization of the electronic medical record system. Mr. died on of a gallbladder infection that would have been easily treated had he received timely care. Instead, the last three months of his life were marred by a series of lapses and missteps, including three mishandled emergencies, that resulted in the denial of medically necessary care.

59. Mr. who suffered from very poorly controlled diabetes (Ex. 31 at ADCM172397), developed alarming symptoms that should have prompted a thorough work up. He submitted an HNR on 4/6/15 complaining of blood in his urine. *Id.* At ADCM173275. Lab tests dated 4/9/15 revealed multiple critically abnormal values demonstrating significant liver dysfunction, but the record contains no indication that these results were ever communicated to Mr. 's physician at the time they were received. The patient's labs were reviewed on 4/16/15 and the critically abnormal tests were acknowledged. *Id.* at ADCM172737. The patient was seen by a gastroenterologist on 4/30/15 but the consultant's report was not reviewed by his physician until three weeks later (ADCM172430), resulting in delayed implementation of critical care recommendations.

60. Mr. was becoming increasingly ill, resulting in custody calling three ICS's in a period of ten days. The first ICS, on 5/27/15, was based on his shortness of breath. The healthcare provider who examined him noted he was short of breath, his abdomen was distended with ascites and he had 3+ edema in his legs (*Id.* At ADCM172790). The provider failed to recognize the severity of this patient's new symptoms and merely ordered him a diuretic and a 1-month followup. *Id.* At ADCM172793.

61. The second ICS was called on 6/4/15, at which point an RN documented that he had full body pain, swelling and hyperactive bowel sounds. Although the nurse writes that the physician examined the patient, there are no exam notes by a physician in the record. The patient was prescribed Tylenol, which was contraindicated in light of his liver failure, and was likely ineffective for his pain. *Id.* at ADCM173216.

62. The following day, Mr. was assessed by an LPN, who performed a complete examination of the patient, despite the fact that this level of care is well out of her scope of licensure. Although she referred the patient's chart for provider review, there is no evidence that the review occurred. *Id.* at ADCM173212.

63. Finally, on 6/6/15, a third ICS was called. The RN noted that Mr. had a critical lab value. At this point, the Nurse Practitioner ordered him transferred to the outside hospital. It is unclear what critical lab value prompted this transfer because there are no orders for labs in this date range (*id.* at ADCM172725), there are no lab reports from this date range in the medical record, the LPN note does not indicate what lab value was critical (*id.* at ADCM173204), and the practitioner who received the critical lab value (NP Mulhern) did not put a note in the chart indicating what critical information was conveyed to her.

64. Overall Mr. s care was disorganized, delayed, haphazard, and inadequate and the sum total of his treatment does not meet the standard of care. His medical record is extremely confusing and I agree with the Mortality Review Committee that his course of care was difficult to follow because of what was documented, what occurred and was not documented, and what was documented in the wrong sections. The provider failed to work up the sudden and significant changes in his health status and the provider's oversight of the healthcare team was delayed and inappropriate. This patient had critical labs that were never addressed, major changes in his bloodwork, multiple ICS responses with ominous physical exam findings that were completely ignored, and consults that gave appropriate guidance that were not reviewed or implemented in a timely fashion to facilitate his workup. While it is clear that he had a number of tests and consults completed during this three month span, the care was so fragmented and scattered that nobody really put together the overall picture of his healthcare issues. By the time he was finally transferred to the hospital, he was so physically sick and compromised that his treatment at the hospital was ineffective and limited and he ultimately had fatal medical complications as a result. The ADC Mortality Review Committee concluded that it could not determine whether this death was preventable. Ex. 30 at ADCM173601. Had Mr. been properly worked up in April 2015, I believe he might have survived.

65. I encountered in the inpatient unit at ASPCTucson. He is an insulin-dependent diabetic who has had a kidney transplant. He has also had a right leg amputation, finger amputation and he was in the IPC with a

diagnosis of Fournier's Gangrene. This diagnosis was given to him by the Corizon physician. There is a note on 12/1/2015 from Dr. Burciaga indicating that he had Fournier's Gangrene and he was to be a direct admit to Mt. Vista Hospital with Dr. D'Silva accepting on 12/1/2015. However, when we toured on 12/2/2015 he was still in his prison bed. This is a problem because Fournier's Gangrene is a surgical emergency that carries a very high morbidity rate. Usually surgery is required to save the patient's life within hours after diagnosis and hyperbaric oxygen treatment is frequently necessary as well. So it is appropriate that Dr. Burciaga sent him to be a direct admit to the hospital; it is completely inappropriate for this emergency case to have waited. In my brief time at Tucson, I was not able to identify the reason for this inexcusable delay. I suspect that it is related to staffing – had Tucson allocated sufficient health care staff to the inpatient unit in which Mr. is housed, someone would have been tasked with ensuring his prompt transfer. The failure to timely transfer him greatly increased his chances of requiring yet another amputation or of dying. This is abysmal care.

66. is another Tucson prisoner I spoke to who failed to receive competent emergency care. He slipped in the shower on 9/6/2015, and an x-ray ordered confirmed a "comminuted depressed tibial plateau fracture and proximal fibula fracture." Inexplicably, he was not referred to Mountain Vista Hospital until four days later on 9/10/15, but the hospital did not admit him because, due to the delay in referral, his fracture had resulted in massive swelling around the knee to the point that surgery was not possible. Moreover, the on-site x-ray was not reviewed by a provider until 9/14/2015 which is well beyond the injury time. Even after his swelling resolved, his care was delayed. By the time he finally had surgery on 10/16/15, his leg had healed improperly and had to be re-broken. When I saw him at Tucson, he was on bedrest, but had not been prescribed medically necessary anticoagulation therapy, placing him at risk of a postsurgical deep venous thrombosis and possible death from pulmonary embolism.

4. Inpatient care

68. When fragile infirmary level patients are not seen sufficiently often, many will suffer harm, and some may die. The case of for example, is one of shocking neglect. Mr. arrived at prison on 9/14/15 with a daily heroin habit and was housed in the ASPC-Tucson infirmary to go through opiate withdrawal. Although he was seen by several nurses over the next few days, who documented that he was experiencing serious withdrawal and was at risk of dehydration due to excessive vomiting, he was apparently never referred to a medical provider, as he should have been. He was ordered medications that were far too weak for his advanced withdrawal, and the medications that were ordered were provided only intermittently. He should have been, but was not, prescribed IV medications in light of his severe vomiting. Staff failed to monitor his condition, failed to order appropriate labs, and failed to refer him to a higher level of care. Consequently, Mr. died unnecessarily days after his arrival at prison, at age 44. The Mortality Review Committee correctly classified this as a preventable death. Ex. 58 at ADCM225738-40.

69. Some patients experience unnecessary pain and injury because they are not seen frequently enough. ASPC-Florence prisoner died on of metastatic colon cancer, after experiencing inexcusable delays in diagnosis. When he was admitted to the hospital shortly before his death, the hospital staff reported that he had a complex decubitus ulcer on his tailbone. Ex. 51 at ADCM018596. A complex ulcer takes time to develop, thus Mr. clearly had been suffering with this painful wound for a considerable time. Shockingly, the ADC nursing documentation during the period leading up to his hospitalization contains not a single mention of the ulcer.

70. Infrequent provider visits result in lapses in care. Mr. ,discussed above, received grossly inadequate care while housed in the Tucson infirmary unit while awaiting his overdue emergency transfer to the hospital. At the time that I saw him, he was receiving vancomycin IV to treat his gangrene pending his hospital transfer. I verified the medication by looking at the label on the IV bag. When I reviewed his electronic medical chart immediately after seeing him, there was no order for vancomycin. No patient, in an inpatient or outpatient setting, should be receiving medications absent a prescription, and why he received this medication without a physician's order is a mystery. Equally important, this medication by itself is grossly inadequate for the treatment of this condition. He should have been on two additional classes of antibiotics in addition to the vancomycin at a minimum.

5. End-of-life care and waivers of treatment

71. End of life planning and compassionate palliative care are important components of the practice of medicine, but they must be done with extreme caution in a correctional setting, with assiduous attention to detail, multiple independent reviewers, meticulous observation of informed consent requirements, and continual review of the appropriateness of the end of life plans given the condition of the patient. This requires spending significant amount of time face-to-face with the prisoner reviewing his care with him, and providing appropriate end of life counseling and guidance. The cases that I reviewed involving DNRs lacked any documentation showing these basic principles were observed. This is not surprising, given the very low staffing levels in the ADC. Complying with these essential patient care standards is time-consuming, and with the limited number of providers on staff it is predictable that these duties would be neglected.

72. The case of a ASPC-Lewis prisoner, is illustrative. Mr. was a 60 year old with a history of hepatitis C who developed pancreatic cancer. His medical care proceeded in a manner to be expected with this diagnosis. His "do not resuscitate" order first appears in the record on 6/10/2015 and it is merely listed in the assessment notes by Dr. Malachinski. Ex 56 at ADCM087345. While I do not have an issue with the implementation of a "do not resuscitate" order in a patient with his diagnosis, I do have an issue with how it was carried out. The listing of this order as a one line entry in an assessment is simply inadequate. There is no evidence of any discussion with the patient or any evidence of an informed choice made by the patient. There is no evidence of a second opinion by a clinician not involved in this patient's care to validate his choice for a do not resuscitate order. This patient's death was inevitable given his diagnosis but this does not excuse the method by which the DNR was implemented and the lack of documentation.

73. Furthermore, in my review of the death charts, there clearly were patients who had significant compromise and predictable decline from terminal illnesses. I was surprised that in most medical records there was no mention of end of life planning and recording of medical directives made while the patient is mentally competent to make

such decisions.

D. Exercise of professional medical judgment

1. Medical records and access to medical histories

74. In my initial investigation, I concluded that the medical records were "a gigantic mess." Doc. 1104-1 at 260. Since then, Corizon has implemented an electronic medical record called eOMIS. When I asked Tucson's medical director, Dr. Lucy Burciaga, to describe the system, she called it "horrific." Unfortunately, she is correct. The system is an unqualified disaster.

75. A reasonable electronic health record unifies medical information in an organized and inter-connected manner which speeds up care and makes documentation easier. This system really does the opposite. For example, when lab reports come back, the providers get a notice in their Outlook email that is not connected to the electronic health record. They have to log into each system and manually navigate between them in order just to evaluate one lab result. This is true with medication renewals as well. A proper system should be interfaced so that internal messages are contained within the system and linked to a process for easy review. Furthermore, the medical director confirmed that there is no ability to communicate within the system about clinical care. They have to utilize Outlook email for this communication which actually produces a separate electronic medical record that is not accessible to anyone except the sender/receiver of the email. This is highly problematic.

76. This medical record system uses templates to create encounter notes. Most of the templates are auto-generated and populated with questionably meaningless data that takes up a significant amount of space. It is difficult to read these notes as they contain bits and pieces of information scattered throughout instead of in one cohesive and consistent location. Another major issue is the presence of ghost encounters in the system that are generated by the system for some reason but the patient was not actually seen. This just confuses the documentation process and makes reading the charts very burdensome.

2. Use of nurses as primary care providers

77. Patients are denied a clinician's professional medical judgment if nurses or other staff are called upon to make decisions they are not qualified to make or exceed professional licensing requirements. I reported that this was a significant problem in my first report, and it continues to occur, placing patients at serious risk of harm or death.

78. As discussed in paragraph 68 above, was in crisis during his brief stay in the infirmary, leading up to his death. He should have been under the care of a provider who was seeing him regularly while he withdrew from his daily heroin habit. Instead, he was repeatedly seen by LPNs and RNs who assessed his condition, but failed to address it or to refer him to a provider who was qualified to treat his life-threatening condition.

79. Patient died on at age 55 at ASPC-Tucson, after his cancer of the head and neck recurred. When he reported his symptoms returning, he was seen for sick call by an LPN on 12/29/2014, rather than an RN, who noted his history of optic nerve cancer, but failed to refer him to a provider. Ex. 71 at ADCM118615-20. Mr. was finally seen by a provider and, on 5/11/15 by an oncologist who diagnosed him with recurrence of his cancer via PET scan. He was ordered to have chemotherapy ASAP. ADCM120514. Although he was finally provided treatment after seeing the oncologist, his recurrent cancer was in an advanced state, and he declined rapidly. While he may have died in any case, the delay in seeing a provider, and subsequently an oncologist, certainly shortened his life. The mortality report indicates that this care met community standards and I disagree. Ex. 83 at ADCM196779-82. The delays in care certainly do not meet community standards, nor does assessment of possible recurrent cancer by a Licensed Practical Nurse.

3. Specialty care

80. The exercise of professional judgment sometimes requires more in-depth knowledge than primary care providers possess. In these cases, the provider must be able to refer patients for specialty consultations. This essential step often was not happening two years ago, when I first reviewed care, and there continue to be major barriers for specialty access. In addition, the specialists who see the prisoners are authorized to recommend treatment, but not to order it. Thus, it is critical that the prison health care system ensures that prison health care providers promptly review the consultant's treatment recommendations and either order the treatment or document why it is not appropriate. This essential coordination is often missing in ADC patient care.

81. The failure to ensure that patients see specialty consultants for medically necessary diagnosis and treatment places patients at an unreasonable risk of harm. Indeed, in some cases, patients will die because they did not have access to medically necessary specialty care. Sixty-five year old for example, was referred multiple times to a cardiologist while at ASPC-Eyman, but the appointments did not occur timely because of multiple operational glitches in the referral process and lack of communication between the referring clinicians and the approval authority. Ex. 45 at ADCM135400. He was ultimately referred for an implantable defibrillator, but he died on before that visit was arranged. Had his diagnostic consults been approved by Utilization Management and scheduled in a timely manner, he would likely still be alive. The ADC Mortality Review reached the same conclusion. *Id.*

82. I spoke to a number of Tucson prisoners regarding longstanding barriers to specialty care, and brought their urgent situations to the attention of ADC officials, and their attorneys. Thirty-two year old , was a patient in the Tucson infirmary when I spoke to him. He had been placed there after he developed a decubitus ulcer on his buttocks as a result of long-standing diarrhea caused by an infection in his GI tract. Although the infection had been identified more than a year earlier, I found no evidence that he had ever been treated for it. Moreover, he had been referred to general surgery to repair the wound on 6/25/15, but has been told that Corizon has not been able to find a surgeon with whom to schedule surgery. In the meantime this otherwise relatively healthy young man has been bedridden for months.

83. 78 years old, has a transplanted kidney and has been on his immunosuppression medications for many years. He developed an allergy to one of his medications that is causing him to have a terrible whole-body rash.

His medical record shows he has submitted many HNR's about his issues and Corizon has not sent him to a transplant physician for evaluation. As a result, he stopped taking his Prograf and Cellsept on 10/29/2015 because the rash had become so intolerable. Instead of sending him to a transplant physician as medically indicated, Corizon referred him for a psychiatric consult to see if he is competent. In conversing with this gentleman it was obvious that he is intellectually keen and well informed about his situation. Competency is not the issue in this case and a referral to psychiatry to assess competency for refusing to take medication is a shameless cover-your-behind maneuver by the prescriber that clearly demonstrates that the provider did not speak to Mr. in any detail, and does not know how to deal with a patient of his complexity. Mr. 's providers have failed to understand that he urgently needs to go see a transplant physician to manage his medications and to assess the kidney. Without this care, he will undoubtedly reject his kidney, which will ultimately hasten his death.

84. Patient is a 47 year old ASPC-Tucson patient with sick sinus syndrome and Wolf-Parkinson-White Syndrome, a condition that causes rapid heartbeat. He has had a pacemaker placed and has had two cardiac ablations. He has had such bad complications from his disease that he filed for a restraining order against Corizon and forced them to house him in IPC because his heart rate fluctuates, and he loses consciousness. He indicates that his cardiology consult to address this was submitted by his provider in August 2015 and he has yet to be seen. Review of his chart demonstrates that despite his multiple issues, his chronic care appointments were just not done and he has not been seen in a timely fashion.

85. Patient , is a 25 year old who developed a slipped disc in his back. While at ASPC-Lewis, he submitted HNRs about this but his care was delayed. Ultimately, he became paralyzed and incontinent before he was finally sent to the hospital for treatment. This constitutes abysmal care. He has a lot of residual nerve damage and can only walk short distances because of weakness and balance issues. When I reviewed his medical record, it stated that he was transferred to Tucson from Lewis in order to receive physical therapy. None had occurred as of my December visit, and he is understandably upset that he has not made progress towards independence.

86. Another Tucson prisoner, underwent an above knee amputation April 2015. No prosthesis had been provided to him, so when I met him he was stuck in a wheelchair despite the fact that he is otherwise physically vigorous and could be up walking which would be much healthier for him and enable him to keep his muscle mass in his legs. He was sent back to the prison following his amputation and was not seen by his provider for five months. Then, on 10/19/15 a consult for a prosthesis was submitted, but that appointment has not yet occurred. When we interviewed the "consult specialist" for Corizon, she verified the consult was approved, but had no explanation for the delay in scheduling the appointment.

87. Finally, Mr. the young man with testicular cancer who I described at the beginning of this report, has experienced unconscionable delays in receiving treatment even after I first brought him to the attention of ADC during the tour in early December 2015. Plaintiffs' counsel randomly met him while walking through a housing unit at Tucson, speaking cellfront with prisoners, and while I was at Tucson I reviewed his medical records and spoke with him. I also raised his case in a meeting with ADC staff and their attorneys on the last day of the tour. Since visiting Tucson, I received updated medical records for him, up until 2/10/16. These records clearly demonstrate the colossal systemic issues that exist within the ADC healthcare system.

88. Mr. was originally diagnosed with testicular cancer by ultrasound on 8/6/15. Ex. 67 at ADCM340110. An urgent request for a CT scan was submitted to Corizon Utilization Management by Dr. Goodman at the time, but that was not completed until 9/23/15. Ex. 67 at ADCM340368. Mr. was subsequently scheduled for an orchiectomy on 10/30/15. In the discharge plans for that surgery, the surgeon (Dr. Daley) requested a two week follow-up after the surgery, along with a CT scan so the pathology could be reviewed and the tumor could be staged appropriately to determine additional care. The specialist's request for a follow-up consult and CT scan was submitted by Dr. Goodman, and she indicated the ordered timelines. Unfortunately, Corizon did not complete the CT scan until 11/24/15, and the post-op follow-up with Dr. Daley was not until 12/2/15, more than a month after the surgery. *Id.* at ADCM340344.

89. Critically, only one out of three pages of the specialty consult report from Dr. Daley inexplicably is included in the medical file. *Id.* at ADCM340349. The pages that are notably missing are those that detail the

diagnosis and the plan. Furthermore, I can find no evidence in the medical record that a provider at the prison reviewed the incomplete specialist report from Dr. Daley, to realize that the most critical components of the note were missing. As such, Mr. has had no care for biopsy-proven, CT-proven, surgical pathology-proven cancer.

90. Since the appropriate documentation does not exist in the chart and we have no idea what the plan was for Mr. 's care, we have to rely on the data that does exist. I know that he had a pure seminoma and that he has CT-proven evidence of mediastinal (chest) adenopathy that measures 2.1 cm x 2.0 cm. *Id.* at ADCM339817. Applying a standard grading scale to this scenario, this patient has a Grade IIB tumor. *See* Oh, W.K., Overview of the treatment of testicular germ cell tumors; Uptodate, Kantoff, PW (ed), Waltham MA (accessed March 28, 2016), available at http://www.uptodate.com/contents/overview-of-the-treatment-of-testicular-germ-celltumors. The current treatment recommendations for a Grade IIB seminoma are surgery to remove tumor (already done) and chemotherapy (not done). *Id.* Seminomas are a highly treatable and generally curable form of testicular cancer, but the appropriate treatment has to be done and it has to be done in a timely fashion. Unfortunately, nothing about Mr. 's care has been timely, only part of the recommendation treatment has been accomplished, and there is no evidence that he is on anybody's radar within ADOC because the last date he had a provider encounter was 10/30/2015—the date of his surgery. Ex. 67 at ADCM339815. He has never been seen by a provider since returning to the facility.

91. We encountered Mr. on my tour of the Tucson facility. I was so concerned at the time after I reviewed his file on-site about his lack of care that I made a request to conduct an exit conference meeting on 12/4/15 to call his situation (and the critical situations of several other patients) to the attention of Corizon administrators and health care staff. I was clear with the ADC attorneys about the purpose of the meeting and the seriousness of the issues. Unfortunately, despite my clarity about the purpose of the exit conference, not a single staff person from Corizon showed up to hear my concerns about Mr. and other prisoners, and my concerns were directed to ADC monitoring staff and attorneys for Defendants. As such, my admonitions for Mr. to have emergency oncology consultation and treatment went unheeded, and he never received appropriate care. I am professionally disturbed by this case because he is a young man who has a very treatable and curable condition that is being totally mismanaged, and Corizon and the ADOC know of his situation. If anybody with clinical training had looked at his chart and tracked his care, the deficits in care would have been obvious. Unfortunately, Corizon's healthcare delivery is so broken that this patient's life is on the line from systemic incompetence despite my detailed description of his problems and his needed care.

92. Mr. also attempted to call his situation to the attention of Corizon officials. He submitted an HNR on 12/29/15 stating "I was supposed to see the oncologist over a month ago for treatment. I need to know what's going on." *Id.* at ADCM340317. This HNR was responded to on 12/29/15 by RN Rynders with "You are scheduled for f/u with the provider." This HNR never made it into the master list of Health Services Requests, (*Id.* at ADCM339817), and as of February 10, 2016 he still had not seen a provider.

93. Mr. submitted another HNR on 1/16/16 that stated "I need to speak to Doctor Goodman ASAP. I was supposed to be scheduled to seen an oncologist over two months ago to start my chemotherapy treatment but I haven't heard a thing back so I need to know what is going on very soon!!!" *Id.* at ADCM340315. This HNR was responded to on 1/18/16 by RN Rynders stating that "You are scheduled to see the Provider." This

HNR is not recorded in the master list of "Health Services Requests" and it appears that it never got implemented, because there is no evidence he ever saw a provider despite the serious nature of the HNR request. *Id.* at ADCM339817.

94. If we triangulate the standard treatment recommendations for his condition with the information that he conveyed in his two separate HNR's about the treatment plan he was expecting, it is completely reasonable to assume that the missing pages of Dr. Daley's consult note contain recommendations for an oncology visit and chemotherapy that have not been carried out. Mr. has notified Corizon with clear language about his dilemma on two separate occasions and despite the dire nature of the notifications, Corizon has never scheduled him for any provider follow-up.

95. Mr. 's case is sadly illustrative of the systemic issues that plague the ADC health care system:

◻◻The specialty consult system is broken.

◻◻Continuity of care does not occur as patients return from outside care.

◻◻The internal provider scheduling process is inadequate.

◻◻The HNR process is broken and does not result in appropriate care.

96. The sum total of all of this is a system that denies prisoners access to care at all levels and needlessly puts them at elevated risk for serious healthcare complications and death. Mr. needs a STAT oncology consultation and all of the treatment ordered by the oncologist. He probably needs to be re-staged, because I am afraid that the extreme delays in his care have resulted in spread of his cancer, and he is probably in a much higher risk category than he would have been in if the care had been accomplished in a timely fashion.

4. Substandard care decisions

97. As I explained in previous reports, treatment decisions must be consistent with community standard of care. As was true two years ago in the Arizona system, the providers continue to make treatment decisions that are clearly substandard and endanger their patients. Because the system lacks a viable quality assurance program to root out and address patterns of poor care, substandard treatment is widespread in the Arizona system, and as a result, some patients suffer harm, while all are subject to an unreasonable risk of harm.

98. Two particularly egregious cases involve patients who both starved to death in June, 2015, while housed in so-called "inpatient" prison units, at ASPC-Florence and at ASPC-Tucson. Mr. was a 57 year old man with a history of pancytopenia (a shortage of all types of blood cells), Hepatitis C, end stage liver disease, and peripheral vascular disease. His long-term management of his end-stage liver disease was poorly done but the patient became acutely ill around 4/23/14, having developed significant ascites (excessive accumulation of fluid in the abdominal cavity). Ex. 32 at ADMC080751. He was sent to see a gastroenterologist for management of his end-stage liver disease nine months later on 1/30/15 and several recommendations were given by the specialist (*id.* at ADCM080898), but ultimately most were not followed by the Corizon providers, or were very delayed. Mr. developed hepatic encephalopathy and was admitted back into the hospital, with swelling so great in his scrotum that he developed scrotal abscesses. *Id.* at ADCM085845.

99. Mr. ultimately experienced gastrointestinal failure that manifested itself with his inability to eat and extreme weight loss, and he died on June 21, 2015. *Id.* at ADCM081372 and ADMC085831. His baseline weight on 3/28/13 was 180 pounds. The last recorded weight in his chart prior to his death was 93 pounds on 4/27/15, which represents almost a 50% decrease in weight. *Id.* at ADCM081647. The healthcare staff at ASPC-Florence failed to address this substantial weight loss and he ultimately died of significant malnourishment that occurred while they watched and documented it. Had the staff managed his end-stage liver disease adequately the gastrointestinal failure would not have occurred and he would have lived a much longer life. I was shocked to see the ADC Mortality Review Committee's conclusion that Mr. 's death was unpreventable and that his care met community standards. *Id.* at ADCM225754, 225756.

100. Mr. was a 64-year-old who had a history of left sided hemiplegia as a result of a gunshot wound to the head. He also had pulmonary fibrosis which was evaluated by a pulmonologist on 11/20/14. At that point in time the pulmonologist requested that Mr. be returned to his clinic in one month in order to initiate treatment. Ex. 36 at ADCM078963. I found no evidence in the chart that this requested follow-up appointment occurred. The failure to treat his pulmonary fibrosis ultimately caused him to develop gastrointestinal failure and severe malnourishment. On 7/29/14 he called attention to his weight loss in a health needs request (*id.* at ADCM079103) wherein Mr. stated, "I have lost a lot of weight, too much, and do not know why or how because I eat all of my meals. I am 5'6" and weigh only 104 pounds. My weight continues to drop and I am unable to gain weight. Please do labs to test for cancer and any other illness that can be causing this. There's something very wrong with me." The medical staff failed to address his weight loss.

101. Mr. was placed in the Tucson infirmary in November 2014, weighing 94 pounds. *Id.* at ADMC079373. On 4/15/15, he was sent out for tubeplacement through his abdominal wall to facilitate feeding. The interventional radiologist felt that the placement of a feeding tube was too risky due to his untreated pulmonary fibrosis. *Id.* at ADCM079335. As a result, his nutritional needs were not addressed and the last recorded weight in this chart was 85 pounds on 5/24/15. *Id.*at ADCM079429. Mr. needlessly died of malnourishment not long after.

102. was another Tucson patient who presented with alarming symptoms, who saw providers sporadically, yet was not evaluated and diagnosed for cancer for many months. In October and November 2014, he was seen for complaints of rapid weight loss, dropping from 175 to 138 pounds in a few months. No work up was initiated. Ex. 50 at ADCM228185. Eight months later, on 7/14/15, he was finally diagnosed with squamous cell carcinoma of the lung. He was referred to an oncologist at that time, and he finally saw an oncologist two months after that, on 9/14/15. Mr. died on . *Id.* at ADCM228168. Although his death may have been inevitable, it is clear that he could have lived longer had his diagnosis not been delayed.

103. Similarly, died at age 32 after experiencing repeated and inexcusable delays by Perryville medical staff in her work up for leukemia. She began submitting HNRs in September 2014 complaining of lumps on her legs. Ex. 53 at ADCM246406. On 5/13/15, she submitted an HNR stating, "you ordered lab work to be done in regards to the lumps on my leg. I have not had it done yet. And I also found 2 more lumps on my pelvis area." *Id.* at ADCM246399. Although her records are confusing, it appears she did not receive a diagnosis of leukemia until 7/8/15, ten months after her initial complaint. *Id.* at ADCM246856; ADCM246116. She died months after her diagnosis, on . What is clear from her records is that her initial work up was inadequate, her labs were delayed, and ultimately, her diagnosis and treatment were delayed, and these serious lapses resulted in hastening her death.

104. , died at ASPC-Eyman on at age 43 of cardiogenic shock (inadequate circulation of the blood), secondary to bacterial endocarditis, an infection of the heart. Although he had been seen at sick call multiple times reporting very alarming symptoms, including that he was vomiting 20 times a day, he never had an adequate work up. His lab results dated 5/27/15 were highly suggestive of an infection, yet they were not signed off by his provider, a physician's assistant, for three weeks,9 and even then, it does not appear that the physician's assistant understood the significance of the abnormal results. Ex. 54 at ADCM086498. The PA's plan to order a variety of tests and follow up with Mr. in two weeks was wholly inadequate. Given Mr. 's fevers, elevated white blood cell count, anemia and history of IV drug abuse, the PA should have been able to diagnose the infection, or at least have recognized the need to confer with a physician for further direction.

105. Mr. 's death was preventable, had his diagnosis been timely. The mortality review committee identified the delay in care, but called it "a difficult diagnosis." Ex. 55 at ADCM120646. Based on the data available, however, I classify this as a missed diagnosis.

106. The case of an ASPC-Lewis prisoner who has also been housed at Yuma and Tucson, is likewise disturbing. I first raised serious concerns about Mr. 's treatment in my November 2013 report, explaining that his HIV had been mismanaged and that he was in "desperate need" of management by an HIV specialist. Doc. 1104-1 at 271-272. Since I first met Mr. he has apparently been seen by an HIV specialist a couple of times. Unfortunately, my review of his chart in early December 2015 makes it clear that his AIDS is still unmanaged. The HIV specialist had recommended follow-up appointments at three month intervals, but it appeared he had not been seen since 6/16/15. At that appointment, the specialist had ordered a critical lab test for determining whether he had developed resistance to any medications, but that apparently had not been done. On 10/16/15, his lab tests revealed a very high viral load, indicating that his prescribed HIV medication was not working and that his virus was continuing to damage his immune system. This ongoing pattern of inadequate treatment is particularly shocking given that, since my first meeting with Mr. I understand that plaintiffs' counsel have submitted advocacy letters to defendants on at least five occasions, notifying them of Mr. 's condition.

107. was in obvious pain when I met him at Tucson in December. According to his medical record, he was referred for a GI consult on 10/12/15 for rectal bleeding. At the time of my visit and interview with him, this consult had yet to occur. He was finally seen by a facility medical provider the day before my site visit, because he had staged a protest and refused to leave the clinic until seen. At that appointment, Mr. was given an

injection of Toradol, which is absolutely contraindicated in a patient with gastrointestinal bleeding of unknown cause and could have killed him by causing his stomach to perforate.

108. , would likely not have died on at age 57 had she been provided competent care. Ms. had a history of chronic obstructive pulmonary disease and congestive heart failure. She was admitted to the Perryville infirmary on 7/6/15, when pulmonary disease became acute. Her situation was never well controlled from that point forward, and she declined fairly rapidly. On 7/7/15, her lab results showed she was in congestive heart failure. Ex. 39 at ADCM107998-7999. She was managed unsuccessfully and incompetently for her breathing problems: she was given three liters of oxygen by nasal cannula, which is a significantly low dose of oxygen delivered in a highly unreliable way. Her blood oxygen level was dangerously low, even on those three liters of oxygen. As such she had significant "air hunger" and struggled to breathe for a long period of time.

109. The Perryville healthcare staff struggled with her for an inordinately long period of time before they finally sent her out to the hospital on 7/12/2015 in full respiratory distress. On 7/12/15 Dr. Seth Stabinsky entered a late note which documents care that he rendered three days earlier, on 7/9/15. This note outlines his logic in treating this patient from a retrospective standpoint. It is interesting that this note was entered shortly after Dr. Stabinsky gave the order to send this patient to the hospital. Given the circumstances and the timing it appears as if this note is a delayed justification and rationalization of poor care. *Id.* at ADCM108024. Ms. died on While this ultimately was not a preventable death, the delays in care and the failure to make an accurate diagnosis over months of management certainly hastened her death.

110. The ADC Mortality Review Committee concluded that died because of inadequate medical care, and I concur. Ms. who was 44 years old when she died on had a history of gastroesophageal reflux disease (GERD), as well as significant mental illness. While at Perryville, she was treated with indomethacin and ibuprofen, two nonsteroidal anti-inflammatory drugs (NSAIDS) that are contraindicated for prisoners with a history of GERD, because they cause ulcers and perforation of the gastrointestinal tract. She received the highest recommended dose of indomethacin and her risk of NSAID ulcer with subsequent perforation was extraordinarily high. Ex. 26 at ADCM228171-8175.

111. Ms. complained on 6/13/15 of constipation and abdominal pain. She was referred to the nursing line, and saw the nurse several times in the following weeks but did not have an abdominal exam. Three weeks later, she bled to death, due to a gastric ulcer. She should never have been prescribed the NSAIDS for any extended period, and the way that she was prescribed it caused her death.

112. Grossly substandard nursing care hastened the death of 51 year old at ASPC-Tucson. Mr. had a history of hepatitis C as well as hypertension and Type II diabetes. He submitted HNRs on 3/16/2015 (Ex. 48 at ADCM040007), 3/22/15 (ADCM 040006) and apparently on 3/25/2015 (not found in chart but referenced in a nurse note at ADCM040047) for swelling and back pain. He was not seen for nurse triage for any of these HNRs. His HNR for back pain on 3/25/15 was answered by nurse Dadasiewicz with "No action needed" and "already scheduled with a provider 3/27/15."

113. On 3/27/15, he saw NP Daye who did not address his back pain but did document shortness of breath. *Id.* at ADCM040163. NP Daye did not order appropriate diagnostic labs or studies for the complaint she listed. On 4/5/15 Mr. was seen on nurse line by RN Patterson who documented a fever and a very low blood oxygen level indicating he was seriously ill. The RN did not notify anyone or intervene, and her assessment of this critical abnormal data is inadequate. *Id.* at ADCM040212-216. She did refer Mr. to the provider line and he was seen by NP Daye on 4/6/15 with a complaint of "IM states is dizzy, headaches, cannot breathe, gets winded walking 2 ft, wants to go to a Dr." Despite this ominous presentation, there is no blood oxygen level recorded on that visit, nor is a respiratory rate. Mr. did have an increased temperature and an increased heartrate, both of which suggest possible infection. NP Daye also documented decreased breath sounds in his lungs which also suggests possible infection. Despite all of this data indicating Mr. was very seriously ill, NP

Daye's plan was to continue with daily weights and abdominal measurements and for him to submit an HNR for any further health needs. *Id.* at ADCM040152-156. He was finally admitted to the hospital later the same day and found to have a high white cell count and an extremely low oxygen level. *Id.* at ADCM040022 and 040025. Mr. was critically ill, well beyond what anyone in the system recognized. He ultimately died of severe bilateral pneumonia and sepsis the following day.

114. The nursing staff, including the Nurse Practitioner, repeatedly failed Mr. As early as 3/25/15 the patient complained of back pain which is a common presentation for pneumonia. Unfortunately his complaint was not evaluated by a clinician, which resulted in a missed opportunity to intervene in a timely fashion and avoid his death. More egregiously, he presented with a fever and a very low blood oxygen level on 4/5/15. These objective findings should have triggered a much more intensive response to determine the reason for such an abnormal finding. Unfortunately, they did not.

115. The provider visit on 4/6/15 with NP Daye is well below the standard of care for this problem. Mr. presented with ominous symptoms of respiratory distress including dizziness, a complaint that he could not breathe, and report that he gets winded within two feet of walking. These complaints at a minimum require an assessment of his respiratory status including respiratory rate and a pulse oximeter reading. These were not done. In addition, he was febrile and with a racing pulse, which should have led to additional inquiry as well. Using the hospital data as a reference point for how sick Mr. presented just hours after he was seen by NP Daye illustrates the inadequacy of NP Daye's assessment and clinical decision-making.

116. The ADC Mortality Review Committee recognizes that "there was some delay in patient care," and recommends that "significant abnormal findings should be communicated to HCP [health care provider] by nursing." Ex. 49 at ADCM120639 –640. Given the magnitude of the errors in this case, this response is grossly inadequate.

E. Delivery of care that is ordered

117. The third major component of an adequate medical care system is the right to treatment. As I explained in my first report, patients must not only be seen by appropriate clinicians and given appropriate diagnoses and treatment orders; they must actually receive the care that is ordered, including medications, diagnostic tests and specialty referrals. As was true when I first visited the ADC prisons, the Arizona system has multiple barriers that interfere with care delivery.

1. Providers' orders

118. Orders written by providers must actually be carried out. Throughout the Arizona system I saw a consistent pattern of ordered care – medications, labs, nursing care, follow-up appointments, and/or specialty referrals – not getting done. This is another symptom of a badly understaffed medical care system.

119. While at ASPC-Tucson, I spoke to a number of patients who were referred for specialty care who never received it, and had predictably poor outcomes. For example, , was bedridden in the infirmary unit with a decubitus ulcer resulting from long-standing diarrhea caused by a C. Difficile infection in his GI tract. His ulcer was not healing because of an exposed vein in the base of the wound that kept bleeding. I asked Mr. why he had not had the relatively common surgery for decubitus ulcers to deal with this problem definitively. He indicated that the Corizon staff had told him they could not find a surgeon willing to treat him. I confirmed in his medical chart that a 6/25/15 surgery referral request for wound care had not been carried out. The surgery that he needs is routine and not that difficult. Any competent plastic surgeon would handle his issue easily. It is difficult to believe that no surgeon is willing to treat him unless the problem is with payment from Corizon for that care.

120. During the Tucson visit, I also observed that the process for alerting providers to diagnostic test results and consult reports for their patients through the electronic medical record had essentially collapsed under its own weight. Because providers daily receive dozens of emails, and because the process for signing off on results was unduly time-consuming and inefficient, many of the providers had simply allowed their mail boxes to fill without reviewing them. I observed that Tucson's NP Daye, for example, had almost 2,500 unread emails in her inbox on the day of my visit, many of which were lab results and specialist's reports. Dr. Burciaga had

approximately 5,600 unread clinical emails in her inbox. Reviewing medical records at the facility, I found numerous examples of cases where patients with abnormal labs were never followed up, and where patients who saw the consultant did not receive the recommended treatment because the consult reports had not been reviewed by the provider.

121. Mr. , discussed above, required monitoring for the immunosuppressive medication, tacrolimus, which he takes to maintain his transplanted kidney. His provider ordered a STAT tacrolimus lab drawn 11/27/15—there was no result in the chart by 12/2/15 which is an unacceptable delay for a STAT lab. That result should be back within hours. On 9/3/15 a regular tacrolimus level was ordered and a result was delivered 9/8/15. This lab result was never reviewed by anyone. The failure to review these lab results, and the failure to obtain timely results for a STAT order, put the patient at significant risk of harm.

122. The failure to follow orders can produce tragic results, as demonstrated in the case of who died on at age 50 at ASPC-Florence. Mr. had a history of renal failure, type II diabetes, cirrhosis, foot amputation, and peripheral vascular disease. It appears that he was significantly compromised when transferred to the Department of Corrections on 6/10/15. He was evaluated by a physician on 6/12/15 and sent immediately to the hospital as a direct admit for a high white blood cell count and a draining left foot amputation wound. Mr. was stabilized at the hospital but noted to be in acute renal failure. That was addressed at the hospital, and he was discharged back to ADC on 6/17/15, and his discharge plan included prescriptions for critical medications. Although these medications were ordered by prison staff on 6/17/15, he did not receive a dose until 6/20/15. Ex. 37 at ADCM107446, 107448. Without these medications, Mr. decompensated quickly and was ultimately admitted into the infirmary. On the infirmary nurses called Dr. Vukcevic at 11:35 to inform him that Mr. was not doing well. Instead of sending this critically ill patient back to the hospital immediately, Dr. Vukcevic instructed nursing staff to apply supplemental oxygen and to continue to observe him. The doctor stated he would be in within an hour to assess the patient. However at 12:55 Mr. was declared dead and the treating physician at the time was Dr. Chris Johnson. *Id.* at ADCM107543. Dr. Vukcevic never came to assess the patient who he blocked from going to the emergency room.

123. This case raises a number of questions. First of all it appears that Mr. was significantly medically compromised at the time and he was transferred to the Department of Corrections and I have no way of knowing where he came from or how it was possible for someone to transfer a patient this sick to ADC. This case also raises questions about the intake process at the ADC reception center and its capacity to identify patients who are too sick to be in a prison environment. Furthermore, this case shows a failure to coordinate care when a very sick patient transfers from the hospital back to the prison. Here, he was ordered critical medication at the hospital as part of his discharge plan but went three days without that medication upon transfer back to the prison, ultimately causing him to destabilize and contributing to his death. I also question the delay in emergency care, and why the physician did not send this patient to the hospital immediately upon hearing that he was having difficulty. Clearly Dr. Vukcevic's instructions were inadequate for this patient, and the delay in obtaining definitive care proved fatal. Given the magnitude of Mr. 's medical conditions his death was inevitable. However it is clear that systemic issues abound in this case and his care was compromised significantly as a result. I concur with the ADC Mortality Review finding that "more timely intervention was clearly warranted." Ex. 38 at ADCM130868.

124. In the charts I reviewed at Tucson, and the charts of deceased prisoners from across the prisons, I saw that labs are routinely ordered but never done, medications ordered but not approved, medications ordered but not administered by the nurses, ADA accommodations ordered but not provided, consults ordered but never approved or scheduled, and follow-up appointments requested by providers but never scheduled. Recommendations from specialists regarding follow-up and additional care were frequently not done or were substantially delayed. Tucson prisoner , , for example, has a condition, inclusion body myositis, which results in significant weakness of his muscles. Tucson referred him to a neurologist, who recommended on 4/16/14 that he be provided a back brace, supportive shoes, elevated shower chair, handicapped bed rails with bars, a multi-vitamin per day, a wedge pillow, an electric hospital bed, and a wheelchair assessment. NP Daye finally ordered

these items for him on 11/10/15, a year and a half later. Corizon's Utilization Management Department has denied all of the requests for these medical devices.

2. Medication administration and monitoring

125. Prescribed medications must be provided to patients in a timely, consistent manner. The ADC monitor reports document consistent and persistent problems delivering medications to patients on time. Performance Measure # 11 requires that new prescriptions be provided to the patient within two business days of the prescription, or the same day, if prescribed STAT. The average scores over the months of February through December, 2015 were below 75% at six of the ten prisons, including at all five of the largest men's prisons. The chart on the next page highlights in yellow each month in 2015 where the prison's compliance level was less than 75%. For each month in 2015, the statewide level of compliance for all of ten institutions.

126. Medications must be renewed regularly and without interruption, and prisoners must be able to transfer housing locations without medication interruptions. ADC monitors' reports show that administration of prescription medication is frequently delayed or missed, and that prescriptions for chronic care medications frequently lapse despite the patients refill requests.

127. As a preliminary matter, I have long maintained that, in a prison or jail setting, an automatic refill system for chronic care and psychotropic medications is critical, and I so advised the parties in this action. ADC's system of requiring patients, some of whom are on psychotropic medications for disabling mental conditions, to file health needs requests to refill their prescriptions practically guarantees they will have gaps in receiving medications. This is particularly true in a system like ADC's, as the Corizon pharmacy responsible for filling the prescriptions is not local, but in Oklahoma.

128. Performance Measure # 14 requires that refills of chronic care and psychotropic medications requested by the patient three to seven days before the medication runs out are filled so that the patient will suffer no lapse. Not one of the ten prisons averaged a passing score (75%) for this measure over the ten months from March to December 2015. (Every facility was given a score of "NA" in February 2015.) Again, non-compliance is shown in yellow in the chart below. Ex. 1 at PLTF-PARSONS-036223.

129. ASPC-Lewis registered a 0% compliance rate for nine of the ten months, and only three small prisons, Phoenix, Safford and Winslow, had an average score of over 50%. Of the five largest prisons, not a single one achieved a passing score at any time during the measured period. As illustrated below, none of the ten prisons achieved a passing average score during the relevant time period. Ex. 1 at PLTF-PARSONS-036223.

130. ADC's record for ensuring that prescriptions for chronic care and psychotropic medications are renewed by the prescribing provider, such that there are no lapses, is also dismal. (Performance Measure # 13.) For the eleven month period of February to December 2015, seven of the prisons, including all of the largest facilities, had average scores well under 75% compliance, as illustrated in the chart on the next page. Ex. 1 at PLTF-PARSONS-036222.

3. Labs, imaging, and other diagnostic tests

131. Diagnostic tests are an essential part of any medical care system. Such tests must be performed timely, based on the provider's order, and must be reviewed and, if abnormal, acted upon promptly. Arizona fails all too often to ensure that labs and diagnostic tests performed are promptly reviewed and acted upon, due in part to the lack of an effective system for reporting such results in the eOMIS system.

132. Once the diagnostic reports are available, the medical provider is required to review the reports, including pathology reports, and act upon those with abnormal values within five calendar days. (Performance Measure # 46.) Nine out of ten of the prisons averaged scores well below passing for this measure, from February to December, 2015. Indeed, the only prison that averaged a passing score was ASPC-Safford, a smaller prison that ADC previously has reported does not house prisoners with high medical needs. *See, e.g.,* Ex. 11 at ADCM226253 (11/30/15) (at Florence's, North unit, just one report of 10 reviewed timely, with half not reviewed a month or more after receipt; Central unit, only half of 10 reports timely reviewed, with three not

reviewed six weeks after receipt); Ex. 16 at ADCM226321 (11/27/15) (at Tucson, in Inpatient Unit, only half of ten records in audit showed timely review); Ex. 13 at ADCM226171 (11/25/15) (at Perryville, San Pedro unit, for ten pap smear tests, only one had result timely reviewed).

133. The failure to act timely on abnormal labs and diagnostic imaging places patients and enormous risk of harm. Given ADC's widespread non-compliance on this measure, it is not surprising that I found numerous examples of patients who were suffering unnecessarily because their providers had failed to act upon their abnormal results. Among them was Mr. (see *infra* at ¶¶ 82 and 119), who tested positive for C. Difficile toxin on 9/18/14. There was no evidence in his record that the results were ever reviewed, or that Mr. was ever treated for this condition. *See also*, Ex. 54 at ADCM086498 (high white blood cell count for Mr. 096480, suggestive of infection performed 5/27/15, not signed off by provider until 6/16/15; patient died eleven days later); (per my onsite chart review, STAT test for immunosuppressant ordered 11/27/15 for Mr. 073659, not performed as of 12/2/15; regular lab ordered 9/3/15, performed 9/8/15, results never reviewed).

III. Conclusion

Medical care in Arizona prisons continues to be inadequate to meet the basic needs of many of the prisoners who experience illness and injury while in custody. Many of the barriers to care that I identified in November 2013, and in my subsequent reports, continue to plague the system. ADC's own audits demonstrate month after month that many of the prisons are failing to comply with critical performance measures, even at the first year level of 75%. Fewer still will meet the current 80% benchmark. The treatment delays and backlogs point to a shortage of health care staff that must be remedied to create an adequate health care system. Defendants should be required (1) to immediately develop a plan to increase nurse and physician staffing to enable each prison to achieve passing CGAR scores of at least 80% for access to RN triage, primary care and chronic care appointments (Performance Measures # 37, # 39 and # 54), timely inpatient encounters (Performance Measure # 66) and timely provider review of diagnostic test results (Performance Measure # 46) ; and (2) to develop a plan to perform a workload study for all health care positions, and to create and implement a staffing plan based upon the results of the study. Additionally, they should be required to develop a plan to automatically refill prescriptions for chronic care and psychiatric diagnoses.

Prenatal Services 57 A Medical Provider will order prenatal vitamins and diet for a pregnant inmate at the inmate's initial intake physical examination.

Prenatal Services 58 Results of an inmate's prenatal screening tests will be documented in the medical record.

Preventative Services 59 Inmates will be screened for TB on an annual basis.

Preventative Services 60 All female inmates ages 21 to 65 will be offered a Pap smear at the inmate's initial intake physical examination.

Preventative Services 61 All female inmates ages 21 to 65 will be offered a Pap smear , every 36 months after initial intake, unless more frequent screening is clinically recommended.

Preventative Services 62 All prisoners are screened for tuberculosis upon intake.

Infirmary Care 63 In an IPC, an initial health assessment will be completed by a Registered Nurse on the date of admission.

Infirmary Care 64 In an IPC, a Medical Provider evaluation and plan will occur within the next business day after admission.

Infirmary Care 65 In an IPC, a written history and physical examination will be completed by a medical provider within 72 hours of admission.

Infirmary Care 66 In an IPC, a Medical Provider encounters will occur at a minimum every 72 hours.

Infirmary Care 67 In an IPC, Registered nurses will conduct and document an assessment at least once every shift. Graveyard shift assessments can be welfare checks.

Infirmary Care 68 In an IPC, Inmate health records will include admission orders and documentation of care and treatment given.

Infirmary Care 69 In an IPC, nursing care plans will be reviewed weekly documented with a date and signature.

Infirmary Care 70 All IPC patients have properly working call buttons, and if not, health care staff perform and document 30-minute patient welfare checks.

Medical Diets 71 Inmates with diagnosed and documented diseases or conditions that necessitate a special diet will be provided the diet, if clinically indicated. When prescribing the special diet, the provider will include the type of diet, duration for which it is to be provided, and any special instructions.

Medical Diets 72 Inmates who refuse prescribed diets for more than 3 consecutive days will receive follow-up nutritional counseling by a QHCP.

Mental Health 73 All MH-3 minor prisoners shall be seen by a licensed mental health clinician a minimum of every 30 days.

Mental Health 74 All female prisoners shall be seen by a licensed mental health clinician within five working days of return from a hospital post-partum.

Mental Health 75 A mental health assessment of a prisoner during initial intake shall be completed by mental health staff by the end of the second full day after the prisoner's arrival into ADC.

Mental Health 76 If the initial mental health assessment of a prisoner during initial intake is not performed by licensed mental health staff, the prisoner shall be seen by a mental health clinician within fourteen days of his or her arrival into ADC.

Mental Health 77 Mental health treatment plans shall be updated a minimum of every 90 days for MH-3A, MH-4, and MH-5 prisoners, and a minimum of every 12 months for all other MH-3 prisoners.

Mental Health 78 All mental health treatment plan updates shall be done after a face-to-face clinical encounter between the prisoner and the mental health provider or mental health clinician.

Mental Health 79 If a prisoner's mental health treatment plan includes psychotropic medication, the mental health provider shall indicate in each progress note that he or she has reviewed the treatment plan.

Mental Health 80 MH-3A prisoners shall be seen a minimum of every 30 days by a mental health clinician.

Mental Health 81 MH-3A prisoners who are prescribed psychotropic medications shall be seen a minimum of every 90 days by a mental health provider.

Mental Health 82 MH-3B prisoners shall be seen a minimum of every 90 days by a mental health clinician.

Mental Health 83 MH-3B prisoners who are prescribed psychotropic medications shall be seen a minimum of every 180 days by a mental health provider. MH-3B prisoners who are prescribed psychotropic medications for psychotic disorders, bipolar disorder, or major depression shall be seen by a mental health provider a minimum of every 90 days.

Mental Health 84 MH-3C prisoners shall be seen a minimum of every 180 days by a mental health provider.

Mental Health 85 MH-3D prisoners shall be seen by a mental health provider within 30 days of discontinuing medications.

Mental Health 86 MH-3D prisoners shall be seen a minimum of every 90 days by a mental health clinician for a minimum of six months after discontinuing medication.

Mental Health 87 MH-4 prisoners shall be seen by a mental health clinician for a 1:1 session a minimum of every 30 days.

Mental Health 88 MH-4 prisoners who are prescribed psychotropic medications shall be seen by a mental health provider a minimum of every 90 days.

Mental Health 89 MH-5 prisoners shall be seen by a mental health clinician for a 1:1 session a minimum of every seven days.

Mental Health

90 MH-5 prisoners who are prescribed psychotropic medications, shall be seen by a mental health provider a minimum of every 30 days.

Mental Health 91 MH-5 prisoners who are actively psychotic or actively suicidal shall be seen by a mental health clinician or mental health provider daily.

Mental Health 92 MH-3 and above prisoners who are housed in maximum custody shall be seen by a mental health clinician for a 1:1 or group session a minimum of every 30 days.

Mental Health 93 Mental health staff (not to include LPNs) shall make weekly rounds on all MH-3 and above prisoners who are housed in maximum custody.

Mental Health 94 All prisoners on a suicide or mental health watch shall be seen daily by a licensed mental health clinician or, on weekends or holidays, by a registered nurse.

Mental Health 95 Only licensed mental health staff may remove a prisoner from a suicide or mental health watch. Any prisoner discontinued from a suicide or mental health watch shall be seen by a mental health provider, mental health clinician, or psychiatric registered nurse between 24 and 72 hours after discontinuation, between seven and ten days after discontinuation, and between 21 and 24 days after discontinuation of the watch.

Mental Health 96 A reentry/discharge plan shall be established no later than 30 days prior to release from ADC for all prisoners who are MH-3 or above.

Mental Health 97 A mental health provider treating a prisoner via telepsychiatry shall be provided, in advance of the telepsychiatry session, the prisoner's intake assessment, most recent mental health treatment plan, laboratory reports (if applicable), physician orders, problem list, and progress notes from the prisoner's two most recent contacts with a mental health provider.

Mental Health 98 Mental health HNRs shall be responded to within the timeframes set forth in the Mental Health Technical Manual (MHTM) (rev. 4/18/14), Chapter 2, Section 5.0.

Mental Health 99 Peer reviews shall be conducted as set forth in the MHTM (rev. 4/18/14), Chapter 1, Section 3.0.

Dental 100 Prisoners on the routine dental care list will not be removed from the list if they are seen for urgent care or pain appointments that do not resolve their routine care issues or needs.

Dental 101 Dental assistants will take inmate histories and vital signs and dental radiographs (as ordered) by the Dentist.

Dental 102 Routine dental care wait times will be no more than 90 days from the date the HNR was received.

Dental 103 Urgent dental care wait times, as determined by the contracted vendor, shall be no more than 72 hours from the date the HNR was received.

CONFIDENTIAL REBUTTAL REPORT OF DR.

Robert L Cohen

I, Robert L Cohen, declare:

1. I am a medical doctor and expert in the field of correctional medicine, with 30 years of experience in the field. I have been appointed by federal courts to serve as a monitor in cases challenging the provision of medical care to prisoners, including in Michigan, New York State, and Florida. I have also been a member of the New York City Board of Corrections since 2009, served as a representative of the National Commission on Correctional Health Care for 17 years, provided primary care to jail inmates at Rikers Island, and published extensively on health care for the incarcerated.

2. I have been retained by plaintiffs' counsel in the Parsons case as an expert in correctional health care. I have been asked to give my opinion about in the adequacy of the Arizona Department of Corrections (ADC) health care delivery system. My billing rate in this action is $300 per hour, with a daily rate for out of town work of $2500.

3. At plaintiffs' request and in order to develop my opinions, I conducted an investigation that included visits to the two largest prison complexes (Lewis and Eyman), interviews with prisoners at those two prisons, including the named plaintiffs, and review of medical charts of prisoners with serious chronic medical diseases, hospitalizations, emergency care and specialty consults for those prisons. 2 In addition, I reviewed the testimony of ADC, Corizon, and Wexford staff, documents produced to plaintiffs' counsel by ADC regarding health care delivery, and various monitoring reports ….2 I also requested to review the medical files of all inmates from those Lewis and Eyman who had died in the previous 12 months. Prior to the tours, the Defendants were given the list of names of charts that I wanted to review. During the tours, however, I was able to review only one deceased prisoners' chart, because ADC policy is to send the medical charts to headquarters after a prisoner's death, and none of the other files were on site at the prisons or otherwise available for me to review. ….I visited, and for Douglas, Safford and Winslow prisons. Finally, I reviewed the records for ten patients who died in ADC custody in 2011 and 2012, and physician reviews of these records prepared at my direction .

4. The methodology I used for selecting the medical charts to review is as follows. First, I reviewed the ADC monitoring reports for the two prisons for the months leading up to the tours. Ten to 15 names of prisoners identified by Defendants' monitors as receiving inadequate chronic, specialty, or emergency care were selected from each list at random. Second, I reviewed the "Monitored Conditions" reports produced by Defendants that listed, as of March 2013, all prisoners housed at the institutions with chronic conditions or diseases including tuberculosis, hypertension, diabetes, cancer, cardiac conditions, COPD/asthma, seizures, HIV, AIDS, Hepatitis C, pregnancy, or other respiratory conditions. Approximately 10 to 12 prisoners with diabetes, five to 10 prisoners with HIV, 10 to 12 prisoners with hypertension, and five to 10 prisoners with seizure disorders were selected at random. Some of the individuals selected had more than one chronic condition, or had been identified in Defendants' monitoring reports. Third, I reviewed the most recent Emergency Transports reports produced by Defendants for the prisons and a sample of about 5 to 10 names was selected at random. I also reviewed the lists of those referred for specialty consults, provided by Defendants and from which names were selected. Fourth, I also reviewed medical charts for some patients that I encountered during my site visits, and an additional chart provided to plaintiffs' counsel by the patient's family. 4 Throughout this report, I cite patient examples illustrating the systemic care deficiencies that I have identified. Rather than include a case study for each in the body of this report, I have attached as Appendix C a patient by patient summary that I prepared after interviewing patients and reviewing medical charts, reflecting a more comprehensive discussion of the charts for the patients cited in this report.

5. The ten files I reviewed for prisoners who had died (excluding the file mentioned in footnote 2), were the selected as follows. Three of the files were chosen because defendants had produced mortality reviews that I could compare to the medical records. The remaining seven were chosen because they were among the most recent deaths for which plaintiffs have received medical records.

6. Based upon my extensive background in correctional medicine, experience as a medical monitor in several states, and my investigation into the conditions in the Arizona prisons, my opinion is that the ADC health care delivery system is fundamentally broken and is among the worst prison health care systems I have encountered.

7. Because of this profoundly deficient system, prisoners with serious medical conditions are regularly deprived of necessary medical care and suffer substantial harm, and even death, as a result. Moreover, all

prisoners in this system are at risk of serious harm and/or death, because the system as a whole is not equipped to provide them with necessary medical care when they experience serious medical needs.

8. The ADC's system, as it currently exists under Corizon's management, is disorganized, under-resourced, understaffed, and completely lacking in the capacity to monitor itself and correct the systemic dysfunction that currently exists. Thus, unless ADC dramatically reverses its course, it will continue to operate in a way that harms patients by denying them necessary care for serious medical conditions.

9. The ADC prisons I visited are unable to sustain the basic delivery of medical care because of limited clinical staffing and the overwhelming number of prisoners who have serious, long-standing, and complicated medical care needs, causing lengthy treatment delays. The long delays in care needlessly compound and aggravate medical conditions that, had they been addressed sooner would have been managed and resolved. The documents I reviewed, including ADC contract monitoring reports, medical records and death reviews, establish that the conditions I observed are typical throughout the state.

10. Prisoners with chronic conditions, including HIV, diabetes, cancer, seizure disorders, hepatitis and hypertension, are particularly at risk in the ADC's system. While many patients with chronic illnesses can be managed and live with relatively stable health, ADC's system lacks an adequate tracking and management system to ensure that patients have regular provider visits and medication renewals. Not surprisingly, I found numerous patients at both prisons who were much sicker than they would have been had they been adequately managed. In fact, there were multiple cases in which the lapses were so shocking and dangerous that I felt ethically obligated as a medical professional to bring them to the immediate attention of the ADC and Corizon staff.

11. Defendants' medication delivery systems are inadequate for the size of the population they serve, and are plagued by short-staffing at a number of their prisons. Too many prisoners, with too few staff and insufficient resources, leads inevitably to medication delays and inadequate treatment documentation. The result is that ADC prisoners receive their medications late or not at all, and suffer as a result, as was evident in my patient interviews and review of charts.

12. Unless medical records and scheduling information are managed, organized, and maintained effectively, appropriate health-care services cannot be provided. ADC lacks the ability to adequately manage and maintain medical records and patient scheduling information.

13. A functioning Quality Assurance program is a critical element in any medical care system, enabling the system to assess and evaluate care provided its patients so that systemic deficiencies may be identified and addressed. To the extent that any medical quality assurance activities are occurring in the ADC, they are plainly inadequate.

14. There are more prisoners requiring specialized placement for medical reasons than Arizona can accommodate. Arizona has not provided adequate medical beds for disabled prisoners, aged inmates, and prisoners who need some form of sheltered living due to their medical or mental health conditions.

15. The clinical spaces that I toured are too small for the prison population, and in all but one or two cases, I never observed any actual medical care being delivered in these spaces. Rather, I observed locked, dark and empty rooms that I was told were exam rooms, but lacked basic medical equipment. Medical equipment was broken, covered in dust, and in some cases based on logs attached to them, had not been repaired or checked in more than a decade.

16. My observations at the prisons and extensive review of documents demonstrate that the gross systemic deficiencies in the ADC's health care delivery system are deeply rooted, long-standing and will require substantial effort to remedy. During the last 15 months, the ADC medical care system has shifted from ADC management, to Wexford and then to Corizon, but privatization has failed to resolve the long-running health care problems. Rather than invest in addressing the serious systemic deficiencies in their program, ADC chose to outsource their system to the lowest bidder, not once, but twice. At no time during this series of management hand-offs has ADC demonstrated the will or capacity to address these deep-seated issues.

BASES FOR MY OPINIONS

I discuss many examples of poor medical care in this report, but I present the case of here because it vividly illustrates the myriad systemic breakdowns that have plagued ADOC, Wexford, and Corizon, over a period of many months, and the impact these breakdowns have on patient care I interviewed Mr. at his cell on Eyman's Browning Unit and reviewed his medical record. Mr. developed severe throat pain in April 2012. He was finally treated on 6/5/12 with amoxicillin for a sore throat. The condition did not respond. On 7/14/12

Mr. placed one of many "health needs requests" (HNRs) complaining of unrelenting pain. He wrote, presciently: "This is a severe, possibly lethal problem and I need someone there to take some action to treat this problem." Mr. was not seen by the nurse practitioner until July 20, six days later. The abscess ruptured spontaneously four days after that. He was seen by a physician at a local hospital who ordered two types of antibiotics, but he received only one. The infection persisted, and Mr. remained in extreme pain. His suffering continued. 19. On 8/17/2012 he was again prescribed a course of two antibiotics and again the medical staff provided only one. He placed an HNR on 8/21/2012 requesting that this problem be addressed. The nursing staff elected to take no action, and to refer the problem to the health care practitioner on 8/24/2012. ADC 135625. That day, the Nurse Practitioner, Jane Houdeshel asked that the medications be "pulled out of RDSA". (unknown abbreviation). ADC 136602. On 9/19/12, Mr. was finally seen by Dr. Joel Cohen, an ENT surgeon, who recommended a tonsillectomy. ADC 136603. Although he was in great pain, and suffering from a persistent infection unresponsive to multiple courses of antibiotics, surgery for removal of his tonsils was not performed for over two months, on 11/20/12. The surgical pathology report was faxed to Dr. Cohen the next day, 11/21/12.

The tonsils showed moderate to poorly differentiated squamous cell carcinoma of the left tonsil, involving full thickness of the submitted material, extending into the muscle, and extending to the margin of the resection. 20. Although Dr. Cohen saw the surgical pathology report (ADC 136593) on 11/21/12, no follow-up was scheduled for the patient. For the next three and a half months, Mr. 's cancer was not treated. 21. On 3/3/13 Mr. placed an HNR. He was not seen for more than three weeks, until 3/28/13. He told Mr. Salyer, the Physician Assistant (PA) that he had been experiencing throat problems since January.

Mr. noticed swollen lymph nodes on the left side of his neck. He told the PA that Dr. Cohen, the ENT surgeon, had told him he had a "Huge ugly tonsil." Mr. Salyer examined Mr. and confirmed that he had adhesions and significantly swollen lymph nodes. On that day, Mr. Salyer requested Corizon approve an ENT urgent consultation because of these findings, but Mr. waited almost seven more weeks to be seen by Dr. Cohen. 22. Dr. Cohen saw Mr. on 5/14/2013. He noted bilateral neck masses. He performed two fine needle aspiration biopsies. Since Dr. Cohen already knew that Mr. had untreated cancer of the tonsil, it is unclear why he performed these biopsies. Dr. Cohen asked for a CT scan of the neck in preparation for radiation therapy. On 6/7/13, Dr. Cohen sought an emergency consultation with an oncologist. 23. On 6/17

/13 Mr. placed another HNR complaining of increasing throat pain, and asking for follow up on the referral for a CT scan and an oncology appointment. ADC 136631. On 6/24/13, one week later, he received his response: "Your consultation has been approved and appointment has been scheduled." The CT scan, which had been urgently recommended on May 14 was not performed until July 2, 2013, four months after Mr. 's HNR complaining about swollen lymph nodes. The CT scan showed "bilateral submandibular complex solid contrast enhancing masses and associated anterior neck lymphadenopathy, likely nasopharyngeal malignancy." In plain English: large solid masses in his salivary glands, swollen lymph nodes, and the diagnosis of nasopharyngeal cancer, a cancer of the upper throat. 24. Remarkably, but entirely consistent with prior delays, this CT report was sent to the Eyman medical staff on 7/2/13 but not reviewed by health care staff until 7/8/13. On that day, Mr. 's scheduled oncology appointment was inexplicably cancelled. He was finally seen by oncology more than a month after the emergency consult was requested. On July 13, PA Ainslie reviewed the oncology recommendations for PET/CT scan, Dental evaluation, Medical Oncology Consultation, and 21st Century Oncology Consultation. ADC 136612. These consultations requests were written on July 13, but were not faxed for approval to the Corizon Clinical Coordinator until 7/15/13.

ADC 136613-616. 25. Two days later, at the time of my visit to Eyman-Browning, on 7/17/13, still had not received any treatment for the cancer. Mr. 's treatment for an extremely painful, life-threatening condition was characterized by consistent failures to provide basic medical care. His pain was ignored for months. His failure to respond to the minimal treatment offered was ignored. Even when he was ordered treatment, he was not provided the ordered medications. Repeated urgent requests for specialty consultation were delayed for weeks and months. Urgent surgical treatment for a painful condition was delayed for months. The extensive cancer left in his neck after his left tonsil was removed was ignored. In March 2013, he noted increasing lymph nodes.

Medical, nursing staff and central office staff all became aware of his untreated cancer, but for the next four months, no treatment was offered. 26. In my more than three decades of doing this work, I have never seen such callous disregard demonstrated over and over again. Beginning in March 2012, medical staffs were fully aware that was in severe pain, and did not treat him. When they finally realized that he had an uncontrolled infection, they delayed treatment. When he required surgery, the surgery was delayed. When he was diagnosed with cancer, his biopsy was ignored. When he sought care for the spreading cancer in March 2013, he again experienced delay after delay. Four months after the rediscovery, he had received no treatment. This is a horrifying example of a failed system that places every seriously ill man and woman it serves at extreme risk. B. Failed Medical Care System 27. Although shocking, Mr. 's case is not anomalous. Instead, it is tragic but predictable outcome of an appallingly poor medical care system that lacks the essential building blocks of an effective health care delivery system and has for years been inadequately staffed, funded and resourced. Moreover the types of lapses and delays I found in Mr. 's case are consistent with the types of problems I found repeatedly in reviewing files and talking with patients. 28. Based on my experience in correctional health care systems, a sound system for a large statewide prison system like Arizona's must include at least the following nine elements: (1) a centralized organizational and management structure; (2) written policies and procedures that are implemented and followed consistently; (3) qualified medical staffing; (4) prompt intake/screening; (5) timely access to primary and specialty medical care, including for the chronically ill; (6) adequate clinical facilities; (7) medication distribution system; (8) a functioning medical records system; and (9) quality assurance, including a viable death review process. ADC's health care delivery system is broken because these essential elements, to the extent they exist, are ill-functioning and are so under-resourced and poorly managed that they are largely ineffective. 29. Despite the fact that these deficiencies are and have been amply demonstrated, including in Wexford's and Corizon's care data, ADC's contract monitoring reports, and individual medical charts, ADC has failed to develop and fund adequate staffing patterns and to allocate sufficient resources necessary to address the longstanding systemic problems. 30. When Wexford Health took over ADC's medical care delivery system, it found it "had to start from the basics and rebuild a dysfunctional program," and advised ADC that this was a task "far beyond the scope of the project described in the RFP." Wexford 000049. Meeting with ADC officials in November, 2012 Wexford staff set forth the myriad system failures it had uncovered, and admitted that "[t]he current class action lawsuits are accurate." Wexford 000130. 31. Based on my investigation, that admission is unfortunately as accurate today with respect to Corizon as it was with respect to Wexford in November, 2012. A survey of cases I reviewed while visiting prisons in July shows no significant changes in care for many prisoner patients who have been the victims of continuing poor care from the Arizona Department of Corrections, Wexford, and now Corizon. To illustrate, and as set forth below and in more detail in Appendix C, 's diabetes has been poorly controlled since November, 2012, his insulin regimen has been chaotic and dangerous for close to a year, and he has not been provided with an ophthalmology consult for close to a year; 's diabetes care has been poorly managed from at least October 2012 until the current time; ' diabetes has been poorly controlled and his medications mismanaged since January, 2013; ' diabetes has been poorly controlled since December, 2012 and medical staff failed to recognize that fact; 's diabetes and hypertension have been poorly managed since November, 2012; has been waiting for cataract surgery since September, 2012, and his pain medications have been mismanaged during that same period of time; , a diabetic, has not had a required eye exam for over two years; has not had the urology specialty consult that was ordered for him on January 1, 2012; has been waiting 18 months for necessary eye surgery; has had care for his HIV disease mismanaged since January, 2013; 's HIV care has similarly been mismanaged since February, 2013; and as described above, has not received treatment for a dangerous cancer that was diagnosed in November, 2012. 32. I also found numerous cases where the medical care mismanagement is clearly solely the responsibility of Corizon, including: 's hypertension has been mismanaged since May, 2013; 's medications were not renewed and critical lab results were not reviewed under Corizon; suffered a delay in getting a necessary urology consultation under Corizon; received no timely cardiology consultation through Corizon after his pacemaker failed; MRSA has been mismanaged by Corizon; has had no clinical or cardiology consultation follow-up under Corizon following an acute heart attack; waited six months to receive treatment for his kidney cancer and relief for the severe pain he suffered from bony metastases; and died because Corizon mismanaged his coccidioidomycosis pneumonia beginning in May, 2013. In all of these cases, these patients' suffered harm and serious risk of harm, needlessly. 33. These continuing and sometimes lethal failures to provide adequate medical care to prisoners with serious and long-standing medical problems demonstrate anew that management of patients with serious medical care problems and complications cannot be done on the cheap. Corizon, like Wexford and the Arizona Department of Corrections before it, has proved again that where corners are cut in providing medical care by having too few professional staff and an inadequate budget, patients will suffer, and sometimes die, because of systemic neglect. Prisoners are getting lost in the medical care system; their serious chronic diseases are not being followed as closely as they should be; and requests for necessary outside medical consultation are going unfilled. 1. Central Management 34. Although the ADC health care services were privatized, ADC is ultimately accountable and responsible for the statewide administration of health care. ADC created a Health Services Contract Monitoring Bureau, mostly comprised of administrators and health care staff who oversaw the delivery of health care by ADC prior to privatization. However, in terms of day-to-day activities, it appears that the contractor Corizon functions largely on its own in terms of deciding how (and whether) to deliver medical care. 35. The failures of the existing management structure are well-illustrated by the ADC's Health Services Contract Monitoring Bureau, which, on a monthly basis, generates lengthy reports regarding compliance with the health care contract at each the prisons. Although these reports consistently document ongoing failures to comply with the contract requirements in many critical areas, including requirements to screen and process sick call requests timely, to implement chronic care treatment plans and to deliver necessary medications, it is not clear who, if anyone, ever reviews these reports. The head of the Bureau testified he does not read the reports on a monthly basis. Gross Dep. 13:17-14:2; see also Campbell Dep. 143:2-5 (Program Evaluation Administrator who supervises contract monitors does not read all of the monthly MGARs). 36. The ADC's most recent Quarterly Monitoring Reports, covering April through June 2013, document Corizon's consistent non-compliance with critical program measurements for sick call and chronic disease management for the state's two largest prisons, Lewis and Eyman. ADC 137754, 137780. These non-compliance findings are repeated in each of the months of July through September, 2013. These findings are entirely consistent with the extreme level of dysfunction that I observed when visiting those two prisons. Indeed, as part of the monthly auditing program, Corizon is required by contract to develop Corrective Action Plans (CAPs) for every performance measure with an unsatisfactory score. However, they frequently fail to produce the CAPs. Headstream Dep. 146:19-148:2 (despite repeated findings of noncompliance, Lewis did not submit CAPs). Defendants also have failed to produce the CAPs for review by Plaintiffs' counsel or me. 37. Despite these repeated failures, ADC management has failed to enforce the CAP requirement. Haldane Dep. 56:12-57:17; 143:12-143:17; Medel Dep. 160:17- 161:15; Campbell Dep. 130:22-131:8. Instead, they continue to generate audit reports month after month that bear witness to gross systemic failures without addressing them, or requiring their contractor to address them. 2. Written Procedures 38. A constitutionally adequate correctional medical care delivery system for a prison system with 33,000 prisoners must have and consistently follow comprehensive written policies and procedures. My review of documents and observations at Eyman and Lewis, and review of the MGAR reports establishes that there is a system-wide practice of not following the ADC and Corizon policies and procedures because, among other things, a failure to provide adequate staffing, supervision and resources to promote compliance. 3. Qualified Staffing 39. The foundation of any sound health care delivery system is staffing adequately trained and in sufficient number to address the patient population's health care needs. Without a sufficient number of clinicians on staff, it is simply impossible to ensure that prisoners receive the care that they require. a. Insufficient Allocated Positions 40. Corizon's current clinical staffing allocation is so alarmingly low that, even if all positions were filled, which is not the case, it would be impossible for the system to delivery adequate health care to the number of prisoners currently in the ADC system. 41. Inadequate clinical staffing has long been a problem for ADC. Institutions were not fully staffed by ADC during the April 2-July 1, 2012 transition period from ADC to Wexford. Pratt Dep. 21:22-22:12. One doctor characterized that time as a period of "a great exodus of staff, both from the mental health and medical areas that weren't being filled." Crews Dep. 18:5-12. 42. Staffing continued to be a problem under Wexford. "It was an understood" that staffing levels at the institutions was one of Wexford's concerns prior to taking over delivery of health care. Pratt Dep. 29:6-10. "A smaller staffing ratio creates a greater risk." (Shaw Dep. 125:5-6) As ADC's Joe Profiri wrote, "Based on the documentation from Mr. Pratt the core problem is staffing. The inadequacy of staffing levels are the root cause of all other deficiencies, none of which can be effectively remediated or sustained with any success until staffing deficiencies are corrected. Wexford should be laser focused on addressing staffing." AGA_Review_00037464. 43. Given that staffing had been identified as a critical issue under ADC and Wexford, I was stunned to learn that Corizon, upon taking over the system in March, 2013, apparently eliminated 30 medical service positions, including almost one third of the staff physician positions and about 15% of the RN positions. AGA_Review_00006402. 44. The next month, ADC monitor, Mark Haldane, reported staffing problems for nurses at Eyman prison. "[T]he tentative schedule for May has large gaps in nursing coverage. It appears that there are days that there is no coverage in any of the cell blocks." AGA_Review_00013126. He further explained, "Even at current staffing levels, nurses are finding ways around standard practice... making errors ...and omitting some tasks. . . . Apparently nursing staff at all Eyman units are being cut." Id. He concluded with, "staffing remains a concern of nursing supervisors at Florence and Eyman and many others (including me)." Id. 45. Currently, the full-time clinician staffing allocated for each of the larger prisons, and Phoenix, with its specialized missions, is extraordinarily thin.5 Douglas complex, which houses approximately 2,200, is allocated no physicians and only a single mid-level practitioner (i.e., a nurse practitioner or physician's assistant). Eyman, Lewis and Yuma, with approximately 5,300, 5,400 and 4,500 prisoners respectively, are each allocated only a single physician and three mid-level practitioners. Tucson houses over 5,000 prisoners, including the sickest prisoners in the system (Robertson Dep. at 32:3-5)Under Corizon, each of the prisons is allocated a Medical Director, and I believe that position must be filled by a physician. I have been told that the Medical Director may have clinical duties. However, given the administrative duties typically demanded of a Medical Director in a prison complex serving several thousand people, it is not possible for the director to have a full clinical schedule, thus I have not included them in my count of clinicians yet has only two physician positions and three mid-level positions. With 4,060 prisoners, Florence has two physician and two mid-level positions. Perryville, which has the only intake unit in the state for women and houses over 3,700 women prisoners, has two physician and five mid-level positions. Phoenix is a smaller facility with approximately 680 prisoners, but it has several specialized missions, with a 40 bed licensed acute mental health unit and a 135 bed licensed intermediate mental health unit, a transitional care unit for mental health inmates, and the state's primary intake unit for men, Phoenix has only a single physician position and four mid-level positions. ADC 153777-153793. b. Failure to Fill Allocated Positions 46. As noted above, staffing at this level would be grossly inadequate for the number of Arizona prisoners if all positions were filled, but Corizon has not been able to fill even these few positions. According to the July 2013 Arizona staffing report, 4.5 of the state's 10 physician positions were vacant. Id. The September 2013 report shows some improvement, but the system is still short almost three full physician positions, and more than four of its ten Medical Director positions are vacant. ADC 155099. 47. In addition, many other key allocated positions have been vacant. July: ADC 153779 (Eyman had no Medical Director, a 37.8% vacancy rate for RNs, and a 60% vacancy rate for RN Supervisors); ADC 153782-83 (Lewis lacked a Medical Director, and had a 32% vacancy rate for RNs) and Bybee Dep. at 50:3-7 (Lewis does not have a Facility Health Administrator); ADC 153791 (Winslow, allocated a full-time medical director and mid-level practitioner has only a half-time director); September: (Douglas has no medical director and only nurse practitioner position is vacant); (Eyman has no medical director); (Lewis has no medical director, and 32% vacancy rate for RNs); (Safford has only 1 LPN for 6.10 positions); (Winslow's one nurse practitioner position is vacant). ADC 155099. Dr. Robertson opined that Corizon has been unable to fill its clinical staff positions because they do not pay enough (Robertson Dep. at 96:9-96:23), and the COO of Corizon testified Corizon has increased the salary matrix for physicians and medical directors but the number of applicants for those positions did not increase after the salary changes. Bybee Dep. at 52:13-53:1. 49. Corizon's staffing deficiencies have been evident and documented at the Eyman complex since the start of their contract in March of this year. 4/9/13 MGAR, ADC 088836 (In 4/13, Eyman site manager reported that he did not have a medical director or director of nursing at Eyman and had only two providers, one physician and one mid-level). ADC's monitor wrote on 4/12/13, "There is no provider on any unit at Eyman Complex today…. Some inmates are going weeks without medications. For example, wrote an HNR stating, 'I have been without my seizure medications since the 23rd of March and I've begun having some bad seizures. My meds were renewed last month. I've written medical and the nurse said she called pharmacy, yet still I have no meds.' . . . . His chart sits on a provider cart on a yard… with no provider. They have been without a provider for 6 weeks." AGA_Review_00015753. Regarding Browning unit, he writes that he had been told their chronic care appointments were "pretty good," but then found their "HNR referrals were backlogged to December." Id. 50. Serious problems are documented at other prisons as well. 4/25/13 MGAR, ADC 088893 ("[Lewis] staffing patterns not supportive of required performance measures at present."), 4/17/13 MGAR, ADC 088995 ("[Staffing at Safford] continues to be an area of potential concern. Corizon has approved fewer nurses than previously were employed."), 4/16/13 MGAR, ADC 089077 ("There has not been a contractor physician at the Winslow or Apache medical units as of this date during the month of April with the exception of one day at each unit that a doctor did chart reviews and saw a total of three inmates"), 4/19/13 MGAR ADC 089081. (Noting that Winslow needs a medical director, mid-level provider, LPN, medical technician, x-ray technician, and a PCT). 51. The ADC has continued to document the staffing problems since then. 7/31/13 MGAR, ADC 137224 (As of July 31, 2013, "although several vacancies have been filled [at Eyman], there are presently no staff working on site in several key positions. These include nursing supervision (3x), Medical Director, Clinical Coordinator, and the Assistant FHA."), 9/5/13 MGAR, ADC 154043 (As of September 5, 2013, the following positions [at Douglas] were not filled: 1 FTE medical director, 1 FTE mid-level practitioner, 1 FTE dental assistant, 0.75 FTE dentist, 0.90 FTE LPN, 0.40 FTE nursing assistant, 0.50 FTE RN…These are critical positions to have unfilled as the staffing plan submitted by Corizon allows for no back-up coverage built into it). 52. The monitoring reports also suggest that Corizon does not employ sufficient temporary staff to meet the medical needs of the inmate population. 4/22/13 MGAR, ADC 088911 ("Current staffing patterns [at Lewis] are affecting nursing and provider lines. All locum and registry nursing has been cut with no noted replacement of F/T staff to cover shortages at present."). 53. Very predictably, inadequate staffing drives appointment backlogs and treatment delays. 4/15/13 MGAR, ADC 088843 ("Provider staffing is woefully inadequate. As of April 12, complex-wide [at Eyman] there were over 450 charts in provider review carts."), 7/22/13 MGAR, ADC 137342 ("Though efforts at increasing current staffing levels [at Lewis] continue, the shortages in all areas to include providers for medical and psychiatry and in areas of nursing clearly compromise the ability of current staff to manage the extensive medical needs of the population."), 4/16/13 MGAR, ADC 089077 (without physician at Winslow, "[c]hart reviews have not been conducted and likely wouldn't be even if a full time physician started today as it would take the rest of the month to catch up on the backlog of inmates needing to be seen and the backlog of chart reviews.").

Intake Screening

54. Prompt intake screening is essential in a correctional setting to ensure, among other things, that patients receive timely medications for serious medical conditions, are screened for communicable diseases and are identified as requiring ongoing attention from specialty consultants. 55. The vast majority of intake screening in the ADC takes place at Phoenix (for men) and Perryville (for women), two prisons that I did not visit. 5. Timely Access to Medical Care 56. In order to ensure that prisoners are able to request medical care when they need it, prisons must have a system for prisoners to make their health care needs known, and for ensuring those requests are evaluated and addressed in a timely manner. For prisoners who suffer from chronic illnesses, the prison must have a system for tracking and scheduling appointments regularly to ensure continuity of care. For those who require care beyond the expertise of their primary care provider, the prison must have a system of referral to specialists. a. Sick Call 57. The ADC has a "sick call process" that patients use by submitting a "health needs request" (HNR) for which they must pay $4 for each request, if they have funds. Under ADC's policies, HNRs are supposed to be collected every day, and for those requests listing symptoms, the patient should be seen by an RN within 24 hours (72 hours for weekends). Health Services Technical Manual, ADC 010827. If the

patient needs further medical attention, he or she is supposed to be scheduled to see the provider (physician or mid-level) within seven days. 58. At the prisons I visited, it was clear these requirements are routinely ignored, causing patients to endure pain and suffering unnecessarily, as demonstrated above in the case, and in many other cases I reviewed. Among other prisoners who experienced harm because of delayed care was . On 5/10/13, he submitted an HNR at Eyman complaining of a cyst in his armpit. He wrote: "Excruciating" "I can hardly move my arm. I think it has to drain. Emergency. Please see me ASAP. I can pay the $4 for this emergency visit. Thanks and God bless." On 5/13/13 he was told that he would be scheduled to the nurses' line. Six days later, he submitted a second HNR stating "Well now it is all infected. I have red streaks running down my arm." ADC 136482. On 5/24/13, two weeks after he submitted the HNR complaining of severe pain from his abscess, he was seen by an RN who confirmed that he had an abscess. Nurse Dorsica cleaned the wound, cultured it, and prescribed an antibiotic, clindamycin 150 mg three times a day and put bacitracin on the wound. Mr. 's infection was cultured as methicillin resistant staph aureus. This is a very serious infection. Treatment of a serious painful bacterial infection should not be delayed for two weeks. 59. a 40 year old man who has hypertension, asthma, epilepsy, and a history of a pituitary tumor, had his last chronic care visit a year before my July 2013 visit to Lewis. His April 20, 2013 HNR stated: "I'm losing my vision, difficulty seeing, experiencing pain and pressure and loss of peripheral vision." In the three months after submitting the HNR, Mr. was not seen by an RN or an MD. 60. right leg has been amputated. He submitted an HNR at Eyman for repair of his right prosthetic leg on May 1, 2012. On September 4, 2012, four months later, his HNR was reviewed, and an appointment with a physician's assistant was scheduled. ADC 136478. Mr. was not seen by the physician's assistant about his broken prosthesis until April 9, 2013, eleven months after he placed his HNR. 61. Named plaintiff Stephen Swartz, 102486, reported that because of the shortage of medical staff at Lewis, it takes prisoners an average of three months to see the doctor from the time they file a HNR. He reports that he submitted an HNR on January 13, 2013, requesting evaluation of a pigmented enlarging mass on his waist. He received no response and continued to submit HNR's. He was finally seen on June 26, 2013, more than five months later. 62. Named plaintiff Joseph Hefner at the Lewis-Barchey Unit, likewise reported he has encountered significant delays in care. When I interviewed him, he had recently had surgery on his left eye for glaucoma. However, following the surgery, he had not gotten the medications he needed or had a follow-up with the ophthalmologist, and he described symptoms that I found very troublesome and indicative of a possibly detached retina. He had pain behind the eyes, floaters, blurriness and spots. He had to file numerous HNRs (ADC 122325-28) but didn't see the prison doctor until July 12. According to Hefner, the prison doctor didn't do any sort of exam, not even pulling out the ophthalmoscope, and told Hefner his eye looked fine. 63. According to Mr. Hefner, nurses' line occurs only twice a week on the yard, and it takes eight weeks to be seen at the nurse's line from the time of filing a HNR. He said after nurses' line, it takes another 4 to 6 weeks to see the doctor. Other prisoners I spoke to at Lewis reported similar delays. 64. Prisoners housed in Eyman's SMU-I and Browning isolation units reported that custody staff will not give prisoners a blank HNR when they ask for them. The process is that the prisoner has to first write a "kite" (an informal letter) to the officers requesting blank HNR forms, and then a couple days later on the graveyard shift, they will be delivered blank forms. Once the prisoner fills out an HNR, they have to give them to custody officers and not the pill nurses or others coming in the unit. This type of custodial involvement is problematic because being forced to disclose medical information to custodial staff violates the prisoners' right to medical privacy. 65. ADC is aware of the failure of prisons to conduct nurse triage within 24 hours of reviewing the HNR, although it appears some staff may have tried to hide the problem. ADC's compliance monitor Terry Allred documented on 5/22/13 that staff had found a backlog of HNRs dating back to December 2012. According to Allred, "it was clearly stated to [the person who discovered it] that the finding was not to be revealed to the audit team." AGA-Review_00017341. 66. MGAR reports likewise amply document the problem. 7/25/13 MGAR, ADC 137185 ("Of 40 medical charts reviewed [at Douglas] (10 at each unit), 18 were not seen within 24 hours of their respective HNR being triaged."); 7/31/13 MGAR, ADC 137201 (Of 50 charts reviewed[at Eyman (10 on each yard), 22 inmates were not seen on nurses line within 24 hours following the triage of their HNR.); 7/30/13 MGAR, ADC 137268 ("Of the 30 inmate medical charts audited (complex wide), only 3 of those noted patient encounters within the required 24 hour period. Of those same 30 inmate medical records, which included 7 '911' or emergent requests, 1 was seen on the same day of submission, while the other 6 were seen on average 6.2 days later."); 8/30/13 MGAR, ADC 137465-66 (Reporting that 32 out of 51 charts reviewed at Eyman indicated that sick call inmates were not being seen within 24 hours of HNR triage); 9/17/13 MGAR, ADC 154348 (Noting that Winslow had a 70% compliance rate with measure requiring inmates to be seen within 24 hours of HNR triage and requesting a corrective action plan); 9/27/13 MGAR, ADC 154050-51 (Reporting that 30 out of 50 charts reviewed at Eyman showed that sick call inmates were not being seen within 24 hours of HNR triage); 9/27/13 MGAR, ADC 154148 ("10 charts pulled from each unit [at Eyman] for the month. The percentage that were not seen within 24 hours of triage: Morey 80%, Stiner 40%, Buckley 50%, Barchey 60%, Rast 90%, Backman 70%, and Eagle Point/Sunrise 90% . . . Of those HNRs which were of the 911 variety: the standard wait time was 1-20 days after triage.") 67. Audits likewise demonstrate the long wait times for provider appointments, following nurse triage. For the month of July, 2013, Corizon reported wait times of up to six months for patients to see their Primary Care Provider (PCP) at Eyman, and up to six weeks at Lewis. ADC 153838. For September, wait times at Eyman remain up to six months, while wait times at Lewis are up to a month. ADC 155093. 68. The ADC's monitoring reports also show regular delays in access to primary care provider clinicians. 4/16/13 MGAR, ADC 088816 ("In almost no cases are sick call referrals seen within 7 days. Rynning Unit [Eyman] has not had a provider for 6 weeks. No unit reported having a provider more than two days per week. Hundreds of HNR appointments/referrals are backlogged at every unit. The backlogged appointments go back to August. Hundreds of charts are on provider carts in the Complex, many at units without a provider to see the patients."); 4/30/13 MGAR, ADC 088893 ("A random audit of 20 nursing patients complex wide [at Lewis] reflected that only about 10% saw the provider within the 7 days period as required."); 4/16/13 MGAR, ADC 089062 ("Referrals to providers from sick call have not been seen within 7 days because Winslow has not had a provider this month."); 7/8/13 MGAR ADC 137403 (Requesting corrective action plan for the failure to have "referrals to providers from sick call being seen within seven (7) days" performance measure at Winslow). These consistent and widespread delays pose a threat of significant harm to the prisoner patients. b. Chronic Care 69. A prison medical care system must provide adequate care to the most challenging of its patients. Those patients are often the sickest, have chronic multi-system diseases, and require close monitoring to keep their complicated diseases from spiraling out of control. Thus, a critical measure of the success, or lack of success, of a prison medical care delivery system is how well that system manages patients with serious diseases that require chronic care. 70. ADC has failed to implement a functioning tracking system that ensures that chronically ill prisoners see their providers on a regular basis. According to Kathy Campbell, the prisons use different systems at different prisons to schedule chronic care appointments, including an electronic program called IHAS, and a system based on index cards. 9/11/13 Campbell Dep.171:20-172:11. Corizon's VP Vickie Bybee acknowledged that IHAS could generate some chronic care tracking report, "if used," but testified that most prisons were not using it. Bybee Dep. 107:7-17. Others testified that the IHAS program was not used consistently or was otherwise flawed. See Headstream Dep. 163:1-21; Dr. Crews Dep. 99:2-13; Mullenix Dep. 36:9-37:4; Fisher Dep. 23:1-15. 71. Without an effective tracking system, seriously ill patients cannot be effectively monitored and managed, and many will deteriorate. This is precisely what I found in the prisoners I interviewed and the files I reviewed. 72. At Eyman and Lewis, I routinely heard prisoners with chronic conditions complain that they were not scheduled for regular appointments. When I was able to review their medical charts, the records often documented these lapses. For example, (Eyman) has Hepatitis C. He told me he sought follow-up for this chronic condition. On December 30, 2012, he placed an HNR in order to see a provider. On January 18, 2013, there was a response sent to Mr. – "Appointment set." As of July 16th, when I reviewed his medical record, six and a half months later, the HNR was unanswered, and there was no documentation that he had seen a provider for a chronic care appointment. 73. Similarly, , Lewis, has HIV infection. Unfortunately his infection is not responding to prescribed treatment. Laboratory studies obtained on April 12, 2013 showed a low CD4 count of 230/mm3, and a high viral load of 3264. Importantly, three months before, on January 18, 2013, the viral load was undetectable. Although Dr. Merchant reviewed the laboratory studies on May 11, 2013, Mr. had not been informed of the deterioration of his condition and no action has been taken to ameliorate it as of the date I reviewed the file. 74. When a person with HIV infection on treatment with previously undetectable viral loads develops a high viral load, this deterioration must be promptly. Resistance can develop to treatment, and can result in rapid deterioration of the patient's clinical status. Mr. already has a very low CD4 count. Should it drop below 200, as is likely given his trend, he will be at high risk for opportunistic infections. It is extremely disturbing that Mr. ' deteriorating condition is not being addressed. Additional studies must be urgently obtained to determine if he is resistant to his current medications, appropriate treatment should be provided, and if Tcells have fallen further, appropriate medications must be provided to prevent opportunistic infections. 75. Diabetes mellitus likewise requires proper management. Without it, the patient's HgA1c levels (hereafter A1c levels) 6 will be elevated, as will his blood sugars. A prisoner-patient whose diabetes is not properly controlled runs the risk of blindness from diabetic retinopathy, and kidney failure from proteinuria (excessive protein in the urine, a complication of diabetes that tells medical staff that the diabetes patient runs the risk of kidney failure). Diabetics require regular eye exams to look for diabetic retinopathy as well as regular kidney function testing for proteinuria. 76. Medical charts that I reviewed for diabetic prisoners revealed a pattern of very poor care resulting in increased morbidity and an elevated risk of death in some cases. See, e.g., (no change in insulin dosage despite persistently high A1c level); (change to insulin dosage caused rise in A1c level, was prescribed wrong types of insulin for his condition); (A1c over 12.9 for a year, no adjustment to insulin); (A1c increases from February to May, but provider documents his control is improving); (referred for The A1c test is a common blood test used to diagnose type 1 and type 2 diabetes and to gauge how well the condition is controlled. The A1c test result reflects the patient's average blood sugar level for the past two to three months. The higher the A1c level, the poorer the blood sugar control and the higher the patient's risk of diabetes complications. The goal for most diabetics is a level less than optometry check on 3/18/12, with no appointment at last chronic care follow up on 5/12/12), (poorly controlled diabetic, incorrectly characterized by provider as "fair" control, with no recent eye exam or tests for proteinuria); (no eye exam for last two years); (no treatment for proteinuria). 77.

I found many other cases where chronic care patients were very poorly managed, whether or not they were regularly seen by their provider. (critical lab studies for HIV delayed, and once done, not reviewed for weeks); (no prescription changes for patient with persistently very high blood pressure values); (on warfarin therapy, INR lab results were consistently reviewed 3-6 weeks after they were drawn.);8 (no chronic care appointment between 2/27/13 and 7/16/13, with INR levels dangerously out of range and abnormal A1c); (failure to prescribe anti-seizure medications; patient has frequent seizures as a result); (medications unchanged for patient with very high blood pressure; intervals too lengthy between visits). 78. ADC's monitoring reports document chronic care inmates often are not seen by the provider every three to six months, as specified in the inmate's treatment plan. 4/26/13 MGAR, ADC 088799 (Douglas inmate with hypertension was last seen in June 2012, was supposed to be seen in August 2012, but had not had a chronic care appointment as of 4/26/13. Douglas inmate with seizures was due to be seen in October 2012, but had not had a chronic care appointment as of 4/5/13. Douglas inmate with seizures was due to be seen in November 2012, but had not had a chronic care As noted above, I have attached as Appendix C my summary of my review of the medical charts for the patients discussed in my report. 8 Warfarin is used to prevent clot formation. It is a drug which is safe only within a very narrow range, and ineffective or very dangerous outside of that range. The degree of anticoagulation is measured by the INR test. Patients on warfarin must have their INR measured frequently, with warfarin dosage adjusted immediately, based on the results of the test. (appointment as of 4/5/13); 4/14/13 MGAR, ADC 088982 (Inmate arrived at Safford on 1/19/12 but he did not receive chronic care appointment for his asthma, hypertension, and Hepatitis C until more than a year later on 3/6/13), 4/19/13, ADC 089065 (At Winslow "multiple [chronic care] charts noted out of compliance in being seen by Provider (every three (3) to six (6) months) as specified in the inmate's treatment plan."); MGAR, ADC 137472-73 (At Eyman in August, 25 out of 50 charts reviewed showed that chronic care patients were not being seen by the provider every three to six months as specified in the inmate's treatment plan), MGAR, ADC 137527-28 (At Lewis in August, 53 out of 76 charts reviewed showed that chronic care patients were not being seen by the provider every three to six months as specified in the inmate's treatment plan); 9/30/13 MGAR, ADC 154059-60 (At Eyman, 24 out of 50 charts reviewed showed that chronic care inmates were not being seen by the provider every three to six months as specified in the inmate's treatment plan); 9/30/13 MGAR, ADC 154059-60 (At Eyman, inmate with previous chronic care appointment on 3/15/12, seen 7/22/13. Inmate with previous chronic care appointment on 2/2/12, seen 9/24/13. Inmate with previous chronic care appointment on 6/11/12, not seen as of 9/16/13); 9/25/13 MGAR, ADC 154152-54 (At

Lewis, 50 out of 71 charts reviewed showed that chronic care patients were not being seen by the provider every three to six months as specified in the inmate's treatment plan). c. Specialty Care 79.

In addition to primary care, some prisoners will require access to specialty providers. A sound prison medical care system must ensure that those prisoners are referred to a specialist on an urgent or routine basis, are timely seen, and then followed up by their provider so that any recommended treatment may be provided. ADC does not have an effective system for ensuring that prisoners receive specialty care when needed. Corizon Vice President Vickie Bybee and others documented this problem on May 10, in an email exchange indicating a backlog of almost 1000 specialty consult referrals that were more than three months old. "We continue to be made aware of consults not processed at the sites in loose filing, in medical records as we see patients." AGA_Review_00016658. 80. In my chart review, I discovered notable failures to refer prisoners for specialty services when they are clearly indicated. For example, , a diabetic, requires yearly eye exams to monitor for diabetic retinopathy, had not had an eye exam for two years. Mr. has HIV infection, and entered the prison with a low T-cell level and a high viral load of 221,310, but was not referred to an HIV specialist until July 2, 2013, five months after his admission to the prison system. Mr. , was diagnosed with a three inch mass in his throat on 5/9/13. When I reviewed his chart more than two months later, I found a CT scan and ultrasound showing the mass, but no diagnosis or referral to a specialist, despite the fact that the mass may be cancerous. 81. Patient charts demonstrate that when ADC prisoners are referred for specialty care, the appointments can be delayed or never occur. A urology consult was ordered for Mr. , 67676, on January 1, 2012, because he had symptoms of a urethral stricture, but the consult had not taken place by my July 2013 visit. , was referred for an ophthalmology consultation on March 5, 2013, and again on July 17, 2013, both for monitoring diabetic retinopathy and for surgical correction of the ectropion, an eye condition which poses a serious risk of infection. In his July 17, 2013 consultation request to Corizon, his provider noted: "left eye pronounced ectropion, irritation of eye, injected sclera . . . This is [a] case which has been delayed approximately 2 years." ADC 136680. Mr. with his failing pacemaker, had cardiology consult requests dating March 22, 2013 and April 29, 2013. ADC 136528. As of July 17, 2013 no consultation had been approved or provided. 82. , also suffered a delay in his specialty referral. injured his hand on August 13, 2012. Although medical staff saw him and advised that his hand was not broken, it remained extremely painful and swollen. An xray, taken four weeks after the injury on September 10, 2012, showed a boxer's fracture of the hand with distal angulation.

The x-ray report was not reviewed by the prison physician, Dr. Merchant until September 21, 2012, ten days later. Dr. Merchant made note of the fracture and requested an orthopedic consultation as soon as possible. Mr. was finally seen at an orthopedic consultation on November 14, 2012, three months after the injury. 83. As set forth above, Mr. endured a seven week delay when waiting for his urgent appointment with the ENT to treat his cancer, a six week wait for an urgent CT scan, and a 33 day wait for a "stat" oncology appointment. Mr. likewise suffered unconscionable delays in his care for cancer. He had complained for months of chest pain, but had received only Tums for indigestion. After several visits to the provider in May and June, 2013, he was sent to the hospital on 6/19/13 when he complained of chest pain and vomiting blood. Mr. told me he was diagnosed with small cell lung cancer. The hospital recommended a PET scan and oncology consult. Both were ordered on 6/27/13, ASAP. However, when I interviewed Mr. a month after his diagnosis, neither the PET scan nor the consult had happened. Small cell cancer is generally treated with chemotherapy, but Mr. had received only pain medication since his diagnosis. 84. When patients do have a consult report, the prison often fails to schedule the necessary follow-up appointment with the providers so that the patient may receive the care recommended by the specialist. For example, named plaintiff Mr. Hefner reported in his Declaration dated November 1, 2012 a long history of eye pain and vision problems, eye surgeries, and delays in his medical care.

Mr. Hefner had cataract surgery on June 13, 2013. He reported that following the surgery he developed flashing lights, floaters, and blurred vision. He submitted an HNR on June 19, 2013 complaining of pain in his eye and difficulty seeing. Mr. Hefner has iritis, an inflammation of the external eye, which causes pain and blurred vision. The ophthalmologist Dr. Heller ordered steroid eye drops and antibiotic eye drops. Mr. Hefner received the steroid eye drops, but not the antibiotic drops. The medical record supports his statement because it shows that the antibiotic order was not acted on until July 15, 2013, the day his attorney and I met with him. That day,

Mr. Hefner was still having difficulty seeing and was in pain. He has been unable to obtain follow-up care for his painful condition. I informed Dr. Winfred Williams, Corizon's regional medical director for Arizona, of my concerns regarding Mr. Hefner's medical problem. 85. Mr. suffered an acute heart attack on 3/27/13. Management of an acute heart attack requires maintenance of anti-platelet therapy. When I reviewed his file at Lewis, I noted that, in the intervening three and a half months, there was no evidence that Mr. has seen a provider during that period, or that he had had any follow-up cardiology consultations. There were also no MARs (medication administration records) for May or June, 2013. This failure to follow up with a patient after a major health event is shocking. 86. , a 47 year old man, was housed at ASPC-Winslow. Mr. suffered severe pain for more than six months before receiving adequate pain medication, and his cancer treatment was deliberately delayed more than four months. Mr. complained of back pain. He was scheduled for evaluation of this complaint on 1/23/13 but the appointment was cancelled because no practitioner was available. He was finally seen for his HNR on 2/21/13 by a nurse, and on 2/26/13 by a nurse practitioner. He failed to respond to treatment for his back pain. The x-ray of his lower spine taken on the 2/26/13 was not filed in the chart on 3/12/13 and the NP ordered another x-ray, which was taken six weeks later, on April 22, 2013. This film showed bony abnormalities consistent with cancer. Corizon denied requests by the Nurse Practitioner for an MRI scan. Mr. suffered increasing pain and lost the ability to Confidential PRSN-RLC 00031 Case 2:12-cv-00601-DJH Document 1104-1 Filed 09/08/14 Page 34 of 364 30 bear weight on his right leg. He could not walk without crutches. 87. The plain x-ray film of the bones taken 4/22/13 was strongly suggestive of cancer. On 5/23/13 CT scans of the Abdomen and Pelvis were ordered to definitively identify the source of the cancer and evaluate its spread. On June 10, 2013, Dr. Moyse noted in the medical record that "Request for CT of Abdomen and Pelvis was denied. Inmate needs to be seen …for follow-up." Finally, almost two months later, on 7/23/13, a CT scan of the Pelvis and hip was performed which showed that Mr. did have cancer, it had spread to both of his hips, and was so extensive that a fracture of his hip was impending. The CT scan of the abdomen was not performed at this time. 88.

A CT scan of the abdomen was performed six weeks later on 9/3/13. It showed that Mr. had cancer of the right kidney, with increasing metastatic bone involvement. It is frightening to read that Corizon denied the MRI scan ordered to determine the source of his cancer, and denied then delayed the critical CT scans for more than four months. During this period, Mr. 's cancer spread, the delay of treatment worsened his chance of effective treatment, and left him to suffer severe cancer pain without treatment. He did not see an oncologist until after August 30, 2013. He was never provided with radiation therapy although radiation therapy has been shown to be effective for relieving bone pain from metastatic kidney cancer. It was not until August 21, 2013, four months after the x-ray showed that he had probable metastatic bone involvement causing his pain, that Mr. was provided with appropriate pain medication. 89. Mr. 's mistreatment demonstrates multiple failures in the Arizona Department of Corrections medical program: delays in responding to an HNR, delays in care because of staff unavailability, disorganized medical records with delays in access to reports, intentional prolonged delays in diagnosis and treatment of cancer by the Corizon specialty care coordinator. These failures were accompanied by severe untreated cancer pain, and according to Corizon medical staff, a terminal prognosis.

A request to the Board of Executive Clemency for early release due to imminent death was submitted by Dr. David Robertson on September 30, 2013. Dr. Robertson noted that Mr. 's right kidney had been removed, and that he would "start chemotherapy in a few weeks." The decision by Corizon to deny the CT and deny the MRI requests when they were aware that Mr. had bone changes indicative of metastatic cancer is terrifying to this reviewer, and demonstrates the grave danger to prisoners who are forced to live under Corizon's medical control. 90. ADC's monitoring reports show that prisoners who are referred for specialty care on an urgent basis, meaning they are supposed to be seen within 30 days of the consult's initiation, are often not seen within that timeframe. 9/30/13 MGAR, ADC 154056 (At Eyman, only 1 out of 12 charts reviewed showed that urgent consultations were being seen within 30 days of the consultation being initiated); 9/25/13 MGAR, ADC 154151 ("There is no urologist available to see inmates with approximately 10-12 inmates with urology consults pending."); 7/12/13 MGAR, ADC 137343 (Reporting that an urgent request to receive an echocardiogram was submitted for Safford inmate on 5/6/13 and the echocardiogram was performed on 7/2/13); 7/30/13 MGAR, ADC 137187 (Inmate received an urgent request for a urology consultation on 7/1/13 which was not approved as of 7/29/13. An unknown inmate received an urgent request for a cardiology consultation on 6/13/13 which was not approved as of 7/29/13); 7/31/13 MGAR ADC 137270 (Listing a sample of 22 urgent consultations requested for Lewis inmates that had not been scheduled within 30 days of the consultation being initiated). 91. The monitoring reports also show that consultation reports often are not timely reviewed by providers for patients returning from specialty care. 9/25/13 MGAR, ADC 154150 (Reporting that only 11 out of 20 charts reviewed showed that consultation reports were being reviewed by the provider within 7 days of receipt); 4/14/13 MGAR, ADC 088981 (Reporting that an outside consultation for a Safford inmate was dated 2/27/13 but was not reviewed by a provider as of 4/11/13), 9/30/13 MGAR, 154056-57 (At Eyman, only 1 out of 12 charts reviewed showed that consultation reports were being reviewed by the provider within 7 days of receipt); 9/25/13 MGAR, ADC 154150 (At Lewis, only 11 out of 20 charts reviewed showed that consultation reports were being reviewed by the provider within 7 days of receipt) 6. Adequate Physical Space 92. Prison health care systems must allocate and equip sufficient space so that medical care can be delivered in a confidential and hygienic setting, and must either maintain sufficient medical beds on-site, or contract for medical beds for those patients requiring inpatient or infirmary level beds. a. Clinic Space 93.

The Eyman and Lewis prison complexes lack sufficient clinical space to provide constitutionally adequate medical care, given the number of prisoners housed at the prisons and the number of prisoners with chronic medical conditions who are at each prison. According to the most recent chronic care reports provided by Defendants, dated March 12, 2013, at Lewis, more than 20% of the total population had one or more chronic condition that needs regular monitoring: 1,187 chronic care patients out of a total population of 5,591.9 ADC 095002-095052. At Eyman, chronic care patients account for an even higher percentage of the prison population: 2,3 out of 5,235 total prisoners, or 41.5%. ADC 094844-094931. (These numbers also show that it is physically and mathematically impossible for timely and minimally adequate chronic care to be provided, given the number of clinicians allocated to the two facilities). 94. As detailed below, the prisons appears to be making minimal use of the limited clinical space. In functioning correctional health care systems, the yard medical clinics are the busiest section of the prison. Nurses and doctor are examining and The daily populations for Lewis and Eyman prison on March 12, 2013 are available on ADC's website at http://www.azcorrections.gov/adc/PDF/count/03122013%20count%20sheet.pdf treating patients; prisoners are lined up inside and outside the clinics awaiting care. Correctional officers would be stationed outside and inside the clinics, escorting prisoners to and from appointments as needed, or providing supervision of the patients waiting at the clinics. Similarly, prison infirmaries, inpatient hospitals, and health care units should be busy places with medical staff on rounds, delivering medications and providing care and assistance with activities of daily living to the infirm and sick. 95.

This was not the case at the two prisons I inspected: the unit clinics were eerily quiet shuttered and dark offices, medical equipment was nonfunctional or covered in dust, and there was no indication that any medical care was being delivered. Indeed, some clinics had the air of a Potemkin village, with clinics and equipment on display, but curiously, neither clinical staff nor patients. This observation has been similarly highlighted in Defendants' monitoring reports. See Eyman, August 2013, ADC 137465 ("it appeared that Meadows, Cook, and Rynning were not conducting NL five days a week.") Lewis, June 2013, ADC 117986 ("A true sick call is not occurring as defined in contract 5 days a week, Monday through Friday on all Lewis units"); Lewis, July 2013, ADC 137268 ("There is no dedicated nursing sick call line being offered on any unit."); 6/24/13 MGAR, ADC 117911 ("[At Douglas] [a]ccording to the FHA, due to the cutback of staff, primarily nurses and med techs, she has had to curtail daily nurse lines at both Mohave and Gila Units to 3 days only.") 96. On the first day of the Lewis tour, I began by inspecting the main medical facility referred to as "the hub," which contains an infirmary-like facility of 11 beds, dental space, and medical space. We were shown the offices designated for the medical providers, none of which had people in them – they were all dark and locked. We walked by the four holding cells for the prisoners awaiting medical care, they were concrete rooms that could probably hold 15-20 prisoners. They were all completely vacant. Similarly, outside the hub were five or six holding cells; each looked like they could seat about 15 or 20 people. There were not any prisoners outside the hub waiting for medical care. 97. The medical hub does not have any negative pressure rooms, which are used to house patients suspected to have tuberculosis or other communicable diseases. Effective isolation of persons with suspected pulmonary tuberculosis, measles, or chickenpox requires that they are placed in airborne infection isolation room. This must be a private room with negative air pressure and a minimum of 6 to 12 air changes per hour. Doors to the isolation room must remain closed, and all persons entering must wear a respirator with a filtering capacity of 95% that allows a tight fit over the nose and mouth.10 Even if a person with suspect tuberculosis is to be transferred to a hospital for treatment, while they are waiting to be transferred they must be housed in a negative pressure room. I later learned that no ADC prison facility has negative pressure rooms. Def's Resp. to Pltf Verduzco's First RFA's, # 179. 98. The Facility Health Administrator ("FHA") showed us two small rooms in the hub that used to be holding cells, but had been converted to private exam rooms.

They were locked, dark, and empty. We went into one of these exam rooms and found that it had no exam tables or any other medical equipment in it, just a cabinet, a book shelf, and a sink. 99. In the maximum security Rast unit, we found the suite of medical offices empty, with all the offices dark and locked. The FHA said that the clinic was closed that day because there were no medical staff. He said, "this was designed to be a free standing full capability medical unit but we only use one exam room." When I asked him why this was the case, the attorney for ADC told him not to answer the question.

General Principles of Infection Control, in UpToDate.com, accessed 11/2/13. UpToDate is an evidence-based, peer-reviewed online medical textbook, written and edited by leading medical experts, which is constantly updated. It is the standard textbook of medicine in the United States today. I requested that they unlock the rooms. The FHA opened up a series of empty rooms he said were exam rooms, but there was no furniture or fixtures other than sinks and empty shelving units. There was an X-ray room, but no X-ray machine in it. The FHA stated that no X-rays were done. We finally got to the one exam room that is in use and had an exam table. There was no paper on the exam table, and there was no soap in the soap dispensers. 101. The medical area in Lewis's Barchey unit only had two offices, and one exam room. The exam table did not have paper on it, and when I asked the nurse on duty and the Director of Nursing where the paper was stored, counsel for Defendants told me I was "browbeating" the witness and threatened to terminate the tour if I asked a single other question of any other line staff. Counsel for Defendants told the Director of Nursing to not answer the question about where the paper is stored.

It is very unsanitary for a health care clinic to not have paper on the exam tables that can be changed after each patient is examined. 102. On July 17-18, 2013, I toured the ASPC-Eyman prison. Unlike Lewis prison, Eyman does not have a central medical hub for the entire complex; each unit has medical space within it. I also inspected living units, interviewed prisoners, and reviewed medical charts. As in Lewis, there was little or no medical care being provided.11 103. In the SMU-1 unit's medical area, we found a small exam room, which had an exam table set up with paper, an ophthalmoscope, and the blood pressure machine was on another wall, with no cuff attached. There was an x-ray viewer, and a sink. A larger exam room was locked, dark and not in use. In this larger room, there wasagurney, but Prisoners in the isolation units have their recreation on small concrete areas adjacent to the cell areas at Eyman complex.

I asked to see the recreation area off the section of the 1-Delta pod where Named Plaintiff Smith was housed. It was about by feet, with feet high walls and a grate overhead obstructing the view of the ky. bout feet he ground over the door, a swastika and the Nazi slogan "Sieg Heil" was painted on the wall in large letters. It looked like it had been there for quite a while and had been painted there – it was worn no ophthalmoscope or blood pressure machine. There was a sink, and a door to the X-ray room. 104. Medical staff told me that the X-ray technician was on site daily, so I asked to go into the X-ray room that was off the exam room. The room was locked, dark, hot and stuffy. The x-ray machine was a very old model. The x-ray table and controls were covered with a thick layer of dust, as was the lead vest that was hanging on the wall. I found a notice on the machine that said it was last inspected on January 2001. Jim Taylor, a Corizon regional vice president, said that the room was not used and prisoners who need X-rays are transported to the Browning Unit. 105. There was a door that said "Darkroom" that was inside the X-ray room. It was a closet approximately feet by feet. To the left against the wall were at least 7 or 8 bankers' boxes stacked up, with stacks of HNRs and other medical documents. To the right were shelves cluttered with half-opened boxes of the various equipment used for blood draws. [See Photograph 1] 106. On the ground to the right, in front of the shelves were two or three fivegallon jugs half-full of brownish liquid. The opposite wall from the door had a crudely cut-out doorway/crawl space to the adjacent office; it was approximately foot high. To the right of the crawl space, was a giant barrel approximately feet high and feet diameter, filled almost to the top with pipettes, blood bags, etc.

The barrel was Photograph of inmate who has had two strokes, and is disabled. He is unable to transfer independently from bed to wheelchair, and from wheelchair to toilet. He had been transferred in and out of L-11, where I interviewed him, and other sites at least five times in the two months prior to my visit. Each time he is sent back to L-11 because he requires nursing support for all activities, secondary to his left-sided paralysis. Because of the stroke, and inability to transfer, he is completely dependent on nursing staff. However, other medical staff at L- 11 treat him as if he is lying, and can transfer, and do not provide him with the basic toileting services he needs. This results in Mr. sitting for prolonged periods in his own urine and feces. Mr. states that he has disciplinary write-ups for failure to put on his underpants, something he is physically unable to do because of his strokes. According to Mr. his transfers to other living units at Lewis, including isolation cells, over the previous six weeks were all related to new prisoners requiring infirmary beds at L- 11. 114. In the same unit, I also interviewed.

Mr. has a painful chronic skin condition called ectodermal dysplasia. Ectodermal dysplasia is a life-threatening condition characterized by a lack of sweat glands. Persons with this genetic disorder are at great risk from overheating and heat intolerance because they cannot sweat and get rid of excess heat. It is an understatement to say Arizona experiences excessive heat. Mr. told me he spent one year in lockdown as punishment for seeking medical treatment. Because his body cannot easily get rid of excess heat, it is vital that Mr. live in a climate controlled environment, such as L- 11, without exposure to high temperatures. Mr. was recently transferred out of L- 11 to Buckley, and then transferred back. The reason he was transferred out was because there was a patient who was being transferred out of a hospital, and no infirmary level beds were available. This is one of multiple examples I have found of a patient being transferred in and out of L-11 because of the shortage of skilled nursing beds or sheltered housing in the Arizona system. At Eyman, I reviewed the case of Mr. who was housed in the general population despite his obvious need for nursing care that was unavailable in that setting. Mr. is a 75-year-old man with multiple serious medical problems, including incontinence of bowel and bladder, diabetes mellitus, coronary artery disease, hypertension, and ADA/mobility issues. His medical conditions required a higher level of nursing care than is available at Eyman, but despite pleas from Dr. Rumsey, the medical director, and the nursing staff, he had not been transferred to a facility with appropriate clinical support. Instead, during the period from June 6, 2013 through July 14, 2013 he was hospitalized six times.

Each time he was sent to the hospital because his complex medical problems required more intensive nursing care than was available at Eyman/Meadows, and each time the hospital sent him back because he required skilled nursing care, not hospitalization. ADC 136687-696. The last note in the medical record when I reviewed it was dated 7/16/13: "Security notified staff that I/M was on his way back to Meadows unit from MVH [Mountain Valley Hospital]. MVH notified that Dr. Rumsey had given a written order the day he was sent out that the inmate was not appropriate to return to this yard due to non-compliance and in need of a higher level of care. Deborah from MVH ok'd for inmate to return to the hospital. Security notified. DON Bito'nn said he is taking care of finding a bed for inmate. Nursing supervisor Meyers notified of the above. /s Shahi, CPN." ADC 136696.

Access to Medication

116. Prisoners must be able to receive necessary medications for their serious medical needs. Defendants' practice and unwritten policy of failing to supervise, manage and support medication distribution has created a system that has been, and currently is, profoundly dysfunctional resulting in serious risk of harm to patients throughout the state. a. Medication Delivery 117. I observed a dangerous medication distribution practice at a unit in Eyman prison complex. Medications are removed from blister packs in the medical area and placed in labeled small cups with prisoners' names written on a separate lid. These cups are then taken to a distribution site in the yard, or to cells of inmates in segregation. There is no way for prisoners to identify if they are receiving the right medications, nor can the nurse assure him/herself that they are dispensing the correct

medication to the correct patient. Because generic forms of same medication can come in different shapes, sizes, and colors, it is never safe to "pre-pour" medications from a labeled container outside of the patient's presence. 118.

An ADC pharmacy monitor discovered at Lewis "2 large trash bags full of medication being returned to PharmaCorr with both expired and adulterated medication cards …. The adulterated patient specific cards… are missing the original Pharmacy label and are being utilized for other patients." AGA_Review_00017096. This utter disregard for accepted medication distribution practices is shocking. 119. ADC also has a dangerous medication distribution practice of having custody officers deliver "Keep on Person," or "KOP" medications, to prisoners. 9/13 MGAR ADC 154168 (at Lewis, KOP delivered by security staff). Corizon staff confirmed during my tours, and in subsequent depositions, that this is still the delivery practice. Gross Dep. 63:22-64:1; Mielke-Fontaine Dep. 278:15 (at Florence). This practice is problematic: custodial officers are not trained health care staff and giving them access to and knowledge of prisoners' prescriptions violates health privacy law and creates an opportunity for that information to be used improperly. 120. ADC has a legacy of dangerous medication distribution practices. Last year at Lewis, more than 100 prisoners were exposed to Hepatitis C after a subcontracted nurse reused a syringe in a vial of insulin. September 21, 2012 letter from Joe Profiri to Karen Mullenix re: Written Cure Notification ADC 027855-856. 121.

Named plaintiff Mr. Polson also told me about medication delivery problems. When I saw him at Lewis in July, 2013, he informed me that he has mania, is Confidential PRSN-RLC 00043 Case 2:12-cv-00601-DJH Document 1104-1 Filed 09/08/14 Page 46 of 364 42 supposed to receive lithium, but frequently is not provided with his medication due to staff shortages. In fact, he had not been given his lithium that morning, and he was acting manic during the interview. Mr. Polson reported in his Declaration dated November 1, 2012 that beginning in 2009 his lithium levels were not regularly checked. My review of his MARs demonstrated that he did not receive eight doses of lithium in April, 2013, and did not receive six doses of this medication in June, 2013. His lithium level was measured on June 13, 2013 and was low, at 0.3 meq/liter. The goal of treatment with lithium is to achieve a serum level of 0.8 to 1.2 meq/liter. No dosage adjustment was made in response to this non-therapeutic serum level.

The low level is likely due to the missed doses, as Mr. Polson suggests. In a patient with known mania, on lithium treatment, inadequate dosage of prescribed lithium can precipitate a manic state. At the time I reviewed his file in mid-July, 2013, Mr. Polson has not seen a psychiatrist since December 2012, a delay of more than seven months. 122. While at Rast unit in Lewis complex, I spoke with named plaintiff Stephen Swartz, who reported that due to a shortage of security staff to escort the pill nurses, the insulin delivery has been late and the diabetic prisoners are having problems getting their shots and food on time. He said the morning pill run can occur anytime between 2 am and 8 am. 123. ADC's recent monitoring reports document widespread and continuing delays in delivering medication to patients. 9/30/13 MGAR, ADC 154085 (Noting that an Eyman inmate's Cymbalta was ordered on 7/29/13 but inmate did not receive the medication until 9/13/13); 9/25/13 MGAR, ADC 154171-73 (At Lewis, 43 out of 70 charts reviewed showed unreasonable delays in inmates receiving prescribed medications); 4/26/13 MGAR, ADC 088809 (Noting delays in inmates receiving keep on person medications at Douglas); 7/30/13 MGAR, ADC 137220 (Giving Eyman a "red" designation for unreasonable delays in inmates receiving prescribed medications); 7/24/13 MGAR, ADC 137207-08 ("Several issues are of concern with this. They include no response from existing D.O.N. on multiple medication issues that have been printed and sent from the online PharmaCorr/Corizon Patient profile. The patient continuity of care may be jeopardized.") 4/18/13 MGAR, AD C088908 (Reporting that, according to staff, medications that arrive at Lewis from the PharmaCorr12 facility on Friday are not delivered to inmates until Tuesday); 4/29/13 MGAR, ADC 088841 (Reporting that none of the non-formulary medication requests found at Eyman were returned within 24 to 48 hours). b. Medication Continuity 124. A sound prison health care system must have processes in place to ensure that prescriptions are timely renewed and refilled.

ADC lacks an effective system to accomplish this. 125. In Rast unit, I spoke to several prisoners, chosen at random, at cellfront. Every single prisoner I spoke to reported gaps of up to six weeks in getting refills of chronic care and psychotropic medication. 126. Medication lapses are a problem for all patients, but can be particularly dangerous for patients with conditions like HIV, where lapses can cause the patient to develop drug-resistance. for example, has HIV infection and requires daily anti-viral medications. His anti-viral therapy (Atripla) lapsed repeatedly during the first half of 2013. Predictably, the forced interruptions in his HIV therapy caused by failure to renew his medications resulted in the deterioration of his clinical condition. His viral load, the main measure of therapeutic success in HIV treatment, had been undetectable.

1. I have reviewed the Confidential Expert Report of Lawrence H. Mendel, D.O., and submit the following Rebuttal Report.

2. The overall message Dr. Mendel presents is that, while Arizona Department of Corrections had problems with health care delivery in the past, Corizon has "fundamentally changed" health care in the Arizona prisons, and "many of the issues raised in the original case have been addressed…." Mendel, 8. According to him, Corizon has transformed the health care delivery system so that the ADC is now operating "within the standard of care for correctional systems." Id. at 49.

3. As a preliminary matter, I am not familiar with the concept of a "standard of care for correctional systems." The duty of a physician is to deliver care to patients consistent with the community standard of care. It appears Dr. Mendel may believe a lesser standard of care applies when a patient is incarcerated. If that is his position, then I strongly disagree. If Dr. Mendel's point is that ADC is delivering health care consistent with the community standard, I also disagree. The delivery system that I observed, and the medical records that I have reviewed, provide no support for such an opinion. The death records for prisoners who died in mid-2012 (the latest date for which I was provided death records) vividly illustrate a deeply entrenched pattern of neglectful and harmful medical care resulting from widespread systemic deficiencies. The medical records I reviewed in July and thereafter, selected at random from lists of prisoners with medical care concerns, showed that prisoners continue to suffer because of unconscionable delays and neglect. This impression was amply supported by my observations while visiting prisons and talking to prisoners, and by my review of deposition transcripts and numerous other documents and records, including defendants' own system audits.

4. That the health care system has not fundamentally changed was made starkly apparent this month, when ADC and Corizon admitted that a Corizon nurse failed to follow standard injection protocols and may have exposed 24 prisoners at ASP-Lewis The nurse administering the insulin pricked the patients' fingers to check their blood sugar and then used the same needle to draw insulin from a multi-use vial, thereby potentially contaminating the insulin provided to other patients. PLTF – PARSONS 031300. Remarkably, as I set forth in my initial report, there was a very similar exposure incident less than 18 months ago at this same prison, where more than 100 prisoners were also possibly exposed to hepatitis B and C due to faulty nurse practices under Wexford, the previous health care contractor. Unfortunately, this type of mistake is predictable, and even to be expected, in a system that is as understaffed and poorly managed as the Arizona Department of Corrections.

5. In my report, I documented numerous examples of failed care illustrating systemic deficiencies that expose ADC prisoners to harm and to risk of harm. Dr. Mendel charges that my report made no effort "to address whether the alleged deficiencies occurred during the period when treatment was provided by ADC, by Wexford, or by Corizon." Mendel, 48. I can only conclude that Dr. Mendel failed to read my report before responding to it. Had Dr. Mendel read my report, he would have observed that, with the exception of the death cases, virtually every patient I described in my report, and in appendix C to my report, suffered from poor care under Corizon, either exclusively, or because Corizon failed to remedy or continued to provide the poor care begun under ADC and Wexford.

6. whose poor medical care I discuss at pages 5-8 of my report, is one of the many prisoners I discussed who has received poor care at ADC, including from Corizon. To recap, was diagnosed with cancer in November, 2012, but defendants did not schedule any follow-up care for for three and a half months, and his cancer was left untreated. Because of badly swollen lymph nodes, he requested to see a doctor by an HNR dated March 3, 2013. A physician's assistant requested that Corizon approve an urgent ENT consultation. Despite the presence of an untreated dangerous cancer, Corizon did not allow to see an ENT surgeon. The ENT surgeon requested a CT SCAN and an emergency consultation with an oncologist; these requests were directed to Corizon. The CT scan

was not performed until July 2, 2013, 4 months after complained by HNR of swollen lymph nodes. The CT SCAN, when finally done, showed a cancer of the upper throat. On Corizon's watch there were further delays in reviewing CT report, and scheduling an appointment with an oncologist. As of July 17, 2013, on Corizon's watch, had still not received any treatment for his cancer. Corizon ignored and failed to treat cancer for more than 4 months. Had Dr. Mendel reviewed my discussion of case, it is inconceivable he would have opined that I made no effort to address whether the atrocious care was provided by Corizon.

7. Dr. Mendel also asserts I made no effort to identify the causes of the "alleged deficiencies." I did - - Corizon is incapable of recognizing and responding to serious medical problems. Cohen, 8. Finally, Dr. Mendel questions whether I have opined that "purported example[ ] of improper care" was the result of "an unfortunate outcome, a simple mistake, provider negligence, or a systemic problem." Mendel, 48. It is clear that poor care is the result of an uncaring system of medical care, indifferent to a life-threatening cancer. I said so in my report: care "is a horrifying example of a failed system that places every seriously ill man and woman it serves at extreme risk." Cohen,

8. That system is now being run by Corizon.

In my initial report, I described the methodology I used to develop my opinions on the adequacy of the ADC health care delivery system. This process included two-day visits to two of ADC's largest facilities, as well as the review of numerous documents, including deposition testimony for ADC, Wexford and Corizon staff; documents produced to plaintiffs by ADC, including ADC's monthly contract monitoring reports, medical records and death reviews for patients who died, medical records for several named plaintiffs, and a randomly selected sample of medical records at the prisons that I visited. I selected the largest number of randomly selected medical records to review on site that was consistent with the time allowed by defendants for the site visit.

9. Dr. Mendel contends that, because the sample sizes at the two prisons I visited were limited, that no valid conclusions about gross systemic deficiencies could be drawn. Dr. Mendel mischaracterizes my report. As indicated above, the chart reviews were one factor that informed my opinions of the overall care. The charts I reviewed, randomly chosen from a sample of prisoners with emergency or chronic medical problems, amply demonstrated a level of dysfunction consistent with my observations while at ASPC-Eyman and ASPC-Lewis, my review of the ADC's own contract monitoring reports and other ADC data, and the ADC deposition testimony. Further, my opinions in this action draw upon my lengthy career in correctional health care, including as the Director of Rikers Island Health Services and as a medical expert in prison conditions cases over the past three decades, and on my review of medical literature.[1]

10. Based upon all of these factors, I state with a high degree of confidence that the ADC health care delivery system is fundamentally broken and among the worst prison health care systems I have seen.

11. My opinion is based upon conditions, documents and records that have existed in the ADC for years and, according to the ADC monitoring reports and other ADC data, continued to exist through the end of September, 2013, which was the latest date for which I received information and records. Dr. Mendel seems to claim that, since September, Corizon has reversed course, and is now providing adequate care. Given the level of disarray I observed in records, documents, deposition transcripts and at the 1 A complete list of the documents that I reviewed for purposes of preparing this rebuttal report is attached as Appendix A. 2 I have learned that defendants recently provided to plaintiffs additional documents that Dr. Mendel relied upon for his expert opinion, in addition to the medical records for prisoners who have died since March 4, 2013. After reviewing them, I may include a discussion of those documents in my supplemental report. Facilities that I visited, and the ADC's recent press release describing the possible exposure of 24 prisoners to hepatitis B and C, I find Dr. Mendel's assertion that the ADC and Corizon have "reached a point where an inmate in ADC custody can expect timely access to appropriate care" (Mendel, 49) to be wholly implausible. RESPONSE TO DR. MENDEL'S OPINIONS Care for Named Plaintiffs

12. During my visits to Eyman and Lewis, I found numerous examples of significantly delayed care that subjected prisoners to harm and risk of harm. My report documents over three dozen recent cases in which

patients should have been seen for acute care, chronic care, and/or specialty care, but did not receive timely care. Many suffered harm as a result and, sadly, I have learned that three of those patients have died since I reviewed their files. (.) Dr. Mendel does not dispute my analysis of these cases except with regards to NPs Swartz, Polson and Hefner.

13. I interviewed named plaintiff Mr. Swartz on July 15, 2013, and reviewed his medical record. Mr. Swartz submitted a health needs request (HNR) on January 13, 2013 requesting evaluation of an enlarging mass on his waist. My review of his medical record confirmed that Mr. Swartz waited five months to have this mass evaluated by a physician. Dr. Mendel's review of Mr. Swartz's medical records re-confirms that this long delay did occur, and further notes that the enlarging mass required surgical removal, which occurred on September 5, 2013.

14. Although Dr. Mendel states that there were no complaints regarding pain in 2013, review of the Mr. Swartz's medical record shows that he did complain of significant facial pain secondary to a 2010 traumatic event. The chart also shows that Mr. Swartz complained about this pain to Dr. Merchant on June 26, 2013. The record indicates that Dr. Merchant was aware of this pain, and ordered pain medication, tramadol, for this chronic pain. Dr. Merchant wrote that control of the chronic facial pain might require prescription of a higher dose of pain medication. This medication had been prescribed previously, but the prescription had run out on April 23, 2013 and had not been renewed. ADC 122468

15. I interviewed named plaintiff Mr. Polson and reviewed his medical record. Mr. Polson reported to me on July 15, 2013 that he frequently was not provided with his ordered lithium carbonate, the medical treatment for his manic psychosis ordered by a psychiatrist. I reviewed his medical record and confirmed that during the three month period April through June, 2013, he had not received 42 out of 182 doses of his medication to prevent recurrence of mania. ADC 122345-122348. His lithium level was checked on June 13, 2013 and was found to be low, 0.3 meq/liter, well below the desired serum level of between .8meq/liter to 1.2 meq/liter. ADC 122344. The purpose of obtaining serum lithium levels is to assure that dosage is adequate, and not toxic. Despite this low level, no adjustment of his lithium dose was made, and no investigation of the cause of the low serum level was carried out. Inadequate doses of lithium carbonate, as reflected by serum level, are less likely to prevent recurrent episodes of mania. Mr. Polson was seen by a psychiatrist on May 13, 2013, who renewed the lithium prescription. However Mr. Polson received no lithium from May 7 through May 20, 2013.3 16. Mr. Polson also complained of chronic ear pain and delays in accessing ordered referrals to outside specialists. Dr. Mendel stated that "none of these claims have been substantiated in the expert reports." Mendel

16. In fact, medical staff from Eyman submitted a referral for Mr. Polson to see an otolaryngologist on June 28, 2011. The purpose of the consultation was to "Please evaluate (R) Hearing Loss, (B) Chronic Ear Pain (no current signs of infection), (and) Deviated Nasal Septum." The consult was finally approved, almost nine months later, on March 19, 2012. The approved consult 3 In my Report, I incorrectly stated that Mr. Polson had not seen a psychiatrist since December, 2012. Cohen, 42. never took place. A copy of the approved consult has a line through it with a handwritten notation marked "No Show." There is no indication on the consult form nor in the medical record of the reason why Mr. Polson was not brought to the appointment. ADC_M000195

17. Named plaintiff Hefner had surgery for removal of a cataract on June 13, 2013. Complications of cataract surgery are rare, but do occur. These complications include bacterial infection. Standard post-operative care includes examination by an ophthalmologist 1 day, seven days, and four weeks postoperatively.4 Mr. Hefner developed disturbing symptoms several days later, including eye pain, flashing lights, and difficulty seeing and submitted an HNR on June 19, 2013. The ophthalmologist ordered steroid eye drops and antibiotic eye drops. The steroid eye drops were provided, but the prescribed antibiotic eye drops, ordered by the ophthalmologist, were not. Mr. Heffner did not receive the ordered antibiotic treatment given until July 15, 2013, four weeks later, the day I interviewed him. I did notify Dr. Winifred Williams, Corizon's regional medical director for Arizona, of my concern that Mr. Hefner was not receiving appropriate post-operative care. Clinic Space 18. The clinic space at Eyman and Lewis prison complexes that I observed was insufficient for the number of prisoners served those prisons, and much of the space that

was allocated appeared to be deserted and little used. At both complexes, I found that many of the clinical exam rooms were "locked, dark and empty." Cohen, 34, 37. 19. Dr. Mendel claims that he was shown the dark and empty rooms that I observed at Lewis, and that he was advised they were located in a unit that is not used because prisoners from that unit receive the majority of their care at "the hub." Mendel, 4 Up-to-date, Cataracts in Adults, referenced January 26, 2014; http://www.uptodate.com/contents/cataract-inadults?source=search_result&search=cataracts+in+adults&selectedTitle=1~150 He further claims that he "was told Dr. Cohen was informed of this information during his tour." Id. Dr. Mendel does not identify who provided him with this false information. While at Lewis, I visited the medical clinics at Rast and Barchey Units. I was advised by staff that all of the unit clinics were identical, and that they were used daily. While in Rast unit, I was told the clinic was not in use at the time of our visit because the pill nurse had to leave the clinic to provide named plaintiff Polson his psychiatric medications, based on our insistence that he receive them. 20. No one ever told me that the clinics were not in use because patients received care at the hub. On the contrary, both FHA Cameron Lewis and Dr. Williams advised me that the Lewis hub clinic was used only for specialty and emergency care, and all sick call and chronic care occurs in the unit clinics. Indeed, this arrangement is consistent with Dr. Mendel's description of the how the clinics are generally set up: In most cases, medical encounters occur on the prison unit where the inmate is assigned. ADC facilities generally consist of multiple units. Most of these units are surrounded by a separate secure perimeter and many have a specific program focus or security level. The provision of care at the prison unit decreases the need to move inmates and reduces the dependency of providers on the custody staff. Mendel, 9. Grievances 21. Dr. Mendel's report includes a section on his grievance review. Defendants did not produce the appeals that Dr. Mendel reviewed until January 30, 2014, making it impossible for me to review them in time to provide informed comment on his findings. However, I disagree with his implied assertion that grievances are a reliable indicator of the strength or weakness of a prison health care system. Grievances can, and should be, a component of quality assurance review. In a functioning health care system, grievances provide a mechanism for identifying individual health care needs which are not being adequately addressed, as well as identifying systemic problems. However, in July 2013, prisoners in the prisons of Arizona consistently informed me that they were aware that the situation regarding health care services was extremely chaotic. Their descriptions of the magnitude of failures to provide them minimal access to nursing sick call, access to physicians, access to specialists, and access to medications was consistent with the findings in the monthly reports filed by Arizona Department of Correction Monitors in their monthly reports. See, e.g., ADC 137185, 137201, 137268, 137465-66, 154050-51, 154148 (delays for nurse triage); ADC 88799, 088982, 137527-28, 154059-60; 154152- 54 (delays for chronic care); ADC 088893, 089063, 137403 (delays for sick call); ADC 154056, 154151, 137343, 137270 (delays for specialty care). Prisoner observations were also consistent with the Wexford presentation to the AZ Department of Corrections on November 7, 2012.

That Power Point presentation also described the systemic failure of the Arizona correctional health care program to provide basic services to prisoners. 22. In my opinion, the relatively low number of appeals, as reported by Dr. Mendel, more likely reflects the prisoners' understanding that the Arizona Department of Correction did not have the capacity to respond the their medical needs. Prisoners described to me that their HNRs would be returned with notations saying that their request for care has been noted, and that they were "scheduled to be scheduled" to be seen. They further reported that these appointments, when they did happen, were long delayed. 23. Dr. Mendel provides an analysis of grievances at only two institutions. The fact that the most serious grievances regarding necessary specialty consultations had been resolved at the time of his review reveals nothing about the significance of the grievance, the actual delay in access to services suffered by the prisoners, and the medical consequences of the delay. Staffing 24. The staffing data Dr. Mendel relies on for October, 2013, which had not been available to me when I prepared my report, shows that the vacancy rates for Medical Case 2:12-cv-00601-DJH Document 1104-1 Filed 09/08/14 Page 145 of 364 10 Directors (must be filled by a physician) and staff physicians have risen sharply since Corizon's takeover. According to ADC's data, in March, 2013, Corizon had a 22% vacancy rate for Medical Directors, and a 20% vacancy rate for staff physicians.

AGA_Review_00019436.5 As of October, 2013, the vacancy rates for these two positions were considerably worse, 52% and 39% respectively. ADC 203041. At that point, the ADC had fewer than 11 full time physicians working at the ten state prisons, a ratio of 1 physician for every 3000+ state prisoners. Moreover, two of the full time physicians working in the prisons are Medical Directors in the larger prisons, and thus are unlikely to have significant clinical duties, which brings the ratio closer to 1 physician for every 3800 prisoners as a practical matter. 25. As of October, 2013 at the five larger prisons (all with prisoner populations greater than 4000), each had a combined vacancy rate of 50% or more for their physician positions, and Florence, with two staff physician and a medical director position, had just .8 of a physician, a 73% vacancy rate. This physician shortage at the larger prisons is particularly problematic because prisons of this size should have a Medical Director with few, if any, clinical duties. 26. According to Dr. Mendel, Corizon has directed "considerable efforts" to recruit providers, with "visible" results. Mendel, 20. In fact, Corizon's recruitment efforts for physician providers have obviously failed spectacularly. 27. Corizon's recruitment for Nurse Practitioner positions has had some success, as the vacancy rate has fallen from 51% in March, 2013, to 9% in October, 2013. That Corizon has filled some of the NP positions does not change my opinion that the ADC lacks sufficient staff to provide care to the 34,000 ADC state prisoners. While NPs are valuable members of a health care team, their scope of practice is more limited than the scope of a physician's practice, and thus, they cannot be substituted for physicians on 5 Had Corizon not reduced the number of staff physician positions that month, the vacancy rate would have been at 45%. (AGA Review_00006402.) a system-wide basis. 28. According to the latest data provided us by Dr. Mendel, there are approximately 45 mid and upper level medical providers working at ADOC facilities (including PRN and registry providers), with a population of 34,073.6 California, with approximately three times the population of prisoners, had 386 medical providers for 123,334 prisoners in August 2014.7 California has over twice the medical staffing ratio as Arizona. Dr. Mendel, appropriately, does not identify a national standard for medical staffing. The current staffing, in my opinion, is not adequate for the size and medical acuity of the prisoner population in Arizona. 29. In addition to recruitment of nurse practitioners, according to Dr. Mendel, Corizon addresses provider and nursing vacancies by contracting with temporary agencies. Mendel, 21. He claims that, during an eight month period, Corizon hired temporary physicians to provide over 4,000 hours of care, or approximately 500 hours per month. This works out to approximately 45 hours per month for each of the 11 state prisons, or one week's coverage. Clearly, this is grossly insufficient to address a systemwide 40-50% vacancy rate for physicians. 30. Moreover, reliance on temporary physicians is not an acceptable or sustainable strategy for covering ADC's long-term and intractable vacancies. Although there is no difference in the kind of medical care that prisoners need from that in the general populations, correctional health systems pose significant barriers to the delivery of minimally necessary care. Physicians who have not worked at the Arizona Department of Corrections need to be trained in the complexities of delivering care in a complex system which is not organized around patient need, but in which there are 6 http://www.azcorrections.gov/adc/reports/capacity/bed_2013/bed_capacity_oct13.pdf. PLTF-PARSONS 031601. 7 http://www.cphcs.ca.gov/docs/special/Public-Dashboard-2013-08.pdf accessed 01/26/14 multiple, and constantly changing barriers to patient access, and to delivery of prescribed treatments. Physicians who have not worked in prisons are often understandably anxious, and overly dependent on correctional staff. They do not know what is allowed and what is forbidden, and thus may allow their clinical decisions to be guided by custody concerns rather than the community standard of care. 31. Additionally, the use of large numbers of temporary physician staff has a significant deleterious effect on the health care of prisoners at the ADC. Effective health care systems are built around providers who monitor their patients on a consistent basis and develop relationships with those who need regular care. This is especially true in the correctional setting for patients with chronic medical conditions. Chronic care of complex medical conditions cannot be effectively provided without continuity of provider, particularly in systems such as the ADC, where medical records are often poorly kept and chaotic. In my experience, having temporary medical staff rotate through clinical positions creates a much greater risk that patients will receive inadequate health care, particularly for their chronic health conditions. Continuity of physician care for patients with chronic illness is associated with decreased hospitalizations and emergency department visits, and improved receipt of preventive services.8 Access to Care/Wait times 32. As Dr. Mendel states, "[a]ccess to care is a quintessential element of correctional healthcare," and lengthy wait times for health care are not acceptable on a long term basis. Mendel, 9-10. Relying on data that was not previously provided to me, he claims that the "statewide provider wait time" has fallen significantly. Id., 10 33. In my opinion, Dr. Mendel's discussion of wait times is based on incomplete data, his analysis of that data is flawed, and his conclusion that wait times 8Cabana MD, Jee SH., Does continuity of care improve patient outcomes?, J Fam Pract. 2004 December;53(12):974-9, PLTF-PARSONS-031892 have fallen statewide is unreliable. The analysis must be based upon several months of data, for each facility, with information provided regarding the numbers of each type of clinical encounter performed. Data must be presented for length of time from request to visit for HNR nurse visits, and for the length of time from request to provider encounter for nurse initiated physician visits. Dr. Mendel does not provide the data required to justify his conclusion.

CONCLUSION

34. Nothing in Dr. Mendel's report changes my opinion that the ADC health care delivery system is fundamentally broken, and that prisoners are at serious risk of harm because the system as a whole is not equipped to provide them with necessary care for their serious medical needs.

CONFIDENTIAL REBUTTAL REPORT OF TODD RANDALL WILCOX

I have reviewed the report of Dr. Lawrence H. Mendel submitted in this case. I believe many of the facts underlying his opinion are unexplained, undocumented, unproven, and in many cases clearly incorrect. I also find his reasoning and medical opinions seriously flawed in several areas. I. Outcome measures Dr. Mendel relies on two sets of outcome measures in drawing his sweeping conclusions about Arizona prison healthcare: data from diabetic patients and mortality rates. I agree that relevant outcome measures can be extremely helpful in evaluating system performance. I would have welcomed the opportunity to review such data for my report, but when I requested it, I was informed by plaintiffs' counsel that it had not been provided. I therefore reviewed with interest Dr. Mendel's outcome measures. I was disappointed in what I saw. Outcome measures are only useful to the extent they are based on reliable data. It is therefore essential to take basic steps to assess the validity of the data before drawing conclusions from it. Unfortunately, Dr. Mendel does not appear to have performed even an elementary review of the numbers he cites. As a result, he has made several key errors and overlooked profound flaws that render his conclusions utterly unreliable. A. Diabetes care Diabetes care, in Dr. Mendel's view, is "the best overall measure of the effectiveness of a correctional healthcare system." Confidential Expert Report of Lawrence H. Mendel, D.O., FSCP, CCHP, December 18, 2013, at 27 (hereafter "Mendel Report"). I agree that it is a reasonable barometer of several interconnected healthcare processes in correctional settings. Dr. Mendel and I differ, however, on how to measure whether a system provides community standard of care in this area. His approach is to look solely at outcome measures -- HgA1c and LDL levels -- and not at any individual patient care, and his results demonstrate the risks of such a limited methodology. 2 The most famous diabetes study ever conducted is called the Diabetic Control and Complications Trial (DCCT). The conventional therapy group for the DCCT, under a treatment regimen very similar to that employed by ADC, had a median HgA1c of 9.1%. The intensive therapy group, with a far superior treatment regimen than that employed in ADC, had a median HgA1c of 7.2%. DCCT Research Group, "The Effect of Intensive Treatment of Diabetes on the Development and Progression of Long-Term Complications in Insulin-Dependent Diabetes Mellitus," New England Journal of Medicine, vol. 329, no. 14 (Sept. 30, 1993). See also "The Diabetes Control and Complications Trial/ Epidemiology of Diabetes Interventions and Complications Study at 30 Years: Overview," Diabetes Care, vol. 37, pages 9-16 (January 2014). This was an academic study that demonstrated that even under tight clinical management very few diabetics can achieve sustained HgA1c levels below 7%. Another important data point is the Geisinger Diabetes Group. Geisinger is a private healthcare network that is the national benchmark for preventative practices and diabetic control in large populations. Their diabetes control program is considered state of the art, and includes many things unheard of in a correctional environment, such as nutritional counseling, individual meal plans, carbohydrate counting, exercise plans, diabetic education, disease support groups, and endocrinology consultations (http://www.geisinger.org/services/endocrinology/diabetes.html). Under the most rigorous medical, dietary, and behavioral management they are able to achieve HgA1c levels of less than 7% in fewer than half of their diabetic patients. Bloom et al., "Redesign of a Diabetes System of Care Using an All-or-None Diabetes Bundle to Build Teamwork and Improve Intermediate Outcomes," Diabetes Spectrum, vol. 23, no. 3 (2010). See also Ali et al., "Achievement of Goals in U.S. Diabetes Care, 1999-2010," New England Journal of Medicine, vol. 368, no. 17 (April 25, 2013) at 1613-24 (after a decade of diabetic management progress, only approximately half of diabetics achieve HgA1c levels of less than 7%). Case 2:12-cv-00601-DJH Document 1104-1 Filed 09/08/14 Page 321 of 364 3 Against this backdrop, Dr. Mendel's claim that more than 70% of diabetics in ADC have achieved HgA1c levels of less than 7% over six months is not credible. The Low Density Lipoprotein (LDL) values presented by Dr. Mendel are similarly difficult to believe. The National Health and Nutrition Examination Survey (NHANES) studies showed only 56.8% of the study group were able to achieve an LDL less than 100. Ali et al., "Achievement of Goals in U.S. Diabetes Care, 1999-2010." Corizon reports, and Dr. Mendel repeats without question or explanation, that 61% of its diabetic management group achieves an LDL less than 100. Mendel Report at 30. The results from academic studies occur under intense dietary and medical management. I saw no evidence of any similar efforts at ADC in my tours and review of the charts. Consequently, results better than the literature are difficult to believe without corroboration. Additional lab data in the documentation produced with Dr. Mendel's report exhibit similar unreliability. In the same Corizon lab monitoring report, HIV management is cited as perfect—100% of HIV patients who have been on HAART (Highly Active Anti-Retroviral Therapy) for 12 weeks or more have an undetectable viral load in the third quarter of 2013. ADC_M000001. This result suggests that every HIV patient in the system is perfectly managed and has a perfect clinical response to treatment. In my clinical experience and to my knowledge of the literature, this result is not an achievable outcome measure across a large population. In my review of HIVpositive patients in ADC I found the care to be disorganized, illogical, poorly executed, and beneath the standard of care in some cases. I found several cases of poor management where HIV viral loads had been ordered but never carried out, and therefore the extent of the mismanagement was not documented objectively. As such, I find the claim of 100% perfection in this difficult and complex patient population to be unbelievable.

Mortality rates

The other outcome measure relied on by Dr. Mendel is the ADC's mortality rate, compared to the national average in prisons and jails. Mendel Report at 31-32. Dr. Mendel's analysis misses the mark: comparisons of crude mortality rates, without controlling for other factors that drive mortality, tell us nothing. The single greatest driver of mortality rates overall is age. Other factors with significant impact on death rates that should be controlled in any cross-population comparison include gender, ethnicity, and length of prison stay. Without controlling for these factors, we cannot draw any conclusions as to why ADC's mortality rate might be lower than the national average. See Curtin and Klein, "Direct Standardization (Age-Adjusted Death Rates)," U.S. Department of Health and Human Services/Centers for Disease Control and Prevention/National Center for Health Statistics (March 1995). Even if comparing the mortality rate of the plaintiff class with the national average in prisons and jails were a useful exercise, Dr. Mendel's conclusions would still be wrong: the mortality rate for the plaintiff class in this case is in fact very close to his cited national average, and rising steadily. We obtain different numbers because his calculations appear to include ADC prisoners in both state-run and private prisons. (It is difficult to tell, since he does a poor job of citing his data sources.) This lawsuit, however, includes only ADC prisoners in state-run facilities. In 2012, there were 84 deaths in state-run facilities, out of an average population of 33,089.1 In 2013, there were 1 I obtained the total number of 2012 deaths in custody from ADC_M000207. That document reports a total of 87 deaths in custody, which includes deaths that occurred in private prisons. I reviewed the accompanying documents for each death and excluded the three that occurred in private prisons, found at ADC_M000268, ADC_M000274, and ADC_M000290. I obtained the average population in state-run facilities for 2012 by taking the average of the monthly population reports issued by ADC in that year. See PLTF-PARSONS-031580-031591   87 deaths in state-run facilities, out of an average population of 33,664.2 Thus the mortality rate for the relevant population was 253.9 per 100,000 in 2012 and 258.4 per 100,000 for 2013. Those figures demonstrate that contrary to Dr. Mendel's statements, the mortality rate in ADC prisons is increasing under Corizon's involvement and it is very near the national average. II. Faulty reasoning Many of Dr. Mendel's sweeping conclusions about healthcare in the ADC are flawed. He argues that care is adequate because staffing is improved, wait times are better, grievances are minimal, and Arizona prisons are accredited by the NCCHC. I examine each of these points in turn, along with his review of the few individual cases he discusses. A. Staffing Dr. Mendel offers a graph to demonstrate staffing improvements. Mendel Report at 20. The graph is confusing and misleading, however. For one thing, the vertical axis is not labeled with any units of measure. I am assuming, from a review of the cited data, that it refers to Full Time Employee Equivalents, but I cannot be sure. For another, Dr. Mendel makes the elementary mistake of graphing his staffing numbers, which are discrete data, using a continuous data method. Staffing numbers go up or down in blocks, not in gradual slopes. It is misleading, for this type of data, to connect the dots and color in the graph beneath the line you create. Moreover, the layering of the different elements (mid-levels, staff physicians, and medical directors) on top of each other improperly aggregates the data, producing a graph that does not match up to any stated 2 I could not obtain the total number of 2013 deaths in custody from the same source as I found 2012 deaths, since the documents produced to me were not complete to the end of the year. I therefore reviewed all the public announcement of 2013 deaths in custody by ADC, excluding executions and deaths occurring at private prisons. PLTF-PARSONS- 031631-031717. I obtained the average population in state-run facilities in 2013 by taking the average of the monthly population reports issued by ADC in that year. See PLTF-PARSONS-031592-031603. For example, if you read this graph literally, in October 2013 ADC had almost 45 units of whatever-is-being-measured of medical directors. That result does not correlate with any data disclosed. Perhaps the most misleading aspect of Dr. Mendel's graph is that it gives the impression that all three important staffing levels – medical directors, physicians, and mid-level providers – have increased significantly under Corizon's management. However, when I looked at the underlying data, I found that that is not the case. Although in this period Corizon did increase the woefully inadequate number of midlevel providers, it also reduced the woefully inadequate numbers of physicians and medical directors. All three job categories remain below the contractually required levels. The graph is also, in one area, dead wrong. Dr. Mendel's graph shows the aggregate staffing level for May 2013 for his three groups at 31 or 32 (my guess at the breakdown, based on a purely visual review of the graph, would be Medical Directors 6, Staff Physicians 10, and Mid-Level Providers 16). He cites ADC117064 for the May 2013 figures, but that document shows the aggregate staffing levels for these groups to be below 25 (Medical Directors 5.5, Staff Physicians 4.5, Nurse Practitioners 14.753). That same document indicates that Corizon has secured only 0.77 FTEs of Medical Director staffing, 0.9 FTEs of physician staffing, and 3.47 FTEs of nurse practitioner staffing from various temporary agencies which still leaves them well short of contract minimums.

B. Access to care

Dr. Mendel states that "significant progress" has been made in recent months, after my tours and document reviews, such that nearly every facility has a "provider wait time" of less than eight days, with a statewide average of seven days. Mendel Report at 3 "Mid-Level Providers" are not listed as a category in this document (ADC117064). The only staffing category that could be considered a mid-level provider is Nurse Practitioner, so that is the number I have used. I looked at the underlying data Dr. Mendel cites and found it questionable at best. According to a document cited by Dr. Mendel, there were no provider HNRs and no wait time at all to see providers at Perryville in the month of May 2013.4 Mendel Report at 10; ADC122017. What can this mean? How is it possible? The same document has no provider information from Lewis at all in May 2013. The same document also shows a four-month wait time to see a provider at Eyman, and Yuma appears to be so shortstaffed with providers that it is projected to take 1-2 months for the system to see a mere 34 patients who have requested provider healthcare. Id. Another document Dr. Mendel cites for his chart (ADC155093) shows no Provider HNRs at Winslow in September 2013. Yet another document (ADC203348) shows no scheduled provider appointments and zero provider wait time at Phoenix in November 2013. The data that Dr. Mendel uses to defend the care at ADC is all over the map, incomplete, internally inconsistent and it exemplifies in one report the systemic issues in this case. Quite simply, Corizon and ADC are unable to describe their own operation accurately with statistical performance numbers. As such, it is illogical to attempt to defend the system using reports that are so glaringly inaccurate and incomplete. A review of the Health Needs Request report for October 2013 (ADC203032), a document not cited by Dr. Mendel, provides some insight into the ongoing Health Needs Request problems in the ADC. According to that report, 17,367 medical HNRs were submitted by prisoners statewide in October 2013. Out of that number, a total of 7,513 (43.3%) were scheduled to see a nurse and 3,478 (20.0%) were then scheduled to see a provider. While the reported decrease in wait times is laudable, the real problem is that the majority of patients requesting healthcare are not seen by anybody. Out of 17,367 requests for treatment, only 7,513 were scheduled to be seen even by a nurse, leaving 4 He fails to define his terms, so it is difficult to tell what exactly he is claiming. What exactly does the "provider wait time" measure? The time from the filing of an HNR to its triage? From the triage to a nurse's line? The nurse's line to a provider line? The entire stretch, from the filing of an HNR until a patient is seen by a provider face-to-face review. We have no information about why they were not seen and do not know if leaving the majority of patients with no face-toface evaluation is appropriate. I strongly suspect it is not.5 Another disturbing aspect of this October 2013 data is what I call "throughput" to the providers – how many patients filing HNRs get seen at a higher level than a nurse? The 20% figure in October 2013 seems extremely low to me, given my experience of patients' written requests and my review of HNRs from ADC prisoners' files. This rate varies by facility: at Douglas, only 12.3% of HNRs result in a provider visit, Tucson runs at 9.7%, and Perryville has only 8.2% provider throughput. To me, the primary issue is not the wait times for those who do see providers but rather overall access to care within the system. This data confirms my opinion that access to healthcare is extremely constrained and staffing is inadequate to meet the demands of the system.

C. Grievances

Dr. Mendel's reliance on grievances as probative evidence of the adequacy of health care is ill-advised. In my experience evaluating and operating correctional healthcare systems I have found that prisoners frequently refrain from filing grievances for many reasons, including fear of retaliation, frustration with what they see as a meaningless process, and low literacy levels. In Arizona, prisoners might feel reluctant to share their healthcare needs on a document that is seen by custody staff. See Deposition of Juliet Respicio-Moriarty, September 23, 2013, at 10:14-11:25. An inadequate grievance tracking process might also yield a smaller number of grievances in the records than were in fact filed. Thus, the fact that only a small number of grievances was produced to Dr. Mendel does not automatically connote satisfaction with the 5 Dr. Mendel makes the questionable assumption that "patient requests have been triaged and prioritized based upon the acuity of the medical need." Mendel Report at 10. He provides no support for this statement. ADC's own monitors have found exactly the opposite to be true, as I did and described at length in my report. 1104-1 Filed 09/08/14 Page 327 of 364 9 responsiveness or efficacy of the system – in fact, it might demonstrate the exact reverse. There is much more we need to know about this information source before we can use it to draw conclusions about the healthcare system. For these reasons, I do not place much credence in an analysis that concludes that a lack of grievances demonstrates satisfaction with the healthcare available. D. NCCHC standards I agree that the National Commission on Correctional Health Care serves a valuable purpose in helping correctional facilities improve healthcare for prisoners. I am well aware of the accreditation process and I agree that in general it is a positive achievement for a facility to become accredited. However, I am also well aware of the significant shortcomings of the accreditation survey process. In Arizona, several of the prisons that are accredited have not been surveyed on site since 2010, and obviously a great deal has changed since then. In addition, while some of the prisons retain accreditation, they are technically on probation because of significant deficiencies found on their last survey. As such, being accredited does not always mean that the healthcare is being delivered in accordance with prevailing standards. A prime example of this disconnect occurred in Maricopa County, Arizona. The jail system there had been accredited for a long time, yet the court ultimately found in Graves vs. Arpaio that many of the core elements of care did not meet prevailing standards and the court ordered remedies to bring the jail into compliance. E. Individual cases Dr. Mendel states that he did review a few of the medical charts that I referred to in my expert report. Unfortunately, it is clear that he performed a very selective review of information and in many cases he missed the entire point for why that patient's management fell beneath the standard of care, as a close examination shows: • Shawn Jensen (032465) had a confirmed elevation in his prostate specific antigen (PSA, a marker of cancer) on August 30, 2006. It took two years and 10 months for ADC to get him seen by a urologist and the biopsy took three years and two months from the initial abnormal lab test. No reasonable clinician would endorse a three-year cancer workup with an elevated PSA as reasonable and meeting the standard of care. The fact that he did not have metastatic disease at the time of his surgery, a fact Dr. Mendel relies on, is hardly a defense for this extraordinarily delayed workup and treatment. Mendel Report at 11-12. In addition, Dr. Mendel disputes my finding that it was inappropriate for a nurse to complete a Foley irrigation for Mr. Jensen. Mendel Report at 12-13. His dispute is based on his misreading of the chart, however. While nurses frequently do manage Foley catheters within their scope of practice, this was a somewhat different case. The Foley catheter was actually a surgical drain strategically placed by the physician. It is well established in the medical community that surgical drains are managed by doctors only; thus, no nurse should have manipulated Mr. Jensen's catheter regardless of level of licensure. • is a diabetic patient who complained of vision loss on 12/12/12. As of my tour on 7/29/13 he had never been seen by an optometrist. In addition, he became critically sick with critically abnormal labs between 3/2013 and 6/2013. His critical lab values were signed off late and no follow-up monitoring was ordered. His diabetes was poorly controlled in prison with a HgA1C of 8.7% on 5/19/2013, which was a significant increase over his long established baseline. He was so sick I felt the need to inform Dr. Williams of the extreme risks to this patient under his current management. Dr. Mendel, however, indicates in his report that he reviewed this patient's chart and makes no mention of the violations of the standard of care. Instead, he appears to defend the care by affirming that he was finally seen by an optometrist. Mendel Report at 23. • Desiree Licci (150051) is a breast and ovarian cancer survivor who began to experience abnormal symptoms in November 2010. It took ADC more than two years to have her seen by an oncologist. Dr. Mendel states "her medical treatment has been consistent with the applicable standards of medical care." Mendel Report at 25. I wholeheartedly disagree. No reasonable clinician thinks that a two-year workup for possible gynecological cancer recurrence is appropriate. Dr. Mendel notes that surgery was scheduled after my visit; I very much hope that this is true and that it has taken place. • Dr. Mendel indicates that he reviewed the care of , who has suffered from a chronic leg wound that has been improperly treated over the course of many months. Dr. Mendel admits that the care was inappropriate but blames Wexford and indicates that the wound appears to be improving. Mendel Report at 40. I am not sure how he came to that conclusion since he never saw the patient. When I reviewed care in August 2013, five months after Corizon took over, it was evident to me that Corizon was continuing a wound care treatment plan that did not meet standard of care for many months with no provider oversight and that wound was allowed to fester and grow to the point that significant reconstructive surgery would be necessary to repair his leg. I very much hope that wound is in fact improving, but I have very little faith in Dr. Mendel's vague statement, especially since the treatment provided clearly had not improved in the two months after I told Dr. Williams of Corizon and the ADC and Corizon attorneys in this case that his care was dangerously deficient.

Confidential Supplemental Report of Todd Randall Wilcox, M.D., M.B.A., C.C.H.P.-A

1 I have reviewed the 125 medical records that Dr. Mendel consulted in developing his opinion about the Arizona prison health care delivery system.1 According to Dr. Mendel, the information he reviewed, including these patients' charts, "shows incontrovertible evidence of [ADC's] ability to identify and resolve major challenges" and to operate "within the standard of care for correctional systems." Mendel Report at 49. Having reviewed the same records, it is my opinion that the evidence contained in them contradicts his wholehearted endorsement of the ADC's healthcare system. In addition, I have also reviewed recent records for named plaintiff Shawn Jensen, and these records likewise reveal a health care system that is seriously flawed. I. Records Reviewed by Dr. Mendel The medical records that constitute one of the bases for Dr. Mendel's expert opinions are notable for several reasons. First, the records clearly contradict and undermine data that Dr. Mendel presented in his initial report and cited in support of his contention that patients with chronic conditions are well controlled. Second, like the records that I reviewed at the Arizona prisons I visited, they revealed ongoing healthcare delivery problems, including poor scheduling and follow-up for ordered tests, lack of timely access to care, uninformed treatment decisions, failure to deliver ordered medications, and inadequate access to specialty care. Because of these serious and ongoing barriers to care, some Arizona prisoners are suffering unnecessary pain and bad outcomes, and all are subject to an unreasonable risk of serious harm. Third, they are an 1 Because defendants did not start to produce these records until ten weeks after Dr. Mendel submitted his report, I was unable to address them in my earlier rebuttal report. There is an unusual number of HIV patients, and the scope of many of the records was limited. Fourth, as was true of all of the ADC patient charts I have reviewed, these records were incomplete and very poorly maintained. A. The Records Dr. Mendel Reviewed Refute Corizon Chronic Care Data Dr. Mendel relies heavily on a single-page report, produced by Corizon, that purports to list

outcome measures for patients with diabetes, patients taking blood thinners, and patients with HIV. ADC_M00001.

The report is the centerpiece of his argument that ADC cares for its patients appropriately. I found the report's outcome measures to be questionable on their face and based on my independent review of Arizona prison medical care, as I described in my rebuttal report. After being provided copies of the medical charts that Dr. Mendel reviewed, I was able to explore his conclusions regarding outcome measures in relation to the information he had to compare them with. I found that the patient charts clearly demonstrate the utter unreliability of the outcome measures. 1. HIV Management According to Corizon's report, in the third quarter of 2013, 100% of HIV positive patients taking antiretrovirals in Arizona prisons had an undetectable viral load. The medical records Dr. Mendel reviewed conclusively establish that this is false. For example, is HIV-positive and also suffers from profound psychosis that is well managed on medications. Like many HIV-positive patients, has been treated with a combination of antiretroviral medications that was, for quite a while, effectively managing his condition. The disease management data in his record demonstrates excellent clinical outcomes for his HIV early in this medical record. On January 30, 2013, his viral load was undetectable and his immune system was in excellent shape with a CD4 count of 498. He was tested again on May 1, 2013, and his viral load then was undetectable and his CD4 was done but the result is illegible. However, after Corizon began providing the healthcare, they apparently adopted a practice of distributing HIV medications as Keep On Person (KOP) medications (i.e., the patient is provided a supply of medications a month at a time to manage on his or her own), rather than administering each dose as was previously done for . There are a number of HNRs in medical record where he complains that he is not receiving his HIV or mental health medications (ADC232654, p. 139; ADC232656, p. 141; ADC232658, p. 143). There are also notes from his mental health provider on September 17, 2013, that indicate the patient reported he has not received his medications "in a while" (ADC232703, p. 188). I attempted to correlate the patient's allegations with the Medication Administration Records (MARs) in his medical record but the recordkeeping is so inadequate as to fall below standard of care for medication administration documentation and they provide no guidance on whether he did or did not receive his HIV medications (Sustiva and Truvada) or his mental health medication (Trilafon). What is bizarre about management is that his critical medications are KOP and some of his other non-critical medications (Benzotropine and Gabapentin) are Direct Observe, and the nurses document his compliance for these non-critical medications daily. If the system makes him come to the window to get his medications every day, why not administer his critical medications to him at the same time. What we do know from the record is that this previously stable patient suffered virologic failure (dramatically increased HIV viral load despite an ongoing HIV treatment regimen) as evidenced by an HIV viral load of 86,708 (log 4.94) on August 22, 2013, and that on the same date his CD4 count crashed to 284, which is a dramatic decrease over just a few months. When HIV-positive patients hit a CD4 of 200, the immune system is generally considered to be so compromised that preventative antibiotics are initiated. Corizon's failure to recognize that psychotic prisoners, and indeed any prisoner with mental illness or developmental delays, may require an individualized medication plan for life-sustaining prescriptions is shocking. What is even more shocking is that after markedly abnormal viral load and decreased CD4 result became known in August, nobody within Corizon investigated why he is failing therapy or attempted to implement any corrective action. This patient is currently being managed by a Physician's Assistant (PA) who does not even make mention of his elevated HIV viral load in the clinic note dated October 8, 2013 (ADC232520, p. 5). Clearly the PA cannot competently manage this complex patient. Based on the medical records in this chart, is currently in danger of rapid progression toward AIDS. Fortunately, the PA has requested an Infectious Disease consult to help manage care. I hope that the ordered consult has occurred and resulted in the appropriate interventions to provide life-saving treatment that has been lacking. The above case demonstrates failures on many levels. The medical care is deficient, mental health care is ineffective, nursing care does not comply with basic standards of nursing documentation, the medication management (nursing and pharmacy) is failing to maintain continuity of care.

The significant increase in this patient's viral load clearly demonstrates the overall failure of management as well as contradicting Corizon's outcome measure. Another case in Dr. Mendel's records with similar results is that of who has been on prescribed HIV medications. He had an HIV viral load of 104,659 (Log 5.02) on September 10, 2013. This lab result is indicative of total virologic failure and no definitive management of that problem is evident in the chart. needs urgent management to avoid potentially damaging long-term consequences. Continuing to provide HIV medications that clearly are ineffective is medically inappropriate and financially wasteful. See also another HIVpositive patient who was on medications during the third quarter of 2013 and did not have in undetectable viral load (ADC234186). These three HIV patients had elevated viral load results reported in the third quarter of 2013. Obviously the lab report that Dr. Mendel relied on that claimed that 100% of HIV patients on medications in the third quarter of 2013 had undetectable viral loads is not accurate, something Dr. Mendel knew or should have known from his record review. 2. Diabetes Management In his report, Dr. Mendel states that he believes that diabetes care is the best overall measure of the effectiveness of a correctional healthcare system (Mendel Report at 27) and that one lab value report can therefore determine the efficacy of the system. I don't agree with that oversimplification of a complex healthcare system any more than I would agree that the health of a patient can be summarized with one vital sign. However, I am willing to entertain his hypothesis and to test it against the patients he reviewed. There were not many diabetic charts to examine. Given his reliance on diabetes as a single measure of success of ADC, it is surprising to me that Dr. Mendel did not select more diabetic patients for his chart review. Remarkably, out of the 125 charts that he claims to have reviewed, only three patients were insulin-requiring diabetics and only three were non-insulin dependent diabetics. The evidence of care contained in these few charts bolsters my opinion of substandard care in Arizona prisons and undermines Dr. Mendel's conclusions. a. Insulin-Requiring Diabetics With respect to the insulin-requiring diabetics, none of them was within acceptable clinical control and appropriate chronic care management. had reasonable blood glucose control (HgA1c of 6.7%) but his blood pressure was significantly elevated (180/98) with no intervention by the medical staff. Blood pressure control is critical to minimize the complications of diabetes and this patient is poorly managed. Furthermore, this patient is on phenytoin for a seizure disorder. Phenytoin is a medication that requires monitoring of blood levels and there is not a single order or result to check his phenytoin level. This case is an example of poor medical management and poor nursing management of a diabetic patient. Based on the information available in this chart, Dr. Mendel's hypothesis that acceptable diabetes care predicts effective healthcare across the board is not supported. Another insulin-requiring diabetic in Dr. Mendel's chart set is . He is a very poorly controlled diabetic with HgA1c levels ranging from 8.9% to 12.9% and he has significant end-organ compromise from his diabetes in the form of diabetic retinopathy, renal failure, and severe neurologic compromise of his feet. Despite his extremely poor control of his diabetes and all of his complications, he is still being managed using only intermediate- and short-acting insulin. This is remarkably rudimentary medical management given what is available in today's healthcare marketplace for patients like this. In this case, the opposite of Dr. Mendel's hypothesis is proven: this patient has very ineffective diabetes care as well as very ineffective medical care. A third insulin-requiring diabetic in this chart series is I am familiar with care from having encountered him on my tours. I reviewed his master chart and I saw him personally to confirm his issues. His overall healthcare was so concerning to me that I specifically identified him to the staff at Yuma and attorneys for the State and Corizon as a patient who was in serious medical trouble. According to the data available in the chart that I reviewed, HgA1c was 8.7% on May 19, 2013. Dr. Mendel indicates that he reviewed this patient's chart, but what was provided to him was a highly truncated version that covers only 44 days of care from October 6, 2013, to November 20, 2013. Apparently he was not shown the earlier care where this young patient's diabetes was completely out of control, his liver function was seriously compromised, and two of his three basic blood cell types (white cells and platelets) were at critically low levels. Instead, Dr. Mendel was shown a few pages of records that did not reveal the extent of this patient's mismanagement. This case fails to support Dr. Mendel's hypothesis as well. b. Non-Insulin Dependent Diabetics One of the diabetics whose chart was reviewed by Dr. Mendel who does not require insulin is His HgA1c on June 5, 2013, was 6.4%. Under Dr. Mendel's theory of care, this result establishes that the rest of his healthcare is adequate. However, review of his chart indicates that this patient is also HIV-positive and seriously mentally ill. The medical record is replete with systemic errors of care. There are multiple examples of the patient's not receiving his critical chronic care medications from the pharmacy on time and being without medication. The Medication Administration Records in this chart are not completed in accordance with the standard of nursing documentation so it is not possible to determine whether and when he received certain medications. In addition, this patient is on HIV medication that should be monitored for efficacy periodically. According to his medical record, his critical HIV labs (CD4 and HIV viral load) were ordered by the clinicians five separate times: June 7, 2013 (ADC245368); September 11, 2013 (ADC245367); November 20, 2013 (ADC245364); December 12, 2013 (ADC245365); and January 25, 2014 (ADC245364). Despite these five orders for labs, not a single lab result is in his chart or mentioned in his clinical notes. The failure of the system to carry out provider orders puts the providers in an impossible situation: they cannot manage their patients safely. This patient's records similarly disprove Dr. Mendel's hypothesis. Is another diabetic who does not require insulin whose chart is on Dr. Mendel's list. While his diabetes care is under good management, he had significantly poor care for his hand fracture in November 2013. At that time he was diagnosed with an open fracture of his fifth metacarpal and he was sent to the emergency room on November 6, 2013. The emergency room stabilized him and sent him back with recommendations for care including pain management and an urgent follow-up visit with the hand surgeon within one week. Unfortunately this was not done. A notation in the chart indicates that this urgent consult was not even requested until November 19, 2013, and it would not be scheduled to occur until December 19, 2013—a full five weeks after the hand surgeon had thought it necessary he be seen. An open fracture requires skilled emergency management to ensure appropriate treatment and to safeguard against a significant bone infection. The treatment in this case falls well below the standard of care for this condition. Again, this is a case where the patient's diabetic management shows success but that success cannot be generalized to the overall success of the healthcare delivery system. The last patient in this series who has diabetes that does not require insulin is She has moderately controlled diabetes and her most recent hemoglobin A-1 C is 7.1% as of January 2014. ADC 239663. Review of her chart demonstrates multiple deficits of care that show substantial delay in her healthcare management. She had labs drawn on October 29, 2013, that showed multiple abnormal values, but those labs were not signed off by a provider within ADC until January 3, 2014. ADC239665. Additional labs were drawn on January 15, 2014 and they also contain significant abnormal results. Those labs were not signed off until February 13, 2014. ADC239661. Again this case does not support Dr. Mendel's hypothesis—her diabetic care might be close to target but the systemic delivery of care in her case is well below the community standard. As I have previously discussed in my rebuttal report, Dr. Mendel relies on HgA1c data produced by Corizon that reports clinical outcomes with diabetics that greatly exceed the best of the best in healthcare—their stated results are just too good to be possible. As we see in the analysis of the charts, the HIV results Corizon reports as perfect turned out not to be nearly as good as they claim and not a single one of the diabetics in this series had acceptable healthcare globally. As such, the evidence simply does not support Dr. Mendel's arguments. B. The Records Dr. Mendel Reviewed Reveal a Broken System After reviewing Dr. Mendel's charts, my prior opinions are strengthened: Arizona prisoners are at serious risk from dangerously inadequate medical care. 1. Patients Suffer From Delayed Care In my review of the healthcare system in Arizona prisons on site tours, on-site chart reviews, off-site chart reviews, and additional documentation review, I have found the most pervasive theme throughout the entire system to be that of delay. I have described in great detail the poor care I found in many cases, with serious delay as a significant component of the treatment deficits. Far from being isolated or anecdotal, it is clearly pervasive, affecting major business practices and healthcare transactions throughout the ADC. Below are some illustrations of this profound deficit that I found within the charts Dr. Mendel reviewed. Illustrates many of the issues faced by patients within the ADC who have serious chronic medical conditions. suffers from Factor VIII Deficiency (Hemophilia A) and frequently has significant bleeding episodes that require Factor VIII infusion to stop. These episodes are extremely painful. The patient has had so many significant bleeding episodes that have required emergency trips to the hospital that the providers within ADC have attempted to stock Factor VIII for emergent use within the prison system. Unfortunately, the pharmacy has been unable to supply this common treatment. As a result, has had multiple episodes where he bleeds significantly into his muscles and develops large painful hematomas (bruises) that ultimately require Factor VIII infusions. To treat his pain, the ADC providers have placed him on Vicodin, a standard oral pain medication. However, as noted on January 4, 2013, by Dr. Laura Brown, the pharmacy that services ADC is unable supply the Vicodin in sufficient amounts, so Dr. Brown put on a pain medication ration that cut his dose down significantly and effectively provided no meaningful pain relief for his condition.

ADC234522. Her instructions about this to the nursing staff are written in a memo and she indicates that "He will just have to toughen up as narcotics are not always available." ADC234783. I find her memo, and the attitude it expresses, to be untenable. She had multiple options available to her for substitute medications, but instead of attempting to advocate for her patient, she resigned herself to the systemic problem and left her patient to suffer needlessly. housed at ASPC-Lewis, is another patient who has experienced significant delays. He originally submitted an HNR on April 21, 2013, for a mass on his neck. He was seen 18 days later on May 9, 2013. An urgent consult for an ultrasound was filled out but not completed until May 21, 2013. Based on the results of that ultrasound, a biopsy was scheduled which took three months to approve and accomplish. The biopsy results showed that he had Hodgkin's Lymphoma. Following that result, the patient was set up on September 24, 2013, with an oncology appointment to develop a plan of care. This appointment took five weeks to set up and the note from that visit with 21st Century Oncology indicates that they will be closing their prisoner clinic and that care will need to be accomplished at another clinic in the future. ADC238026. The patient was eventually seen in another oncology clinic on November 6, 2013, for his lymphoma. In total, it took ADC seven months to work up and initiate treatment on an obvious case of Hodgkin's Lymphoma. That deviates significantly from the standard of care for this condition and places this patient at serious risk of harm. Unfortunately, this case is remarkably similar to that of as described in Dr. Cohen's 2/24/14 Supplemental Expert Report. In that case, developed a neck mass that was suspicious for Hodgkin's Lymphoma in October 2012. He received no treatment for his highly treatable condition, and died Cohen Supplemental Report at 19-25. is a patient with a number of complicated issues. He has severe coronary artery disease, he is suffering with chronic unstable angina, he has had four stents placed previously, and he has a left below-knee amputation. His chart epitomizes ADC's delay in care in managing a complicated chronically ill patient. He was seen by orthopedics in May 2011 and they recommended a bilateral shoulder MRI to evaluate his bilateral shoulder pain. That order was not placed into the system until almost seven months later in January 2012. It took another six months for the order to be carried out: it was completed on June 15, 2012. The MRI showed significant rotator cuff tears bilaterally and an orthopedic consult was entered into the system on August 1, 2012, to evaluate the possibility of surgery for this patient. It has taken 16 months for him to finally see orthopedics back in return and he had a completed orthopedic consult on December 19, 2013. It has taken ADC 31 months to do a simple work-up for bilateral rotator cuff tears in a patient who is significantly compromised as a result of his leg amputation. That is unreasonable and far below the standard of care. Even after 31 months the problem has yet to be resolved and the surgery has not been completed. In addition, was not supplied with baby powder, the usual method of avoiding damaging friction between his skin and the sleeve of his prosthesis. As a result, he had breakdown of his prosthesis which ultimately caused breakdown of his skin on the stump in his leg. This is a terrible and easily avoidable outcome for this highly compromised patient. Dr. Merchant admitted that the patient's medications and his management have been inappropriate due to a pharmacy error. (ADC245917). On April 10, 2013, a consult for the repair of his prosthesis to minimize the damage to his stump was entered. That prosthesis repair was completed on January 10, 2014 -- a full nine months after it was put in to the system. That is unreasonable and caused to suffer needless pain. Additional examples of delay and fragmentation of care in Dr. Mendel's records include numerous cases where patients have been unable to receive timely diagnostic imaging to receive required treatment. See, e.g., (recurrent shoulder dislocations; MRI took three months to schedule); (xray order to be completed on August 7, 2013; not done, no results in chart); (complained of acute ankle pain on June 8, 2013; took two and a half months for x-ray); (June 25, 2013, order for a thyroid ultrasound; never completed); (diagnosed with a left testicular cyst, referred for repeat ultrasound; never done). Similarly, providers order lab tests, often essential to the management of chronic illnesses, and they are not completed or they are done late. See, e.g., (HIV-positive patient had appropriate monitoring lab work ordered on April 3, 2013, but not drawn until four months later; additional lab work ordered on February 5, 2013, but never drawn); (pregnant patient arriving in ADC had a blood sugar of 155, which is significantly high and requires monitoring and workup; a lab test was ordered but never completed and no further monitoring was done for her gestational diabetes mellitus for three months); (HIVpositive patient with multiple HIV labs ordered but never completed); (HIV-positive patient had labs ordered May 16, 2013, but no record that they have been drawn or completed; he remains on medication, which is irresponsible treatment); (HIV-positive patient with viral load ordered on June 19, 2013; no result in chart); (HIV-positive patient with no labs ordered for first six months in prison and two-month delay after labs finally ordered); (mentally ill HIV-positive patient on HIV medication with no monitoring since January 1, 2013). When labs are done and the results are abnormal, follow-up is often untimely or non-existent. See, e.g., (three separate positive tests for blood in his stool on February 13, 14, and 15, 2013; no follow-up for very ominous finding); (chest x-rays done to monitor his lung disease with documented abnormalities; took three weeks before provider signed off on result); (unusual laboratory finding on complete white count (monocytosis) required a pathologist to determine the validity of the results; test has never been completed and the evaluation of this patient's potentially ominous lab results remains incomplete). The records also document numerous delays for patients seeking primary care for serious conditions. See, e.g., (submitted HNRs for genitourinary issues; no record of healthcare professional evaluation or treatment); (submitted HNR for care for acute shoulder injury, not seen for three weeks); (Hepatitis C patient submitted 10 HNRs over 13 months regarding his condition; never seen by provider in response); (patient with cardiac rhythm abnormalities and palpitations waited for eight months for a provider to see him regarding his stated complaint); (complained of chest pain; not seen for five days and then only by a nurse and never worked up appropriately for the chest pain); (year and a half wait for a provider evaluation for knee and ankle pain following surgery, despite numerous HNRs). Some patients who require specialty consult care are unable to receive it. See, e.g., (cardiac patient referred for appropriate cardiology consult denied with no justification); (patient with history of lung cancer denied oncology evaluation for possible recurrence, in the one-month period of records provided); (patient with left testicular cyst referred for urology consult on May 11, 2012, but there is no evidence in the chart that the consult has been completed); (HIV-positive patient referred to Infectious Diseases on April 10, 2013; September 9, 2013; September 17, 2013; and October 2, 2013, all without success). Prisoners with serious chronic conditions must be provided their life–sustaining medications on a consistent basis. The records Dr. Mendel reviewed show that medication lapses happen too often in Arizona prisons, and because ADC's medication administration records are rarely complete, it is impossible to verify whether prescriptions that are timely renewed are actually provided to the patients. Medication lapses are particularly problematic for patients receiving treatment for HIV, as lapses in these medications can lead to acceleration of the disease, development of resistance, increased side effects, and difficulty in disease management long-term. See, e.g., (multiple instances where HIV medications were not delivered timely); (multiple medication lapses, including a three-week period in the fall of 2012, when CD4 count plummeted from 600 to 300). ADC Patients Reviewed During Expert Site Visits Continue to Receive Poor Care During my visits to ADC facilities during the summer of 2013, I encountered a number of medically compromised patients who were in danger because of the poor health care they were receiving. These patients included , a very fragile patient with end-stage liver disease at Yuma. At the time I met him he was very poorly managed and had complications from his disease that had resulted in multiple hospitalizations. Dr. Mendel reviewed his chart, but he was apparently provided with only 44 days of medical history spanning October 7 to November 20, 2013. However, within that small amount of charting, it is clear that care continues to be inadequate. During that time, he had a critical ammonia level that took five days for anyone to evaluate (ADC240336). That is clinically unacceptable and it places the patient at grave risk. This is purely a systemic process issue and staffing issue and it is emblematic of the problems that exist within the ADC. is another Yuma prisoner who has received grossly substandard care for his complicated condition and is now suffering complications as a result. suffers from a very serious type of Crohn's Disease which causes fistulas (tunnels) to develop through the walls of his intestines and into other organs. He has been hospitalized many times for this condition and he has required many surgeries. When I saw him, I was surprised to discover that he was not on Remicade, the standard medication used for this condition. He reported to me that he had been started on Remicade, but Corizon had denied it long-term due to cost. The denial was confirmed in his medical record. I was so concerned about him after reviewing his chart and talking with him that I identified him to prison and Corizon staff and attorneys as a very at-risk patient who needed sophisticated care beyond what was available at Yuma. Specifically, he needed Remicade and a gastroenterology/surgery treatment team experienced with managing fistulizing Crohn's Disease. Unfortunately none of my recommendations were heeded and continues to have substantial problems as evidenced by his record in this chart review. As with Dr. Mendel only reviewed a few weeks of medical records for this very complicated patient. It is evident, however, even from the small timeframe of records provided, that continues to suffer the consequences of poor care. Since I met him over the summer, he has developed a significant fistula between his rectum and his bladder and has had a major infection as a result. He has not been restarted on his Remicade and at this point is probably not even a candidate for that medication given his complications. He very badly needs to be transferred to a prison near a major medical center that has experience with dealing with his condition. Remaining in Yuma under the inexperienced care available there will be a death sentence for him. In my initial report, I referred to the case of an AIDS patient who had been referred to an Infectious Disease Specialist in May, but had not seen one by the time of my site visit to Yuma in July. According to Dr. Mendel, was finally seen by the appropriate specialist on August 21, 2013, and the Yuma staff had implemented the consultant's recommendations. Dr. Mendel concluded that was receiving "appropriate specialty care" and had not been harmed by the delayed access to care. Again, Dr. Mendel was provided with only a fraction of the actual medical record: October 6 to November 20, 2013. As a result, he did not see the records that documented truly substandard and dangerously incompetent HIV management, the failure to send him to the consultants, the failure to draw the appropriate labs, and the patient's ongoing suffering as a result of this mismanagement. He is another patient I felt compelled to raise with Corizon and ADC staff and attorneys because his life was truly at risk. After months of delay, they had him seen by an HIV specialist and his care was moving ahead appropriately until the very end of this chart that was produced when the local provider decided to stop all of his HIV medications. This was clearly the wrong decision and the reason for it is unclear. I hope it was only a temporary hiatus as this patient is at extreme risk for serious complications and death. C. Limited Records Sample While he criticized plaintiffs' expert reports for the size of their records sample, Dr. Mendel considered fewer records from the seven prisons that he visited than Dr. Cohen and I reviewed. In his first supplemental report, Dr. Mendel wrote that his practice is to "request records from nurse's and provider's lines for a randomly selected day, approximately two weeks prior to [the] visit." Mendel Supp. Report at 4. He further stated that he typically chose 12 or more records from each category. Id. However, based upon the records he provided plaintiffs, the most records he reviewed for any prison was 31 (Yuma), and at Phoenix, he reviewed only 7Additionally, the disease spectrum contained in the medical records does not correlate with normal disease prevalence. Specifically, there were an abundance of HIVpositive patients and a dearth of diabetic patients. It is unclear how Dr. Mendel arrived at these charts but the selection does not appear to be random. Finally, many of the records provided were quite limited, covering only one or two months of care for prisoners who had long treatment histories. Most of the short records were for patients whose complete records I had reviewed for my report and identified as experiencing serious care deficiencies. These limited record excerpts reviewed by Dr. Mendel did not provide sufficient information from which to draw meaningful conclusions about the totality of care for these patients in the Arizona system. D. Organization of Medical Records In Dr. Mendel's report, he states that he found the records to be "organized in a manner used by many other correctional systems." He does note that he found some isolated documentation issues but he opines that this was not a systemic pattern. While I do agree that the use of tabs is common in paper charts across medical systems and that is the system used in ADC, I found it extremely difficult to review these charts and come to an understanding of the documentation and the flow of the healthcare experience. Whenever I evaluate medical records for their adequacy I try to place myself in the position of a treating clinician using the medical record to care for patient. In that sense I find the ADC records extraordinarily difficult to use, inaccurate, incomplete, and illegible. The deficiencies are severe enough to compromise patient care. The poor quality of the medical records must inescapably have a substantial impact on the productivity of the providers. It is even difficult simply to figure out the elements of the care being provided, given how poorly the documentation is maintained. Many of the providers and nurses within the ADC system have illegible handwriting. Illegible care plans are dangerous, and practically guarantee that follow-up care will be missed. If you can't read it, you can't follow it. The nursing documentation contained in the charts is atrocious. Most of the documentation is in the form of the Medication Administration Records (MARs), which is the record that is supposed to document the Seven Rights of Medication Administration: right patient, right route, right drug, right amount, right time, right documentation, and right to refuse. ADC medication administration records do not comply with the above national standard for nursing care. On the whole, the MARs are a mess. Clearly the practices vary from facility to facility throughout ADC and some nurses do document within the standard of care, whereas others take phenomenal shortcuts and there is no meaningful information that can be derived from reviewing their documentation on the medication administration record. In addition, many charts are missing several months of medication administration, so there is no way for a clinician to determine compliance. Without knowing medication compliance, a provider cannot assess why a treatment plan is not succeeding. In my review of Dr. Mendel's charts I attempted to go back and verify many treatment failures using the MARs. I found them to be wholly inaccurate, incomplete, and unusable. As such the nursing documentation within the ADC falls substantially short professional standards overall.

Recent Medical Records for Shawn Jensen Dr. Mendel maintains that plaintiffs' experts have identified few cases where access to care has been a factor in the outcome of a class member's care. Mendel Report at 11. He then sets forth the case of named plaintiff Shawn Jensen, who experienced a three-year delay before his prostate cancer was diagnosed and treated in 2009. Dr. Mendel concludes that "[t]here were … no issues as a result of any delay," implying that the delay was not significant. Id. at 12. As set forth in my rebuttal report, a three-year delay for a cancer work-up cannot be endorsed as reasonable. Furthermore, review of recent records show clearly that the initial delay actually did cause problems that are only now being manifested. Since submitting my rebuttal report, I have been provided and reviewed Mr. Jensen's more recent medical records. I was alarmed to find that the pattern of neglect and delay evident in the years leading up to Mr. Jensen's 2010 prostatectomy has continued, even after Mr. Jensen began showing clinical signs of recurrent cancer. Indeed, more than one year after the likely recurrence was identified, a medically reasonable treatment plan to address his probable recurrence of prostate cancer has not been developed or implemented by a qualified specialist. Instead, Mr. Jensen has once again experienced long delays in being given needed tests and approvals to see specialists. These delays increase the probability that the cancer will be more widespread and harder to treat, they put Mr. Jensen at increased risk that metastatic lesions will compromise other organ systems, and they place Mr. Jensen at increased risk for pain and decreased quality of life. Why and When to Treat Prostate Cancer Prostate cancer is the second leading cause of cancer death in American men, behind only lung cancer, killing approximately 30,000 men a year. While prostate cancer grows more slowly than other cancers, this does not mean that it should be ignored or untreated. It is a type of cancer that often metastasizes to nearby internal organs and the bones, and can result in devastating and crippling injuries or death. For example, prostate cancer, if untreated, can metastasize to the liver, causing acute liver failure, which is incredibly painful and usually results in death. Additionally prostate cancer cells often metastasize to the bones closest to the prostate: the hips, pelvis, spine, or femur (thighbone). A metastatic lesion on such critically important weight-bearing bones can lead to catastrophic results, including crippling fractures. After a man has been treated for prostate cancer, the standard of follow-up care is to measure his serum prostate-specific antigen (PSA) every three months to detect for signs of possible recurrence of the cancer, since many recurrences following initial treatment can be successfully treated. The PSA is an excellent tumor marker in men with an established diagnosis of prostate cancer, and is particularly useful because the majority of recurrences following radical prostatectomy or radiation treatment for localized prostate cancer are asymptomatic. When the PSA level exceeds 0.1, it means that it is probable that there is persistent or recurrent disease. There are certain risk factors associated with more aggressive prostate cancers, as well as a more aggressive recurrence of prostate cancer. The risk of recurrence is higher in men who have a family history of prostate cancer, are older, or are overweight. Another well-established risk factor is if a man is a Vietnam veteran who was exposed to Agent Orange or other defoliants, as these chemicals increase the risk of developing soft tissue cancers, including prostate cancer. Men with these risk factors need careful follow-up and very close monitoring. I am told Mr. Jensen was exposed to Agent Orange while serving in Vietnam. He is also older (65) and overweight. B. Failure to Monitor and Treat Mr. Jensen for Recurring Cancer Despite Mr. Jensen's significant risk factors for cancer recurrence, ADC has failed to appropriately monitor him, and once he showed clear signs of relapse, has failed to provide him timely and necessary treatment. ADC has failed to perform PSA tests every three months since Mr. Jensen's 2010 surgery. It appears that Mr. Jensen had only two PSA tests performed through early 2013, and one of those tests was performed only after Mr. Jensen requested it. ADC004538, PLTF-PARSONS-32162. This failure to test his PSA level every three months is unacceptable and below the standard of care. A copy of the test results was not his medical file, but other documents in his medical file reference his level to be 1.2 in

February 2013. ADC123383. Given Mr. Jensen's elevated risk factor for recurrence and the fact that the PSA level was 12 times higher than what would have been the normal limit after a prostatectomy (1.2 versus 0.1), upon receiving the February 6, 2013, results, the provider should have immediately referred him to a qualified specialist for examination and to develop and implement a cancer treatment plan that best meets his needs and level of cancer. The two most common options for the cancer treatment plan would be either to provide full pelvic radiation therapy or to initiate androgen deprivation therapy using a drug like leuprolide (Lupron). The typical dosage of Lupron is a shot that is administered every three months. Neither of these courses of treatment was adopted. Instead, Mr. Jensen saw Dr. Catsoros, a primary care provider, on February 19, 2013. At that appointment, despite the elevated PSA score, Dr. Catsoros failed to refer Mr. Jensen to an oncologist. He wrote that Mr. Jensen's degree of control of the cancer was "good" and that his clinical status was "improved." ADC123382. A week later, Dr. Catsoros ordered another PSA test. ADC123381. The second PSA test confirmed that Mr. Jensen's PSA level was indeed 1.2. ADC123330. Dr. Catsoros apparently made a request for a urology consultation on April 1, 2013, but Mr. Jensen did not see an urologist until May 20, 2013. ADC130312, ADC123318-328. The urologist's assessment was worsening prostate cancer, and he ordered an abdominal CT scan and a bone scan to stage Mr. Jensen's cancer and to determine if he had any bony metastatic disease. The purpose of the testing was to determine his status at that point in time and to develop a treatment plan for him. The urologist requested that Mr. Jensen return within three weeks to review, and reported to Corizon that he needed to be evaluated by oncology to determine the type of cancer treatment. ADC123320, ADC123328. Mr. Jensen was tested again on June 5, 2013, after he submitted an HNR, and the level had increased to 1.9. ADC123329. Mr. Jensen had a bone scan and CT scan on June 7, 2013. ADC123309-123311. Fortunately, the scans did not show evidence that the cancer had metastasized to his bones. Although Mr. Jensen had the appropriate staging testing completed, nobody used the results of that testing to implement an appropriate treatment plan for him. The prison nurse practitioner sent a consultation request to Corizon headquarters on June 20, 2013, requesting the Mr. Jensen have follow up specialist appointments with a urologist and nephrologist. ADC123291-123292. He did not see Dr. Banti, the urologist, until July 17, 2013, more than two months after the previous appointment and almost a month after the consultation was requested. ADC222285-222286. Dr. Banti's plan called for Lupron at 22.5 mg and a PSA test in three months, a clinically reasonable plan. ADC222286. Unfortunately, there is no evidence in the medical record through January 2014 that this plan was ever implemented. In the months following, Mr. Jensen's PSA continued to rise. As of August 7, 2013, it was 2.22, and by October 9, 2013, was 2.93. ADC222295, ADC222290. Mr. Jensen was seen by a different urologist, Dr. Goldberg, on October 29, 2013, who diagnosed prostate cancer, and reported back to Corizon that Mr. Jensen needed a bone scan "ASAP." ADC222262. This second bone scan was required because no treatment was initiated after his previous bone scan, and they had to see if the delay in care had resulted in metastasis of the cancer to his bones. Still, his PSA continued to rise. On December 11, 2013, it measured 4.21. ADC222288. On December 18, 2013, Mr. Jensen had his bone scan. ADC222255. Again, fortunately, no evidence of cancer was found in his bones. Case 2:12-cv-00601-DJH Document 1104-1 Filed 09/08/14 Page 361 of 364 27 By this point in his care, Mr. Jensen falls into another high-risk category (in addition to the Agent Orange exposure, age and weight) for the development of metastatic disease. In the tracking of his PSA levels, his doubling time (the time for PSA level to double in value) is approximately six months. This short doubling time should be particularly concerning to those caring for him, but I found no mention in the medical record that anybody has taken this new high risk factor into consideration. Furthermore, it is clear from the pathology report that when his initial radical prostatectomy was completed in 2010, the margins of the surgical resection contained tumor. This is yet another high risk factor for recurrence. It was known from the onset and documented that Mr. Jensen was a high risk for a recurrence, and yet I see no evidence in the record that anybody has acknowledged this or has taken it into consideration in referring him for the development of a treatment plan. ADC123294. By the end of 2013, Mr. Jensen still had not been examined by an oncologist. On January 9, 2014, his file was apparently reviewed by Dr. Richard Kosierowski, who is an oncologist that Corizon contracts with nationally to provide guidance and second opinions regarding care plans for cancer patients in the Corizon system. PLTFPARSONS-031985. Dr. Kosierowski apparently reviewed Mr. Jensen's chart and denied care without examining the patient and without accurate facts. Dr. Kosierowski states that Mr. Jensen "appears to have been on Lupron" and denies the prison provider's request for a urology consultation. Id. Dr. Kosierowski clearly has some questions and concerns about Mr. Jensen's care and his current status. These were set forth in his note, and yet as of today there is no documentation that he resolved these concerns or followed up on the patient's management. As a result, Mr. Jensen has been left in limbo awaiting a decision from a physician he has never seen. As of January 24, 2014, Mr. Jensen had not been examined by an oncologist, nor has he had a cancer treatment plan developed. Mr. Jensen filed HNRs on January 20 and 29, 2014, asking to have his PSA tested again and to see a cancer specialist. PLTFPARSONS 031981-31983. I am especially concerned that Mr. Jensen reported in early February that he has sharp pains in his left hip because that is the most common clinical symptom for the presentation of a metastatic lesion in the bone. PLTF-PARSONS 031984. I have been informed that Mr. Jensen reported very recently that he has yet to be seen by an oncologist and nobody has implemented a cancer treatment plan for him. In reviewing the records available to me in this case it is clear that Mr. Jensen's care regarding his prostate cancer is dangerously mismanaged, disorganized, and delayed, and falls well below the standard of care. III. Conclusion I have reviewed hundreds of medical records in this action, met dozens of patients whose care I needed to clarify following their chart reviews, toured five facilities to understand the care delivery process, met with ADC and Corizon staff, and reviewed extensive documentation of external evaluations and contract monitoring. I have also reviewed Dr. Mendel's reports endorsing the care provided by ADC. It is clear that the deficiencies within the Arizona prison healthcare system exist on both a systemic level as well as an individual care level. Throughout the system there are multiple deficiencies that cause medically necessary.

I, Todd Wilcox, declare: I have personal knowledge of the matters set forth herein and if called as a witness I could competently so testify. I. Introduction and background This report assesses Arizona's prison medical care by reviewing the system's building blocks (such as adequate staff and facilities) and its performance in four broad categories: timely access to care, the exercise of professional medical judgment, delivery of care that is ordered, and processes to minimize preventable negative outcomes. I found major deficiencies in all of these primary drivers of healthcare, as I discuss in detail below. A. Qualifications I have worked as a physician in jail and prison environments for 17 years. My opinions in this case are derived from extensive experience in the design, administration, and delivery of correctional healthcare as well as the national standards that govern the field. I actively practice in correctional healthcare as the Medical Director of the Salt Lake County Jail System and I am frequently called upon as a consultant to assist facilities and organizations nationally in improving their delivery of care, including Maricopa County (Phoenix, AZ), California Department of Corrections and Rehabilitation, Mississippi Department of Corrections, Pima County (Tucson, AZ) Department of Institutional Health, Seattle-King County Jail System (Seattle, WA), the National Commission on Correctional Health Care (Chicago, IL), the National Institutes of Corrections, the American Jail Association, the American Correctional Association, and The Rand Corporation. I am one of a select group of individuals to have achieved the advanced level of certification in correctional healthcare (CCHP-A) from the National Commission on Correctional Health Care and I frequently present to national audiences on pertinent topics in this field of medicine. I am the president-elect of The Society of Correctional Physicians and I am currently the chairman of the National Commission on Correctional Health Care's Committee on Physician Certification. My curriculum vitae is attached as Appendix A. The cases in which I have been deposed and/or given trial testimony in the last four years are listed in Appendix B, along with my rate of compensation for my work on this case and publications subsequent to those listed on my curriculum vitae. B. Information sources I undertook an extensive investigation to develop my opinions expressed in this report. I reviewed thousands of pages of documents produced by the State in this case, as well as documents produced by Wexford and Corizon. I reviewed well over a hundred partial and full healthcare records of Arizona prisoners and carried out several dozen patient interviews. I reviewed depositions of prisoners, Arizona Department of Corrections (ADC) staff, and Wexford and Corizon staff as well as Defendants' Responses to Plaintiff Verduzco's First Set of Requests for Admission. These documents are listed in Appendix C. In addition, I reviewed documents during the course of my tours, such as binders and loose filing and notices posted on the walls. I describe these documents in the course of this report. I toured five prison complexes in Arizona: Phoenix, Perryville, Yuma, Florence, and Tucson. At each complex, I viewed the majority of the clinical and support facilities where medical care was prepared and delivered, including inpatient units, exam rooms, urgent care facilities, medication rooms, medical records rooms, and medical supply rooms. I also witnessed pill call at Yuma's Cheyenne Unit and I toured one food preparation unit. I reviewed numerous healthcare records, logs, and binders (such as descriptions of medical diet options and medication administration processes).

Methodology

I reviewed several dozen patient healthcare records at every prison I toured. I did not review a random sample; instead, I chose to look at files of specific types of prisoners. This is because when evaluating a healthcare delivery system, it is not generally as helpful to examine care for healthy people as it is to look at the treatment of sick people, particularly those with complex or chronic conditions that require coordination, communication, and judgment. Therefore, I attempted to focus on records of people with diabetes, hypertension, HIV, kidney failure, hepatitis, and infections. I reviewed records for cancer patients and pregnant women, and for people who had been identified on ADC's monitoring reports as not receiving tests or specialty care or experiencing other problems with care. I reviewed records for the class representatives. I also looked through lab reports, diagnostic test logs, and Health Needs Requests on site at each facility to identify patients who had objective findings that were concerning and then I asked for their charts to be pulled for my review and if I found areas of concern I would frequently request that the patient be pulled for me to interview to confirm my findings. I felt it was important to speak directly with the patients in order to gather additional information and to make my own professional medical judgment with respect to the acuity of their illness as best I could without being able to examine them except visually. I also randomly spoke to prisoners on my tours about their healthcare challenges and I routinely reviewed their medical files in order to verify the information they gave me. I asked prisoners about information I heard from staff, and staff about information I heard from prisoners. I was able to verify information I gathered through consulting multiple sources and triangulating the information available to me. On the tours of the institutions, my goal was to observe general living conditions for the patients and the working conditions for medical care staff. I performed a basic check to see if the standard equipment was present and to get a broad sense of how the PA Physician's assistant RN Registered nurse

II. Opinions

In my opinion, the medical care provided in Arizona prisons is significantly below community standards and places patients at serious risk of harm. In order to provide community standard of care in a correctional setting, a system must be in place – complete with centralized management, policies and procedures, adequate staff and clinical space and budget – that allows patients reasonable access to healthcare providers, professional clinical judgment on their case, delivery of the care that is ordered, and selfcorrecting processes designed to minimize preventable negative outcomes. I discuss defendants' systemic deficiencies in each of these major categories in the following sections. I identified these deficiencies in my reviews of patient healthcare records and interviews with patients as well as in the documents produced by the State and others and the depositions of various staff and administrators. I toured five of the ten prison complexes in the Arizona system and undertook thorough reviews of the care at those institutions. My findings in this report are systemwide, however, and not just confined to those five complexes. I am confident in making systemic findings for several reasons. First, the deficiencies in care were consistent across the prisons that I toured. I found some variations and distinctions, but overall the prison complexes I toured were subject to the same serious problems, as described throughout this report. Second, those problems were of a system-wide nature, caused by deficits in organizational structure, staffing, and quality assurance measures that are not the responsibility of individual prisons to develop. In addition, I have seen testimony that policies and practices are statewide, as are the deficits. Third, I reviewed many dozens of healthcare records of prisoners who had been housed at prisons around the state. I have therefore reviewed care from a wide range of prisons beyond what I toured. Finally, I have reviewed numerous documents attesting to poor care and serious deficits the system. These documents are listed in Appendix C and I allude to them throughout the report. Before I move on to a methodical review of the elements of the healthcare delivery system, I would like to discuss an emblematic case. One patient I met in my investigation experienced so many errors in so many areas that his case serves as an introduction of sorts to the remainder this report. whom I met in Yuma's La Paz unit on August 1, 2013, has experienced horrendous care in ADC with potentially disastrous consequences. On April 19, 2013, he received a diagnosis of advanced colon cancer as a result of an emergency department visit for abdominal pain. As of August 1, it had not even been staged. Staging is critical for cancer cases and it requires a number of diagnostic tests in order to know how extensive the cancer is at the time of diagnosis. All treatment plans for cancer depend heavily on staging because the treatment plans vary widely based on the severity and spread of disease. On a fundamental level, the staging process answers the question regarding whether the cancer is locally contained or whether it has metastasized to involve organ systems other than where the cancer started. The failure to stage this new cancer diagnosis guaranteed that care could not proceed because no treatment plan could be formulated. His medical records contain a referral for consultation, but it had not yet been done in early August. This is a patient for whom every day counts, and more than 100 days had passed since initial diagnosis without even taking the first step toward a treatment plan. There were numerous serious errors in his care. It is a screening failure: he should have had a screening colonoscopy at age 50 (he is 51 currently). It is an access to care failure: on December 12, 2012, he complained of lumps and bowel problems but received no follow-up; on January 10, 2013, a physician's assistant saw him for his complaints of lumps in stomach and change in bowel habits on the provider line but did not perform a rectal exam or perform a test for blood in his stool; on January 21, 2013, his labs showed that he was anemic with strong evidence of iron deficiency, which is very common in colon cancer cases, but the physician's assistant did nothing to evaluate these abnormalities further when he signed off the labs. On March 7, 2013, a prison doctor ordered a screening test for colon cancer that came back positive (occult blood positive); the test result was sent to the facility doctor for review and no action was taken to evaluate this abnormal critical lab further. Staff did not know he had cancer until April 19, when they found a huge tumor and obstructed bowel. They should have known far earlier. was not referred to oncology until May 8 and not seen until July 5. The PET and CT scans ordered at that time to accomplish the staging had not been done by early August. His case also shows additional treatment planning failures: he has no teeth and cannot open his mouth well and he has a deformity of his gumline. As a result, it is not possible to fit him with dentures without completing some dental surgery to enable the dentures to fit properly. In cancer patients it is critical to maintain nutrition, weight, and hydration to help them deal with their treatment. Dealing with his eating limitations is a long-term planning issue. I saw no evidence of any such planning in his file, and he told me there had been none, to his knowledge. Instead of treating him so he can effectively masticate, the prison system has left him untreated and edentulous. I saw him again at the end of October when I toured Tucson and he was edentulous and he appeared much more gaunt and in significant pain. He informed me that he had seen the oncologist on October 24, 2013, and that chemotherapy had finally been ordered. He was six months after initial diagnosis of his cancer and treatment had yet to begin. Moreover, his case shows medication failures: he has severe pain from his advanced colon cancer and obstructed bowel. At Yuma, he was given Vicodin (hydrocodone / acetaminophen) four times a day, which is a short-acting pain killer that is medically inappropriate for chronic cancer pain. To make matters worse, the Facility Health Administrator at Yuma executed a written order dated June 21, 2013, that I saw posted that mandated that all pain medication be crushed prior to administration, which greatly reduces the duration of effectiveness of an already short-acting medication. As such, his pain regimen was inappropriate and ineffective for the severity of his disease. Finally, his case raises serious ethical concerns: when I saw him again by chance in Tucson he told me that his pain regimen had been changed to longer acting medications but that the nursing staff refused to give him his pain medications until he signed a broad waiver of care that was initiated by his assigned nurse with no physician involvement. By his account, this waiver – which I reviewed, and on its face find unethical and deeply disturbing – was offered to him under troublingly coercive circumstances. I discuss the profound ethical and legal violations inherent in this situation below, in Section II.B.6. In sum, this patient's experience displays the incompetence, heartlessness, and deliberate indifference I found throughout the system as a whole. is dying a needless, painful, and preventable death. A. Essential building blocks to a correctional healthcare delivery system It is well established that functional healthcare delivery systems are comprised of certain building blocks that allow them to provide effective care. As all competent healthcare administrators know, the failure to carefully design, implement, and maintain these building blocks can cause a system to devolve quickly into chaos and substandard care. In the Arizona system, I found ample evidence that most of these elements are either missing or profoundly flawed. 1.

Centralized organization/management structure It is axiomatic that a functional system must be well structured, with clear lines of authority, oversight, and accountability. The healthcare delivery system in Arizona prisons has none of these characteristics. Instead, it has experienced years of chaos. The State ran its own healthcare system for many years, before contracting to the lowest bidder in July 2012. Wexford, the company that won the contract, by ADC's own account failed utterly to implement a healthcare system that met minimum constitutional requirements, and was replaced in early March 2013 by Corizon, the next lowest bidder. Corizon has run healthcare in the Arizona prisons since that time. (a) ADC to Wexford to Corizon It is clear from the documents and depositions I have reviewed that medical care has been systematically deficient during these transitions. With ADC in charge prior to July 2012, healthcare reportedly suffered from many of the same deficits I see in the present system and discuss throughout this report, including failures in intake screening, with "grossly incomplete" transfer summaries, poor documentation of medical histories, and failure to provide preventive care (WEXFORD000023-25)2 ; medical records that were disorganized, incomplete, and sometimes lost (27, 68); chaotic and unreliable chronic care (29, 73); poor care for HIV patients, with incorrect dosages and medication combinations that placed patients at risk for developing drug-resistant HIV (35); a backlog of thousands of referrals for outside specialty consultations dating to 2008 (39-40); lack of negative airflow infirmary beds (43); care "below acceptable standards" (46), inadequate or nonexistent quality improvement programs and "[w]idespread quality deficiencies" (54); nurses practicing outside the scope of their licenses (59); and "longstanding medication administration practices that were not only dangerous and outside accepted scope of practice, but also threatened nurses' licensure" (66-67). In sum, "The ADC system is broken, and does not provide a constitutional level of care." WEXFORD000003; see also ADC048247- 48250. More specifically, "[a]fter working within the ADC inmate health care system for four months, Wexford Health finds the current class action lawsuits to be accurate." WEXFORD000003; see also WEXFORD000130 (same), WEXFORD000075 (as of 2 the citations in this sentence are to documents produced by Wexford, with the Bates number prefix WEXFORD0000. For the sake of efficiency, I do not repeat the prefix for each citation. November 2012, "[p]rocesses and practices outlined in detail in the ADC's current class action lawsuits remain present; the ADC has not shared any improvement plans with Wexford Health"). At least one high-level ADC official admits to problems pre-dating Wexford's arrival. ADC's Medical Program Administrator admits that chronic care was a problem when ADC ran its own medical care because of short-staffing. Deposition of David Robertson, August 26, 2013 (Robertson Depo), at 65:1-65:6. Wexford's eight-month tenure in Arizona was rife with serious problems. On September 21, 2012, ADC sent a "Written Cure Notification" to Wexford's Director detailing 20 significant areas of non-compliance, including, again, the same problems outlined in this report: lack of basic building blocks of a healthcare delivery system (inadequate staffing leading to treatment failures; inadequate quality assurance measures; poor communication between field staff, prison administrators, and Wexford); failure to provide timely access to care (patients not getting seen, patients' health needs requests and grievances ignored, chronic care patients not identified); and failure to provide care that is ordered (medication delivery failures, interruptions, discontinuations and changes; specialty care not provided). ADC027854- ADC027860. All deficiencies were identified at all ten ADC complexes. Id. at ADC027863-ADC027869. Wexford, in response, did not dispute the deficiencies; instead, they placed the blame on ADC, stating that they could not cure them in 90 days and that most "are long-standing issues, embedded into ADC health care policy and philosophy, and which existed well before Wexford Health assumed responsibility for the program." ADC027941-ADC027942. In March 2013, Corizon assumed responsibility for healthcare in Arizona prisons. This report is grounded on information dated since that time, although I include older data when relevant. The current fundamental failures I describe are nearly identical to Wexford's portrait of ADC (WEXFORD000001-131) and to ADC's portrait of Wexford. ADC027854-27860. Corizon has clearly has not managed to turn this ship aroundThere are surface differences between ADC and Wexford and Corizon, but care has been egregiously bad for years, under direct supervision of all three. I can state this confidently not only because of the finger-pointing reports from ADC and Wexford, but also because the types of problems I found and describe in this report – such as the widespread failure to follow policies, provide timely care, and deliver appropriate medications -- are chronic ones that do not develop overnight. I have also seen compelling evidence, in patients' charts and in the documents and depositions I have reviewed, that the problems are of long standing. Privatization is inherently risky in the correctional realm, as Joe Profiri, ADC's Contract Bed Operations Director, points out: the profit motive leads to corners being cut. AGA_Review_00037464 ("Wexford by design will maintain minimum staffing to maximize profits"). It also leads to dilatory and inadequate responses to serious and lifethreatening treatment failures: I agree with Mr. Profiri that Wexford (and Corizon as well, from my review) has displayed a lack of urgency to repair the problems, which "is all to[o] often a component missing with privatization." AGA_Review_00037465. As Mr. Profiri stated, "Wexford's failure[s] in many ways are our failures." AGA_Review_00037462. The same is true of Corizon, and any private company the State contracts with to provide essential services. ADC is ultimately responsible for the lengthy catalogue of deficiencies and damage I describe in this report. (b) Current oversight: the MGAR system The oversight structure Arizona uses to monitor Corizon and ensure that care is delivered in its prisons is the Monthly Green-Amber-Red (MGAR) reporting process. In this system, certain performance measures -- such as timeliness of sick call, scheduling of urgent specialty consultations, and appropriate medical records filing -- are selected each month. Not all measures are monitored all the time. Declaration of Kathleen Campbell, Dkt. No. 707-1, October 28, 2013, at ¶ 4. The ADC monitor measures compliance for the selected performance measures, and enters a finding of green, amber, or red to Case 2:12-cv-00601-DJH Document 1104-1 Filed 09/08/14 Page 226 of 364 12 indicate compliance levels. Id. The computerized system automatically generates an emailed request for a corrective action plan (CAP) to Corizon to address each individual deficient finding. Id. at ¶ 7. Any CAP is entered into the MGAR system, but the monitor does not know unless he or she looks for it in the system, and the CAP for each individual performance measure is stored separately, making the review of a large number of CAPs onerous. Id. at ¶¶ 8, 11-12. The MGAR process, while providing extensive evidence of the deficiencies of Wexford's and Corizon's performance, is a failure as a management oversight structure. While the MGAR reports are helpful for pointing out certain errors and omissions, they are not effective measures of compliance. At least one monitor agrees: the Perryville monitor testified that MGARs are "probably not" a fair representation of compliance. Haldane Depo, 136:20-137:5. The Corizon Vice President for Operations testified that she did not think the MGARs were a meaningful quality assurance process. Deposition of Vickie Bybee, October 10, 2013, at 6:17-6:18, 90:10-90:14; 91:7-91:20. There are several reasons for this. First, monitors have no meaningful standards. The MGARs list performance standards and rate them on a color based system (green, yellow, and red) to indicate compliance levels. The scoring is arbitrary, there are no scoring standards, and the results do not conform to anything that resembles meaningful performance grading. Deposition of Kathleen Campbell, September 11, 2013, at 71:8- 71:12 (no scoring criteria). The deficiencies associated with this process are demonstrated by the monitors themselves: Deposition of Arthur Gross, September 9, 2013, at 107:6-107:12 (individual monitors decide based on own judgment when a deficiency changes from amber to red); Deposition of Marlena Bedoya, September 10, 2013, at 113:15-113:24, 158:24-159:13 (decisions about severity and significance of data reported in MGARs based on personal feelings; Tucson monitor has no rubric); Deposition of Jenny Mielke-Fontaine, September 20, 2013, at 98:24-99:1, 238:16-238:21 (difference between amber and red is "subjective"), 229:9-229:24 (MGAR "is a Case 2:12-cv-00601-DJH Document 1104-1 Filed 09/08/14 Page 227 of 364 13 subjective tool"), 317:10-317:16 (no policy directs monitors on number of charts to review); Deposition of Anthony Medel, September 17, 2013, at 64:5-65:8, 192:25-193:8 (no personal rules for Yuma monitor about what colors correspond to what percentages compliance); Deposition of Mark Haldane, September 18, 2013, at 162:6-163:21 (although specific performance standard not met, it was marked green by Perryville monitor because "other deficiencies [are] of higher priority" and "if everything is a priority, then nothing is a priority"), 164:2-164:10, 165:12-166:14 (green rating for one item despite noncompliance over 30% because "progress [was] being made"). Second, the rating system is unreliable. I found deplorable treatment errors and systemic deficiencies in care at the Yuma complex, but the ADC monitor has never given Corizon a red mark because he does not believe they have warranted it. Medel Depo, 116:22-116:23. He rated one item amber that had a 44% compliance score, down from 55% the previous month. Medel Depo, 215:12-220:13. The same monitor was unable to explain why he rated Corizon better on staffing in June 2013 than in July 2013, despite the fact that staffing numbers were better in July. Medel Depo, 209:7-213:21. Third, some monitors also lack the necessary skills to be effective. Mark Haldane, the Perryville monitor, has no formal health training at all. Haldane Depo, 13:9-13:11. Arthur Gross, ADC Assistant Director over the Health Monitoring Bureau which is responsible for the monitoring, has no clinical medical training.

Deposition of Arthur Gross, September 9, 2013, 10:4-10:14. Compounding all these problems is the fact that the individuals in charge of the healthcare system do not take the monitors or their reports seriously. Mr. Gross, the Health Monitoring Bureau chief, does not read the monthly MGAR reports or any CAPs from Corizon. Gross Depo, 13:17-14:2 (MGARs), 97:4-97:9 (CAPs). ADC's Medical Program Administrator similarly does not read the monthly MGAR reports. Robertson Depo, 79:13-79:16, 120:6-120:12. He knows so little about the process that he believes that if a monitor identifies a specific problem as amber status in an MGAR, it is the monitor's responsibility to follow up on the problem and see that it is addressed (a responsibility disavowed by the monitors, as I discuss below). Robertson Depo, 83:11- 83:21. Although MGARs are inadequate measures of compliance, they do contain valuable information about deficiencies; many of my conclusions are informed by the problems they describe. However, I see no evidence that the MGAR process has contributed to any solutions for these problems, primarily because there is no evidence that the monitors or anyone else takes appropriate action to correct problems, even if they find chronic noncompliance. Bedoya Depo - Tucson, 160:8-160:21 (not the monitor's responsibility to take action if a measure is in noncompliance for consecutive months), 220:17-221:3 and 221:9-221:12 (monitor can't fix problems); Haldane Depo – Perryville, 78:5-78:17 (his responsibility is to report the problem; he can't force compliance), Haldane Depo – Perryville, 63:22-65:4, 176:25-178:23, 65:8-65:24 (monitor's role is to "keep reporting it, and if it's important to somebody above my level, then they can get it corrected. If it's not that big of a deal, if nobody cares, then it probably isn't my job to care either"), 53:12-56:1 ("no powers to force [Corizon] to do anything"); MielkeFontaine – Florence, 212:23-213:5 (Corizon's job, not hers, to solve problems), 213:6- 213:10 (no change to her responsibilities if she finds repeated, chronic noncompliance). The utility of these reports is further limited because monitors do no analysis: they do not investigate causes of noncompliance. Bedoya Depo - Tucson, 196:4-196:7 (no investigation of causes for noncompliance; Mielke-Fontaine Depo – Florence, 112:4- 112:7 (not her job to look at past performance), 299:8-299:9 (no analysis of MGAR data), 196:7-197:23 (found poor compliance with patient access to care in July 2013, but did no follow-up or analysis). There are also areas of oversight that the MGARs do not even address. For example, ADC does not monitor whether Corizon performs adequate training or orientation for staff. Gross Depo, 95:17-95:20. The MGAR process does not address whether informed consents have been obtained. Deposition of Kathleen Campbell, September 23, 2013, at 52:19-53:6. The monitor for the Phoenix complex, where all male ADC prisoners undergo intake screening, does not know the requirements for intake medical screening; her job is merely to "monitor if they have complied with completing all the forms. . . . Medical, clinically what they're to be doing. . . that's not my area." Deposition of Helen Valenzuela, August 23, 2012 (Valenzuela Depo), 87:20-89:20. The monitoring ultimately is ineffective. The CAP process is, essentially, a farce: chronic noncompliance is simply reported over and over and over again, and to the extent CAPs are even produced, nobody appears to review them to see if they are effective. Campbell Depo (September 11, 2013), 90:11-90:13 (statewide nursing monitor did not track whether she or the nurses she supervised ever received a CAP); Winland Depo, 41:16-41:23 (statewide pharmacy monitor has never seen a CAP); Haldane Depo – Perryville, 54:1-55:12 (CAPs had "canned responses" that "in many instances [were] not responsive to the issue that was raised"), 56:12-57:17, 143:3-143:17; Mielke-Fontaine Depo – Florence, 101: 6-101:9, 102:2-102:18 (doesn't know whether CAPS required for amber or red findings). The persistent deficiencies that plague ADC institutions highlight the inefficacy of the review process. 2. Consistently followed policies and procedures Policies and procedures are fairly standardized across correctional healthcare systems. In the Arizona system, I was struck by the widespread violation of the policies and the lack of oversight and accountability that would compel compliance. Basic healthcare policies – such as those governing sick call timelines, chronic care management, healthcare records filing, and specialty consultations -- are violated in the Arizona system to a distressing degree. For the sake of space, I will not repeat here the evidence set forth throughout this report, particularly in Sections II.B.1, II.B.2, II.C.2, II.C.3, II.C.4, II.D.1, and II.D.2. Case 2:12-cv-00601-DJH Document 1104-1 Filed 09/08/14 Page 230 of 364 16 In addition to its abysmal record in following its own policies, Arizona also lacks some critical written policies. The following are all policy omissions that fall below community standard of care for correctional healthcare systems: (all citations are to Defendants' Responses to Plaintiff Verduzco's First Set of Requests for Admission, June 11, 2013): ADC policy does not require diabetic prisoners be referred to ophthalmology if healthcare staff detect the presence of retinopathy (Response 211); ADC policy does not require that healthcare staff consult with an HIV specialist prior to initiating, changing, or discontinuing medications for HIV positive prisoners (Response 241); ADC policy does not require that prisoners with COPD be given an annual pneumonia or flu shot (Responses 199-202); ADC policy does not require that prisoners on anticoagulants have their blood tested every 4 weeks to measure their INR levels, and if the level is not within the therapeutic range that they be monitored every 7 calendar days (Responses 193-196); ADC does not have a tuberculosis control program at each prison complex (Response 167); ADC policy does not require that prisoners with symptoms of pertussis be single-celled (Response 171); ADC policy does not require that prisoners with symptoms of influenza be single-celled (Response 173); ADC policy does not require that healthcare staff always have a sharps container within arm's reach when using a needle or sharp instrument to reduce the possibility of blood-borne pathogen exposure (Response 189); ADC policy does not require prisoners suspected or confirmed to have chicken pox be isolated in a negative pressure room (Response 179); and ADC policy does not require prisoners with tuberculosis symptoms or positive tuberculosis tests be isolated in a respiratory isolation room (ADC does not have a respiratory isolation room, and states that if a provider suspects a prisoner has tuberculosis, that inmate will be sent to the hospital) (Responses 169-170). Arizona lacks other policies that, while not strictly necessary in order to provide community standard of care, are nonetheless good practice. Because their absence contributes to the deficiencies in the system and because adoption of these policies be helpful as one aspect of system reform, I set them out as recommendations but not requirements: ADC policy does not require that prisoners on anticoagulants be examined by a healthcare clinician at least every 90 days (Response 197); ADC policy does not require prisoners with chronic obstructive pulmonary disease and forced expiratory volume 1 score < 50% be seen by a clinician at least every 90 days (Response 203); ADC policy does not require prisoners with cirrhosis be given at the time of diagnosis a baseline screening esophagogastroduodenoscopy for the diagnosis of esophageal and gastric varices (Response 229); ADC policy does not require prisoners with cirrhosis be screened with an abdominal ultrasound at least every 180 days (Response 231); ADC policy does not require prisoners with cirrhosis be examined by a clinician at least every 90 days (Response 233); ADC policy does not require prisoners with chronic Hepatitis C be given annual blood tests for their levels of aspartate transaminase, gamma glutamyl transpeptidase, bilirubin, platelets, and international normalized ratio level (Response 235); ADC policy does not require prisoners with chronic Hepatitis C be screened with an abdominal ultrasound at least every 180 days (Response 237); ADC policy does not require prisoners whose seizures are managed with anti-epileptic drugs be examined by a healthcare clinician at least every 180 days (Response 253). 3. Adequate staffing Staff are the backbone for medical care delivery. There is no dispute that there is a medical staffing crisis in the Arizona prisons. The ADC Assistant Director over the Health Monitoring Bureau admits that "there are shortages of providers that need to be addressed" (Gross Depo, 97:22-23), and that as of June 2013, "the staffing patterns were insufficient. They were at 53 percent of staffing positions." Gross Depo, 115:7-9. The evidence to support his conclusion is overwhelming.3 Robertson Depo, 88:14-88:16, 90:8-90:15 (in April 2013 at Florence South Unit, staffing problems caused 3 The numbers of prisoners in these individual units is relevant to the compliance numbers I describe. For the sake of efficiency, I have not included the population Case 2:12-cv-00601-DJH Document 1104-1 Filed 09/08/14 Page 232 of 364 18 the unit to be more than 500 behind on chronic care with at least 100 charts pending review), 93:15-93:21 (only one part-time physician at Tucson when the contract indicated that two should be employed); 95:9-95:13 (monitors are always pressing for more staff); 104:3-104:11 (staff shortages are "an outstanding issue" at all prisons); Haldane Depo - Perryville, 45:6-46:2 (Perryville is persistently noncompliant with requirement that referrals from sick call to providers be seen within 7 days because they "don't have the staff to meet that requirement, and it's almost never met"), 222:15-223:5 ("staffing shortages throughout the complex" and "nurses [were] reporting that without the ability to use registry staff or overtime and with nurse hours being cut beginning the week of 4/28/13, they do not have the ability to fill all shifts "); Deposition of Jeffrey Sharp, October 9, 2012, at 50:20-51:1 (according to Perryville physician, not enough medical staff at complex to provide adequate care). As of September 27, 2012, 35% budgeted full-time equivalent healthcare positions and 47% of all budgeted full-time equivalent medical provider positions statewide were vacant. ADC035214, ADC049045-49055. ADC's own monitoring reports describe that widespread understaffing leads to inadequate care and delays in care. See, for example, ADC154342 (September 30, 2013) (nurses at Tucson frequently get called off, leaving the unit understaffed for total care patients); ADC154338 (September 28, 2013) (open positions at Tucson lead to missed sick call deadlines and chronic care backlogs); ADC154210-11 (September 18, 2013) (Perryville San Pedro does not have an RN and Perryville San Carlos has only one pill nurse); ADC154210 (September 18, 2013) (vacancies throughout Perryville "affect the ability of existing staff to meet the needs of all" patients); ADC137395 (July 29, 2013) (Tucson's open positions include 1.5 LPNs, 3.7 nursing assistants, 1.5 physicians, 4.1 RNs, 1 RN supervisor, and 1 regional director); ADC137335 (July 29, 2013) (open positions per the contract staffing pattern at Phoenix leave staffing insufficient to meet number for every housing unit in every reference in this report. Instead, I attach as Exhibit D a recent ADC population report to give some context to these numbers. prisoner needs); ADC137309 (July 26, 2013) (for at least one year, Perryville has had only one nurse on duty between 0500 and 0700, and she conducts diabetic lines, leaving no nurse to respond to emergencies or the use of restraints); ADC137445 (July 25, 2013) (Yuma lacks 0.5 LPN, 3 full-time nurse practitioners, 0.4 nursing assistants, 1 physician, and 0.6 RNs); ADC137260 (July 26, 2013) (Florence is only 80% staffed); ADC137445 (July 25, 2013) (Yuma is not fully staffed and not able to meet the needs of the prison population); ADC137259 (July 19, 2013) (Florence Globe has only one RN working on assignment, and labs had not been drawn since March); ADC088885 (April 30, 2013) (Florence South has no regularly scheduled healthcare provider); ADC089055 (April 29, 2013) (Tucson staff vacancies include 1 nurse practitioner, 1 RN supervisor, 2 staff RNs, 7 nursing assistants, 1 psychologist, 2 mental health registered nurses, 1 physician, and 1 regional director); ADC088949 (April 30, 2013) (Perryville lacks a Director of Nursing, Assistant Director of Nursing, and a nursing supervisor); ADC088886 (April 29, 2013) ("Florence complex has onl[y] one HCP and two mid level providers at this time" and "[a]ll units have numerous in[ma]tes overdue for chronic care visits and referrals"); ADC088930 (April 29, 2013) (Perryville lacks dedicated medical records staff in three units); ADC088976 (April 28, 2013) (upper management at Phoenix Aspen does not permit overtime and the use of agency despite an "extremely high back load number of intakes, resulting in medical and medical records staff working until midnight); ADC089108 (April 26, 2013) (At Yuma, "staffing is not adequate/effective to meet[] the facility's needs"); ADC088951 (April 24, 2013) (April schedule at Perryville shows no or partial coverage by CNA some days leaving one RN for 5-7 infirmary patients, two of which are high acuity and one of which requires two-person transfer); ADC088885-86 (April 23, 2013) (according to nurses, nurse shifts at Florence are unfilled because hours are being cut, and they are prevented from using registry staff or overtime); ADC089057 (April 17, 2013) (Tucson infirmary has six total or almost total care inmates and only one day shift, part-time second aid staff); ADC088885 (April 16, 2013) (per Florence Central staff, use of overtime or registry nurses is not permitted resulting in May schedule coverage gaps in the infirmary, on Sundays, and in cell blocks on some days); ADC088852 (April 14, 2013) (no provider on site during March at Florence Globe); ACD088771 (April 5, 2103) (Phoenix has only one mid-level staff member providing "all the patient care at this facility"); and ACD088750 (April 3, 2013) (Florence has only two full-time medical providers for all units and one part time medical provider for South and Kasson). Some staffing problems appear to have grown worse under Corizon's management. The Tucson Medical Director reacted with dismay in February 2013 to the news that Corizon would cut back significantly on the already over-extended providers: "Our skeleton just lost a foot and tibia." AGA_Review_00001721. He explained that he "[a]nticipate[s] the already overloaded backlog to get worse over the next few months" and warned that "[a]ll providers are telling me they are mentally, emotionally and physically exhausted already and so am I. . . . there is absolutely no way we can provide contract required coverage w/ current staffing." Id. Nursing coverage appears be similarly strained under Corizon: an ADC monitor noticed in April 2013 that Florence Central's May schedule showed "days that there is no coverage in any of the cell blocks"; Eyman's Cook Unit showed nursing hours cut by 40 hours per week. AGA_Review_00013126. The monitor noted that "[e]ven at current staffing levels," nurses were cutting corners to keep up with their work, including presigning medication administration reports, failing to take patients' vital signs, and failing to update problem lists in medical records. Id. See also AGA_Review_00001704 (Corizon cut pharmacy technical staff in half at Tucson, down to four pharmacy technicians for more than 5000 patients); AGA_Review_00009347 (as of March 28, 2013, pharmacy staff at Tucson too small to ensure prisoners are provided medications on release: "the current system IS NOT working"). I saw evidence of inadequate staffing on my tours. At Tucson, the Medical Director's concerns from February, quoted above, were clearly justified: there were only two physicians in the complex, one of whom is the medical director and thus has administrative duties in addition to seeing patients. The other is part-time. These numbers are completely inadequate for a prison with 5,000 prisoners. One patient in the infirmary (called IPC, or inpatient care unit), , told me he hardly ever sees a doctor, which does not surprise me. Nursing care suffered from similar deficits: there were only two RNs for 40 patients in the IPC. 4 I saw some of the results of Tucson's staffing deficiency on my tour: a large number of lab results and consult results and x-ray reports, some of which showed significant abnormalities, that had not been filed or reviewed for four to six weeks (described in more detail below in Section II.D.3). At Perryville, I saw a notation in a healthcare record for a heart patient named : her chronic care follow-up form dated April 2, 2013, by D.O. DL Palmer indicated that "I have concerns of patient on this yard – no weekend nurse coverage." Staffing shortages endanger patients. Sharp Depo, 52:23-52:25, 53:1-9 (according to Perryville physician, the staffing problems can create delays in providing medical care which can create a serious medical risk). They do this in a variety of ways: they lead to excessive delays in access to care (Section II.B, below), healthcare staff acting outside the scope of their licenses (Section II.C.3, below), the failure to carry out providers' orders (Section II.D.1, below), and the failure to review and file diagnostic test results (Section II.D.3, below). 4 Nursing staff is spread thin in other Tucson units as well: I saw a chart on my October 25 tour which laid out the nurse staffing per unit: in Cimmaron, 1 RN 2 LPNs; in Winchester, 1 RN 2 LPNs;in the Minors Unit, no RN 1 LPN (for passing out meds only); in Santa Rita, 2 RNs 1 LPN; in Rincon, 2 RNs 1 LPN; in Whetstone D, 1 RN 2 LPN; in Whetstone E, 0 1 LPN; in Manzanita D, 2 RNs 1 LPN. There are not enough nurses to meet the needs of these patients. Adequate physical facilities My observation of the physical facilities at prisons I toured showed me that basic elements are there: equipment, exam rooms, storage facilities, lab draw rooms, medication storage rooms were generally acceptable and generally clean.5 While the form was usually acceptable, the scale of the physical facilities is far too small: the clinic areas I toured in Perryville, for example, were surprisingly small and the infirmary – the highest level of care for the entire women's prison of over 3600 women – had only seven beds. At the time of my tour, only three were filled. I could not help wondering where all the sick women were, because in that large a population, many more infirmary beds are needed. I was also shocked at the extremely small medication rooms in the prisons I toured. They simply do not have the capacity to address the medical needs of the number of people they are intended to serve. Further, even undersized physical facilities are drastically underutilized, as was clear both from my personal observations and from the serious deficits in care evident in the healthcare records and from the interviews with prisoners. For one thing, there is no possible way staff are identifying and treating the medical needs of the population, given how few medications are being dispensed. I saw in Florence North an open metal case filled with medication bins. The population in this unit was 1078 at that time, and in a population that size I would have expected to see many more medications than were in the bins on the shelves of this metal case. Similarly, in Yuma, on a yard of 1000 inmates there were only three medication bins, far too small for the population. Because of the 5 There are scattered problems with physical facilities for patient living and care, however. A Perryville physician testified about conditions in Lumley Unit Building 30, with prisoners living in cells exposed to the weather, with no climate control in the heat of the Arizona summers, and a small exam room on the end of the building for medical care delivery: "I was kind of shocked . . . that the prisoners would live like that and I would be expected to provide medical care in that physical facility." Sharp Depo, 82:20-83:19. I viewed that unit and agree that the facilities and patient living conditions are substandard: the cells are indeed exposed to the heat and the outdoor elements and the exam room is airless and lacks basic equipment and facilities for medical care delivery. Dramatic lack of evidence of medication I saw on my first day of touring Yuma, I specifically requested to attend a medication pass to verify my concerns. On my second day I attended medication pass on Yuma's Cheyenne Unit which had a population of approximately 800 prisoners. Pill line started at 11:58 am and was complete by 12:12 pm and a total of seven patients received medications that I observed. It is simply not possible to believe that the healthcare needs of the prisoner population are adequately met when less than 1% of the population receives medications from pill line. It is not just the paucity of medications being dispensed that leads me to believe that the medical facilities are underutilized. I toured five prison complexes over a total of approximately eight days and saw hardly any encounters with nurses or primary care providers, hardly any patients in waiting areas, and hardly any medication being delivered. Aside from a few scattered finger sticks, a very few patients with providers, one short pill call, and a dozen prisoners waiting to be seen outside one clinic, I saw no evidence of care being delivered on my tours. Instead, I saw staff in their offices or moving around the prison and many empty exam rooms that clearly were not in routine use. On all of the tours I looked in the biohazard waste disposal cans present in the exam and treatment areas. These are generally not emptied daily in medical care settings and they contained scant biohazard waste material. This is not a definitive finding but it is an observation across the system that correlates with the general paucity of care I observed. It is simply impossible that so few people are in need of medical care at these prisons. In prisons the size of those I toured, even ones holding a primarily healthy population, I would expect the clinics to be a bustle of activity, with patients being seen, waiting to be seen, having vital signs taken, obtaining medications, being tested, and so forth. I was surprised to hear that ADC does not have a negative-pressure rooms or respiratory isolation rooms; their policies state that any prisoners requiring such housing are sent to outside hospitals. Responses 169-70 and 179, Defendants' Responses to Verduzco's First Set of Requests for Admission. A system this size should have these facilities. In a correctional facility there are multiple reasons why patients would need respiratory isolation as part of a precautionary step while they are assessed or treated. It is simply not reasonable in a system of this size to send all of these patients to the hospital. Many of these patients require extended isolation while the disease workup is completed. If Arizona does send all of the patients who legitimately need this type of isolation to the hospital, the cost would be extraordinary and wasteful. B. Timely access to care Having discussed some of the building blocks of a medical care delivery system, I turn now to consider the four broad categories of care. The most important major category of a functional medical care delivery system is access to care: the seemingly simple task of getting patients to see nurses and providers. Arizona fails this fundamental task. I have seen a shocking number of delays in access to care or even complete denials of care in Arizona's prisons. Some delays I saw were catastrophic and entirely preventable; other delays were less damaging to patients simply through luck of the draw: if a tumor turns out to be benign, a lengthy delay in providing a biopsy does not result in morbidity or mortality. However, the systematic failure to provide timely access to care places all patients at an unreasonable risk of serious harm. Patients with significant injuries or illnesses in the Arizona prison system are not safe: they are at serious risk of preventable negative outcomes. One typical example of delayed access to care provides an introduction to the topic. at Perryville found a lump in her breast on February 27, 2013. She filed an HNR immediately, saying the lump was "very sore." She was initially seen by a nurse on February 28 and a nurse practitioner on March 7. She had a mammogram performed on April 3 that resulted in an urgent consult being submitted by the facility doctor on that same date. There are several notes in her chart from her facility doctor that trace the care: May 6 (biopsy re-faxed to Dr. Irving); May 15 (still waiting for approval for biopsy); May 21 (no biopsy yet); May 22 (verbal approval for consult); Case 2:12-cv-00601-DJH Document 1104-1 Filed 09/08/14 Page 239 of 364 25 May 29 (official approval still pending doctor left message again); June 5 (doctor discussed case with supervising doctor still awaiting official consult approval); June 11 (doctor called and informed that patient was scheduled with surgeon); June 18 (patient sees surgeon for pre-op evaluation); June 20 (consult written to obtain biopsy per surgeon's recommendation); July 1 (local doctor sees patient again no biopsy yet); July 18 (patient has biopsy of breast mass); July 22 (patient given results of biopsy). The patient had Grade III invasive ductal breast cancer and it took five months to get a simple tissue diagnosis because of profound delays in access to care, even with her local physician actively advocating for her. The string of delays and incompetent treatment decisions is a catastrophe for . She now faces a much more invasive and toxic treatment regimen with the probability of much more extensive surgery needed to address her advanced cancer than if she had been worked up expeditiously. The delays also greatly increase the risk of recurrence and metastasis of the cancer than if the cancer had been dealt with immediately upon discovery. 1. Sick call/HNR system Correctional healthcare systems are resource-limited environments. In that setting, the most critical component of a sick call system is triage and it must be done face to face by an appropriately licensed healthcare provider (RN or above in Arizona), it must be done within 24 hours of receipt of the health needs request (HNR) and it must contain the basic elements of an assessment including brief history, vital signs, exam, and a disposition. This is the doorway to care, and patients must be seen quickly, sorted out, and provided quick referrals to urgent care or provider appointments as needed. Arizona's sick call and HNR system is not effective and patients face lengthy, sometimes life-threatening, delays in obtaining care. Pursuant to Arizona's policies, prisoners in need of medical care must file written HNR forms, which are required to be triaged within four hours of the time they are stamped as received. ADC010827. The patients are to be seen the same day for urgent needs; otherwise, they are to be seen by nurses for sick call ("nurse line") within 24 hours of the triage (or up to 72 hours if it is a weekend and clinically appropriate). Id. If higher level attention is warranted, patients must be seen by providers within seven days after that ("provider line"), as monitored on the MGARs. My review of healthcare records, documents, and depositions and my interviews with patients demonstrated to me that Arizona has a system-wide deficiency in providing an effective sick call process. The barriers to access at the front end are significant. Prisoners with serious conditions, including extremely fragile patients with chronic conditions, simply cannot get seen by the appropriate medical personnel. Because this element is so critical, I expended significant effort to understand the HNR process on my tours, in my staff interviews, in my patient interviews, and in my chart reviews. What I discovered is that a triage system does not exist anywhere I visited. The existing sick call system consists of prisoners submitting HNRs to a mailbox; the HNRs are collected and answered several days after submission with the universal answer consisting of some variant of "you will be scheduled." There were no signs of triage, no face-to-face assessment in a timely fashion, no vital signs, and no disposition. I was unable to track individual HNRs through the process from submission to a provider visit and most of the charts I reviewed had stacks of HNRs that did not result in healthcare visits. I did find sporadic evidence of what was termed "nursing sick call lines" that were conducted by LPNs long after the HNRs are submitted. LPNs are not legally allowed to perform "assessments" on patients so those nursing sick call visits are ineffective and the LPNs are practicing outside of their legal scope of practice. The patients I interviewed assured me, however, that the prison system is unerringly effective at charging them the fee for submitting an HNR and it happens very quickly even though the healthcare encounter they pay for often does not happen quickly or may not ever occur. An excellent example of the consequences of an inadequate triage system and using nurses outside of their scope is the case of that I discuss in Section II.C. The documentation of Arizona's failure to provide patients with timely access to care is overwhelming. ADC's Assistant Director over the Health Monitoring Bureau acknowledges that prisoners are not being seen in the appropriate time frames after the HNR is triaged by the nurse, and says he told Corizon to correct this problem. Gross Depo, 66:24-67:11. ADC's monitors document extreme backlogs in HNR and nurse and provider lines. See, for example, ADC154280 (September 30, 2013) (in September, Tucson had 11 missed sick call lines, 357 HNR backlog, 226 provider chart review backlog, 303 nurse line backlog, and a 535 provider line backlog); ADC154338 (September 28, 2013) (open positions at Tucson lead to missed sick call deadlines and chronic care backlogs); ADC137626 (August 28, 2013) (at Tucson, 20 missed sick call lines, backlog of HNRs (439), charts requiring provider review (252), backlog for nurse lines (317) and provider lines (393)); ADC137395 (July 29, 2013) (Tucson has backlogged charts needing provider reviews); ADC137360-61 (July 29, 2013) (Tucson Whetstone had 231 unprocessed HNRs, a provider line backlog at 322, and a nurse sick call backlog at 169, with similar statistics for Winchester, Cimarron, Rincon West Medical, Catalina, and Manzanita, and Santa Rita); ADC137309 (July 26, 2013) (Perryville San Carlos and Santa Maria have provider review chart backlogs); ADC088949 (April 30, 2013) ("[p]rovider lines, nurse lines, and chronic care appointments are each backlogged to varying degrees" at Perryville); ADC089000 (April 28, 2013) (April had only 29 provider line visits, with over 140 prisoners waiting to be seen, and a 227 prisoner backlog for the nurse line at Tucson Cimarron); ADC088745 (April 4, 2013) (at Florence Central, 36 HNRs were awaiting nurse line); Valenzuela Depo, 139:5-139:13 (sick call not occurring according to policy at Phoenix). Arizona nurses consistently fail to see patients within 24 hours of the HNR review. Haldane Depo - Perryville, 206:3-206:15, 34:5-34:12 (requirement "almost never met at Lumley"); Bedoya Depo – Tucson, 159:20-24, 186:17-24 (timeliness is common problem); ADC154281-85 (September 29, 2013) (56 of 80 Tucson charts reviewed show noncompliance); ADC154096-97 (September 30, 2013) (Florence units 82% noncompliant); ADC154183 (September 24, 2013) (in September to date, 36% of sick call appointments untimely in Perryville); ADC137583 (August 30, 2013) (at Phoenix, nearly all files show noncompliance); ADC137497 (August 30, 2013) (at Florence, nearly all files show noncompliance); ADC137629 (August 29, 2013) (Tucson prisoner had multiple HNRs for surgical, prescription, and medical device issues all of which have not been addressed); ADC137627 (August 29, 2013) (67 of 80 Tucson charts reviewed show noncompliance); ADC137497-98 (August 21, 2013) (32 of 44 Florence files noncompliant); ADC137363-65 (July 31, 2013) (at Tucson, 57 of 80 files noncompliant); ADC137259 (July 30, 2013) (Florence Central and South have stacks of HNRs waiting to be seen on sick call and by the provider); ADC137395 (July 29, 2013) (2-3 week wait for Tucson prisoners who file HNRs); ADC137419-20 (July 23, 2013) (widespread noncompliance in Yuma files); ADC089002 (April 29, 2013) (Tucson patient not seen for more than a month after HNR); ADC088848 (April 15 and 27, 2013) (at Florence, most charts reviewed show noncompliance); ADC089085 (April 26, 2013) (noncompliance on multiple yards at Yuma); ADC088915 (April 23, 2013) (custody levels and housing at Perryville Lumley interfere with compliance); ADC088847-48 (April 14 and 27, 2013) (36 of 54 records reviewed at Florence Globe show noncompliance). ADC prisoners frequently do not see a provider within seven days of sick call. Haldane Depo, 45:13-46:2 (Perryville is persistently noncompliant with requirement that referrals from sick call to providers be seen within seven days because they "don't have the staff to meet that requirement, and it's almost never met"); ADC137632 (August 29, 2013) (37 of 44 Tucson charts reviewed noncompliance); ADC137556 (August 26, 2013) (Perryville noncompliant); ADC137424-25 (July 23, 2013) (widespread noncompliance at Yuma); ADC089087 (April 26, 2013) (same); ADC088852 (April 18, 2013) (Florence East sick call referrals seen in April were old as January 26); ADC088852 (April 14, 2013) (Florence Globe prisoners not seen in 7 days as there was no provider in March). Some of the delay derives from the failure to conduct sick call consistently five days a week. See ADC154137 (September 30, 2013) ("[s]ick call is not being conducted 5 days a week at any unit on Florence complex. . . . Chronic condition back log of appointments is growing. Many inmates are not seen as ordered or required by disease management guidelines"); ADC154183 (September 24, 2013) (in September, only Perryville Lumley held sick call 5 days per week to date); ADC137497 (August 30, 2013) (sick call does not appear to be running 5 days a week on any unit in Florence); ADC137259 (July 30, 2013) (Florence sick call is not completed daily, requiring prisoners to continually reschedule); ADC137360 (July 29, 2013) (28 sick call lines were missed in July in Tucson); ADC088885 (April 30, 2013) (sick call line in Florence Central not run Monday to Friday); ADC089000 (April 29, 2013) (sick call not conducted 5 days a week at Tucson Rincon Minors); ADC089000 (April 28, 2013) (sick call not conducted 5 days a week at Tucson Cimarron); ADC088847 (April 27, 2013) (Florence Kasson demonstrated no evidence of a sick call nurses line during April); ADC089085 and ADC089108 (April 26, 2013) (multiple yards without sick call at Yuma); ADC088746 (April 4, 2013) (sick call was not conducted in Florence East Monday through Friday per policy); ADC088745 (April 4, 2013) (sick call was not conducted in Florence Central Monday through Friday per policy). These findings are consistent with what I heard from prisoners, who described waits of weeks or months after submitting HNRs for conditions that should have been addressed in a far more timely fashion. In the healthcare records I reviewed, I saw numerous examples of HNRs that were ignored or had extremely delayed responses. For example, in Tucson had testicular cancer and completed a course of chemotherapy at the end of 2012. He filed repeated HNRs seeking follow-up care. Despite his persistent attempts to receive care through the HNR process, his first follow-up appointment after chemotherapy did not occur until June 11, 2013. A CT scan was ordered at that time and done on July 17, 2013, and he was finally seen in follow-up on September 25, almost a year after completing chemotherapy. The Arizona Cancer Center requested that he been seen again within one month but as of late October 2013 that visit has not occurred, and did not appear to be scheduled in the medical record. All of this delay has potentially life-threatening consequences for and yet the delays in care are attributable completely to the caregivers, not to this well informed and very concerned patient. At Perryville, I found in my chart reviews a pregnant woman named whom staff had clearly forgotten about – as of July 31, 2013, she hadn't been seen since early May, when she arrived at the prison. An ultrasound consult was ordered for her on May 22, 2013, which is standard of care for pregnant women, but the ultrasound had not been completed. It is shockingly negligent not to obtain an ultrasound in a high-risk pregnant woman and the consequences are potentially dire for her and her baby. She told me that her due date was September 18. 6 Clearly the HNR system in Arizona is broken. An appropriate way to run such a system would be for every HNR have a serial number on it, which gets a logged into a system by number and date. The log can then be reviewed closely to make sure that there are timely follow ups to medical needs set forth in the HNR. Under Arizona's current practice, nobody tracks HNRs electronically. Responses 36 & 37, Defendants' Responses to Plaintiff Verduzco's First Set of Requests for Admission (June 11, 2013); see also Mielke-Fontaine Depo – Florence, 221:5-221:11 (the only way Florence monitor knows about the timeliness of the triaging of HNRs is by pulling the patients' charts), 317:22-317:25 (monitor would not know if a patient is not seen in response to an HNR). 6 I told the Perryville Director of Nursing the patient's name and number and urged her to have the patient seen and given the ultrasound that had been ordered two and a half months ago. She said "thank you" and walked away without writing the name down. medication renewal process. In looking at the medication administration records in his chart, it is obvious that he has had big breaks in therapy and that he has been getting less than his four medications and that all of the medications are out of sync with each other. The consequence for the patient is that treatment with less than all four of the medications at the same time induces resistance in the HIV virus and his immune system is failing because of incomplete therapy. All of this is unnecessary, but if Arizona continues to rely on this rudimentary HNR process that is horribly broken, cases like this will continue to be the norm. 2. Chronic care Chronic care clinics are a major focus of healthcare in any correctional setting. Preventive care is essential with chronic care patients; it is impossible to provide community standard of care without regularly scheduled appointments that allow providers to track the progress of these patients and ensure appropriate treatment modification are made. Insulin dependent diabetes is a good example. The standard of care is to schedule most of these patients for visits every three months. Providers will examine the patients, review how things have been going, update their care records, and obtain the basic healthcare screening needs. Various tests are employed at regular intervals, and providers can appropriately weigh risk and treatment options. In Arizona prisons, the chronic care is haphazard at best. There is no meaningful computerized tracking system for appointments for chronic care inmates who are supposed to see a provider every six months, just a physical appointment book.7 Robertson Depo, 136:16-136:25. Not surprisingly, chronic care prisoners in ADC 7 According to Corizon Arizona Regional Medical Administrator Dr. Williams, Corizon has been using the IHAS database to track chronic care, but "it's our impression that the database is not complete," so they are developing a new system called Care Log. Williams Depo, 30:18-31:20, 32:20-32:24. The new database will not track how often chronic care patients are seen by providers, however. Id. at 36:24-37:3 commonly do not see providers every three to six months as specified by their treatment plans; some chronic care patients go for years without seeing a provider. See, for example, ADC154294-96 (September 30, 2013) (at Tucson, widespread noncompliance in charts reviewed); ADC154228-29 (September 27, 2013) (15 of 43 Phoenix charts reviewed show noncompliance); ADC154108-10 (September 27, 2013) (74% noncompliance at Florence); ADC137587 (August 2013) (41% noncompliance at Phoenix); ADC137502-03 (August 21, 2013) (noncompliance rate ranges from 70% to 90% at Florence); ADC137637-40 (August 19, 2013) (noncompliance at Tucson); ADC137395 (July 29, 2013) (examinations past due for chronic care patients at Tucson); ADC137309 (July 26, 2013) (chronic care appointments not timely completed at Perryville); ADC088861 (April 27, 2013) (8 of 9 Florence South chronic care files reviewed demonstrate noncompliance); ADC088860 (April 27, 2013) (5 of 5 Florence Central files reviewed showed noncompliance); ADC089091 (April 27, 2013) (chronic care patients at Yuma Dakota and La Paz not seen as specified in treatment plans); ADC089091 (April 24, 2013) (Yuma Cheyenne prisoner who had open heart surgery in 2005 had not been seen by chronic care); ADC088958 (April 21, 2013) (noncompliance at Phoenix Aspen); ADC089017 (April 20, 2013) (Tucson prisoner with chronic seizures last saw chronic care provider on 11/10/11); ADC088927 (April 12 and 16, 2013) (at Perryville, 2 of 9 San Carlos charts and 7 of 11 San Pedro charts show noncompliance); ADC088772 (April 5, 2013) (some chronic care patients at Phoenix have not been seen for years). Moreover, ADC has severe appointment backlogs for many chronic care prisoners. ADC154137 (September 30, 2013) (at Florence, "[c]hronic condition back log of appointments is growing" and therefore "many inmates are not seen as ordered or required by disease management guidelines"); ADC154338 (September 28, 2013) (open positions at Tucson lead to chronic care backlogs); ADC088885 (April 30, 2013) (Florence South is 500+ behind on chronic care appointments with at least 100 charts to review); ADC088885 (April 30, 2013) (Florence North's mid-level provider is 150+ behind on chronic care appointments and has 100+ charts to review); ADC088885 (April 30, 2013) (Florence East's assigned healthcare provider is 250+ behind on chronic care appointments and has approximately 75-80 charts to review); ADC088949 (April 30, 2013) (Perryville chronic care appointments are backlogged); ADC088885 (April 30, 2013) (Florence Central is behind 400+ chronic care appointments); ADC089108 (April 26, 2013) (Yuma La Paz has a 3-4 month backlog of chronic care visits); ADC088746 (April 4, 2013) (chronic care at Florence East is 250+ appointments behind and 58+ charts were on a cart awaiting review). Many chronic care patients are simply not managed according to ADC policy. See, for example, ADC154298-300 (September 30, 2013) (at Tucson, 9 of 10 Rincon/HU9 charts, 5 of 10 Rincon charts, 6 of 10 Manzanita charts, 7 of 10 Catalina charts, 8 of

10 Winchester charts, 6 of 10 Santa Rita charts showed that disease management guidelines were not developed and implemented for chronic disease or other conditions not classified as chronic care); ADC154112-13 (September 27, 2013) (Florence develops and implements disease management guidelines only 26% of the time for chronic disease and other conditions not classified as chronic care); ADC154230 (September 27, 2013) (28 of 49 Phoenix charts reviewed demonstrated noncompliance with disease management guidelines for chronic disease or other conditions not classified as chronic care); ADC088862 (April 27, 2013) (25 of 36 Florence chronic care files reviewed showed noncompliance with disease management guidelines). My chart reviews and patient interviews bore out this data. I saw chronic care problems at Phoenix, especially for patients with seizures and diabetes, particularly in the coordination of insulin and finger sticks. See also AGA_Review_00006398 (March 5, 2013, email notes multiple chronic care patient forms missing important information and two significantly late chronic care appointments at Phoenix). At Florence, chronic care was similarly bad. had deficient and very sporadic attention for his poorly controlled diabetes, with blood sugars consistently in the 300s and some over 400 with no notes from the provider or nurses. At those blood sugar levels the patient could very easily slip into diabetic ketoacidosis, a life- threatening condition brought about by abnormally high sugars. I saw no acknowledgement that the nurses appreciated that risk or attempted to intervene to reduce it. Day after day his sugars ran high with no intervention. In addition, these out-of-control sugar levels cause accelerated damage to his other major organs so the longer he stays out of control the faster his other systems will fail. His long-term blood work returned a Hemoglobin A1C level on September 3, 2013, of 10.9% which indicates extremely poor blood sugar control. In looking at his medical records, he was housed at Lewis earlier in his incarceration where his sugars were well controlled and his Hemoglobin A1C was 6.4%, indicating ideal management. He clearly can be managed successfully; he just needs proper care. He put in an HNR on August 14: "want to see doctor to see why my sugars levels are so high" but he has yet to be seen as of the end of October. I saw records for a Florence patient with diabetic retinopathy ( ), who had only one chronic care visit on June 27, 2013. His records appropriately indicated he should be seen every 60 days, but as of October 16, 2013, no follow-up visit had been scheduled. A patient with HIV ( ) at Florence had labs and a visit on January 13, 2013 (as far as I could tell from the file); the six-month follow-up that was requested (and is appropriate) was not done as of October 16, 2013. These deficiencies present a serious danger because we know that those patients are fragile and at risk for developing significant complications. With this group of patients, more than anywhere else, an ounce of prevention is worth a pound of cure, because many complications of these diseases are preventable if clinicians keep a careful watch on them. Emergency care The problems described above with staffing and the HNR/sick call process also present barriers to appropriate responses to medical emergencies. See, for example, ADC137365 (July 31, 2013) (Tucson prisoner submitted an emergency HNR for chest pains on 6/15/13 and was not seen until 7/9/13). Custody staff play an essential role in providing first response emergency services. Given the fact of incarceration, they are simply the only people around who can do so. It is essential for prisoner health and safety that these staff be properly trained and responsive to medical emergencies. I saw many examples in the documents produced by the State of just the opposite: dereliction of emergency response duty by custody staff, often with dire results. ADC 49423-24 (Employee Disciplinary Letter suspending sergeant 8 hours without pay: "As a supervisor you are required to respond to emergency incidents on your unit. You failed to respond to this emergency ICS for twenty five minutes after it was initiated. You also failed to generate the travel orders for this inmate to be transported which delayed her from obtaining medical treatment"); ADC 49438-39 (Employee Disciplinary Letter demoting sergeant to CO II for having an inmate perform CPR on another inmate who subsequently died); ADC 49440-42 (Employee Disciplinary Letter suspending CO II 40 hours without pay for "leaving the inmate experiencing a medical emergency, unattended, sitting on the floor"). I also saw multiple failures of custody staff to perform basic safety and welfare check on prisoners as required by ADC policy. These failures also endanger the health of prisoners. ADC 024177 – 83 (officer saw prisoner lying with head towards wall and legs draped over bunk's edge at 6:25 a.m., was called to other duties, and returned hours later to find inmate same position, dead, with rigor mortis set in: "another officer is 'supposed to' cover her post. However that does not always happen, and the issue has been addressed as it is 'a constant battle'" (024180)); ADC 49412-14 (disciplinary letter suspending CO II 40 hours without pay for failing to conduct and log hourly security Case 2:12-cv-00601-DJH Document 1104-1

Filed 09/08/14 Page 251 of 364 37 checks after prisoner found dead); ADC O24972 – 024973 (prisoner died of lung cancer in cell; body was stiff and cold when found); ADC049457-58 (disciplinary letter suspending CO II 80 hours without pay for falsifying records and lying to investigators about conducting security, health, and welfare checks of bathroom after prisoner found unresponsive in bathroom); ADC049471-73 (disciplinary letter firing CO II after prisoner found dead in cell, strangled by cellmate, with rigor mortis setting in; investigation determined staff did not observe living breathing flesh during his checks); ADC049474- 75 (disciplinary letter suspending CO II for 40 hours without pay for same violation, same incident); ADC049465-68 (disciplinary letter demoting lieutenant to sergeant for failure to post a replacement officer on unit for an hour, during which prisoner committed suicide). Staffing failures in ADC emergencies are not confined to custody staff. In one particularly disturbing case, on March 11, 2013, a prisoner in Tucson was found "covered in blood and feces" with "three lacerations from his neck and one laceration to his inner right forearm above the wrist" and "incomprehensible" speech. AGA_Review_ 00007169. Custody staff requested medical assistance, but the night nurse apparently did not have a vehicle and the Complex Shift Commander "had no staff available to pick up medical personnel." AGA_Review_00007168. An ambulance was called and arrived 16 minutes later. AGA_Review_00007169. For this patient, every minute counted and the lack of quick medical response might have had troubling consequences. Apparently, this is not the only time such a barrier to effective emergency response has been noted. AGA_Review_00007168 ("it seems like this also happened in the case of as well where they couldn't respond"). At Perryville in August 2012, three prisoners overdosed in the course of several hours, but not one was sent to the hospital. AGA_Review_00038450. According to one staff at the institution, "one provider . . . said she medically cleared two over the phone – which was not true. One LPN requested guidance from the RN and was denied any and (Florence Central infirmary and HU8 prisoners are not receiving required physician rounds or follow up, and approximately 160 charts are awaiting provider review for labs, reports, medication renewals, and the like); ADC089057 (April 16, 2013) (Tucson prisoner had 33 falls in the infirmary since November 2012, the last of which required a craniotomy); ADC088887 (April 28, 2013) (as of 4/25/13, prisoners in the Florence infirmary and HU8 had not been seen for at least six days); ADC089057 (April 17, 2013) (Tucson infirmary has six total or almost total care inmates and only one day shift, part time second aid staff); ADC089057 (April 17, 2103) (Tucson infirmary has no supervising nurse 24 hours a day); ADC088951 (April 24, 2013) (April schedule at Perryville shows no or partial coverage by CNA some days, leaving one RN for 5-7 infirmary patients, two of which are high acuity and one of which requires two person transfer. 5. Custody involvement Custody support is essential to achieve physical access to care. In Arizona they act as gatekeepers to care, both preventing patients from reaching medical staff and intervening to try to get patients seen by medical staff (which demonstrates access problems as well as raising privacy concerns). In the absence of a functional sick call system, custody staff act as gatekeepers for medical care: patients must persuade them that they need help in order to get to medical staff. Many prisoners described having to beg custody staff to help them get medical care. For example, at Perryville went into labor in June 2013. She told me that her water broke in the morning, but staff refused to take her to the hospital. She reported that nurses refused to believe that her water broke, even though they tested the liquid and it tested positive for amniotic fluid. After having contractions all day, she reported, she started to scream at about 7:45 p.m., and officers called 911 and had her taken to the hospital, where she gave birth. also at Perryville, told me that she went into labor on July 27, 2013. She reported that at approximately 11 a.m. she told a correctional officer she was in labor, only to be told to "wait until the contraction is over, I'll bring a wheelchair." At noon, she says, she was rolled to medical, where she waited for over an hour; by the time an ambulance was called and arrived, her contractions were one minute apart. She told me she got to the hospital at 1:55 p.m. and had the baby 20 minutes later. Throughout, she says, she was never checked for dilation. Medical staff seem to have almost entirely abdicated responsibility to custody staff to get these women to the hospital to give birth. is a young otherwise healthy patient I met at Florence North Unit, who has had multiple methicillin-resistant staph aureus (MRSA) outbreaks in 2013. He told me that when he developed his second outbreak in May 2013 he walked immediately to the medical office on his yard to seek care because he knew what the problem was as a result of his previous outbreak a few months earlier. The medical department refused to see him even for basic triage and told him to turn in an HNR to be seen. told me that he knows how fast these MRSA infections spread so he immediately appealed the refusal to the Deputy Warden on the custody side and after proving to the Deputy Warden that he had turned in an HNR and showing him his rapidly advancing infection, the Deputy Warden had him escorted to medical and demanded that they care for him. The medical staff did ultimately care for him after correctional officer insistence for that episode but follow-up care that was ordered by the providers in his medical record has not been carried out and no attempt to eradicate the MRSA from his system has been undertaken so he can avoid future infections. Reliance on custody staff as gatekeepers to such a degree is a dangerous practice. Unlicensed, unqualified people are making medical decisions. It also raises patient privacy concerns, as does the practice in ADC of having custody officers dispense keep on-person (KOP) medications at some prisons. Gross Depo, 63:22-64:1; MielkeFontaine Depo – Florence, 278:11-278:15 (Florence). 6. End-of-life care and waivers of treatment I encountered one situation that is worth describing in detail, since to me it is emblematic of the utter disregard for patient care presented by the Arizona prison system, as well as serious problems with understaffing and lack of oversight. In the Inpatient Care Unit at the Tucson complex, I chose two patients to interview because they were both alert and talkative; I knew nothing about them beforehand. After hearing their medical concerns, I reviewed their healthcare records. Both of their records had on prominent display a blanket cessation of care form. This type of document is commonly called a "do not resuscitate" (DNR) form, but these were far broader: they included a waiver of ongoing care, lab work, intravenous medication and sustenance, and the like. These forms were filled out by the nurse in the unit and signed by the nurse and the patients. There were no informed consents documented by a physician or competency evaluations by a psychiatrist Surprised and concerned about such comprehensive waivers of treatment without the protections that standard of care requires in such situations, I went back to talk to the patients. The first patient ( ) acknowledged his signature on the form and identified it as "the form I had to sign before the nurse would give me any pain medications." I asked him to clarify and he told me that when he came to that unit he was in so much pain from his colon cancer that he was crying in bed at night and couldn't sleep. He requested his pain medications and the nurse told him that she was worried that his pain medications might kill him so she wouldn't give him any pain medications until he signed the form. I clarified the information a third time with him and had him repeat his story to be sure I fully understood. The second patient ( ) has end stage liver disease that results in occasional increases in his blood ammonia level which results in hepatic encephalopathy. He was recently in the hospital for hepatic encephalopathy and during that time he was not conscious of his surroundings or what was happening to him, as is typical in such situations. He does not remember being at the hospital or any of the care he received. At the hospital, they executed a DNR upon admission, as is standard practice with conscious patients, despite his inability to comprehend his actions. The attorney for the State on my tour informed me that the hospital DNR was merely carried forward to the Arizona prison system and that the one I saw in his file, signed in ADC custody, was simply "extra." I am extremely concerned, based on the documentary evidence I reviewed, that this patient executed the hospital DNR while he was totally incompetent with a sky-high ammonia level. In my opinion, no reasonable physician would honor such a document. After his condition stabilized at the hospital, he was returned to Tucson and signed the comprehensive waiver of care order I saw in his file. I asked him if he knew what the form was for. He told me that could not read the form when he signed it because he didn't have his glasses, and had no understanding of what it was. I explained the form to him and he indicated that those were not his desires. As with the first patient, there is no record of any physician or psychiatrist involvement in this process. I hesitate to generalize from two data points, but it is at the very least striking and disturbing that two such blatant violations of patients' rights to treatment and to agency in end-of-life decisions could exist with no apparent review or oversight. Any medical professional should be disturbed on a on medical, psychological, ethical, emotional, humanistic, and legal level by the mere existence of these forms in these patients' files, lacking as they do any informed consent, provider involvement, or indicia of review, much less the patients' accounts of coercive circumstances under which they were signed. I believe that this practice has a great deal to do with the severe and profoundly irresponsible understaffing I observed in these high-acuity care settings. I also suspect that many more patients in this unit have such forms in their files and that it is essentially a work reduction technique by an overwhelmed understaffed nursing group with extremely limited physician engagement. I did see an indication of other questionable practices in Tucson relating to DNRs and end of life care. Shawn Jensen (032465), a class representative, testified in his declaration of November 6, 2012, that he and others had been presented with living wills, healthcare power of attorney forms, and DNR forms in Tucson in March 2012. According to Mr. Jensen, prisoners were given no education about the forms and no assistance with reading them; no healthcare staff were available to answer their questions; patients were simply told to complete them. Prisoners who were monolingual Spanish speakers were provided with forms only in English. This report makes it all the more urgent to investigate such matters thoroughly and to ensure patients in Arizona's custody are provided individual education and information about their options. End of life planning and compassionate palliative care are important components of the practice of medicine, but they must be done with extreme caution in a correctional setting, with assiduous attention to detail, multiple independent reviewers, meticulous observation of informed consent requirements, and continual review of the appropriateness of the end of life plans given the condition of the patient. None of that was present in Tucson. The circumstances surrounding the clear violations of these patients' rights suggest that the problem is widespread and places patients at serious risk of denial of care. I am deeply concerned that I do not know, and am unable to discover the depth and breadth of this problem, given the limitations placed on my ability to investigate in this case. C. Exercise of professional medical judgment The heart of a functional healthcare delivery system is the ability of the appropriate clinicians to exercise their professional medical judgment regarding patient care. In order for that to happen, providers must first be able to see patients and second must be equipped with the appropriate information to diagnose and treat them. Nurses cannot dictate care in the same way; I am extremely concerned about the degree to which Arizona relies on nurses practicing outside the scope of their licenses to provide basic care. I am similarly concerned about the degree to which providers are denied access to consultations from appropriate specialists, thereby forcing them to make patient care decisions outside the scope of their expertise. Finally, I saw extensive evidence that providers often simply make very bad treatment decisions, and sometimes disastrously bad ones, to the serious detriment of their patients. 1. Access to care The issues I discussed above relating to timely access to care in Section II.B are relevant in this context. Patients must be seen and care needs identified, both on intake and throughout their prison terms. If access to care is poor, the system blocks professional judgment from operating. In Arizona prisons, access to care for many patients is so poor that they are forced to rely on the "professional medical judgment" of custody staff, as described above in Section II.B.5. If they can persuade officers, sergeants, or lieutenants that they need treatment, those staff will sometimes break through the barriers set up by the healthcare delivery system. 2. Medical records and access to medical histories Providers cannot render a professional medical judgment without appropriate medical data. If a provider sees a diabetic without access to the blood sugar data because it hasn't been filed yet, or without results because they have not arrived, he or she is treating the patient with a blindfold, lacking appropriate information about the condition. Without a full medical record, providers don't have adequate information to render a professional medical judgment. The problem is compounded for complex or chronic care patients. If the charts lack historical information on the patient, filed in a logical place, it makes treating that patient very difficult, if not impossible. Arizona's Assistant Director over the Health Monitoring Bureau agrees. Gross Depo, 122:25-123:6 (it is important to have paperwork properly filed so that the information can be in a chronological order for others to read and interpret). The charts I reviewed at all the prisons were inadequate to convey current patient care. Simply put, they were a gigantic mess. There was often no way to track the care logically through the chart; it was generally very hard to tell medical histories and medication administration. Medication orders should be consistent with the medical administration records (MARs), but in the Arizona charts I reviewed, I saw very little correlation between the orders and the MARs. It was often unclear who had ordered a medication and when that medication needed to be renewed. While half of the medication record might be in the medical chart, half of it might be somewhere else (for example in a Pharmacorr binder), which makes no sense. A treating clinician picking up a chart to review before an appointment or a provider trying to design a treatment plan would have no idea what the medications the patient is taking. This is a patient safety issue. It is no wonder Arizona makes the prisoners submit medication refills via HNRs -- none of the healthcare staff can tell when something needs to be renewed based on the records I reviewed. I was not surprised to read the reports from ADC monitors of record-keeping delays and errors. See, for example, ADC154302 (September 30, 2013) (46 of 80 Tucson charts reviewed showed that medical records were not current, accurate, or chronologically maintained with all the documents filed in the designated location); ADC137309 (July 26, 2013) (Perryville San Carlos has a large amount of unsecured and incorrectly sectioned filing); ADC088931 (April 29, 2013) (Perryville San Pedro and San Carlos have significant backlogs of MARs in loose filing); ADC088930 (April 29, 2013) ("[l]oose filing at [Perryville] San Carlos can be measured in feet. Unfiled MARs date back to January"); ADC088915-18 (April 23, 2013) (large amount of loose filing at Perryville Santa Maria, San Carlos, and Lumley prevented an accurate assessment of sick call); ADC088929 (April 18, 2013) (medical records not current, accurate, and chronologically maintained with all documents filed in the designated location at multiple Perryville units). The monitors have also consistently found that prisoner medical records often lack necessary information, as was my experience. See, for example, ADC154383-84 (September 30, 2013) (at Yuma, 7 of 10 Cibola charts, 9 of 10 Dakota charts, 5 of 10 Cheyenne charts, 4 of 10 Cocopah charts, and 7 of 10 La Paz charts reviewed were not noted daily with time, date, and name of the person taking the orders off); ADC137393 (July 31, 2103) (medication errors at Tucson are not all documented); ADC137256-7 (July 30, 2013) (non-formulary medication approval or denial not in charts at Florence); ADC137443 (July 29, 2013) (31 of 50 Yuma charts reviewed have missing initials on dates indicating that the medicine was not administered); ADC137236 (July 14, 2013) (hospital-setting open reduction notation missing for a Florence prisoner's oral surgery on 6/21/13); ADC088887 (April 28, 2013) (on 4/11, there were no daily nursing notes on any charts reviewed in Florence); ADC088874 (April 18, 2013) (staff report Florence East does not report or document appointment no-shows); ADC088864-65 (April 14, 2013) (0 of 10 files Florence Central files reviewed had provider orders taken off and daily annotated with time, date, and name of person taking the orders off); ADC088856 (April 14, 2013) (4 of 10 Florence Globe charts reviewed revealed consultation reports were not timely reviewed by providers). It was not a surprise to me to read that a fivefoot stack of unfiled records was found in the Tucson complex in February 2013. AGA_Review_00004833. According to the monitors, medication administration records (MARs), an essential aspect of record-keeping, are frequently not completed to standard nursing practices: they often lack doses, routes, frequencies, start dates, and nurses' signatures. See, for example, ADC154407-08 (September 30, 2013) (at Yuma, 9 of 10 Cibola MARs, 9 of 10 Cocopah MARs, 10 of 10 Cheyenne MARs, 10 of 10 Dakota MARs, and Case 2:12-cv-00601-DJH Document 1104-1 Filed 09/08/14 Page 261 of 364 47 9 of 10 La Paz MARs noncompliant); ADC154327-332 (September 30, 2013) (at Tucson, 10 of 10 IPC/HU9 charts, 6 of 10 Rincon charts, 10 of 10 Manzanita charts, 10 of 10 Catalina charts, 10 of 10 Whetstone charts, 8 of 10 Minors/CDU charts, 10 of 10 Winchester charts, 6 of 10 Santa Rita charts, and 7 of 10 Cimarron charts reviewed had noncompliant MARs); ADC154306 (September 30, 2013) (16 of 32 Tucson MARs noncompliant); ADC154137 (September 30, 2013) ("MARs are not being completed correctly at any unit on Florence complex"); ADC154115-16 (September 30, 2013) (33 or 34 Florence MARs noncompliant); ADC154245 (September 27, 2013) (MARs at Phoenix are not compliant, and "nurse signatures do not match initials on MARs, prescription information crossed out and written over without initiating a new MAR entry"); ADC154205-07 (September 26, 2103) (at Perryville, 10 of 10 MARs at San Carlos, Santa Cruz, Lumley, PU/SM/PI, and San Pedro noncompliant); ADC154385-86 (September 1, 2013) (42 of 46 Yuma MARs noncompliant); ADC137591 (August 28, 2013) (medication at Phoenix is administered without a retrievable record of the recipient); ADC137656-59 (August 26, 2013) (at Tucson, 8 of 10 MARs at Rincon, 6 of 10 MARs at Santa Rita, 6 of 10 MARs at Manzanita, 8 of 10 MARs at Whetstone, 6 of 12 MARs at Catalina, 5 of 10 MARs at Winchester, 8 of 8 MARs at Minors, 9 of 10 MARs at CDU, 7 of 10 MARs at IPC/HU9, and 9 of 10 MARs at Cimarron not compliant); ADC137331 (July 31, 2013) (conflicting MARs for allergies for Phoenix prisoner); ADC137331 (July 31, 2013) (MAR for Phoenix prisoner has blank spaces on administration of antibiotics, no start date shown, and no diagnosis); ADC137295 (July 24, 2013) (Perryville MARs may be inaccurate); ADC137254-5 (July 30, 2013) (9 of 10 Florence East MARs, 10 of 10 Florence North MARs, and 10 of 11 Florence South MARs noncompliant); ADC137442-43 (July 29, 2013) (at Yuma, 8 of 10 La Paz MARs, 8 of 10 Cibola MARs, 10 of 10 Dakota MARs, 7 of 10 Cheyenne MARs reviewed were noncompliant); ADC137373-74 (July 24, 2013) ("the MARs are so messed up" at Tucson Santa Rita); ADC137303 (July 16, 2013) (Perryville Santa Maria, Santa Rosa, and Piestewa Unit MARs noncompliant); ADC137303 (July 19, 2013) (Perryville San Pedro and Lumley MARs noncompliant); ADC088880-81(April 28, 2013) (multiple blank dates in most MARs reviewed at Florence); ADC089105 (April 27, 2013) (MARs at Yuma Dakota, Cocopah, and La Paz noncompliant); ADC089093 (April 27, 2013) (multiple MARs completed incorrectly at Yuma La Paz and Dakota); ADC088742 (April 4, 2013) (many MARs at Florence incomplete or filled out incorrectly). I reviewed historic MARs in the medical records I read as well as active MARs in the different medical treatment areas of the facilities I visited. As suggested by the monitoring reports, I found that they are a documentation disaster. For example, in the chart of , whom I discussed above, I counted eight different MARs for August 2013. Each of the MARs contained some of his ordered medications, but each one was different from the rest by one or two medications. I was unable to figure out what medications he was actually supposed to be on because the MARs overlapped so much and there were no orders in the chart to use as a reference. It is no wonder the patient complained about not getting all of his HIV medications; clearly, nobody knew what to do. I also saw examples of obvious nursing disregard for medication orders. is a Florence patient who is on court-ordered treatment for injectable long-acting Haldol Decanoate via a Psychotropic Medication Review Board (PMRB) order. There was an indication in the MAR that the patient was due for his shot on October 23, 2013. I visited the facility on October 25 and the nurse in that unit indicated that she did not know if the medication had been given since it was not properly recorded. We found the medication on the shelf unused. Similarly, was ordered Haldol Decanoate to be administered on October 18, 2013, by PMRB order indicating that he "can't refuse." Nobody could determine whether he had received his critical medication because a temporary nurse had been on shift that day and none of the nurses knew how to contact her to determine whether she gave the medication or not. The issue remained unclarified for at least a week prior to my October 25 tour and nobody was able to resolve the issue and provide me an answer as to whether this critically mentally ill patient had been treated. Another example of medication misadventure is the case of who is currently being treated with Enbrel, a Tumor Necrosis Factor inhibitor that is quite expensive. He saw the specialist and an order was written on October 9, 2013, to change his Enbrel dosing to a new dose. The nurse made a notation in the MAR that the new dose was not to start until November 1 despite the fact that the medical order in the physician's written order section of the medical record clearly states that the new dosing was to begin October 9. The nurse overruled a specialist's medical management of a fragile patient in clear violation of scope of practice and medical oversight, but undetectable in this system unless someone is looking closely. Also not surprisingly, ADC has major backlogs for provider chart review. See, for example, ADC154226 (September 27, 2013) (0 of 11 Phoenix charts reviewed showed that consult reports were reviewed by the provider within 7 days of receipt); ADC137360-61 (July 29, 2013) (Tucson Whetstone had 106 charts awaiting provider review, with serious backlogs also at Winchester, Cimarron, Rincon West Medical, Catalina, Manzanita, and Santa Rita); ADC137395 (July 29, 2013) (Tucson has backlogged charts needing review); ADC137369-71 (July 26, 2013) (Tucson Rincon, Catalina, Manzanita, and Santa Rita each have dozens of consult reports awaiting review); ADC137309 (July 26, 2013) (Perryville San Carlos and Santa Maria have provider review chart backlogs); ADC137236-37 (July 14 and 30, 2013) (most reviewed Florence South, Central, and North charts not timely reviewed by provider); ADC137236 (July 14, 2013) (Florence prisoner's 5/4/13 hospital discontinued orders were not reviewed as of 7/11/13); ADC137259 (July 30, 2013) (every Florence unit except Kasson has 70+ charts waiting to be reviewed); ADC088943 (April 30, 2013) (at Perryville, the medical director is providing direct care to inmates in addition to her responsibilities and has not been able to conduct monthly or quarterly chart reviews); ADC088746 (April 4, 2013) (Florence East charts with labs, x-ray reports, hospital notes, and consultant notes dating back to early February have not been reviewed). In addition, there are problems at least in Perryville with getting information back from outside hospital stays, which makes post-inpatient planning, at a time when a patient is particularly fragile, very difficult. ADC 52804 ("there continues to be a delay in receiving hospital documentation, discharge information and/or recommendations. Staff are unaware who is responsible for this task"); ADC 52823 ("[t]his continues to be an issue for the provider to receive the hospital records, information &/or recommendations. It has occurred that the provider had not received these records by the time of the inmate's hospital follow up appt with the provider. It is unclear to staff, including providers – who actually is responsible for this task to be completed in a timely manner"); ADC 52782-83 ("[t]he hospital admission, care provided, tests done, discharge recommendations or follow up is not provided to the staff/providers, per staff – in a timely manner. It is unclear who is responsible for this task"); ADC 52760 ("[h]aving hospital record information, discharge information &/or recommendations is difficult to obtain in a timely manner. Staff state their frustrations with this task and it is unclear who is actually responsible for this task"). In my review of medical records areas on my tours I found many examples of records that had not yet been reviewed by providers and the data that they were supposed to review was quite old. For example, in Tucson I found entire shelves of medical records that contained loose filing that was over a month old waiting for providers to review. I reviewed the records myself and found many abnormal lab results and radiology findings that had yet to be acted upon. In addition, I found fifty-six lab results and radiology results in a file that indicated that the charts could not be found. As such, the abnormal results were just sitting there with no place to be filed and no action taken on the abnormalities. Use of nurses as primary care providers Patients are denied a clinician's professional medical judgment if nurses or other staff are called upon to make decisions that standard of care – and sometimes professional licensing requirements – reserve for primary care providers. This happens all too often in the Arizona system. See ADC137397 (Tucson infirmary patients are not being seen every 72 hours by doctor or mid-level provider, as policy requires, but are instead seen by LPN, CNA, or RN). In Yuma, I saw extensive evidence of this practice: LPNs doing RN work and RNs doing primary care provider work that should only be done by physicians, physicians' assistants, or nurse practitioners. My review of medical records for in the Dakota Unit ( ) provides one example. experienced horrible follow-up after a hospital stay for three days with gastrointestinal bleeding at the end of May 2013. The day after his return, he complained of chest and abdominal pain. He was seen only by an LPN, with no provider follow-up. (He was frequently seen by an LPN, including for chronic care appointments). Other Arizona prisons also have this problem. I saw RNs reviewing labs and ordering treatment for end stage renal disease patient , in Florence. My review of medical records of at Yuma showed multiple violations of nursing scope of practice. has end-stage AIDS and he is a very complicated patient. He has been seen multiple times by LPNs for healthcare and the LPNs have diagnosed him and treated him for problems such as upper respiratory infections and a chronic rash. I requested to see this patient and it is clear that the LPNs' and RNs' management of him is medically incorrect, as described in more detail in Section II.C.4. They are well outside of the scope of their practice and they are far over their heads in even trying to assess a patient of this complexity. Sadly, he has suffered serious harm as a result of their mismanagement, all as a result of nurses attempting to practice medicine. The dialysis program is essentially run by a nurse on a day-to-day basis. I reviewed all of the dialysis charts (approximately 12) at Florence and a nurse orders the labs, interprets the labs, decides on what changes need to be made on the dialysis prescription, and writes orders for post-dialysis management. This is boldly beyond the scope of practice for a nurse. The nephrologist overseeing the dialysis care within the system has inappropriately delegated prisoner dialysis treatment to a nurse and technicians. Another example of nurses practicing beyond their scope is the nurse who attempted to provide postoperative management to Shawn Jensen (032465), who underwent a robotic radicle prostatectomy on July 15, 2010, and discharged on July 18, 2010, with instructions to follow up in three weeks for Foley removal. On July 20, 2010, and July 31, 2010, Mr. Jensen submitted two HNRs reporting leaking from his catheter site. He was finally seen on August 1, 2010, at which time the nurse offered him pads. He was again seen the following day, and instead of referring the patient to the provider for appropriate post-operative management of an indwelling catheter in a surgical site the nurse attempted to complete what she believed to be a Foley irrigation by "twist[ing] the catheter, manipulate[ing] the catheter, push[ing] it in further" in order to "try[] to get it to drain better." No improvement was documented. Fortunately, Mr. Jensen was already scheduled to be seen by the urologist on August 5, 2010, at which time he reported to the hospital with no urine in his leg bag and "soaked towels in his perineal area [in an attempt] to keep himself dry"; the urine had leaked through the towels into his orange jumpsuit. The cystogram completed at the hospital showed that the catheter was "located anterior and outside the bladder," and his urine had been leaking into his abdominal cavity. As a result of this botched procedure by the nurse, Mr. Jensen required emergency surgery to repair the tear in his bladder neck and remove the Foley from his abdomen. Mr. Jensen has continued to experience severe complications, and require a number of operations, as a result of the nurse's inappropriate manipulation of an indwelling surgical drain. Another example of nurses practicing beyond their scope is the case of Charlotte Wells (247188). On February 20, 2010, days after Ms. Wells received heart surgery to address her blocked artery, she complained of chest pain again at 7:15pm. ADOC0005180-81. At that time, she was seen by a nurse who treated her based on phone conversations with Dr. Enciso, the covering doctor that day. Id. She was never examined and appropriate diagnostic assessments were not completed. Her pain reportedly improved with treatment and she was sent back to the yard. Id. Medical standards of care indicate that patients who have recently received a stent are at high risk for getting a blood clot and having a heart attack post-procedure. Thus, any chest pain in a recently stented patient is usually very concerning and should be evaluated thoroughly by a medical provider instead of a nurse. I found another dramatic example of nurses practicing outside of their legal scope of practice in the chart of . There is a remarkable note in his chart dated July 12, 2013, indicating that telephone orders supposedly written by the Family Nurse Practitioner at 0430 the previous day were not written by or given by the Family Nurse Practitioner. It appears that the nurse on call decided to give this patient prescription medications without appropriate provider orders and she forged the order in the chart. When I looked at the provider orders, there were no orders in the chart corresponding to this incident, suggesting that someone had removed them from the record. In general, these practices not only violate licensing requirements but they can all too easily result in bad outcomes. They also provide evidence of poor staffing in the Arizona system. The following nightmarish example details how such a practice can seriously injure patients. is a patient I chose to interview randomly in the infirmary in Tucson. He related the following history, which I confirmed from a review of his healthcare records. On July 20, 2013, this previously healthy 42-year-old patient complained of neck and back pain and was seen by an LPN. He had a fever of 99.1 and the LPN did not examine him or consult anyone about him. She determined that he was OK and sent him back to his unit. It was a violation of the scope of practice for this staff member to make decisions about his care, and indeed the LPN made a drastically poor decision to provide no follow-up. Two days later, the patient again complained of back and neck pain and was again assessed by an LPN, who failed to take his temperature and decided to give him an injectable non-steroidal pain medication (Toradol). It was again a violation of the LPN scope of practice to assess this patient. This time, he was scheduled to see a provider on the following day. At that time, the RN found he had a temperature of 100.0 degrees and gross neurological deficits. He was sent to an outside emergency room, where it was found that he has an abscess of his neck muscles and epidural spinal abscess. He was sent to University Hospital for surgery and then transferred to St. Luke's Hospital for several months and then returned to Tucson IPC, where I saw him bed-bound, with no physical therapy and no prevention from complications of bed rest, foot drop on the left leg, fixed flexion contractures in the left hand, and an indwelling Foley catheter that had been in place for weeks. This case is a tragedy across the board. The fact that the healthcare system used LPNs out of scope virtually guaranteed a delay in diagnosis. LPNs are not taught to do physical examinations; they are not taught pathophysiology; and they have no experience assessing sick patients, developing a plan to work up the problem, and pursuing a proper diagnosis. As a result, likely suffered much more significant neurological damage than necessary because of the delay in diagnosis. is now experiencing a different type of neglect. He is bed-bound, no care is rendered to him to help him gain strength and range of motion, and he is slowly and needlessly dwindling physically. The nursing staff have placed a Foley catheter into his bladder; in my experience and based on the factors he presents, this decision was likely made because they grew tired of helping him urinate into a bottle. This places him at unnecessary risk for developing additional infections, all because there are not enough staff to help him with basic bodily functions. He also returned from the hospital with a hard cervical collar in place, which is a very unusual long-term intervention and it runs significant risk of causing long term impairment. I asked him if any of the physicians had seen him to discuss his need to wear the C-collar and he replied that nobody had discussed any plans with him in the six weeks that he has been back. I reviewed his chart and could find no clinical indication for continued use of a hard C-collar. This case is a tragedy of errors. Even now, given all that has happened, he could still make a modest recovery and retain the ability to perform activities of daily living, but he is being completely ignored in his bed by the staff and quickly losing what remains of his physical capabilities. I was so moved by his neglect that I called his case out to Corizon Arizona Regional Medical Director Dr. Williams and the attorneys for the State and Corizon in the hope they would intervene on his behalf. 4. Specialty care The exercise of professional judgment sometimes requires more in-depth knowledge than primary care providers possess. In these cases, the provider must be able to refer patients for specialty consultations. This essential step often does not happen in Arizona. Haldane Depo - Perryville, 204:19-205:4, 45:13-46:2 (referrals have been an "issue of noncompliance," "pretty much . . . every month"); Sharp Depo, 47:18-48:2 (concerns with specialty referrals that have "loomed larger with time" and continue to present). Patients are harmed as a result. I saw numerous examples of people whose cases clearly required input from specialists or a more advanced understanding of their complex needs but yet they were not referred for that care. For example, in Yuma's La Paz Unit, has end-stage liver disease, with very little liver function left. He is very fragile and has a complex case that is being mismanaged. When I saw him in early August 2013, he needed to see a hepatologist urgently. He never had, although he had been in ADC for more than three years. Similarly, is HIV positive and housed in the Tucson complex. His medications are not renewed regularly, resulting in gaps of up to a month without them (a grievance I saw in his file dated December 4, 2012, signed by Director Ryan, agrees he went without HIV medications for 30 days). As I discussed earlier, HIV medication management has to be done correctly and patients need to receive all of their HIV medications every day without gaps or the virus can mutate and further damage the immune system. CD4 count (a common measure of the strength of his immune system) dropped dramatically due to the medication mismanagement. If the virus has become resistant, the medications might need to be entirely changed. Despite his poor care and obvious deterioration, he has never been seen by an HIV specialist. housed in the Manzanita Unit IPC in Tucson, is an extremely fragile 31-year-old patient with lupus and multiple sclerosis; the intersection of these two major diseases makes him an extremely complicated patient in need of specialty care. He has been seen by a rheumatologist on telemedicine, but not enough, and some of the recommendations of the specialist have been ignored. In a wellfunctioning system he would be seen regularly by multiple specialists and have regular labs to measure the effect of the medications. He is not getting such care and as a result, his life expectancy will be shortened and he will likely become debilitated. Another example, is a patient who has lupus. It had initially been incorrectly diagnosed as Sjogren's disease in 2007. He saw a rheumatologist via telemedicine in 2011 who diagnosed lupus, but he did not see a rheumatologist again (by telemedicine) for two years, which is far too long. Even when referrals are actually made, they are all too often delayed so long as to place the patients at serious risk of harm. I addressed the case of consultations have never happened. A repeat order for a dermatology consultation was written on July 22, 2013. Although the biopsy removed some of the growth, cancer cells remained in the margins and if they are not removed, the cancer will continue to grow and metastasize. If left untreated this condition is potentially fatal and can cause deformity and pain. I met Shawn Jensen (032465), a class representative in this case, in ASPC-Tucson. He had been waiting for a CT scan for an aneurysm in his heart that was first ordered in July 2010; it was finally done the day before my tour. Fortunately, there were no significant negative findings, but the delay of more than three years for this test placed Mr. Jensen at unreasonable risk of harm and caused him prolonged and unnecessary distress. in Florence has newly diagnosed significant rectal cancer. He had a consult written to oncology on September 24, 2013, for initial evaluation. This consult is essential for his care, but as of October 16, 2013, I saw no evidence in his file that it was approved, scheduled, or completed. Similarly, , also at Florence, has a large hepatic cyst. He had received excellent care prior to incarceration and his physician wrote a letter on July 8, 2013, outlining the care plan for the patient's multiple significant problems. That care plan included a cardiology consult and a general surgery consult to evaluate his large hepatic cyst for surgical treatment. A cardiology consult was written by a physician's assistant within the prison on September 3, 2013, but he did not write a general surgery consult despite the fact that it was recommended in the same letter. Both specialty consults are essential for his care, but as of October 16, 2013, I saw no evidence in his file that the cardiology was approved, scheduled, or completed and the general surgery consult had been completely disregarded and never initiated. Referrals do not appear to be tracked in any meaningful way. Mielke-Fontaine Depo – Florence, 251:9-251:19 (no list of urgent consultations at a facility; only way to find out is to look at the file for each consult ordered). Corizon Arizona Regional Medical Director Dr. Williams, along with one colleague, reviews all utilization management requests, including for off-site specialty care. Deposition of Winfred Williams, October 10, 2013 (Williams Depo), at 16:7-16:13. The requests are entered into a computer system, as are approvals and denials, and appointment schedulers at the prisons are informed of the approvals. Id. at 84:6-84:15, 85:25-86:5, 90:7-90:19. An effective healthcare delivery system requires more, however: it must have the capacity to track referrals with a time line for completion and provider notification. The time line is essential because time frames vary: some referrals need to go immediately, others must be completed quickly but are not immediate, and still others can be completed on a longer time line or can happen when there is room in the schedule. Referrals must also be tracked so that cancellations, which are an unfortunate reality in correctional medicine due to factors such as court dates and institutional emergencies, are minimized and referrals are rescheduled promptly as needed. I see no evidence of these essential measures in the Arizona prisons. Neither ADC nor Corizon requires that providers who make specialty referrals be notified about whether the referral was approved. Williams Depo, 87:3-14; Responses 257 and 259, Defendants' Responses to Verduzco's First Set of RFAs (all healthcare staff referrals to outside contractors must be reviewed and approved by a committee of healthcare and ADC administrative staff , but ADC policy does not require the committee to notify the referring healthcare staff whether the referral was approved or denied); Responses 260 and 262, Defendants' Responses to Verduzco's First Set of RFAs (Corizon policy requires all healthcare staff referrals to outside specialty contractors be reviewed and approved by a committee of healthcare staff, but Corizon policy does not require the committee to notify the referring healthcare staff whether the referral was approved or denied). Not surprisingly, the primary care providers are not in fact always notified of the status of referrals. Sharp Depo, 71:19-72:4, 72:5-24 (physician who practiced at Eyman, Florence, and Perryville testified he would not always be notified whether a specialty referral was approved and this was a "concern about adequacy of care"). This is a problem because it is the job of the primary care physicians to track the continuity of care for patients under their care. They are expected to manage the patient up to the point of the referral, assess the new information obtained from the referral, and then implement a new care plan for the patient based on the referral. If they don't know the status of a referral, how can they reasonably manage their patients in this chaotic resource-limited environment? Even when notified, providers often do not review referral reports in a timely manner. ADC154105 (September 30, 2013) (13 of 42 Florence files reviewed show consultation reports were not reviewed by the provider within seven days of receipt); ADC137428 (July 29, 2013) (5 of 9 Yuma La Paz charts reviewed do not have consultation reports reviewed by provider within seven days of receipt). Although referrals are not effectively tracked, ADC monitors have catalogued extensive delays that serve to bolster my opinion that this aspect of care in Arizona prisons is completely broken and just missing in many cases. See, for example, ADC137629 (August 29, 2013) (Tucson prisoner's 7/11/13 urgent orthopedic consult request for foreign body in knee with repeated infections has not been addressed); ADC137628 (August 29, 2013) (Tucson prisoner with basal cell cancer not scheduled to go out for treatment despite numerous HNRs requesting such); ADC137365 (July 31, 2013) (Tucson prisoner submitted an emergency HNR for chest pains on 6/15/13 and was not seen until 7/9/13); id. (July 31, 2013) (Tucson prisoner with an aortic aneurysm measuring 4.2 cm on 6/16/11 and 4.7 cm on 10/25/12 had an urgent cardiology consultation dated 5/28/13, but apparently had not been seen as of 7/10/13); ADC137238 (July 30, 2013) (Florence prisoner had an urgent surgery requested on 5/30 and had not been seen as of 7/25); ADC137236 (July 30, 2013) (Florence prisoner had an urgent consultation written on 5/30/13 and was not seen as of 7/25/13); ADC137425 (July 23, Case 2:12-cv-00601-DJH Document 1104-1 Filed 09/08/14 Page 275 of 364 61 2013) (a Yuma provider's telephone order for two prisoners with abscesses was not "signed" as of 7/15); ADC137369 (July 11, 2013) (Tucson prisoner received a cardiology consult on 6/6/13 for syncopal episodes, was referred for a walking EKG and follow-up appointment with cardiology, but was not sent for an EKG; another Tucson prisoner's cardiology follow-up approved 2/7/13 but not seen by 7/3/13; a third Tucson prisoner with testicular mass and urethral stricture seen by urology on 1/30/13, consults submitted 3/26/13, but not yet seen/scheduled; a fourth Tucson prisoner's urgent colonoscopy consult was written 12/31/12, approved 3/13/13, but not yet scheduled); ADC137322 (July 8, 2013) (an urgent consultation for a Phoenix prisoner was written on 5/15/13, entered on 5/24/13, and had not been scheduled as of 7/8/13); ADC088863 (April 30, 2013) (Florence North prisoner who was exposed to HIV positive blood on 4/24 had no progress note or SOAPE note documenting the incident nor an indication that the prisoner was seen by medical after exposure); ADC089013 (April 29, 2013) (an urgent cardiology consult for a prisoner at Tucson Whetstone written on 6/7/12 was not reviewed by a provider until 3/8/13); ADC088858 (April 27, 2013) (prisoner's recommended left heart catheter/angiogram was not addressed at Florence South); another prisoner delayed in beginning radiation therapy for prostate cancer at Florence North); ADC088856 (April 27, 2013) (prisoner at Florence North with urgent oncology request on 2/25/13 was not seen until 4/10/13, with consult re-written on Corizon form on 3/29/13); ADC088746 (April 4, 2013) (Florence Central appears "out of compliance for scheduling specialty care appointments"); ADC037152 (October 2012) (Tucson prisoner had "urgent cardiology written 8/16/12 approved 9/14/12 not scheduled as of 10/1/12"; another "[i]nmate was seen by cardiology on 3/28/12 requested 2D Echo and adenosine stress test. If these test[s] are abnormal consider cardiac catheterization, otherwise f/u in one year. Dr. DeGuzman has ordered Consult urgent on 4/30/12. Inmate has not been seen [as of October 2012 review]. There is no indication the studies have been approved to be done"); ADC 52782-83 (November 2012) (Perryville prisoners are not being referred out in a timely manner for specialist reviews, and outside medical consultations are not reviewed in a timely manner by prison healthcare providers, including "consult report dated 09/27 and was signed on 11/13/12"). Urgent consults are often not seen as required within 30 days. See, for example, ADC154103 (September 30, 2013) (8 of 10 urgent consults at Florence noncompliant); ADC154226 (September 27, 2013) (2 of 3 Phoenix urgent consults noncompliant); ADC137428 (July 29, 2013) (5 of 9 Yuma La Paz charts reviewed noncompliant). In my review of the medical records across all of the facilities I visited, the failure to schedule consult appointments in a timely fashion was rampant in the charts. On the whole I found the on-site physician consultation requests to be medically appropriate and it is clear that the breakdown is at the system level with delays, obfuscations, alternate treatment plans, and frequently total disregard for the consultation requests. In most of the cases I reviewed, the failure to accomplish the consultation was a clear violation of the standard of care for the disease being treated. 5. Substandard care decisions To this point, I have discussed the exercise of professional judgment in terms of what is needed to get the patient in front of the provider and to get the provider the tools needed to make treatment decisions. There is another element, however: those treatment decisions must be consistent with community standard of care. In the Arizona system, all too often the providers make treatment decisions that are clearly substandard and endanger their patients. Because human error is a reality of life, a responsible healthcare delivery system builds in methods to find and correct such problems. 9 A rigorous quality assurance 9 The fact that human error is inevitable does not make it excusable. The errors and omissions I describe in this section are serious and harmful; some, in my opinion, are actionable. My point here, however, is that because people are fallible, particularly in chaotic systems such as I have seen in Arizona, a responsible health care system must be prepared to find and address mistakes before they impact patient care. Case 2:12-cv-00601-DJH Document 1104-1 Filed 09/08/14 Page 277 of 364 63 program, a functional patient feedback loop (such as through HNRs and grievances), and high-quality staff who communicate well with one another and are supported by a responsive system that delivers assistance in the form of appropriate diagnostic testing and timely specialty referrals are all essential elements to correct for the known factor of human error. As discussed elsewhere in this report, Arizona lacks all of these elements. The results, for some of the many patients who are placed at severe risk, are described below. at Perryville experienced terrible medical judgment in wound care. She told me she was returned to the prison on June 12, 2013, after delivering by a Caesarian section in an outside hospital. She reported that she noticed her wound was leaking and infected after only a few days and she asked for attention at the medical unit several times but was sent away each time, finally being told, by an officer, "if you come back again without an appointment, we'll write you a ticket." As a result, she said she was on the yard for two weeks with an open incision (she was later told it was more than an inch deep.) Finally, she was taken to the infirmary, where the wound started to heal. As of July 30, when I saw her, medical staff were packing the wound with sugar -- the kind of packets you use for coffee. This treatment was documented in her medical records. I have never anything like it in my years practicing medicine and it definitely does not conform to the standard of care. At ASPC-Phoenix, I saw the healthcare records for whose name had appeared on the HIV chronic care list. The chart clearly stated that he is not HIV+, and that he had purportedly lied about that status in 2008. However, test results in the file that were several years old showed that he has an active case of syphilis, and there was no indication in the file that anyone had done anything about his illness. , in Yuma, urgently needs wound care that works; his current inadequate treatment has transformed a treatable infection into a huge, gaping wound that requires immediate plastic surgery and reconstruction on his leg. This has lost his ability to walk as a result of a year's worth of mismanagement of a simple wound and inept treatment. When I spoke with him on August 2, 2013, his wound was being treated with silvadene, which is silver in a cream, typically used for initial burn treatment. It is a ridiculous choice for this purpose and its chronic use does not conform to the standard of care. Also at Yuma, I interviewed and reviewed the charts for a 69-year-old with hypertension. On June 10, 2013, at 1:15 a.m., he complained of chest pain. An RN evaluation by L. Sanders told him to "drop HNR" and "return[] to dorm." At 7:50 a.m., he complained of chest pain again, and this time RN A. Gutierrez appropriately sent him to the emergency room. He had a heart attack. In sum, medical staff lost six and a half hours during this patient's heart attack through RN error and lack of effort. Fortunately, he lived, but the risk of injury or even mortality was high.

also in Yuma, has out-of-control diabetes. In December 2012, in county jail, he was found to have a very low blood platelet count, possibly as a result of medication he was given (Depakote). At that time, it was 62, which is an alert to medical staff. On March 5, 2013 (after he had arrived in ADC), it was at 49 and his white blood cell count was at a critical low. His liver function was normal on that date. These test results were not reviewed for five days, which is far too long for such abnormal findings, and nothing was done even after they were reviewed. On May 17, 2013, his lab values had changed radically and he had substantially high liver enzyme readings. These results were not read until June 6, an even longer and less excusable delay, and again, nothing was done as a result. These abnormal lab results showed serious liver dysfunction and dysfunction in the production of the cells of the blood system and should have been quickly addressed. In addition, he has lost vision in his eyes due to his diabetes but no retinal exam has been completed, his blood sugars are routinely out of control with no attempts at management, and he is not on an ACE inhibitor to protect his kidneys, which is a clear violation of the standard of care case is error compounded on error, with critical physical exam findings and critical lab values that as of August 2, 2013, were unaddressed, and routine chronic disease management that has been poorly designed and implemented. in Yuma's Cheyenne Unit, has a severe case of Crohn's Disease, which is fistulizing: his bowel walls are breaking down and fecal matter leaks out into other areas, which is life threatening. He is an extremely fragile patient, at serious risk, who requires constant vigilance. He was admitted to the hospital with a significant fistula and abscess where he was stabilized and then transferred to Florence where he recovered. The hospital started him on Remicade (a tumor necrosis factor inhibitor) which is the standard of care for management of fistulizing Crohn's Disease. By his report he received two doses. However, when he was transferred back to Yuma, Corizon declined to continue his Remicade and switched him to asacol. Since starting the asacol he has decompensated several times and ended up back in the hospital. The cardinal error in this case was stopping the Remicade, apparently because of a central office utilization review decision. Remicade is a unique medication that is the standard of care for this patient's disease and the only thing that really works to reduce the development of fistulas. Once it is started, it must be maintained since it is usually not possible and medically dangerous to restart Remicade in patients because of extreme risk of allergic reaction upon re-exposure to this medication. As such, it is very unfortunate that the poor decision-making within the system probably has eliminated as a treatment option the only medication that really works by exposing him to Remicade for a couple of doses and then stopping it. In Tucson, complained of swelling in his chest for more than a year. He was told repeatedly by medical staff that it was only a cyst, but when it was finally biopsied in March 2013, it was found to be Stage IVB Hodgkin's Lymphoma. No care was pursued until May 2013. The cancer is now untreatable because it is so far advanced. in Tucson, is 17 years old. He has shotgun pellets in his knee and a plate in his femur that is probably infected. His infections have been partially treated through antibiotics and dressing changes, but the underlying problem is the plate, which clearly needs to be removed. He was seen by an orthopedic surgeon at the hospital, who ordered that he be seen again on September 19, 2013. As of October 24, he did not have an appointment. He has only 10 degrees range of motion in his knee, and will likely be disabled at a young age because of this failure to provide adequate care. also in Tucson, has heart problems, but there is not a single EKG in his healthcare records. He has an artificial heart valve which requires anticoagulation medication. He is on a high dose of Coumadin which has failed to produce an appropriate amount of thinning of his blood. His treatment plan was not changed for over a year even though there is ample lab evidence in the chart that his plan is failing. He is also on ibuprofen, which is contraindicated with Coumadin. Desiree Licci (150051) suffers from a prolapsed uterus, Stage III cystocele, and Stage III rectocele, and a hysterectomy was recommended by Dr. Irving. ADC122691, ADC122684. However, since Ms. Licci does not objectively fit the classic criteria for a hysterectomy, her subjective complaints and reports of pain were not considered. Ms. Licci has a history of breast and ovarian cancer. In late 2010, she began to experience a series of symptoms, including fatigue, pain, and congestion, and she also began to feel multiple masses on her arms, breasts, eyelid and mouth. In November 2010, her provider attributed her symptoms to Hepatitis C. In February 2011, her provider noted that the question of whether her symptoms indicated a reoccurrence of cancer was a question for experts. ADC005459. Ms. Licci continued to experience symptoms that were increasing in severity. She submitted a number of HNRs requesting care. See, e.g., ADC0010810, 0010808, 0010799. On May 14, 2011, in response to her HNR regarding the lump in her arm, she was told that the "Hep C issue" would be addressed first. ADC005905. In response to another HNR submitted May 14, 2011, Case 2:12-cv-00601-DJH Document 1104-1 Filed 09/08/14 Page 281 of 364 67 regarding a visit with oncology, the response notes "all in good time. You have multiple problems. Consult to oncology written on 5/18/11." ADC005906. After a number of attempts to get treatment for her symptoms and lumps, she finally received a properly administered CT scan in September 2011 which revealed numerous masses in her reproductive system. ADOC0010633-34. Ms. Licci then received an MRI in March 2012 which confirmed multiple masses in her reproductive system. Ms. Licci was finally seen by an oncologist in February and May 2012, who concluded that she had a "simple cyst," without conducting any type of biopsy in this cancer survivor. She needs be evaluated by a gynecologist for proper management of her reproductive system issues. D. Delivery of care that is ordered The third major component of an adequate medical care system is the right to treatment. Patients must not only be seen by appropriate clinicians and given appropriate diagnoses and treatment orders; they must actually receive the care – medications, labs and other diagnostic tests, special diets -- that is ordered. Teamwork, communication, and good documentation are essential to ensure that care that is ordered is actually provided to patients. I have observed multiple barriers in the Arizona system that interfere with care delivery. 1. Providers' orders Orders written by providers must actually be carried out. Throughout the Arizona system I saw a consistent pattern of ordered care – medications, labs, nursing care, follow-up appointments, specialty referrals – not getting done. This is another symptom of a badly understaffed medical care system. In Florence North and East, I was also struck by the divide between nursing and medical staff in terms of orders not being carried out. For example, I talked with a patient with MRSA and multiple episodes of serious staph infections. There were orders to medical staff to call him in for a wound check to see if he had healed from his infections, but he was never brought in to be seen. in Tucson, has prostate cancer that was partially treated. His doctor appropriately recommended that his prostate be reduced chemically with Casodex to allow him to function normally without a Foley catheter, which he has had for 14 months. The recommendation was denied, which subjects this patient to needless pain and suffering. housed in the Manzanita IPC in Tucson, is an extremely fragile 31-year-old patient with lupus and multiple sclerosis; the intersection of these two major diseases makes him a very complicated patient in need of specialty care. Some of the recommendations of the specialist he has seen have been ignored. is housed in the Florence infirmary because he has very aggressive multiple sclerosis (MS). He has been evaluated by an outside neurologist (Dr. Ales Hlubocky) who described his situation as "very active MS, disease is aggressive impacting ADL's significantly." On August 13, 2013, Dr. Hlubocky recommended Tysabri infusions because of the severity of the disease and because of its aggressive appearance on neurological imaging. So far the Tysabri has not been approved and there is a notation in the patient's record that Corizon is seeking to find a second neurologist to seek an alternative to the Tysabri treatment that has been recommended. As of October 15, 2013, no Tysabri has been administered to the patient, no follow-up has occurred with his neurologist, no appointment has been scheduled with the second neurologist, and the patient is bed-bound. His disease continues to progress without any treatment and he has now lost the ability to feed himself because his hand tremor is so severe that he cannot get food into his mouth. The other prisoners on his unit help feed him because the IPC where he is housed is so short-staffed with nurses that this is his only option despite the fact that in my understanding it is technically against ADC policy. Without treatment he will continue to lose function, lose vision, lose the ability to sit and care for his basic body needs, and his life span will be significantly shortened. Throughout my chart reviews it was common to see labs ordered but never done, medications ordered but not approved, medications ordered but not administered by the nurses, ADA accommodations ordered but not provided, consults ordered but never approved or scheduled, follow-up appointments requested by providers but never scheduled, and medical diets ordered but not received. In the Arizona prison system prisoners invest a tremendous amount of time, effort, money, and suffering into finally getting to see a provider; it is such a tragedy that when those providers do order appropriate healthcare interventions, the system is all too often not accurate, expeditious, or motivated to ensure that the care is delivered. 2. Medication administration and monitoring Prescribed medications must be provided to patients in a timely, consistent manner. Medications must be renewed regularly and without interruption, and prisoners must be able to transfer housing locations without medication interruptions. The system must ensure appropriate monitoring of efficacy and side effects. Arizona fails in all these areas, as high-level administrators acknowledge. Robertson Depo, 143:23-144:9 (ADC's Medical Program

Administrator describes gap in delivery of medications under Corizon, including the delivery of HIV medication); Gross Depo, 61:20-62:2 (ADC Assistant Director over the Health Monitoring Bureau notes that ADC has identified problems with medication management, including refill, reordering, and dispensing), 62:22-63:4 (there are problems both with the pharmacy refilling the medications and because doctors aren't rewriting prescriptions as needed); Williams Depo, 54:6-54:25, 56:21-56:24 (Corizon Arizona Regional Medical Director admits to problems with Corizon's pharmacy services, with "some discrepancy between the expiration report and the patients actually being on medications"). The ADC monitors' reports show that administration of prescription medication is frequently delayed or missed. ADC154207 (September 26, 2013) (16 of 24 Perryville MARs showed unreasonable delays in prescription medication distribution); ADC137255 (July 30, 2103) (Florence prisoner hospitalized after not receiving antibiotics following surgery); ADC137432 (July 30, 2013) (prisoner at Yuma Cheyenne presumably went without psych medication when his 5/28/13 HNR was not addressed until 6/19/13); ADC137443 (July 29, 2013) (31 of 50 Yuma charts reviewed have missing initials on dates indicating that the medicine was not administered); ADC137390 (July 29, 2013) (Tucson prisoner went 20 days without medication despite filing HNR alerting staff to upcoming medication expiration dates) ADC137294-5 (July 24, 2013) (pill line delays at Perryville); ADC137293 (July 24, 2013) (boxes of undistributed medications were found on multiple occasions at Perryville); ADC137264 (July 14, 2013) (Florence prisoner (163888) had an order for intravenous Primaxin [antibiotic] upon discharge from the hospital, and although this was brought to the attention of nursing staff on 7/5/13, there was still no medication as of 7/8/13); ADC137305 (July 5, 2013) (at Perryville San Carlos, three inmates who were prescribed antibiotics did not receive them); ADC089051 (April 30, 2013) (Tucson prisoner's (15141) Rifaximin marked not available from 4/1/13 to 4/24/13); ADC088880-81(April 28, 2013) (8 of 10 reviewed MARs at Florence North had multiple blank dates indicating medications not administered); ADC088880-81 (April 28, 2013) (6 of 10 reviewed MARs at Florence Kasson had multiple blank dates indicating medications not administered); id. (April 28, 2013) (10 of 10 reviewed MARs at Florence East had multiple blank dates indicating medications not administered); ADC088880-81 (April 28, 2013) (8 of 10 reviewed MARs at Florence Central had multiple blank dates indicating medications not administered); ADC088973 (April 21, 2013) (multiple prisoners at Phoenix Aspen did not have medications for April); ADC088744 (April 4, 2013) (MARs at Florence Kasson listed medications that were not available to prisoners for multiple days in a row in March); ADC088742 (April 4, 2013) (minimum of 47 patients in Florence East who were consistently absent from "watch swallow" medication line). Case 2:12-cv-00601-DJH Document 1104-1 Filed 09/08/14 Page 285 of 364 71 Corizon policy requires prisoners to file an HNR to request that chronic care prescription medication be refilled (Response 31, Defendants' Responses to Verduzco's First Set of RFAs), a practice that practically guarantees patients will face medication interruptions. They do: prisoners consistently reported to me that it takes a week or more to get refills. At Tucson, I saw many HNRs for medication renewal that were over a month old; they had not been reviewed by a prescriber so they were not refilled. The ADC monitors have documented extensively that prescriptions are commonly allowed to expire before being reordered or renewed and expired medication continues to be distributed. ADC154137 (September 30, 2013) ("[m]edications are not being ordered prior to expiration on any unit on Florence complex"); ADC154333 (September 30, 2013) (Tucson staff reordered 0 of the 140 formulary prescriptions reviewed either on or prior to expiration, and only 5 after expiration); ADC137603 (August 29, 2013) (only 66% of chronic care medications in Phoenix are being reviewed prior to expiration); ADC137576 (August 20, 2013) (medicine renewal compliance is 67% at Perryville); Winland Depo, 129:6-129:11 (127 prescriptions identified as expired in Phoenix); ADC137339 (July 19, 2013) (Phoenix Aspen notes 64 expired medications cards in with current administered medications); id. (July 31, 2013) (multiple units at Phoenix document currently using medications that have expired); ADC137256 and ADC137240 (July 30, 2013) (51 of 375 Florence prescriptions were renewed after expiration); ADC137395 (July 29, 2013) (medications are not ordered, filled, or refilled on time at Tucson); ADC137240 (July 29, 2013) (medications are improperly refrigerated and not timely renewed at Florence); ADC137306 (July 29, 2013) (71 of 165 Perryville prescriptions expired prior to renewal date); ADC137430 (July 25, 2013) (a "more diligent approach to filling and refilling expired medication must be adopted" in Yuma); ADC137333 (July 25, 2013) (52 of 103 prescriptions reviewed at Phoenix expired prior to renewal date); ADC137323-29 (July 24, 2013) (64 expired medicine cards from April 2013 to July 2013 are in the currently used bins at Phoenix); ADC137313-14 (July 12 , Case 2:12-cv-00601-DJH Document 1104-1 Filed 09/08/14 Page 286 of 364 72 16, and, 19, 2013) (expired medication in use in KOP and DOT bins at Perryville San Pedro, Lumley Santa Cruz, Santa Rosa, Santa Maria, and Piestewa); ADC137306 (July 15, 2013) (at Perryville, 86 of 154 prescriptions reviewed expired prior to their renewal date and 20 of 154 prescriptions ran reviewed out of medication prior to their renewal date); ADC137306 (July 15, 2013) (review of Perryville July 1-8 stop date report showed chronic condition medication expiration dates were not being reviewed prior to expiration); ADC137259 (July 30, 2013) (medications at Florence are expiring before being reordered); ADC088890 (April 15, 2013) (numerous medications in the "Man Down" bag at Florence were expired, some for over one year); ADC089106 (April 27, 2013) (many delays in receiving medication at Yuma); ADC088947 (April 22, 2013) (43 of 112 reviewed mental health and chronic care prescriptions at Perryville were expired without renewals). Some of the medication delivery problems are caused by staffing deficits. For example, Corizon slashed in half the number of pharmacy technicians at Tucson. AGA_Review_00001704-1705. This has caused problems such as those documented above in this Section. It has also led to problems not monitored in the MGAR process: for example, as of March 28, 2013, pharmacy staff at Tucson were unable to ensure prisoners are provided medications on release. AGA_Review_00009347 -9349. 3. Labs, imaging, and other tests Diagnostic tests are an essential part of any medical care system. Arizona fails all too often to provide labs, x-rays, CT and PET scans, and other tests that are ordered by providers as crucial diagnostic tools. Some tests that are ordered are simply never done. In Florence, I noticed in the chart of one patient with Hepatitis C ( ) that there was no record of his current viral load even though there was an order to draw that lab on August 19, 2013. When I asked for any records indicating his current viral load, I was told by Corizon Arizona Regional Medical Director Dr. Williams that there were no results in the file because it had not been done. It is important in treating Hepatitis C patients to understand their viral load because it correlates with the severity of the disease and determines the success of treatment. In Tucson, , who is HIV positive, had appropriate labs ordered but never drawn (as confirmed by the Corizon attorney on the tour), so his providers know nothing about where he is in the disease process and cannot effectively treat him. He is admitted into the Inpatient Care Unit where he has had a number of medical complications that have required care but the medical doctors do not even have the basic healthcare information about his underlying condition even though it is prominently listed as an active problem in his chart. This is just bad healthcare. Another Tucson patient, has basal cell cancer (a skin tumor). He was given a definite diagnosis in a biopsy on May 1, 2012, and at the same time an order was placed for a CT scan of his neck. The CT scan was not done until February 5, 2013. If left untreated this condition is potentially fatal and can cause deformity and pain. Even if lab tests are done, they are sometimes not timely filed or reviewed, which renders them useless for patient care. In the clinic at Santa Rita unit in Tucson, I saw a great deal of loose filing of lab results and consult results and x-ray reports which were upwards of four to six weeks old and had clearly never been looked at by anyone – they were not organized into the patients' files and there were no signatures indicating review or any follow up. Such delays can be dangerous to patients: I looked at many of the unreviewed lab reports and found significant abnormal levels. If lab results are not reviewed promptly, they do the patient no good – they might as well not have been ordered. These errors speak to lack of staff and provider availability. My findings are bolstered by the testimony of ADC's own staff. See Sharp Depo, 54:21-56:5 (according to Perryville physician, it currently takes 2-4 weeks to get x-ray reports from radiologist; such delays can and have posed a serious risk to patients); ADC137319 (July 31, 2013) (no regular medical provider line in Phoenix, resulting in untimely review of laboratory results); ADC088856 (April 14, 2013) (review of imaging and lab results at Florence Globe was delayed, including an x-ray result that was received on 2/27/13 and not reviewed until 4/5/13 and an abnormal lab dated 3/14/13 and still not reviewed as of 4/5/13). See also Maryann Chisholm (200825) for delays in reviewing lab work and consult orders. 4. Special medical diets Medical diets are necessary as part of the overall care plan for some patients. Healthcare providers order these special medical diets just like medications because in many instances a proper medical diet is more efficacious at treating a problem than prescription medications. As such, I always pay attention to making sure that certain types of patients receive appropriate diets because it is so essential to successful disease management. I was shocked to discover that Arizona prisons have extremely limited disease-specific diets. The most common special diet in a correctional facility is a calorie-controlled diabetic diet. This does not exist in the Arizona prison system. I pulled diet binders that listed the diets available, I pulled diet order forms that were used for ordering diets, I pulled lists of medical diets that the kitchen was preparing for individual patients and not a single mention of a diabetic diet was found. This is inconceivable to me as a clinician as it eliminates one of the most important variables in managing diabetics—moderating the amount of sugar (carbohydrates) they consume. Florence's Deputy Warden for Operations, Julie Jackson, attempted to explain the medical diet issue to me and indicated that a few years ago medical diets were eliminated in favor of a universal "heart healthy diet" in the ADC. She explained that the heart healthy diet was used for almost all medical diets regardless of condition and it has greatly simplified the process of producing food in the prisons. She informed me that the diabetics were all given the heart healthy diet and they did just fine on it. Based on her assertions I sought to find evidence of the universal diet's effectiveness. I reviewed blood sugar logs for diabetic patients, chronic care notes for diabetics, and standard diabetic laboratory monitoring results in the medical records. What I discovered, not surprisingly, is that while the universal heart healthy diet may be convenient for corrections, it is not effective in managing diabetic patients. A very high percentage of the insulin-dependent patients had sugar levels that were poorly controlled. For example, when came into the system, his Hemoglobin A1c level (an indicator of long-term blood sugar control covering about 90 days of time) was 7.6%, which indicates that he was in reasonably good control prior to incarceration. After he moved to Florence and began the heart healthy diet plan, his finger stick blood glucose readings jumped up consistently to the 300 to 400 range and his Hemoglobin A1cs increased to 10.3 and 10.6 on respective tests. As determined by the objective evidence he went from being a well-controlled diabetic to a very poorly controlled diabetic, at risk for severe disease complications.[10] The insulin was the same and the patient is the same; the primary variable that changed was the diet. I saw many examples of this phenomenon and while I did not have the time in the prisons or access to the documentation I need to examine the entirety of the medical diet dilemma, I see it as a major issue that deserves more study since I believe that the inappropriate diet issues in the prison contribute dramatically to the disease issues that I did study in detail. E. Protection from preventable negative outcomes Healthcare administrators know that a significant number of negative outcomes can be prevented through carefully implemented quality assurance, patient feedback, and

[10] Another breakage in the system is that if a blood sugar goes above 400, nursing staff are ordered to call a medical doctor so that action can be taken. I routinely saw blood sugars over 400, up to 500, with no notes, no assessment, and medical staff simply giving insulin and calling it good treatment with no provider involvement despite medical orders to call. I saw no indication that anyone had called a provider about blood sugar readings

screening mechanisms. I saw no evidence that any of these measures have been meaningfully implemented in the Arizona system. 1. Quality assurance People make mistakes. This is an unavoidable fact of human nature. In order to find and correct errors before they harm patients, healthcare administrators establish quality assurance mechanisms. An effective quality assurance process requires structured and systemic review of healthcare processes throughout the whole system. This is typically done by identifying a problem to be investigated, developing a hypothesis, performing a review of a statistically significant number of charts by a qualified individual or group to assess the evidence of care, calculating appropriate statistics to prove or disprove the hypothesis, formulating proposed action plans to improve the item being reviewed if necessary, developing policy and procedure to implement the new action plans, and then reassessing the results of the changes in the future to determine that the identified problems have actually been corrected. I saw no evidence that such system exists in ADC, which does an inadequate job of providing this essential aspect of healthcare delivery. The MGAR monitoring system is no substitute for a true quality assurance program. It is merely an incident reporting tool with no analysis of cause and effect and it simply is not an adequate tool to assess healthcare quality in any way. Dr. Winfred Williams, the Corizon Arizona Regional Medical Director, oversees and supervises doctors in the system, including peer review based on chart reviews. Williams Depo, 9:1-9:4, 12:20-13:5. He looks at "clinical outcomes data," including information about patient HIV viral loads and insulin levels and the like, from the laboratory database to measure performance. Id. at 17:25-18:6, 20:16-20:22, 21:22-23:4. Corizon also conducts quality assurance studies with review performance measures analogous to the MGARs.[11] Id. at 24:23-26:1. From Dr. Williams's own description of his processes, however, it is clear to me that they are not an adequate quality assurance mechanism. For one thing, he does not have enough information. He has only seen a few MGAR reports, he does not receive official reports from medical directors, and he does not receive any reports that review delays in patient care. Williams Depo, 16:17-16:21, 15:11-15:17, 21:2-21:10. Weekly conference calls with providers (id. at 15:18-16:6) and occasional trips to the field (id. at 14:1-14:6) are no substitute for methodical information-gathering. Nor is a review of lab numbers in a database: such data give you some information about patient health, but they do not pinpoint deficits with quality of care. (If a patient's numbers are subnormal, is the problem in delayed access to care? Medication delivery? Interaction with other medications?) Without reviewing patient charts, it is impossible to tell whether the medical care delivery system is working and if not, where the problem lies. Moreover, without reviewing additional data and performing thorough reviews at the site, it is impossible to tell what these numbers are missing. For example, how many patients should have had labs drawn but did not? The answer cannot be found in reviewing lab results. The fact that Dr. Williams is unaware of serious care delivery problems in the system he oversees demonstrates the inadequacy of any quality assurance mechanisms currently in use. Although he believes he can determine the rate at which chronic care patients are timely seen by assessing the computerized lab data (id. at 46:16-50:18), his belief is clearly misplaced: as of October 2013, he did not know that in June 2013, some 11 I was not provided with any of these studies. My understanding is the Corizon has not produced them in this litigation. I would be happy to review any such studies, but I am confident, based on the evidence I have seen and documented in this report, that any quality assurance measures Corizon is taking are ineffective. chronic care appointments at Eyman were overdue by many months – and several for over a year. Id. at 57:6-58:2, 59:24-60:4. He did not know that in July 2013, 68% of chronic care appointments at Eyman were late. Id. at 60:6-64:14 (actual question and response at 64:1-64:14). Most chillingly, Dr. Williams is either unaware of or unpersuaded by the serious staffing deficits I cataloged in Sections II.A.3 and II.B.2, above: he believes that Corizon currently has adequate providers to meet chronic care guidelines: "from what I've seen when I've been out to the sites, I notice that the patients are being seen and provider lines are being done. And patients are scheduled." Williams Depo, 45:9-45:23. See also Bybee Depo, 8:13-8:16, 24:24-25:12 (Corizon vice president of operations for Arizona believes that Corizon has enough providers to see patients 7 days after nurse's line). 2. Grievance process Patient grievances are an important source of information for healthcare administrators and practitioners. They are another essential element of quality assurance programs in correctional settings. Of course, patients file many meritless grievances, but the meritorious ones make the process worthwhile: in any system, people can slip through the cracks and the grievance process affords an opportunity for them to be heard, for errors to be corrected, and for oversights to be addressed. The healthcare grievance process does not work in Arizona prisons. For one thing, neither ADC nor Corizon tracks grievances electronically. Responses 38 & 39, Defendants' Responses to Verduzco's First Set of RFAs. Without that capability, the feedback loop cannot be effective, and staff and administrators cannot learn from their mistakes. An effective grievance process relies on statistical analysis of patterns to uncover issues that need to be addressed. Extracting any meaningful quality data from grievances is simply not possible without any tracking, categorization, or analysis of the grievances as an overall data set. In Arizona, problems conveyed on grievances come in one by one, unit by unit, prison by prison and they are addressed individually without any ument 1104-1 Filed 09/08/14 Page 293 of 364 79 sense of the larger healthcare delivery process within the Arizona Department of Corrections. The grievance system also is unreliable when responses are significantly delayed. I have seen some evidence of delays in Arizona. ADC036793 (ASPC-Perryville Grievances Performance Measures: "[a]s of October 15, 2012, there were 260 informal grievances [and] 7 formal grievances that had not been answered. Of the informal grievance, only 23 were compliant with this standard" requiring a response within 15 working days of receipt per Department Order 802); ADC089042 (April 27, 2013) (7 past due inmate grievances and 28 overdue incomplete inmate letter responses to date at Tucson); ADC088938 (April 29, 2013) (10 of 32 informal grievances due by 4/29 at Perryville were not answered within the allotted time and approximately 60 informal grievances awaiting site managers signatures). 3. Screening Correctional healthcare systems must have an initial screening process to catch urgent or emergent needs (for example, major injuries from the arrest process) and then a secondary, more thorough screening that is an actual clinical encounter to address medications, infectious disease control, and the like. Arizona's intake screening process, which takes place for male prisoners at the Phoenix facility, is faulty. ADC's Phoenix monitor has repeatedly told Corizon of intake compliance problems. Valenzuela Depo, 108:7-108:21. These problems include physical exams not occurring in a timely fashion. ADC088954 (April 28, 2013) (5 of 10 charts reviewed at Phoenix C area had not had a physical examination completed by a medical provider by the second day of the intake process); ADC088998 (April 29, 2013) (as of 4/29/13, 8 minors at Tucson Rincon Minors yard had not had a physical exam by a provider completed within two days of the intake process); AGA_Review_00009556 (as of March 31, 2013, 14 Phoenix intake charts show no timely physical exam). Case 2:12-cv-00601-DJH Document 1104-1 Filed 09/08/14 Page 294 of 364 80 Another problem involves lab testing: "lab results are not consistently transferred with the inmate in his medical records to his permanent yard in a timely manner creating a situation of unavailability of laboratory results to medical staff at the inmate's permanent facility." AGA_Review_00009559-9560 (listing multiple lab results not filed or not reviewed by provider) (emphasis in original). Perhaps the main constraint on intake processing is that the space set aside for it -- Alhambra Unit at Phoenix -- is very small. Since Alhambra can house only a limited number of prisoners awaiting transfer, when new buses arrive there is serious pressure to move people out as quickly as possible, as documented on a series of frantic emails I reviewed between ADC and Corizon staff in June 2013. AGA_Review_00021332- 21333 ("Alhambra only has a capacity of 336 beds. Intake continues to be extremely high. As of right now we are negative 90 inmates, with only 17 ready to move. We need at least 48 more scheduled out for today. Medical has 190 roll overs and tomorrow we have 103 arrivals putting Alhambra at almost 130 negative"). As one staff member put it, "We can not operate intake this way." Id. ADC ascribes the hold-up to Corizon: "[m]ovement out of Alhambra is being impeded by the current medical process. Inmates are getting backed up there without bed space to house them." AGA_Review_00021381-21382 (also noting large numbers of prisoners awaiting medical processing; "it's like this almost daily"). As a result, prisoners are rushed through the process and it is not always adequately completed. For example, physicians' orders are substandard: Dr. Robertson, ADC's Medical Program Administrator, determined that "notes are scanty and some are even copied for a presigned progress note and place[d] in chart with minor modifications. (This is unacceptable.)" AGA_Review_00018506. I agree. Dr. Robertson also points out that other providers do not trust Alhambra's intake labs, a "serious" issue that "needs to be looked at." Id. Untrustworthy labs could be another symptom of rushed processing. These are problems of long standing. Dr. Fisher from Wexford found that transfer summaries coming out of Phoenix for men were "grossly incomplete," with many sections left completely blank. Deposition of Neil Fisher, October 8, 2013 (Fisher Depo), at 16:18-17:8, 88:21-89:16; WEXFORD000023. Transfer summaries from Perryville for women were "better, but still challenged." WEXFORD000023. This meant that providers lack a patient's full medical and social history. Id. at 107:19-108:17. Wexford detailed extensive deficiencies in the screening process in November 2012, including the failure to implement a proper intake screening process and the failure to provide tuberculosis testing and preventive care. WEXFORD000023-25. Corizon has not cured all of these deficiencies. According to the ADC monitor for Phoenix, Corizon has been notified repeatedly of problems but has not addressed them in a meaningful or lasting way. ADC118026 ("[t]he health services intake process is problematic in medically processing inmates and entering the information on a timely basis resulting in a serious delay of ADOC inmates being moved or transferred out to other facilities. Corizon upper management at the Phoenix Complex have been previously and currently made aware of this on several occasions and were provided with suggestions for making improvements. They have shown a momentary attention to address the problems with the intake process; however, it is temporary with limited to no follow up to assure correction"). In sum, "[i]t seems there exists an attitude of ignoring the ineffective current medical intake process combined with a non urgency to maintain timely intake medical inmate processing." Id III. Conclusion Medical care in Arizona prisons is simply inadequate to meet the basic needs of many of the prisoners who experience illness and injury while in custody. Throughout my investigation, I found evidence of a system in disarray: poor management structure and lines of authority; systematic violations of policies and procedures as well as omitted policies that are necessary for patient care; staff spread far too thin to provide for patients' needs; malfunctioning sick call process and consequent significant barriers to care; dangerously inadequate chronic care patient management; serious concerns regarding emergency and inpatient care; signs of custody interference with care; disturbing waivers of treatment at least in the Tucson infirmary; a widespread failure to provide patients with appropriate provider medical judgment due to chaotic and disorganized medical records, nurses acting outside of the scope of their licenses, denial of specialty care consultations, and substandard decision-making; inability to provide patients with medically necessary medications and diagnostic tests; and the inability to self-correct or to address known risks of harm through quality assurance, grievance, and screening mechanisms. All of these problems are chronic but also current. All of them harm patients. My follow-up experience with two patients I met during my tours is symptomatic to me of the system's failures. I discussed the case of in Section II.C.5 on substandard care decisions. He is the Yuma patient in urgent need of wound care: his inadequate treatment had transformed a treatable infection into a large pus-filled gaping wound that required immediate vascular surgery with reconstructive plastic surgery on his leg. After I interviewed him on August 2, 2013, I arranged for to show his wound to Corizon's Arizona Regional Medical Director Dr. Williams as well as the lawyers for the State and for Corizon on the tour and I described for them why the current long-standing wound management for him was incorrect and what steps need to be pursued quickly to address this treatable problem. I understand that wrote to the Prison Law Office in September and again on October 23, 2013, reporting that he still had not received meaningful care for his wound. According to the copy of the grievance I was shown, dated October 22, 2013, was taken on September 17 to Yuma Regional Medical Center where he was given an IV drip and other aggressive treatment and told by a plastic surgeon that he would require several surgeries. This finding is consistent with what I would expect the wound I saw in August continued to be incompetently treated to that point. According to , three days after arriving at the hospital he was moved to the Tucson prison, where he was denied any treatment for several days and was then returned to Yuma, where he is once again on the same inadequate treatment regimen: bandage changes three times a week. I have not been able to review healthcare records because they have not been produced by the State, although they were requested after my tour, so I cannot verify his account. If what he relates is true, however, it is outrageous and demonstrates deliberate indifference to his serious medical needs. What started off as a manageable problem has turned into a catastrophe for this patient as a result of a year of incompetent wound care management. Without adequate treatment, there is a very real possibility that he may require amputation to control the infection. The second patient is whom I discussed in Section II.C.4 regarding failure to provide him with specialty care. has end-stage AIDS and is a very sick and fragile patient. After I met with him and reviewed his chart at Yuma, I told Dr. Williams and the attorneys for the State and for Corizon that his case was being seriously mishandled by the facility providers with a treatment plan that fell well short of the standard of care. He needed urgently to see an HIV specialist to correct fundamental treatment errors and omissions. I pointed out that on May 23, 2013, an infectious disease consult had been ordered, but it had never been completed. I have been provided with a copy of medical chart through October 7, 2013. From the documentation, I see that he was in fact seen by an HIV specialist on August 19, 2013, several weeks after I informed Dr. Williams of his dangerously mishandled care. The specialist confirmed my initial findings and ordered a panel of diagnostic tests necessary to evaluate the patient in light of his failed treatment and to reset the treatment plan as best as possible. A follow-up appointment with the HIV specialist one month later was also ordered.

SUPPLEMENTAL EXPERT REPORT OF ELDON VAIL

I. INTRODUCTION

1. I have been asked to submit a supplemental report based on my review of documents covering the period September 27, 2013 through April 1, 2014, as well as a second inspection of isolation units in three Arizona Department of Corrections (ADC) prisons. Those inspections took place on August 11-13, 2014. I spent one day at the Arizona State Prison Complex (ASPC)-Perryville, one day at ASPC-Florence, and one day at ASPC-Eyman. I previously inspected these same prisons over a five day period July 29-August 2, 2013.

2. During the 2014 inspections I traveled with a rather large entourage, consisting of attorneys for each party in this case, ADC administrators, an additional expert for the Plaintiffs, an expert for the Defendants, a variety of custody staff and at times, a video crew, (apparently using the opportunity of this inspection to shoot a video of ADC prisons for presentation at an upcoming meeting of the Association of State Corrections Administrators (ASCA)). The size of the entourage was, at times, between fifteen and twenty people. This is significant because it greatly slowed movement throughout the facility and sometimes, in my opinion, inhibited interaction with prisoners. The entourage stayed

together at Perryville but split into two groups later in the day at Florence and Eyman.

3. At each prison complex, ADC administrators had orchestrated presentations for the entourage, which I will address later in this report. The purpose of those presentations was apparently to illustrate the changes and progress ADC believes they have achieved in the management of inmates held in their isolation units during the past year. Inmates sometimes behaved as one would expect in the presence of so many ADC officials and facility guests and said they appreciated the program or class they were siting in, especially when asked leading questions by ADC officials or Defendants' expert, Dr. Seiter. Other times that veneer faded quickly and hard questions were asked of ADC officials. My subsequent conversations at the cell front with a few of the inmates who were participating in classes we interrupted with ADC's entourage expressed much more skepticism on the value of the programs when ADC officials were not present.

II. ASSIGNMENT

4. I have been retained by Plaintiffs to evaluate and offer my opinion regarding the policy and operational practices of the Arizona Department

of Corrections (ADC) regarding the use of isolation units. I understand that the Court has defined the isolation sub-class in this case as "All prisoners who are now, or will in the future be, subjected by the ADC to isolation, defined as confinement in a cell for 22 hours or more each day or confinement in the following housing units: Eyman—SMU I; Eyman—Browning Unit; Florence—Central Unit; Florence—Kasson Unit; or Perryville—Lumley Special Management Area."

5. The particular focus of my review has been and continues to be on the conditions of confinement for inmates housed in isolation in the units identified in the Court's Order and on whether or not the inmates, especially mentally ill inmates, living in those units suffer serious harm or are subject to a substantial risk of serious harm. The defendants take issue with the use of the word "isolation" to describe the conditions under which many of the mentally ill live in the ADC. Within the corrections industry several different words are used to describe these living conditions. In addition to "isolation," some of the most frequently used terms are "segregation," "super-max," and "solitary confinement." I use the word "isolation" throughout this Report. It was the first word I learned to describe these conditions when I started working in corrections in 1974. The Defendants use it as well in their curriculum for *Understanding Mentally Ill Inmates* on page 54: "Also, staff should know that placing this inmate in isolation may

6. The particular focus of my most recent inspection and this report is to opine on whether or not the ADC has made sufficient changes in the operation of their isolation units to reduce the risk of serious harm to the prisoners held in their isolation units.

III. FOUNDATION FOR EXPERT OPINION

7. I have previously submitted three reports and a declaration in this case. In my first report I detailed my experience and qualifications. Attached to this report, as **Exhibit 1** is a copy of my resume, updating my work as a correctional consultant and expert witness. During the past two years I have been retained as an expert witness or correctional consultant in ten different states. In several cases I have been asked to opine on practices in isolation units, including the states of Mississippi, California, and New York, where an interim settlement agreement has been reached and negotiations are ongoing. I testified in Federal court in *Coleman v. Brown* in California and *Graves v. Arapio* in Arizona, both class action lawsuits regarding issues related to incarcerated mentally ill inmates. With both parties concurring in my selection, I was also appointed and completed a

Special Master assignment for the judge in *Corbett v. Branker*, a case related to the Use of Force (UOF) against inmates held in isolation in a prison in North Carolina.

8. I considered information from a variety of sources in preparing this report. This includes information provided by the parties, court filings submitted by the parties, deposition testimony and declarations, and ADC

training actually worsen his psychosis due to isolation, boredom, and lack of stimuli." materials, records, and internal reports covering the period of September

27, 2013 through April 1, 2014. A complete list of the materials I reviewed in this matter is attached hereto as **Exhibit 2,** and may be referred to in footnotes and/or other references within this report.

9. In addition to a handful of UOF videos I viewed for previous reports, for this report I viewed approximately thirty-three additional videos of Use of Force (UOF) incidents with inmates who are mentally ill and/or housed in ADC isolation units. With the exception of one of those events, I was able to view the related Serious Incident Reports (SIR's). I also read SIR's for an additional thirty-eight UOF events for which videos were not provided. Based on the wording in at least eight of those SIR's, videos were taken but not produced to the Plaintiffs.

10. As referenced above, I also relied on my findings in the three days of inspections I conducted at the isolation units. During my recent inspection at Perryville-Lumley I was able to interview approximately twenty-five inmates, mostly at their cell front, with six in a confidential setting. At Florence I interviewed approximately fifty-three inmates and at Eyman approximately forty-seven. Most of these interviews took place at the cell front. In the interest of the limited time I had at these large facilities, there were no confidential interviews at Eyman or Florence. During these interviews I asked inmates for their observations of changes in their conditions of confinement. I frequently told them I wanted to know if things had gotten better and, if so, how. The Eyman-Browning unit seems to have a different practice for videoing UOF events than do the other units I inspected. Situations where cameras were used at other facilities identical to ones I read about at Browning were not video recorded.

11. At each prison complex I was able to inspect the maximum custody cells, the shower areas, and the new recreation and program areas. At Florence I inspected CB 1, CB 2, CB 4, CB 5, CB 7, and Kasson. At Eyman I inspected Browning and SMU 1.

12. The inspection took place in August of this year. I understand that the court had cut off discovery as of April 1, 2014. My observations from the inspection are obviously after that date and do inform the opinions in this report.

IV. OPINIONS

13. It is my opinion that the problems I identified with the conditions of confinement in ADC's isolation units in my previous reports persisted during the period in question – September 27, 2013 through April 1, 2014 –and they will continue to persist without a major overhaul of policy and practice. Therefore, I stand by the opinions I have previously expressed in this case. While acknowledging that the ADC is attempting to change some aspects of the way they use isolation within their prison system, it is my opinion that the changes currently implemented are rudimentary, entirely insufficient and unlikely to be sustained. Given the culture of the prisons I found in my extensive review of documentation and encountered a year ago during my five-day inspection – which has only been reinforced by this year's inspection and my review of updated discovery documents – it is my opinion that it will take years and not a period of a few weeks or months to effectively reduce the substantial risk of serious harm created for prisoners by the conditions of confinement in ADC's isolation units.

14. More specifically, the ADC policy for isolating inmates continues to be over-broad and fails to exclude individuals with mental illness or systematically take into account their needs.

15. Changes to the conditions of confinement for some inmates have been marginally improved but this is largely for those prisoners that either do not need or never needed confinement in segregation units to begin with. The conditions of confinement for the majority of inmates in isolation in ADC facilities, including inadequate mental health monitoring, inappropriate use of chemical spray, inadequate nutrition, inadequate

exercise, limited property, extreme social isolation, and other hardships, are both unnecessary and counter-productive to good prison security, as well as harmful for all inmates, but especially for the mentally ill.

16. ADC routinely and inappropriately uses chemical agents, such as Oleoresin Capsicum (OC) products, against mentally ill inmates without considering the impact on the inmate and the effective management of the inmate population. This includes systemic use of force (UOF) practices that result in unnecessary use of force and needless pain, suffering, and humiliation for the inmate population.

17. My additional opinions are stated in the body of this report.

V. ADC STILL OVERUSES ISOLATION WHICH UNNECCESSARILY SUBJECTS PRISONERS TO SUBSTANTIAL RISK OF SERIOUS HARM

18. The publication of DI 326, signed by Director Ryan on March 27, 2014, is the biggest change in written instruction within the ADC regarding maximum custody since my last inspection of ADC facilities. Unfortunately, DI 326 failed to address the fundamental flaws in the ADC's classification policy that I identified in my previous reports.

19. I do not argue that qualified consultants have validated ADC's classification policy. However, there is no representation that the consultants who validated the policy were familiar with or even considered the actual conditions of confinement that inmates who score maximum custody are subjected to in the ADC. As I said in a previous report, A prison system's classification scoring system, no matter if it has or has not been validated, bears no necessary relationship to the actual conditions of confinement found in that system's prisons. The practice in ADC assumes that inmates who are maximum custody must be placed in isolation. Most jurisdictions make a distinction between assigning an inmate to their highest level of general population confinement and placing someone in isolation or segregation. Arizona does not. All maximum inmates are placed in isolation. To illustrate by way of an outrageous example, if the ADC decided to house all inmates who score minimum custody in their isolation units it would not violate the validity of the classification instrument itself.

20. ADC continues to subject too many inmates to the risk of harm of placement in isolation who do not need such secure confinement. In his deposition, Director Ryan indicated that one of the drivers in ADC's decision to make changes in their management of inmates in isolationappears to be the work of the Association of State Corrections Administrators (ASCA).7 The resolution published by ASCA wisely says, "ASCA is committed to the universal classification principle of managing inmates in the least restrictive way necessary to carry out its mission." In continuing to house some inmates in isolation who do not require such secure placement, the ADC continues to expose those inmates to an unnecessary risk of harm. Based on my experience as Secretary of Corrections in Washington, some of those held in isolation in the ADC that do not require such restrictive placement are inmates with life sentences, validated Security Threat Group (STG) members, and even some inmates sentenced to death. The publication of DI 326 did not touch this issue and those inmates remain routinely assigned to maximum custody and placement in isolation within the ADC.

21. DI 326 also does not address the overuse of isolation for inmates who are mentally ill. I documented in my previous reports the dangers of housing the mentally ill in isolation and my own work to keep the mentally ill out of those units and instead house them in a secure treatment environment. DI 326 makes no move to create treatment units for the mentally ill and continues to house them under conditions creating a substantial risk of serious harm.

22. DI326 supposedly addresses two distinct populations—the mentally ill and the non-mentally ill. But the Directive does not exclude seriously mentally ill from the isolation units; nor does it make any clear distinctions between treatment and therapy programs for the mental ill and cognitive programs designed for the non-mentally ill. The mentally ill need treatment for their mental illness. While time out of cell in a cognitive program may alleviate some of the extreme isolation and idleness suffered by prisoners in isolation, for someone who is seriously mentally ill, and who may be hearing voices, having hallucinations, or experiencing other mental decompensation, attending a class in Money Management, for example, has little therapeutic value. There is almost no detail in DI 326 about the level of treatment to be afforded mentally ill prisoners in isolation. As discussed below, I found that the existing programs, policies and practices (whether part of DI 326 or not), for all prisoners in isolation, and especially the mentally ill, do not adequately alleviate the suffering and risk created by the conditions of confinement in these units.

23. In my opinion the failure to fundamentally reconsider who needs to be housed within the isolation units of ADC ensures that many will continue to suffer needlessly, and is in fact contrary to good prison security and the above language from the ASCA resolution.

VI. CONDITIONS OF CONFINEMENT IN THE ISOLATION UNITS CONTINUE TO CREATE A SUBSTANTIAL RISK OF SERIOUS HARM

24. One of the stated purposes of DI 326 says, This Director's Instruction is being implemented to facilitate a process that requires inmates in maximum custody to work through a program utilizing a step system providing the opportunity to participate in jobs, programs and other out of cell activities. Based on behavior and programming, inmates may progress from controlled based housing where movement outside a cell is without restraint equipment. The directive, which was only effective March 27, 2014, goes on to describe the process for Intake and Assessment into maximum custody and the Step Program, the critical element that would allow the prisoner to progress from isolation into a less restrictive environment. The details of the Step Program for each sub group held in isolation are then detailed in the directive.

25. Despite the fact that ADC has not moved to create treatment units for the mentally ill, the directive does indicate a plan to cluster some mentally ill inmates in certain housing locations. I had the opportunity to inspect most of those units and found them entirely inadequate to provide a suitable environment for the mentally ill. The fact that DI 326 does not even 10 DI 326, Purpose section (ADC261959). provide a mental health program for women at the Perryville SMA unit is especially troubling.

26. CB 4 at Florence is one of the units designated to house the mentally ill. DI 326 indicates, "Cell Block 4 Program houses male general population inmates requiring a less controlled housing environment, while still receiving enhanced programming and socialization skill building. Most of the beds will be reserved for the SMI population."

27. I was able to speak with thirteen inmates in CB 4 at the front of their cells. Their descriptions of the conditions of confinement in that unit were not substantially different than they were when I inspected the unit a year ago. Four of the inmates complained about and showed me that their toilets were broken and/or leaking. Others complained of inadequate cleaning supplies and dirty showers. This is similar to the accounts I heard from inmates in 2013, which suggests a lack of attention to the most basic needs of the inmates housed in these units. None of the inmates I spoke with could tell me if they participated in any groups. Two of the inmates told me they had just gotten jobs. Several others wanted one. In my inspection of CB 4 I found no evidence of an established, functioning mental health program or indeed any program for any inmates – and certainly nothing that would be remotely adequate for fragile prisoners designated as SMI (seriously mentally ill). This lack of programming was confirmed in the 11 Under DI 326 the only option for women at SMA is evaluation by mental health staff within 72 hours or transfer to the inpatient unit at Flamenco Unit, the George Ward. ADC261963-64. In practice this means that women with serious mental illness, like named plaintiff Christina Verduzco, who I interviewed during both my inspections, linger in the isolation units without adequate treatment, until they decompensate to such a level that they are temporarily transferred to Flamenco to be "stabilized" and returned to isolation – where they start to decompensate again. 12 DI 326, 4.1.1.3 (ADC261963). testimony of Carson McWilliams, the Interim Division Director of Prison Operations, who conceded in July 2014 that the program in CB 4 was not yet operational.

28. During my inspection of CB 4 I did find some inmates who talked about improved opportunities for exercise in the new recreation areas. These improvements were very recent. The best estimate of when this accessbegan to be provided was about July 1, 2014. Some inmates, however, had still not participated in the new recreation program. The fact that even rudimentary changes in the availability of exercise have yet to be accomplished for prisoners in CB 4 even though the physical enclosures and exercise field have been built illustrates that ADC's claims about changes to programming and conditions of confinement in the isolation units are not supported – especially in a unit they claim is specifically designated for the seriously mentally ill.

29. DI 326 describes CB 1 as a placement for mentally ill inmates housing, "…male general population inmates who require a less controlled housing environment, while still receiving enhanced programming and socialization skill building." CB 2 is not specifically mentioned in DI

326 but my understanding is that it is the least restrictive placement for male non-mentally ill inmates. One would expect to find more programming in these units. When asked in his deposition about the level of programming in CB 1 and CB 2, Mr. McWilliams expands his answer to include CB 1 through CB 4, "If you're talking about your core area of the CB 1 through 4, probably more than 50 percent of the inmates."15

13 McWilliams Dep., 7/1/14, 85:19-86:6. 14 DI 326., 4.1.1.2 15 McWilliams Dep., 7/1/14, 80:16-81:4.

30. As I indicated above, I inspected CB 4 and interviewed inmates there. Programming for mentally ill inmates in that unit is nowhere near 50%. I also inspected CB 1 and CB 2 and interviewed a total of fourteen inmates in those two units. Mr. McWilliams' estimate of the percentage of prisoners who are programming may be more accurate for those two units. But the availability of programming for only 50% of the population in units that are supposed to be the most program-rich in the system – and which I was repeatedly told have been in operation for years – is still entirely inadequate. Of the inmates I interviewed, only half had jobs, some who worked as much as six hours a day. In my opinion someone who can perform on the job for up to six hours a day should be in a general population unit in a lower custody status. But this also indicates that many prisoners do not have jobs, and since just half of the inmates (under ADC's own estimate) even have access to programming (and this is generally just one hour a week), this means that there is still a great deal of isolation and idleness in these units. For example, in my cell front interview I also encountered inmates in CB 1 and 2 who were not in groups but wanted them; inmates who would be releasing directly to the street in the very near future who did not have jobs; and inmates who spoke of the lack of respect they receive from the officers and the poisonous environment this creates, especially for the mentally ill.

31. A few of the inmates in these two units talked about their concerns with the food. Current ADC policy and practice reduces the caloric intake for inmates in isolation. I have previously stated my opinion that ADC's policy of only providing two meals a day and lowering caloric intake is ill Fizer Dep. 145:8-25. advised, increases isolation, and contributes to the unnecessarily harsh conditions in the isolation units. During my most recent inspections I again heard repeated complaints about the amount and quality of the food and the need for inmates to supplement food with commissary purchases in order to stave off hunger – if they are lucky enough to have funds in their account. In CB 1 and 2, I also heard from the prisoners with new jobs, who asked me, since more of them had jobs now, would the caloric content of their meals be increased? I told them I could not answer that question but I thought it was a good one.17 If ADC is actually serious about providing increased job opportunities, increased exercise opportunities, and increased out-of-cell programming, it is difficult to understand why they have taken no action to alter food policies that deny prisoners adequate nutrition.

32. CB 5 is designated for the Restricted Status Housing Program (RSHP). Along with CB 7, it is one of the most severely isolating units I have seen in the ADC. There is a solid steel door with a small window to the hallway that is very difficult to converse through. The window to the outside offers a view only of the concrete backside of the window in the next cell. DI 326 describes the RSHP as the unit housing inmates who have committed one of the "Forbidden Three Acts (serious assaults on staff, serious inmate on

inmate assaults with a weapon and multiple inmates assaulting an inmate with serious injury)." One of the things ADC staff took back from their visits to Washington state's Intensive Management Units was the concept of the "Forbidden Three." They took the concept and applied it completely different way than it is used in Washington. In Arizona they created a new isolation unit with more restrictive conditions of confinement for certain prisoners than they ever had before. In Washington it is used as a tool to manage STG issues in the close custody general population without placing prisoners in solitary confinement. As in my first inspection, inmates continue to be universally extremely critical of the "Mega-sack" lunch and the fact that it was supposed to suffice for two meals a day. DI 326, 5.2

33. I interviewed seven inmates in CB 5 who were in the RSHP program. A couple of the inmates were more positive, citing the opportunity to attend groups. In contrast to most of the other units I inspected, a higher percentage of prisoners appeared to be receiving access to some programs in this unit. And given the stark conditions in this unit and the lack of a

coherent way out of isolation that has existed historically in the ADC, it is not surprising that the population here would express satisfaction with any access to a program or out-of-cell time. But most inmates at RSHP also told similar stories to inmates in other ADC isolation units. They reported that recreation was sometimes canceled and that the officers ignore them. Concerns with the operation of the program also emerged. For example, one person had lost his step level for simply kicking his cell door. There is a great deal of uncertainty in the prisoner population about what happens to an individual if they can successfully complete the RSHP. In my opinion it is unclear whether this program will lead to improved behavior and a successful return to lower custody for prisoners, or just an increased level of isolation in the ADC system that traps prisoners in a spiral of behavioral dysfunction partially caused or amplified by conditions which subject individuals to the debilitating effects of extreme social isolation.

34. Inmates in CB 7 were confined in an identical cellblock to CB 5 but much less in the way of programming than inmates in the RSHP. Only one

of the inmates I spoke with participated in a group. No one had a job. Others complained of vermin in the units and problems with responsiveness of their assigned counselor. The levels of extreme social isolation and idleness I noted in Florence Central during my first inspection were unchanged here.

35. DI 326 says that, "Kasson Wing One Program houses male inmates requiring significant mental health interventions." Of the twelve inmates I interviewed at the cell front at Kasson, only one said he participated in groups twice a week. All the rest said they either had access to a group once a week or not at all. About half that I interviewed said they did not have one-on-one contact with mental health professionals. The rest said they had such access once a month or greater. Two inmates in the unit told me they had a job. One inmate in this unit told me that conditions are getting worse, citing staff behavior. Another told me of the bad relationships he had with staff. A third told me that custody officers and treatment staff are not working together. Two inmates told me they expected to be released directly to the streets from isolation within the next couple of months. In my experience such comments reflect an attitude on the part of staff that is not conducive to helping inmates get better and improve their behavior, or to learn the necessary skills to keep them from returning to prison.

36. With the exception of the two inmates who had jobs, the conditions of confinement for this group of the mentally ill "requiring significant mental DI 326, 4.1.1 health interventions" means that except for recreation and showers, most are only out of their cells for one additional hour each week. That's a far cry from what Mr. McWilliams says in his deposition when he describes Kasson as, "very treatment oriented." 37. By way of comparison to another jurisdiction, similarly situated mentally ill inmates in the California Department of Corrections and Rehabilitation (CDCR) are required to have weekly contact with an assigned primary clinician, either individually or in a group, individual clinical contact at least every other week, and ten hours per week of scheduled structured therapeutic activities (not including regular exercise opportunities). The program at Kasson falls far, far short of this, including for some inmates who get no groups at all.

38. DI 326 says, "ASPC-Eyman, Browning Unit has the least amount of out of-cell activities."23 DI 326 goes on to say, "Male sex offenders requiring

any level of control can be housed in SMU I." 24 This includes sex offenders who suffer from mental illness. I had the opportunity to speak at the cell front to 8 of these inmates.

39. Only one of these inmates reported that he goes to a mental health group once a month although others wanted to go. One-to-one access to mental health professionals was reported as very limited—either at the cell front or to a single meeting with a doctor for a medication review. Inmates complained about unresponsive and abusive treatment by some custody staff.

40. In the BMU, another unit housing the mentally ill at Eyman, including inmates who repeatedly engage in self-harm, I spoke with five inmates. These inmates reported the ability to attend a group once a week or once a month. One-on-ones, if they occurred, took place at the front of the cell and not in a confidential setting. This group seemed particularly disturbed with self-reports of suffering from schizophrenia, depression, and hearing voices. They all appeared to be heavily medicated.

41. Records of available mental health resources for mentally ill inmates in all of Eyman-SMU 1 illustrate there were a total of three hundred and twentytwo mentally ill inmates. The corresponding program schedule shows ten different mental health groups running each week. Two of those groups are scheduled to last for three hours and eight of them are scheduled for an hour and a half. Assuming each of those programs was filled and fully functional and assuming a group size of eight, that would involve a total of sixty eight inmates in one group each week, leaving the remaining two hundred and fifty four without any opportunity for group treatment.

42. In his testimony for ADC, Division Director McWilliams affirmed his previous statement that SMU I ran only seven inmate programs, including

a mental health group, starting in January 2014. As a result of this programming, Director McWilliams admits that just 192 SMU I inmatesare offered one hour of out-of-cell programming a week. This represents just 20% of the SMU I population according to Director McWilliams. ADC_P000868-Eyman SMU 1 Mental Health Inmate List ADC_P000867 Eyman Mental Health Program Schedule During my inspection of Eyman SMU I, I saw the two classrooms set up

for inmate programming. In each of these areas there were about 8 restraint chairs used for the group programming, although surprisingly the ongoing classes we saw usually were not fully subscribed. 28 McWilliams Dep., 7/1/14, 103:1-19.

Director McWilliams also affirmed his previous declaration that about 110 inmates may participate in mental health groups at any one time – but that is a "best case scenario" and according to him, as of June 30, 2014 there were about 480 mental health inmates at SMU I.29

43. Division Director of Prison Operations, Carson McWilliams, in his deposition also acknowledges that the program at Eyman (and Browning) is in its infancy. Speaking of the changes taking place, McWilliams states, "But in SMU 1 and Browning, it didn't really get as widespread as it is now until about I'd say over the last six months." I am hard pressed to consider the program as "widespread" when so many inmates are still not allowed to even participate due to a lack of resources. And even under ADC's "best case scenario" programming is wholly inadequate for all SMU I prisoners, and especially the mentally ill.

44. This lack of a developed program adequate to meet the size of the population in all of these units undermines the stated purpose for the implementation of DI 326. Even under Director McWilliams' "best case scenario" in these units, there is insufficient programming and out-of-cell time, and given my findings during inspections in August, 2014, I found it doubtful that the programming numbers recited by Director McWilliams in both his declaration and at deposition were actually accurate. If there is very limited, little, or no opportunity to participate in programs or jobs in the unit where an inmate is assigned, there is little opportunity for the inmate to progress out of isolation. The minor, sporadic changes to the operation of these units are not alleviating the conditions that put inmates at risk of harm, even though some did say the increased opportunity to actually go outside for exercise made things better. If the alleged programs at Florence-CB 4 and at Eyman-SMU 1 for inmates with mental illness have barely begun, at Kasson, where ADC has concentrated prisoners with severe mental health problems for some time and alleged the presence of an actual treatment program, it is clear that the resources in no way match the level of need. It is also clear that the scanty programming ADC alleges it is implementing is wholly inadequate for the mentally ill populations in all these units.

45. When questioned about resources Mr. McWilliams explains in his deposition that the ADC has not hired any new staff nor have they modified their contract with Corizon in order to actually implement DI 326.31 However well-intentioned he or anyone else is within the ADC, without additional resources the lack of

treatment and profound levels of idleness and social isolation I described in previous reports and found during my most recent inspection cannot be alleviated.

46. The problem of insufficient resources figures into the implementation of DI 326 for other populations as well. As I have previously said, the ADC makes the mistake of placing Security Threat Group (STG) members in isolation simply because they meet the ADC definition of "validated." Other jurisdictions, including Washington, Mississippi, and New York, do not follow this mistaken policy. Rather, inmates are placed in segregation because of their actual behavior and not because they are simply members of an STG.

47. According to testimony in Mr. Ryan's deposition, there are two ways for validated STG members to try and get out of isolation. One is to

McWilliams Dep., 14:22-16:11. 20 "renounce" their STG membership and tell staff what they know about the operation of the gang. For some, this ill-advised policy can be perceived as a death sentence and few are likely to pursue this lengthy avenue to get out of isolation only to spend the rest of their prison sentence in protective custody or worse. The other avenue is to participate in in the STG stepdown program.

48. The STG inmates at I spoke with at Eyman-Browning were simply not interested in the renunciation avenue. They were, however, very interested in participating in the STG step-down program. During our inspection of Browning we were told there were approximately 350 STG inmates held in isolation at that facility. According to Mr. McWilliams deposition, there is currently only room for ten inmates to participate in this program at any given time—a program that takes six months to complete. Mr. McWilliams then acknowledges a desire to expand the program so that 20 inmates can participate, a promise he also made to inmates who questioned him about this problem during our tour. It is not clear how the ADC will be able to expand the program to twenty participants given their lack of additional resources but it would be an initial positive step if they do. They should expand beyond twenty so that they provide an opportunity for this group of inmates to get out of isolation that matches the number of inmates motivated to attempt to do so. I do not know if they even have that information. Since the program lasts six months, if would take five years to process one hundred inmates through the program. That's better than the ten years it will take at the current level of resource devoted to this program but it is still woefully inadequate.

Ryan Dep., 130:10-130:13; 171:17-175:4. 33 McWilliams Dep., 129:12-129:18. 21

49. For too many inmates in Florence and Eyman, the opportunity for exercise was still their only opportunity to leave their cell; and this opportunity is still only three days a week for 2 hours at a time. The other four days too many inmates are simply left in their cells. During this inspection I once again heard repeated accounts from prisoners of frequent cancellation of exercise. Inmates in some units reported that exercise is cancelled about once a week, while those in other units estimated that exercise is cancelled about once every other week. This means that unless the prisoner is one of the few who have some other program, they are left in their cell for five days a week.

50. Defendants produced Detention Logs for only three of the named plaintiffs since my last report. The time frames of those logs are different for each prisoner, with dates from July 2011 through March of 2014. A review of those logs for eleven weeks from December 30, 2013 through March 30, 2014 shows that one prisoner never once received or was offered the opportunity for out of cell exercise consistent with ADC policy. For another prisoner, from the logs made available for the same time period, only once out of seven weeks did she receive or was offered the opportunity for out of cell exercise. (No records for 2014 were offered for the third prisoner.) These records evidence no change from the past practices I documented in my previous reports.

51. I also inspected Perryville-Special Management Area (SMA) where women inmates are housed in isolation. This is the smallest isolation unit in ADC. At the time of my inspection we were told that the population ADC262182-262203 Gamez-Indiv IM Detention Logs-2013-12-30 to 2014-03-30 35 ADC262216-262283 Verduzco-Indiv IM Detention Logs-2013-08-12 to 2014-03-30 22 count at SMA included about 75 inmates that day. In comparison to last year's inspection there were some improvements. First, in the unit for suicide watch most exposed to the hot Arizona sun, they had installed a screen outside the cellblock to cut down the direct

sunlight into the cell doors. Also the new program classrooms look to be appropriately sized to the inmate population. The increased access to group outdoor recreation for some inmates was seen as an improvement. The program space at the SMA appears to be of adequate size for the ADC to provide services for the population that they hold in isolation at that prison.

52. But interviews with the inmates show that many problems remain. Like at every prison complex we visited, the ADC administration had a program planned to show us their changes. Upon our arrival at the SMA it began with a visit to a classroom where we joined inmates being assembled for a group session. I later got a chance to speak to one of the women participating in this program at the cell front where staff could not overhear our conversation. She told me that this group usually met on Fridays but they were called out to meet today because of our tour. She also told me this is the first time this group had met in three weeks.

53. Her account was consistent with what I heard from other women at the SMA. I previously indicated I interviewed twenty-five inmates at this facility. However, five of them were on suicide watch and I only asked them about their present situation and not about their ongoing activities in the facility. Of the twenty remaining, seven of them told me they either did not participate in groups or had no one-on-ones with clinical staff. Those who indicated that they did have one-on-one contact with mental health providers told me that these were scheduled monthly. Of all my 23 interviewees, only one prisoner told me she went to group weekly and only one said she went twice a week. Only two women told me they had jobs.

54. An exhibit from Mr. McWilliams deposition contains more detailed

evidence. The actual program attendance rosters for groups offered at the SMA for March 13, 2014 through May 9, 2014 were produced. Backing out the number of inmates on those rosters not allowed to attend the group session because they were stage 1 of the program, the average number of hours available for out-of-cell group programming for these eight weeks was sixteen. The population held in isolation at the SMA when I last inspected the facility was seventy-five. Clearly sixteen hours for seventy five inmates is not sufficient to allow inmates to work their way out of isolation as promised by DI 326 and it is in no way adequate to alleviate the extreme social isolation on this unit for the vast majority of women housed there.

55. Inmates at the facility highlighted multiple concerns with the operation of the isolation units at SMA but two of them were frequent enough to require inclusion in this report.

56. The first has to do with the newly installed windows in the cell doors. The installation of the new windows is described by ADC as, "Innovative

physical and environmental changes to enhance observation and mental health treatment" and, to increase "communication between staff and inmates" and "inmate socialization." I would add that the new windows in the cells at SMA also increase natural light into the cells. But the unintended consequence is the report from inmates that they are receiving institutional rule violations for indecent exposure, disciplinary tickets that they were not receiving prior to the installation of those windows.

57. In my first report I documented my concerns about so many male officers supervising women prisoners at the SMA, especially those on suicide

watch. That problem has been compounded with the installation of the new windows causing me to reiterate those concerns. The ADC does not allow an inmate in isolation to temporarily hang a towel or piece of cloth over the door while they are using the bathroom. In my experience this is not uncommon for a very short period of time in some isolation units in other jurisdictions. In a facility for women with so many male officers it should be allowed. Instead, according to the reports from the inmates, they are now receiving discipline charges for indecent exposure when they are using the toilet or attempting a "bird bath" in their sink. This simple violation of basic human dignity should be addressed and corrected at the Perryville facility.

58. The other issue raised by inmates in the SMA (and in the male facilities as well) is their concern that they can lose their step level in the program for behavior that does not seem significant. Inmates at Perryville told me of step levels being lost because of standing in the wrong place, for painting on eye brows, for tying shoes

strings together, for turning their head while waiting in line, and for talking in the chow hall line. According to DI 326, progressing through these stage levels is the only way for inmates to work their way out of isolation. It is critical that any decision to drop an inmate back a level to a more extreme level of isolation be based on significant reasons and not the whims of the officers. Otherwise, the system loses all credibility and any efficacy it might have. For inmates with mental illness, complete and immediate compliance with all the rules they are expected to follow in a prison can be very difficult. For precisely that reason step programs do not always work with the mentally ill. Those administering those programs must take a prisoner's mental illness into account when making decisions regarding step levels, especially when one insignificant violation can send the prisoner back to the beginning to start all over again. However, DI 326 itself makes no allowance for the mentally ill within the step program in this manner and based on the reports of inmates in the isolation units it is clear that losing a step level can occur for behaviors that are not significant. At the same time these same behaviors for the mentally ill can be very difficult to control so that they are being severely punished due to their disease.

59. To emphasize this last point and related to the issue of the turning of a head and talking in line, during our inspection we witnessed step 2 and 3 inmates who are allowed to eat two meals a day in the chow hall standing in line outside in a formation resembling military attention in the midday Arizona sun while waiting for lunch. It seemed particularly odd to require inmates, especially mentally ill inmates, to be expected to behave in this manner. In my experience many mentally ill inmate simply don't have that capacity. As a tour group we all stood and watched this curious formation. If it was part of ADC's effort to illustrate progress in their program for inmates in isolation it produced a mixed reaction for this expert. While I was pleased to see some prisoners able to come out of their cell to eat two meals a day in a group setting, the point of being required to stand in a military formation where misbehavior might result in loss of a step level and a return to more extreme levels of isolation seems particularly counterproductive.

60. ADC's efforts to illustrate changes for those of us inspecting their prisons for men produced similar mixed results. At Florence we were taken to the big yard where several inmates from CB 3 were taking advantage of the opportunity for unrestrained movement. I had the opportunity to inspect this same area a year ago when inmates from CB 1 were present. The difference in the inmates this year was striking. Last year the prisoners were open and willing to converse. This year the inmates avoided eye contact and when approached, often refused to speak with us. This may have been the result of the size of the entourage and the number of ADC officials present. In my experience the lack of eye contact and unwillingness to engage in conversation reflects very poor relations between staff and inmates.

61. We were then shown a reasonably stocked prison library that is apparently a feeder library for several prisons. We were told that inmates on step 3 are allowed direct access to the library ten at a time. When we asked how often that opportunity is provided to access the library we were told that frequency has yet to be determined since they were still moving inmates into CB 4, another indicator of how new—and potentially temporary—these programs are within the ADC.

62. Then, still at Florence, we were shown other elements of their new program. We were led into groups that were in session. During the first group we encountered, questioning revealed it was the first session of this group ever--another indications that these programs are in their inception and potentially staged for the inspection.

63. We interrupted another group, this one for inmates in CB 2, and Director McWilliams addressed the inmates. What quickly ensued were some very good questions from the inmates in the classroom. Inmates wanted to know what impact attendance in the programs had on their classification and if it would change their points in that system. It is troubling that the answer to such a fundamental question was not common knowledge among the inmate population—which underscores the limited extent and recent/nascent implementation of the programs. But Director McWilliams did not answer that question directly (it is my understanding that group attendance does not impact classification points). Instead he told the group that he is considering overriding inmates in CB 1 through 4 to close custody so he can provide them with education programs. Apparently state law prohibits maximum custody inmates from participating in educational programs

unless they require special education. In my opinion such a move clearly supports my position that the ADC holds prisoners in isolation that don't need to be there. How such a move would impact the conditions of confinement beyond being able to attend education classes is not known, as Director McWilliams did not address it, and it was clear from his remarks to the inmates and subsequent remarks to the expert group that this idea is just that – an idea.

64. There were similar experiences at Eyman. In the Browning unit we were ushered into a classroom where a group of prisoners in restraints were participating in a class. Later during my inspection I had the chance to speak directly to two of the inmates who had been in the classroom that we had interrupted. I discovered that one of the two spoke no English even though the class was being conducted only in English. It had been previously asked during the tour if any of the program material had been translated to Spanish since the ADC has so many Hispanic inmates and the answer was "no." I am sure the non-English speaking person appreciated the hour out of his cell to attend the group but I am equally sure he wasn't picking up much from attending the class.

65. In that same classroom Director McWilliams spoke extensively of ADC's efforts to reform their system. He was asked about data. He indicated that they are collecting data but said that as of yet they do not have enough data to draw any conclusions. This is additional proof of how new and sporadic these programs are and how unknown the outcomes might be. I asked whether or not they intended to track inmates who returned to isolation after completing their programs and it was apparent this was not something they had previously contemplated. My impression is that Director McWilliams may have accepted this data point as a good measurement of their program's success and I hope and recommend that they pay attention to this critical data element. Unless they do there will be really no way to tell if their programs are successful.

66. When I was working in the WDOC, we launched two programs aimed at getting inmates off of Intensive Management Status (IMS)—the equivalent of Arizona's isolation population—one at the Washington State Penitentiary in Walla Walla and one at the Clallam Bay Corrections Center. Researchers from the University of Washington (UW) tracked outcomes of both programs. We lost the program at Walla Walla (it has since been reconstituted) as well as our twenty-year contract for collaborative relationship with the UW due to lack of funding caused the global economic collapse of 2008.

67. The outcomes for the program were impressive. The evaluation of the program at Walla Walla was open and candid. It concluded that inmates who went through the program were four times more likely to not return to isolation than those in a control group.

68. The program at Clallam Bay is still in existence to this day. As our contract with the UW was ending, the lead researcher authored a memo that indicated inmates who completed the program were six times more likely not to return to isolation than those in a control group. The last time I spoke to the manager of this program at Clallam Bay he told me that 80% of program graduates were not returning to segregation.

69. Conditions of confinement in the ADC are still very stark and isolating, partly because of physical plant design and the age and deterioration of some facilities, and partly because of the way those units are operated. Prisoners, especially those with mental illness continue to be placed at substantial risk and too many actually experience harm. What actual treatment for the mentally ill exists (as opposed to their limited access to cognitive programs that may or may not be of any help to the seriously mentally ill) is sporadic and not of sufficient "dosage" to provide for real treatment. While the ADC program described in DI 326 has some The fact that so many of the completed suicides in ADC continue to be in the isolation units points not only to the substantial risk created by the conditions there, especially for the mentally ill, but also to ADC's continuing inability to alleviate those risks. For example, between September 27, 2013 and April 1, 2014 all of ADC's completed suicides took place in the isolation units. (ADC364245; ADC423967; ADC424945). It is also now clear looking at new death records produced by the Defendants that eight of the ten suicides which occurred in the ADC during the time Corizon has been responsible for healthcare (March 2013 to April 1, 2014) occurred in the isolation units of SMU I, Browning Unit, and Florence Central. This is incredibly disproportionate to the ADC population held in the isolation units, but ample evidence of the terrible risks created by the conditions of

confinement there. encouraging elements for some of ADC's prisoners in isolation, even if fully implemented it in no way provides the type of clinical care and setting that would be appropriate for seriously mentally ill inmates. At the same time, as I have demonstrated with examples throughout this report, the step program is very new, only roughly conceived, barely implemented, and incapable of reaching more than a small minority of inmates at current capacity levels, especially given the overuse of isolation within the ADC. No one has any idea what the outcomes of the program will be for another year or two. It is premature to say they are even on the right track. It is a program more on paper than in practice and it is even insufficient as written because it does not focus on alleviation of social isolation and the risk of harm to prisoners created by the conditions of confinement in ADC's isolation units. There have been some small improvements in some of the units for some of the inmates, but in my opinion the program is not fully thought-out, funded, and by the continued admission of the Defendants, especially Director McWilliams, it is clearly "a work in progress"

VII. THE ADC USES FORCE PREMATURELY AND UNNECESSARILY AGAINST MENTALLY ILL INMATES CREATING A PATTERN OF UNNNECESSARY PAIN, HUMILITATION, AND SUFFERING

70. There is nothing more revealing about the skill level and training of correctional staff than how they respond to the difficult challenge of potential UOF situations, especially with mentally ill inmates. I have been able to view thirty-three videos of UOF incidents and the written reports McWilliams Dep. 98:11.31 for thirty-two of them. My analysis of some of the critical elements of those videos is attached to this report as **Exhibit 3**.

71. My analysis reveals that the ADC has no system in place to use a mental health intervention to attempt to de-escalate a potential use of force situation. Of the thirty-three videos produced by ADC, it is my opinion that a mental health intervention should have taken place in at least twenty-five of them. Instead, the ADC initiates use of force against mentally ill prisoners in the absence of any imminent threat when an attempt at de-escalation may well have allowed them to avoid using force at all.

72. In any use of force situation corrections staff must make an assessment of the level of threat presented. They must ask themselves if there is an imminent threat that requires force to be used immediately. "Time" and "circumstance" are often on the side of corrections staff and must be considered, especially when the prisoner is locked in a cell.

73. The most common reason for initiating a UOF from these videos is because the inmate is refusing to cooperate with a direction to submit to restraints and/or submit to a strip search and come out of his/her cell. Most frequently the need for removing the inmate from the cell is to complete a routine cell search. Other reasons include: the inmate has a doctor's appointment; the inmate is being assigned to another cell; or the inmate is being moved to another institution. There is simply no imminent threat involved in such situations and no reason to resort to force without first attempting other methods to de-escalate the situation. To use chemical agents, such as pepper spray on the mentally ill in those situations is not only fundamentally wrong, in my experience it is likely to have a negative impact on the inmate's perception of staff, a critical ingredient in running a safe and secure institution and in getting the inmate to trust the staff enough to participate in treatment for their mental illness. Below I detail some of my findings from the documents and videos that are summarized in Exhibit 3.

74. At Lumley a mentally ill prisoner was naked in her cell. The written report says that she was, "refusing to be placed in belly chains/uncover face and hands while on continuous mental health watch." She is sprayed twice. Prior to the spray being used the camera documenting the event failed to give a view into the cell. After she is sprayed twice, less than four minutes into the video, the camera shows the inmate lying on the floor, moving and partially covered by her suicide smock. About eight minutes into the video she says she needs more air and her hands and face are exposed. Ten minutes into the video she gets to her feet but then falls in the cell. The officers report that she did not hit her head. A voice over the radio can be heard saying, "Inmate has decided to start flopping around and fall on the ground," indicating that the speaker believes the inmate's behavior is simply willful. The officers who can see into the cell then say she is again covering up. About four minutes later she is sprayed a third time. A couple of minutes later a cell extraction team consisting of five officers enters the cell. The inmate offers no resistance while the officers place her in restraints. The officers are

clearly being affected by the amount of spray that had previously been administered into the cell, as they are not equipped with proper respirators. The inmate is placed on a gurney and restrained, face down. She is taken about thirty feet to a medical exam room where she is given a shot. Medical staff then take off of her stomach and place her on her side. Twenty-seven minutes into the video medical staff decides it is necessary to call 911 and they place a collar around her neck. Twenty-six minutes after being sprayed, medical staff begin to decontaminate her eyes of the effects of the pepper spray.

75. There are three videos with this same SIR number, labeled 1 of 3, 2 of 3 and 3 of 3. In the above paragraph I described the events in video 1 of 3. Video 2 of 3 is a direction continuation of video 1 of 3 as medical staff continues to treat the inmate until an outside ambulance arrives and she is taken to a hospital. On this second video you can hear the nurse tell the EMT/ambulance staff that the inmate was psychotic before she hit her head, that she has no idea where she is, and that she did indeed hit her head.

76. But video 3 of 3 is a bit of a mystery. The events in the video are not referenced in the related Serious Incident Report. Videos one and two occurred around 9 o'clock in the morning. In video 3 of 3 the same officers are on duty, the inmate is in the same cell but it is dark outside.

My best guess is that the events in this video occurred early that same day in December of 2013. Whatever the actual time of the events, in this video the same inmate is shown to be naked in her cell, ordered to submit to restraints for a "cell integrity" check. She is talking to herself or perhaps responding to voices or hallucinations. Less than a minute into the video she is sprayed. Two minutes into the video she falls onto the floor. The officers say she did not hit her head. A couple of minutes later she submits to restraints and is removed from the cell and taken to the shower for decontamination. She is then placed back into her cell. There is no evidence that her cell was decontaminated or that she was seen by medical after being sprayed. In the last view we have of the inmate she continues to talk to people who are not there while making sweeping gestures with her hands.

77. This woman is clearly in distress and suffering from serious mental illness. There is no evidence in any of the videos of an actual imminent risk of self-harm or a threat to others. In video 3 of 3 it is demanded that she immediately submit to restraints so that officers can conduct a "cell integrity" check. In video 1 of 3, at first the issue is that the officers cannot see her face and hands. Then it becomes necessary to get her out of her cell because she has been sprayed and may be injured. During this video she is so out of touch with reality and unable to respond to the shouted demands of the officers that officers eventually give up on spraying and go into the cell to remove her.

78. In his declaration, Director McWilliams discusses the issue of inmates who will not uncover their face or hands. ADC employs the use of a pressurized $H2O$ canister devise similar to a fire extinguisher to gain compliance from Mental Health inmates who will not respond to orders issued by correctional personnel to uncover the inmate's head or body so that the correctional personnel can complete a safety or welfare check to determine that the inmate is alive, breathing and not injured. The uncomfortable but non-lethal deployment of a strong stream of water most often simply annoys the inmate to the point that the inmate will uncover his or her body or head in order that a safety and welfare check can be completed. As above with the use of chemical agents, a supervisor must authorize the use of the $H2O$ canister device and the use of the canister is videotaped. Additionally, the use of the H2Ocanister must be documented in an Incident Report.

79. In all the UOF videos that I have watched, in all the Serious Incident Reports that I have read, in the written use of force policies of the ADC, this is the first and only time I have heard of this method being used. It would have been preferable to what the mentally ill and actively psychotic prisoner in the above paragraphs was subjected to. Even better might have been a loud bang on the door to make sure she was OK, followed up by a conversation with mental health staff. Instead she was sprayed multiple times, fell twice, and wound up having to be taken to an outside hospital for medical care that could not be provided at the facility. The ADC does not just subject mentally ill prisoners to the risk of harm—sometimes they cause it.

80. Four levels of authority within the Perryville chain of command reviewed this incident (the space for the Warden to sign was left blank).49 None of those reviews offered any criticism of the events that took place. In

my experience, this lack of supervisory oversight is clear and convincing evidence that the entire facility condones this kind of mistreatment of mentally ill prisoners and regularly approves of the unnecessary use of force.

81. In another incident, this one at Browning Unit, there is a very short video where a supervisor gives an introduction saying that they are preparing to use force on an inmate who is refusing to cuff up for a "blanket check", a procedure I take to be a type of cell search.50 The next video opens at the cell front of the mentally ill inmate. He is lying on his bunk covered with a suicide smock. After talking to the inmate for a minute and a half, he is sprayed. Officers, once again not equipped with proper respirators, show the effects of the spray. Less than four minutes later the inmate is sprayed a second time. About twelve minutes after that the video ends with the camera operator coughing and walking away from the cell with the camera pointed to the ground. The third video begins with the introduction of the cell extraction team. The inmate is still lying on his bunk. He is sprayed a third time. Four minutes into this third video five officers rush into the cell and pin the inmate to his bed with a shield. The officers cough uncontrollably from the impact of the spray. One of them has to leave the cell. Eventually three more must leave the cell. The inmate is then placed in restraints on a gurney as one of the remaining officers yells, "Where did everybody go?" The inmate is naked and wheeled out of the cell, strapped face down to the gurney, and taken outside. The officers continue to argue about who left the cell. The inmate refuses medical treatment. He asks for help because the restraints are hurting his hand. The officers take a few minutes before they adjust the cuffs. He is wheeled back inside and the officers run him into a door while strapped to the gurney. He is unstrapped from the gurney but is unable to stand up on his own so the officers assist him into the shower. The officers get him a chair but refuse to allow it to be placed into the shower so he can be decontaminated. He is physically supported by the officers and placed back into his cell. The written report says he refused decontamination. Based on the video evidence, that is not accurate. The inmate could not even stand up enough so the officers could remove his restraints. They ultimately had to lay him on his bunk so that the restraints could be removed. Had they been willing to take the simple step of placing the plastic chair into the shower the prisoner could have been de-contaminated – and the inmate's pain could have been alleviated.

82. Use of force against this mentally ill inmate was unnecessary here. There was nothing in the inmate's behavior throughout this incident to suggest he was any kind of threat to himself or to others. Rather, he is mentally ill with some clear physical challenges that are evident from watching him struggle to move in these videos. There was nothing in his behavior to justify the need for the use of force.

83. Again, after four levels of review of this incident within the Eyman chain of command, the Deputy Warden concludes with, "Force was reasonable and necessary." It is clear that the inability to recognize unnecessary use of force against individuals with mental illness exists at more than one institution in the ADC. Indeed, based on the evidence, I believe it is a systemic problem.

84. Director McWilliams states in his Declaration that, "Prior to scheduling a planned cell extraction in a mental health unit or for a known mental health inmate, the shift commander contacts mental health staff or a psychologist for special handling instructions, if any, unless the situation dictates otherwise." I can see nothing in these videos or in the related documentation in the SIRs56 that suggest "the situation dictates otherwise." In all of these situations, officers should have contacted mental health staff prior to using force – but none of them did. If they had made such a consultation, perhaps the situation could have been avoided altogether.

Better yet, if mental health staff, especially a mental health staff that had worked with and developed a relationship with the inmate and understood his/her mental health issues had been deployed to the scene, it is entirely possible that this use of force could have been avoided altogether.

85. In another incident an inmate on suicide watch at Kasson refused to submit to restraints for a medical appointment. He was speaking with the officer and was asking questions, trying to understand his situation. The officer was completely insensitive to the inmate's questions and continued to speak from his script, speaking over the inmate and directing him to submit to restraints or he would be sprayed. While still speaking to the officer the inmate was abruptly sprayed. Throughout the incident the inmate was polite and respectful. It is

impossible to tell from the written report or the video why the decision to resort to use of force without trying other alternatives was used. There was nothing about the prisoner's behavior that suggested an imminent threat. This use of force was unnecessary.

86. Once again, the review process through the chain of command—this time at Eyman—deemed the use of force "reasonable and unnecessary" the third facility demonstrating an utter lack of understanding of effective techniques to manage an inmate in distress—this time a prisoner on suicide watch, presumably for his own protection.

87. Again Mr. McWilliams Declaration statements fall far short of the operational reality of the ADC when he says, "In all applications involving the use of force, patience is emphasized and consideration must be given to alternative solutions, such as waiting the inmate out, before initiating or escalating the use of force." In this last example and in too many others, nothing could be further from the truth.

88. There is a pattern and a practice of the unnecessary use of pepper spray against the mentally ill on psychotropic medications within each of the ADC facilities that I inspected. I offer only one example from each facility in this report. As I illustrate in **Exhibit 3**, it is my opinion that in twentyfive of the incidents where I have been provided the SIR's and the video evidence, force was used prematurely and without proper consultation, and more importantly, intervention by a mental health professional.

89. The ADC policy on use of force says:

In Mental Health care facilities, correctional staff shall notify and/or request intervention by Mental Health staff if the inmate or staff are not in imminent danger. When Mental Health staff are not available, the shift commander shall contact the assigned mental health staff.

The purpose of notification of mental health staff is not clear in the policy, nor is their definition of "Mental Health care facilities." If such notifications do occur, one has to ask the question about the purpose of such a notification. It appears to have no impact on the ultimate use of force in ADC. Mental health interventions are another matter. It is clear they are not occurring. If they were, many if not most of the use of force incidents against the mentally ill could be avoided.

90. The California Department of Corrections and Rehabilitation (CDCR) recently revised their use of force policy, establishing in great detail the requirements to avoid using force whenever possible against mentally ill inmates. The CDCR defines an imminent threat as:

An imminent threat is any situation or circumstance that jeopardizes the safety of persons or compromise the security of the institution, requiring immediate action to stop the threat. Some examples include, but are not limited to: an attempt to escape, on-going physical harm or active physical resistance.

This definition establishes the threshold for allowing the immediate use of force. If this threshold is not met, then controlled ("planned" in Arizona parlance) use of force is the required avenue. In my opinion, for each of the UOF events in Exhibit 3 that I have labeled as "premature," this threshold was not met and each of those events within the ADC should have been planned, creating the potential that force would not have to have been used at all.

91. The CDCR policy goes on to extensively describe the requirements for controlled use of force. Some elements of that policy that are critical include:

 All controlled uses of force shall be preceded by a cool down period to allow the inmate an opportunity to comply with custody staff orders. The cool down period shall include clinical intervention (attempts to verbally counsel and persuade the inmate to voluntarily exit the area) by a licensed mental health practitioner and may include similar attempts by custody staff...

 If it is determined the inmate does not have the ability to understand orders, chemical agents shall not be used without authorization from the Warden...

🅐 If it is determined an inmate has the ability to understand orders but has difficulty complying due to mental health issues, or when a licensed mental health practitioner believes the inmate's mental health issues are such that the controlled

use of force could lead to a substantial risk of decompensation, a licensed mental health practitioner shall propose reasonable strategies to employ in an effort to gain compliance.

🅐 The cool down period may also include use of other available resources/options such as dialogue via religious leaders, correctional counselors, correctional officers and other custody and non-custody staff that have established rapport with the inmate.

🅐 A decision to use chemical agents for the extraction should be based on more than passive resistance to placement in restraints or refusal to follow orders. If the inmate has not responded to staff for an extended period of time, and it appears that the inmate does not present an imminent physical threat, additional consideration and evaluation should occur before the use of chemical agents is authorized.

92. It is clear from these excerpts from the CDCR policy that they are doing all they can to avoid the unnecessary use of force against the mentally ill.

This policy was developed as a result of federal litigation. The ADC policy that makes reference to "notification" of mental health staff and interventions that in practice are not occurring does not even begin to provide adequate protection for the mentally ill in comparison. At the same time, the actual practices of staff in these use of force incidents makes clear that they have not been adequately trained either on use of force or on treatment of mentally ill prisoners. As a result, the toxic environment created by ADC's policy and practice of using force on individuals with mental illness and on psychotropic medications in the isolation units creates a substantial risk of harm for all prisoners in those units.

93. In addition to the problem of using force unnecessarily against thementally ill by the ADC, there are other problems with their use of force practices, problems that subject mentally ill prisoners to prolonged pain and discomfort, humiliation, and that are potentially dangerous.

94. One of ADC's most dangerous practices is the restraining of prisoners to a gurney face down, apparently following every use of force, including

exposure to pepper spray. As documented in **Exhibit 3**, this practice occurred every time during UOF events at the male facilities, with only two exceptions. Prisoners are left in this position for considerable periods of time, sometimes for a half hour or more, most often as they wait for medical evaluation and/or treatment following a use of force event. As I have previously reported, this practice is associated with positional asphyxia and is contrary to sound correctional practice. Put simply by the National Institute of Justice, "As soon as the suspect is handcuffed, get him off his stomach." ADC policy and practice fails to follow this basic directive.

95. In 2002, a disability rights organization from California published a study about the dangers of the prone restraint (face down) position and positional asphyxia. Their study "...concluded that the prone restraint position was a significant contributing factor in the demise of the individuals restrained." The study goes on to recommend,

🅐 Individuals must never be placed in the prone position when restrained;

🅐 Temporary prone containment should only be attempted when all other techniques are ineffective to prevent imminent serious harm and when there are sufficient safeguards in place to protect the individual from positional asphyxiation;

🅐 Restraint and containment must be viewed as the result of a treatment failure, not a treatment intervention; and

🅐 All first responders must be educated regarding the risks of positional asphyxiation with prone restraint. This is not the routine practice at Lumley, although it does occur at that facility See **Exhibit 3**. 64 Supplemental Report of Eldon Vail, February 24, 2014, paragraph 6 US Department of Justice, National Law Enforcement

Technology Center, Positional Asphyxia—Sudden Death, June 1995, page 2, available at https://www.ncjrs.gov/pdffiles/posasph.pdf. Disability Right California, The Lethal Hazard of Prone Restraint: Positional Asphyxiation, April 2002, Publication #7018.01, page 3

96. Acknowledging that there is other research that reaches different conclusions, I do not know of another jurisdiction that routinely allows and apparently expects officers to keep prisoners in the prone restraint position for long periods of time following a UOF event.

97. In addition to the practice being potentially dangerous, it is also humiliating to prisoners. Typically, after the use of pepper spray, unless the inmate is actively resisting, the use of the gurney is unnecessary.

Simply escorting the inmates in restraints to the shower for decontamination is the common practice. This reduces the risk to the prisoner of harm, as he or she does not have to be lifted from the gurney to a standing position. In more than one of the videos I viewed from ADC the struggle to lift prisoners either on to of off of the gurney is evident.

Allowing the prisoner to walk to the shower can be the beginning of a return to normalcy as it actually places the officer in a position to help the inmate through the process of decontamination.

98. In **Exhibit 3,** I also document the very short amount of time spent on proper decontamination procedures by ADC officers for inmates subjected to pepper spray. Very rarely did the decontamination last for more than a minute. Such short exposure to cold water following exposure to pepper spray is contrary to my own training and experience, as well asgeneral knowledge about proper decontamination procedures.

99. One of the main manufacturers of pepper spray products publishes a Material Safety Data Sheet (MSDS) which instructs, "Flush with cool water for at least 15 minutes, or until relieved." Based on the UOF documents and videos produced by ADC, I found that mentally ill prisoners in the ADC who have been subjected to pepper spray are instead most likely to receive decontamination relief from running water for a mere sixty seconds or less. In fourteen cases staff discontinued decontamination after only twenty seconds or less. In only four cases did staff actually permit the inmate to be decontaminated by water for more than ninety seconds. In no cases did I see the 15-minute decontamination suggested by manufacturers of pepper spray. The result of these professionally inadequate practices is pain and suffering by prisoners that is simply unnecessary and entirely avoidable.

100. Compounding the problem is the practice at the male facilities of taking the inmates to medical, restrained face down on the gurney, for an evaluation before decontamination procedures are implemented. I have never seen or heard of such a routine practice in other corrections departments. The result is that prisoners are left to suffer for no legitimate purpose. The typical practice would be to take a prisoner directly to the shower for decontamination as soon as the prisoner is in restraints, and thereafter take the prisoner to medical for evaluation once the decontamination is complete.

101. In ADC, the inmates are sometimes not even taken off the gurney and allowed to decontaminate in the shower. Instead they are wheeled into the shower on the gurney and the backs of their heads are showered.

This is not effective when the prisoner has been sprayed in the face or all over the body.

102. One of the most egregious examples of ADC's decontamination practices can be found on the video for a UOF event at Central.69 The prisoner was alleged to have spit on staff. After being removed from the cell, placed in restraints, and strapped to the gurney face down he was wheeled down a hallway to wait to see medical staff. While lying in the hallway, several minutes after he exited the cell, the officers decided to put a spit mask on him. The prisoner repeatedly says he cannot breathe and begs for help from the officers but they leave the spit mask on. Finally he is given the opportunity to be decontaminated. The officers refuse to remove the spit mask while they place the inmate in the shower. He struggles and becomes panicky and is only allowed to be in the shower about ten seconds. His experience in the shower looked and sounded like it was akin to waterboarding. The way this prisoner was handled following a UOF event is a graphic example of ADC's often brutal mistreatment of mentally ill prisoners.

103. The brutal treatment of prisoners with mental illness in ADC's isolation units is graphically illustrated by a typical UOF scenario for such prisoners in the ADC. Too often a prisoner's mental illness may impact his/her ability to follow, or in some instances even understand, orders to "cuff up" from custody staff for a routine cell search. In ADC's isolation

units, such a failure of comprehension by the mentally ill too frequently leads to being subjected to pepper spray, and thereafter being placed in restraints, face down on a gurney, while they wait to see medical staff. The prisoner may or may not be decontaminated from the spray at all and even if decontaminated, the process will nearly always be insufficient to ameliorate the effects of the chemical spray. These prisoners are then typically infracted for their alleged "misbehavior" and receive additional sanctions—in effect being punished for their mental illness—extending their incarceration and/or keeping them in the isolation units where they should never be in the first place.

104. Prisoners are also sometimes subjected to verbal abuse and demeaning treatment during UOF events by ADC staff. Although there are examples of this behavior from all facilities, this is a significant problem at Lumley, revealing a staff that are dramatically unprepared and untrained to work with the mentally ill.

105. For example, at Lumley an inmate is sprayed in her cell for the second time after the start of the video. Thereafter, she is immediately ready to cuff up. The Lieutenant (Lt.) then stops the officer from immediately cuffing her and leaves her in her cell a little longer as she suffers the impacts of the spray. A few minutes later the Lieutenant shows up in the medical exam room where the restrained inmate has been taken to wait for medical staff. She is suffering the typical effects of the spray including a very runny nose. Her breasts are exposed in the presence of male officers. No one makes any attempt to cover her. About ten minutes into the video the Lt. begins to yell at the inmate. He tells the inmate to stop spitting on his floor, telling her to instead spit on herself. The inmate follows the Lt.'s orders. The Lt. decides the medical exam is over and grabs the inmate by her clothing, holding the top of the back of her coveralls as if she were a rag doll and escorts her back to her cell. The Lt. is rough and rude with the inmate as he removes her restraints. If the Lt.'s behavior was directed towards a child it would border on child abuse.

Such treatment has no place in a correctional facility. The fact that such conduct is exhibited by a Lieutenant is even more troubling as it signals to line staff that prisoners may be treated with disrespect, violence, and brutality without consequences.

106. In another incident at Lumley, an officer sprays an inmate who is locked in her cell. After this Use of Force is deployed a senior officer asks the officer who did the spraying if that was her first spray. Acknowledging that it was and in view of other inmates, the two officers fist bump to celebrate this apparent "rite of passage" with the senior officer saying "cherry's popped." The same Lt. I mentioned above then appears and moves female officers out of the way so he can escort the restrained inmate to medical. The blanket that was wrapped around her immediately falls to the ground. The inmate is then naked and a female officer wraps her back in the blanket. After reaching the medical exam room the Lt. is verbally abusive of the inmate. At one point he says, "I'm not a doctor, I'm not a psych. All we do is spray and control you. We're gonna do this all day long if you don't pay attention. If you've got asthma, take care of yourself." He then says, "I don't think you have asthma, you are breathing better than me."

107. In addition to the fact that the Lt. has no business offering his opinion on the inmate's medical condition, his statement of his role directed towards the inmate tells her she can expect no help or no understanding from him or presumably from anyone under his supervision.

As the Lt. himself proclaims, the staff are there simply to "spray and control."

108. In yet another incident involving the same Lt. the video begins with the mentally ill inmate wrapped only in a blanket in the medical exam room. She has already been subjected to pepper spray. The inmate is directed by a male officer to walk back to her cell. The inmate takes a couple of steps and falls. The officers make disparaging comments about her fall as if she is faking. She is lifted to her feet and the Lt. says, "Quit your little game playing. Nobody believes you." While being escorted back to her cell an officer says, "She's got some

B.O. and shit." She isplaced back in her cell and is slow to follow the officer's orders to "cuff up," typical behavior for a mentally ill prisoner. The Lt. says, "Get the big can," referring to a pepper spray dispenser that will put more spray into the cell than the personal size canister the officers carry on their duty belt. As the inmate struggles to turn around and get her arms through the cuff port so that her restraints can be removed another officer says, "Pull her fucking arms out." The Lt., who is now in possession of the "big can," expresses his disappointment that the inmate has complied with the officer's orders so he cannot spray her again. Perhaps realizing that he's just said something highly damning of his professional ethics and conduct, he then says, "Damn, you might want to edit that."

109. The behavior of the officers in the incident is completely inappropriate, unprofessional, and demeaning to the mentally ill inmate. In my experience it is likely to lead to more problems with the same inmate down the road. It is clear that she cannot trust the officers, as there are no controls on their language or behavior and no understanding of how to manage a mentally ill inmate. Sadly, the Lt. condones and encourages this brutal and unprofessional conduct with the example he sets with his own words and actions.

110. In one more example of the behavior of the same Lumley Lt., the video begins with the restrained inmate being lifted and placed face down on a gurney. The Lt. tells the inmate to "shut up" and calls her an "idiot."

While escorting her on the gurney, the Lt. calls her an "asshole." A couple of minutes later the inmate, who is securely strapped to the gurney and presents no threat to the Lt., asks him for a "little respect" and if he would take his hand off of the back of her head. The Lt. says, "Keep your head down or I will hold it down" and pushes her head into the gurney witheven more force. The inmate complains that she cannot breathe. There is along walk to the compound sally port. When the camera catches up to give an accurate view of the scene the Lt.'s hand is still on the back of the inmate's head, pushing her face down into the gurney.

111. The Lt. was verbally and physically abusive to this prisoner. In the first example I cite he is borderline physically abusive as he removes the restraints from the inmate he has placed back into her cell. In all of the examples (and there are more I have not detailed here) he is verbally abusive. What is even more tragic is that he is a Lieutenant and should be modeling proper behavior for his staff. Unfortunately, he is indeed a role model, but his example is leading ADC staff in the wrong direction, teaching them to harass and disrespect mentally ill inmates, demonstrating an utter lack of understanding or skill in how to safely manage this disabled population.

112. The SIR records for three of these incidents (it was not produced for SIR 13-14780) show they were all viewed by facility administration. None of those administrators identified or raised any of the concerns that I have documented with my examples. It is quite simply clear that no one in that review process has even a remote understanding that the behavior of their staff is counter-productive to managing mentally ill inmates, or any inmate for that matter. Humiliating and demeaning treatment and sometimes even physical abuse is condoned and allowed. The officers and supervisors in these videos know they are on camera yet they still behave with impunity towards the inmates. It scares me to think about what happens when the camera is not rolling.

113. As an experienced corrections administrator who has reviewed use of force videos in my own jurisdiction for more than twenty years, if I was aware of the behavior of the Lt. I have described, he would no longer be employed in my agency. Yet there is apparently no questioning of hisperformance or that of other officers. The abuse is authorized – and obviously condoned. There is no question in my mind that the administration and officers of the ADC are completely unprepared and ill trained to manage their large population of mentally ill prisoners, and that their current policies and practices ensure that they will remain so. Theresults of this tragic and knowing misconduct is that prisoners are not only placed at substantial risk of serious harm in the isolation units – they arebeing hurt and will continue to be hurt without extensive changes to current policy and practice.

VIII. INSUFFICIENT TRAINING TO MANAGE THE MENTALLY ILL WITHIN THE ADC

114. In his deposition testimony Director McWilliams describes how the ADC prepared with training for the implementation of their proposed program. He says they trained, "all line staff working in mental health pods to

have awareness in handling mental health issues, as well as interacting with mental health inmates." He says, "We did a series of trainings over the past year and a half." He indicates that "70, 80 percent" were trained at Browning, "a little higher" at SMU 1 and Central as well as "probably all their staff" at Perryville. He says that "hundreds" were trained.

115. When asked how that training was integrated into actual practice, his basic response is, "I know the staff certainly have told me that they think it's great training and it has been very effective in helping them with their jobs." When asked what the ADC administration does to ensure their staff are actually implementing the training, he says they do it by "walking and talking."

116. It is clear from the examples I have cited that the training has not been effective. Unnecessary use of force practices, demeaning comments towards and abusive treatment of mentally ill inmates, subjecting those inmates to pepper spray and then putting them on display strapped face down to a gurney, with either an inadequate de-contamination from pepper spray or a de-contamination that has yet to even occur is not consistent with any training for managing the mentally ill of which I am familiar. Nor is giving a small percentage of the mentally ill an extra hour out of their cells each week to attend a class. The information I have relied on to write this report—and much more—is available to ADC administrators. The fact that ADC supervisors fail to recognize the depth of their problem with line staff from their "walking and talking" tells me that ADC simply has not begun to implement the kind of cultural changes necessary to reform its practices in managing mentally ill inmates. I can only conclude that in the "walking and talking" ADC supervisors are reinforcing their historical bad practices since they seem to accept uncritically the current state of affairs.

117. In describing the training offered, Director McWilliams says, "It wasn't just one training class. I believe we had a series of about a dozen to 15 different classes, you know, that entailed this information. And some of it was about direct supervision. Some of it was even about keeping yourself focused and in good mental health space because it's very stressful work. So it's a combination of things."

118. Director McWilliams' deposition that I quote from was taken on July 1, 2014. He testified that their training initiative to support their proposed program has been going on for the past year and a half, presumably back to January 1, 2013. The annual training plan for the fiscal year 2013 was made available to me. Assuming the fiscal year ended on June 30, 2013, six months of the training to support their proposed program should be reflected in that plan. It is not. Instead the only training listed on their plan regarding the mentally ill is a two-hour course offering called, Signs and Symptoms of Mentally Inmates, and a one-hour offering, in Suicide Prevention.80 Whether or not the more ambitious mental health

training to implement their new program was listed on their training plan for 2014 is unknown, as it was not produced. What was produced was a Restrictive Housing Training Report that indicates the training was completed between February and April of 2014,81 indicating to me that the training has not been going on for the past year and a half but for three months around the time that DI 326 was allegedly implemented.

119. Some of their instructional material for their new training was made available to me. Of the three documents related to suicide prevention training only one was specifically for corrections. It is a four page document that does wisely say inmates are at highest risk for suicide, "When placed in a special housing unit, e.g., restrictive housing."

120. Other training material made available included course outlines and related slides for courses entitled *Tactical Communication, Flexible Supervision Strategies, Officer Role in Influencing Behavior, Managing Inmate Behavior, Managing Differences in the* Unit and *Establishing Yourself in the Housing Unit*. Each of these courses is credited to the National Institute of Corrections (NIC) curriculum *How to Run a Direct Supervision Housing Unit*.

121. I am familiar with the NIC. They have trained me and I have trained for them. The NIC courses, which ADC represents as preparing their staff to work with the mentally ill, are off on two counts. First, from the course material referenced above, none of them are about training staff to work with mentally ill inmates. Second, these courses were designed to teach officers to work in a direct supervision jail, not the restricted

housing isolation units in a state prison. "Direct supervision" is in fact the opposite of an isolation unit. Typically the officer is stationed in the middle of the pod and during most hours of the day the inmates move freely to and from their cells. How the ADC thinks this course curriculum will help their staff better interact and supervise mentally ill inmates in an isolation unit is beyond my comprehension.

122. Other course material offered, as being part of the preparation for ADC's proposed program are *Crisis Intervention in Maximum Custody*, *Effectively Responding to Stressors*, *Group Dynamics* and *Inmate Programs the Basics*.

123. The course outline for *Crisis Intervention in Maximum Custody* includes some rudimentary information about how the officers' personal style connects with the opportunity to de-escalate conflicts with inmates. It is fine as far as it goes but it contains absolutely no specific information about working with the mentally ill.

124. The course outline for *Effectively Responding to Stressors* describes a fine program, focused on helping corrections staff develop skills to manage the impact the job has on their personal lives. Unfortunately it also contains no information about working with the mentally ill, nor is there any particular focus on working in the isolation units.

125. *Inmate Programs the Basics* is an overview of the new programs that are to be offered for inmates in isolation in ADC. It also includes five pages telling staff about the importance of informal interactions with inmates as opportunities to influence their behavior but once again, there is absolutely no information related to building officer skills to work with the mentally ill.

126. Director McWilliams' representations to the contrary, if this is the curriculum they have relied upon to train their officers to work with the mentally ill in their isolation units, it cannot possibly accomplish that goal.

There is nothing about working with mental illness in their training offerings.

127. In my own experience overseeing the training for line staff to work in the new mental health program we developed at McNeil Island Corrections Center, we offered intensive training. The staff we hired were about two-thirds former correctional officers and one third with other background or experience, often in working with the mentally ill. Training was extensive and ongoing and ranged from an explanation of the basics of behavior one could expect from a prisoner who was schizophrenic, depressed or suffering from a variety of diagnosis, to tangible experiences about what a mentally ill person might actually experience if they were hearing voices. Part of the training, which I was selected to demonstrate the first time it was offered, was to put on a set of headphones that allowed you to hear what was being said by the person in front of you but also delivered "voices" through the headphones. Then, the trainer barked orders, giving the trainee (me) a clear understanding of why it sometimes takes a mentally ill person some time to figure out what they are being ordered to do and to organize their thoughts so they could respond accordingly. I am convinced this technique had a powerful impact on those who experienced it, as it did for me. This type of hands-on training is necessary to actually change staff behavior and skills when working with the mentally ill. None of the training materials produced by ADC provides this type of necessary skill-building.

128. Also offered by the ADC, as part of their training is *Group Dynamics*, which was targeted for their Correctional Officer III's (C.O. III) to prepare them to deliver the groups and classes to the inmates. It is a fine course outline for learning how to lead a group but contains nothing

about program content. When questioned during our tour of Browning about what other training is offered regarding program content, Director McWilliams indicated that the only training provided was the *Group Dynamics* course. (The unfortunate C.O. III who was teaching the class we interrupted had to admit he had not yet taken the class, yet he had been teaching the class for some time and indicated that he was the primary instructor for nearly all of Browning's group programs.) Director McWilliams then offered that the course content was not that complex and most could learn it as it was being delivered.

129. I am unfamiliar with many of the specific group programs the ADC currently says it offers to prisoners. When asked by Defendants' expert, Dr. Seiter, if the programs were "evidenced-based," the gold standard by

which current correctional programs are measured, Director McWilliams could not give an affirmative answer. I, however, am familiar with one of the programs they offer, *Thinking for a Change*.

130. *Thinking for a Change* is an NIC product that is an evidenced-based program. I am familiar with it because we offered it in Washington State. NIC has historically offered Technical Assistance Grants to prepare employees to teach the program and it requires a certification process to become an instructor. If this training or certification was provided to staff in the ADC to deliver this program, Mr. McWilliams was apparently not aware of it and no documentation was produced to demonstrate that any such certification has taken place.

131. In my training and experience evidenced-based programs only work when they are instructed consistent with the program model, a process often referred to as "fidelity to the model." Instructor performance needs to be routinely monitored by an outside auditor to make certain the program is being delivered correctly. This is a practice that we utilized in the State of Washington and I recently saw it in place in the Department of Corrections and Community Supervision (DOCCS) in New York State.

The absence of the outside audit means it is very likely that, over time, the quality of the program will slide and no longer rise to the threshold of being evidence-based. If this is not in place in Arizona, and I do believe that it is not since it is not referenced in any of the material produced by the Defendants, it is likely that none of the programs they offer can truly make the claim to be evidenced-based.

132. Based on the evidence and admissions I found during my facility inspections, and the training material for line staff and C.O. III's produced by Defendants as evidence that they have moved to better prepare their staff to work with the mentally ill in isolation, it is clear to me that ADC has completely and utterly failed to provide adequate training and supervision for staff working with prisoners in the isolation units, especially the mentally ill.

CONCLUSION

133. Director McWilliams emphasizes in his deposition that ADC's recent attempt to make changes for inmates held in their isolation units were not motivated by the *Parsons* case. If they were not then one must ask the question of why Arizona officials believe it is time to make any changes at all. In any case, these changes must be seen as a response (although wholly inadequate) to the substantial risk of serious harm created by the conditions of confinement in ADC's isolation units which occasioned this litigation.

134. Directors Ryan and McWilliams both make reference to ASCA as influencing their thinking about how to reform the practices of their isolation units. When asked during his deposition if DI 326 is based on the ASCA Guiding Principles, Director McWilliams says, "It's not based on [sic] solely. There's a combination of things that went into 326. It was some information that we compiled and other agencies around the country, particularly the state of Washington."

135. None of their responses give a clear meaning to their reasons for change. I have come to the conclusion that Arizona prison officials likely have no idea why they are proposing to make changes other than the knowledge that they are being sued, and that their current practices are out-of-step with both law and policy that finds the extreme isolation practiced by ADC is harmful for the mentally ill and all prisoners – and too often counterproductive for safety and security. Unfortunately, it is clear that ADC has failed both to develop an adequate plan to address the persistent and serious problems in its isolation units and to even understand fully what steps they must take to eliminate the serious risk of harm – and the actual harm – they are creating in these units.

136. The reason to reform restricted housing practices is to reduce the substantial risk of harm those units present to all prisoners and especially the mentally ill. These are risks that I have documented in my previous reports. Arizona never acknowledges that the collective body of research accumulated over the past few decades has shown the substantial risk of harm caused by placing prisoners in isolation. Instead, they fail to take the most basic measures, for example, excluding seriously mentally ill from isolation units and ensuring that therapeutic, clinical programs are available to house such prisoners in the alternative.

137. Among the steps necessary for meaningful change to occur within the ADC isolation units are, at least, the following elements:

Stop placing inmates in isolation who do not need to be there and exclude seriously mentally ill inmates from the isolation units.

Create secure treatment units for mentally ill inmates separate and apart from a regular isolation unit for those that need some type of segregation housing.

These units must provide adequate structured and unstructured time out-of-cell and appropriate clinical treatment. Management of those units must be the shared responsibility of custody and clinical staff.

Actually train the custody staff to work effectively in those units.

Hold staff accountable who are abusive to the mentally ill and all prisoners.

For inmates that are not mentally ill, but who require placement in segregation, provide program and exercise opportunities that get them out of their cell at least five days a week, and ensure conditions of confinement that do not contribute to or constitute extreme social isolation, such as inadequate nutrition, inadequate mental health monitoring, and inadequate property.

Provide sufficient resources for ADC's STG step-down programs to meet the need.

Reform the use of force practices and policy to emphasize mental health intervention and de-escalation similar to the CDCR policy appended to this report.

Provide adequate decontamination from pepper spray when it must be used.

Conform to national guidelines for the prone restraint position.

CITES AND AUTHORITIES

This section outlines judicial decisions. The number of violations by authorities indicate that human rights violations are endemic. The mere fact that due to PLRA, the ICCPR violations, because prisoners are required to provide a higher standard of proof, the complainants have not prevailed, is of no import. The violations are there but due to PLRA prisoners have been denied relief. Janis, Kay, and Bradley, European Convention On Human Rights Law (3rd. ed. 2008)

VICTOR ANTONIO PARSONS, ET AL., PLAINTIFFS, VS. CHARLES L. RYAN, ET AL., DEFENDANTS. NO. CV12-0601-PHX-NVW UNITED STATES DISTRICT COURT FOR THE DISTRICT OF RIZONA289 F.R.D. 513 (2013)

I. Background

ADC currently incarcerates approximately 33,000 inmates in ten complexes statewide: Douglas, Eyman, Florence, Lewis, Perryville, Phoenix, Safford, Tucson, Winslow, and Yuma (Doc. 321, Ex. 2, Decl. of Def. Richard Pratt ¶¶ 3-5). Plaintiffs filed this action in March 2012, presenting five claims for relief stemming from Defendants' alleged deliberate indifference in the provision of overall health, medical, dental, and mental health care and to unconstitutional conditions of confinement in the ADC's isolation units [2] (Doc. 1 at ¶¶ 140-149). Plaintiffs seek declaratory and injunctive relief, including an Order compelling Defendants to develop a plan to provide Plaintiffs and the proposed class and subclass with constitutionally adequate health care and protection from unconstitutional conditions of confinement in ADC's isolation units.

2   Defendants take issue with the term "isolation" cell or unit as they argue it implies a total inability to communicate with others (Doc. 326 at 6). For consistency, the Court will use the terminology supplied by Plaintiffs, but such use does not amount to an opinion about the substance of Plaintiffs' isolation claims.

Plaintiffs seek class certification for one Class and one Subclass. The proposed Class definition is "all prisoners who are now, or will in the future be, subjected to the medical, mental health, and dental care policies and practices of the ADC" (Doc. 248 at 6). The proposed Class representatives are Plaintiffs Parsons, Jensen, Swartz, Brislan, Rodriguez, Verduzco, Thomas, Smith, Gamez, Chisholm, Licci, Hefner, Polson, and Wells. The proposed Subclass definition is "all prisoners who are now, or will in the future be, subjected by the ADC to isolation, defined as confinement in a cell for 22 hours or more each day or confinement in the following housing units: Eyman-SMU 1; Eyman-Browning Unit; Florence-Central Unit; Florence-Kasson Unit; or Perryville-Lumley Special Management Area" (*id.*). The proposed Subclass members are Plaintiffs Gamez, Swartz, Brislan, Rodriguez, Verduzco, Thomas, Smith, and Polson.

II. Governing Standard

The Court's authority to certify a class action is found in *Federal Rule of Civil Procedure 23*. Plaintiffs first bear the burden of establishing the four requirements articulated in *Rule 23(a)*: (1) the class is so numerous that joinder of all members is impracticable; (2) there are questions of law or fact common to the class; (3) the claims or defenses of the representative parties are typical of the claims or defenses of the class; and (4) the representative parties will fairly and adequately protect the interests of the class. Additionally, Plaintiffs must also establish one of the requirements found in *Rule 23(b)*. In this case, Plaintiffs allege that class certification in this case is appropriate pursuant to *Rule 23(b)(2)*, which requires a demonstration that "the party opposing the class has acted or refused to act on grounds that apply generally to the class, so that final injunctive relief or corresponding declaratory relief is appropriate respecting the class as a whole." *FED. R. CIV. P. 23(b)(2)*.

When analyzing whether class certification is appropriate, the Court must conduct "a rigorous analysis" to ensure that "the prerequisites of *Rule 23(a)* have been satisfied." *Wal-Mart Stores, Inc. v. Dukes, 131 S. Ct. 2541, 2551-52, 180 L. Ed. 2d 374 (2011)* (citing *Gen. Tel. Co. of the Sw. v. Falcon, 457 U.S. 147, 161, 102 S. Ct. 2364, 72 L. Ed. 2d 740 (1982)*). As discussed below, the Court finds that certification of the Class and the Subclass is appropriate.

III. *Rule 23(a)* Analysis

A. Numerosity

Defendants do not dispute that the numerosity requirement is satisfied by ADC's overall inmate population of more than 33,000 and isolation population of approximately 3,000. Indeed, there is no doubt that joinder of all members of the potential Class and Subclass would be impracticable, if not impossible. *See Sepulveda v. Wal-Mart Stores, Inc., 237 F.R.D. 229, 242 (C.D. Cal. 2006)* (acknowledging that joinder will be impracticable for very large classes). The numerosity requirement is satisfied.

B. Commonality

1. Governing Standard

To establish commonality, Plaintiffs must demonstrate that there are "questions of law or fact common to the class." *FED. R. CIV. P. 23(a)(2)*. Plaintiffs need not demonstrate that all questions are common to the class; rather, class claims must "depend upon a common contention . . . [that is] capable of classwide resolution." *Wal-Mart, 131 S. Ct. at 2551*. "Even a single [common] question" will suffice to satisfy *Rule 23(a)*. Id. at 2556 (citation omitted). In the civil rights context, commonality is satisfied "where the lawsuit challenges a system-wide practice or policy that affects all of the putative class members." *Armstrong v. Davis, 275 F.3d 849, 868 (9th Cir. 2001)*.

In assessing commonality, "it may be necessary for the court to probe behind the pleadings before coming to rest on the certification question." *Gen'l. Tel. Co. of Sw. v. Falcon, 457 U.S. 147, 160, 102 S. Ct. 2364, 72 L. Ed. 2d 740 (1982)* ("[T]he class determination generally involves considerations that are enmeshed in the factual and legal issues comprising the plaintiff's cause of action.") (quotation omitted). That said, although the Court must consider the underlying merits of Plaintiffs' claims to ascertain whether commonality exists, it is not the Court's function at this juncture to "go so far . . . as to judge the validity of these claims." *USW v. ConocoPhillips Co.*, 593 F.3d 802, 808-09 (9th Cir. 2010) (quoting *Staton v. Boeing Co.*, 327 F.3d 938, 954 (9th Cir. 2003)). Thus, Plaintiffs' motion for class certification is not an opportunity to hold "a dress rehearsal for the trial on the merits." *Messner v. Northshore Univ. HealthSystem*, 669 F.3d 802, 811 (7th Cir. 2012). The prohibition on requiring Plaintiffs to establish their claims at the class certification stage was recently reinforced by the Supreme Court in *Amgen Inc. v. Connecticut Retirement Plans and Trust Funds*, U.S. , 133 S. Ct. 1184, 185 L. Ed. 2d 308, 2013 WL 691001 (2013), at *7 ("*Rule 23* grants courts no license to engage in free-ranging merits inquiries at the certification stage.")

Plaintiffs maintain that the common question to all Class and Subclass members is whether Defendants are deliberately indifferent to their health and safety in violation of the *Eighth Amendment*. Thus stated, the common question is too broad. As detailed below, the Court construes the common question as it relates to the practices Plaintiffs identified in their Complaint.

To support their motion, Plaintiffs rely on the factual allegations in their Complaint (Doc. 1 at ¶¶ 26-100), voluminous evidence obtained thus far during discovery, declarations of four experts (Doc. 240, Exs. B-E), and declarations of the named Plaintiffs (Doc. 249, Exs. F-S). Plaintiffs argue that the facts derived from this evidence soundly establish the existence of a "system-wide practice or policy that affects all of the putative class members" for both the Class and Subclass. *See Ortega- Melendres v. Arpaio*, 836 F. Supp. 2d 959, 989 (D. Ariz. 2011) (quoting *Armstrong*, 275 F.3d at 868). More specifically, Plaintiffs contend that as to the Class systemic deficiencies exist in the provision of medical, dental, and mental health care that expose all inmates to a substantial risk of serious harm. With respect to the Subclass, Plaintiffs maintain that the conditions of confinement in ADC's isolation units place inmates--and particularly mentally ill inmates--at a substantial risk of serious harm.

2. Facts

i. Medical Care

Wexford Health Sources was the private entity providing health care services to ADC inmates pursuant to the Arizona legislature's mandate from July 1, 2012 through March 3, 2013 (Doc. 321, Ex. 2, Decl. of Def. Richard Pratt ¶ 8). Effective March 4, 2013, Corizon, Inc. took over for Wexford as ADC's health care provider. While private contractors are responsible for the delivery of health care, the Court noted in its October 10, 2012 Order denying Defendants' Motion to Dismiss that Defendant Ryan "has a continuing duty to ensure that those to whom he delegated functions or duties performed those duties appropriately" (Doc. 175 at 10). Plaintiffs' medical care expert, Dr. Robert Cohen, opines that prior to and since privatization, Defendants "have neglected the serious medical needs of the Arizona state prisoners by failing to manage, support, supervise and administer medical care to prisoners in the ten state complexes. Because of this neglect, these prisoners are at serious risk of harm, and in some cases, death." (Doc. 240, Ex. C, Decl. of Robert L. Cohen, M.D. ¶ 5). Included in Dr. Cohen's review was ADC's September 21, 2012 "Written Cure Notification" to Wexford's Director (Doc. 240, Ex. EE at ADC027858-ADC027859). The Cure Notification detailed twenty significant areas of non-compliance and required corrective action within 90 days pursuant to the contract between ADC and Wexford. The deficiencies included:

o   Inadequate staffing levels in multiple program areas at multiple locations;

o   Staffing levels creating inappropriate scheduling gaps in on-site medical coverage;

o   Staffing levels forcing existing staff to work excessive hours, creating fatigue risks;

o   Quantitative decrease in routine institutional care: backlog of prescription medication expiration review;

- o Incorrect or incomplete pharmacy prescriptions;

- o Inappropriate discontinuation/change of medication;

- o Inconsistent non-formulary medication approval process;

- o Inconsistent or contradictory medication refill and/or return procedures;

- o Inadequate pharmacy reports;

- o Inconsistent documentation of Medication Administration Records;

- o Inconsistent provision of release, transfer, and/or renewal medications;

- o Inability to readily identify specific groups of inmates or chronic conditions based upon medications prescribed (e.g., diabetes);

- o Inadequate/untimely communication between field staff, corporate staff, and ADC;

- o Lack of responsiveness and/or lack of awareness of incident urgency and reporting requirements;

- o Quantitative decrease in routine institutional care: backlog of chart reviews;

- o Quantitative decrease in routine institutional care: backlog of provider line appointments;

- o Quantitative decrease in routine institutional care: untimely handling of Health Needs Requests;

- o Quantitative decrease in routine institutional care: backlog/cancellation of outside specialty consultations;

- o Unresponsive approach to ADC inquiries on patient information; and

- o Unresponsive approach to inmate grievance process (id.).

All twenty deficiencies were identified at all ten ADC complexes (*id.* at ADC027863-ADC027869). Further underscoring this evidence is Wexford's response to the Cure Notification, which argued that ADC's expectation that all deficiencies would be cured within 90 days was unreasonable. Wexford explained that "the majority of the problems Wexford now faces are long-standing issues, embedded into ADC health care policy and philosophy, and which existed well before Wexford Health assumed responsibility for the program" (*id.*, Ex. FF at ADC027941-ADC027942). The Cure Notification relied on much of the same evidence Plaintiffs submit in support of their motion, which obviates the need to repeat it here.

Additionally, six named Plaintiffs present specific allegations related to his or her own medical treatment and the delays experienced in receiving medical care.

o Plaintiff Swartz suffered extensive injuries after being attacked by other inmates and experienced significant delays in seeing an ophthalmologist, never saw a plastic surgeon to whom he was referred, was not prescribed adequate pain medication for months, experienced months long delays in receiving prescription refills, and suffers permanent facial paralysis and is unable to completely close his left eye (Doc. 249, Ex. L, Decl. of Pl. Stephen Swartz ¶¶ 4-9).

o Plaintiff Desiree Licci was treated at ADC for cancer in 2001 and began experiencing troubling symptoms in fall 2010 (Doc. 249, Ex. N, Decl. of Pl. Desiree Licci ¶¶ 3-4). Despite several referrals to an oncologist, Plaintiff Licci waited for over one year to see a specialist and has not received a biopsy to rule out cancer despite numerous masses evident on CT scans (*id.* ¶¶ 5-26).

o Plaintiff Shawn Jensen had six years of highly elevated PSA tests but was not diagnosed with prostate cancer until October 2009 when it had progressed to Stage 2 (Doc. 249, Ex. O, Decl. of Pl. Shawn Jensen ¶¶ 5-7). Plaintiff Jensen experienced delays in receiving GnrH antagonist therapy (to lower testosterone levels) and did not receive surgery until July 2010 (*id.* ¶¶ 8-9). Thereafter, Plaintiff Jensen experienced extreme difficulty with his catheter and was leaking urine (*id.* ¶¶ 14-

15). On August 1, 2010, Assistant Cordova could not ascertain what was causing the leakage and attempted to push the catheter further into Plaintiff Jensen's urethra. This incident resulted in permanent catastrophic damage to Plaintiff Jensen's urethra and bladder, requiring six additional surgeries (*id.* ¶¶ 16-43, 45).

o Plaintiff Joseph Hefner experienced a negative reaction to expired eye medication, causing acute glaucoma (Doc. 249, Ex. P, Decl. of Pl. Joseph Hefner ¶¶ 5-6). Plaintiff Hefner experienced delays in receiving prescriptions and in seeing a physician after being assaulted by inmates (*id.* ¶¶ 7-9).

o Plaintiff Charlotte Wells had a history of heart problems and chronic chest pain but she did not see a heart specialist until she was sent to the hospital (Doc. 249, Ex. Q, Decl. of Pl. Charlotte Wells ¶ 3). Tests conducted revealed an 80% blockage in her artery, and a stent was implanted (*id.* ¶ 4). Plaintiff Wells continues to suffer from an irregular heartbeat, a leaky valve, problems with blood pressure, and chest pain (*id.* ¶ 11).

o Plaintiff Joshua Polson developed multiple ear infections during incarceration (Doc. 249, Ex. R, Decl. of Pl. Joshua Polson ¶ 19). From 2009 on, he filed multiple health needs requests describing the pain in his ears but it takes days or weeks to see a provider (*id.*). He has tested positive for MRSA (methicillin-resistant staph aureus) and the antibiotics provided do not eradicate the ear infections (*id.*). At one point, Plaintiff Polson experienced pain and blood running from his left ear but the nurse said the bleeding was caused by a scratch (*id.* ¶ 20). Plaintiff had a hearing test in March 2010 that found he was deaf in his right ear (*id.* ¶ 19).

iv. Subclass -- Conditions of Confinement in Isolation Units

With respect to the effects of the conditions of confinement in ADC's isolation units, Plaintiffs submit the declaration of Dr. Craig Haney (Doc. 240, Ex. E, Decl. of Craig Haney). He opines:

> Contrary to sound correctional practice and the weight of psychological and psychiatric opinion, ADC currently houses seriously mentally ill prisoners in its isolation units. ADC's failure to have and implement policy that excludes these prisoners from these units places these prisoners at an unreasonable risk of harm . . . [C]onditions of extreme isolation can create enormous harm in even previously healthy individuals. ADC's apparent failure to put in place careful mental health monitoring policies for all prisoners subject to the extremely isolated conditions in their maximum security/isolation units, places all prisoners subject to such conditions at an unreasonable risk of harm (*id.* ¶ 54).

Plaintiffs argue that the conditions in ADC's isolation units that pose a substantial risk of serious harm to inmates are:

o Lack of exercise;

o Lack of educational programming;

o Constant cell illumination;

o Limited access to property; and

o Infrequent and reduced calorie meals (*id.* ¶ 44).

3. Analysis

Based upon the above evidence, the question common to all members of the Class and the Subclass is whether Defendants' practices are deliberately indifferent to inmates' health and safety in violation of the *Eighth Amendment* and subjection to unconstitutional conditions of confinement in isolation units. *See Farmer v.*

Brennan, 511 U.S. 825, 828, 114 S. Ct. 1970, 128 L. Ed. 2d 811 (1994). Further, the answer to that question is "apt to drive the resolution of the litigation" and would form the basis for whether an injunction directing Defendants to remedy any unconstitutional conditions is appropriate. *Wal-Mart, 131 S. Ct. at 2551* (citation omitted).

To maintain an *Eighth Amendment* medical-care claim, Plaintiffs must demonstrate "deliberate indifference to serious medical needs." *Jett v. Penner, 439 F.3d 1091, 1096 (9th Cir. 2006)* (citing *Estelle v. Gamble, 429 U.S. 97, 104, 97 S. Ct. 285, 50 L. Ed. 2d 251 (1976)*). There are two prongs to the deliberate-indifference analysis: an objective standard and a subjective standard. First, a prisoner must show a "serious medical need." *Jett, 439 F.3d at 1096* (citations omitted). A "'serious' medical need exists if the failure to treat a prisoner's condition could result in further significant injury or the 'unnecessary and wanton infliction of pain.'" *McGuckin v. Smith, 974 F.2d 1050, 1059 (9th Cir. 1992),* overruled on other grounds, *WMX Techs., Inc. v. Miller, 104 F.3d 1133, 1136 (9th Cir. 1997)* (en banc) (internal citation omitted).

Second, a prisoner must show that the defendant's response to that need was deliberately indifferent. *Jett, 439 F.3d at 1096.* The state of mind required for deliberate indifference is subjective recklessness; however, "the standard is 'less stringent in cases involving a prisoner's medical needs . . . because the State's responsibility to provide inmates with medical care ordinarily does not conflict with competing administrative concerns.'" *Snow v. McDaniel, 681 F.3d 978, 985 (9th Cir. 2012)* (quoting *McGuckin, 974 F.2d at 1060*). The deliberate-indifference prong is met if the prisoner demonstrates (1) a purposeful act or failure to respond to a prisoner's medical need and (2) harm caused by the indifference. *Id.* Further, prison officials are deliberately indifferent to a prisoner's serious medical needs if they deny, delay, or intentionally interfere with medical treatment. *Wood v. Housewright, 900 F.2d 1332, 1334 (9th Cir. 1990).*

i. Health Care Class

Defendants' response raises three main contentions against commonality: (1) Plaintiffs' allegations are nothing more than "a conglomeration of specific practices . . . based on isolated instances" that deviate from ADC's established and constitutional policies (Doc. 326 at 7); (2) Plaintiffs' claims necessarily turn on fact-specific inquiries which precludes a commonality finding (*id.* at 26-27); and (3) many of the Plaintiffs failed to allege any harm resulting from an alleged constitutional violation, which is facially insufficient to establish deliberate indifference (*id.*).

All three of these arguments, however, miss the mark in a class action seeking only injunctive and declaratory relief. First, Defendants' oft-repeated contention that Plaintiffs' allegations are inconsistent with ADC policies misunderstands the substance of Plaintiffs' claims. Plaintiffs' claim is that *despite* ADC stated policies, the actual provision of health care in its prison complexes suffers from systemic deficiencies that rise to the level of deliberate indifference.

Similarly, Defendants erroneously focus on Plaintiffs' perceived failure to allege actual harm. But Defendants rely on cases in which plaintiffs sought monetary damages. When seeking only injunctive relief, a plaintiff need not wait until he suffers an actual injury because the constitutional injury *is* the exposure to the risk of harm. *Brown v. Plata, 131 S. Ct. 1910, 1926 n.3, 179 L. Ed. 2d 969* (citing *Farmer, 511 U.S. at 834*).

For the same reason, assessing commonality does not require a fact-specific inquiry into each Plaintiff's allegations. It matters not that each inmate may suffer from different ailments or require individualized treatment because commonality may be met where "the claims of every class member are based on a common legal theory, even though the factual circumstances differ for each member." *Walsh v. Ford Motor Co., 130 F.R.D. 260, 268 (D. D.C. 1990)* (citing *Hanlon v. Chrysler Corp., 150 F.3d 1011, 1019 (9th Cir. 1998)*).

Nor does the Supreme Court's decision in *Wal-Mart* defeat commonality. *Wal-Mart's* analysis on commonality arose in a legally and factually inapposite context. Commonality in *Wal-Mart* was defeated because the putative class members--female *Wal-Mart* employees--alleged that they had been improperly denied promotions pursuant to a discriminatory corporate practice but, in fact, promotion decisions were discretionary and were handled independently by the numerous Wal-Mart managers. *Wal-Mart, 131 S. Ct. at 2547-48*. This practice vitiated the conclusion that Wal-Mart acted pursuant to a centralized policy. *Id. at 2554*. That lack of commonality contrasts with this case, where all inmates are subjected to Defendants' actions or lack thereof, because they have the sole responsibility for health care policy.

Despite the distractions presented by Defendants that do not defeat commonality, the crucial question is whether there is sufficient evidence of systemic issues in the provision of health care or whether Plaintiffs' allegations are simply many examples of isolated instances of deliberate indifference. A policy, practice, or custom may be inferred from widespread practices or evidence of repeated constitutional violations for which the errant officials are not reprimanded. *Menotti v. City of Seattle, 409 F.3d 1113, 1147 (9th Cir. 2005)* (citing *Nadell v. Las Vegas Metro. Police Dep't., 268 F.3d 924, 929 (9th Cir. 2001))*. When examining liability for an improper custom or practice, courts should look at whether the practice at issue is one of sufficient duration, frequency, and consistency such that the alleged conduct may be the "traditional method of carrying out policy." *Trevino v. Gates, 99 F.3d 911, 918 (9th Cir. 1996)*.

In answering this narrow question, the Court finds that ADC's September 21, 2012 Cure Notification to Wexford and Wexford's response thereto is probative evidence that tips the balance in favor of concluding that the problems identified in the provision of health care are not merely isolated instances but, rather, examples of systemic deficiencies that expose all inmates to a substantial risk of serious harm (Doc. 240, Ex. EE; Doc. 243, Ex. FF). This is particularly true in view of ADC's contention in the Cure Notification that twenty critical failures existed at all ten ADC complexes. This evidence is what sets this case apart from Defendants' citations to other cases where class certification was denied. In those cases, there was simply insufficient evidence propelling the plaintiffs' isolated allegations of mistreatment into a plausible claim of systemic deficiencies in those facilities. In contrast, the evidence here suggests that the root cause of the injuries and threats of injuries suffered by Plaintiffs is the systemic failures in the provision of health care generally.

Further, the Court finds that Plaintiffs' expert declarations, largely unrebutted at this juncture, are sufficient to establish that ADC's practices or customs in the provision of health care rise to the level of deliberate indifference that places inmates at a substantial risk of serious harm. The Court reiterates that its conclusion is not an opinion that Plaintiffs will ultimately succeed on the merits of their claim. Rather, it is a finding that their initial evidence is sufficient to establish that a common question exists as to all putative Class members. *See Baby Neal v. Casey, 43 F.3d 48, 56 (3d Cir. 1994)* ("[C]lass members can assert such a single common complaint even if they have not all suffered actual injury; demonstrating that all class members are *subject* to the same harm will suffice.") (emphasis in original). Put another way, the Court finds that the allegations of systemic deficiencies in ADC's provision of health care are sufficient to establish "a system-wide practice or policy that affects all of the putative class members." *Armstrong, 275 F.3d at 868*.

The evidence cited above is the "significant proof" that ADC is operating under a policy of providing deficient health care. *See Wang v. Chinese Daily News, 709 F.3d 829, No. 08-55483, 2013 U.S. App. LEXIS 4423, *10 (9th Cir. March 4, 2013)*. The Court also finds that litigating the adequacy of ADC's health care to all inmates "depend[s] on a common contention . . . of such a nature that it is capable of classwide resolution --- which means that determination of its truth or falsity will resolve an issue that is central to the validity of each one of the claims in one stroke." *2013 U.S. App. LEXIS 4423 at *9* (citing *Wal-Mart, 131 S. Ct. at 2551*).

Defendants' limited disputes about the substance of Plaintiffs' allegations "amount to an attempt to hold 'a mini-trial on the merits' prior to certification, which is simply impermissible." *Connor B. ex rel. Vigurs v. Patrick, 272 F.R.D. 288, 296 (D. Mass 2011)* (citing *In re PolyMedica Corp. Sec. Litig., 432 F.3d 1, 16 (1st Cir. 2005))*.

Based on Plaintiff's showing of systemic deficiencies at all ten ADC facilities, the Court finds that commonality exists with respect to the allegations in Plaintiff's Complaint that the following practices constitute deliberate indifference to all inmates. Those practices, with citations to the named Plaintiffs' declarations detailing their exposure to them, are as follows:

1. Failure to provide timely access to health care (Chisholm Decl. ¶¶ 17-18; Swartz Decl. ¶¶ 4-9; Licci Decl. ¶¶ 3-29; Jensen Decl. ¶¶ 5-45; Hefner Decl. ¶¶ 5-9; Wells Decl. ¶¶ 3-5, 11; Polson Decl. ¶¶ 19-21).

2. Failure to provide timely emergency treatment (Jensen Decl. ¶ 15; Hefner Decl. ¶ 6; Wells Decl. ¶¶ 3-5).

3. Failure to provide necessary medication and medical devices (Gamez Decl. ¶ 20; Chisholm Decl. ¶¶ 17-18; Swartz Decl. ¶¶ 7; Smith Decl. ¶¶ 7-13; Licci Decl. ¶¶ 3- 29; Jensen Decl. ¶¶ 5-45; Hefner Decl. ¶¶ 5-9; Wells Decl. ¶¶ 3-5, 11; Polson Decl. ¶¶ 19-21).

4. Insufficient health care staffing (i.e. physicians, psychiatrists, dentists, physicians' assistants, registered nurses, and other qualified clinicians) (Rodriguez Decl. ¶ 7; Smith Decl. ¶ 6; Polson Decl. ¶ 17; Verduzco ¶ 14).

5. Failure to provide care for chronic diseases and protection from infectious disease (Chisholm Decl. ¶¶ 17-18; Licci Decl. ¶¶ 3-29; Jensen Decl. ¶¶ 5-45; Wells ¶¶ 3-5, 11; Polson Decl. ¶¶ 19-21).

6. Failure to provide timely access to medically necessary specialty care (Swartz Decl. ¶¶ 4-9; Licci Decl. ¶¶ 3-29; Jensen Decl. ¶¶ 5-45; Hefner Decl. ¶¶ 5-9; Wells ¶¶ 3-5, 11; Polson Decl. ¶¶ 19-21).

7. Failure to provide timely access to basic dental treatment (Chisholm Decl. ¶¶ 19--25; Swartz Decl. ¶ 14; Wells Decl. ¶¶ 13-20; Polson Decl. ¶¶ 7-12).

8. Practice of extracting teeth that could be saved by less intrusive means (Chisholm Decl. ¶¶ 22, 25; Swartz Decl. ¶ 14; Wells Decl. ¶¶ 13-20).

9. Failure to provide mentally ill prisoners medically necessary mental health treatment (i.e. psychotropic medication, therapy, and inpatient treatment) (Brislan Decl. ¶¶ 4-10; Gamez Decl. ¶¶ 3-23; Chisholm ¶¶ 3-9; Rodriguez ¶¶ 7-8; Swartz ¶¶ 10-13; [*523] Thomas Decl. ¶¶ 4-9; Polson Decl. ¶¶ 14-16; Verduzco ¶¶ 12-16).

10. Failure to provide suicidal and self-harming prisoners basic mental health care (Brislan Decl. ¶¶ 4-10; Swartz ¶¶ 10-13; Thomas Decl. ¶¶ 4-9; Verduzco ¶¶ 12-16).

ii. Subclass

Plaintiffs also allege that the conditions of confinement in ADC's isolation units pose a substantial risk of serious harm to all inmates and particularly to mentally ill inmates. Further, it is undisputed that ADC does not require a face-to-face mental health evaluation prior to placing an inmate in isolation. In opposition, Defendants reiterate their argument that to determine whether these conditions pose an unconstitutional risk of harm, the Court must assess each individual class member's exposure to the alleged conditions. The Court disagrees, however, for the same reasons outlined above, particularly when considering the effects of these conditions in the aggregate instead of each condition on its own. This is true even though all Subclass members may not be mentally ill because the risk of harm stemming from the allegedly unconstitutional conditions is the same for all inmates, even though the conditions may, in fact, impact the mentally ill in a more significant way. *See Rodriguez v. Hayes, 591 F.3d 1105, 1122 (9th Cir. 2009); Baby Neal, 43 F.3d at 56.*

Thus, the Court finds that commonality exists as to the following allegedly unconstitutional conditions in ADC's isolation units:

1. Inadequate psychiatric monitoring because of chronic understaffing (Brislan Decl. ¶ 8; Gamez Decl. ¶¶ 6, 22; Rodriguez Decl. ¶ 7; Swartz Decl. ¶ 10; Smith Decl. ¶ 6; Thomas Decl. ¶ 5; Polson Decl. ¶ 17).

2. Use of chemical agents against inmates on psychotropic medications (Brislan Decl. ¶ 8; Verduzco Decl. ¶ 9).

3. Lack of recreation (Brislan Decl. ¶ 11; Rodriguez Decl. ¶ 13; Thomas Decl. ¶ 6; Polson Decl. ¶ 18).

4. Extreme social isolation (Brislan Decl. ¶ 11; Gamez Decl. ¶ 24; Rodriguez Decl. ¶ 14; Smith Decl. ¶ 15; Thomas Decl. ¶ 6).

5. Constant cell illumination (Brislan Decl. ¶ 11; Rodriguez Decl. ¶ 12).

6. Limited property (Rodriguez Decl. ¶ 14).

7. Insufficient nutrition (Gamez Decl. ¶ 24; Rodriguez Decl. ¶ 13; Thomas Decl. ¶ 11).

C. Typicality

"The commonality and typicality requirements of *Rule 23(a)* tend to merge." *Wal- Mart, 131 S. Ct. at 2551 n. 5* (quoting *Falcon, 457 U.S. at 158-59*). In *Armstrong*, the Ninth Circuit explained that "named plaintiffs' injuries [need not] be identical with those of the other class members, only that the unnamed class members have injuries similar to those of the named plaintiffs, and that the injuries result from the same, injurious course of conduct." *Armstrong, 275 F.3d at 869.*

Defendants point out that not all of the named Plaintiffs have similar injuries. While true, the relevant inquiry is whether the named Plaintiffs have injuries typical to the class and not to each other. Nor is Defendants' reliance on *Schilling v. Kenton County, Ky., CV No. 10-143-DLB, 2011 U.S. Dist. LEXIS 8050, 2011 WL 293759, at *10 (E.D. Ky. Jan. 27, 2011)*, helpful because certification of this class does not require a merits-based inquiry to determine membership. Rather, as explained above, it is ADC's practices that determine whether inmates are exposed to a substantial risk of serious harm, irrespective of what their individual health care needs or circumstances may be. The Court finds the typicality factor is satisfied.

D. Adequacy of Representation

Finally, *Rule 23(a)(4)* requires that class representatives fairly and adequately represent the interests of the entire class. "This factor requires: (1) that the proposed representative Plaintiffs do not have conflicts of interest with the proposed class, and (2) that Plaintiffs are represented by qualified and competent counsel." *Wal-Mart, 603 F.3d at 614.*

Defendants only challenge the adequacy of Plaintiff Parsons, pointing out that he was released on parole (Doc. 326 at 36). The Court agrees that Parsons' release undermines his adequacy as a Class representative and he will be dismissed.

IV. *Rule 23(b)(2)*

Plaintiffs are also charged with satisfying one of the requirements in *Rule 23(b)* which applies when "the party opposing the class has acted or refused to act on grounds that apply generally to the class, so that final injunctive relief or corresponding declaratory relief is appropriate respecting the class as a whole." *FED. R. CIV. P. 23(b)(2)*. In this case, Plaintiffs allege that *Rule 23(b)(2)* is met because Defendants are obligated to provide constitutionally adequate health care and are aware of the systemic deficiencies in ADC's health care but have not taken corrective action.

Defendants focus again on the alleged factual differences among the class members and insist that these differences defeat certification under *Rule 23(b)(2)*. But as the Ninth Circuit explained in *Walters v. Reno*:

> [a]lthough common issues must predominate for class certification under *Rule 23(b)(3)*, no such requirement exists under *23(b)(2)*. It is sufficient if class members complain of a pattern or

practice that is generally applicable to the class as a whole. Even if some class members have not been injured by the challenged practice, a class may nevertheless be appropriate.

> *145 F.3d 1032, 1047 (9th Cir. 1998)* (citing 7A Charles Alan Wright, Arthur R. Miller & Mary Kay Kane, *Federal Practice & Procedure* § 1775 (2d ed. 1986)).

Plaintiffs' claims for injunctive relief stemming from allegedly unconstitutional conditions of confinement are the quintessential type of claims that *Rule 23(b)(2)* was meant to address. As discussed above, the claims of systemic deficiencies in ADC's health care system and unconstitutional conditions of confinement in isolation units apply to all proposed class members. And while the Court is certainly cognizant that any proposed injunction must also meet *Rule 65(d)*'s specificity requirement, the Court does not find that any proposed injunction here would be crafted "at a stratospheric level of abstraction." *Shook v. Bd. of County Comm'rs, 543 F.3d 597, 604 (10th Cir. 2008).* Even *Shook* recognized that plaintiffs are not "required to come forward with an injunction that satisfied *Rule 65(d)* with exacting precision at the class certification stage." *Id. at 606.* Further undermining Defendants' argument is their failure to introduce any authority supporting the notion that the proposed injunction in this case violates *Rule 65(d).* Indeed, the Ninth Circuit explained in *Rodriguez* that *Rule 23(b)(2)* certification is appropriate when "all class members seek the exact same relief as a matter of . . . constitutional right." *Rodriguez, 591 F.3d at 1126.*

This conclusion is bolstered when considering the effects of a potential injunction. The remedy in this case would not lie in providing specific care to specific inmates. Rather, the level of care and resources would be raised for all inmates. Thus, if successful, a proposed injunction addressing those practices would therefore prescribe "a standard of conduct applicable to all class members." *Shook, 543 F.3d at 605.* This case is "a paradigm of because injunctive relief for some inmates would necessarily result in injunctive relief for all inmates. *Colon v. Passaic County, 2009 U.S. Dist. LEXIS 45151, 2009 WL 1560156, at *5 (D. N. J. May 27, 2009)* (certifying a class of prisoners seeking injunctive and declaratory relief for allegedly unconstitutional conditions of confinement) (citations omitted).

The boundaries outlined in this Order and Plaintiff's preliminary outline of injunctive relief presented in their Complaint are sufficient at this stage to meet *Rule 23(b)(2)*'s requirements.

THE PRISON LITIGATION REFORM ACT

The Court is required to screen complaints brought by prisoners seeking relief against a governmental entity or an officer or an employee of a governmental entity. *28 U.S.C. § 1915A(a).* The Court must dismiss a complaint or portion thereof if a plaintiff has raised claims that are legally frivolous or malicious, that fail to state a claim upon which relief may be granted, or that seek monetary relief from a defendant who is immune from such relief. *28 U.S.C. § 1915A(b)(1)-(2).*

A pleading must contain a "short and plain statement of the claim *showing* that the pleader is entitled to relief." *Fed. R. Civ. P. 8(a)(2)* (emphasis added). While Rule 8 does not demand detailed factual allegations, "it demands more than an unadorned, the-defendant-unlawfully-harmed-me accusation." *Ashcroft v. Iqbal, 556 U.S. 662, 678, 129 S. Ct. 1937, 173 L. Ed. 2d 868 (2009).* "Threadbare recitals of the elements of a cause of action, supported by mere conclusory statements, do not suffice." *Id.* "Pro se plaintiffs proceeding [in forma pauperis] must . . . be given an opportunity to amend their complaint [prior to dismissal of the case] unless it is absolutely clear that the deficiencies of the complaint could not be cured by amendment." *Franklin v. Murphy, 745 F.2d 1221, 1228 n. 9 (9th Cir. 1984).* The United States Court of Appeals for the Ninth Circuit has instructed, courts must "continue to construe *pro se* filings liberally." *Hebbe v. Pliler, 627 F.3d 338, 342 (9th Cir. 2010).* A "complaint [filed by a *pro se* prisoner] 'must be held to less stringent standards than formal pleadings drafted by lawyers.'" Id. (quoting *Erickson v. Pardus, 551 U.S. 89, 94, 127 S. Ct. 2197, 167 L. Ed. 2d 1081 (2007) (per curiam)).*

Although *pro se* pleadings are liberally construed, *Haines v. Kerner, 404 U.S. 519, 520-21, 92 S. Ct. 594, 30 L. Ed. 2d 652 (1972),* conclusory and vague allegations will not support a cause of action. *Ivey v. Board of Regents of the University of Alaska, 673 F.2d 266, 268 (9th Cir. 1982).* Further, a liberal interpretation of a civil rights complaint may not supply essential elements of the claim that were not initially pled. *Id.*

"[A] complaint must contain sufficient factual matter, accepted as true, to 'state a claim to relief that is plausible on its face.'" *Id.* (quoting *Bell Atlantic Corp. v. Twombly, 550 U.S. 544, 570, 127 S. Ct. 1955, 167 L. Ed. 2d 929 (2007)).* A claim is plausible "when the plaintiff pleads factual content that allows the court to draw the reasonable inference that the defendant is liable for the misconduct alleged." *Id.* "Determining whether a complaint states a plausible claim for relief [is] . . . a context-specific task that requires the reviewing court to draw on its judicial experience and common sense." *Id. at 679.* Thus, although a plaintiff's specific factual allegations may be consistent with a constitutional claim, a court must assess whether there are other "more likely explanations" for a defendant's conduct. *Id. at 681.*

The Prison Litigation Reform Act (PLRA) requires an inmate to exhaust prison grievance procedures before filing suit in federal court. *See 42 U.S.C. § 1997e(a); Jones v. Bock, 549 U.S. 199, 202, 127 S. Ct. 910, 166 L. Ed. 2d 798 (2007); Jones v. Norris, 310 F.3d 610, 612 (8th Cir. 2002).* Exhaustion under PLRA is mandatory. *Jones, 549 U.S. at 211.* "[T]o properly exhaust administrative remedies, prisoners must 'complete the administrative review process in accordance with the applicable procedural rules,' rules that are defined not by the PLRA, but by the prison grievance process itself." *Id., 549 U.S. at 218* (quoting *Woodford v. Ngo, 548 U.S. 81, 88, 126 S. Ct. 2378, 165 L. Ed. 2d 368 (2006)).* Compliance with a prison's grievance procedures is, therefore, all that is required by the PLRA to properly exhaust. *Id.* Thus, the question of whether an inmate has properly exhausted administrative remedies will depend on the specifics of that particular prison's grievance policy. *See Id.* The prisoner must complete the administrative review process in accordance with the applicable rules. *See Woodford v. Ngo, 548 U.S. 81, 92, 126 S. Ct. 2378, 165 L. Ed. 2d 368 (2006).* Exhaustion is required for all suits about prison life, *Porter v. Nussle, 534 U.S. 516, 523, 122 S. Ct. 983, 152 L. Ed. 2d 12 (2002),* regardless of the type of relief offered through the administrative process, *Booth v. Churner, 532 U.S. 731, 741, 121 S. Ct. 1819, 149 L. Ed. 2d 958 (2001).* The defendant bears the initial burden to show that there was an available administrative remedy and that the prisoner did not exhaust it. *Albino v. Baca, 747 F.3d 1162, 1169, 1172 (9th Cir. 2014);*

The defendant bears the ultimate burden of proving failure to exhaust. *See Brown v. Valoff, 422 F.3d 926, 936 (9th Cir. 2005).* If the defendant initially shows that (1) an available administrative remedy existed and (2) the prisoner failed to exhaust that remedy, then the burden of production shifts to the plaintiff to bring forth evidence "showing that there is something in his particular case that made the existing and generally available administrative remedies effectively unavailable to him." *Albino, 747 F.3d at 1172.* Confusing or contradictory information given to a prisoner is relevant to the question "of whether relief was, as a practical matter, 'available.'" *Brown, 422 F.3d at 937.* Administrative remedies will be deemed unavailable and exhaustion excused if the inmate had no way of knowing the prison's grievance procedure, if the prison improperly processed an inmate's grievance, if prison officials misinformed an inmate regarding grievance procedures, if the inmate "did not have access to the necessary grievance forms within the prison's time limits for filing the grievance," or if prison staff took any other similar actions that interfered with an inmate's efforts to exhaust. *Albino, 747 F.3d at 1173.* If a prisoner has failed to exhaust available administrative remedies, the appropriate remedy is dismissal without prejudice. *Wyatt v. Terhune, 315 F.3d 1108, 1120 (9th Cir. 2003), overruled in part on other grounds by Albino, 747 F.3d 1162.*

"[A] [§ 1983] suit against a state official in his or her official capacity is not a suit against the official but rather is a suit against the official's office," *i.e.,* against the State. *Will v. Mich. Dept. of State Police, 491 U.S. 58, 71, 109 S. Ct. 2304, 105 L. Ed. 2d 45 (1989).* The State is not a "person" amenable to suit under § 1983. *Id.* The state and its agencies are immune from suit pursuant to the *Eleventh Amendment. Quern v. Jordan, 440 U.S. 332, 340-45, 99 S. Ct. 1139, 59 L. Ed. 2d 358 (1979); see Lawson v. Shelby Cnty., Tenn., 211 F.3d 331, 335 (6th Cir. 2000)* ("[T]he [Eleventh] Amendment prohibits suits against a 'state' in federal court whether for injunctive, declaratory or monetary relief."). The only exceptions to a state's immunity are (1) if the state has consented to suit or (2) if Congress has properly abrogated a state's immunity. *S & M Brands, Inc. v. Cooper, 527 F.3d 500, 507 (6th Cir. 2008). See Berndt v. Tennessee, 796 F.2d 879, 881 (6th Cir. 1986)* (noting that Tennessee has not waived immunity to suits under § 1983); *Hafer v. Melo, 502 U.S. 21, 25, 112 S. Ct. 358, 116 L. Ed. 2d 301 (1991)* (reaffirming that Congress did not abrogate states' immunity when it passed § 1983). The only other exception is when the *Ex parte Young* exception applies. *See S&M Brands, 527 F.3d at 507.* Under this exception, "a federal court can issue prospective injunctive and declaratory relief compelling a state official to comply with federal law." *Id.* (quoting *Will, 491 U.S. at 71 & n.10*).

Qualified immunity protects officials who acted in   an objectively reasonable manner and shields a government official from liability when his or her conduct does not violate "clearly established statutory or constitutional rights of which a reasonable person would have known." *Harlow v. Fitzgerald, 457 U.S. **800**, 818, 102 S. Ct. 2727, 73 L. Ed. 2d 396 (1982).* Qualified immunity is a question of law, not a question of fact. *McClendon v. Story County Sheriff's Office, 403 F.3d 510, 515 (8th Cir. 2005).* Thus, issues concerning qualified immunity are appropriately resolved on summary judgment. *See Mitchell v. Forsyth, 472 U.S. 511, 526, 105 S. Ct. 2806, 86 L. Ed. 2d 411 (1985)* (the privilege is "an immunity from suit rather than a mere defense to liability; and like an absolute immunity, it is effectively lost if a case is erroneously permitted to go to trial.").

To determine whether defendants are entitled to qualified immunity, courts generally consider two questions: (1) whether the facts alleged or shown, construed in the light most favorable to the plaintiff, establish a violation of a constitutional or statutory right; and (2) whether that right was so clearly established that a reasonable official would have known that his or her actions were unlawful. *Pearson v. Callahan, 555 U.S. 223, 232, 129 S. Ct. 808, 172 L. Ed. 2d 565 (2009); see also Saucier v. Katz, 533 U.S. 194, 201, 121 S. Ct. 2151, 150 L. Ed. 2d 272 (2001).* Defendants are entitled to qualified immunity only if no reasonable fact finder could answer both questions in the affirmative. *Nelson v. Correctional Medical Services, 583 F.3d 522, 528 (8th Cir. 2009).* Deference to the expertise of prison officials in matters of prison security is not absolute. *Cutter v. Wilkinson, 544 U.S. 709, 725 n. 13, 125 S. Ct. 2113, 161 L. Ed. 2d 1020 (2005); United States v. Williams, 791 F.2d 1383 (9th Cir. 1986).*

Standard for Injunctive Relief - A request for injunctive relief requires that a plaintiff make a showing of "real or immediate threat" of injury. *Hodgers-Durgin v. De La Vina, 199 F.3d 1037, 1042 (9th Cir. 1999)* (quoting *O'Shea v. Littleton, 414 U.S. 488, 502, 94 S. Ct. 669, 38 L. Ed. 2d 674 (1974)).* Plaintiff is entitled to preliminary injunctive relief only if he/she shows either: "(1) a likelihood of success on the merits and the possibility of irreparable injury; or (2) the existence of serious questions going to the merits and the balance of hardships tipping in [the movant's] favor." *MAI Sys. Corp. v. Peak Computer, Inc., 991 F.2d 511, 516-517 (9th Cir. 1993)* (quoting *Diamontiney v. Borg, 918 F.2d 793, 795 (9th Cir. 1990)).* Under either formulation of the test, the movant must demonstrate a significant threat of irreparable injury. *AGCC v. Coalition for Economic Equity, 950 F.2d 1401, 1410 (9th Cir. 1991).*

Further, in unusual circumstances where the preliminary injunction relates to the inmate's access to the district court, the district court need not consider the merits of the underlying complaint in considering whether to grant a preliminary injunction. *Diamontiney v. Borg, 918 F.2d 793, 796 (9th Cir. 1990).*

Preliminary Relief Different From Ultimate Relief - The purpose of preliminary injunctive relief is to preserve the status quo or to prevent irreparable injury pending the resolution of the underlying claim on the merits. Therefore, the party seeking preliminary injunctive relief "must necessarily establish a relationship between the injury claimed in the motion and the conduct asserted in the complaint." *Devose v. Herrington, 42 F.3d 470, 471 (8th Cir. 1994)* (*Eighth Amendment* claim cannot provide basis for preliminary injunction against alleged acts in retaliation for filing claim). Thus, Plaintiff must ordinarily seek injunctive relief related to the merits of his underlying claim. "A district court should not issue an injunction when the injunction in question is not of the same character, and deals with a matter lying wholly outside the issues in the suit." *Kaimowitz v. Orlando, Fla., 122 F.3d 41, 43 (11th Cir. 1997).*

To state a claim under § 1983 against a private entity performing a traditional public function, such as providing medical care in a prison, a plaintiff must allege facts to support that his constitutional rights were violated as a result of a policy, decision, or custom promulgated or endorsed by the private entity. *See Tsao v. Desert Palace, Inc., 698 F.3d 1128, 1138-39 (9th Cir. 2012); Buckner v. Toro, 116 F.3d 450, 452 (11th Cir. 1997).* Because there is no respondeat superior liability under § 1983, a defendant's position as the employer of someone who allegedly violated a plaintiff's constitutional rights. , "[A] plaintiff must allege facts, not simply conclusions, that show that an individual was personally involved in the deprivation of his civil rights." *Barren v. Harrington, 152 F.3d 1193, 1194 (9th Cir. 1998)*. For an individual to be liable in his official capacity, a plaintiff must allege that the official acted as a result of a policy, practice, or custom. *See Cortez v. County of Los Angeles, 294 F.3d 1186, 1188 (9th Cir. 2001)*. Further, there is no *respondeat superior* liability under § 1983, so a defendant's position as the supervisor of someone who allegedly violated a plaintiff's constitutional rights does not make him liable. *Monell v. Dep't of Soc. Servs., 436 U.S. 658, 691, 98 S. Ct. 2018, 56 L. Ed. 2d 611 (1978); Taylor v. List, 880 F.2d 1040, 1045 (9th Cir. 1989)*. A supervisor in his individual capacity "is only liable for constitutional violations of his subordinates if the supervisor participated in or directed the violations, or knew of the violations and failed to act to prevent them." *Taylor, 880 F.2d at 1045*. To state a claim for failure to train, a plaintiff must allege facts to support that the alleged failure amounted to deliberate indifference. *Canell v. Lightner, 143 F.3d 1210, 1213 (9th Cir. 1998)*. A plaintiff must allege facts to support that not only was particular training inadequate, but also that such inadequacy was the result of "a 'deliberate' or 'conscious' choice" on the part of the defendant. *Id. at 1213-14; see Clement v. Gomez, 298 F.3d 898, 905 (9th Cir. 2002)* (a plaintiff must allege facts to support that "in light of the duties assigned to specific officers or employees, the need for more or different training is [so] obvious, and the inadequacy so likely to result in violations of constitutional rights, that the policy[]makers . . . can reasonably be said to have been deliberately indifferent to the need." (quoting *City of Canton v. Harris, 489 U.S. 378, 390, 109 S. Ct. 1197, 103 L. Ed. 2d 412 (1989)*)).

JAMES JACKSON ELLSWORTH, PLAINTIFF, VS. CORIZON HEALTH, INC.,1 ET AL., DEFENDANTS. *2012 U.S. Dist. LEXIS 53276 (AZ. April 16, 2012)*

(SEE ALSO DISCUSSION UNDER ACCESS TO COURTS)

II. Plaintiff's Motion for Summary Judgment re: Exhaustion of Remedies

Plaintiff asserts that he is entitled to summary judgment on Defendants' affirmative defense that Plaintiff failed to exhaust his available administrative remedies. He argues that he was excused from the exhaustion requirement under the plain terms of Arizona Department of Corrections (ADC) Department Order 802.01, § 1.8, which Plaintiff asserts exempts emergency complaints from the formal grievance procedure. Plaintiff further asserts that, even though he was not required to exhaust administrative remedies, he did exhaust his administrative remedies by following the ADC's grievance procedure.

Defendants respond that "Plaintiff's conclusory statements citing to D.O. 802 are not enough to prove that his specific medical complaints constituted an 'emergency condition' within the meaning of D.O. 802" and that Plaintiff has failed to present evidence demonstrating that his prostate cancer presented an emergency medical condition under D.O. 802. Defendants further assert that D.O. 802.01, §1.8 does not obviate an inmate's obligation to exhaust the ADC's grievance and appeals procedures in the event of an emergency, but "simply allows an inmate to bring an emergency to the attention of staff, by any available means, rather than to rely on the written grievance procedure to alert staff to an emergency." (Doc. 137 at 6.)

Defendants next assert that the Grievance Appeal Response signed by Director Ryan on February 28, 2014 does not show that Plaintiff exhausted his administrative remedies because "Plaintiff does not provide any documents that were submitted by him as part of the grievance process related to the Grievance Appeal Response signed by Director Ryan on February 28, 2014, or any additional documents related to the other grievances submitted by Plaintiff." (Doc. 140 at 5.)

B. Exhaustion

Under the Prison Litigation Reform Act, a prisoner must exhaust "available" administrative remedies before filing an action in federal court. *See 42 U.S.C. § 1997e(a); Vaden v. Summerhill, 449 F.3d 1047, 1050 (9th Cir. 2006); Brown v. Valoff, 422 F.3d 926, 934-35 (9th Cir. 2005)*. The prisoner must complete the administrative review process in accordance with the applicable rules. *See Woodford v. Ngo, 548 U.S. 81, 92, 126 S. Ct. 2378, 165 L. Ed. 2d 368 (2006)*. Exhaustion is required for all suits about prison life, *Porter v. Nussle, 534 U.S. 516, 523,*

122 S. Ct. 983, 152 L. Ed. 2d 12 (2002), regardless of the type of relief offered through the administrative process, *Booth v. Churner, 532 U.S. 731, 741, 121 S. Ct. 1819, 149 L. Ed. 2d 958 (2001)*.

The defendant bears the initial burden to show that there was an available administrative remedy and that the prisoner did not exhaust it. *Albino v. Baca, 747 F.3d 1162, 1169, 1172 (9th Cir. 2014)*; *see Brown, 422 F.3d at 936-37* (a defendant must demonstrate that applicable relief remained available in the grievance process). Once that showing is made, the burden shifts to the prisoner, who must either demonstrate that he, in fact, exhausted administrative remedies or "come forward with evidence showing that there is something in his particular case that made the existing and generally available administrative remedies effectively unavailable to him." *Albino, 747 F.3d at 1172*. The ultimate burden, however, rests with the defendant. *Id.* Summary judgment is appropriate if the undisputed evidence, viewed in the light most favorable to the prisoner, shows a failure to exhaust. *Id. at 1166, 1168*; *see Fed. R. Civ. P. 56(a)*.

If summary judgment is denied, disputed factual questions relevant to exhaustion should be decided by the judge; a plaintiff is not entitled to a jury trial on the issue of exhaustion. *Albino, 747 F.3d at 1170-71*. But if a court finds that the prisoner exhausted administrative remedies, that administrative remedies were not available, or that the failure to exhaust administrative remedies should be excused, the case proceeds to the merits. *Id. at 1171*.

C. Facts regarding Exhaustion

ADC Department Order 802.06 outlines the formal inmate medical grievance process. (Doc. 113-2 at 5.) An inmate may appeal a response to a formal inmate medical grievance to the Director. (*Id.* at 6.) The decision of the Director for medical grievance appeals is final and constitutes exhaustion of all remedies for inmate medical grievances within ADC. (*Id.* at 7.) Section 802.01 entitled "General Information" provides, in part, that "[i]nmates are not required to use the formal Inmate Grievance Procedures to submit a verbal or written emergency complaint." (*Id.* at 3.) An emergency is defined as "a condition which, if processed through the normal grievance time frames, would subject the inmate to substantial risk of medical harm, personal injury or cause other serious and irreparable harm." (*Id.*) The Department Order further provides that "[a]ny emergency complaint received by staff shall be immediately evaluated through the chain of command to determine whether it is an emergency as defined in 1.8.1 of this section and requires immediate response outside of the Inmate Grievance Procedure time frames."

D. Discussion

Plaintiff argues that he was excused from the exhaustion requirement under the plain terms of ADC Department Order 802.01, § 1.8, which provides that "[i]nmates are not required to use the formal Inmate Grievance Procedures to submit a verbal or written emergency complaint." The emergency complaint procedure, however, is not a model of clarity. Section 1.8 clearly states that inmates are not required to use the formal grievance process in the case of an emergency,[4] but provides no further information as to exhaustion of remedies in the case of an emergency. The consequences of this ambiguity are on display in this case.

4   The Court is unconvinced by Defendants' argument that an inmate must still follow the formal grievance process even after submitting an emergency complaint. It is Defendants who are able to define the grievance process and how administrative remedies are exhausted and, thus, any ambiguity in their policy should be construed in favor of Plaintiff. *See Woodford, 548 U.S. at 90* (proper exhaustion requires using all steps that the agency holds out, and doing so properly).

Plaintiff provides a "consultation request" signed by Dr. Kessler, which states that Plaintiff told him that it was important to establish care with a urologist for treatment of his prostate cancer. (Doc. 25-9 at 1.) He argues that this evidence shows he orally pursued treatment for his prostate cancer and, therefore, was exempt from the formal administrative grievance process. Defendants argue that Plaintiff has not shown that his condition constituted an emergency within the meaning of Section 1.8.1, which provides that an emergency is "a condition which, if processed through the normal grievance time frames, would subject the inmate to substantial risk of medical harm, personal injury or cause other serious and irreparable harm." The Department Order, however, does not state who decides which conditions are "medical emergencies" or what happens when, after evaluation, a complaint is deemed to not constitute an emergency.

Despite the substantial ambiguity in the emergency complaint grievance process, Plaintiff is entitled to summary judgment on Defendants' exhaustion of administrative remedies affirmative defense because the uncontroverted evidence shows that he exhausted his claims to the Director's level. Plaintiff provides a January 13, 2014 response from Director Ryan responding to Plaintiff's request for "immediate and thorough treatment for [his] cancer or immediate release to get treatment by a competent doctor due to the life threatening nature of [his] cancer." (Doc. 114-2 at 1-2.) Defendants state that Plaintiff has failed to show that he exhausted his claims in this action because he did not provide any of the grievance documents that led to Director Ryan's final decision with his Motion for Summary Judgment. But Defendants point to nothing in their policy requiring Plaintiff to name every defendant or explicitly set forth his legal claims in his grievances. *Morton v. Hall, 599 F.3d 942, 946 (9th Cir. 2010)* (The level of detail in an administrative grievance necessary to properly exhaust a claim is determined by the prison's applicable grievance procedures, but "when a prison's grievance procedures are silent or incomplete as to factual specificity, a grievance suffices if it alerts the prison to the nature of the wrong for which redress is sought."). Plaintiff provides evidence that he exhausted his claims related to the fact that he was not being provided immediate and thorough treatment for his cancer. Defendants have not met their burden of demonstrating that Plaintiff did not exhaust his claims, and cannot shift the burden to Plaintiff by claiming that Plaintiff has not produced enough evidence to demonstrate that he did exhaust. *See Albino, 747 F.3d at 1172* (the ultimate burden of proof as to exhaustion remains with the defendant). Plaintiff has provided unrebutted evidence that he exhausted his administrative remedies, and thus, the Court finds that Plaintiff is entitled to summary judgment on the exhaustion defense.

ALDRICK JOSEPH LAPORTE, PLAINTIFF, VS. CORIZON HEALTH, INC., ET AL., DEFENDANTS. CIVIL ACTION NO. 14-CV-12231 UNITED STATES DISTRICT COURT FOR THE EASTERN DISTRICT OF MICHIGAN, SOUTHERN DIVISION

A. Plaintiff's Factual Allegations

Plaintiff alleges that in December of 2001, before he was incarcerated, he was in an automobile accident, which resulted in torn ligaments and a severed perineal nerve. (Docket no. 1 ¶9.) In February of 2002, his doctor told him that he could "expect pain forever due to the nerve damage in his leg" and that he could control the pain with medication and by wearing proper "braces, shoes, etc." (*Id.* ¶10.)

Plaintiff was incarcerated in October of 2003, and in January of 2004, he hyperextended his leg and fell. He was then transferred to another prison, where he fell again, in April or May of 2004. At that time, the prison doctor determined that Plaintiff should be seen by a specialist, but the Regional Management Office (RMO) denied the request. Plaintiff did have an MRI taken of his knee, which revealed a "chronically torn" ACL. Plaintiff claims that he was told by the prison doctor that CMS (which Plaintiff contends is not Corizon) "did not want to pay for ACL surgery;" thus, he was given pain medication. Plaintiff claims that his leg continued giving out. (*Id.* ¶11.)

Plaintiff alleges that over the next seven years, he was given various pain medications through the Pain Management Committee (PMC), with varying levels of success; he notes that he continued to fall due to his ACL injury and that he broke his pinky finger trying to prevent one of the falls. (*Id.* ¶12.) Ultimately, Plaintiff began taking Ultram, which "displayed some success" in alleviating his pain but did not help with his falling. (*Id.*) In 2011, Plaintiff tried to get a refill of his Ultram, but Dr. Borgerding denied the refill and ordered Plaintiff to return to the PMC for evaluation. (*Id.* ¶13.) The PMC changed Plaintiff's medication, which Plaintiff alleges caused him additional pain. (*Id.*)

In 2012, Plaintiff was transferred to another prison, at which time he requested a knee sleeve and new shoes. Plaintiff alleges that from that time through the time he filed his Complaint, several physical therapists ordered braces and shoes, but each time, Dr. Borgerding denied the request. (*Id.* ¶¶ 14-19.) One Physical Therapist even provided Plaintiff with a brace found in the back room of the clinic, but the brace was not fitted properly, so it "ate the skin off plaintiff's leg." (*Id.* ¶16.) Plaintiff alleges that he now suffers from "holes in his leg, severe pain/burns from brace rubbing and deformity." (*Id.* ¶17.)

Plaintiff claims that Defendants Corizon and Borgerding are liable for violating his *Eighth Amendment* rights "in refusing to medical care for a condition that is serious and ongoing;" that Defendant Corison showed "deliberate indifference resulting from somewhere between mere negligence (carelessness) and actual malice (intent to cause harm)" because it "plac[ed] the craven for profits above providing needed medical care;" that Defendant Borgerding "evidences his deliberate indifference and recklessness, and his actions falls (sic) somewhere between mere negligence and actual malice" because of his "outright denials of treatment;" that Defendants Corizon and Borgerding "disregarded the excessive risk to Plaintiff's health, safety, and wellbeing;" that all the Defendants violated the *Eighth Amendment* when they failed to provide adequate care; and that Defendants Corizon and Borgerding committed "the tort of negligence under the law of Michigan." (*Id.* ¶¶ 21-26.)

C. Analysis

Through its Motion for Judgment on the Pleadings, Defendant asserts that (1) Plaintiff has failed to exhaust his administrative remedies; (2) Plaintiff's claims related to medical care prior to June 5, 2011, are barred by the applicable statute of limitations; and (3) Plaintiff's Complaint fails to state a claim. (Docket no. 21.) As noted, Plaintiff has not filed a Response.

1. Exhaustion of Administrative Remedies

Defendant first argues that Plaintiff has failed to properly exhaust his administrative remedies. The Prison Litigation Reform Act (PLRA) of 1995 requires that a prisoner exhaust all administrative remedies before filing a *Section 1983* action. Specifically, the statute provides, "no action shall be brought with respect to prison conditions under *section 1983* . . . , or any other Federal law, by a prisoner confined in any jail, prison or other correctional facility until such administrative remedies as are available are exhausted." *42 U.S.C. § 1997e(a)*. But "while the preferred practice is for inmates to complete the grievance process prior to the filing of an action and to attach to their complaint documentation of that fact, 'because the exhaustion requirement is not jurisdictional, district courts have some discretion in determining compliance with the statute.'" *Curry v. Scott, 249 F.3d 493, 502 (6th Cir. 2001)*(citations omitted). Notably, the Sixth Circuit "requires an inmate to make 'affirmative efforts to comply with the administrative procedures,' and analyzes whether those 'efforts to exhaust were sufficient under the circumstances.'" *Risher v. Lappin, 639 F.3d 236, 240 (6th Cir. 2011)* (citing *Napier v. Laurel Cnty., Ky., 636 F.3d 218, 224 (6th Cir. 2011)*(internal quotation marks and citation omitted)).

The MDOC Policy Directive regarding prisoner grievances requires a prisoner to file a Step I grievance within five days of attempting to resolve the grievable issue with prison staff. MDOC Policy Directive 03.02.130(V). The prisoner must then proceed through Steps II and III of the grievance process and receive a Step III response to complete the process. *See Muttscheler v. Martin, No. 12-1221, 2013 U.S. Dist. LEXIS 99025, 2013 WL 3730095, at *3-5 (W.D. Mich. July 15, 2013)*.

As part of its Motion, Defendant has provided the Court with Plaintiff's Step III Grievance Record going back to May of 2009. (Docket no. 21-2.) In that time, Plaintiff has filed seven grievances; Defendant argues that only four of those grievances related to Plaintiff's medical care, and none of those grievances exhausts Plaintiff's claims against Defendant. (Docket no. 21 at 13, 20-23.) The undersigned agrees. February 5, 2014, Plaintiff alleged that Defendant Borgerding (in his position as RMO) denied his request for medical shoes, even though the shoes were prescribed by one of the doctors at the prison. (*See* docket no. 21-2 at 7.) In grievance no. URF-13-05-1474-24b, filed by Plaintiff on May 13, 2013, Plaintiff requested a prison transfer. (*See id.* at 14.) In grievance no. LMF-11-08-1792-12d1, filed by Plaintiff on August 19, 2011, Plaintiff alleged that Defendant Borgerding's decision to send Plaintiff to the PMC on July 26, 2011, was inappropriate. (*See id.* at 20.) In grievance no. LMF-11-08-1728-12d3, filed by Plaintiff on August 12, 2011, Plaintiff alleged that the PMC's decision to take him off his medication was unethical. (*See id.* at 26.) And in grievance no. LMF-11-02-0325-

12e4, filed by Plaintiff on February 2, 2011, Plaintiff alleged in general that the "MDOC PHS" improperly denied him athletic shoes. (*See id.* at 34.)

"The point of the PLRA exhaustion requirement is to allow prison officials 'a fair opportunity' to address grievances on the merits, to correct prison errors that can and should be corrected and to create an administrative record for those disputes that eventually end up in court." *Reed-Bey v. Pramstaller, 603 F. 3d 322, 324 (6th Cir. 2010)* (citation omitted). Thus, compliance with the PLRA requires that prisoners file a grievance against the person(s) they ultimately seek to sue. *Curry v. Scott, 249 F.3d 493, 505 (6th Cir. 2001).* In the first four of the above-referenced grievances, although Plaintiff does mention Defendant Borgerding and the PMC, Plaintiff makes no mention of Defendant Corizon. And as Defendant contends, although Plaintiff does mention "PHS" in the grievance he filed in February of 2011, the allegations against Corizon in his Complaint do not relate to Corizon's failure to provide proper shoes. (*See* docket no. 1.) Moreover, according to grievance records, Plaintiff ultimately received tennis shoes. (Docket no. 21-2 at 31.) Therefore, Plaintiff has not exhausted his administrative remedies with regard to Defendant Corizon, and his claims should be dismissed.

EARL FARMER, PLAINTIFF, V. C.L. "BUTCH" OTTER; RANDY BLADES; MS. WAMBLE-FISHER; CATHY STEFFEN; CORIZON MEDICAL SERVICES; IDAHO STATE DEPARTMENT OF CORRECTION; AND IDAHO STATE BOARD OF CORRECTION, DEFENDANTS. CASE NO. 1:14-CV-00345-BLW UNITED STATES DISTRICT COURT FOR THE DISTRICT OF IDAHO

BACKGROUND

1. Introduction

Plaintiff Earl Farmer is a prisoner in the custody of the Idaho Department of Correction (IDOC), currently incarcerated at Idaho State Correctional Institution (ISCI). On August 21, 2014, Farmer filed his Complaint against several defendants, including Corizon, LLC (misnamed Corizon Medical Services), Shell Wamble-Fisher, and Randy Blades, alleging that Defendants failed to protect him from physical and sexual assault by other inmates and were deliberately indifferent to his mental health. *Compl.*, Dkt. 3. Farmer asserted civil rights claims under *§ 1983*, as well as unidentified state law claims.

On November 5, 2014, the Court issued an Initial Review Order dismissing several defendants and all but one claim: an *Eight Amendment* cruel and unusual punishment claim for deliberate indifference to Farmer's mental health care needs against Defendants Blades, Wamble-Fisher, and Corizon. *Initial Review Order*, Dkt. 7. The Court summarized Farmer's only remaining claim as follows:

> Plaintiff asserts that IDOC policy allows only 6 mental health counseling sessions, regardless of the individual prisoner's mental health needs. He also alleges that he requested more sessions from Defendants Blade and Wamble-Fisher, as well as from individual medical providers employed by Corizon, Inc., the private entity that provides medical treatment to the inmates; however, he was not allowed any more than the 6 sessions provided by policy.

Id. at 9.

SPECIFICALLY, FARMER ALLEGES THAT DEFENDANTS WERE DELIBERATELY INDIFFERENT TO HIS MENTAL HEALTH WHEN IT DID NOT FOLLOW THE STANDARDS AS PROVIDED FOR IN CORIZON'S CONTRACT WITH THE IDOC. *COMPL.*, P. 6, DKT. 3. HE ALLEGES THAT HE REQUESTED TO HAVE MENTAL HEALTH COUNSELING, BUT HIS REQUEST WAS REFUSED DUE TO BUDGETARY CONCERNS. *ID.* FARMER FURTHER ALLEGES THAT DEFENDANTS DID NOT PROVIDE HIM NEEDED MENTAL HEALTH CARE BECAUSE IT ONLY HAS ONE PSYCHOLOGIST AND NO PSYCHIATRIST ON STAFF. *ID.* AT 6-7. IN ADDITION, FARMER ALLEGES THAT HIS MENTAL HEALTH ISSUES HAVE NOT BEEN PROPERLY DIAGNOSED BY A COMPETENT LICENSED MENTAL HEALTH PROFESSIONAL, AND THAT HE HAS NOT BEEN PLACED ON A MENTAL HEALTH PROGRAM OR PATHWAY THAT FITS HIS NEEDS. *ID.* AT 7. BECAUSE, HE RECEIVED INADEQUATE MEDICAL CARE, FARMER CLAIMS HE WAS PLACED IN A LIVING ENVIRONMENT WHERE HE WAS PHYSICALLY ATTACKED BY ANOTHER INMATE IN JANUARY 2014. *ID.*

Defendant Corizon and Defendants Blades and Wamble-Fisher have filed separate motions for summary judgment. Corizon argues that Farmer's Complaint should be dismissed because he failed to exhaust administrative remedies within the prison system for the allegations in this Complaint. Blades and Wamble-Fisher argue the merits of the claim--that Farmer was and is being provided appropriate mental health services.

ANALYSIS

1. CORIZON'S MOTION FOR SUMMARY JUDGMENT FOR FAILURE TO EXHAUST

A. EXHAUSTION REQUIREMENTS

The defendant bears the ultimate burden of proving failure to exhaust. *See Brown v. Valoff, 422 F.3d 926, 936 (9th Cir. 2005)*. If the defendant initially shows that (1) an available administrative remedy existed and (2) the prisoner failed to exhaust that remedy, then the burden of production shifts to the plaintiff to bring forth evidence "showing that there is something in his particular case that made the existing and generally available administrative remedies effectively unavailable to him." *Albino, 747 F.3d at 1172*. Confusing or contradictory information given to a prisoner is relevant to the question "of whether relief was, as a practical matter, 'available.'" *Brown, 422 F.3d at 937*. Administrative remedies will be deemed unavailable and exhaustion excused if the inmate had no way of knowing the prison's grievance procedure, if the prison improperly processed an inmate's grievance, if prison officials misinformed an inmate regarding grievance procedures, if the inmate "did not have access to the necessary grievance forms within the prison's time limits for filing the grievance," or if prison staff took any other similar actions that interfered with an inmate's efforts to exhaust. *Albino, 747 F.3d at 1173*.

If a prisoner has failed to exhaust available administrative remedies, the appropriate remedy is dismissal without prejudice. *Wyatt v. Terhune, 315 F.3d 1108, 1120 (9th Cir. 2003), overruled in part on other grounds by Albino, 747 F.3d 1162*.

B. GRIEVANCE PROCEDURE

Idaho has adopted a grievance procedure for inmates in its custody. *Whittington Aff.* ÷ 3, Dkt. 18-3. The IDOC grievance procedure consists of a three-step process: (1) the inmate seeks an informal resolution of the matter by completing an Offender Concern Form; (2) the inmate completes a Grievance Form if informal resolution cannot be accomplished; and (3) the inmate appeals any unfavorable response to the grievance. *Id.* ÷ ÷ 5-8. Once all three steps are completed, the offender grievance process is exhausted. *Id.* ÷ 9.

As an inmate incarcerated by the Idaho Department of Corrections, the Offender Grievance Process has been available to Famer. *Id.* ÷ 4; *Grievance and Informal Resolution Procedure for Offenders*, Dkt. 18-4. Farmer fully exhausted two grievances by completing all three steps: Grievance II 130001139 and Grievance II 140001240. *Whitting Aff.* ÷ 11. Grievance II 130001139 concerned the Prison Rape Elimination Act. *Id.* ÷ 13. In Grievance II 140001240, Farmer complained on November 17, 2014, after this suit was filed, that the IDOC and Corizon refused to provide him a parole plan for mental health aftercare (after his release) due to cost. *Id.* ÷ 14. In particular, he wanted the IDOC and Corizon to provide him mental health assistance after his release. *Id.* Farmer also filed a third grievance, which he apparently did not fully complete: Grievance II 130001073. In this last Grievance, Farmer requested counseling or therapy from an outside specialist, but that grievance did not allege that he was denied adequate mental health care due to cost. *Id.* ÷ 12. Farmer concedes that he received six additional counseling sessions as a result of the grievance. *Id.; Compl.* at 15, Dkt. 3.

Corizon now moves for summary judgment on the grounds that Farmer has failed to exhaust his administrative remedies because none of the grievances Farmer submitted raised the issues contained in the Complaint.

C. FARMER'S FAILURE TO EXHAUST ADMINISTRATIVE REMEDIES

The record demonstrates that Farmer did not exhaust his administrative remedies through the grievance process any of the allegation raised in his Complaint. In his Complaint, Farmer alleges that Corizon was deliberately indifferent to his mental health when it did not follow the standards as provided for in Corizon's contract with the IDOC. *Compl.*, p. 6, Dkt. 3. He alleges that he requested to have mental health counseling, but his request was refused due to budgetary concerns. *Id.* Farmer further alleges that Corizon does not provide him needed mental health care because it only has one psychologist and no psychiatrist on staff. *Id.* at 6-7. In addition, Farmer alleges that his mental health issues have not been properly diagnosed by a competent licensed mental health professional, and that he has not been placed on a mental health program or pathway that fits his needs. *Id.* at 7. Because he allegedly received inadequate medical care, Farmer claims, he was placed in a living environment where he was physically attacked by another inmate in January 2014. *Id.*

Yet, Farmer never filed a grievance alleging that: (1) Corizon did not follow the mental health standards as provided for in its contract with the IDOC; (2) his mental health care was inadequate due to staffing; (3) his mental health issues have not been properly diagnosed by a competent mental health professional; (4) he has not been placed on a mental health program or pathway that fits his needs; and (5) due to inadequate mental health care, he was placed in a living environment where he was physically assaulted by another inmate in January 2014. *Whittington Aff.* ÷ 15. Because Farmer did not raise any of these specific issues contained in his Complaint in a grievance, the claims in his Complaint are unexhausted and must be dismissed. *Woodford, 548 U.S. at 85.*

Farmer, however, argues that (1) Grievance II-130001073 includes the issues in the Complaint; (2) Grievance II-140001240 is "a continuation" of Grievance II-130001073; (3) Defendant Shell Wamble-Fisher did not allow his Concern Forms or Grievances to be processed between January 2013 and late 2014; and (4) Prison Rape Elimination Act ("PREA") claims do not need to be addressed through the grievance process. *Pl.'s Resp.*, Dkt. 21. The Court disagrees with each of these arguments and will address each in turn.

First, Grievance II-130001073, filed September 9, 2013, does not address the issues raised in the Complaint. Rather, with this grievance, Farmer requested counseling from an outside specialist. This grievance was granted at the Level II response, and Farmer received six outside counseling sessions. But Farmer's contends in his Complaint that he was denied counseling sessions beyond the six sessions provided in response to this Grievance. In other words, this Grievance 1240 did not raise the same issues as those raised in the Complaint..

SECOND, GRIEVANCE 1240 IS NOT A CONTINUATION OF GRIEVANCE II-130001073, AS FARMER CONTENDS. IN GRIEVANCE 1073, FARMER COMPLAINED THAT THE IDOC AND CORIZON REFUSED TO PROVIDE HIM A PLAN FOR MENTAL HEALTH CARE *AFTER* HIS RELEASE FROM PRISON BECAUSE OF COST. WHETHER ADDITIONAL CARE SHOULD HAVE BEEN PROVIDED *WHILE* FARMER REMAINED IN PRISON, WHICH IS WHAT FARMER CONTENDS IN HIS COMPLAINT, IS AN ENTIRELY DIFFERENT ISSUE FROM WHETHER FARMER SHOULD RECEIVE CARE *AFTER* HIS RELEASE, WHILE HE IS ON PAROLE. MOREOVER, THE IDAHO GRIEVANCE POLICY REQUIRES THAT EACH GRIEVANCE ADDRESS ONLY A SINGLE ISSUE AND THERE CANNOT BE "CONTINUING" GRIEVANCES. *GRIEVANCE AND INFORMAL RESOLUTION PROCEDURE FOR OFFENDERS*, P. 9, DKT. 18.

However, even if Grievance 1073 did arguably encompass the allegations in Farmer's Complaint, it was not filed until after the Complaint was filed, and therefore Farmer did not exhaust his administrative remedies prior to initiating this action. *See 42 U.S.C.* ~ 1997e(a); *see also Hall v. Reinke*, No. 1:13-cv-118-REB, 2014 U.S. Dist. LEXIS 136372, 2014 WL 4793955, at *6 (D. Idaho Sept. 25, 2014) (unpublished) ("A claim may be exhausted prior to filing suit or during suit, *so long as exhaustion was completed before the first time the prisoner sought to include the claim in the suit*.") (emphasis added). If Corizon did not know about the specific problem, they could not attempt to remedy it.

Third, there is no evidence that Wamble-Fisher denied Farmer access to the grievance process. The only evidence Farmer provides is a series of documents that appear to come from an unrelated whistle-blower case; Farmer argues that these documents demonstrate Wamble-Fisher's lack of credibility and propensity to alter documents. But these documents do nothing to show that Wamble-Fisher somehow impeded *Farmer's* access to the grievance process. Indeed, the fact that Farmer filed five concern forms and grievances in 2013, and two more in 2014 belies his allegations that Wamble-Fisher prevented him from filing a grievance during this same time frame. Farmer does not explain how he filed these five concern forms or grievance but failed to file a single grievance raising the same concerns raised in his Complaint.

However, even assuming that Farmer's allegations were true, it would not matter because Farmer did not have to go through Wamble-Fisher to file a grievance. The Idaho Grievance Policy makes clear that if a staff member does not respond to an Offender Concern Form within seven days, the inmate can elect to submit another Offender Concern Form to another staff member or use the grievance process. *Grievance and Informal Resolution Procedure for Offenders*, p. 3. Dkt. 18. So, if Wamble-Fisher ignored or impeded Farmer's concern forms or delayed the grievance process as Farmer alleges, he could have simply bypassed that step and filed a grievance in a lockbox that is provided for all inmates to use for confidential offender/grievance/appeal forms. *Id.*, p. 6.

Finally, several problems exist with Farmer's argument that his claim qualifies as a "PREA" claim and thus does not need to be exhausted. Congress enacted the PREA to address the problem of rape in prison by creating national standards to prevent, detect, and respond to prison rape. *See, e.g. Hatcher v. Harrington, No. 14-00554 JMS/KSC, 2015 U.S. Dist. LEXIS 13799, 2015 WL 474313, at *4 (D. Haw. Feb. 5, 2015)*. Neither Farmer's deliberate indifference claim at issue here nor any of the grievances he filed in 2013 and 2014 raise concerns about sexual abuse or prison rape (which he contends occurred in 1997); instead, his claims and grievances involve issues with access to mental health counseling. Thus, it is not clear that Farmer's claim would qualify as a PLRA. Indeed, it is questionable that PREA even creates a private cause of action that can be brought by an individual plaintiff. *Hatcher v. Harrington, No. 14-00554 JMS/KSC, 2015 U.S. Dist. LEXIS 13799, 2015 WL 474313, at *5 (D. Haw. Feb. 5, 2015)* (listing cases) ("Nothing in the PREA explicitly or implicitly suggests that Congress intended to create a private right of action for inmates to sue prison officials for noncompliance with the Act."). Finally, many courts have held that the PREA's reporting requirements do not supersede the PLRA's exhaustion requirements. *See, e.g., Omaro v. Annucci, 68 F. Supp. 3d 359, 2014 WL 6068573, at *4 (W.D.N.Y. 2014)* ("Nothing in the text or legislative history of the PREA suggests that it was intended to abrogate the PLRA's exhaustion requirement."); *Lamb v. Franke, No. 2:12-cv-367-MO, 2013 U.S. Dist. LEXIS 22708, 2013 WL 638836, at *2 (D.Or. Feb. 14, 2013)* (unpublished) ("The PREA does not impose an alternative remedial scheme, nor does it supersede PLRA's exhaustion requirement.").

In sum, Farmer was required to exhaust his administrative remedies before filing suit but failed to so. Accordingly, the Court will grant Corizon's motion for summary judgment.

JASON KEEL, PLAINTIFF, VS. CORIZON MEDICAL SERVICES, ET AL., DEFENDANTS. CAUSE NO. 3:14-CV-1492 UNITED STATES DISTRICT COURT FOR THE NORTHERN DISTRICT OF INDIANA, SOUTH BEND DIVISION

BACKGROUND

Jason Keel, a former inmate at the Miami Correctional Facility ("Miami"), brought this action on May 2, 2014, pursuant to *42 U.S.C. § 1983*. (DE #1.) The Court screened the complaint pursuant to *28 U.S.C. § 1915A*, and granted him leave to proceed on a claim that Dr. Mitcheff, the regional medical director for Corizon Medical Services[1], refused to treat Keel's hand problems in March 2014. (DE #6.) And, because Keel alleged that he is still receiving inadequate medical care with respect to his hand, he was also granted leave to proceed on a claim for injunctive relief against Dr. Mitcheff, pertaining to his current medical needs. (*Id.*)

1   A private company which provides medical care at Indiana   Department of Correction facilities.

In his motion for summary judgment, Dr. Mitcheff argues that Keel has failed to exhaust his available administrative remedies prior to filing suit as required by the Prisoner Litigation Reform Act ("PLRA") and, therefore, these claims must be dismissed. Keel was provided with a "Notice of Summary Judgment Motion" as required by *N.D. Ind. L.R. 56-1* and a copy of both *Federal Rule of Civil Procedure 56* and *Local Rule 56-1*. (DE #36.) That notice clearly informed him that unless he disputed the facts presented by the defendant, the court could accept those facts as true. *Fed. R. Civ. P. 56(e)* ("If a party . . . fails to properly address another party's assertion of fact . . . the court may . . . consider the fact undisputed for purposes of the motion."). It also told him that unless he submitted evidence creating a factual dispute, he could lose this case. *Fed. R. Civ. P. 56(a)* ("The court shall grant summary judgment if the movant shows that there is no genuine dispute as to any material fact and the movant is entitled to judgment as a matter of law."). Keel has filed his response (DE #46) and Defendant filed a reply (DE #47). The motion is therefore fully briefed and ripe for adjudication.

Facts

At all relevant times, and pursuant to Indiana Department of Correction ("IDOC") policy, Miami has an Offender Grievance Process under which an inmate can grieve a broad range of issues related to their conditions of confinement. (DE #34-1, Ex. A ¶ 7; Ex. B.) All inmates are made aware of the grievance process during orientation and a copy of the process is available in the law library. (Ex. A ¶ 7; Ex. B.) The process begins with the inmate attempting to resolve the matter informally with staff. (Ex. A ¶ 9.) If the issue cannot be resolved informally, the inmate must file a formal grievance within 10 days of the underlying incident. (*Id.* ¶ 9; Ex. B.) If the grievance is not resolved to the inmate's satisfaction, he must file an appeal within 10 working days of the grievance response. (*Id.* ¶ 8; Ex. B.) The grievance manager reviews the appeal and submits a response. (*Id.* ¶ 7; Ex. B.) An inmate has not fully exhausted the Offender Grievance Process until he completes all three steps of the process and receives a response from the Department's Offender Grievance Manager. (*Id.* ¶ 10; Ex. B.) Moreover, exhausting the grievance procedure requires timely pursuing each step of the informal and formal process. (*Id.*)

On October 21, 2013, Keel filed Grievance No. 79052, complaining about the medical care he received from Dr. Kream, Dr. Loveridge and Nurse Shalala. (DE #46 at 11.) He fully exhausted that grievance on December 18, 2013. (*Id.* at 6.) According to the grievance records kept and maintained at Miami, Keel has initiated three (3) grievances in 2014 that have been fully exhausted: Grievance Numbers 81396, 81760 and 82172 (Ex. A, ¶ 11; Ex. C.) In Grievance No. 81396, Keel complained about prison staff losing his property in conjunction with a move to the infirmary. (Ex. A ¶ 12; Ex. C.) This grievance was not fully exhausted until May 22, 2014. (*Id.*) In Grievance No. 81760, he complained about his medical care, including being in continuous pain and not being able to exercise. (*Id.*) Notably, this grievance complained about Dr. Mandaret, not Dr. Mitcheff. It was not fully exhausted until June 3, 2014. (*Id.*) In Grievance No. 82172, he complained about not being able to obtain information from the state medical licensing board. (*Id.*) This grievance was not fully exhausted until May 29, 2014. (*Id.*)

Pursuant to the Prison Litigation Reform Act ("PLRA"), prisoners are prohibited from bringing an action in federal court with respect to prison conditions "until such administrative remedies as are available are exhausted." *42 U.S.C. § 1997e(a)*. An inmate must exhaust before bringing his lawsuit, and efforts to exhaust while the case is pending do not satisfy *42 U.S.C. § 1997e(a). Ford v. Johnson, 362 F.3d 395, 398 (7th Cir. 2004)* ("exhaustion must precede litigation"); *Perez v. Wisconsin Department of Corrections, 182 F.3d 532, 535 (7th Cir. 1999)* (compliance with *42 U.S.C. § 1997e(a)* is a "precondition to suit"). For exhaustion purposes, an inmate is deemed to have "brought" the action on the date when his complaint is tendered for mailing. *Ford, 362 F.3d at 400.*

The failure to exhaust is an affirmative defense on which the defendant bears the burden of proof. *See Jones v. Bock, 549 U.S. 199, 216, 127 S. Ct. 910, 166 L. Ed. 2d 798 (2007); Dole v. Chandler, 438 F.3d 804, 809 (7th Cir. 2006).* The U.S. Court of Appeals for the Seventh Circuit has taken a "strict compliance approach to exhaustion." *Dole, 438 F.3d at 809.* Thus, "[t]o exhaust remedies, a prisoner must file complaints and appeals in the place, and at the time, the prison's administrative rules require." *Pozo v. McCaughtry, 286 F.3d 1022, 1025 (7th Cir. 2002).* "[A] prisoner who does not properly take each step within the administrative process has failed to exhaust state remedies." *Id. at 1024.*

Here, Dr. Mitcheff argues that Keel did not properly exhaust his administrative remedies before filing suit. As outlined above, the record reflects that Keel exhausted three grievances in 2014 and none were related to Mr. Mitcheff's March 2014 treatment of his hand.

Keel nevertheless maintains that he exhausted his administrative remedies by pointing to a grievance he filed on October 21, 2013. (DE #46 at 6.) However, that grievance was filed four months before Dr. Mitcheff allegedly denied him medical treatment for his hand. In addition, that October 2013 grievance did not relate to Dr. Mitcheff's treatment of Keel's hand. Thus, the October 2013 grievance is insufficient to demonstrate that Keel exhausted his administrative remedies for his claims against Dr. Mitcheff in this case. Therefore, the undisputed facts show that Keel did not exhaust his administrative remedies regarding his claims that Dr. Mitcheff denied him medical treatment for his hand in March 2014 and beyond.

WILLIAM R. TUBBS, PLAINTIFF V. CORIZON, INC.; ET AL., DEFENDANTS 5:13CV00377-BSM-JJV UNITED STATES DISTRICT COURT FOR THE EASTERN DISTRICT OF ARKANSAS, PINE BLUFF DIVISION

(SEE ALSO DISCUSSION UNDER MEDICAL CARE)

I. INTRODUCTION

William R. Tubbs ("Plaintiff") is an inmate of the Arkansas Department of Correction ("ADC") and he alleges the named Defendants[1] exhibited deliberate indifference toward his serious medical needs. (Doc. No. 52.) Pending before the Court is Defendants' Motion for Summary Judgment. (Doc. No. 167.) Plaintiff has not responded to this Motion and the time for doing so has passed.

1   Only Defendants Estella Bland, Corizon, LLC, Annette Esaw, Laura Morgan, Amanda Pevey, and Sherie Rice remain. All other Defendants have been dismissed. (Doc. No. 174.)

III. ANALYSIS

Plaintiff alleges Defendants violated his rights by (1) denying him a cane; (2) failing to refer him to a provider in January 2013; and (3) not giving him appropriate doses of pain medication for back pain. (Doc. No. 52 at 7-9.) Defendants argue (1) Plaintiff failed to exhaust his administrative remedies against Defendants Morgan, Pevey, and Corizon, LLC; (2) he only exhausted claims related to a July 23, 2013, encounter against Defendant Bland; and (3) the record establishes that none of the named Defendants were deliberately indifferent to Plaintiff's medical needs. For the reasons below, I conclude Defendants are entitled to summary judgment.

A. Exhaustion of Administrative Remedies

The Prison Litigation Reform Act (PLRA) requires an inmate to exhaust prison grievance procedures before filing suit in federal court. *See 42 U.S.C. § 1997e(a)*; *Jones v. Bock, 549 U.S. 199, 202, 127 S. Ct. 910, 166 L. Ed. 2d 798 (2007)*; *Jones v. Norris, 310 F.3d 610, 612 (8th Cir. 2002)*. Exhaustion under the PLRA is mandatory. *Jones, 549 U.S. at 211*. "[T]o properly exhaust administrative remedies, prisoners must 'complete the administrative review process in accordance with the applicable procedural rules,' rules that are defined not by the PLRA, but by the prison grievance process itself." *Id., 549 U.S. at 218* (quoting *Woodford v. Ngo, 548 U.S. 81, 88, 126 S. Ct. 2378, 165 L. Ed. 2d 368 (2006)*). Compliance with a prison's grievance procedures is, therefore, all that is required by the PLRA to properly exhaust. *Id.* Thus, the question of whether an inmate has properly exhausted administrative remedies will depend on the specifics of that particular prison's grievance policy. *See Id.* Plaintiff's claims are governed by Administrative Directive 12-16. (Doc. No. 169-1 at 3.) An inmate who believes he has been wronged is first required to file an informal resolution. (*Id.* at 7-10.) If the inmate is unsatisfied with the outcome of the informal resolution, he may proceed to the formal grievance procedure which entitles him to a response, first from the appropriate medical personnel, and then, if desired, from the ADC Deputy Director. (*Id.* at 10-14.) Inmates must be specific as to their issues and any personnel involved. (*Id.* at 7.)

The record shows Plaintiff exhausted eight grievances[2] during the time period relevant to this suit. (Doc. No. 169-1 at 2.) Defendants   state none of these grievances properly exhausted any claims against Defendants Morgan, Pevey, or Corizon, LLC. I agree. Neither Morgan nor Corizon, LLC is explicitly referenced in the eight grievances. Plaintiff only names "Pevey" in grievance CU-13-2065. (*Id.* at 45.) Defendants state this is not a reference to Defendant Pevey, who is a nurse, but rather an ADC Garment Factory Supervisor of the same name. (Doc. No. 169 at 4 n.1.) A review of CU-13-2065 supports their assertion. Plaintiff states he sought permission from Glover and "Pevey", his garment factory supervisors, "not to come back to P.M. work do (sic) to my pain." (Doc. No. 169-1 at 45.)

2   These grievances are numbered: CU-13-00237, CU-13-00568, CU-13-00637, CU-13-01058, CU-13-01226, CU-13-01514, CU-13-02064, and CU-13-02065. (Doc. No. 169-1 at 2.)

With respect to Defendant Bland, only grievance CU-13-2064 exhausts relevant claims against her. (*Id.* at 41.) These claims relate to a July 23, 2013, encounter where Plaintiff complained of severe pain but was allegedly not given sufficient pain medication. (*Id.*) Defendant Bland was also referenced in CU-13-01226, but no actual claim was stated against her. (*Id.* at 35.) Rather, this grievance stated Defendant Esaw had not provided Plaintiff with a cane which Bland had previously authorized. (*Id.*)

Based on the foregoing, I recommend Defendants Morgan, Pevey, and Corizon, LLC be dismissed for Plaintiff's failure to exhaust administrative remedies. Additionally, any claims against Defendant Bland which do not arise from the July 23, 2013, encounter should also be dismissed on this basis.

HAROLD DAVEY CASSELL ADC # 073885, PLAINTIFF V. CORRECT CARE SOLUTIONS, LLC AND CORIZON, INC., DEFENDANTS 5:14CV00403-DPM-JJV UNITED STATES DISTRICT COURT FOR THE EASTERN DISTRICT OF ARKANSAS, PINE BLUFF DIVISION

(SEE ALSO DISCUSSION UNDER MEDICAL CARE)

I. INTRODUCTION

Harold Davey Cassell ("Plaintiff") is an inmate of the Arkansas Department of Correction ("ADC"). He alleges that Corizon, LLC[1] and Correct Care Solutions, LLC ("Defendants") have exhibited deliberate indifference to his serious medical needs. (Doc. No. 1.) Specifically, Plaintiff suffers from Hepatitis-C and contends that Defendants failed to treat his condition with the drugs Victrelis and Incivek when both were approved by the Food and Drug Administration in 2011. (*Id.* at ¶¶ 12-15.) He claims Defendants were also deliberately indifferent when they failed to administer the drugs Olysio and Savaldi, which were approved in 2013. (*Id.* at ¶¶ 23-26.) Defendants have now motioned for summary judgment (Doc. No. 27) and Plaintiff has responded (Doc. No. 32).

1 This Defendant is currently listed as "Corizon, Inc" on the docket. The Clerk shall alter the listing to reflect the appropriate name.

III. ANALYSIS

Defendants raise three arguments in support of their Motion for Summary Judgment. First, they argue that Plaintiff failed to exhaust his administrative remedies against Defendant Correct Care Solutions prior to filing this suit. Second, they contend that Defendants, both of whom are corporations, cannot be held liable for the alleged misconduct of their employees pursuant to a theory of *respondeat superior*. Finally, Defendants argue that Plaintiff has now been provided with Havaroni, one of the newest drug treatments for Hepatitis-C, and that he suffered no injury as a result of any delay in treatment. For the reasons stated hereafter, I conclude that Defendants' Motion should be granted.

A. Exhaustion of Administrative Remedies

The Prison Litigation Reform Act (PLRA) requires an inmate to exhaust prison grievance procedures before filing suit in federal court. *See 42 U.S.C. § 1997e(a); Jones v. Bock, 549 U.S. 199, 202, 127 S. Ct. 910, 166 L. Ed. 2d 798 (2007); Jones v. Norris, 310 F.3d 610, 612 (8th Cir. 2002).* Exhaustion under the PLRA is mandatory. *Jones, 549 U.S. at 211.* "[T]o properly exhaust administrative remedies, prisoners must 'complete the administrative review process in accordance with the applicable procedural rules,' rules that are defined not by the PLRA, but by the prison grievance process itself." *Id., 549 U.S. at 218* (quoting *Woodford v. Ngo, 548 U.S. 81, 88, 126 S. Ct. 2378, 165 L. Ed. 2d 368 (2006)).* Compliance with a prison's grievance procedures is, therefore, all that is required by the PLRA to properly exhaust. *Id.* Thus, the question as to whether an inmate has properly exhausted administrative remedies will depend on the specifics of that particular prison's grievance policy. *See Id.*

Here, Plaintiff's claims are governed by Administrative Directives 12-16 and 14-16. The relevant procedures for medical grievances are consistent across both directives, which require an inmate who believes he has been wronged to file an informal resolution. (Doc. No. 28-2 at 5-6.) If the inmate is unsatisfied with the outcome of the informal resolution, he may proceed to the formal grievance procedure which entitles him to a response, first from the Health Service Administrator, and then, if desired, from an ADC Deputy, Chief Deputy, or Assistant Director. (*Id.* at 8-11.) Inmates must be specific as to their issues and any personnel involved. (*Id.* at 5-6.)

Defendants state that Correct Care Solutions did not begin their contract with the ADC until January 1, 2014. (Doc. No. 29 at 9.) Plaintiff does not appear to dispute this assertion. From January 1, 2014, until this suit was filed on October 30, 2014, Plaintiff filed thirteen medical grievances.[2] (Doc. No. 28-4 at 1-2.) After review of these grievances, I conclude Plaintiff failed to properly exhaust the claims which he now brings against Correct Care Solutions. Notably, none of the grievances makes any reference to Victrelis, Incivek, Olysio, or Savaldi, the drugs which Plaintiff now alleges should have been administered to him. Instead, the grievances raise various issues which are not relevant to this case: (1) CU-14-00162 complained of anal bleeding, possibly related to hemorrhoids, and alleged that the medication prescribed for this ailment had been ineffective; (2) CU-14-00255 complained that non-party Lasonya Griswold found no need for a medical follow-up despite a diagnostic result indicating that Plaintiff's platelet levels had dropped; (3) CU-14-00477, CU-14-00536, and CU-14-00803 each complain about non-party Laura Morgan's failure to adhere to ADC grievance policy; (4) CU-14-00804 complains that Plaintiff was not afforded an opportunity to discuss the results of a colonoscopy with medical staff; (5) CU-14-00805 and CU-14-00850 allege that Correct Care Solutions and unit medical staff denied him a follow-up with an outside specialist to discuss various medications which that specialist had prescribed; (6) CU-14-00932 and CU-14-01045 allege that non-party Dana Peyton was untruthful in her responses to Plaintiff's earlier grievances; (7) CU-14-01514 asks for the results of a blood test; and (8) CU-14-01515 complains that he has not received boots which medical staff indicated would be prescribed for him. (Doc. No. 28-3 at 4-45.)

2   The affidavit of Medical Grievance Coordinator Shelly Byers notes, however, that only twelve of these grievances were actually exhausted. (Doc. No. 28-4 at 1.) She states that Plaintiff failed to fully appeal grievance CU-14-01567. (*Id.*)

For his part, Plaintiff argues that some of the medical conditions raised in the grievances, most notably the anal bleeding, are "extraheptic manifestations" and therefore related to Plaintiff's Hepatitis-C. (Doc. No. 32-3 ¶¶ 2-3, 7-8.) Accepting this argument as true, Plaintiff still failed to raise the issues which underlie this case, namely whether Correct Care Solutions was deliberately indifferent in failing to prescribe certain drugs to combat his Hepatitis-C. Plaintiff also contends that those grievances which raise issues of inadequate procedure are indicative of an effort by Correct Care Solutions to "cause external impediment" and "deny prisoners due process to the grievance procedure." (*Id.* ¶¶ 5-6.) These arguments are unsupported by any substantive evidence. Moreover, even if prison staff failed to respond adequately or truthfully to Plaintiff's grievances, there is no indication that anyone prevented Plaintiff from grieving and exhausting the claims he raises in this suit. Finally, Plaintiff states that he apprised Correct Care Solutions of his situation by way of a letter sent by his counsel to the Regional Director. (Doc. No. 32-3 at 36.) This communication was not part of the official grievance procedure, however, and cannot substitute for a properly exhausted grievance.

Based on the foregoing, I recommend that Defendant Correct Care Solutions be dismissed for failure to exhaust administrative remedies.

DWAYNE R. STEPHENSON, PLAINTIFF, VS. CORIZON MEDICAL SERVICES, DR. YOUNG, NP POULSON, ET AL., DEFENDANTS. Case No. 1:14-cv-00460-BLW UNITED STATES DISTRICT COURT FOR THE DISTRICT OF IDAHO

DEFENDANTS' MOTION FOR SUMMARY JUDGMENT: EXHAUSTION OF ADMINISTRATIVE REMEDIES

IN THE PENDING MOTION FOR SUMMARY JUDGMENT, THE CORIZON DEFENDANTS ARGUE THAT PLAINTIFF FAILED TO EXHAUST HIS ADMINISTRATIVE REMEDIES COMPLETELY BEFORE FILING HIS LAWSUIT, MANDATING DISMISSAL WITHOUT PREJUDICE. FOR THE REASONS THAT FOLLOW, THE COURT AGREES.

1. PLAINTIFF'S ALLEGATIONS AND UNDISPUTED MATERIAL FACTS

PLAINTIFF FILED HIS COMPLAINT ON OCTOBER 28, 2014. HE CONTENDS THAT, AFTER UNDERGOING A NECK SURGERY IN OCTOBER 2013, SOMETHING IN HIS NECK "SNAPPED," AND THEREAFTER HE SUFFERED CONTINUOUS PAIN. HE ASSERTS THAT THE

MEDICAL PROVIDERS AT THE PRISON--DEFENDANTS DR. MURRAY YOUNG AND NURSE PRACTITIONER WILLIAM POULSON, WHO WORK FOR CORIZON, LLC --HAVE REFUSED TO GIVE HIM PROPER DIAGNOSES AND TREATMENTS AFTER THAT DATE.

IN MARCH 2014, PLAINTIFF SIGNED FORMS GIVING PERMISSION FOR INMATE REPRESENTATIVES IN AN ONGOING CLASS ACTION LAWSUIT TO DISCUSS HIS MEDICAL ISSUES WITH IDAHO DEPARTMENT OF CORRECTION (IDOC) MEDICAL SERVICES ADMINISTRATOR RONA SIEGERT AND OTHERS AT STATUS MEETINGS WHERE THE MONITORING OF THE PROVISION OF MEDICAL SERVICES IS DISCUSSED AMONG IDOC OFFICIALS, CORIZON OFFICIALS, INMATES, LAWYERS, AND OTHER INTERESTED REPRESENTATIVES. THE PERMISSION FORM STATES:

> I understand that this form is not a substitute for a . . . grievance form. . . . I am also still required to follow the concern/grievance process if I want to grieve this issue.

(Plaintiff's Exhibit, Dkt. 17-2, p. 1.)

On October 6, 2014, Plaintiff filed a grievance on the same medical issues, which was denied. On November 5, 2014, he filed an appeal, but his appeal form was returned because the handwriting was partially illegible, and he resubmitted it. The response was returned to Plaintiff on November 12, 2014. However, Plaintiff filed his Complaint in this matter on October 28, 2014, before the appeal was completed.

3. IDOC Grievance Process

The IDOC has a simple grievance process, consisting of three stages. First, an inmate with a concern must seek resolution of the problem by filling out an offender concern form, addressed to a staff person capable of resolving the issue. If the issue cannot be resolved through the use of a concern form, the inmate must then file a grievance form. The grievance is then resolved by a Level 1 Initial Response, which is reviewed by a Level 2 Reviewing Authority Response, and then returned to the inmate. If the grievance did not resolve the issue satisfactorily, the inmate must file an appeal, which is reviewed and decided by a Level 3 Appellate Authority Response. When all three of these steps--concern form, grievance form, and grievance appeal--are completed, the administrative grievance process is exhausted. (Affidavit of Jill Whittington, Dkt. 13-3.) The procedure requires that the grievance and appeal forms be handwritten legibly; if they are not, they are returned to the inmate with instructions to make the writing legible. (IDOC Grievance Procedures, Dkt. 13-4, p. 10.)

4. Discussion and Conclusion

The law is clear that (1) the particular prison grievance procedures must be followed as specified in the prison's written policies; and (2) a claim cannot be included in a civil rights complaint unless it was exhausted before the time it is first included in the lawsuit. Here, Plaintiff attempted to informally resolve his problem by taking it to the class action medical monitoring meeting. However, nowhere does Plaintiff point to any procedures that state that this method is an acceptable alternative to filing a prison grievance, or to any official statement by a prison administrator letting him know that he had satisfied the grievance procedures in an alternative manner and had the green light to file a lawsuit without using the established grievance procedures. The form itself contradicts his argument.

The fact that completion of the grievance process was delayed because Plaintiff submitted a partially illegible appeal was his own fault, and he was simply required to rewrite it and resubmit it, which he did. A legible appeal is a reasonable requirement, because prison officials cannot know of the problem if they cannot read the grievance appeal. However, after resubmitting the grievance appeal in a legible form, Plaintiff then was required to wait for a response from his grievance appeal before filing his lawsuit, which he did not do.

One of the reasons prisoners must follow the internal grievance system is to allow prison officials to fix problems internally, without the need for filing a costly, time-consuming lawsuit. Another reason is to provide them with legal notice, so that a lawsuit can be filed if officials do not fix the problem at the grievance or appeal stage. Yet another reason is to aid prisoners in the rehabilitative process--they are in prison for failing to follow society's rules, and the sooner they understand the importance of rules and learn how to follow them with exactness, the better able they are to function within the prison society and, if released, within the society at large. The bottom line is that "before" means before.

The undisputed material facts show Plaintiff did not follow the rules of administrative exhaustion. The United States Supreme Court has clarified that exactness in following the administrative exhaustion rules is required. No adequate excuse for failing to follow the rules is evident from the record. The Court rejects Plaintiff's argument that he did not first present his claim in his lawsuit at the time he first presented the lawsuit for filing--simply because his lawsuit was "conditionally" filed by the Clerk of Court. It is not the category in which the Clerk accepted and filed the lawsuit that is at issue, but the fact that Plaintiff presented it for filing at that time.

Therefore, this case must be dismissed without prejudice. However, because Plaintiff is still within the statute of limitations period on his more current lack-of-care claims, he may re-file his lawsuit immediately, based upon any completed grievances, and so Defendants' procedural victory may be short-lived.

ROBERT SCHILLEMAN, PLAINTIFF, V. CORIZON HEALTH INCORPORATED, ET AL., DEFENDANTS. NO. CV 14-01825-PHX-DLR (BSB) UNITED STATES DISTRICT COURT FOR THE DISTRICT OF ARIZONA

II. Plaintiff's Motion for Summary Judgment re: Exhaustion of Remedies

Plaintiff asserts that he is entitled to summary judgment on Defendants' affirmative defense that Plaintiff failed to exhaust his available administrative remedies. He argues that he was excused from the exhaustion requirement under the plain terms of Arizona Department of Corrections (ADC) Department Order 802.01, § 1.8, which Plaintiff asserts exempts emergency complaints from the formal grievance procedure. Plaintiff further asserts that, even though he was not required to exhaust administrative remedies, he did exhaust his administrative remedies by following the ADC's grievance procedure.

Defendants respond that "Plaintiff's conclusory statements citing to D.O. 802 are not enough to prove that his specific medical complaints constituted an 'emergency condition' within the meaning of D.O. 802" and that Plaintiff has failed to present evidence demonstrating that his prostate cancer presented an emergency medical condition under D.O. 802. Defendants further assert that D.O. 802.01, §1.8 does not obviate an inmate's obligation to exhaust the ADC's grievance and appeals procedures in the event of an emergency, but "simply allows an inmate to bring an emergency to the attention of staff, by any available means, rather than to rely on the written grievance procedure to alert staff to an emergency." (Doc. 137 at 6.)

Defendants next assert that the Grievance Appeal Response signed by Director Ryan on February 28, 2014 does not show that Plaintiff exhausted his administrative remedies because "Plaintiff does not provide any documents that were submitted by him as part of the grievance process related to the Grievance Appeal Response signed by Director Ryan on February 28, 2014, or any additional documents related to the other grievances submitted by Plaintiff." (Doc. 140 at 5.)

B. Exhaustion

Under the Prison Litigation Reform Act, a prisoner must exhaust "available" administrative remedies before filing an action in federal court. *See 42 U.S.C. § 1997e(a); Vaden v. Summerhill, 449 F.3d 1047, 1050 (9th Cir. 2006); Brown v. Valoff, 422 F.3d 926, 934-35 (9th Cir. 2005).* The prisoner must complete the administrative review process in accordance with the applicable rules. *See Woodford v. Ngo, 548 U.S. 81, 92, 126 S. Ct. 2378, 165 L. Ed. 2d 368 (2006).* Exhaustion is required for all suits about prison life, *Porter v. Nussle, 534 U.S. 516, 523, 122 S. Ct. 983, 152 L. Ed. 2d 12 (2002),* regardless of the type of relief offered through the administrative process, *Booth v. Churner, 532 U.S. 731, 741, 121 S. Ct. 1819, 149 L. Ed. 2d 958 (2001).*

The defendant bears the initial burden to show that there was an available administrative remedy and that the prisoner did not exhaust it. *Albino v. Baca, 747 F.3d 1162, 1169, 1172 (9th Cir. 2014); see Brown, 422 F.3d at 936-37* (a defendant must demonstrate that applicable relief remained available in the grievance process). Once that showing is made, the burden shifts to the prisoner, who must either demonstrate that he, in fact, exhausted administrative remedies or "come forward with evidence showing that there is something in his particular case that made the existing and generally available administrative remedies effectively unavailable to him." *Albino, 747 F.3d at 1172.* The ultimate burden, however, rests with the defendant. *Id.* Summary judgment is appropriate if the undisputed evidence, viewed in the light most favorable to the prisoner, shows a failure to exhaust. *Id. at 1166, 1168; see Fed. R. Civ. P. 56(a).*

If summary judgment is denied, disputed factual questions relevant to exhaustion should be decided by the judge; a plaintiff is not entitled to a jury trial on the issue of exhaustion. *Albino, 747 F.3d at 1170-71.* But if a court finds that the prisoner exhausted administrative remedies, that administrative remedies were not available, or that the failure to exhaust administrative remedies should be excused, the case proceeds to the merits. *Id. at 1171.*

C. Facts regarding Exhaustion

ADC Department Order 802.06 outlines the formal inmate medical grievance process. (Doc. 113-2 at 5.) An inmate may appeal a response to a formal inmate   medical grievance to the Director. (*Id.* at 6.) The decision of the Director for medical grievance appeals is final and constitutes exhaustion of all remedies for inmate medical grievances within ADC. (*Id.* at 7.) Section 802.01 entitled "General Information" provides, in part, that "[i]nmates are not required to use the formal Inmate Grievance Procedures to submit a verbal or written emergency complaint." (*Id.* at 3.) An emergency is defined as "a condition which, if processed through the normal grievance time frames, would subject the inmate to substantial risk of medical harm, personal injury or cause other serious and irreparable harm." (*Id.*) The Department Order further provides that "[a]ny emergency complaint received by staff shall be immediately evaluated through the chain of command to determine whether it is an emergency as defined in 1.8.1 of this section and requires immediate response outside of the Inmate Grievance Procedure time frames."

D. Discussion

Plaintiff argues that he was excused from the exhaustion requirement under the plain terms of ADC Department Order 802.01, § 1.8, which provides that "[i]nmates are not required to use the formal Inmate Grievance Procedures to submit a verbal or written emergency complaint." The emergency complaint procedure, however, is not a model of clarity. Section 1.8 clearly states that inmates are not required to use the formal grievance process in the case of an emergency,[4] but provides no further information as to exhaustion of remedies in the case of an emergency. The consequences of this ambiguity are on display in this case.

4   The Court is unconvinced by Defendants' argument that an inmate must still follow the formal grievance process even after submitting an emergency complaint. It is Defendants who are able to define the grievance process and how administrative remedies are exhausted and, thus, any ambiguity in their policy should be construed in favor of Plaintiff. *See Woodford, 548 U.S. at 90* (proper exhaustion requires using all steps that the agency holds out, and doing so properly).

Plaintiff provides a "consultation request" signed by Dr. Kessler, which states that Plaintiff told him that it was important to establish care with a urologist for treatment of his prostate cancer. (Doc. 25-9 at 1.) He argues that this evidence shows he orally pursued treatment for his prostate cancer and, therefore, was exempt from the formal administrative grievance process. Defendants argue that Plaintiff has not shown   that his condition constituted an emergency within the meaning of Section 1.8.1, which provides that an emergency is "a condition which, if processed through the normal grievance time frames, would subject the inmate to substantial risk of medical harm, personal injury or cause other serious and irreparable harm." The Department Order, however, does not state who decides which conditions are "medical emergencies" or what happens when, after evaluation, a complaint is deemed to not constitute an emergency.

Despite the substantial ambiguity in the emergency complaint grievance process, Plaintiff is entitled to summary judgment on Defendants' exhaustion of administrative remedies affirmative defense because the uncontroverted evidence shows that he exhausted his claims to the Director's level. Plaintiff provides a January 13, 2014 response from Director Ryan responding to Plaintiff's request for "immediate and thorough treatment for [his] cancer or immediate release to get treatment by a competent doctor due to the life threatening nature of [his] cancer." (Doc. 114-2 at 1-2.) Defendants state that Plaintiff has failed to show that he exhausted his claims in this action because he did not provide any   of the grievance documents that led to Director Ryan's final decision with his Motion for Summary Judgment. But Defendants point to nothing in their policy requiring Plaintiff to name every defendant or explicitly set forth his legal claims in his grievances. Morton v. Hall, 599 F.3d 942, 946 (9th Cir. 2010) (The level of detail in an administrative grievance necessary to properly exhaust a claim is determined by the prison's applicable grievance procedures, but "when a prison's grievance procedures are silent or incomplete as to factual specificity, a grievance suffices if it alerts the prison to the nature of the wrong for which redress is sought."). Plaintiff provides evidence that he exhausted his claims related to the fact that he was not being provided immediate and thorough treatment for his cancer. Defendants have not met their burden of demonstrating that Plaintiff did not exhaust his claims, and cannot shift the burden to Plaintiff by claiming that Plaintiff has not produced enough evidence to demonstrate that he did exhaust. See Albino, 747 F.3d at 1172 (the ultimate burden of proof as to exhaustion remains with the defendant). Plaintiff has provided unrebutted evidence that he exhausted his administrative remedies, and thus, the Court finds that Plaintiff is entitled to summary judgment on the exhaustion defense.

CARL RUPERT SMITH, #137 787, PLAINTIFF, V. CORIZON HEALTH SERVICES, ET AL., DEFENDANTS. CIVIL ACTION NO. 2:15-CV-20-MHT UNITED STATES DISTRICT COURT FOR THE MIDDLE DISTRICT OF ALABAMA, NORTHERN DIVISION

This 42 U.S.C. § 1983 action involves a dispute over the of medical care and treatment afforded Plaintiff, an inmate incarcerated at the Staton Correctional Facility in Elmore, Alabama. Plaintiff names as defendants Corizon, LLC, Darryl Ellis, Michele Sagers-Copeland, and Domineek Guice. Plaintiff seeks damages and injunctive relief for the alleged violation of his constitutional rights. Doc. No. 1.

Defendants filed an answer, special report, and supporting evidentiary materials addressing Plaintiff's claims for relief. In these documents, Defendants argue this case is due to be dismissed because prior to filing this cause of action Plaintiff failed to properly exhaust an administrative remedy available to him through the prison system's medical care provider, Corizon, Inc., prior to initiation of this case. Doc. No. 13, at 12-15. Defendants base their exhaustion defense on Plaintiff's failure to submit any medical grievances regarding the claims presented. Id., Sagers-Copeland Affidavit. In addition, Defendants maintain, and the evidentiary materials, including Plaintiff's medical records, indicate that Plaintiff received appropriate medical treatment during the time relevant to the matters alleged in the instant complaint. See Doc. No. 13, Ellis, Sagers-Copeland, & Guice Affidavits & Exh. A. On April 13, 2015, the court provided Plaintiff an opportunity to file a response to Defendants' report in which he was advised to "specifically address Defendants' argument that he [] failed to exhaust his available administrative remedies as required by 42 U.S.C. ˜ 1997e(a) of the Prison Litigation Reform Act ('PLRA')." Doc. No. 17 at 1 (footnote omitted). On May 5, 2015, the court granted Plaintiff's request for additional time to file his response. Doc. No. 19. Plaintiff has filed no response within the time allowed by the court.

"[A]n exhaustion defense . . . is not ordinarily the proper subject for a summary judgment [motion]; instead, it should be raised in a motion to dismiss, or be treated as such if raised in a motion for summary judgment." Bryant v. Rich, 530 F.3d 1368, 1374-75 (11th Cir. 2008) (internal quotations omitted); Trias v. Fla. Dep't of Corr., 587 F. App'x 531, 534 (11th Cir. 2014) (District court properly construed defendant's "motion for summary judgment as a motion to dismiss for failure to exhaust administrative remedies"). Therefore, the court will treat Defendants' report as a motion to dismiss.

I. STANDARD OF REVIEW

In addressing the requirements of 42 U.S.C. § 1997e regarding exhaustion, the Eleventh Circuit has recognized that "[t]he plain language of th[is] statute makes exhaustion a precondition to filing an action in federal court." Higginbottom v. Carter, 223 F.3d 1259, 1261 (11th Cir. 2000) (per curiam) (quoting Freeman v. Francis, 196 F.3d 641, 643-44 (6th Cir. 1999)). This means that "until such administrative remedies as are available are exhausted," a prisoner is precluded from filing suit in federal court. See id. (affirming dismissal of prisoner's civil rights suit for failure to satisfy the mandatory exhaustion requirements of the PLRA); Harris v.

Garner, 190 F.3d 1279, 1286 (11th Cir. 1999) ("reaffirm[ing] that *section 1997e(a)* imposes a mandatory requirement on prisoners seeking judicial relief to exhaust their administrative remedies" before filing suit in federal court), *modified on other grounds, 216 F.3d 970 (11th Cir. 2000)* (en banc); *Miller v. Tanner, 196 F.3d 1190, 1193 (11th Cir. 1999)* (holding that under the PLRA's amendments to ˜ *1997e(a)*, "[a]n inmate incarcerated in a state prison . . . must first comply with the grievance procedures established by the state department of corrections before filing a federal lawsuit under *section 1983*"); *Harper v. Jenkin, 179 F.3d 1311, 1312 (11th Cir. 1999)* (per curiam) (affirming dismissal of prisoner's civil suit for failure to satisfy the mandatory exhaustion requirements of ˜ *1997e(a)*); *Alexander v. Hawk, 159 F.3d 1321, 1328 (11th Cir. 1998)* (affirming dismissal of prisoner's *Bivens* action under ˜ *1997e(a)* for failure to exhaust administrative remedies prior to filing suit in federal court).

Leal v. Ga. Dep't of Corr., 254 F.3d 1276, 1279 (11th Cir. 2001). The court has, therefore, determined that "the question of exhaustion under the PLRA [is] a 'threshold matter' that [federal courts must] address before considering the merits of the case. *Chandler v. Crosby, 379 F.3d 1278, 1286 (11th Cir. 2004).* Because exhaustion is mandated by the statute, [a court has] no discretion to waive this requirement. *Alexander v. Hawk, 159 F.3d 1321, 1325-26 (11th Cir. 1998)." Myles v. Miami-Dade Cnty. Corr. and Rehab. Dep't, 476 F. App'x 364, 366 (11th Cir. 2012).* The court will "resolve this issue first." *Id.*

When deciding whether a prisoner has exhausted his remedies, the court should first consider the plaintiff's and the defendants' versions of the facts, and if they conflict, take the plaintiff's version of the facts as true. "If in that light, the defendant is entitled to have the complaint dismissed for failure to exhaust administrative remedies, it must be dismissed." *Turner v. Burnside, 541 F.3d 1077, 1082 (11th Cir.2008) (citing Bryant, 530 F.3d at 1373-74).* If the complaint is not subject to dismissal at this step, then the court should make "specific findings in order to resolve the disputed factual issues related to exhaustion." *Id. (citing Bryant, 530 F.3d at 1373-74, 1376).*

Myles, 476 F. App'x at 366. A district court

may resolve disputed factual issues where necessary to the disposition of a motion to dismiss for failure to exhaust [without a hearing]. *See [Turner, 541 F.3d at 1082].* The judge properly may consider facts outside of the pleadings to resolve a factual dispute as to exhaustion where doing so does not decide the merits, and the parties have a sufficient opportunity to develop the record. *Bryant, 530 F.3d at 1376.*

Trias, 587 F. App'x at 535.

Upon review of the complaint, Defendants' special report, and the evidentiary materials filed in support thereof, the court concludes that Defendants' motion to dismiss is due to be granted.

II. DISCUSSION

Plaintiff challenges the adequacy of medical care received at the Staton Correctional Facility for a heart condition. *Doc. No. 1.* In response to the complaint, Defendants deny that they provided Plaintiff with constitutionally inadequate medical care and argue this case is subject to dismissal because Plaintiff failed to exhaust the administrative remedy provided by the institutional medical care provider prior to filing this complaint as required by the Prison Litigation Reform Act, *42 U.S.C. § 1997e(a). Doc. No. 13, Sagers-Copeland Affidavit, Exh. A.* As explained, federal law directs this court to treat Defendants' response as a motion to dismiss for failure to exhaust an administrative remedy and allows the court to look beyond the pleadings to relevant evidentiary materials in deciding the issue of proper exhaustion. *Bryant, 530 F.3d at 1375.*

The Prison Litigation Reform Act compels exhaustion of available administrative remedies before a prisoner can seek relief in federal court on a ˜ *1983* complaint. Specifically, *42 U.S.C.* ˜ *1997e(a)* states that "[n]o action shall be brought with respect to prison conditions under *section 1983* of this title, or any other Federal law, by a prisoner confined in any jail, prison, or other correctional facility until such administrative remedies as are available are exhausted." "Congress has provided in ˜ *1997e(a)* that an inmate must exhaust irrespective of the forms of relief sought and offered through administrative remedies." *Booth v. Churner, 532 U.S. 731, 741 n.6,*

121 S. Ct. 1819, 149 L. Ed. 2d 958 (2001). "[T]he PLRA's exhaustion requirement applies to all inmate suits about prison life, whether they involve general circumstances or particular episodes, and whether they allege excessive force or some other wrong." *Porter v. Nussle, 534 U.S. 516, 532, 122 S. Ct. 983, 152 L. Ed. 2d 12 (2002)*. Exhaustion of all available   administrative remedies is a precondition to litigation and a federal court cannot waive the exhaustion requirement. *Booth, 532 U.S. at 741; Alexander, 159 F.3d at 1325; Woodford v. Ngo, 548 U.S. 81, 126 S. Ct. 2378, 165 L. Ed. 2d 368 (2006)*. Moreover, "the PLRA exhaustion requirement requires proper exhaustion." *Id. at 93*.

> Proper exhaustion demands compliance with an agency's deadlines and other critical procedural rules [as a precondition to filing suit in federal court] because no adjudicative system can function effectively without imposing some orderly structure on the courts of its proceedings . . . . Construing ˜ 1997e(a) to require proper exhaustion . . . fits with the general scheme of the PLRA, whereas [a contrary] interpretation [allowing an inmate to bring suit in federal court once administrative remedies are no longer available] would turn that provision into a largely useless appendage.

Id. at 90-91, 93. The Supreme Court reasoned that because proper exhaustion of administrative remedies is necessary an inmate cannot "satisfy the Prison Litigation Reform Act's exhaustion requirement . . . by filing an untimely or otherwise procedurally defective administrative grievance or appeal[,]" or by effectively bypassing the administrative process simply by waiting until the grievance procedure is no longer available to her. *Id. at 83-84; Bryant, 530 F3d at 1378* (quoting *Johnson v. Meadows, 418 F3d 1152, 1158 (11th Cir. 2005)* ("To exhaust administrative remedies in accordance with the PLRA, prisoners must 'properly take each step within the administrative process.'"); *Johnson, 418 F.3d at 1157* (inmate who files an untimely grievance or spurns the administrative process until it is no longer available fails to satisfy the exhaustion requirement of the PLRA); *Higginbottom, 223 F.3d at 1261* (inmate's belief that administrative procedures are futile or needless does not excuse the exhaustion requirement). "The only facts pertinent to determining whether a prisoner has satisfied the PLRA's exhaustion requirement are those that existed when he filed his original complaint." *Smith v. Terry, 491 F. App'x 81, 83 (11th Cir. 2012)* (per curiam).

The record is undisputed that the health care provider for the Alabama Department of Corrections provides a grievance procedure for inmate complaints related to the provision of medical treatment. *Doc. No. 13, Sagers-Copeland Affidavit*. Defendants submitted evidence which reflects that when inmates are processed into the custody of the Alabama Department of Corrections they are informed of the process and procedure for obtaining medical care and medication and are also educated about the availability of the medical grievance process whereby they may voice complaints regarding any medical treatment sought or received during their incarceration. *Id*. Inmate grievance forms are available to inmates at Staton to submit a grievance related to the provision of health care, inmate grievances are answered within approximately ten days of receipt of the grievance, and the inmate grievance form provides information about how an inmate may appeal the response he receives to his initial inmate grievance. *Id*. A written response to a formal grievance appeal is provided in approximately ten days of receipt. *Id*. Inmates are provided with a copy of the completed grievance and/or grievance appeal containing the health service administrator's response. *Id*. Defendants state Plaintiff has submitted no medical grievances or medical grievance appeals of any kind nor did he ever request any assistance in notifying the Staton medical staff of any complaints, concerns or grievances he possessed relative to the medical care he has received at Staton. *Id.; Exh. A*.

The court granted Plaintiff an opportunity to respond to the exhaustion defense raised by Defendants in their motion to dismiss but he did not do so. *Doc. No. 17*. The court, therefore, finds that a grievance system is available at Staton for Plaintiff's claims, but he failed to exhaust the administrative remedy available to him. Plaintiff does not dispute his failure to submit any grievances related to the provision of his medical care at Staton, and the unrefuted record before the court demonstrates he failed to properly exhaust an administrative remedy available to him at Staton regarding his allegation of inadequate medical care prior to seeking federal relief, a precondition to proceeding in this court on his claims. Any grievances filed after initiation of this federal cause of action have no bearing on Plaintiff's proper exhaustion of the administrative remedy provided by the facility's medical provider. *Terry, 491 F. App'x at 83.*

Accordingly, Defendants' motion seeking dismissal for Plaintiff's failure to exhaust available administrative remedies should be granted, and such dismissal should be without prejudice. *See Ngo, 548 U.S. at 87-94; Bryant, 530 F.3d at 1374-1375* (dismissal for failure to exhaust an administrative remedy when the remedy remains available is not an adjudication of the merits and is without prejudice); *Woodford, 548 U.S. at 87-94.*

JAMES COLEN #604910, PLAINTIFF, V. CORIZON MEDICAL SERVICES, ET AL., DEFENDANTS. CIVIL ACTION NO.: 14-12948 UNITED STATES DISTRICT COURT FOR THE EASTERN DISTRICT OF MICHIGAN, SOUTHERN DIVISION

I. BACKGROUND

Colen's claims stem from medical care related to an injury he sustained in 2010, when he allegedly broke his foot playing basketball. When he was first evaluated by defendant Rogers, he was diagnosed with a sprain and given an ace bandage. [R. 13, PgID 82]. Over the next two and a half years, he continually kited various medical providers for assistance for increasing pain in his foot, swelling, and new pain in his knee, but he was told that his pain was either a sprain or simply arthritis and he was given minimal care. X-rays taken much later revealed knee deterioration requiring replacement, arthritis, and an old foot fracture that had not healed properly. [*Id.*, PgID 83-92]. Colen had knee replacement surgery in 2014, but continued to experience foot pain that remained untreated. [*Id.* 93-94].

Colen's amended complaint alleges that the MDOC Defendants' conduct violated his *Eighth* and *Fourteenth Amendment* rights, and constituted intentional infliction of emotional distress and gross negligence. [R. 13]. The MDOC Defendants now move for summary judgment, alleging that Colen failed to properly exhaust his administrative remedies. This Court disagrees.

III. ANALYSIS

Colen filed five arguably relevant grievances between April and October 2013, but the Court will address only one because it is dispositive. In grievance ARF-13-09-2586-12d1, Colen addressed the entire medical history that gave rise to his amended complaint, stating, "I am continually being denied medical treatment for the injury sustained on my foot where I have broken bones and torn ligaments which have worsened over the last two years." [*Id.*, PgID 323]. He emphasized, "I have tried unsuccessfully to resolve my condition with the Health care staff, and the Adrian Administration. Nothing is being done to correct my foot, knee and leg, and I am in excruciating pain." [*Id.*]. He alleged that "Health Care and the Adrian Staff are being deliberately indifferent by purposefully ignoring my request [to see a specialist and receive injections] and ailment." [*Id.*]. MDOC resolved this grievance on its merits. [*Id.*, PgID 320-22]. In fact, MDOC informed Colen on January 31, 2014, that its denial of this Step III grievance represented an exhaustion of his administrative remedies. [*Id.*, PgID 320].

Nonetheless, the MDOC defendants now argue that grievance ARF-13-09-2586-12d1 was not properly exhausted because Colen did not specify the names of those involved, in violation of MDOC policy. [R. 40, PgID 297]. But, that argument was rejected by the Sixth Circuit in *Reed-Bey v. Pramstaller, 603 F.3d 322, 324-25 (6th Cir. 2010)*, because the state failed to follow its own procedural rule requiring the prisoner to name those involved, and instead decided the otherwise defaulted claims on the merits. "When prison officials decline to enforce their own procedural requirements and opt to consider <u>otherwise-defaulted claims on the merits, so as a</u> general rule will we." *Id. at 325.*

Since MDOC decided grievance ARF-13-09-2586-12d1 on its merits, in disregard for the requirement that he name all those involved, this Court should decide the merits of his claims, too.

DAVID WILSON (ADC#138042), PLAINTIFF V. DON NELSON, CORIZON LLC, JAMES PRATT, JOHN HAROLD AND JIM MCLEAN, DEFENDANTS CIVIL NO. 6:13-CV-06036 UNITED STATES DISTRICT COURT FOR THE WESTERN DISTRICT OF ARKANSAS, HOT SPRINGS DIVISION

(SEE DISCUSSION UNDER MEDICAL CARE)

I. BACKGROUND

During the time at issue here Plaintiff was incarcerated in the Arkansas Department of Corrections Diagnostic Unit in Pine Bluff ("Diagnostic Unit") and the Ouachita River Unit in Malvern, Arkansas ("ORU"). Plaintiff filed his Complaint in the Eastern District of Arkansas on March 29, 2013. ECF. No. 2. His Complaint was transferred to this District on April 15, 2013 after the ADC was dismissed as a Defendant. ECF. No. 3.

In his Complaint, Plaintiff named Don Nelson (ADC Head of Construction), Corizon, James Pratt (Corizon employee), John Harold (ADC Construction Supervisor), and Jim McLean (ADC Construction Supervisor). ECF No. 1. On October 29, 2013, the Court ordered service on the Medical Defendants in care of the law firm Humphries and Lewis, and the ADC Defendants in care of the Arkansas Board of Correction. ECF No. 9. Humphries and Lewis accepted service on behalf of Corizon, Inc. but declined to accept service for James Pratt, as he had been terminated from Corizon on August 22, 2013. ECF No. 11. Subsequently, the Court ordered James Pratt to be served at the address provided by Humphries and Lewis. ECF No. 24. Humphries, Odum, and Eubanks[1] subsequently filed a Notice of Appearance on behalf of both Corizon and James Pratt. ECF No. 22, 38.

1   It appears that this is the same law firm, as the address of PO Box 20670, White Hall, AR is used consistently despite the changes in named partners.

In his Complaint, Plaintiff alleges his *Eighth Amendment* right to be free from cruel and unusual punishment were violated in relation to back, arm, hip, and knee injuries he suffered when he fell through a prison barracks ceiling while doing electrical work on his ADC job assignment.

III. DISCUSSION

Plaintiff argues the ADC Defendants failed to properly train and supervise him, resulting in his fall and injuries. He argues the Medical Defendants repeatedly delayed or denied medical care after he was injured.

The ADC Defendants argue Summary Judgment should be granted as to Plaintiff's claims against them because he failed to file a grievance against them, his claim is based on the theory of respondeat superior, and his claims are barred by both qualified and sovereign immunity. ECF No. 61. The Medical Defendants argue Summary Judgment should be granted as to Plaintiff's claims against them because Plaintiff did not exhaust his claims against Corizon, James Pratt had no direct involvement or authority in the medical consultation process, and his claim fails as a matter of law because he was treated for those conditions deemed medically necessary. ECF Nos. 91, 92.

A. Plaintiff Failed to Exhaust His Administrative Remedies Against The ADC Defendants

The Prison Litigation Reform Act ("PLRA"), mandates exhaustion of available administrative remedies before and inmate files suit. *Section 1997e(a)* of the PLRA provides: "[n]o action shall be brought with

respect to prison conditions under *section 1983* of this title, or any other Federal law, by a prisoner confined in any jail, prison, or other correctional facility until such administrative remedies as are available are exhausted." *42 U.S. C. § 1997e(a).*

In *Jones v. Bock, 549 U.S. 199, 127 S. Ct. 910, 166 L. Ed. 2d 798 (2007)*, the Supreme Court concluded that "exhaustion [as required by the PLRA] is not *per se* inadequate simply because an individual later sued was not named in the grievances." *Id. at 219.* "[T]o properly exhaust administrative remedies prisoners must complete the administrative review process in accordance with the applicable procedural rules." *Id. at 218* (internal quotation marks and citation omitted). The Court stated that the "level of detail necessary in a grievance to comply with the grievance procedures will vary from system to system and claim to claim, but it is the prison's requirements, and not the PLRA, that define the boundaries of proper exhaustion." *Id.*

In this case, Plaintiff admits that he never filed a grievance against the ADC Defendants. He argues that he did not do so because the Administrative Directive 09-01, section III G, 4 states that job assignments are non-grievable. ECF No. 90-10.

This section does state that a number of matters are not grievable:

1. Parole;

2. Release;

3. Transfer;

4. Job assignments unless in conflict with medical restrictions;

5. Disiplinaries;

6. Anticipated Events (i.e. events or activities which may or may not occur in the future);

7. Matters beyond the control of the Department of Correction, including issues controlled by State or Federal law or regulation.

AD 12-16.III.G. Items that are grievable include:

1. A policy applicable within his or her unit/center of assignment that personally affects the inmate;

2. A condition in the facility that personally affects the inmate;

3. An action involving an inmate(s) of his or her facility that personally affects the inmate;

4. An action of an employee(s), contractor(s), or volunteer(s) at his or her facility that personally affects the inmate;

5. An incident occurring within his her facility that personally affects the inmate.

AD 12-16.III.B. Reading these two provisions together, it is clear from the plain language of this policy that an inmate is prevented from grieving exactly what work assignment he or she may receive, unless the assignment conflicts with medical restrictions. It does not prevent an inmate from grieving an injury that he or she believes was the result of a faulty policy, action, condition, or incident simply because it occurred during a work assignment.

Nor does Plaintiff's subjective belief that he could not grieve the incident excuse his failure to exhaust his Administrative remedies against these Defendants. The Eighth Circuit has repeatedly held that a court is not permitted "to consider an inmate's merely subjective beliefs, logical or otherwise, in determining whether administrative procedures are "available.'" *Lyon v. Vande Krol*, 305 F.3d 806, 809 (8th Cir. 2002)(citing *Chelette v. Harris*, 229 F.3d 684, 688 (8th Cir.2000), cert. denied, 531 U.S. 1156, 121 S. Ct. 1106, 148 L. Ed. 2d 977 (2001)).

Because Plaintiff did not exhaust his Administrative remedies against the ADC Defendants his claim against them is barred by *Section 1997e(a)* of the PLRA.

<u>B. Plaintiff Failed to Exhaust His Administrative Remedies Against Corizon</u>

Corizon argues Plaintiff failed to exhaust his administrative remedies against them because he did not explicitly name the company in his grievances and that, despite delays, Plaintiff ultimately received all medically necessary treatment. Because Plaintiff failed to name Corizon in the grievances exhausted before he filed his complaint, he failed to exhaust his Administrative remedies against the company.

The Eighth Circuit has held "the PLRA's exhaustion requirement is satisfied if prison officials decide a procedurally flawed grievance on the merits." *Hammett v. Cofield*, 681 F.3d 945, 947 (8th Cir. 2012). In *Hammett*, Plaintiff's grievance appeals were untimely, but otherwise complete. Therefore, the Court reasoned that the policies underlying the exhaustion requirement were met when the institution waived the procedural timing requirements and instead decided the claims on the merits. *Id.* Specifically, the Court noted that the benefits of exhaustion: are fully realized when an inmate pursues the prison grievance process to its final stage and receives an adverse decision on the merits, even if the decision-maker could have declined to reach the merits because of one or more procedural deficiencies. A complete administrative record exists, and a reviewing court will have the benefit of the agency's institutional perspective. This rule also takes into account the likelihood that prison officials will benefit if given discretion to decide, for reasons such as fairness or inmate morale or the need to resolve a recurring issue, that ruling on the merits is better for the institution and an inmate who has attempted to exhaust available prison remedies.

Id. at 947-48.

Failure to name a party is more than a "mere procedural flaw" when it prevents the agency from fully addressing the merits of the grievance and thereby defeats the purpose of the exhaustion requirement. *Burns v. Eaton, 752 F. 3d 1136, 1141 (8th Cir.2014).* In *Burns*, the Plaintiff failed to name an officer in a grievance about an incident, and his amended complaint about that incident later added facts not in the original incident grievance against that second officer. *Id.* Although the prison had decided the greivance on the merits, the Court of Appeals held that the failure to name the second officer rendered it "completely unexhausted" against that second officer because although the officers were both involved in the incident, "they had different responsibilities and took different actions." *Id.* "Thus, this was not a case where prison officials declined to enforce their own procedural requirements and opted to consider otherwise-defaulted claims on the merits. *Id.* (internal quotations omitted)(quoting *Reed-Bey v. Pramstaller, 603 F.3d 322, 325 (6th Cir.2010)).* "Rather, the amended complaint against [the second officer] asserted a new greivance . . . completely unexhausted." *Id. at 1141-42.* (internal quotations omitted.). Therefore, the policy concerns underlying the exhaustion requirement were not met.

Several later unpublished Eighth Circuit cases by different panels, while not binding on this Court, appear at first glance to be split over whether failure to name is always more than a "mere procedural flaw." *See Morrow v. Kelley, 2013 U.S. Dist. LEXIS 173437, 2013 WL 6500616 (E.D. Ark Dec. 11, 2013)* for discussion of these cases. However: overwhelming recent precedent has harmonized these Eighth Circuit opinions by focusing on whether - despite the procedural flaw- prison officials reached and decided the merits of the specific claims asserted against each defendant. To make that determination, the Court must look beyond the prisoner's grievances and examine the issues that the prison officials reviewed and decided during the administrative appeal process. This approach is consistent with the *Hammett* opinion and the purposes of the PLRA's exhaustion requirement.

Colten v. Hobbs, 2014 U.S. Dist. LEXIS 42090, 2014 WL 1309069 (E.D. Ark. Mar. 28, 2014)(internal quotations omitted)(quoting Morrow, 2013 U.S. Dist. LEXIS 173437, 2013 WL 6500616 (E.D.Ark. Dec. 11, 2013) and citing Jones v. Bond, 2013 U.S. Dist. LEXIS 171490, 2013 WL 6332681 (E.D.Ark. Dec. 5, 2013); Hooper v. Kelley, 2013 U.S. Dist. LEXIS 155522, 2013 WL 5881613 (E.D.Ark. Oct. 30, 2013); Scott v. Burl, 2013 U.S. Dist. LEXIS 183431, 2013 WL 5522404 (E.D.Ark. Oct. 1, 2013); Wallace v. Warner, 2013 U.S. Dist. LEXIS 140668, 2013 WL 5531280 (E.D.Ark. Sept. 30, 2013)). Using this approach, "the Courts have consistently dismissed named defendants who were not otherwise identified in exhausted grievances, either by their names, descriptions of their positions, or the conduct which led to the complaint at issues. Leggett v. Corizon, Inc., 2014 U.S. Dist. LEXIS 147916, 2014 WL 5325170 (E.D. Ark. Oct. 17, 2014).

In this case, the record shows Plaintiff completed the grievance process for three grievances prior to filing his complaint. ECF. Nos. 69-1, 70-1-56.)These are OR-12-1350. OR-12-1408, and OR-12-1580. ECF Nos. 69-7, ECF 70-1-56.

OR-12-1350 was filed on October 10, 2012. ECF No. 70-57. It concerned the delay in getting a post-MRI followup on his hip, and named Mr. Pratt. It did not name Corizon. Therefore it will be discussed below in the section for Mr. Pratt.

OR-12-1408 WAS FILED ON OCTOBER 25, 2102. ECF NO. 70-60. IT CONCERNED THE FACT THAT ANOTHER INMATE'S MEDICAL INFORMATION WAS IN HIS MEDICAL JACKET. HE WANTED TO BE ABLE TO REVIEW HIS OWN MEDICAL INFORMATION AND WAS

CONCERNED ABOUT OTHER INMATES SEEING HIS INFORMATION. IT DID NOT NAME CORIZON OR ANY SPECIFIC PERSONNEL. THE RESPONSE ON OCTOBER 19, 2012 APOLOGIZED FOR THE MISFILING, AND INSTRUCTED PLAINTIFF TO FILE A NEW REQUEST TO REVIEW HIS RECORDS.

OR-12-1580 WAS FILED ON DECEMBER 18, 2012. ECF 70-1-61. THIS GRIEVANCE STATED "I HAVE REPEATEDLY NOT BEEN SEEN AND/OR RECEIVED THE NEEDED MEDICAL TREATMENT IN A TIMELY MANNER SINCE I FELL ON CONSTRUCTION AND BROKE MY RIGHT HIP, HURT MY RIGHT KNEE, AND FRACTURED MY RIGHT ELBOW ON 4-7-10." ID. THE FIRST RESPONSE TO THIS GREIVANCE WAS DATED JANUARY 15, 2013, THE DAY BEFORE HE SAW ORTHOPEDIC SURGEON DR. CROWELL ON JANUARY 16 FOR HIS MRI FOLLOWUP AND WAS INFORMED THAT HE NEEDED A HIP REPLACEMENT. THIS GRIEVANCE WAS FOUND TO BE WITHOUT MERIT. SPECIFICALLY, IT STATED THAT "YOU HAVE BEEN SEEN FOR THIS ISSUE IN SICK CALL AND BY A PROVIDER. YOU CURRENTLY ARE SCHEDULED TO SEE AN ORTHOPEDIC PROVIDER ON 1/16/2013. YOUR GRIEVANCE IS WITHOUT MERIT." ID. PLAINTIFF APPEALED ON JANUARY 17, 2013. HE REPEATS THAT HE HAS NOT BEEN SEEN AND/OR RECEIVED TREATMENT IN A TIMELY MANNER FOR HIS INJURIES, PROVIDED SEVERAL TIME DELAY EXAMPLES, AND THAT DR. CROWELL TOLD HIM THAT HIS HIP NOW NEEDS TO BE REPLACED - "HOPEFULLY IN A TIMELY MANNER." IT DID NOT NAME CORIZON OR ANY SPECIFIC PERSONNEL. ON MARCH 11, 2013, HIS APPEAL WAS FOUND TO BE WITHOUT MERIT, NOTING THAT HE HAD RECEIVED A HIP REPLACEMENT ON FEBRUARY 22, 2013. THE APPEAL NOTICE ALSO STATES "YOU MUST BE SPECIFIC AS TO THE SUBSTANCE OF THE ISSUE, INCLUDING THE DATE, THE STAFF INVOLVED, PLACE, AND WITNESSES. . . .YOU DID NOT GRIEVE A SPECIFIC INCIDENT OR PROVIDE DATES WITHIN THE TIME FRAME ALLOWED BY POLICY." ID. AT 63.

Because Plaintiff did not name Corizon in these grievances, and further did not provide sufficient detail as required by policy, he failed to exhaust his Administrative remedies as to Corizon. Although the grievances did proceed through the greivance appeals process, the failure to name and to provide sufficient detail on the grievances prevented the agency from fully addressing the merits of the grievance, thereby defeating the purpose of the exhaustion requirement.

C. PLAINTIFF FULLY EXHAUSTED HIS CLAIM AGAINST JAMES PRATT

PLAINTIFF DID NAME JAMES PRATT IN OR--12-1350, FILED ON OCTOBER 12, 2012. IN THIS GREIVANCE HE STATED THAT:

I received an MRI of my right hip on 7-25-12 and I was told that I should be seen within two weeks . On 8-7-12 I was seen at sick call and was told that they would check on this matter. On 8-20-2012 I sent Mr. Pratt a request to check on this matter. On 9-4-12 I sent Mr. Pratt another request on this matter. I was seen at sick call on 9-18-12 and was told that they would check on this matter. I would like to know when I will be seen by Dr. Crowell to discuss the results of the MRI that was taken of my right hip.

ECF No. 70-57.

ON NOVEMBER 2, 2012, MR. PRATT SIGNED A HEALTH SERVICES RESPONSE WHICH STATED:

Ms. McGrath did review your MRI results and has submitted a consult to Dr. Crowell. There was not enough information present to approve the consult. The request was returned to Ms. McGrath. Ms. McGrath met with you on 10/25/12 and prescribed medications to address any problems your knee may be causing you. Your greivance is with merit but resolved. If you have any other problems with your knee drop a sick call request so the nurses can get you back to see Ms. McGrath.

ECF No. 70-58.

ON NOVEMBER 6, 2012 PLAINTIFF APPEALED THE RESPONSE STATING:

I disagree with this decision because I have not been seen by Dr. Crowell for a consult to discuss the results of the MRI that was taken on 7-27-12 on my right hip as the greivance states. I do not understand why being seen by Ms. Graft [sic] and being prescribed medications to address my pain I have with my knee stops me from being seen by Dr. Crowell to discuss the results of the MRI on my right Hip that Dr. Crowell ordered and I received on 7-27-12.

ECF No. 70-58.

ON DECEMBER 28, 2012 THIS APPEAL WAS FOUND TO BE "WITH MERIT" "DUE TO THE DELAYS." ECF No. 70-59.

THUS, IT IS CLEAR THAT PLAINTIFF FULLY EXHAUSTED HIS ADMINISTRATIVE REMEDIES AGAINST MR. PRATT FOR THIS GRIEVANCE.

SHAWN HODGES, Plaintiff, v. CORIZON, CORIZON OF MICHIGAN, PRISON HEALTH SERVICES, INC., HARRIET A. SQUIER, M.D., ASTER BERHANE, M.D., JOSHUA A. BUSKIRK, P.A., DANIEL A. HEYNS, and GEORGE PRAMSTALLER, Defendants. Civil Action No. 14-11837 UNITED STATES DISTRICT COURT FOR THE EASTERN DISTRICT OF MICHIGAN, SOUTHERN DIVISION

2. The Corizon Defendants Have Not Met Their Burden on Exhaustion

Next, the Corizon Defendants argue that, with respect to his claims against Dr. Squier, Dr. Berhane, and P.A. Buskirk, Hodges failed to properly exhaust his administrative remedies, as required by the Prison Litigation Reform Act ("PLRA"), 42 U.S.C. §1997e(a). (Id. at 14-18).

a. The Applicable Law and Grievance Procedure

Under the PLRA, a prisoner may not bring an action, "under [§1983] or any other Federal law," to challenge his conditions of confinement until all available administrative remedies have been exhausted. 42 U.S.C. §1997e(a); Woodford v. Ngo, 548 U.S. 81, 85, 126 S. Ct. 2378, 165 L. Ed. 2d 368 (2006) . This "exhaustion" requirement serves two main purposes: it promotes efficiency by encouraging the resolution of claims at the agency level before litigation is commenced, and it protects administrative authority by allowing the agency an opportunity to correct its own mistakes before being haled into federal court. See Woodford, 548 U.S. at 89. The Supreme Court has held that this "exhaustion requirement requires proper exhaustion." Id. at 93. Proper exhaustion requires "compliance with an agency's deadlines and other critical procedural rules." Id. at 90. Failure to exhaust is an affirmative defense that must be raised by a defendant, and on which the defendant bears the burden of proof. See Jones v. Bock, 549 U.S. 199, 216, 127 S. Ct. 910, 166 L. Ed. 2d 798 (2007); Vandiver v. Corr. Med. Servs., Inc., 326 F. App'x 885, 888 (6th Cir. 2009).

In determining whether a plaintiff has properly exhausted his claim, the only relevant rules "are defined not by the PLRA, but by the prison grievance process itself." Jones, 549 U.S. at 200. In Michigan's correctional facilities, prisoner grievances are governed by MDOC Policy Directive 03.02.130 ("Prisoner/Parolee Grievances"). (Doc. #14-2). A state prisoner must first complete the process outlined in the Policy - including pursuing a grievance through "all three steps of the grievance process" - before he can file a lawsuit challenging the alleged unlawful conduct. (Id. at ¶B). If the prisoner cannot resolve his dispute with the staff member involved, he has five business days to file a Step I grievance. (Id. at ¶¶P, V). "Information provided [in the Step I grievance] is to be limited to the facts involving the issue being grieved (i.e., who, what, when, where, why, how). Dates, times, places, and names of all those involved in the issue being grieved are to be included." (Id. at ¶R). If the prisoner is dissatisfied with the Step I response, he may submit a Grievance Appeal to the Step II Grievance Coordinator within ten business days after receipt of the Step I response, or if no timely response is received, within ten business days of the date the response was due. (Id. at ¶BB). If the grievant is dissatisfied with, or does not receive, a Step II response, he has ten business days within which to file a final appeal at Step III. (Id. at ¶FF). Again, an inmate may only pursue a claim in court if he has complied with his obligations at each of these three steps. (Id. at ¶B).

b. The Key Grievances Filed by Hodges

After thoroughly reviewing the documents attached to Hodges' complaint, as well as those submitted by the Corizon Defendants as attachments to their reply brief, it is apparent that Hodges filed numerous grievances between the time he injured his right wrist (in November 2010) and the filing of his complaint in this case (in May 2014). With respect to Dr. Squier, Dr. Berhane, and P.A. Buskirk, the Corizon Defendants focus on three grievances - Grievance Nos. SRF-2011-11-1630-12D1 (the "SRF Grievance"), JCF-2012-01-0127-28G (the "JCF Grievance"), and LMF-2012-02-0450-28E (the "LMF Grievance") - and argue that none of these grievances was properly exhausted. (Doc. #14 at 16). Thus, in order to determine whether Hodges' claims against Dr. Squier, Dr. Berhane, and P.A. Buskirk are properly exhausted, a thorough examination of these grievances is required.[5]

5   In his response brief, Hodges also mentions Grievance No. JCF-2013-09-1592-12E2. (Doc. #22 at 13). In this grievance, Hodges asserted that his Special Accommodation Notices - pertaining to a bottom bunk, extra

bedding, etc. - were expiring and "JCF Medical staff" and Corizon were not "promptly making sure" he did not suffer. (Doc. #24-5 at 26). Because the incidents described in this grievance are not at issue in this lawsuit, however, the fact that Hodges pursued this grievance to Step III does not serve to exhaust any of the claims in his complaint.

(1) The Grievances Highlighted by the Corizon Defendants

(a) The SRF Grievance

In the SRF Grievance, dated November 10, 2011, Hodges makes numerous allegations about the medical care he did and did not receive related to his wrist. While it is true that most of his complaints in that grievance seem to relate to the alleged failure to treat his broken wrist in late 2010, rather than the failure to provide radiation treatment for his tumor in late 2011, importantly, the grievance does specifically challenge the delayed radiation for the tumor in his hand. (Doc. #1-5 at 2-3). Hodges, after specifically referencing that "in August 2011 the Doctor told me that I had a Tumor in my hand and in September of 2011, the Doctor told me that I had [a malignant form of cancer]," stated, "I am now at a very critical stage in which I need medical attention A.S.A.P. ..." (Id.) (emphasis added). Indeed, the grievance respondent summarized Hodges' Step I grievance as follows (in pertinent part): "I had an MRI & CT Scan & surgery in August & I was told I had a tumor in my hand. The doctor told me I had cancer cells. Because PA Buskirk denied me urgent medical treatment & I waited 5 months, I am now at a critical stage." (Doc. #24-5 at 97).

In responding to this Step I grievance, RN Alton reviewed Hodges' electronic medical record and summarized the care he was provided at SRF between November 2010 and September 2011 (when he was transferred to Alger Correctional Facility ("LMF")). (Id. at 97-98). RN Alton concluded that there "was no evidence of denied medical treatment" and denied the SRF Grievance at Step I. (Id.). In his Step II appeal, Hodges reiterated that he was challenging P.A. Buskirk's alleged refusal to act on Dr. Haverbush's "recommendation for radiation after surgery in my hand as right now had (PVNS) with malign[ant] giant cell tumor and cancer." (Doc. #1-5 at 7). Hodges further clarified, "all this time since surgery I am [being denied] radiation at SRF by Buskirk, P.A. ...." (Id.). In RN Lamb's Step II response, however, Hodges was advised that there was no evidence that he was denied urgent treatment following his wrist injury. (Doc. #24-5 at 94). With respect to Hodges' allegation that P.A. Buskirk was denying him radiation, the grievance response indicated, "New issues[6] raised at Step II Appeal will not be addressed in this response." (Id.). Hodges subsequently filed a Step III appeal, which was denied, this time on the basis that: (a) Hodges originally grieved P.A. Buskirk's failure to respond to his letters - as opposed to his failure to provide medical treatment - and Buskirk was not required by policy to do so; and (b) the grievance was untimely, as it was dated November 10, 2011 but referred in "the body of his grievance [to] issues from November 2010," and Hodges had not "provided reasoning for the substantial delays."[7] (Doc. #24-5 at 92).

6   As discussed in the preceding paragraph, Hodges' complaint about being denied the recommended radiation treatment was not a "new issue" presented for the first time at Step II of the grievance process.

7   There is an inherent inconsistency in these two bases for denying the grievance: if Hodges actually was grieving P.A. Buskirk's failure to respond to his letters, as the Step III grievance response concluded, then he was not challenging "issues from November 2010."

In their motion, the Corizon Defendants argue that the SRF Grievance was not properly exhausted because it was rejected on procedural grounds as untimely. (Doc. #14 at 16). The applicable Policy Directive provides that a "Step I grievance must be filed within five business days after the grievant attempted to resolve the issue with appropriate staff." (Doc. #14-2 at ¶P). However, under the MDOC's own grievance policy, although a grievance "may be rejected" if "filed in an untimely manner," it "shall not be rejected if there is a valid reason for the delay, e.g., transfer." (Id. at ¶G(3) (emphasis added)). Here, the SRF Grievance was deemed untimely because Hodges had purportedly not "provided reasoning for the substantial delays." (Doc. #24-5 at 92). There are several problems with this conclusion, however.

First, looking only at the face of Hodges' grievance, it is not at all clear that this grievance was untimely, as Hodges grieved in part P.A. Buskirk's failure to respond to a letter dated November 7, 2011 (just three days before the date of the grievance). (Doc. #1-4 at 67). It also addressed the denial of the radiation treatment which had been recommended only a few months prior to Hodges' submission of the grievance. Moreover, the fact that the SRF Grievance was not rejected at Steps I or II of the grievance process further calls into question the Corizon Defendants' timeliness argument (as does the fact that the "MDOC Prisoner Step III Grievance Report" attached to the Corizon Defendants' reply brief indicates that this grievance was "Denied" at Step III, not "Rejected"). (Doc. #24-5 at 7).

But, even assuming that the SRF Grievance was untimely, the Step III contention that Hodges failed to "provide reasoning" for any delay in its filing is inaccurate. Indeed, Hodges explained in the grievance that he had undergone surgery and been diagnosed with PVNS, and it was apparent from the MDOC records that he had been transferred between facilities more than once in the intervening time period. Both of these facts could have provided a valid explanation for any delay in filing the SRF Grievance, had they been considered. See, e.g., Boling v. Corr. Med. Servs.., 2007 U.S. Dist. LEXIS 80479, 2007 WL 3203133, at *5 (E.D. Mich. Oct. 31, 2007) (hospital stay and medical condition were valid reasons for delay in filing grievance); Coleman v. Gullet, 2013 U.S. Dist. LEXIS 81885, 2013 WL 2634581, at *11 (E.D. Mich. June 10, 2013) (plaintiff's transfer was conceivably a valid reason for the delay in appealing a grievance).[8]

8 Additionally, the SRF Grievance was addressed - to some extent, at least - on the merits at Steps I, II, and III. Courts have held that, under certain circumstances, procedural objections to timeliness can be waived where a grievance is addressed on the merits. See, e.g., Christian v. Michigan Dep't of Corr. - Health Servs., 2013 U.S. Dist. LEXIS 136311, 2013 WL 5348832, at *5 (Sept. 24, 2013) ("[W]hen the prison elects to address a grievance on the merits rather than invoke a procedural bar to the grievance, the prisoner has exhausted his claim.") (quoting Allen v. Shawney, 2013 U.S. Dist. LEXIS 80822, 2013 WL 2480658, at *4 (E.D. Mich. June 20, 2013)); Flentall v. Lange, 2011 U.S. Dist. LEXIS 27695, 2011 WL 1045443, at *4 (W.D. Mich. Jan. 31, 2011).

In sum, resolving all reasonable inferences in Hodges' favor, as must be done at the motion to dismiss stage, the Corizon Defendants fail to satisfy their burden of proof on this affirmative defense, and the Court cannot conclude that Hodges failed to exhaust the SRF Grievance against P.A. Buskirk.

(b) The JCF Grievance

On or about October 25, 2011, Hodges was transferred from LMF to the G. Robert Cotton Correctional Facility ("JCF") in Jackson, Michigan. (Doc. #1 at ¶¶126-27). Once there, Hodges filed the JCF Grievance on January 13, 2012, specifically asserting that, while he was incarcerated at LMF, Dr. Berhane "was denying/delaying requests for an off-site referral with an orthopedic specialist, acting alone or in concert with others." (Doc. #1-4 at 1). He also asserted that P.A. Buskirk delayed treating him following his November 2010 injury. (Id.). And, he alleged that "Dr. Berhaney (and the others) simply threw their hands up in the air, without trying to help me get further treatment [for] my wrist or the cancer." (Id.). The JCF grievance was rejected at Step I on January 17, 2012, because "JCF lacks jurisdiction over medical treatment at LMF." (Id. at 2). Hodges was further advised: "You may re-submit your complaint and send it to the Grievance Coordinator at LMF using ID Mail. However; JCF takes medical issues/complaints very seriously. Because of this, a copy of your complaint has been forwarded to the JCF HUM for review." (Id.). Although there is no clear evidence that Hodges resubmitted this grievance to LMF, there is at least some indication - based on a letter Hodges sent to the "JCF Mail Room, JCF Grievance Coordinator and ECF/DWH Mail Room" - that he attempted to do so. (Doc. #1-5 at 158). That letter provides as follows:

On January 27, 2012, I was admitted at the University of Michigan Hospital for a lung biopsy. I stayed there for roughly a day to day and a half and was then transported to [Duane Waters Health Center ("DWH")]. I was admitted to DWH until February 8, 2012, when I was discharged back to JCF.

During this period of time, I am certain a piece of interdepartmental (I.D.) mail was returned to my housing unit in error. As I was not in the housing unit, but had been admitted at the U of M, the mail was dropped back in the B Unit mail box. To this date, that white envelope, addressed to the grievance coordinator at Alger, has not found its way back to me.

If any mail was temporarily held during my transition from JCF to U of M, from U of M to DWH, then DWH to JCF, please forward it to me now. I am most grateful for your attention in this matter. (Id.). The Court has located no response to this letter in the record, nor does it appear that the JCF Grievance was pursued to Step II or Step III (and it is not listed on the "MDOC Prisoner Step III Grievance Report"). (Doc. #24-5 at 3-7).

In their motion, the Corizon Defendants argue that the JCF Grievance was properly rejected - and, thus, was not exhausted - because Hodges "submitted [it] to JCF staff, who lacked jurisdiction over grievances pertaining to SRF and LMF." (Doc. #14 at 16). Although this fact might be correct, it is not dispositive under the circumstances. From the contents of Hodges' letter quoted above, it appears to the Court that Hodges attempted to send this grievance to LMF and that, for some unexplained reason, it was neither accepted nor returned to him for further action. That Hodges apparently was in and out of two different hospitals during the relevant time period - during which time he learned that his cancer had metastasized to his lungs - certainly might explain some of the confusion surrounding re-submission of this grievance and, indeed, could have provided a "valid reason" for any delay in filing the grievance with LMF. Where the MDOC's own grievance policy provides that a grievance shall not be rejected if there is a valid reason for the delay (Doc. #14-2 at ¶G(3)), the Court cannot conclude that Hodges failed to exhaust the JCF Grievance against Dr. Berhane.

(c) The LMF Grievance

It appears that after Hodges learned that LMF had not received the JCF Grievance, he submitted the LMF Grievance. (Doc. #1-4 at 2). The LMF Grievance largely tracked the prior JCF Grievance. In the LMF Grievance, dated February 18, 2012, Hodges again asserted that, while he was incarcerated at LMF, Dr. Berhane delayed and/or denied "requests for off-site referral with an orthopedic specialist, acting alone or in concert with others." (Doc. #1-3 at 15). As with the JCF Grievance, Hodges also alleged that, "Dr. Berhane (and the others) simply threw their hands up in the air, without trying to help me get further treatment for my hand/wrist or the cancer therein." (Id.). The LMF Grievance was rejected as untimely at Step I, however, and Hodges was advised that the grievance investigation reveals that "you have exceeded your time limits in filing a grievance on issue(s) that concern you, and at the same time provided no reasonable circumstance beyond your control that would have prevented you from filing this grievance in a timely fashion." (Id. at 10; Doc. #24-5 at 90). Hodges submitted a Step II appeal, explaining that he had been taking medication for his wrist pain, which produced side effects (including drowsiness, difficulty focusing, etc.). (Doc. #1-3 at 6). He further indicated that he had only recently learned who was (at least partially) responsible for denying his requests for referral to a radiation oncologist and then had been hospitalized for a period of time. (Id. at 6-7). Hodges' appeal was denied at Step II because (1) investigation revealed that Hodges was "provided continuous medical care while at [LMF]" and there was "no evidence of deliberate indifference" to a serious medical need, and (2) the grievance was untimely.[9] (Id. at 21). Hodges appealed to Step III, again arguing that he should be "granted considerable leeway in pursuing medically related appeals," given the medication he was taking, the pain he was experiencing, and the other difficulties his condition presented. (Id. at 23). The grievance was denied at Step III. (Id. at 13).

9 As to the untimeliness rejection, the Step II response indicates that Hodges'"Step II Appeal was due to the Grievance Coordinator on 3/26/12; however it was not received until 4/2/12." (Doc. #1-3 at 21). Pursuant to applicable MDOC policy, however, "Grievances and grievance appeals at all steps shall be considered filed on the date sent by the grievant." (Doc. #14-2 at 5, ¶S). Here, Hodges' Step II appeal is dated March 21, 2012, and he indicates this appeal was mailed prior to the due date (March 26, 2012). The fact that Hodges was housed at JCF at the time his appeal was mailed to LMF may explain why it was not received at that facility until April 2, 2012. Thus, the evidence before the Court shows that Hodges' Step II appeal was timely filed pursuant to MDOC policy and should not have been rejected on timeliness grounds.

The Corizon Defendants argue that the LMF Grievance was properly rejected as untimely and, thus, was not properly exhausted. Again, however, the MDOC's own grievance policy provides that a grievance "shall not be rejected if there is a valid reason for the delay, e.g., transfer." (Doc. #14-2 at ¶G(3)). In this case, it does not appear that any consideration was given as to whether there was a valid reason for Hodges' delay in filing the grievance; rather, the Step I grievance response indicates only that Hodges "provided no reasonable circumstance beyond [his] control that would have prevented [him] from filing this grievance in a timely fashion." (Doc. #1-3 at 10).

In appealing this untimeliness rejection, however, Hodges provided multiple explanations for the delay in filing this grievance. For example, he mentioned his ongoing medical treatment and medication, which he indicated caused drowsiness and "prohibit[ed] focus." (Id. at 6). He also indicated that he had been delayed in obtaining the names of the staff to be included in the grievance. (Id.). Moreover, it bears keeping in mind that Hodges first filed a nearly-identical grievance at JCF in January 2012; this grievance was rejected because JCF "lack[ed] jurisdiction over medical treatment at LMF." (Doc. #1-4 at 2). It appears that Hodges then immediately attempted to send this grievance to LMF, as instructed, but for reasons outside his control - he was hospitalized for nearly two weeks after a lung biopsy - and other reasons not entirely clear, the grievance was not immediately sent to LMF. Thus, there is at least a question of fact as to whether this grievance was properly rejected at Step I as untimely, and, consequently, the Court cannot conclude that Hodges failed to exhaust the LMF Grievance against Dr. Berhane.

(d) Exhaustion as to Dr. Squier

In summary, a genuine issue of material fact exists as to whether Hodges properly exhausted the SRF Grievance, the JCF Grievance, and the LMF Grievance. These grievances name only P.A. Buskirk and Dr. Berhane, however, and the Corizon Defendants argue that Hodges' failure to specifically name Dr. Squier in these grievances bars his claims against her. (Doc. #14 at 17).

It is true that proper exhaustion of administrative remedies means "using all steps that the agency holds out, and doing so properly." Woodford, 548 U.S. at 90. And, the applicable MDOC Policy Directive provides that grievances must include "[d]ates, times, places, and names of all those involved in the issue being grieved." (Doc. #14-2 at ¶R). The Sixth Circuit, however, has cautioned courts against being too technical when deciding whether a prisoner's grievance has been properly exhausted. See LaFountain v. Martin, 334 Fed. Appx. 738, 2009 WL 1546376, at *2 (6th Cir. 2009) ("It is sufficient for a court to find that a prisoner's [grievance] gave prison officials fair notice of the alleged mistreatment or misconduct that forms the basis of the constitutional or statutory claim made against a defendant in a prisoner's complaint."). Notably, then, "[a]lthough the [MDOC] policy requires a grievance to include specific names, those requirements are relaxed when the purpose of the grievance has been achieved." Hall v. Raja, 2010 U.S. Dist. LEXIS 77651, 2010 WL 3070141, at *3 (E.D. Mich. Aug. 2, 2010). In other words, "The exhaustion requirement was not designed as a web to ensnare unsophisticated prisoners in procedural technicalities, but rather to prevent inmates from using the federal courts as their first forum to resolve grievances." Hall v. Raja, 2009 U.S. Dist. LEXIS 126333, 2009 WL 6315346, at *5 (E.D. Mich. Aug. 28, 2009) (emphasis in original).

As set forth above, in both the JCF Grievance and the LMF Grievance, Hodges alleged that Dr. Berhane, "acting alone or in concert with others," denied his requests for off-site referral to an orthopedic specialist as well as treatment for his cancer. (Docs. #1-3 at 15, 1-4 at 1). Neither of these grievances was rejected for lack of specificity, nor was Hodges asked to identify who the "others" were. Moreover, the Step II response to the LMF Grievance specifically indicated that: "Investigation into this matter has revealed you were provided continuous medical care while at this facility. There is no evidence of deliberate indifference to your health care needs as you have claimed." (Doc. #1-3 at 21). Presumably, then, Hodges' medical record and/or history were reviewed - which would have revealed Dr. Squier's decision to monitor Hodges, rather than send him to a radiation oncologist.

On the present record, then, the Court cannot say that Hodges failed to comply with the "spirit and purpose of the administrative exhaustion rules" with respect to Dr. Squier. Hall, 2010 U.S. Dist. LEXIS 77651, 2010 WL 3070141, at *3. There is no indication that Dr. Squier ever provided direct patient care to Hodges; thus, it is certainly reasonable to infer that, at the time he filed these grievances, he had no way of knowing that she was the individual who he now alleges was making the ultimate decision not to refer him to a radiation oncologist. For these reasons, despite the fact that neither the JCF Grievance nor the LMF grievance specifically named Dr. Squier, the Court finds that, on the current record, a reasonable jury could find that these grievances gave Dr. Squier fair notice of the claims against her. See, e.g., Stevenson v. Mich. Dep't of Corr., 2008 U.S. Dist. LEXIS 16459, 2008 WL 623783, at * (W.D. Mich. Mar. 4, 2008) (grievance naming specific individuals and "all those equally involved" was substantially similar to the facts alleged in Plaintiff's complaint and, thus, "gave Defendants sufficient notice to address and resolve the claim that Plaintiff brings against them in his complaint"); Contor v. Caruso, 2008 U.S. Dist. LEXIS 24937, 2008 WL 878665, at *3 (W.D. Mich. Mar. 28, 2008) (noting that "prisoners may not be able to learn the names of all persons involved in a situation given prisoners' limited access to information" and concluding that grievance sufficiently put prison officials on notice); Austin v. Corr. Med. Servs., 2008 U.S. Dist. LEXIS 77008, 2008 WL 4426342, at *5 (W.D. Mich. Sept. 26, 2008) (grievance naming "the Medical Service Department here at M.C.F." was sufficient to exhaust claims against the named defendants).

For all of these reasons, the Court finds that the Corizon Defendants' motion to dismiss based on exhaustion grounds should be denied, and Hodges should be permitted to proceed with his Eighth Amendment denial-of-medical-care claims against Dr. Squier, Dr. Berhane, and P.A. Buskirk.

JAMES MERRION, PLAINTIFF VS. CORIZON HEALTH, INC., ET AL., DEFENDANTS. Civil Action No. 1:13-CV-1757 UNITED STATES DISTRICT COURT FOR THE MIDDLE DISTRICT OF PENNSYLVANIA

(SEE DISCUSSION UNDER MEDICAL CARE)

C. The Prison Litigation Reform Act ("PLRA") Does Not Apply

Defendants argue that they are entitled to summary judgment because Plaintiff is subject to the PLRA, and was required to exhaust his administrative remedies prior to filing suit. According to Plaintiff, because he was not incarcerated when he filed suit, the PLRA does not apply to him. Pursuant to the plain language of the statute, as well as controlling case law from the Third Circuit Court of Appeals, we must agree with Plaintiff.

The PLRA states that "[n]o action shall be brought with respect to prison conditions . . . by a prisoner confined in any jail, prison, or other correctional facility until such administrative remedies as are available are exhausted." 42 U.S.C. § 1997e(a) (emphasis added). In Ahmed v. Dragovich, 297 F.3d 201 (3d Cir. 2002), the Third Circuit explicitly held that the PLRA does not apply to former prisoners who file suit after their release. Id. at 210. "Any other view would be inconsistent with the spirit of the PLRA, which was designed to deter frivolous litigations by idle prisoners." Id. (emphasis added). The Third Circuit noted that every court of appeals to have considered this issue has arrived at the same conclusion. Id. at 210 n.10 (collecting cases). Defendants' contention that Plaintiff should be considered a prisoner because he was subject to electronic monitoring is unavailing. A "prisoner" is defined in the statute as "any person incarcerated or detained in any facility who is accused of, convicted of, sentenced for, or adjudicated delinquent for, violations of criminal laws or the terms and conditions of parole . . . ." 28 U.S.C. § 1915(h) (emphasis added). Because Plaintiff was not "incarcerated or detained in any facility" when he filed suit, he is not bound by the PLRA's exhaustion requirement. See Kerr v. Puckett, 138 F.3d 321, 323 (7th Cir. 1998) (finding PLRA not applicable to lawsuit filed by inmate after he was released on parole).

LAWRENCE MARTIN ADC # 106491, PLAINTIFF v. CORIZON CORRECTIONAL MEDICAL SERVICES; et al., DEFENDANTS 5:13CV00364-KGB-JJV UNITED STATES DISTRICT COURT FOR THE EASTERN DISTRICT OF ARKANSAS, PINE BLUFF DIVISION

(SEE ALSO ARGUMENT UNDER MEDICAL CARE)

B. ADC Defendants

1. Administrative Exhaustion

The Prison Litigation Reform Act (PLRA) requires an inmate to exhaust prison grievance procedures before filing suit in federal court. See 42 U.S.C. § 1997e(a); Jones v. Bock, 549 U.S. 199, 202, 127 S. Ct. 910, 166 L. Ed. 2d

798 (2007); Jones v. Norris, 310 F.3d 610, 612 (8th Cir. 2002). Exhaustion under the PLRA is mandatory. Jones, 549 U.S. at 211. "[T]o properly exhaust administrative remedies, prisoners must 'complete the administrative review process in accordance with the applicable procedural rules,' rules that are defined not by the PLRA, but by the prison grievance process itself." Id., 549 U.S. at 218 (quoting Woodford v. Ngo, 548 U.S. 81, 88, 126 S. Ct. 2378, 165 L. Ed. 2d 368 (2006)). Compliance with a prison's grievance procedures is, therefore, all that is required by the PLRA to properly exhaust. Id. Thus, the question as to whether an inmate has properly exhausted administrative remedies will depend on the specifics of that particular prison's grievance policy. See Id.

ADC Directive 12-16 governs exhaustion of Plaintiff's claims. (Doc. No. 181-3.) The directive requires inmates to submit an informal resolution, a formal grievance, and an appeal to the Assistant and/or Deputy Director level in order to fully exhaust a claim. (Doc. No. 181-4 ÷ 5.) According to the affidavit of Barbara Williams, ADC Inmate Grievance Supervisor, Plaintiff exhausted four grievances -- CU-13-01340, CU-13-01435, CU-13-01608, and CU-13-02109 -- which are relevant to the claims underlying this action. (Id. ÷ 8.) She states that none of these grievances identified Defendants Selvey, Warner, Brown, or Puckett and, therefore, no claims against them were exhausted. (Id.) The Court agrees.

Directive 12-16 clearly states a requirement that inmates must be specific as to the personnel involved in any grieved incident. (Doc. No. 181-3 at 5.) The Court has reviewed the grievances in question and confirmed that these four Defendants are not specifically named or otherwise referenced therein. (Doc. Nos. 181-5 - 181-8.) Plaintiff has not offered any argument to the contrary. Accordingly, the Court recommends that Defendants Selvey, Warner, Brown, and Puckett be dismissed without prejudice due to Plaintiff's failure to exhaust administrative remedies against them. See Barbee v. Correctional Medical Services, 394 Fed. Appx. 337, 338 (2010) ("Once the court determined that the claims were unexhausted, it was required to dismiss them without prejudice.").

2. Qualified Immunity[5]

[5] In their brief, ADC Defendants raise a separate argument that the weight of evidence does not support a violation of Plaintiff's Eighth Amendment rights. Analysis of that argument overlaps with a discussion of qualified immunity, and the Court elects to evaluate immunity first because "Qualified immunity is immunity from suit rather than a mere defense to liability, and therefore, immunity issues should be resolved at the earliest possible stage of the litigation." Saucier v. Katz, 533 U.S. 194, 201, 121 S. Ct. 2151, 150 L. Ed. 2d 272 (2001).

Qualified immunity protects officials who acted in an objectively reasonable manner and shields a government official from liability when his or her conduct does not violate "clearly established statutory or constitutional rights of which a reasonable person would have known." Harlow v. Fitzgerald, 457 U.S. 800, 818, 102 S. Ct. 2727, 73 L. Ed. 2d 396 (1982). Qualified immunity is a question of law, not a question of fact. McClendon v. Story County Sheriff's Office, 403 F.3d 510, 515 (8th Cir. 2005). Thus, issues concerning qualified immunity are appropriately resolved on summary judgment. See Mitchell v. Forsyth, 472 U.S. 511, 526, 105 S. Ct. 2806, 86 L. Ed. 2d 411 (1985) (the privilege is "an immunity from suit rather than a mere defense to liability; and like an absolute immunity, it is effectively lost if a case is erroneously permitted to go to trial.").

To determine whether defendants are entitled to qualified immunity, courts generally consider two questions: (1) whether the facts alleged or shown, construed in the light most favorable to the plaintiff, establish a violation of a constitutional or statutory right; and (2) whether that right was so clearly established that a reasonable official would have known that his or her actions were unlawful. Pearson v. Callahan, 555 U.S. 223, 232, 129 S. Ct. 808, 172 L. Ed. 2d 565 (2009); see also Saucier v. Katz, 533 U.S. 194, 201, 121 S. Ct. 2151, 150 L. Ed. 2d 272 (2001).[6] Defendants are entitled to qualified immunity only if no reasonable fact finder could answer both questions in the affirmative. Nelson v. Correctional Medical Services, 583 F.3d 522, 528 (8th Cir. 2009).

[6] Courts are "permitted to exercise their sound discretion in deciding which of the two prongs of the qualified immunity analysis should be addressed first in light of the circumstances in the particular case at hand." Nelson v. Correctional Medical Services, 583 F.3d 522, 528 (8th Cir. 2009) (quoting Pearson v. Callahan, 555 U.S. at 236).

After reviewing the record, the Court finds that the facts shown, construed in a light most favorable to Plaintiff, do not establish a violation of his rights. ADC Defendants state that Plaintiff received his medical classification based on determinations made by licensed medical personnel. (Doc. No. 181-13 ÷ 7.) In turn, his job assignment was based on the restrictions, or lack thereof, specified by his medical classification. (Id.) The Court is convinced that the overwhelming weight of evidence indicates that "inside lawn duty" did not exceed Plaintiff's physical abilities, as determined by medical staff. The record indicates that Plaintiff's work day was not particularly strenuous or long. Defendant Swygart avers that Plaintiff was primarily assigned to pick up trash, none of which exceeded his nineteen-pound lifting restriction. (Id. ÷ 10-11.) He was not made to work more than his four-hour restriction, and he was provided frequent breaks for water and rest. (Doc. Nos. 183-13 ÷ 10-12, 183-14.)

Even assuming, for the sake argument, that Plaintiff's medical classification was made erroneously, ADC Defendants would still not be liable. It is established that, where a defendant lacks medical expertise, they cannot be held liable for the diagnostic decisions of medical staff. See Camberos v. Branstad, 73 F.3d 174, 176 (8th Cir. 1995). Plaintiff's medical classification fits squarely within the category of a "diagnostic decision" and there is no evidence indicating that any ADC Defendant had the medical expertise to reach a different conclusion. As such, they were completely justified in relying on the determinations of the medical staff.

Based on the foregoing, the Court finds that Defendants Jones, Lay, May, Swygart, and Wood are entitled to qualified immunity and Plaintiff's claims against them should be dismissed.

3. Official Capacity Claims

Lastly, any official capacity claims for damages against the ADC Defendants should also be dismissed. These claims are akin to claims against the state itself. See Kentucky v. Graham, 473 U.S. 159, 166, 105 S. Ct. 3099, 87 L. Ed. 2d 114 (1985). It necessarily follows that these official capacity damage claims are barred by the Eleventh Amendment. Will v. Mich. Dep't of State Police, 491 U.S. 58, 70-71, 109 S. Ct. 2304, 105 L. Ed. 2d 45 (1989).

KENNETH R. HARRISON, #160623, Plaintiff, v. CORIZON MEDICAL SERVICES, Defendant. CIVIL ACTION NO. 2:14-CV-1251-MHT UNITED STATES DISTRICT COURT FOR THE MIDDLE DISTRICT OF ALABAMA, EASTERN DIVISION

I. INTRODUCTION

In this 42 U.S.C. § 1983 action, Kenneth R. Harrison ("Harrison"), a former state inmate, challenges the medical treatment provided to him for an atrial septal defect ("ASD"), congenital heart condition, during his incarceration in the Alabama prison system. Complaint - Doc. No. 1 at 3.[1] Specifically, Harrison contends that after his appointment with a free-world cardiologist in April of 2014 the defendant acted with deliberate indifference to his heart condition. Harrison names Corizon Medical Services as the sole defendant in this cause of action. He seeks monetary damages for the alleged violation of his constitutional rights. Id. at 4.

1 Harrison was released from state custody on February 1, 2015.

The defendant filed a special report and supporting evidentiary materials addressing Harrison's claims for relief. In these documents, the defendant adamantly denies that it acted with deliberate indifference to Harrison's heart condition. The defendant further asserts that the complaint is due to be dismissed because prior to filing this cause of action Harrison failed to properly exhaust an administrative remedy available to him during his incarceration in the Alabama prison system. Defendant's Special Report - Doc. No. 6 at 6-7. The defendant bases its exhaustion defense on Harrison's failure to file a grievance in accordance with the grievance procedure provided by Corizon regarding the claims raised in the instant complaint. Id. at 7.

"[A]n exhaustion defense . . . is not ordinarily the proper subject for a summary judgment; instead it should be raised in a motion to dismiss, or be treated as such if raised in a motion for summary judgment." Bryant v. Rich, 530 F.3d 1368, 1374-75 (11th Cir. 2008) (internal quotations omitted); Trias v. Fla. Dep't of Corr., 587 F. App'x 531, 534 (11th Cir. 2014) (holding that the district court properly construed defendant's "motion for summary judgment as a motion to dismiss for failure to exhaust administrative remedies"). The court will therefore treat the defendant's report as a motion to dismiss. Bryant, 530 F.3d at 1375; Order of February 12, 2015 - Doc. No. 9 (advising Harrison that the defendant's report will be treated as a dispositive motion and explaining the manner in which to respond to such a motion).

II. STANDARD OF REVIEW

The Eleventh Circuit has determined that

the question of exhaustion under the PLRA [is] a "threshold matter" that [federal courts must] address before considering the merits of the case. Chandler v. Crosby, 379 F.3d 1278, 1286 (11th Cir. 2004). Because exhaustion is mandated by the statute, [a court has] no discretion to waive this requirement. Alexander v. Hawk, 159 F.3d 1321, 1325-26 (11th Cir. 1998).Myles v. Miami-Dade Cnty. Corr. and Rehab. Dep't, 476 F. App'x 364, 366 (11th Cir. 2012). Based on the foregoing, the court will "resolve this issue first." Id.

When deciding whether a prisoner has exhausted his remedies, the court should first consider the plaintiff's and the defendants' versions of the facts, and if they conflict, take the plaintiff's version of the facts as true. "If in that light, the defendant is entitled to have the complaint dismissed for failure to exhaust administrative remedies, it must be dismissed." Turner v. Burnside, 541 F.3d 1077, 1082 (11th Cir. 2008) (citing Bryant, 530 F.3d at 1373-74). If the complaint is not subject to dismissal at this step, then the court should make "specific findings in order to resolve the disputed factual issues related to exhaustion." Id. (citing Bryant, 530 F.3d at 1373-74, 1376). Myles, 476 F. App'x at 366.

Consequently, a district court may resolve disputed factual issues where necessary to the disposition of a motion to dismiss for failure to exhaust [without a hearing]. See [Turner, 541 F.3d at 1082]. The judge properly may consider facts outside of the pleadings [i.e., evidentiary materials submitted in support of the special report] to resolve a factual dispute as to exhaustion where doing so does not decide the merits, and the parties have a sufficient opportunity to develop the record. Bryant, 530 F.3d at 1376. Trias, 587 F. App'x at 535.

Upon review of the undisputed facts of this case as evidenced by the evidentiary materials filed by the defendant, the court concludes that the defendant's motion to dismiss is due to be granted.

III. DISCUSSION

Harrison challenges the constitutionality of medical treatment he received for a heart condition. In response to the complaint, the defendant denies Harrison's allegations and further argues that this case is subject to dismissal because Harrison failed to properly exhaust the available administrative remedy prior to filing this complaint as required by the Prison Litigation Reform Act, 42 U.S.C. § 1997e(a).

The Prison Litigation Reform Act compels exhaustion of available administrative remedies before a prisoner can seek relief in federal court on a § 1983 complaint. Specifically, 42 U.S.C. § 1997e(a) states that "[n]o action shall be brought with respect to prison conditions under section 1983 of this title, or any other Federal law, by a prisoner confined in any jail, prison, or other correctional facility until such administrative remedies as are available are exhausted." "Congress has provided in § 1997e(a) that an inmate must exhaust irrespective of the forms of relief sought and offered through administrative remedies." Booth v. Churner, 532 U.S. 731, 741 n.6, 121 S. Ct. 1819, 149 L. Ed. 2d 958 (2001). "[T]he PLRA's exhaustion requirement applies to all inmate suits about prison life, whether they involve general circumstances or particular episodes, and whether they allege excessive force or some other wrong." Porter v. Nussle, 534 U.S. 516, 532, 122 S. Ct. 983, 152 L. Ed. 2d 12 (2002). Exhaustion of all available administrative remedies is a precondition to litigation and a federal court cannot waive the exhaustion requirement. Booth, 532 U.S. at 741; Alexander v. Hawk, 159 F.3d 1321, 1325 (11th Cir. 1998); Woodford v. Ngo, 548 U.S. 81, 126 S. Ct. 2378, 165 L. Ed. 2d 368 (2006). Moreover, "the PLRA exhaustion requirement requires proper exhaustion." Woodford, 548 U.S. at 93 (emphasis added).

Proper exhaustion demands compliance with an agency's deadlines and other critical procedural rules [as a precondition to filing a civil action in federal court] because no adjudicative system can function effectively without imposing some orderly structure on the courts of its proceedings. . . . Construing § 1997e(a) to require proper exhaustion . . . fits with the general scheme of the PLRA, whereas [a contrary] interpretation [allowing an inmate to bring suit in federal court once administrative remedies are no longer available] would turn that provision into a   largely useless appendage.

548 U.S. at 90-91, 93. The Court reasoned that because proper exhaustion of administrative remedies is necessary an inmate cannot "satisfy the Prison Litigation Reform Act's exhaustion requirement . . . by filing an untimely or otherwise procedurally defective administrative grievance or appeal[,]" or by effectively bypassing the administrative process simply by waiting until the grievance procedure is no longer available to him. 548 U.S. at 83-84; Johnson v. Meadows, 418 F.3d 1152, 1157 (11th Cir. 2005) (inmate who files an untimely grievance or simply spurns the administrative process until it is no longer available fails to satisfy the exhaustion requirement of the PLRA). "The only facts pertinent to determining whether a prisoner has satisfied the PLRA's exhaustion requirement are those that existed when he filed his original complaint." Smith v. Terry, 491 F. App'x 81, 83 (11th Cir. 2012) (per curiam) (emphasis added).

The record in this case is undisputed that the defendant provides a grievance procedure for inmate complaints related to the provision of medical treatment. The defendant explains the procedure and relevant facts as follows:

. . . The initial orientation process with the ADOC correctional system includes educating inmates as to the availability of the grievance process. The existence   of this grievance procedure is well-known among the prison population, as indicated by the fact that the medical staff at Ventress receives inmate requests and/or inmate grievances on a daily basis. The physicians, nurse practitioners, nurses and other medical personnel at Staton [and other facilities] attempt to resolve all inmate concerns prior to an "inmate grievance" being submitted.

The grievance process is initiated when an inmate submits a Medical Grievance form to the HSA through the institutional mail system. After reviewing the Medical Grievance, the HSA [or her designee] then provides a written response [to the grievance] within approximately ten (10) days of receipt of the Inmate Grievance. The written response to a Medical Grievance is included on the bottom portion of the same form containing an inmate's Medical Grievance. Below the portion of the form designated for the "Response," the following notation appears:

IF YOU WISH TO APPEAL THIS REVIEW YOU MAY REQUEST A GRIEVANCE APPEAL FORM FROM THE HEALTH SERVICES ADMINISTRATOR. RETURN THE COMPLETED FORM TO THE ATTENTION OF THE HEALTH SERVICE ADMINISTRATOR. YOU MAY PLACE THE FORM IN THE SICK CALL REQUEST BOX OR GIVE IT TO THE SEGREGATION SICK CALL NURSE ON ROUNDS.

As stated in the Medical Grievance forms, the second step of the grievance process involves the submission of a formal Medical Grievance Appeal, at which time the inmate may be brought in for one-on-one communication with the medical staff, HSA and/or the Director of Nursing. A written response to a formal Medical Grievance Appeal is provided within approximately ten (10) days of receipt. Medical Grievance and Medical Grievance Appeal forms are available from the Health Care Unit and the correctional shift commander office at [each facility]. Inmates are instructed to place completed Medical Grievance and Medical Grievance Appeal forms in the sick call boxes located [in the facility]. The HSA reviews the grievances daily, provides a written response within approximately ten (10) days at the bottom of the form and returns a copy of the completed forms to the inmate. The HSA encourages inmates who have complaints about the medical care they have sought or received at [the facility] to utilize this grievance process. Mr. Harrison did not submit any Medical Grievances or Medical Grievance Appeal [regarding the treatment provided for his heart condition] during the course of his incarceration at Staton.

Defendant's Exhibit 1 (Aff. of Darryl Ellis, Director of Nursing for Staton) - Doc. No. 6-1 at 5-6; Defendant's Exhibit 6 (Aff. of Loris Baugh, Health Services   Administrator at Kilby) - Doc. No. 6-6 at 2 ("The grievance process at [the relevant correctional facilities] is identical and I am the individual typically responsible for overseeing and responding to grievances at Kilby. During his incarceration at Kilby, Mr. Harrison did not submit any grievance of any kind.").

Upon review of the arguments set forth by the defendant, the court entered an order which provided Harrison an opportunity to file a response to these arguments in which he was advised to "specifically address the defendant's assertion[] that . . . [h]is claims are due to be dismissed because he failed to exhaust his available administrative remedies as required by 42 U.S.C. § 1997e(a) of the Prison Litigation Reform Act ('PLRA')" prior to filing this federal civil action. Order of February 12, 2015 - Doc. No. 9 at 1. The time allowed Harrison to file his response expired on February 26, 2015. Id. at 2. As of the present date, Harrison has filed no response to this order.

The evidentiary materials filed by the defendant demonstrate that Harrison failed to file the requisite grievance prior to initiation of this federal civil action. Harrison does not dispute his failure to exhaust the administrative remedy available to him in the prison system prior to filing this case. In addition, there is nothing before the court which justifies Harrison's failure to exhaust the grievance procedure provided by Corizon. It is likewise clear that the administrative remedy provided by the defendant is no longer available to Harrison due to his release from prison. Under these circumstances, dismissal with prejudice is appropriate. Bryant, 530 F.3d at 1375 n.1; Johnson, 418 F.3d at 1157; Marsh v. Jones, 53 F.3d 707, 710 (5th Cir. 1995) ("Without the prospect of a dismissal with prejudice, a prisoner could evade the exhaustion requirement by filing no administrative grievance or by intentionally filing an untimely one, thereby foreclosing administrative remedies and gaining access to a federal forum without exhausting administrative remedies."); Berry v. Kerik, 366 F.3d 85, 88 (2d Cir. 2004) (footnotes omitted) (inmate's "federal lawsuits . . . properly dismissed with prejudice" where previously available administrative remedies had become unavailable). Consequently, the court concludes that this case is subject to dismissal with prejudice as Harrison failed to properly exhaust an administrative remedy available to him during his prior term of incarceration which is a precondition to proceeding in this court on his complaint.

NORMAN GRAY, # 108144, Plaintiff, v. CORIZON HEALTH SERVICES, et al., Defendants. Case No. 1:14-cv-947 UNITED STATES DISTRICT COURT FOR THE WESTERN DISTRICT OF MICHIGAN, SOUTHERN DIVISION

This is a civil rights action brought by a state prisoner under 42 U.S.C. § 1983. Plaintiff filed this lawsuit on September 15, 2014, regarding conditions of his confinement at the Muskegon Correctional Facility (MCF). The defendants are Corizon Health Services (Corizon) and Dr. William D. Nelson. Plaintiff alleges that defendants violated his rights under the Eighth Amendment's Cruel and Unusual Punishments Clause.[1]

1   Plaintiff's complaint refers to defendant Corizon as "Corizon Health Services, Inc." His pleading also contains passing references to the First and Fourteenth Amendments. The Eighth Amendment's Cruel and Unusual Punishments Clause applies to the states through the Fourteenth Amendment's Due Process Clause. See Graham v. Florida, 560 U.S. 48, 53, 130 S. Ct. 2011, 176 L. Ed. 2d 825 (2010). Plaintiff has not alleged any facts supporting a claim under the Fourteenth Amendment's Equal Protection Clause or the First Amendment.

Dr. Nelson

Plaintiff alleges that in December 2013 and January 2014, Dr. Nelson found that plaintiff had a suspected case of tuberculosis and ordered that he be transported to Muskegon Mercy Hospital spread of tuberculosis. (Compl. at Page ID 3). According to plaintiff, hospital tests revealed that he did not have tuberculosis, but did have a possible fungal infection in his lungs. Plaintiff was sent back to prison with prescription medication for the suspected fungal infection. When follow-up x-rays suggested that plaintiff's lung problem was getting worse, plaintiff was transported back to the hospital for a CT scan and a lung biopsy. In July 2014, Mercy Hospital Staff informed plaintiff of the diagnosis of lung cancer. (Id.).

Corizon

Plaintiff alleges that Corizon is Dr. Nelson's employer and a conclusion that the medical care that plaintiff received was delayed, inadequate, and inconsistent. (Id. at Page ID 4-5). Plaintiff seeks an award of damages. (Id. at Page ID 6).

The matter is now before the court on defendants' motion for summary judgment based on the affirmative defense provided by 42 U.S.C. § 1997e(a). For the reasons set forth herein, I recommend that defendants' motion for summary judgment (docket # 11) be granted and that all plaintiff's claims against defendants be dismissed without prejudice.

Proposed Findings of Fact

The following facts are beyond genuine issue. Plaintiff filed this lawsuit on September 15, 2014, while he was an inmate at the Muskegon Correctional Facility (MCF). The defendants are Dr. William D. Nelson and Corizon Health Services, Inc. (Corizon).

Plaintiff concedes that he did not exhaust any claim against defendants through the MDOC's grievance process before he filed this lawsuit. (Plf. Brief at 2-3, docket # 19, Page ID 68-69).

Discussion

Defendants have raised the affirmative defense that plaintiff did not properly exhaust his administrative remedies against them as required by 42 U.S.C. § 1997e(a). Plaintiff argues that he should be excused from the exhaustion requirement "because of a serious illness, see medical records." (Plf. Brief at 3, Page ID 69). Plaintiff did not submit any medical evidence in support of his argument. Thus, there is no evidence before the court that plaintiff's medical condition prevented him from utilizing the MDOC's grievance process. Exhaustion is mandatory. Woodford, 548 U.S. at 85. "[N]o unexhausted claim may be considered." Jones v. Bock, 549 U.S. at 220. Plaintiff did not properly exhaust any claim against defendants before he filed this lawsuit. I find that defendants have carried their burden on the affirmative defense and are entitled to dismissal of all of plaintiff's claims.

TELLY ROYSTER, PLAINTIFF V. CORIZON, ET AL., DEFENDANTS CIVIL NO. 3:CV-13-1449 UNITED STATES DISTRICT COURT FOR THE MIDDLE DISTRICT OF PENNSYLVANIA

I. Introduction

Plaintiff, Telly Royster, filed this civil rights action pursuant to 42 U.S.C. § 1983. He is currently confined at the Greene State Correctional Institution (SCI-Greene), in Waynesburg, Pennsylvania. He names 31 defendants who are either employed by the Pennsylvania Department of Corrections (DOC) at SCI-Camp Hill, in Camp Hill, Pennsylvania, or by Corizon, the contract medical care providers at SCI-Camp Hill, Mr. Royster's former place of confinement. Mr. Royster claims defendants violated his Eighth Amendment rights by delaying his receipt of his migraine medication. He also claims some of the defendants retaliated against him by rewriting his migraine script after he complained about the delay. (Doc. 1-1, Comp.)

Presently before the court is Mr. Royster's Second Motion to Compel. (Doc. 72.) Mr. Royster seeks to compel the defendants to produce the name of all inmates (and their current locations) that were housed with him in the same area of SCI-Camp Hill's Special Management Unit (SMU). He also seeks the defendants to produce copies of his medical and grievance records requested in discovery free of charge. Finally, Mr. Royster claims "Defendants are refusing to cooperate in any manner to plaintiff's discovery request". (Doc. 73, ECF p. 1.) Defendants urge the court to deny the motion based on Mr. Royster's failure to specify which of their discovery responses he finds lacking, why he should be entitled to free copies of discovery documents, or any facts to support his conclusory allegation that they are intentionally thwarting his discovery efforts. (Doc. 74.) In his reply brief, Mr. Royster claims to be "dissatisfied with every response and objection made by defendants" to his discovery requests. (Doc. 77.) However, Mr. Royster has not supplied a copy of defendants' responses. (Id.) Additionally, he interjects that he should be permitted to correspond with any inmates housed at SCI-Camp Hill, not just the ones housed in the same housing unit, because conferring with them may "lead to admissible evidence". (Doc. 77.)

II. Standard of Review

Fed. R. Civ. P. 37(a) allows a party to file a motion to compel discovery where the opposing party fails to respond adequately to document request propounded pursuant to Fed. R. Civ. P. 34. Fed. R. Civ. P. 37(a)(3)(B)(iv). Pursuant to Fed. R. Civ. P. 26(b)(1), a party "may obtain discovery regarding any nonprivileged matter that is relevant to any party's claim or defense." Fed. R. Civ. P. 26(b)(1). Relevant information sought in discovery need not be admissible at trial, as long as it "appears reasonably calculated to lead to the discovery of admissible evidence. (Id.) Relevance is generally "construed broadly to encompass any matter that bears on, or that reasonably could lead to other matter that could bear on, any issue that is or may be in the case." Oppenheimer Fund, Inc. v. Sanders, 437 U.S. 340, 351, 98 S.Ct. 2380, 2389, 57 L.Ed.2d 253 (1978). The moving party bears the initial burden of showing that the requested discovery is relevant. Morrison v. Phila. Hous. Auth., 203 F.R.D. 195, 196 (E.D.Pa. 2001).

While generally liberal, permissible discovery is not without limitations, it "should not serve as a fishing expedition." Provine v. Ambulatory Health Services, Inc., No. 13-334, 2014 U.S. Dist. LEXIS 702, 2014 WL 47771, *2 (M.D. Pa. Jan. 6, 2014). It is well established that the scope and conduct of discovery are within the sound discretion of the trial court. In re Cendant Corp. Sec. Litig., 343 F.3d 658, 661-62 (3d Cir. 2003). "Rulings regarding the proper scope of discovery, and the extent to which discovery may be compelled, are matters consigned to the Court's discretion and judgment." McConnell v. Canadian Pacific Realty Co., 280 F.R.D. 188, 192 (M.D. Pa. 2011). A court's decision regarding the conduct of discovery will be disturbed only upon a showing of an abuse of discretion. Ohntrup v. Makina Ve Kimya Endustrisi Kurumu, 760 F.3d 290, 296 (3d Cir. 2014).

III. Discussion

A. SCI-Camp Hill's SMU D-Pod Housing Logs for March 2012[1]

1 "Identify each inmate housed on D-pod of the SMU in March of 2012. Produce the document(s) used to answer this interrogatory." (Doc. 73, ECF p. 2).

In his Complaint, Mr. Royster claims that between March 2011 and April 2012 he was regularly denied migraine medication. In his motion to compel he argues that defendants have objected to his prior requests to correspond with inmates who were not housed in the same housing area. He claims that defendants refused to produce documents indicating who those inmates were. (Doc. 73.) Without addressing the merits of Mr. Royster's allegations, defendants argue that "Plaintiff has failed to identify a discovery request which sought" the identification of these inmates, suggesting they never received a request for production of documents asking for the logbook. However, attached to Mr. Royster's brief in support of his Motion to Compel is a document entitled "Interrogatories and Production of Documents on Sgt. Flinn." (Doc. 73, ECF p. 2.) The document is dated October 18, 2014. (Id.) If this is a properly served discovery request, Mr. Royster must supply the court with proof of proper service of this request, defendants' response to his discovery request, and advise the court why the response is inadequate or otherwise improper. Without this information the court cannot accurately assess Mr. Royster's motion to compel. Mr. Royster's motion to compel the production of SCI-Camp Hill's SMU D-Pod housing log for March 2012 is denied without prejudice.

B. Defendants are not Required to Produce Gratis Discovery.

Mr. Royster seeks defendants to provide him with free copies of his medical and grievance records he requested via discovery. Although Mr. Royster proceeds in forma pauperis, there "is no provision in the [in forma pauperis] statute for the payment by the government of the costs of deposition transcripts, or any other litigation expenses, and no other statute authorizes courts to commit federal monies for payment of the necessary expenses in a civil suit brought by an indigent litigant." Tabron v. Grace, 6 F.3d 147, 159 (3d Cir. 1993). Thus, with respect to discovery documents, defendants have the obligation to produce them for Mr. Royster's inspection. To the extent he seeks copies of these documents, he should consult prison policies which will allow him, provided he follows the policy guidelines, to go into debt for the purpose of making photocopies of legal documents. Accordingly, Mr. Royster's motion to compel defendants to provide him with free copies of his medical and grievance records is denied.

C. Defendants Non-Compliance with Discovery.

Fed. R. Civ. P. 37(b) permits a court to impose sanctions for a party's noncompliance with discovery obligations. Mr. Royster's allegations that defendants "are refusing to cooperate in any manner" with his discovery requests is not persuasive. Mr. Royster has failed to carry his burden to demonstrate that the defendants have either failed to respond to his discovery requests or have failed to produce documents responsive to a document request. In fact, Mr. Royster has failed to point to any specific discovery request that defendants have failed to answer. While "dissatisfied" with defendants' responses, he is not guaranteed satisfying discovery responses, he is guaranteed complete answers or objections to his properly served interrogatories or documents requests. To date Mr. Royster has not demonstrated any dilatory or obstructive behavior by defendants in responding to properly served discovery requests. Therefore, Mr. Royster's allegations of defendants' non-cooperation with discovery, standing alone, cannot support the imposition of sanctions.

DENIAL OF MEANINGFUL ACCESS TO COURTS

Courts require litigants provide citations to authority that support their positions. Even though appointed counsel clearly fail to provide adequate representation, prison systems, to deny litigants the opportunity to present their claims, refuse to provide them with access to cases law and use paralegals, not authorized to assist them in presenting arguments and case law, violating the right to equal opportunity. These decisions reflect violations of the right to equal access to the courts.

STATE OF ARIZONA, APPELLEE, V. HECTOR E. APARICIO VASQUEZ, APPELLANT. *2015 ARIZ. APP. UNPUB. LEXIS 1484* (DECEMBER 8, 2015)
FACTS AND PROCEDURAL BACKGROUND

In June 2013, Vasquez backed a truck out of a parking space and ran into the victim's car. The victim testified that Vasquez--who got out of the driver's side of the truck--smelled of alcohol, was stumbling, and appeared to be drunk.

Phoenix Police officers who arrived at the scene noticed that Vasquez's eyes were bloodshot and watery, and that his breath smelled moderately of alcohol. Vasquez acknowledged hitting the other car, and he told an officer that he drank a few beers before driving and that his license was suspended. A Motor Vehicle Division report confirmed that Vasquez's license was suspended at the time.

About one and a half hours after the collision, a police phlebotomist drew two samples of Vasquez's blood. Testing showed a blood alcohol concentration ("BAC") of 0.098.

The State charged Vasquez with two class 4 felony counts of aggravated DUI: (1) driving while impaired to the slightest degree with a suspended license, *see Ariz. Rev. Stat. ("A.R.S.") §§ 28-1381(A)(1),-1383(A)(1)*, and (2) driving with a BAC of at least 0.08 with a suspended license, *see A.R.S. §§ 28-1381(A)(2),-1383(A)(1)*. After a five-day trial, a jury found Vasquez guilty as charged.

After a subsequent trial to determine whether Vasquez had prior convictions, the superior court found that Vasquez had one historical prior felony conviction: a conviction of aggravated DUI in 1995. *See A.R.S. § 13-105(22)(a)(iv)*. The court sentenced Vasquez as a category two repetitive offender to concurrent, presumptive terms of 4.5 years, with credit for 405 days of presentence incarceration. Vasquez timely appealed.

We have reviewed the record for reversible error, *see Leon, 104 Ariz. at 300*, and we find none. Vasquez was present and represented by counsel at all stages of the proceedings against him. The record reflects that the superior court afforded Vasquez all his constitutional and statutory rights, and that the proceedings were conducted in accordance with the Arizona Rules of Criminal Procedure. The court conducted appropriate pretrial hearings, and the evidence presented at trial supported the jury's verdicts. Vasquez's sentences fall within the range prescribed by law, with proper credit given for presentence incarceration.

After the filing of this decision, defense counsel's obligations pertaining to Vasquez's representation in this appeal will end after informing Vasquez of the outcome of this appeal and his future options, unless counsel's review reveals an issue appropriate for submission to the Arizona Supreme Court by petition for review. *See State v. Shattuck, 140 Ariz. 582, 584-85, 684 P.2d 154 (1984)*. Vasquez shall have 30 days from the date of this decision to proceed, if he desires, with a *pro se* motion for reconsideration or petition for review.

STATE OF ARIZONA, APPELLEE, V. MARK RYAN GERI, Appellant. *2015 Ariz. App. Unpub. LEXIS 1483 (December 8, 2015)*
FACTS AND PROCEDURAL HISTORY

We view the facts in the light most favorable to sustaining the trial court's judgment and resolve all reasonable inferences against Geri. *State v. Fontes, 195 Ariz. 229, 230 ¶ 2, 986 P.2d 897, 898 (App. 1998).*

At dawn one morning in February 2013, an apartment security guard saw two men on the roof of a neighbouring strip mall. Although he could not see the facial features of either person, the guard noted that one man--later identified as Geri--wore a lighter colored jacket and the other wore a darker colored jacket. The man in the dark jacket descended from the roof and received a duffle bag from Geri. After lowering the bag, Geri also descended and both men took off on bicycles. The security guard called 911 to report what he had witnessed.

Within one minute of receiving the call, police officers in the area observed two men matching the security guard's description exit the strip mall's rear parking lot. The officers stopped the men and had them sit on the curb where Geri and the other man, who was still carrying the duffle bag, identified themselves. Inside the duffle bag the officers discovered a copper pipe, folded and broken in several spots.

Another team of officers climbed onto the roof where the security guard saw Geri. There, the officers found that the copper drainage pipes on several air conditioning units had been broken off and that the remaining pipes had "broke, jagged" edges that were shiny, indicating that the break had occurred recently. The officers later noted that the weathering on the roof's pipes matched that of the pipes found in the duffle bag and that the two pipes were the same size. The State subsequently charged Geri with one count of third degree burglary.

Before the jury trial, the State requested a hearing pursuant to *Arizona Rule of Evidence 609*, which provides that the State may impeach a testifying defendant with his prior convictions if the probative value of those convictions outweighs their prejudicial effect. The State alleged that Geri had four prior felony convictions. The trial court did not conduct the hearing, but because Geri elected to not testify, defense counsel did not raise any objection to that. The State also alleged other aggravating circumstances, including the taking of property, the presence of an accomplice, the expectation of the receipt of pecuniary gain, and victim financial harm.

After the State rested its case-in-chief at the trial, defense counsel moved for an Arizona Rule of Criminal Procedure 20 judgment of acquittal, but the trial court denied the motion. Then, before closing arguments, Geri moved to remove his counsel, arguing that counsel "did not do his job" because counsel failed to ask the witnesses any of the pages of questions that Geri gave him to ask. The trial court denied Geri's motion. After deliberating, the jurors convicted Geri of third degree burglary. The jurors also found that the State had proved the aggravating factors of expectation of the receipt of anything of pecuniary value and the presence of an accomplice.

At the subsequent sentencing hearing conducted in compliance with *Arizona Rule of Criminal Procedure 26*, Geri admitted to having four prior felony convictions, which the trial court accepted. The trial court then sentenced Geri to eight years' imprisonment with 147 days' presentence incarceration credit. Geri timely appealed.

DISCUSSION

We review Geri's conviction and sentence for fundamental error. *See State v. Gendron, 168 Ariz. 153, 155, 812 P.2d 626, 628 (1991).*

Counsel for Geri has advised this Court that after a diligent search of the entire record, he has found no arguable question of law. We have read and considered counsel's brief and fully reviewed the record for reversible error. *See Leon, 104 Ariz. at 300, 451 P.2d at 881.* We find none. All of the proceedings were conducted in compliance with the Arizona Rules of Criminal Procedure. So far as the record reveals, Geri was represented by counsel at all stages of the proceedings, and the sentence imposed was within the statutory limits. We note that although Geri effectively claimed ineffective assistance of counsel at trial, we do not address that issue on direct appeal. *State v. Spreitz, 202 Ariz. 1, 3 ¶ 9, 39 P.3d 525, 527 (2002).* Such claims can only be addressed in a post-conviction proceeding pursuant to *Arizona Rule of Criminal Procedure 32. See State ex rel. Thomas v. Rayes, 214 Ariz. 411, 415 ¶ 20, 153 P.3d 1040, 1044 (2007).* We decline to order briefing, and we affirm Geri's conviction and sentence.

Upon the filing of this decision, defense counsel shall inform Geri of the status of his appeal and of his future options. Defense counsel has no further obligations unless, upon review, counsel finds an issue appropriate for submission to the Arizona Supreme Court by petition for review. *See State v. Shattuck*, 140 Ariz. 582, 584-85, 684 P.2d 154, 156-57 (1984). Geri shall have 30 days from the date of this decision to proceed, if he desires, with a pro per motion for reconsideration or a petition for review.

JON HOUSER, PLAINTIFF, VS. CORIZON, SCOTT LOSSMANN, GARTH GULICK, CATHERINE WHINNERY, GLEN BABICH, AND MARK SPELICH, DEFENDANTS. CASE NO. 1:13-CV-00006-EJL UNITED STATES DISTRICT COURT FOR THE DISTRICT OF IDAHO

BACKGROUND

Plaintiff filed this action on January 4, 2013 alleging that Defendants were deliberately indifferent in responding to his medical needs. The Court reviewed the Complaint pursuant to *28 U.S.C. §§ 1915* and *1915A* and allowed Plaintiff to proceed on his *Eighth Amendment* claims against Defendants. Initial Review Order (Dkt. 4). The Court then considered whether to dismiss some claims for failure to exhaust administrative remedies. The Court allowed Plaintiff to proceed on Counts 1, 2, 3, 4, 6, 8 and 9 of his Complaint and dismissed without prejudice Counts 5 and 7. Order (Dkt. 43).

Plaintiff now has the assistance of counsel and seeks to file an Amended Complaint. Plaintiff's counsel filed a three-paragraph memorandum to support the requested amendments, arguing only that an amended complaint will "streamline the case, clarify the allegations and causes of action, . . . and allow for a more orderly litigation of this matter." (Dkt. 49, p. 2). Defendant Mark Spelich does not object to the amendments. (Dkt. 50). However, Defendants Glen Babich, M.D., Corizon, LLC, Scott Lossmann, M.D., Catherine Whinnery, M.D., and Garth Gulick, M.D. (collectively the "Medical Provider Defendants"), oppose several of the proposed amendments. (Dkt. 51). Unfortunately, Plaintiff's counsel did not respond to the Medical Provider Defendants' opposition or substantive arguments. For the reasons set forth below, the Court will grant in part, and deny in part, Plaintiff's Motion.

B. Discussion

1. Proposed Claims and Allegations Reiterating Dismissed Claims Should be Excluded from the Proposed Amended Complaint.

Count 5 of the original Complaint alleged deliberate indifference in Defendants Gulick and Lossman "rushing [Plaintiff] into surgery for his (L) knee before having him seen by a Mental Health provider." Dkt. 1, p. 17. Count 7 of the original Complaint alleged deliberate indifference in Defendants Gulick, Lossmann, and Spelich failing to remove Plaintiff from Hepatitis C treatment after the first MRSA outbreak. Dkt. 1, p. 17.

Paragraphs 77 and 79 of the proposed Amended Complaint repeat the same claims made in Counts 5 and 7, which the Court dismissed for failure to exhaust.[1] (Dkt. 43). Accordingly, amending the Complaint to reiterate these dismissed claims would be futile. Additionally, to the extent paragraphs 62 and 64 of the proposed Amended Complaint include factual allegations that relate solely to claims made in paragraphs 77 and 79 (recycled from dismissed Counts 5 and 7 of the original Complaint), those allegations also should be excluded from any Amended Complaint.

1 Plaintiff conceded that Count 5 was unexhausted, Order (Dkt. 43, p. 10), and the Court found Plaintiff failed to exhaust Count 7. Order (Dkt. 43, pp. 14-15). Even though both counts were dismissed without prejudice, Order (Dkt. 43, p. 16), Plaintiff has not argued that he would be able to demonstrate exhaustion if he were allowed to amend his Complaint to include the dismissed counts. Thus, on the record before the Court, nothing has changed to prompt the Court to reconsider its earlier ruling that Counts 5 and 7--containing claims that are repeated in paragraphs 77 and 79 of the proposed Amended Complaint--should be dismissed.

2. Plaintiff May Not Amend His Complaint to Add or Continue State Law Medical Malpractice Claims That Did Not go Through the Required Prelitigation Review.

Plaintiff's attempt to allege malpractice claims against Dr. Lossmann, Dr. Whinnery, and Dr. Babich in the proposed Amended Complaint is futile because he did not undergo the required prelitigation review, and Plaintiff has not provided any argument that such review is not required. *See Idaho Code § 6-1001* (requiring prelitigation consideration of personal injury and wrongful death claims and stating those proceedings are "compulsory as a condition precedent to litigation"). For the same reasons, his claims against Dr. Gulick are limited to the actual issue that underwent prelitigation review-- Dr. Gulick's alleged failure to fully inform Plaintiff of the consequences of three surgeries performed between April and May of 2011. Burke Aff., Ex. A (Dkt. 52). In short, Plaintiff's Amended Complaint should include only medical malpractice claims that went through prelitigation review, a prerequisite imposed by Idaho law.

3. The Amended Complaint May Include a Negligent Training and Supervision Claim Against Corizon.

The Medical Provider Defendants argue that Plaintiff's third cause of action against Corizon--for negligent retention, training and supervision--fails to state a claim because Plaintiff has not identified by name any employee whose specific conduct is at issue. However, the Idaho caselaw relied upon by Defendants to support this argument deal with the requirements for establishing a genuine issue of material fact at the summary judgment and/or trial stages of proceedings. In this case, Plaintiff has not had the assistance of counsel in obtaining discovery and crafting the case. Hence, the issue presented is whether the Complaint may be amended with the assistance of counsel now that it has passed the initial review stage. At this point in the proceedings, the Court finds amendment to include the third cause of action against Corizon is not futile, and the Court will apply its discretion and the liberal amendment policy of *Rule 15* to allow the proposed amendment in this regard.[2]

2 This does not, of course, mean that Plaintiff is excused from ultimately proving his claim on the merits, or that his third cause of action will survive a motion to dismiss or motion for summary judgment. Those questions are for another day.

MICHAEL L. ARNOLD, PLAINTIFF, VS. CORIZON, INC., ET AL., DEFENDANTS. Case No. 1:15-cv-62 SNLJ UNITED STATES DISTRICT COURT FOR THE EASTERN DISTRICT OF MISSOURI, SOUTHEASTERN DIVISION

Plaintiff requests counsel because he says he has no knowledge of the law or how to litigate a claim and because he is not permitted to seek help from other inmates. Plaintiff says he lost his last case before this court, No. 1:13-cv-121 SNLJ, because he was not appointed an attorney. That case, however, was dismissed for failure to exhaust administrative remedies. Plaintiff claims he has since exhausted his administrative remedies, and the present case is a refiling of the same claims at issue in 1:13cv121.

The appointment of counsel for an indigent *pro se* plaintiff lies within the discretion of the Court. Indigent civil litigants do not have a constitutional or statutory right to appointed counsel. *Stevens v. Redwing, 146 F.3d. 538, 546 (8th Cir. 1998); Edgington v. Mo. Dept. of Corrections, 52 F.3d. 777, 780 (8th Cir. 1995); Rayes v. Johnson, 969 F.2d. 700, 702 (8th Cir. 1992).* The standard for appointment of counsel in a civil case involves the weighing of several factors which include the factual complexity of a matter, the complexity of legal issues, the existence of conflicting testimony, the ability of the indigent to investigate the facts, and the ability of the indigent to present his claim. *See McCall v. Benson, 114 F.3d 754 (8th Cir. 1997); Stevens, 146 F.3d. at 546; Edgington, 52 F.3d. at 780; Nachtigall v. Class, 48 F.3d 1076, 1081-82 (8th Cir. 1995); Johnson v. Williams, 788 F.2d. 1319, 1322-1323 (8th Cir. 1986).*

In this matter, the Court finds that appointment of counsel is not mandated at this time. The plaintiff appears able to litigate this matter. This action appears to involve straightforward questions of fact rather than complex questions of law, and plaintiff appears able to clearly present and investigate his claim. The Court will continue to monitor the progress of this case, and if it appears to this Court that the need arises for counsel to be appointed, the Court will do so.

WAYNE DOUGLAS MERKLEY, PLAINTIFF - APPELLANT, V. STATE OF IDAHO; CORIZON HEALTH SERVICES INCORPORATED, DEFENDANTS - Appellees. 2015 U.S. App. LEXIS 17000 (September 25, 2015)

Idaho state prisoner Wayne Douglas Merkley appeals pro se from the district court's order denying his motion for leave to proceed in forma pauperis ("IFP") in his *42 U.S.C. § 1983* action alleging various constitutional claims and claims under the Americans with Disabilities Act. We have jurisdiction under *28 U.S.C. § 1291*. We review for an abuse of discretion. *Escobedo v. Applebees, 787 F.3d 1226, 1234 (9th Cir. 2015)*. We reverse and remand.

The district court denied Merkley's motion to proceed IFP because it concluded that Merkley did not make a sufficient showing of indigency. However, there was inadequate support in the record to conclude that Merkley had access to sufficient funds to pay the court costs and his basic needs. *See id. at 1234* (explaining that a district court abuses its discretion when it "rules on an issue without giving a party an opportunity to explain, or without adequate support on the record"). The record shows that Merkley received approximately $130.00 per month, but does not show how much his monthly expenses were and what items he purchased at the prison's commissary. Accordingly, we reverse the judgment and remand for further proceedings.

JAMES JACKSON ELLSWORTH, PLAINTIFF, VS. CORIZON HEALTH, INC.,[1] ET AL., DEFENDANTS. 2012 U.S. DIST. LEXIS 53276 (AZ. APRIL 16, 2012)

> 1   This is the accurate name of the defendant formerly knows as Prison Health Services, Inc., as more fully explained in this court's recent order. See Ord. (Doc. 66) at 1-2.

Background

Plaintiff is an inmate housed at the Mohave County Jail ("the Jail"), alleging a violation of his *Eighth Amendment* right to be free from cruel and unusual punishment. More specifically, plaintiff alleges that he was denied certain medical treatment relating to his diagnosis of multiple sclerosis, allegedly because the Jail's protocol did not allow it. See Co. (Doc. 1) at 3, ¶ 3.

By order entered February 23, 2012, the Magistrate Judge denied four motions by plaintiff. On March 16, 2012, plaintiff filed a motion for "review" of that Order, directed to three of those four motions. See Mot. (Doc. 65). In particular, plaintiff is challenging the Magistrate Judge's denial of his motions to: (1) compel compliance with a subpoena directed to a non-party entity (Doc. 43); (2) extend the time for completion of discovery (Doc. 48); and (3) "'join' parties[2] to this matter[.]" Ord. (Doc. 56) at 1:24.

> 2   As explained in Ellsworth v. Prison Health Services, CV-11-8070, actually, plaintiff was seeking to add non-parties to this action. See Ord. (Doc. 66) at 2, n.2.

Additionally, plaintiff seeks review of the Magistrate Judge's order, filed March 7, 2012, denying plaintiff's motions to compel compliance with subpoenas *duces tecum* directed to three other non-party entities (Docs. 41; 44; and 45). See Ord. (Doc. 63) at 4:4-10. On April 3, 2012, plaintiff filed a separate motion seeking "[r]eview" of that order. Mot. (Doc. 67) at 1:9.

Discussion

With one exception, all of the rulings to which plaintiff objects directly pertain to discovery. Hence, those rulings are non-dispositive matters within the meaning of *Fed.R.Civ.P. 72(a)*. See *Gabriel Techs. Corp. v. Qualcomm Inc., 2012 U.S. Dist. LEXIS 33417, 2012 WL 849167, at *2 (S.D.Cal. Mar. 13, 2012)* (citing *Maisonville v. F2 Am., Inc., 902 F.2d 746, 748 (9th Cir. 1990)*) ("Discovery orders are ordinarily considered non-dispositive because they do not have the effect of dismissing a cause of action.") Plaintiff's challenge to the denial of his motion to "join parties" also is non-dispositive as it is not among the eight types of motions explicitly excluded from determination by *28 U.S.C. § 636(b)(1)(A)*. Nor is that motion "analogous to a motion listed in th[at] [excepted] category[.]" See *United States v. Rivera-Guerrero, 377 F.3d 1064, 1067 (9th Cir. 2004)* (citation omitted) (emphasis omitted). Thus, plaintiff's joinder motion "falls within the non-dispositive group of matters which a magistrate may determine." See *id. at 1068* (citation omitted). Given the non-dispositive status of the motions which plaintiff Ellsworth is challenging, *Rule 72(a)* and *28 U.S.C. § 636(b)(1)(A)* provide the governing legal standards.

Timeliness

Pursuant to *Rule 72(a) of the Federal Rules of Civil Procedure*, "[a] party may serve and file objections to [a] [nondispositive pretrial order of a magistrate judge] within 14 days after being served with a copy[]" of that order. *Fed.R.Civ.P. 72(a)*. "The district judge in the case *must* consider *timely* objections and modify or set aside any part of the order that is clearly erroneous or is contrary to law." Id. (emphasis added); see also *28 U.S.C. § 636(b)(1)(A)* ("A judge of the court may reconsider any pretrial matter under this subparagraph (A) where it has been shown that the magistrate judge's order is clearly erroneous or contrary to law.") However, "[a] party may not assign as error a defect in the order not timely objected to." *Fed.R.Civ.P. 72(a)*.

In the present case, the court construes plaintiff's motions for "review," as objections to the Magistrate Judge's rulings on nondispositive matters, as *Rule 72(a)* allows. Plaintiff's objections were not timely filed, however. As just stated, objections pursuant to that Rule must be filed and served within 14 days after being served with a copy of a magistrate judge's order. On March 26, 2012, plaintiff filed his objections to the February 23, 2012 order. Computing the time for service in accordance with *Rule 6*, plaintiff had until March 12, 2012 in which to file his objections.[3] Plaintiff did not meet that filing deadline though.

3   In accordance with *Fed.R.Civ.P. 6(a)(1)(A)*, February 23, 2012, the entry date of the order, is excluded from computing plaintiff's time to file objections. Beginning to count on February 24, 2012, and adding three days for service pursuant to *Fed.R.Civ.P. 6(d)*, means that the 14 day time frame ended on March 11, 2012. Because March 11, 2012, was a Sunday, that time frame is extended until Monday, March 12, 2012. See *Fed.R.Civ.P. 6(a)(1)(C)*.

Plaintiff also did not meet the filing deadline with respect to the Magistrate Judge's March 7, 2012 order. Computing the time for service in accordance with *Rule 6*, plaintiff had until March 26, 2012 in which to file his objections to that order.[4] Yet, plaintiff did not file his objections until April 3, 2010. Untimeliness alone is a sufficient basis for denying both of plaintiff's motions for "review." See *Matthewson v. Ryan, 2012 U.S. Dist. LEXIS 20848, 2012 WL 510318, at *2 (D.Ariz. Feb. 16, 2012)* (citing, *inter alia, Simpson v. Lear Astronics Corp., 77 F.3d 1170, 1174 (9th Cir.1996)*) ("The absence of a timely objection precludes later assignment of error in this court or in any higher court of the non-dispositive rulings of a magistrate judge.")

4   In accordance with *Fed.R.Civ.P. 6(a)(1)(A)*, March 7,, 2012, the entry date of the order, is excluded from computing plaintiff's time to file objections. Beginning to count on March 8, 2012, and adding three days for service pursuant to *Fed.R.Civ.P. 6(d)*, means that the 14 day time frame ended on March 24, 2012. Because March 24, 2012, was a Saturday, that time frame is extended until Monday, March 26, 2012. See *Fed.R.Civ.P. 6(a)(1)(C)*. **State agents consistently insist procedures not provided for be utilized. In Robert Schilleman, Plaintiff, v. Corizon Health Incorporated, et al., Defendants. *2015 U.S. Dist. LEXIS 161675* (December 2, 2015) the court states in part:**

In a March 26, 2015 Order, the Court found that Plaintiff stated the following claims in his First Amended Complaint: (1) *Eighth Amendment* claims against Corizon in Counts One and Three; (2) an *Eighth Amendment* claim against Ryan in Count One; (3) *Eighth Amendment* claims against Defendants Hegmann, Mulhorn, Medical Director, Medical Providers, Montano, Facility Health Administrators, and Fansler in Count Two; and (4) state law negligence claims against Defendants Hegmann, Mulhorn, Medical Director, Medical Providers, Montano, Facility Health Administrators, and Fansler in Count Three. (Doc. 23.) The Court noted that because unnamed Medical Director, Medical Providers, and Facility Health Administrators could not be served, Plaintiff should seek to amend his complaint to add the proper names of those Defendants when they were discovered. (*Id.* at 15.)

Plaintiff seeks leave to add claims against Patrick Arnold, Duc Vo, Winfred Williams, Cynthia Ripsin, Kent Ainslie, "Facility Health Administrators, ASPC-Eyman," "Corizon's Clinical Coordinator assigned to the ASPC-Eyman (Cook Unit)," and "Corizon's Regional Medical Director responsible for the ASPC-Eyman (Cook Unit)."

A. Legal Standard

Although the decision to grant or deny a motion to amend is within the discretion of the district court, "*Rule 15(a)* [of the Federal Rules of Civil Procedure] declares that leave to amend 'shall be freely given when justice so requires'; this mandate is to be heeded." *Foman v. Davis, 371 U.S. 178, 182, 83 S. Ct. 227, 9 L. Ed. 2d 222 (1962).* "In exercising its discretion[,] . . . 'a court must be guided by the underlying purpose of Rule 15--to facilitate decision on the merits rather than on the pleadings or technicalities . . . . Thus, 'Rule 15's policy of favoring amendments to pleadings should be applied with extreme liberality.'" *Eldridge v. Block, 832 F.2d 1132, 1135 (9th Cir.1987)* (citations omitted). Motions to amend should be granted unless the district court determines that there has been a showing of: (1) undue delay; (2) bad faith or dilatory motives on the part of the movant; (3) repeated failure to cure deficiencies by previous amendments; (4) undue prejudice to the opposing party; or (5) futility of the proposed amendment. *Foman, 371 U.S. at 182.* "Generally, this determination should be performed with all inferences in favor of granting the motion." *Griggs v. Pace Am. Grp., Inc., 170 F.3d 877, 880 (9th Cir. 1999).* Significantly, "[t]he party opposing amendment bears the burden of showing prejudice," futility, or one of the other permissible reasons for denying a motion to amend. *DCD Programs Ltd. v. Leighton, 833 F.2d 183, 187 (9th Cir. 1987); see Richardson v. United States, 841 F.2d 993, 999 (9th Cir. 1988)* (stating that leave to amend should be freely given unless the opposing party makes "an affirmative showing of either prejudice or bad faith").

Here, there is no evidence of undue delay, bad faith, repeated failure to cure, or undue prejudice. Defendants assert that allowing Plaintiff leave to amend to add additional allegations against additional Defendants would be futile because Plaintiff fails to state a claim upon which relief can be granted against those Defendants. Accordingly, the Court will examine whether Plaintiff states claims upon which relief may be granted in his Second Amended Complaint.

B. Futility

1. Count One

Plaintiff continues to assert *Eighth Amendment* claims against Defendants Corizon and Ryan in Count One. Consistent with the Court's findings in its March 26, 2015 Order, Plaintiff states an *Eighth Amendment* claim against Defendants Corizon and Ryan in Count One of his Second Amended Complaint.

. . . .

2. Count Two

In Count Two, Plaintiff seeks to add an *Eighth Amendment* claim based on deliberate indifference to serious medical needs against Defendants Kent Ainslie, Unknown FHAs, Unknown Clinical Coordinators, the Corizon Regional Medical Director, Patrick Arnold, Duc Vo, Winfred Williams, and Cynthia Ripsin. Having reviewed Plaintiff's allegations in Count Two, the Court finds that Plaintiff states an *Eighth Amendment* claim against Defendants Kent Ainslie, Unknown FHAs, Unknown Clinical Coordinators, the Corizon Regional Medical Director, and Patrick Arnold, Duc Vo, Winfred Williams, and Cynthia Ripsin in Count Two. The Court will therefore allow Plaintiff to amend his complaint to add his *Eighth Amendment* claims in Count Two against Defendants Kent Ainslie, Patrick Arnold, Duc Vo, Winfred Williams, and Cynthia Ripsin. However, to the extent Plaintiff seeks to add Corizon's Clinical Coordinator, Unknown Facility Health Administrators, and Corizon's Regional Medical Director, he must seek to amend his claims against those Defendants when he discovers their proper names for the same reasons set forth in the Court's March 26, 2015 Order.

Additionally, Plaintiff reasserts *Eighth Amendment* claims against Defendants Hegmann, Mulhorn, and Montano in Count Two. Consistent with the Court's findings in its March 26, 2015 Order, Plaintiff states an

Eighth Amendment claim against Defendants Hegmann, Mulhorn, and Montano in Count Two of his Second Amended Complaint.

Finally, after Plaintiff filed his proposed Second Amended Complaint, which included claims against Fansler, the parties stipulated to the dismissal of Fansler from this action (Doc. 142). Accordingly, the Court will deny Plaintiff's Motion to Amend as moot to the extent he asserts claims against Fansler in his Second Amended Complaint.

3. Count Three

Plaintiff asserts a state law negligence claim against all Defendants in Count Three. Having reviewed Plaintiff's allegations in Count Three, the Court finds that Plaintiff states state law negligence claims against all Defendants in Count Three. The Court will therefore allow Plaintiff to amend his complaint to add his state law negligence claims in Count Three against Defendants Corizon, Ryan, Montano, Hegmann, Mulhorn, Arnold, Vo, Williams, Ripsin, and Ainslie. However, to the extent Plaintiff seeks to add Corizon's Clinical Coordinator, Unknown Facility Health Administrators, and Corizon's Regional Medical Director, he must seek to amend his claims against those Defendants when he discovers their proper names for the same reasons set forth in the Court's March 26, 2015 Order.

The Court will therefore direct the Clerk of the Court to file Plaintiff's Second Amended Complaint currently lodged at Doc. 130-2. The Court will further direct the Clerk of the Court to dismiss Defendants Fansler, Corizon's Clinical Coordinator, Unknown Facility Health Administrators, and Corizon's Regional Medical Director from the Third Amended Complaint and this action without prejudice.

LEONARD DEWITT, PLAINTIFF-APPELLANT, V. CORIZON, INC., ET AL., DEFENDANTS -APPELLEES. NO. 13-2930 UNITED STATES COURT OF APPEALS FOR THE SEVENTH CIRCUIT

I. BACKGROUND

Because the district court decided this case on a motion for summary judgment, we recite the facts in the light most favorable to the nonmoving party, Dewitt. *See Greeno v. Daley, 414 F.3d 645, 652 (7th Cir. 2005).* Dewitt's eye problems began in 2007 during his first incarceration at the Wabash Correctional Facility, which is a part of the Indiana Department of Corrections ("IDOC"). The IDOC contracts with Appellee Corizon, Inc. to provide medical care to Indiana prisoners. Dewitt submitted the first of many Requests for Healthcare to Corizon stating something was very wrong with his bloodshot left eye and his vision was "like looking through a dirty piece of plastic." Corizon's eye doctor diagnosed him with astigmatism and presbyopia (old-age nearsightedness causing slightly blurry vision), and prescribed eyeglasses.

Three months later, Dewitt submitted another Request for Healthcare after being transferred to a local work-release facility. IDOC medical staff contacted the Plainfield Correctional Facility to set up an appointment for him since the work-release facility did not have any specialists on staff. But Appellee Patty Wirth said that no appointment would be available for three months, so IDOC medical staff sent Dewitt to a prison physician who noted no obvious abnormalities in his left eye.

In May 2008, Dewitt was released on parole. A doctor determined that Dewitt had a form of glaucoma in his left eye and he was advised in late 2008 to undergo laser-eye surgery to prevent any future attacks. He underwent a surgical procedure on his right eye in early 2009 to remove part of the iris to decrease eye pressure. His left eye continued to have higher than normal intra-ocular pressure.

Dewitt was again incarcerated in 2009, this time at the Putnamville Correctional Facility, where he filed another Request for Healthcare, noting exceptional irritation in his left eye. He was referred to Wishard Hospital where an ophthalmologist prescribed medicated eye drops in order to decrease the pressure. The ophthalmologist told Dewitt if they did not work, he might need to have the eye or portions of it removed. The drops did not work, and, believing he had no real alternative, Dewitt submitted another Request for Healthcare in November to have his left eye removed.

Dewitt received treatment both inside and outside the facility over the next several months, and filed another Request for Healthcare to have his eye removed in February 2011. Corizon's regional medical director, Appellee Dr. Michael Mitcheff, viewed removal as an extreme last resort and suggested a more conservative approach, including medicated eye drops and pain medication. Dewitt was prescribed medication, including a 90-day prescription for Vicodin by defendant Dr. Naveen Rajoli, ultimately received a glaucoma evaluation at the Midwest Eye Institute and eye removal was recommended. In May 2012, he underwent surgery to remove part of his left eye's ciliary body.

Dewitt filed suit under *42 U.S.C. ~ 1983* against Corizon, Wirth, and Mitcheff, asserting that they were deliberately indifferent to his glaucoma condition. He also sued Dr. James Stewart and Dr. Rajoli, but Stewart was dismissed from the suit and Dewitt does not mention Rajoli in his brief. In April 2012, Dewitt moved for assistance of counsel, stating his vision problems combined with his tenth-grade education made it difficult for him to conduct discovery and litigate his case. The district court denied his request, finding that Dewitt's claims were not overly complex or meritorious, that Dewitt was familiar with his claims and able to present them, and he was "within the spectrum of most indigent parties." Six months later, Dewitt moved again for assistance of counsel, repeating his earlier statements. He also complained that Appellees had abused discovery rules and delayed their responses. The court denied this request using the same language as the first denial and without addressing the alleged discovery abuses.

After Appellees moved for summary judgment, Dewitt filed a "reply" to Appellees' reply in support of summary judgment, and a request under *Federal Rule of Civil Procedure 56(f)* (now *Rule 56(d)*) for further discovery. He again begged the court to recruit counsel so he could conduct discovery. The district court did not address Dewitt's *Rule 56(d)* motion, but granted Appellees' motion for summary judgment, in part, because Dewitt failed to show Corizon had any "official policy or custom" to delay medical treatment and because Dr. Mitcheff exercised reasoned professional judgment. Dewitt now appeals.

II. ANALYSIS

Though Dewitt argues the merits of the summary judgment order, we do not reach that issue because we hold that Dewitt should have had an attorney throughout the litigation. There is no right to recruitment of counsel in federal civil litigation, but a district court has discretion to recruit counsel under *28 U.S.C. § 1915(e)(1). See Henderson v. Ghosh, 755 F.3d 559, No. 13-2035, 2014 U.S. App. LEXIS 11816, 2014 WL 2757473, at *4 (7th Cir. June 18, 2014)* (per curiam). If an indigent plaintiff has made a reasonable attempt to obtain counsel and then files a motion for recruitment of counsel, the district court should ask "whether the difficulty of the case--factually and legally--exceeds the particular plaintiff's capacity as a layperson to coherently present it to the judge or jury himself." *Pruitt v. Mote, 503 F.3d 647, 655 (7th Cir. 2007)* (en banc). We acknowledge this is a "difficult decision" since "[a]lmost everyone would benefit from having a lawyer, but there are too many indigent litigants and too few lawyers willing and able to volunteer for these cases." *Olson v. Morgan, 750 F.3d 708, 711 (7th Cir. 2014)*. So we review the denial of the recruitment of counsel for an abuse of discretion and will re-verse only if the plaintiff was prejudiced by the denial--*e.g.*, if there is a reasonable likelihood that the recruitment of counsel would have made a difference in the outcome of the litigation. *See Santiago v. Walls, 599 F.3d 749, 765 (7th Cir. 2010)*. In so deciding, our case law is clear that a plaintiff can be prejudiced by the lack of counsel pretrial just as easily as during the briefing or trial itself. *See id. at 765* (noting prejudice when plaintiff "was incapable of engaging in any investigation[] or locating and presenting key witnesses or evidence" (quoting *Pruitt, 503 F.3d at 659*)); *see also Henderson, 2014 U.S. App. LEXIS 11816, 2014 WL 2757473 at *7* (finding prejudice where plaintiff "was incapable of obtaining the witnesses and evidence he needed to prevail on his claims"); *Bracey v. Grondin, 712 F.3d 1012, 1017 (7th Cir. 2013)* ("Complexities anticipated (or arising) during discovery can justify a court's decision to recruit counsel").

The first question, then, is whether the district court abused its discretion in denying the motions for recruitment of counsel. In his first motion, Dewitt requested the recruitment of counsel because of his tenth-grade education, the fact that he was incarcerated and unable to investigate and discover relevant facts. He also pointed out that he was "now totally blind in his left eye and the vision in his right eye is impaired." He discussed the medical complexity of his case, his reliance on "jailhouse lawyers," and his inability "to comprehend with any legal understanding, the discovery rules and the Defendants [sic] motions." The court denied the motion and stated that "the claims by the plaintiff are not of sufficient complexity or merit as to surpass the plaintiff's ability to properly develop and present them," and that "the plaintiff is within the spectrum of 'most indigent parties' because he has and will have a meaningful opportunity to present his claim, he has demonstrated familiarity with his claims and the ability to present them." The court stated that it had considered the complexity of the case and Dewitt's ability to litigate the case--without delving into any of Dewitt's personal characteristics or the specifics of the case--before denying the motion.

The court abused its discretion by failing to explain its reasoning and failing to address all the relevant arguments Dewitt raised. For example, the court characterized Dewitt as fitting within the spectrum of most pro se litigants and said it had considered his personal characteristics, but it did not identify those characteristics. However, the court did not address the challenges that Dewitt, as a blind and indigent prisoner with a tenth-grade education and no legal experience, faced in being able to investigate crucial facts and depose witnesses, doctors, and other allegedly resistant prison personnel. *See Pruitt, 503 F.3d at 655* (noting the court "should review any information submitted in support of the request for counsel, as well as the pleadings, communications from, and any contact with the plaintiff"); *see also Navejar v. Iyiola, 718 F.3d 692, 696 (7th Cir. 2013)* (noting judge should have considered plaintiff's "limited education, mental illness, language difficulties, and lack of access to fellow prisoners or other resources for assistance after his transfer from Stateville"). Moreover, the court's statement that Dewitt "has demonstrated familiarity with his claims and the ability to present them" does not demonstrate that the district court specifically examined Dewitt's personal ability to litigate the case, versus the ability of the "jailhouse lawyer" who Dewitt said in his motion was helping him. The analysis should be of the *plaintiff's* ability to litigate *his own* claims, and the "fact that an inmate receives assistance from a fellow prisoner should not factor into the decision whether to recruit counsel." *Henderson, 2014 U.S. App. LEXIS 11816, 2014 WL 2757473 at *5.*

Nor did the court explain why the claims were not of "sufficient complexity" to merit recruitment of counsel. In fact, the case presents complicated medical matters, involves varying recommended courses of treatment by numerous physicians, and required discovery into what constitutes reasonable care for medical professionals. Though not every deliberate indifference case is so complex and beyond the individual plaintiff's capacity as to warrant the recruitment of counsel, this one was. *See Henderson, 2014 U.S. App. LEXIS 11816, 2014 WL 2757473 at **6-7* (noting case required recruitment of counsel because it "involves complex medical terms and concepts," requires proof of the "defendants' state of mind" and proof of doctor's knowledge of a substantial risk of harm and disregard of that risk). *But see, e.g., Olson, 750 F.3d at 711-12* (holding no abuse of discretion in denying recruitment of counsel motion for medical indifference case when disputed issue was whether defendant knew of plaintiff's physical condition); *Romanelli v. Suliene, 615 F.3d 847, 854 (7th Cir. 2010)* (finding no abuse of discretion in denying motion in medical indifference case when neither side contested that plaintiff was ill). We are aware that the appointment of counsel in civil cases can pose challenges for judges, who ask lawyers to volunteer their time to take these assignments, and the attorneys who are asked by the judges and who ultimately take the assignments. As a way to combat those issues, we again highlight the work done by the Pro Bono Program for the United States District Court for the Northern District of Illinois Trial Bar, which mandates that members of the Trial Bar serve as an appointed attorney in pro se civil or appellate matters. *See N.D. Ill. L.R. 83.35; N.D. Ill. L.R. 83.11(g). See also Henderson, 2014 U.S. App. LEXIS 11816, 2014 WL 2757473 at *3 n.1; Synergy Assocs. v. Sun Biotechnologies, Inc., 350 F.3d 681, 684 (7th Cir. 2003).* While other districts in this circuit have similar procedures, *see C.D. Ill. L.R. 83.5(J), N.D. Ind. L.R. 83-7, S.D. Ind. 4-6, 83-7,* the mandatory nature of the Northern District of Illinois's program ensures that judges are not put in the position of repeatedly asking the same counsel to take on appointments, and attorneys are not put in the position of being asked time and again to take cases by the judges in front of whom they appear on a regular basis.

In Dewitt's second motion to recruit counsel, Dewitt made basically the same arguments while adding that "Defendants are intentionally abusing the discovery rules, they have delayed their responses to the Plaintiff's interrogatories so as to gain an upper hand with the closing of the deadlines the Court has imposed, and [are] now claiming that they have no obligation to answer further interrogatories." The court denied Dewitt's motion without addressing this new argument. Though the district court need not address every point raised in recruitment motions, it must address those that bear directly on whether "the difficulty of the case--factually and legally--exceeds the particular plaintiff's capacity as a layperson to coherently present it to the judge or jury himself." *Pruitt, 503 F.3d at 655.* That includes whether Dewitt was capable of putting a stop to alleged discovery abuses. *See, e.g., Henderson, 2014 U.S. App. LEXIS 11816, 2014 WL 2757473 at *6* (finding court erred by not considering substantive issue, namely appellant's personal capabilities, that was raised in recruitment motion).

Moreover, in his *Federal Rule of Civil Procedure 56(f)* (now *56(d)*) "reply" to Appellees' reply in support of summary judgment, Dewitt requested more time for discovery as well as the recruitment of counsel to aid him in conducting such discovery. Although this was not a separate formal motion requesting counsel, the court should have addressed it. *See McNeil v. United States, 508 U.S. 106, 113, 113 S. Ct. 1980, 124 L. Ed. 2d 21 (1993)* ("[W]e have insisted that the pleadings prepared by prisoners who do not have access to counsel be liberally construed"); *Santiago, 599 F.3d at 765* (noting "the magistrate judge's methodological lapse in failing to give full consideration to each factor constitutes an abuse of discretion"); *Pruitt, 503 F.3d at 658.*

Finding that the district court abused its discretion does not end our inquiry. We must now determine whether Dewitt was prejudiced. Based on the reasons the court gave in granting the motion for summary judgment, we find Dewitt was. For example, the district court determined that Dr. Mitcheff exercised "reasoned professional judgment" inconsistent with deliberate indifference. But could a lawyer have helped Dewitt present sufficient facts to create a genuine issue about why the doctor declined to follow a specialist's recommendations or advised a continuation of ineffective treatments that prolonged his pain? We think there is a reasonable likelihood counsel could have aided here and made a difference in the outcome. *See Greeno, 414 F.3d at 658* (holding case was "legally more complicated than a typical failure-to-treat claim because it require[d] an assessment of the adequacy of the treatment that [plaintiff] did receive, a question that will likely require expert testimony"); *Ortiz v. Webster, 655 F.3d 731, 735 (7th Cir. 2011)* (analyzing complexities of deliberate indifference claims).

Counsel also could have assisted Dewitt in addressing his concerns about the alleged discovery violations. Dewitt filed a motion to compel, to which Appellees responded that they had replied to all outstanding discovery. The court found the issue moot based on Appellees' response and denied the motion. Yet, two months later, Dewitt stated in his second motion for recruitment of counsel that Appellees were not complying with all discovery requests. That was still a problem when Dewitt filed his *Rule 56(f)* request for more time to conduct discovery. We do not make any determinations on the merits of Dewitt's allegations relating to discovery abuses, but find that had Dewitt had counsel to navigate through discovery, there is a reasonable likelihood that he could have better advocated his position and changed the outcome of the litigation. *See Santiago, 599 F.3d at 765-66* (noting Appellant's "later attempts to conduct relevant discovery were not successful" and "[t]he treatment afforded him by the defendants was not, it is safe to say, the same treatment that would have been afforded a member of the bar").

Finally, we observe the district court disregarded Dewitt's request under *Federal Rule of Civil Procedure 56(f)* seeking more time to conduct discovery before the court ruled on Appellees' motion for summary judgment. While a district court has broad discretion to deny such motions, *see Kalis v. Colgate-Palmolive Co., 231 F.3d 1049, 1056 (7th Cir. 2000)*, it is improper to decide summary judgment without first ruling on a pending 56(f) motion. *Doe v. Abington Friends School, 480 F.3d 252, 257 (3d Cir. 2007).*

IVES T. ARTIS, PLAINTIFF, VS. BYUNGHAK JIN, MEDICAL DIRECTOR (INDIVIAUL COMPASITY); CORIZON HEALTH, FORMERLY PRISON HEALTHCARE SERVICES (OFFICIAL COMPASITY), DEFENDANTS. CIVIL ACTION NO. 13-1226 UNITED STATES DISTRICT COURT FOR THE WESTERN DISTRICT OF PENNSYLVANIA

A. FACTUAL AND PROCEDURAL BACKGROUND

Plaintiff's Complaint (ECF No. 4) and Amended Complaint (ECF No. 59)(supplementing allegations contained in original Complaint) allege that in July 2010, Plaintiff sustained an injury to his left ankle, which was followed by a three-year course of inadequate medical treatment, while incarcerated at SCI-Greene. Plaintiff alleges that the treatment received was based upon economic nonmedical factors and resulted in three years of pain and the exacerbation of his condition.

In particular, Plaintiff alleges that his medical treatment included physical therapy beginning in November 2010; outside shoes for comfort in January 2011; high dosages of acetaminophen for a year; at least four sets of x-rays from July 12, 2010, through April 24, 2012, (in lieu of his request for an MRI); an eight-month course of Vicodin from February 2012 through October 2012; and, on April 16, 2012, an MRI which revealed arthritic changes, mild swelling, small fracture fragments and apparent ligament tears in his left ankle. (ECF No. 4, pp. 5-6). Plaintiff alleges that he was then prescribed air cushioned shoes, two ankle braces and pain medication, but these treatments were revoked for three months while he was housed in the Restrictive Housing Unit ("RHU"), causing him to suffer in pain.[1] Plaintiff alleges that these prescribed aids were returned to him on January 3, 2013, upon his release from the RHU, and that he was provided a walker for mobility due to his deteriorating condition three weeks later. Plaintiff alleges that the walker was defective, causing him to fall, but a new walker was not provided. Defendant Park allegedly ordered a wheelchair for Plaintiff, but this order was rescinded by Dr. Jin as not necessary.

[1]   Attached to Plaintiff's Complaint are copies of several grievances filed in accordance with the Pennsylvania Department of Corrections' administrative review process (ECF No. 1-2). The grievances indicated that Plaintiff's medication was "adjusted" after he was caught selling his Vicodin and that his air cushioned shoes and braces were removed while he was housed in the RHU for security reasons and as not medically necessary while restricted to his cell for 23 hours per day. (ECF No. 1-2, pp. 25, 28).

Plaintiff alleges that he was then seen and treated by an orthopedic specialist at Allegheny General Hospital, who conducted a second MRI, and confirmed that the injuries to his left ankle persisted despite a course of conservative treatment, and that his right ankle also suffered from osteoarthritis. (ECF No. 4, pp. 6-7).

Plaintiff alleges that he underwent surgery on his left ankle in June 2013, but only after the Pennsylvania Department of Corrections changed corporate medical providers. After surgery, Plaintiff alleges Dr. Jin continued to delay or deny treatment during his recovery, by waiting 6 days to provide a blood thinner to prevent a blood clot (Plaintiff does not allege he suffered a blood clot) and by forcing him to use crutches to support his left ankle, when his right ankle suffered from arthritis.

Thereafter, Plaintiff filed a Motion for Injunction, seeking a transfer to a different facility so that he could be treated by a new doctor. (ECF No. 6). Plaintiff's Motion was denied as not meeting the heightened standard required for a preliminary injunction. (ECF No. 8). Plaintiff filed a second Motion for a Preliminary Injunction and Motion for Temporary Restraining Order on August 6, 2014, again seeking a transfer to a different facility. (ECF No. 39). In resolving the Motion, this Court ordered the production of certain of Plaintiff's medical records to determine whether Plaintiff was receiving any required treatment for his ankle post-surgery (ECF No. 43).. The records establish that while Plaintiff continued to complain of pain and request authorization to wear air cushioned shoes instead of prison issued boots, it was determined that there was no medical need for special accommodations because he had an "old, healed injury," and "[p]ain is expected." (ECF No. 50-1). The records also reveal that Plaintiff is non-compliant with psychiatric medication, and that for ongoing pain, he was provided with knee high compression stockings. It was determined that his ankle injury appeared "fully recovered." (ECF No. 50-1, p. 6). The records reveal Plaintiff insisted that he required surgery on his right ankle, but there are no indications in his records from any medical provider, including his treating orthopedist at Allegheny General Hospital, to support this request. Id. at p. 8.

In resolving the Motion for a Preliminary Injunction, it was determined that Plaintiff had been moved to a new facility, and therefore the requested injunctive relief was denied as moot. See, No. 13-1226, (W.D. Pa. September 11, 2014).

Defendants, through their Motions to Dismiss, contend that the allegations contained in Plaintiff's Complaint and the evidence of record produced in conjunction with the Motion for Preliminary Injunction, establish that Plaintiff was provided consistent but conservative medical treatment for his ankle injury and, accordingly, there is no evidence of deliberate indifference to his condition. Defendants also argue that Plaintiff has failed to exhaust available administrative remedies and thus his claim is barred pursuant to the Prison Litigation Reform Act ("PLRA"), *42 U.S.C. § 1997e(a)*.

1. Defendants Jim and Park

Plaintiff alleges that Defendants Jin and Park violated his *Eighth Amendment* right to be free from "cruel and unusual punishment" because Defendants were "deliberately indifferent" to his serious medical needs. In particular, Plaintiff alleges Defendants failed to properly investigate his foot pain by failing to conducting additional tests, including an MRI, and failing to promptly schedule appropriate surgical treatment, in the face of his continued pain and evident decline in mobility.

In this case, the Court assumes that Plaintiff's ankle pain constituted a serious medical need. However, the records attached to his Complaint as well as to his brief in opposition to the Motion to Dismiss establish that the treatment provided prior to surgery was consistent with a conservative treatment plan, and that several different treatment options were attempted including physical therapy, medication, and supportive braces, crutches and a walker. When surgery was provided, Plaintiff's medical records indicate that surgery was not the only treatment option available to provide relief, and that more conservative options such as those already implemented would be appropriate.[2] (ECF No. 73-1, p.3). Under these circumstances, it is apparent that the record in this case shows only a difference over opinion over the course of proper medical treatment, rather than a complete denial of medical care. In such situations, the United States Court of Appeals for the Third Circuit has held that courts should not second guess medical judgments to constitutionalize claims which sound in state tort law. *U. S. ex rel. Walker v. Fayette Cnty., Pa., 599 F.2d 573, 575 n.2 (3d Cir. 1979)*(citing *Westlake v. Lucas, 537 F.2d 857, 860 n. 5 (6th Cir. 1976)*). Thus, because Plaintiff has failed to allege facts evidencing deliberate indifference giving rise to a constitutional claim under *Section 1983*, it is recommended that the Motion to Dismiss filed on behalf of Defendants Park and Jin be granted.[3]

2 Plaintiff has provided a copy of his medical records from the date of his admission to Allegheny General Hospital for left ankle surgery. The "Indications for Procedure" note that "[t]reatment options were discussed with the patient including both nonoperative and operative treatment options. The patient had attempted conservative measures in the past and had failed." (ECF No, 73-1, p.3).

3 In his brief in opposition to the Motion to Dismiss, Plaintiff references the Universal Declaration of Human Rights as a basis for his claims against Defendants. However, Plaintiff cannot sustain such claims because the Universal Declaration of Human Rights is a non-binding declaration that provides no private rights of action. *Sosa v. Alvarez--Machain, 542 U.S. 692, 734, 124 S. Ct. 2739, 159 L. Ed. 2d 718 (2004)* (explaining that Universal Declaration is simply a statement of principles and not a treaty or international agreement that would impose legal obligations.).

2. Defendant Corizon Health

Defendant Corizon Health is identified in Plaintiff's Complaint as providing medical staff to Pennsylvania correctional institutions "through an independent contract." ECF No. 4, p. 7. Plaintiff alleges that Corizon "employed and conducted regulations and ta[c]tics to save money." Id. For *§ 1983* purposes, Corizon Health "cannot be held responsible for the acts of its employees under a theory of respondeat superior or vicarious liability." *Natale v. Camden County Corrections Facility, 318 F.3d 575, 584 (3d Cir. 2003)*. However, the United States Court of Appeals for the Third Circuit has held that a contracted health care provider, such as Corizon Health, could be held liable if the plaintiff shows that there was a relevant policy or custom, and that the policy or custom caused the constitutional violation plaintiff alleges. Specifically, there are three situations where acts of a government employee may be deemed to be the result of a policy or custom of the governmental entity for whom the employee works, thereby rendering the entity liable under *§ 1983*. The first is where "the appropriate officer or entity promulgates a generally applicable statement of policy and the subsequent act complained of is simply an implementation of that policy." The second occurs where "no rule has been announced as policy but federal law has been violated by an act of the policymaker itself." Finally, a policy or custom may also exist where "the policymaker has failed to act affirmatively at all, [though] the need to take some action to control the agents of the government 'is so obvious, and the inadequacy of existing practice so likely to result in the violation of constitutional rights, that the policymaker can reasonably be said to have been deliberately indifferent to the need.'" *Id. at 584* (footnote and citations omitted). The same standard applies to claims against a private corporation that is functioning as a "state actor." See *Weigher v. Prison Health Services, 402 F. App'x 668, 669-70 (3d Cir.2010)*.

Here, Plaintiff has not alleged facts giving rise to a constitutional violation or suggesting that any decision to refuse or delay medical treatment to Plaintiff was the result of an actionable policy, practice, or custom of Corizon Health. Rather, Plaintiff broadly speculates that the course of treatment was the result of an unspecified policy to "save money," but fails to allege any supportive facts sufficient to "nudge [his] claims ... across the line from conceivable to plausible." *Iqbal, 556 U.S. at 680-81*. Accordingly, it is recommended that the Motion to Dismiss filed on behalf of Corizon Health be granted.

3. Futility

If a civil rights complaint is subject to *Rule 12(b)(6)* dismissal, a district court must permit a curative amendment unless such an amendment would be inequitable or futile. *Fletcher--Harlee Corp. v. Pote Concrete Contractors, Inc., 482 F.3d 247, 251 (3d Cir. 2007)*. In this case, Plaintiff's allegations, coupled with the medical records he has provided to the Court in conjunction with his Complaint and brief in opposition to the Motions to Dismiss, unequivocally demonstrate that Plaintiff has received care consistently, but he disagrees with the propriety and adequacy of the care received. Because Plaintiff cannot sustain a § 1983 claim under these circumstances, leave to amend would be futile. Accordingly, it is recommended that Plaintiff's Complaint and Amended Complaint be dismissed with prejudice.

AMILCAR GABRIEL, PLAINTIFF-APPELLANT, VS. JIM HAMLIN, BOB DOERR, ALLEN WISELY, BRIAN RUIZ, M.D. AND WEXFORD HEALTH SOURCES, INC., DEFENDANTS-APPELLEES. NO. 06-3636 UNITED STATES COURT OF APPEALS FOR THE SEVENTH CIRCUIT

STATEMENT OF THE CASE

This lawsuit involves actions under 42 U.S.C.§l983 for knowing exposure of the plaintiff prisoner to dangerous work conditions, and denial of medical care. Plaintiff suffered burns when he was working in the kitchen at Big Muddy River Correctional Center, and his leg went into a kettle of scalding water when he fell, causing serious burns. Plaintiff claimed that he was knowingly exposed to dangerous work conditions, and that he was denied proper medical care for his burns, infections and pain.

The case was first set for trial to commence on July 12, 2005, and was rescheduled by the court to August 23, 2005. (Doc.57) On July 18, 2005 the defendants filed a motion to continue trial, (Doc.68), which the court granted and reset the trial for Tuesday through Thursday of the weeks of September 19 and 26, 2005. (Doc. 69) On September 12, 2005 the district court, on its own motion, rescheduled the trial from Tuesday through Thursday the weeks of September 19 and September 26, 2005 to Monday through Friday of the week of September 19, 2005. (Doc.77)

On September 14, 2005 plaintiff filed his first and only motion to continue trial, setting forth that the plaintiff's expert was not able to testify the week of September 19, 2005, and in the alternative for voluntary dismissal without prejudice. (Doc.81) On September 15, 2005 the court denied plaintiff's motion to continue trial, denied the motion for voluntary dismissal without prejudice, and dismissed the actions with prejudice for want of prosecution. (Doc.85; Short. Appendix)

On September 27, 2005 plaintiff filed a timely Rule 60(b) motion to reconsider the dismissal, (Doc.87), which was denied on September 5, 2006. (Doc.92) Plaintiff appeals the dismissal with prejudice, the denial of the motion to continue trial or voluntary dismissal without prejudice, and the denial of his Rule 60(b) motion.

STATEMENT OF FACTS

Allegations of the Complaint

The amended complaint alleged that on December 4, 2000 the plaintiff was a resident at Big Muddy River Correctional Center, and was employed in the prison kitchen. (Doc.16, Amended Complaint, Count I, Par.10) Defendants, Jim Hamlin and Bob Doerr, were employed as food service supervisors in the kitchen. (Id., pars. 11-12)

Jim Hamlin assigned Mr. Gabriel to the job of cleaning the exhaust system in the kitchen on a weekly basis. (Id., Count I, par.11) In order to clean the exhaust system, it was necessary to reach portions over an area where there were two (2) large pots of scalding hot water, by leaning over them or standing over them.

Count I alleged that Jim Hamlin and Bob Doerr knew that the plaintiff would have to reach over the pots of scalding hot water to clean the exhaust system, but did not provide any ladder or other means of safe access to the area, and observed the plaintiff on many occasions cleaning the exhaust system by standing over the pots. (Id., pars.14-15)

Count I further alleged that, fearing for his safety, Mr. Gabriel began to empty the pots of scalding hot water before cleaning the exhaust system, and then refilling them after completing the work. (Id., par.17) Jim Hamlin and Bob Doerr disregarded the substantial risk to the plaintiff's safety, ordered him not to empty the pots of scalding hot water again, and forced him to risk serious injury when he cleaned the exhaust system. (Doc.16, Count I, pars.19-20)

The defendant, Brian Ruiz, M.D. was employed by Wexford Health Sources and performed medical services under their contract with the Illinois Department of Corrections as a physician at Big Muddy River Correctional Center. (Doc.16, Count II, par.11) Allen Wisely was the health care administrator. (Id. par.12)

On December 4, 2000 the plaintiff, Amilcar Gabriel, sustained second and third degree burns to his right leg when he fell while cleaning the exhaust hood and his leg went into a pot of scalding hot water. He was taken to the health care unit, where he became a patient of Dr. Ruiz. (Id., pars. 13-14)

Count II further alleged that it was the duty of the defendants, Allen Wisely, Brian Ruiz, M.D. and Wexford Health Sources, under 730 ILCS 5/3-7-2(d) to provide necessary medical care and treatment to Mr. Gabriel. (Doc.16, Count II, par.16)

Dr. Ruiz treated Mr. Gabriel's burns at the prison, and refused to send him to an outside hospital. Although he knew that the plaintiff had sustained serious burns to his leg, Dr. Ruiz only wrapped the wounds and sent plaintiff back to his housing unit the next day. (Id., par.19) Mr. Gabriel could barely walk and was in severe pain. (Id., par.20). He asked Dr. Ruiz for a wheelchair because of his difficulty walking and the severe pain, but Dr. Ruiz denied the plaintiff's request for a wheelchair. (Id., pars. 21-22)

During a period from December 4, 2000 through August, 2001, the plaintiff was under the care of Dr. Ruiz and sought treatment for his burns, infections and severe pain from Dr. Ruiz. (Id. par.15) Count II further alleged that the defendants disregarded the plaintiff's serious medical need, and refused to send plaintiff to an emergency room to provide necessary medical care to the plaintiff for his serious burns and pain. (Id., par.17)

Dr. Ruiz refused to provide the plaintiff with effective pain medication, and gave him only regular over-the-counter motrin and aspirin tablets on December 4 and December 5, 2000. (Id. par.18)

On December 18, 2000 the plaintiff was returned to the health care unit because the burns had not begun to heal well, and complications and infection had begun. (Doc.16, Count II, par. 24) Plaintiff asked Dr. Ruiz to send him to an outside specialist, but Dr. Ruiz denied plaintiff's request for care by an outside specialist. (Id., pars. 25-26) Mr. Gabriel asked Dr. Ruiz for strong pain medication for his severe pain, and Dr. Ruiz denied the plaintiff's request. (Id., par. 27)

Plaintiff remained in the health care infirmary until February 16, 2001, a total of fifty-eight (58) days, during which time the only pain medication Dr. Ruiz ordered was over-the-counter Ibuprofen until December 28, 2000 and over-the-counter Motrin until February 2, 2001. (Doc.16, Count II, par.28) Dr. Ruiz discontinued pain medication and refused to authorize any pain medication for the plaintiff between February 2 and March 5, 2001, and he received no medication for his pain after March, 2001 other than two doses of Motrin in July, 2001. (Id., pars. 33-34)

Allen Wisely, as acting health care unit administrator, investigated the plaintiff's complaints, knew of the plaintiff's severe burns, knew that the burns had become infected and that plaintiff was in great pain, but did nothing to obtain medical care for the plaintiff's pain, a consultation with a specialist or other assistance. (Id., pars. 31-32)

Plaintiff's terrible pain and suffering was not addressed until Dr. Ruiz left Big Muddy River Correctional Center, and other physicians, including Dr. Garcia, took over his care in September or October, 2001. (Id., par.37)

Proceedings Below

The plaintiff filed a pro se complaint under 42 U.S.C.§1983, alleging violation of his civil rights by the defendants in requiring him to work in conditions which presented a substantial risk of serious bodily injury and by the denial of prompt necessary medical care for his injuries and pain. (Doc.1) On September 16, 2002, after leave was given for Barbara J. Clinite to file her appearance for the plaintiff, plaintiff filed an amended complaint. (Doc.16)

Discovery was extended by order entered on March 26, 2004, in part because the depositions of defendant, Dr. Ruiz, and Dr. Garcia had not been taken. Dr. Garcia was the subsequent treating physician at the correctional center, had left the state of Illinois, and was difficult to locate and depose.

On August 4, 2004 the defendants filed a motion to bar plaintiff's expert witnesses, (Doc.45), and plaintiff filed a response, arguing that the deposition of Dr. Garcia had not been taken, and was necessary for his expert to finalize opinions. (Doc.50) The court entered an order barring plaintiff's experts. (Doc.69) Magistrate Judge Frazier based the order barring plaintiff's experts on the fact that plaintiff had not provided the expert's report.

Plaintiff filed a motion on August 26, 2004 seeking to reopen discovery and for leave to disclose his expert's report after the deposition of Dr. Garcia. (Doc.52) The motion set forth that the failure to provide a report from the expert was due to the fact that Dr. Garcia had not given his deposition. The motion sought time to depose Dr. Garcia, time for plaintiff's expert to review the deposition, and time to provide his expert's report.

In the motion to reopen discovery, Par.8, plaintiff stated that he had served unsigned Supplemental Answers to Interrogatories disclosing his expert, but without a report, on May 25, 2004, and provided signed answers two weeks later. (Doc. 52, Ex.B) Plaintiff identified Richard Lewan, M.D. as his expert. The court entered an order on August 31, 2004 granting plaintiff's motion, and stated that "Plaintiff's expert shall review this deposition and provide his report on or before November 19, 2004." (Doc.53; Short Appendix)

Plaintiff complied with the court's order and served his Rule 26 Expert Opinion Witness Disclosure with Dr. Lewan's preliminary draft report on the defendants on October 25, 2004, within the time ordered. After reviewing the deposition of Dr. Garcia, Dr. Lewan had no changes in his opinions and, therefore, the preliminary draft was allowed to stand as his report in the case.

In his Rule 26 Expert Opinion Witness Disclosure plaintiff set forth the following regarding Dr. Lewan's opinion testimony:

"SUBJECT MATTER: discussion of the medical notes and reports in DOC records, including nurses' notes; discussion of Plaintiff's burns, infections and treatment given; explanations of medical terms; discussion of materials reviewed; discussion of pain behavior, discussion of pain medications used and not used, but available; discussion of Plaintiff's pain at various times; and other matters set forth in his preliminary report attached hereto.

OPINIONS/CONCLUSIONS: It is Dr. Lewan's opinion that 800 mg. Tylenol or Motrin was totally inadequate treatment for the Plaintiff's pain - so wholly inadequate as to be cruel. As a result Plaintiff suffered intense unnecessary pain and suffering. Notes in the medical chart, and the nature of the condition under treatment, showed that the Plaintiff's pain was genuine, and his pain behaviors showed that his complaints were genuine. The refusal to provide effective pain treatment showed deliberate indifference to Mr. Gabriel's well-being. See also preliminary report attached hereto."

Dr. Lewan's report also criticized the defendants for not referring Mr. Gabriel to a specialist for treatment of infection and pain.

None of the Defendants requested a deposition of Dr. Lewan. On August 12, 2004 the parties filed the final pretrial order. (Doc. 49) On February 14, 2005, a pretrial conference was held, at which the court informed counsel that trial would be conducted on Tuesday through Thursday of each week, starting July 12, 2005 and being completed the following week. (Doc.57)

On October 29, 2004 the deposition of Dr. Garcia was taken and was available for presentation at trial. On March 16, 2005 the plaintiff's trial testimony was taken by video deposition. Plaintiff's counsel contacted Dr. Lewan, and arranged for him to testify during the July trial dates.

On June 24, 2005 the district judge changed the starting trial date from July 12 to August 23, 2005. (Doc. 62) Counsel for plaintiff contacted Dr. Lewan and arranged for his testimony at the August trial. On July 18, 2005 the defendants Hamlin and Doerr filed a motion to continue trial, (Doc.68), which the court granted and reset the trial to start September 20, 2005. (Doc.69)

Counsel for plaintiff contacted Dr. Lewan to arrange his testimony for September 27, 2005 and scheduled witnesses based on the trial being conducted Tuesday through Thursday of the weeks of September 19 and 26, 2005.

On September 12, 2005 the district court, on its own motion, rescheduled the trial from Tuesday through Thursday the weeks of September 19 and 26, 2005 to Monday through Friday of the week of September 19, 2005. (Doc.77) Counsel for plaintiff immediately contacted Dr. Lewan and was informed that he could not testify or give a deposition the week of September 19, 2005, but was available September 27, 2005. (Doc.81)

On September 14, 2005 plaintiff filed his first and only motion to continue trial, setting forth that his expert was not able to testify the week of September 19, 2005, and in the alternative for voluntary dismissal without prejudice. (Doc.81) In the motion plaintiff stated that Dr. Lewan is the only live witness, other than the defendants, plaintiff would present at trial, set forth the opinions shown in the opinion witness disclosure, and discussed the importance of his testimony. (Doc.81)

On September 15, 2005 the court denied plaintiff's motion to continue trial, denied the alternative motion for voluntary dismissal without prejudice, and dismissed the actions with prejudice for want of prosecution. (Doc. 85; Short.Append) The order stated that the plaintiff's motion to continue trial was based upon the unavailability of Dr. Lewan, and that plaintiff's expert witnesses had been barred by an order entered by Magistrate Judge Frazier.

Plaintiff then filed a timely Rule 60(b) motion for reconsideration, pointing out the later order granting leave to reopen discovery and disclose the expert's report. (Doc. 87) The court denied the motion for reconsideration, because plaintiff had not taken Dr. Lewan's deposition for use at trial. (Doc.92)

SUMMARY OF ARGUMENT

The plaintiff respectfully submits that the district judge erred in dismissing his actions with prejudice for want of prosecution, because plaintiff had diligently prepared his case for trial, and confirmed his expert's availability to testify during the July, August and the original September trial dates. The court's action in changing the trial dates only one week before trial meant that the trial would not continue into the second week as originally scheduled, when Dr. Lewan planned to testify.

A dismissal for want of prosecution is a harsh sanction and should be used sparingly, only in extreme situations where there is a clear record of delay or conduct which is contumacious. *Grun v. Pneumo Abex, Corp., 163 F.3d 411, 425 (7th Cir.l998)*

In the instant case, other than the unavailability of Dr. Lewan, plaintiff was prepared for trial, and there was no record of a course of delay which would call for a sanction of dismissal with prejudice.

The plaintiff further respectfully submits that the district court abused its discretion in denying the plaintiff's motion to continue trial. It was the first and only motion by plaintiff to continue trial, after the court had continued it from July to August because of a conflict in the court's schedule, and after a defense motion to continue trial had been granted.

The plaintiff's motion was necessary because the trial judge changed the dates only a week before trial, and instead of rescheduling the trial to a later date, scheduled it to take place in one week, instead of the two weeks original ordered. As a result, plaintiff's expert would not have been able to testify.

While a district court has inherent power to manage its docket and schedule trials, the court must balance the need to control its docket with the rights of litigants. *Arthur Pierson Co., Inc. v. Provini Veal Corp., 887 F.2d 837, 839* (7th Cir.1989)

Plaintiff respectfully submits that the denial of his motion to continue the trial was an abuse of discretion, because there were reasonable grounds for the motion.

In addition, the plaintiff combined with the motion to continue trial an alternative motion for voluntary dismissal without prejudice.

As a general rule, a defendant must demonstrate plain legal prejudice in order to prevent a voluntary dismissal of a claim. *Quad/Graphics, Inc. v. Fass, 724 F.2d 1230, 1233* (7th Cir. 1983); *Tyco Laboratories, Inc., v. Koppers Co., Inc., 627 F.2d 54,56* (7th Cir.1980) Plaintiff legal prejudice requires more than the prospect of another lawsuit. *Stern v. Barnett, 452 F.2d 211,213 (7th Cir.1971)*

Plaintiff respectfully submits that the denial of the motion for voluntary dismissal without prejudice was an abuse of discretion, because there was no plain legal prejudice to be suffered by the defendants, and the prejudice suffered by the plaintiff from the denial of the motion was substantial.

FEDERAL RULE OF CIVIL PROCEDURE 41

"(a) Voluntary Dismissal: Effect Thereof.

(1) *By Plaintiff, by Stipulation.* Subject to the provisions of Rule 23(e), of Rule 66, and of any statute of the United States, an action may be dismissed by the plaintiff without order of court (i) by filing a notice of dismissal at any time before service by the adverse party of an answer or of a motion for summary judgment, whichever first occurs, or (ii) by filing a stipulation of dismissal signed by all parties who have appeared in the action. Unless otherwise stated in the notice of dismissal or stipulation, the dismissal is without   prejudice, except that a notice of dismissal operates as an adjudication upon the merits when filed by a plaintiff who has once dismissed in any court of the United States or of any state an action based on or including the same claim.

(2) *By Order of Court.* Except as provided in paragraph (1) of this subdivision of this rule, an action shall not be dismissed at the plaintiff's instances save upon order of the court and upon such terms and conditions as the court deems proper. If a counterclaim has been pleaded by a defendant prior to the service upon the defendant of the plaintiff's motion to dismiss, the action shall not be dismissed against the defendant's objection unless the counter-claim can remain pending for independent adjudication by the court. Unless otherwise specified in the order, a dismissal under this paragraph is without prejudice.

(b) Involuntary Dismissal: Effect Thereof.

For failure of the plaintiff to prosecute or to comply with these rules or any order of court, a defendant may move for dismissal of an action or of any claim against the defendant. Unless the court in its order for dismissal otherwise specifies, a dismissal under this subdivision and any dismissal not provided for in this rule, other than a dismissal for lack of jurisdiction, for improper venue, or for failure to join a party under Rule 19, operates as an adjudication upon the merits.

(c) Dismissal of Counterclaim, Cross-Claim, or Third Party Claim.

The provisions of this rule apply to the dismissal of any counterclaim, cross-claim, or third-party claim. A voluntary dismissal by the claimant alone pursuant to paragraph (1) of subdivision (a) of this rule shall be made before a responsive pleading is served or, if there is none, before the introduction of evidence at the trial or hearing.

(d) Costs of Previously-Dismissed Action.

If a plaintiff who has once dismissed an action in any court commences an action based upon or including the same claim against the same defendant, the court may make such order for the payment of costs of the action previously dismissed as it may deem proper and may stay the proceedings in the action until the plaintiff has complied with the order."

ARGUMENT

I. STANDARD OF REVIEW

In reviewing a dismissal for want of prosecution the issue is whether the trial court abused its discretion. *Grun v. Pneumo Abex Corp., 163 F.3d 411, 424 (7th Cir.1999)*

A dismissal for want of prosecution will be reversed only if it was a mistake, or if the judge did not consider factors essential to the exercise of sound discretion. *Sharif v. Wellness International Network, 376 F.3d 720, 725 (7th Cir.2004)*

Also, in reviewing the denial of a motion to continue trial, the reviewing court applies an abuse of discretion standard. *Brooks v. United States, 64 F.3d 251, 256 (7th Cir.1995)* Matters of trial management are for the district judge, and the court of appeals intervenes only when it appears that the trial judge acted unreasonably. *Mraovic v. Elgin, Joliet & Eastern Ry.Co., 897 F.2d 268, 270-71 (7th Cir.1990)*

In reviewing the decision whether to grant or deny a motion for voluntary dismissal without prejudice, the court of appeals will not reverse the denial of the motion, absent an abuse of discretion. *United States v. Outboard Marine Corp., 789 F.2d 497, 502 (7th Cir.1986); Kovalic v. DEC Intern, Inc., 855 F.2d 471, 473 (7th Cir.1988)*

II. THE DISTRICT COURT SHOULD NOT HAVE DISMISSED THE ACTIONS WITH PREJUDICE FOR WANT OF PROSECUTION

This appeal presents a situation in which a trial judge dismissed plaintiff's actions with prejudice for want of prosecution, because plaintiff was unable to proceed to trial without the testimony of his expert, Dr. Lewan. The dismissal order does not mention any other delay, failure to appear or failure to comply with court deadlines and orders.

Initially, the trial judge denied plaintiff's motion to continue trial or for voluntary dismissal without prejudice under a mistaken impression that plaintiff's experts were barred from testifying. (Doc.85; Short Append) After the plaintiff filed his motion for reconsideration, pointing out the later order reopening discovery and granting leave for plaintiff to disclose his expert's report, the trial judge denied the motion for reconsideration based upon the fact that plaintiff had not taken a deposition of Dr. Lewan for use at trial. (Doc.92, Short Append)

Plaintiff respectfully submits that the trial judge erred in dismissing his actions with prejudice for want of prosecution, because plaintiff had diligently prepared his case for trial, and there was no record of delay or contumacious conduct by the plaintiff.

A dismissal for want of prosecution is a harsh sanction   and should be used sparingly, only in extreme situations where there is a clear record of delay or conduct which is contumacious. *Grun v. Pneumo Abex, Corp., 163 F.3d 411, 425 (7th Cir.1998)*

In *Sharif v. Wellness International Network, 376 F.3d 720, 725 (7th Cir.2004),* the Court reversed a dismissal for want of prosecution, where counsel had actively participated in the case,   and there was no record that counsel needlessly delayed the case.

In reversing a dismissal with prejudice for want of prosecution in *GCIU Employer Retirement Fund v. Chicago Tribune Co., 8 F.3d 1195* (7th Cir.l993), based upon the plaintiff's failure to promptly seek entry of judgment after an appeal was dismissed for lack of a final judgment, the Court held that the dismissal was an abuse of discretion. Although twenty-two (22) months had passed while the parties negotiated, the Court found that the plaintiff's conduct was not contumacious and:

"...the Fund did not fail to respond adequately to discovery requests, did not repeatedly miss deadlines, and did not engage in 'a continuing pattern of delay, non-cooperation and disobedience,' ... and did not display a 'distinct lack of prosecutorial intent dat[ing] back to the inception of the case[,]' as in *Daniels, 887 F.2d at 786;* and it did not disregard pre-trial orders, did not request numerous continuances, did not fail to file pre-trial orders, and did not 'flagrant[ly] abuse judicial time and resources...'" *(8 F.3d at 1199-1200)*

Plaintiff respectfully submits that the same is true in the instant case. Counsel for plaintiff had diligently prepared his case for trial, taking a deposition of Dr. Garcia, subsequent treating physician, for trial, and the video deposition of Mr. Gabriel for trial, serving request to admit facts, (Doc.61), and timely filing the pre-trial order. After his case was set for trial to start on July 12, 2005, plaintiff notified his expert, filed petition for writs of *habeas corpus* for inmate witnesses to testify by video conference at trial, (Doc.60), sent subpoenae to other witnesses and filed a motion in limine (Doc.58).

Plaintiff had confirmed his expert's availability to testify during the July, August and the original September trial dates. The court's action in changing the trial dates only one week before trial meant that the trial would not continue into the second week as originally scheduled, when Dr. Lewan planned to testify.

Plaintiff respectfully submits that dismissing the case with prejudice for want of prosecution was too harsh a sanction, based only on the fact that plaintiff had not taken a deposition of Dr. Lewan earlier to have it available just in case the court changed the trial dates to a time when Dr. Lewan could not appear to testify. Plaintiff's expert had cooperated and arranged to testify each time the trial was continued to a *later* date.

Taking a deposition of Dr. Lewan would have been expensive, involving travel to Wisconsin and the doctor's fee for preparation and giving the deposition. While the expense would have been reasonable if plaintiff was having difficulty in arranging Dr. Lewan's appearance when he was contacted for the July, August and original September trial dates, each time he was given sufficient notice Dr. Lewan agreed to arrange his schedule so that he could testify in open court.

In addition, Dr. Lewan's live testimony was of great importance, as he was the primary witness on liability and damages, and the only live in court witness plaintiff was going to call, other than the defendants. Using a deposition of Dr. Lewan would have left plaintiff with no live in court witnesses, and the advantage to the defendants in countering with numerous live witnesses would have been unfair to the plaintiff.

Dr. Lewan's testimony was needed to present to the jury a discussion of the medical notes and his opinions. Without Dr. Lewan's testimony and opinion that the lack of care and pain treatment was so wholly inadequate as to be cruel, and his opinions and discussion of notes reflecting deliberate indifference, plaintiff's cause of action likely would not have survived a motion for directed verdict at the close of plaintiff's case.

Plaintiff respectfully submits that it was through no fault of the plaintiff that Dr. Lewan could not testify at trial the week of September 19, 2005, but rather the result of circumstances which required the court to change the trial dates with extremely short notice.

It is well established that district courts have inherent authority to dismiss a case *sua sponte* for a plaintiff's failure to prosecute. *GCIU Employer Retirement Fund v. Chicago Tribune, 8 F.3d 1195, 1199* (7th Cir.l993) However, the authority is not unfettered. (Id.) The district court must balance the competing interests of keeping a manageable docket against deciding cases on their merits. (*Id. at 1199*)

Under the circumstances, plaintiff respectfully submits that the trial judge acted unreasonably in punishing the plaintiff for not having taken a deposition of Dr. Lewan. Other than the unavailability of Dr. Lewan, plaintiff was prepared for trial, and there was no record of a course of delay which would call for a sanction of dismissal with prejudice.

Therefore, plaintiff's respectfully submits that it was error to dismiss the actions with prejudice for want of prosecution.

III. IT WAS AN ABUSE OF DISCRETION TO DENY THE MOTION TO CONTINUE TRIAL

The plaintiff further respectfully submits that it was an abuse of discretion for the district court to deny the plaintiff's motion to continue the trial. Plaintiff diligently prosecuted his case, prepared for trial and confirmed his expert's availability for trial in July, 2005, August, 2005 and the week of September 26, 2005.

On June 24, 2005 when the court continued the trial to August 23, 2005, (Doc.62), plaintiff's counsel contacted Dr. Lewan and arranged for his testimony at the August trial. However, defendants Jim Hamlin and Bob Doerr filed a motion to continue the trial. (Doc.68) Although plaintiff was inconvenienced, he did not file objections. The court continued the trial to September 20, 2005. (Doc.69)

Counsel for plaintiff contacted Dr. Lewan in August to arrange for his in court testimony on September 27, 2005.

On September 8, 2005 counsel for plaintiff received a phone message, telephoned Judge Stiehl's clerk and was told that the judge wanted to change the trial dates to start September 19, 2005 and finish in that one week. Counsel stated that her expert was not available that week and she was asked to check on taking a deposition for trial. Counsel immediately phoned Dr. Lewan and was told that he had no openings the week of September 19, 2005 for either trial or deposition and was "totally booked". (Doc.81)

On September 12, 2005 the court e-mailed notice to the parties that trial was rescheduled to begin September 19, 2005. (Doc. 77)

Plaintiff respectfully submits that when the trial judge found that there was a problem having the trial continue into the week of September 26, 2005, it would have been reasonable to continue the trial to a later date. However, by changing the trial dates one week before trial to Monday through Friday of the week of September 19, 2005, the trial judge did not provide sufficient time for the plaintiff's expert to reschedule his testimony.

Because Dr. Lewan was the plaintiff's retained opinion witness whose testimony was essential to establishing deliberate indifference to plaintiff's serious medical need, and because he was the only witness, other than the defendants, who was going to appear in open court to testify for plaintiff, it was very important for plaintiff to be able to present his testimony live in open court.

Had it not been for the last minute change in trial dates, plaintiff would have proceeded to trial, and would have been able to present Dr. Lewan's live testimony in open court. Therefore, plaintiff respectfully submits that Dr. Lewan's unavailability on short notice to testify the week of September 19, 2005 was a reasonable and compelling basis for a continuance of the trial.

A district court has substantial inherent power to control and manage its docket and schedule trials. *Arthur Pierson & Co., Inc. v. Provini Veal Corp., 887 F.2d 837, 839* (7th Cir.1989) However, in exercising its power, the court is required to "strike a balance between the needs for judicial efficiency and the rights of litigants." *Arthur Pierson & Co., Inc. v. Provini Veal Corp., 887 F.2d at 839; In re Strandell, 838 F.2d 884, 886* (7th Cir.1987)

In the instant case, the plaintiff respectfully submits that the district court did not balance the interests of the plaintiff with the court's need to manage its docket. The court gave little, if any, consideration to the fact that the plaintiff had adjusted to prior continuances by the court on its own motion, and on the defendants' motion to continue trial, and one week prior to the original September trial dates was fully prepared to proceed as originally scheduled. The delay from the first trial date in July, 2005 was not due in any part to conduct or motion by the plaintiff, and had it not been for the last minute change in the September trial dates, plaintiff would have had no need to request a continuance.

In the case at bar, the defendants would have suffered no legal prejudice had the motion been granted. The defendants had been planning on the trial taking place during two weeks, into the week of September 26, 2005, and presenting their case the second week. Therefore, when the court moved the dates to the one week of September 19, 2005, the defendants had to change their plans anyway.

Plaintiff respectfully submits that he submitted reasonable grounds for the motion, and that the trial judge acted unreasonably in denying the plaintiff's motion to continue trial, because plaintiff had not previously sought a continuance or unreasonably delayed the case, the defendants would not have been prejudiced, and the court could have continued the trial to a later date to avoid the conflict in the court's schedule.

For the above reasons, plaintiff submits that the denial of the motion to continue trial was an abuse of discretion.

IV. IT WAS AN ABUSE OF DISCRETION TO DENY THE PLAINTIFF'S MOTION FOR VOLUNTARY DISMISSAL

The plaintiff combined with the motion to continue trial an alternative motion under Fed.R.Civ.Pro. 41(a) for voluntary dismissal without prejudice. (Doc.81) Plaintiff respectfully submits that the district court abused its discretion in denying the alternative motion for voluntary dismissal without prejudice.

Rule 41(a) provides that after a defendant has filed an answer or motion for summary judgment, the plaintiff may voluntarily dismiss the action without prejudice, by order of court and upon such terms and conditions as the court deems proper. *Marlow v. Winston & Strawn, 19 F.3d 300, 303* (7th Cir.1994)

In the instant case, plaintiff sought a voluntary dismissal without prejudice only if the court denied his motion to continue trial. A continuance would have enabled all parties to proceed to trial at a later date, and avoid the need for a second lawsuit. Plaintiff had no real choice if the continuance were not granted, because he could not proceed to trial without the testimony of Dr. Lewan.

Plaintiff respectfully submits that, because the motion to continue trial was denied, the court should have allowed the voluntary dismissal without prejudice, rather than dismiss the action with prejudice for want of prosecution. While all parties would have been inconvenienced by another lawsuit, any prejudice to the defendants would have been small compared to the prejudice to plaintiff by the dismissal with prejudice.

As a general rule, a defendant must demonstrate plain legal prejudice in order to prevent a voluntary dismissal of a claim. *Quad/Graphics, Inc. v. Fass, 724 F.2d 1230, 1233* (7th Cir. 1983); *Tyco Laboratories, Inc., v. Koppers Co., Inc., 627 F.2d 54, 56* (7th Cir. 1980); *Kovalic v. DEC International, Inc., 855 F.2d 471, 474* (7th Cir. 1988)

In exercising its discretion, a district court should follow the principle that voluntary dismissal should be allowed unless the defendant will suffer some plain legal prejudice other than the prospect of another lawsuit. *Stern v. Barnett, 452 F.2d 211, 213* (7th Cir. 1971); *Tyco Laboratories, Inc. v. Koppers Co., Inc., 627 F.2d 54, 56* (7th Cir.1980)

The Court has, in the past, discussed certain factors to be considered in determining whether a defendant would suffer plain legal prejudice if an action is voluntarily dismissed without prejudice. They include:

"...the defendants's effort and expense of preparation for trial, excessive delay and lack of diligence on the part of the plaintiff in prosecuting the action, insufficient explanation for the need to take a dismissal, and the fact that a motion for summary judgment has been filed by the defendant." (*Pace v. Southern Express Co., 409 F.2d 331, 334* (7th Cir.1969).)

The factors to be considered are a guide to the exercise of discretion by the court, not a mandate. *Kovalic v. DEC Intern, Inc., 855 F.2d 471, 474* (7th Cir.1988)

In the case at bar, the defendants did not demonstrate any plain legal prejudice which they would have suffered if the action were voluntarily dismissed without prejudice. There was no evidence of excessive delay and lack of diligence by plaintiff, and plaintiff submitted a reasonable explanation for the need to take a voluntary dismissal without prejudice. There was no pending motion for summary judgment.

The other factor set forth in *Pace v. Southern Express Co., 409 F.2d 331, 334* (7th Cir.1969), is the defendants' effort and expense of preparing for trial, which alone would not constitute plain legal prejudice, since the prospect of another lawsuit is not enough. *Stern v. Barnett, 452 F.2d 211, 213* (7th Cir. 1971) In a second lawsuit much of the expense and time spent preparing for trial in the first one would be useful and beneficial.

The fact that discovery had been completed would not mean that the defendant would suffer plain legal prejudice. In *Tyco Laboratories, Inc. v. Koppers Co., Inc., 627 F.2d 54, 56* (7th Cir.1980), the Court rejected the argument that the fact that discovery had been done meant that the defendant would suffer plain legal prejudice.

Furthermore, in the instant case, the prejudice, if any, to the defendants could have been minimized by the fact that discovery they have taken in this action could have been used in a refiled action, and most of their time invested in the defense would still have been useful.

In addition, Rule 41(d) provides that if the case is refiled, the court may make an order for payment of costs of the action previously dismissed as may be deemed proper. Generally, the terms and conditions of a voluntary dismissal without prejudice include reasonable expenses and fees for work which would not be beneficial to or used in a refiled case. *Cauley v. Wilson, 754 F.2d 769, 772* (7th Cir. 1985)

In *Marlow v. Winston & Strawn, 19 F.3d 300* (7th Cir. 1994), as in the case at bar, the plaintiff filed a motion for voluntary dismissal without prejudice, and the court dismissed the case with prejudice. In reversing, the court of appeals emphasized that Rule 41(a) preserves a plaintiff's right to take a voluntary nonsuit and start over so long as the defendant is not harmed. *(19 F.3d at 303;* See also, *McCall-Bey v. Franzen, 777 F.2d 1178, 1184* (7th Cir. 1985)

Plaintiff respectfully submits that the district court abused its discretion in denying the plaintiff's motion for voluntary dismissal without prejudice and dismissing the case with prejudice.

KENNETH F. LEONARD, PLAINTIFF/APPELLANT, V. FLORIDA DEPARTMENT OF CORRECTIONS, WEXFORD HEALTH SOURCES, INC., DAVID HARRIS, G. SOMODEVILLA, A. PIPIN, J.L. GREEN, AND G.J. SMITH, DEFENDANTS/APPELLEES. 06-11223-FF UNITED STATES COURT OF APPEALS FOR THE ELEVENTH CIRCUIT

B. Statement of Facts.

At the time of filing his Complaint and "Emergency" Motion for Temporary Restraining Order and/or Preliminary Injunction, Mr. Leonard was incarcerated at the Dade Correctional Institution. In both pleadings, as well as in the Complaint previously filed against Defendant John Holmes, a correctional officer at Dade Correctional Institution, Mr. Leonard claims that the Appellees failed to provide him with special shoes in violation of his Eighth Amendment constitutional rights.

Indeed, in the first Exhibit attached to his "Emergency" Motion for Temporary Restraining Order and/or Preliminary Injunction, the Inmate Grievance of July 18, 2005 (Dkt. 6), Mr. Leonard refers to special passes for Brogans. Brogans are state-issued boots. The response to the above-mentioned Inmate Grievance indicates that "Plaintiff states that Plaintiff had already received a pair of Brogans." The second Exhibit attached to Plaintiff's "Emergency" Motion for Temporary Restraining Order and/or Preliminary Injunction (Dkt. 6) refers to the fact that Plaintiff received Bobos. Again, said Exhibit does not indicate that Mr. Leonard cannot have Brogans; it reflects that if the Bobos shoes are the incorrect size, he may exchange them on Thursdays. The remainder of Plaintiff's Complaint, and his "Emergency" Motion for Temporary Restraining Order and/or Preliminary Injunction, appear to be directed to allegations of all inmates as a class at Dade Correctional Institution, which is improper absent class certification. The aforementioned Exhibits demonstrate that Mr. Leonard could access sick call regarding orthopedic shoes, that he was already in possession of Brogan shoes, and that if the Bobos shoes were too small, they would be replaced.

Since the filing of the pleadings at issue, Mr. Leonard has been transferred and is now incarcerated at Avon Park Correctional Institution.

C. Standard of Review

In addition to the standard of review set forth in Appellant's Initial Brief, Appellees submit that the standard of review is abuse of discretion for the District Court's denial of Plaintiff's "Emergency" Motion for Temporary Restraining Order and/or Preliminary Injunction. *See, Swatch Watch, F.A. v. Taxor, Inc., 785 F.2d 956 (11th Cir. 1986).*

SUMMARY OF THE ARGUMENT

The District Court appropriately denied Plaintiff's "Emergency" Motion for Temporary Restraining Order and/or Preliminary Injunction because the Plaintiff did not fulfill the prerequisites necessary for the issuance of a preliminary injunction, and the Plaintiff's claims did not rise to the level of an emergency. Moreover, denial of the "Emergency" Motion for Temporary Restraining Order and/or Preliminary Injunction was appropriate as Mr. Leonard alleges simply that he was deprived of adequate footwear, but does not allege facts indicative of an Eighth Amendment violation.

The District Court appropriately dismissed Plaintiff's claims for failure to state a claim upon which relief may be granted as Plaintiff's claims do not rise to the level of a violation of an Eighth Amendment constitutional right pursuant to *42 U.S.C. § 1983.* Additionally, dismissal of Plaintiff's Complaint was appropriate as Plaintiff improperly brought forth multiple causes of action on the same claim.

ARGUMENT AND CITATION OF AUTHORITY

A. The District Court Was Correct in Denying Plaintiff's "Emergency" Motion for Temporary Restraining Order and/or Preliminary Injunction.

1. The Allegations in the "Emergency" Motion for Temporary Restraining Order and/or Preliminary Injunction are Insufficient to Rise to the Level of "Emergency" and Mr. Leonard's Claims Do Not Establish the Prerequisite Elements Needed for the Issuance of a Permanent Injunction or Temporary Restraining Order.

It is axiomatic that the prerequisites for the issuance of a preliminary injunction are: (1) the inadequacy of a remedy at law; (2) the likelihood of irreparable injury if not issued; and (3) the probability of success in the action by the party seeking relief. *Aoude v. Mobil Oil Corp., 862 F.2d 890, 892 (1st Cir. 1988).* Mr. Leonard filed two separate Complaints and therefore, clearly has not established the inadequacy of a remedy at law.

Moreover, it is essential that the facts upon which Mr. Leonard bases his right to relief must be essentially undisputed or appear with such substantial clarity that the Court can weigh and determine the probability of success. *Bass v. Holberman, 295 F. Supp. 358, 361 (D.C. N.Y. 1968).* In order to grant injunctive relief, the relief requested must also be a presently existing actual threat. To this point, it is noted as follows:

The dramatic and drastic power of injunctive force may be unleashed only against conditions generating a presently existing actual threat; it may not be used simply to eliminate the possibility of a remote future injury, or a future invasion of rights, by those rights protected by statute or by the common law.

Holiday Inns of America, Inc. v. B&B Corporation, 409 F.2d 614, 618 (C.A. Vir. 1969). Further, it has long been established that an injunction will not be issued merely to allay the fears and apprehensions or to soothe the anxieties of individuals which may well exist without substantial reasons and may be absolutely groundless. *U.S. v. Dogan, 206 F. Supp. 446, 446 (D.C. Miss. 1962).* Here, Mr. Leonard has neither established a likelihood of success nor has he established irreparable injury. The evidence Mr. Leonard relied upon at the District Court level was two exhibits attached to his "Emergency" Motion for Temporary Restraining Order and/or Preliminary Injunction. Contrarily, however, both exhibits showed that: (i) Mr. Leonard could access sick call regarding orthopedic shoes, (ii) he was already in possession of Brogan shoes, and (iii) if the Bobos shoes were too small, they would be replaced. Accordingly, these allegations clearly do not demonstrate the likelihood of success or irreparable harm. For these reasons alone, Plaintiff's "Emergency" Motion for Temporary Restraining Order and/or Preliminary Injunction should have been denied.

2. Mr. Leonard Has Not Demonstrated a Deprivation of Constitutional Rights.

The Courts have carved out an exception to the requirement of irreparable injury in the prerequisites enumerated above for the issuance of a preliminary injunction where the alleged deprivation of constitutional rights is involved. In the case at bar, however, Mr. Leonard cannot establish that he has suffered a constitutional violation. In order to support a claim of an Eighth Amendment violation, a plaintiff must demonstrate acts or omissions sufficiently harmful to evidence deliberate indifference to serious medical needs. *Olsen v. Stotts, 9 F.2d 1475, 1476-77 (10th Cir. 1993)*. Mr. Leonard simply alleges that he has been deprived of adequate footwear. It cannot reasonably be disputed that this allegation is not indicative of a serious medical need giving rise to an Eighth Amendment violation.

B. The District Court Was Correct in Dismissing Plaintiff's Complaint.

1. Plaintiff Has Failed to State a Claim Upon Which Relief May Be Granted.

The allegations in Plaintiff's Complaint were brought pursuant to *42 U.S.C. § 1983* and Plaintiff argued that Defendants/Appellees failed to provide him with special shoes. In order to state an Eighth Amendment violation, Plaintiff must show acts or omissions sufficiently harmful to evidence deliberate indifference to serious needs. *Olsen v. Stotts, supra.* Appellant's claims relate solely to the inadequacy of footwear. In considering claims brought pursuant to Section 1983 regarding footwear, courts have indeed determined that such claims do not demonstrate "deliberate indifference" to an inmate's "serious medical needs." For example, in a case involving an inmate's claim that being forced to work in hard soled boots exacerbated an ankle injury, the Fifth Circuit Court of Appeals, in affirming the District Court's dismissal of the inmate's claim as frivolous, found that the inmate's claim does not involve a medical problem that is serious nor does it involve deliberate indifference. *Banuelos v. McFarland, 42 F.3d 232 (5th Cir. 1995)*. Moreover, the Seventh Circuit Court of Appeals, in upholding the District Court's finding that preliminary injunction was not warranted, found that "reasonable measures" had been taken by the prison and that a prisoner was not entitled to the medical treatment of his choice relating to a claim of deliberate indifference to his serious medical needs by the prison's refusal to prescribe the inmate footwear for lumps and ulcers on his feet. *Hall-Bey v. Ridley-Turner, 154 Fed. Appx. 493 (7th Cir. 2005)*. In the case at bar, even if all allegations together are taken as true, these claims do not rise to the level of a violation of an Eighth Amendment constitutional right.

2. An Individual's Claims May Not Be Split and All Grounds Upon Which a Single Claim is Based Must be Asserted and Included in One Action.

Plaintiff filed one Complaint in April 2005 against Defendant John Holmes, a correctional officer at Dade Correctional Institution. Subsequently, Plaintiff filed a second Complaint on July 25, 2005, alleging the same claims against Defendants/Appellees herein. Thereafter, on August 15, 2005, Plaintiff filed the "Emergency" Motion for Temporary Restraining Order and/or Preliminary Injunction with the same exact allegations as set forth in the previously-filed two Complaints.

Plaintiff improperly brought forth two actions on the same claim - and both cases are before the United States District Court for the Southern District of Florida. Under controlling law, it is improper for Plaintiff to split his causes of action. In fact, it has been held that all parts of a single claim or cause of action should be advanced in one single claim. *McConnell v. Travelers Indemnity Company, 346 F.2d 219 (5th Cir. 1965)*. Here, Mr. Leonard failed to do so. Accordingly, Plaintiff's Complaint was appropriately dismissed by the District Court.

JAMES E. SKINNER, PLAINTIFF, VS. CHARLES L. RYAN, ET AL., DEFENDANTS. No. CV-12-1729-PHX-SMM (LOA) UNITED STATES DISTRICT COURT FOR THE DISTRICT OF ARIZONA *2014 U.S. Dist. LEXIS 91711* (July 7, 2014)

I. Background

Plaintiff, a maximum security inmate housed in maximum security units of maximum security prison complexes within the Arizona Department of Corrections, filed a First Amended Complaint on October 2, 2012. (Docs. 8; 141 at 1) Plaintiff raised two grounds for relief against seventeen separate defendants. In Count I, Plaintiff alleged he is being deprived of basic necessities in violation of the *Eighth Amendment*, including inadequate plumbing in his cell, unsanitary conditions in his cell and other areas, and the failure to provide cleaning supplies to address the unsanitary conditions. Plaintiff claims that, for nine months, he was housed in a cell in which the base of the toilet leaked every time it was used, which caused flooding, and he was not provided adequate supplies to address the problem. He further claims that when he was eventually moved to a different cell in a different housing unit, the walls of the cell appeared to have blood and dried feces on them. He claims that, during the several months he was there, he repeatedly requested supplies to clean his cell but received adequate supplies on only one occasion. Plaintiff also claims that outdoor recreation cages and an outer stairwell were covered with cat waste and pigeon droppings. He claims these contaminants were then tracked back into his cell. Plaintiff claims he informed Defendants of these issues but they failed to take any action to resolve the problems.

In Count II, Plaintiff alleged that prison officials retaliated against him in violation of the *First Amendment* for filing a previous federal civil rights lawsuit. The District Judge screened the First Amended Complaint in accordance with *28 U.S.C. § 1915A(a)* on February 19, 2013. (Doc. 9) The District Judge dismissed Count II for failure to state a claim, along with three defendants, but ordered fourteen defendants to answer the allegations in Count I.[1] (Doc. 9 at 15) Plaintiff seeks unspecified compensatory and punitive damages, along with declaratory and injunctive relief. (Doc. 8 at 20)

---

1 Thirteen defendants have answered. The fourteenth, Rita Duarte, was dismissed without prejudice, on March 13, 2014, for failure to serve pursuant to *Fed.R.Civ.P. 4(m)*. (Doc. 134)

II. Motion to Compel

In the February 6, 2014 Motion to Compel, Plaintiff identifies thirty-three interrogatories to which he claims Defendants failed to adequately respond. (Doc. 113) He asks the Court to order more complete responses. Defendants argue in the response that their responses are sufficient and any objections asserted are proper.

A. Legal Standards for Discovery

Federal Rule of Civil Procedure 26(b)(1) provides that "[p]arties may obtain discovery regarding any nonprivileged matter that is relevant to any party's claim or defense . . . Relevant information need not be admissible at the trial if the discovery appears reasonably calculated to lead to the discovery of admissible evidence. All discovery is subject to the limitations imposed by *Rule 26(b)(2)(C)*." *Fed.R.Civ.P. 26(b)(1)*. These limitations reflect that, in addition to being relevant, discovery must also be proportional to the issues and needs of the case. *Kaiser v. BMW of North America, LLC, 2013 U.S. Dist. LEXIS 63855, 2013 WL 1856578, at *3 (N.D. Cal. May 2, 2013)* (citing *Fed.R.Civ.P. 26(b)(2)(C)*). Rule 26(b)(2)(C) provides:

> On motion or on its own, the court must limit the frequency or extent of discovery otherwise allowed by these rules or by local rules if it determines that:
>
> (i) the discovery sought is unreasonably cumulative or duplicative, or can be obtained from some other source that is more convenient, less burdensome, or less expensive;
>
> (ii) the party seeking discovery has had ample opportunity to obtain the information by discovery in the action; or
>
> (iii) the burden or expense of the proposed discovery outweighs its likely benefit, considering the needs of the case, the amount in controversy, the parties' resources, the importance of the issues at stake in the action, and the importance of the discovery in resolving the issues.

Thus, the court must "strike[ ] the proper balance between permitting relevant discovery and limiting the scope and burdens of the discovery to what is proportional to the case." *Kaiser, 2013 U.S. Dist. LEXIS 63855, 2013 WL at *3*. Moreover, "[b]road discretion is vested in the trial court to permit or deny discovery, and its decision to deny discovery will not be disturbed except upon the clearest showing that denial of discovery results in actual and substantial prejudice to the complaining litigant." *Hallett v. Morgan, 296 F.3d 732, 751 (9th Cir. 2002) (citing Goehring v. Brophy, 94 F.3d 1294, 1305 (9th Cir. 1996)).*

B. Application

1. Defendant Heet

Plaintiff first challenges two interrogatory responses from Defendant Assistant Deputy Warden Heet. The Court finds Defendant Heet's responses are sufficient. In response to Plaintiff's question, Heet identifies the procedure by which an inmate can request a mop from the floor officer. Plaintiff's motion complains that Heet failed to identify "all documents specifically referenc[ing the] mopping of cells" is without merit in light of the vagueness of the request. (Doc. 114-2 at 2) Likewise, Heet sufficiently responded that documentation of cell cleaning was completed on pod sheets and correctional service journals. The Court will not compel further responses from Defendant Heet.

2. Defendant Barrios

Next, Plaintiff challenges Defendant Deputy Warden Barrios's responses to certain interrogatories. Defendant Barrios sufficiently responded to interrogatories four and five. Regarding Plaintiff's request for mopping procedures, Barrios referenced housing unit post orders, which specify expectations for cell cleaning. Regarding Plaintiff's extremely broad request to identify any and all documents pertaining to sanitation at Plaintiff's housing unit, Barrios identified correctional service journals, and the information contained therein. He also referred to individual inmate detention records, which document inmate receipt of cleaning supplies. The Court will not compel additional responses.

With regard to interrogatories 12 and 13, Barrios properly responded to the questions, which pertained to the steps taken to ensure compliance with cell cleaning procedures. The Court will not order further responses to those questions, nor to interrogatory 22, which again deals with oversight.

3. Defendant Hetmer

Next, Plaintiff challenges Defendant Hetmer's responses to interrogatories 16, 17 and 24. The Court finds that Hetmer's response to the questions about mopping and cleaning procedures at Central Unit to be sufficient. He explains there is a cell cleaning schedule that is overseen by sergeants on each shift and cell block tours are done to ensure compliance with cell cleaning. He also states that Plaintiff was scheduled to receive cleaning supplies on Thursdays during the day shift. Likewise, Hetmer's identification of five separate work orders between August and December 2011 pertaining to the toilet in Plaintiff's cell was a proper response to Plaintiff's question. The Court will not compel any additional responses from Defendant Hetmer.

4. Defendant Kane

Plaintiff next challenges Defendant Kane's responses to interrogatories 16, 21 and 22. The Court finds Kane, the Central Unit Assistant Deputy Warden, properly responded to Plaintiff's question concerning compliance with sanitation procedures. Kane addressed how cleaning schedules were posted on bulletin boards and how walk-throughs are performed to observe conditions and operations. Regarding who was responsible for reviewing cell inspection records, Kane referred Plaintiff to a policy, presumably one that explains the cell inspection review policy. Plaintiff does not assert otherwise. Finally, Kane properly referred Plaintiff to records previously disclosed to Plaintiff pursuant to a request for production when asked to identify all cell inspection records. The Court finds no basis to compel additional responses from Defendant Kane.

5. Defendant Ryan

Plaintiff next challenges Defendant Ryan's responses to interrogatories 10, 13, 15, 16, 17, 19 and 23. Director Ryan's response to Plaintiff's question regarding the potential for, or incidents of, a MRSA ("methicillin-resistant staphylococcus aureus") infection was sufficient. Defendant Ryan, the Director of the Arizona Department of Corrections, said he knows it has occurred, the potential exists, but he is not familiar with specific conditions that may increase or diminish the risk. Regarding Plaintiff's four questions pertaining to cleaning supplies and cell cleaning schedules, Director Ryan properly explained that the day-to-day operations of the Arizona prisons, including cell cleaning issues, are delegated to the wardens and he has little knowledge of those issues. In response to another interrogatory regarding a specific grievance response, Director Ryan referred Plaintiff to the response, explaining that it speaks for itself. Lastly, in response to another extremely overbroad question in which Plaintiff asks Director Ryan to identify specific documents, Director Ryan responds that he does not have sufficient personal knowledge to respond because the documents pertain to the day-to-day operation of the prisons which is delegated to the wardens. The Court finds no basis to compel additional responses from Defendant Ryan.

6. Defendant Fizer

Lastly, Plaintiff challenges Defendant Deputy Warden Fizer's responses to interrogatories 4, 5, 7, 8, 9-14, and 16. In the first and second questions, Plaintiff asked Fizer to explain any and all priorities and funding issues that Fizer referenced in a response to Plaintiff regarding a request to repair or replace his toilet. He also asked about the cost of repairing and replacing a toilet. In addition to objecting, Fizer responded that there are a multitude of demands on prison budgets that Plaintiff does need not know about, including that the replacement of a toilet in Plaintiff's housing unit costs more than $4,000 each. While this seems to be an incredibly high figure, it is Fizer's response and may be properly used at trial for impeachment if it is not accurate. Without more evidence, it is not the province of the trial court to determine the credibility of an adverse party's answers to discovery requests at the discovery stage provided such answers are complete and responsive to the discovery request. Fizer's response is sufficient for now.

"Complete and accurate responses to discovery are required for the proper functioning of our system of justice. . . [and] parties have a duty to provide true, explicit, responsive, complete and candid answers to discovery[.]" *Wagner v. Dryvit Systems, Inc., 208 F.R.D. 606, 609-610 (D. Neb. 2001)* (citations omitted). "Providing false or incomplete discovery responses violates the Federal Rules of Civil Procedure and subjects the offending party and its counsel to sanctions." *Id. at 610.* One of the primary "purpose[s] of discovery is to make a trial 'less a game of blind man's bluff and more a fair contest with the basic issues and facts disclosed to the fullest practicable extent possible'. . . ." *Equal Rights Center v. Post Properties, Inc., 246 F.R.D. 29, 32 (D.D.C. 2007)* (citations omitted). Moreover, *Rule 26(e)(2), Fed.R.Civ.P.,* mandates that a party "[i]s under a duty seasonably to amend a prior response to an interrogatory . . . if the party learns that the response is in some material respect . . . incorrect and if the additional or corrective information has not otherwise been made known to the other parties during the discovery process or in writing." If there is intentional bad faith in answering discovery requests, sanctions may be appropriate as "[l]itigation is not a game. It is the time-honored method of seeking the truth, finding the truth, and doing justice." *Haeger v. Goodyear Tire & Rubber Co., 906 F.Supp.2d 938, 940 (D. Ariz. 2012).*

Plaintiff also asked whether the Central Unit was "adequately funded" during the relevant time frame and if not, whether Fizer notified others. Fizer's response referring to his previous response in which he said he did not believe the Central Unit had a funding problem. Additionally, in response to Plaintiff's question regarding whether the Central Unit tracked work orders, Fizer's responded "yes," and directed Plaintiff to work orders produced pursuant to a request of production. Fizer's responses are sufficient.

In response to Plaintiff's question about the number of times a work order was submitted on the toilet in Plaintiff's cell from ninety days before Plaintiff arrived in the cell to when it was repaired or replace, Fizer objected, stating it would require speculation on his part. He further stated that as the deputy warden, he did not keep track of such things. The Court will not compel Fizer to respond further to something about which he does not have specific knowledge.

Regarding Plaintiff's question about the identities of any inmates housed in the cell after it was "initially realized" that the toilet needed to be repaired, Fizer properly objects on vagueness grounds. Also, Fizer correctly explains that as a maximum security inmate, Plaintiff is not entitled to the "name(s) and number(s)" of any inmates housed in the cell, as his question requests, for legitimate security and appropriate penological reasons. Courts are required to consider the competing interests of the parties in deciding discovery requests and defer to the expertise of prison officials in matters of prison security. *Cutter v. Wilkinson, 544 U.S. 709, 725 n. 13, 125 S. Ct. 2113, 161 L. Ed. 2d 1020 (2005); United States v. Williams, 791 F.2d 1383 (9th Cir. 1986).*

Plaintiff also asked about Central Unit's procedures for mopping the cells. In response, Fizer explains the cell cleaning process at Central Unit, including the existence of a cleaning schedule, distribution of supplies, and oversight to ensure compliance. Fizer's response is sufficient. Similarly, Fizer's response that he does not have first-hand knowledge of what specific cleaning supplies are available for inmate use, is also sufficient. Plaintiff apparently does not believe Fizer is providing a truthful response, but the Court has no basis to conclude Fizer is not being truthful.

With regard to Plaintiff's overly broad request in Interrogatory No. 13 for "any and all ADC documents you were aware of that in any way relates to cell sanitation to include policies, procedures, protocols, post orders, logs, correctional standards, directives, audit reports, Arizona and Federal law, schedules, individual inmate detention records, budget records, supplies purchasing records, [and] supplies inventory records," the Court will order no further response. Plaintiff's request is disproportional to the issues in this case. The same is true with regard to Plaintiff's request for an equally-long laundry list of documents pertaining to sanitation of the outside areas of the Central Unit. Fizer will not be directed to respond to these two requests in Interrogatories No. 13 and 14.

Finally, Plaintiff is dissatisfied with Fizer's response to his request to explain the circumstances that led to Plaintiff's removal from the "Max Phase Program." Fizer stated he has no personal knowledge pertaining to the information requested. Fizer claims that "[a]part from the problems with [Plaintiff's] discovery (i.e. compound lines of inquiry, asking for production of documents in an interrogatory, and failing to identify the 'relevant time frame'), [Plaintiff] is simply upset that Fizer either does not remember or lacks the personal knowledge [Plaintiff] believes he should remember or know." (Doc. 141 at 8) The Court has no basis or evidence to conclude Fizer is not being truthful and will not order a further response. The Court, therefore, finds no basis to compel additional responses from Defendant Fizer.

UNFETTERED DESTRUCTION OF EVIDENCE

Rule 801(a) Federal Rules Of Evidence provides that a (statement) is (1) an oral or written assertion" and e.mails are statements within the meaning of this rule. When a person prepares a document, every draft, prior to the final document, is a statement.

Policies, practices and conduct of employees of prison systems and Corizon are often under litigation. As such they are aware that these documents are evidence and must be preserved. Arizona as a matter of public policy has adopted Department Order 102 which reads in part:

1.8.1.1 Due to the volume of the e-mail messages and associated storage space requirements noted above, the e-mail system shall purge messages automatically according to the following schedule:

1.8.1.1.1 "Trash" - container items purged every 14 calendar days. The system shall empty the messages from the mailbox. Users may use self-service recovery in order to retrieve a purged message for an additional 14 days.

1.8.1.1.2 "Sent Items" – items purged every 90 calendar days. After 90 calendar days, these messages shall be placed in a folder called "Sent Items," directly under the "Deleted Items" folder. They shall be held there for an additional 14 days before being purged.

1.8.1.1.3 Any e-mail message a mailbox owner intends to save indefinitely shall be placed in the designated "E-mail Retention Folder" (or user defined subfolders below this folder) which resides under "Managed Folders." Messages may also be retained by archiving the message to an archive file on the user's network home directory or "H" drive. Managed Folders and archived folders shall be exempt from automated cleanup.

1.8.1.1.4 Staff shall periodically review e-mail messages in their system folders to prevent the "E-mail Retention Policy" from deleting important e-mail(s) from their inbox, sent items, etc.

1.8.1.1.5 "Inbox" – Items regardless of whether or not they have been opened are purged every 90 calendar days. After 90 calendar days, the system shall place these messages in a folder called "Inbox" directly under the "Deleted Items" folder. They shall be held there for an additional 14 days before being purged.

1.8.2 Users may also retain messages by saving the message to an archive file on the network home directory or "H" drive. Messages retained in this way shall not be counted in the 2.6 GB storage quota.

1.8.3 Users may contact Network Services Support at ittechsupport@azcorrections.gov for assistance.

1.8.4 The "Calendar", "Task", and "Notes" in the messaging system are user controlled and are not purged automatically. To avoid storage problems, users shall delete or archive these items regularly. When a permanent record is necessary, the item shall be archived. In all other instances, the item shall be purged.

It has made the deliberated choice to destroy these evidence adverse to Arizona. As Justice Marshall stated in Ake v Oklahoma, 470 U.S. 68, 77 (1985) "mere access to the courthouse doors does not by itself assure a proper functioning of the adversary process." Being on notice "that documents and in its possession are relevant to litigation, or potential litigation, or are reasonably calculated to the discovery of admissible evidence" Wm. T. Thompson Co v General Nutrition Corp., 593 F. Supp. 1443, 1455 (C.D. Ca. 1984) Arizona has put in place the practice of destroying evidence.

It "is under a duty to preserve what it knows or reasonably should know, is relevant to the action, is reasonably calculated to lead to the discovery of admissible evidence, is reasonably likely to be requested during discovery" concerning its practices and employees.

"Even where an action has not been commenced and there is only a potential for litigation, the litigant is under a duty to preserve evidence which it knows or reasonably should know is relevant to the action." Fire Insurance Exchange v Zenith Radio Corp., 747 P.2d. 911, 914 (NV. 1987)

As prisoners are victims of this destruction of evidence the courts reward Arizona not withstanding that there is "convincing evidence that those responsible for the document destruction were aware at the time it took place that...litigation was a serious threat " Bowmar Instrument Corp v Texas Instruments, 25 Fed. Rules. Serv. 2d (Callaghan) 423, 427, 428 (N.D.Ind. 1977)

In Medellin v. Texas, 552 U.S. 491, 128 S. Ct. 1346, 1356 n.2, 170 L. Ed. 2d 190 (2008). JUSTICE BREYER, with whom JUSTICE SOUTER and JUSTICE GINSBURG join, dissenting states: "the Constitution's Supremacy Clause provides that "all Treaties . . . which shall be made . . . under the Authority of the United States, shall be the supreme Law of the Land; and the Judges in every State shall be bound thereby." Art. VI, cl. 2. The Clause means that the "courts" must regard "a treaty . . . as equivalent to an act of the legislature, whenever it operates of itself without the aid of any legislative provision." Foster v. Neilson, 2 Pet. 253, 314 (1829) (majority opinion of Marshall, C. J.).

Supreme Court case law stretching back more than 200 years helps explain what, for present purposes, the Founders meant when they wrote that "all Treaties . . . shall be the supreme Law of the Land." Art. VI, cl. 2. In 1796, for example, the Court decided the case of Ware v. Hylton, 3 Dall. 199. A British creditor sought payment of an American's Revolutionary War debt. The debtor argued that he had, under Virginia law, repaid the debt by complying with a state statute enacted during the Revolutionary War that required debtors to repay money owed to British creditors into a Virginia state fund. Id., at 220–221 (opinion of Chase, J.). The creditor, however, claimed that this state-sanctioned repayment did not count because a provision of the 1783 Paris Peace Treaty between Britain and the United States said that "'the creditors of either side should meet with no lawful impediment to the recovery of the full value . . . of all bona fide debts, theretofore contracted'"; and that provision, the creditor argued, effectively nullified the state law. Id., at 203–204. The Court, with each Justice writing separately, agreed with the British creditor, held the Virginia statute invalid, and found that the American debtor remained liable for the debt. Id., at 285. The key fact relevant here is that Congress had not enacted a specific statute enforcing the treaty provision at issue. Hence the Court had to decide whether the provision was (to put the matter in present terms) "selfexecuting." Justice Iredell, a member of North Carolina's Ratifying Convention, addressed the matter specifically, setting forth views on which Justice Story later relied to explain the Founders' reasons for drafting the Supremacy Clause. 3 J. Story, Commentaries on the Constitution of the United States 696–697 (1833) (hereinafter Story). See Vázquez, The Four Doctrines of Self-Executing Treaties, 89 Am. J. Int'l L. 695, 697–700 (1995) (hereinafter Vázquez) (describing the history and purpose of the Supremacy Clause). See also Flaherty, History Right?: Historical Scholarship, Original Understanding, and Treaties as "Supreme Law of the Land", 99 Colum. L. Rev. 2095 (1999) (contending that the Founders crafted the Supremacy Clause to make ratified treaties self-executing). But see Yoo, Globalism and the Constitution: Treaties, NonSelf-Execution, and the Original Understanding, 99 Colum. L. Rev. 1955 (1999).

Justice Iredell pointed out that some Treaty provisions, those, for example, declaring the United States an independent Nation or acknowledging its right to navigate the Mississippi River, were "*executed*," taking effect automatically upon ratification. 3 Dall., at 272. Other provisions were "executory," in the sense that they were "to be carried into execution" by each signatory nation "in the manner which the Constitution of that nation prescribes." *Ibid. Before* adoption of the U. S. Constitution, all such provisions would have taken effect as domestic law *only if* Congress on the American side, or Parliament on the British side, had written them into domestic law. *Id.,* at 274–277. But, Justice Iredell adds, *after* the Constitution's adoption, while further parliamentary action remained necessary in Britain (where the "practice" of the need for an "act of parliament" in respect to "any thing of a legislative nature" had "been constantly observed," *id.,* at 275–276), further legislative action in respect to the treaty's debt collection provision *was no longer necessary* in the United States. *Id.,* at 276–277. The ratification of the Constitution with its Supremacy Clause means that treaty provisions that bind the United States may (and in this instance did) also enter domestic law without further congressional action and automatically bind the States and courts as well. *Id.,* at 277.

"Under this Constitution," Justice Iredell concluded, "so far as a treaty constitutionally is binding, upon principles of *moral obligation,* it is also by the vigour of its own authority to be executed in fact. It would not otherwise be the *Supreme law* in the new sense provided for." *Ibid.;* see also Story, *supra,* §1833, at 697 (noting that the Supremacy Clause's language was crafted to make the Clause's "obligation more strongly felt by the state judges" and to "remov[e] every pretense" by which they could "escape from [its] controlling power"); see also The Federalist No. 42, p. 264 (C. Rossiter ed. 1961) (J. Madison) (Supremacy Clause "disembarrassed" the Convention of the problem presented by the Articles of Confederation where "treaties might be substantially frustrated by regulations of the States"). Justice Iredell gave examples of provisions that would no longer require further legislative action, such as those requiring the release of prisoners, those forbidding war-related "future confiscations" and " 'prosecutions,'" and, of course, the specific debt-collection provision at issue in the *Ware* case itself. 3 Dall., at 273, 277.

Some 30 years later, the Court returned to the "selfexecution" problem. In *Foster,* 2 Pet. 253, the Court examined a provision in an 1819 treaty with Spain ceding Florida to the United States; the provision said that "'grants of land made'" by Spain before January 24, 1818, "'shall be ratified and confirmed'" to the grantee. *Id.,* at 310. Chief Justice Marshall, writing for the Court, noted that, as a general matter, one might expect a signatory nation to execute a treaty through a formal exercise of its domestic sovereign authority (*e.g.,* through an act of the legislature). *Id.,* at 314. But in the United States *"a different principle"* applies. *Ibid.* (emphasis added). The Supremacy Clause means that, here, a treaty is "the law of the land . . . to be regarded in Courts of justice as equivalent to an act of the legislature" and "operates of itself without the aid of any legislative provision" unless it specifically contemplates execution by the legislature and thereby *"addresses itself to the political, not the judicial department." Ibid.* (emphasis added). The Court decided that the treaty provision in question was *not* self-executing; in its view, the words "shall be ratified" demonstrated that the provision foresaw further legislative action. *Id.,* at 315.

The Court, however, changed its mind about the result in *Foster* four years later, after being shown a less legislatively oriented, less tentative, but equally authentic Spanish-language version of the treaty. See *United States* v. *Percheman,* 7 Pet. 51, 88–89 (1833). And by 1840, instances in which treaty provisions automatically became part of domestic law were common enough for one Justice to write that "it would be a bold proposition" to assert "that an act of Congress must be first passed" in order to give a treaty effect as "a supreme law of the land." *Lessee of Pollard's Heirs* v. *Kibbe*, 14 Pet. 353, 388 (1840) (Baldwin, J., concurring).

Since *Foster* and *Pollard,* this Court has frequently held or assumed that particular treaty provisions are self executing, automatically binding the States without more. See Appendix A, *infra* (listing, as examples, 29 such cases, including 12 concluding that the treaty provision invalidates state or territorial law or policy as a consequence). See also Wu, Treaties' Domains, 93 Va. L. Rev. 571, 583– 584 (2007) (concluding "enforcement against States is the primary and historically most significant type of treaty enforcement in the United States"). As far as I can tell, the Court has held to the contrary only in two cases: *Foster, supra,* which was later reversed, and *Cameron Septic Tank Co.* v. *Knoxville,* 227 U. S. 39 (1913), where specific congressional actions indicated that Congress thought further legislation necessary. See also Vázquez 716. The Court has found "self-executing" provisions in multilateral treaties as well as bilateral treaties. See, *e.g., Trans World Airlines, Inc.* v. *Franklin Mint Corp.,* 466 U. S. 243, 252 (1984); *Bacardi Corp. of America* v. *Domenech,* 311 U. S. 150, 160, and n. 9, 161 (1940). And the subject matter of such provisions has varied widely, from extradition, see, *e.g., United States* v. *Rauscher,* 119 U. S. 407, 411– 412 (1886), to criminal trial jurisdiction, see *Wildenhus's Case,* 120 U. S. 1, 11, 17– 18 (1887), to civil liability, see, *e.g., El Al Israel Airlines, Ltd.* v. *Tsui Yuan Tseng,* 525 U. S. 155, 161–163 (1999), to trademark infringement, see *Bacardi, supra,* at 160, and n. 9, 161, to an alien's freedom to engage in trade, see, *e.g., Jordan* v. *Tashiro,* 278 U. S. 123, 126, n. 1 (1928), to immunity from state taxation, see *Nielsen* v. *Johnson,* 279 U. S. 47, 50, 58 (1929), to land ownership, *Percheman, supra,* at 88–89, and to inheritance, see, *e.g., Kolovrat* v. *Oregon,* 366 U. S. 187, 191, n. 6, 198 (1961).

Of particular relevance to the present case, the Court has held that the United States may be obligated by treaty to comply with the judgment of an international tribunal interpreting that treaty, despite the absence of any congressional enactment specifically requiring such compliance. See *Comegys* v. *Vasse,* 1 Pet. 193, 211–212 (1828) (holding that decision of tribunal rendered pursuant to a United States-Spain treaty, which obliged the parties to "undertake to make satisfaction" of treaty-based rights, was "conclusive and final" and "not re-examinable" in American courts); see also *Meade* v. *United States,* 9 Wall. 691, 725 (1870) (holding that decision of tribunal adjudicating claims arising under United States-Spain treaty "was final and conclusive, and bar[red] a recovery upon the merits" in American court).

All of these cases make clear that self-executing treaty provisions are not uncommon or peculiar creatures of our domestic law; that they cover a wide range of subjects; that the Supremacy Clause itself answers the selfexecution question by applying many, but not all, treaty provisions directly to the States; and that the Clause answers the self-execution question differently than does the law in many other nations. See *supra,* at 5–9. The cases also provide criteria that help determine *which* provisions automatically so apply—a matter to which I now turn.

The case law provides no simple magic answer to the question whether a particular treaty provision is selfexecuting. But the case law does make clear that, insofar as today's majority looks for language about "self execution" in the treaty itself and insofar as it erects "clear statement" presumptions designed to help find an answer, it is misguided. See, *e.g., ante,* at 21 (expecting "clea[r] state[ment]" of parties' intent where treaty obligation "may interfere with state procedural rules"); *ante,* at 30 (for treaty to be self-executing, Executive should at drafting "ensur[e] that it contains language plainly providing for domestic enforceability").

The many treaty provisions that this Court has found self-executing contain no textual language on the point (see Appendix A, *infra*). Few, if any, of these provisions are clear. See, *e.g., Ware,* 3 Dall., at 273 (opinion of Iredell, J.). Those that displace state law in respect to such quintessential state matters as, say, property, inheritance, or debt repayment, lack the "clea[r] state[ment]" that the Court today apparently requires. Compare *ante,* at 21 (majority expects "clea[r] state[ment]" of parties' intent where treaty obligation "may interfere with state procedural rules"). This is also true of those cases that deal with state rules roughly comparable to the sort that the majority suggests require special accommodation. See, *e.g., Hopkirk* v. *Bell,* 3 Cranch 454, 457–458 (1806) (treaty pre-empts Virginia state statute of limitations). Cf. *ante,* at 21 (setting forth majority's reliance on case law that is apparently inapposite). These many Supreme Court cases finding treaty provisions to be self-executing cannot be reconciled with the majority's demand for textual clarity. Indeed, the majority does not point to a single ratified United States treaty that contains the kind of "clea[r]" or "plai[n]" textual indication for which the majority searches. *Ante*, at 21, 30. JUSTICE STEVENS' reliance upon one ratified and one *un*-ratified treaty to make the point that a treaty *could* speak clearly on the matter of selfexecution, see *ante*, at 2 and n. 1, does suggest that there are a few such treaties. But that simply highlights how few of them actually *do* speak clearly on the matter. And that is not because the United States never, or hardly ever, has entered into a treaty with self-executing provisions. The case law belies any such conclusion. Rather, it is because the issue whether further legislative action is required before a treaty provision takes domestic effect in a signatory nation is often a matter of how that Nation's domestic law regards the provision's legal status. And that domestic status-determining law differs markedly from one nation to another. See generally Hollis, Comparative Approach to Treaty Law and Practice, in National Treaty Law and Practice 1, 9–50 (D. Hollis, M. Blakeslee, & L. Ederington eds. 2005) (hereinafter Hollis). As Justice Iredell pointed out 200 years ago, Britain, for example, taking the view that the British Crown makes treaties but Parliament makes domestic law, virtually always requires parliamentary legislation. See *Ware, supra*, at 274–277; Sinclair, Dickson, & Maciver, United Kingdom, in National Treaty Law and Practice, *supra*, at 727, 733, and n. 9 (citing *Queen v. Secretary of State for Foreign and Commonwealth Affairs, ex parte Lord ReesMogg,* [1994] Q. B. 552 (1993) (in Britain, "'treaties are not self-executing'")). See also Torruella, The *Insular Cases*: The Establishment of a Regime of Political Apartheid, 29 U. Pa. J. Int'l L. 283, 337 (2007). On the other hand, the United States, with its Supremacy Clause, does not take Britain's view. See, *e.g., Ware, supra*, at 277 (opinion of Iredell, J.). And the law of other nations, the Netherlands for example, directly incorporates many treaties concluded by the executive into its domestic law even without explicit parliamentary approval of the treaty. See Brouwer, The Netherlands, in National Treaty Law and Practice, *supra,* at 483, 483–502.

The majority correctly notes that the treaties do not explicitly state that the relevant obligations are selfexecuting. But given the differences among nations, why would drafters write treaty language stating that a provision about, say, alien property inheritance, is selfexecuting? How could those drafters achieve agreement when one signatory nation follows one tradition and a second follows another? Why would such a difference matter sufficiently for drafters to try to secure language that would prevent, for example, Britain's following treaty ratification with a further law while (perhaps unnecessarily) insisting that the United States apply a treaty provision without further domestic legislation? Above all, what does the absence of specific language about "selfexecution" prove? It may reflect the drafters' awareness of national differences. It may reflect the practical fact that drafters, favoring speedy, effective implementation, conclude they should best leave national legal practices alone. It may reflect the fact that achieving international agreement on *this* point is simply a game not worth the candle. In a word, for present purposes, the absence or presence of language in a treaty about a provision's self-execution proves nothing at all. At best the Court is hunting the snark. At worst it erects legalistic hurdles that can threaten the application of provisions in many existing commercial and other treaties and make it more difficult to negotiate new ones

The case law also suggests practical, context-specific criteria that this Court has previously used to help determine whether, for Supremacy Clause purposes, a treaty provision is self-executing. The provision's text matters very much. Cf. *ante*, at 17–19. But that is not because it contains language that explicitly refers to self-execution. For reasons I have already explained, Part I–B–1, *supra*, one should not expect *that* kind of textual statement. Drafting history is also relevant. But, again, that is not because it will explicitly address the relevant question. Instead text and history, along with subject matter and related characteristics will help our courts determine whether, as Chief Justice Marshall put it, the treaty provision "addresses itself to the political . . . department[s]" for further action or to "the judicial department" for direct enforcement. *Foster*, 2 Pet., at 314; see also *Ware*, 3 Dall., at 244 (opinion of Chase, J.) ("No one can doubt that a treaty may stipulate, that certain acts shall be done by the Legislature; that other acts shall be done by the Executive; and others by the Judiciary").

In making this determination, this Court has found the provision's subject matter of particular importance. Does the treaty provision declare peace? Does it promise not to engage in hostilities? If so, it addresses itself to the political branches. See *id.*, at 259–262 (opinion of Iredell, J.). Alternatively, does it concern the adjudication of traditional private legal rights such as rights to own property, to conduct a business, or to obtain civil tort recovery? If so, it may well address itself to the Judiciary. Enforcing such rights and setting their boundaries is the bread-andbutter work of the courts. See, *e.g.*, *Clark* v. *Allen*, 331 U. S. 503 (1947) (treating provision with such subject matter as self-executing); *Asakura* v. *Seattle*, 265 U. S. 332 (1924) (same).

One might also ask whether the treaty provision confers specific, detailed individual legal rights. Does it set forth definite standards that judges can readily enforce? Other things being equal, where rights are specific and readily enforceable, the treaty provision more likely "addresses" the judiciary. See, *e.g.*, *Olympic Airways* v. *Husain*, 540 U. S. 644 (2004) (specific conditions for air-carrier civil liability); *Geofroy* v. *Riggs*, 133 U. S. 258 (1890) (French citizens' inheritance rights). Compare *Foster, supra*, at 314–315 (treaty provision stating that landholders' titles "shall be ratified and confirmed" foresees legislative action).

Alternatively, would direct enforcement require the courts to create a new cause of action? Would such enforcement engender constitutional controversy? Would it create constitutionally undesirable conflict with the other branches? In such circumstances, it is not likely that the provision contemplates direct judicial enforcement. See, *e.g.*, *Asakura, supra*, at 341 (although "not limited by any express provision of the Constitution," the treaty-making power of the United States "does not extend 'so far as to authorize what the Constitution forbids' ").

Such questions, drawn from case law stretching back 200 years, do not create a simple test, let alone a magic formula. But they do help to constitute a practical, context-specific judicial approach, seeking to separate run-ofthe-mill judicial matters from other matters, sometimes more politically charged, sometimes more clearly the responsibility of other branches, sometimes lacking those attributes that would permit courts to act on their own without more ado. And such an approach is all that we need to find an answer to the legal question now before us.

.......*First*, the language of the relevant treaties strongly supports direct judicial enforceability, at least of judgments of the kind at issue here. The Optional Protocol bears the title "Compulsory Settlement of Disputes," thereby emphasizing the mandatory and binding nature of the procedures it sets forth. 21 U. S. T., at 326. The body of the Protocol says specifically that "any party" that has consented to the ICJ's "compulsory jurisdiction" may bring a "dispute" before the court against any other such party. Art. I, *ibid.* And the Protocol contrasts proceedings of the compulsory kind with an alternative "conciliation procedure," the recommendations of which a party may decide "not" to "accep[t]." Art. III, *id.*, at 327. Thus, the Optional Protocol's basic objective is not just to provide a forum for *settlement* but to provide a forum for *compulsory* settlement.

Moreover, in accepting Article 94(1) of the Charter, "[e]ach Member . . . undertakes to comply with the decision" of the ICJ "in any case to which it is a party." 59 Stat. 1051. And the ICJ Statute (part of the U. N. Charter) makes clear that, a decision of the ICJ between parties that have consented to the ICJ's compulsory jurisdiction has "*binding force* . . . between the parties and in respect of that particular case." Art. 59, *id.*, at 1062 (emphasis added). Enforcement of a court's judgment that has "binding force" involves quintessential judicial activity.

True, neither the Protocol nor the Charter explicitly states that the obligation to comply with an ICJ judgment automatically binds a party *as a matter of domestic law* without further domestic legislation. *But how could the language of those documents do otherwise?* The treaties are multilateral. And, as I have explained, some signatories follow British further-legislation-always-needed principles, others follow United States Supremacy Clause principles, and still others, *e.g.*, the Netherlands, can directly incorporate treaty provisions into their domestic law in particular circumstances. See Hollis 9–50. Why, given national differences, would drafters, seeking as strong a legal obligation as is practically attainable, use treaty language that *requires* all signatories to adopt uniform domestic-law treatment in this respect?

The absence of that likely unobtainable language can make no difference. We are considering the language for purposes of applying the Supremacy Clause. And for that purpose, this Court has found to be self-executing multilateral treaty language that is far less direct or forceful (on the relevant point) than the language set forth in the present treaties. See, *e.g.*, *Trans World Airlines*, 466 U. S., at 247, 252; *Bacardi*, 311 U. S., at 160, and n. 9, 161. The language here in effect tells signatory nations to make an ICJ compulsory jurisdiction judgment "as bind- ing as you can." Thus, assuming other factors favor self-execution, the language *adds*, rather than *subtracts*, support.

Indeed, as I have said, *supra*, at 4, the United States has ratified approximately 70 treaties with ICJ dispute resolution provisions roughly similar to those contained in the Optional Protocol; many of those treaties contemplate ICJ adjudication of the sort of substantive matters (property, commercial dealings, and the like) that the Court has found self-executing, or otherwise appear addressed to the judicial branch. See Appendix B, *infra*. None of the ICJ provisions in these treaties contains stronger language about self-execution than the language at issue here. See, *e.g.*, Treaty of Friendship, Commerce and Navigation between the United States of America and the Kingdom of Denmark, Art. XXIV(2), Oct. 1, 1951, [1961] 12 U. S. T. 935, T. I. A. S. No. 4797 ("Any dispute between the Parties as to the interpretation or application of the present Treaty, not satisfactorily adjusted by diplomacy, shall be submitted to the International Court of Justice, unless the Parties agree to settlement by some other pacific means"). In signing these treaties (in respect to, say, alien land ownership provisions) was the United States engaging in a near useless act? Does the majority believe the drafters expected Congress to enact further legislation about, say, an alien's inheritance rights, decision by decision? I recognize, as the majority emphasizes, that the U. N. Charter uses the words "undertakes to comply," rather than, say, "shall comply" or "must comply." But what is inadequate about the word "undertak[e]"? A leading contemporary dictionary defined it in terms of "lay[ing] oneself under obligation . . . to perform or to execute." Webster's New International Dictionary 2770 (2d ed. 1939). And that definition is just what the equally authoritative Spanish version of the provision (familiar to Mexico) says directly: The words "compromete a cumplir" indicate a present obligation to execute, without any tentativeness of the sort the majority finds in the English word "undertakes." See Carta de las Naciones Unidas, Articulo 94, 59 Stat. 1175 (1945); Spanish and English Legal and Commercial Dictionary 44 (1945) (defining "comprometer" as "become liable"); *id.*, at 59 (defining "cumplir" as "to perform, discharge, carry out, execute"); see also Art. 111, 59 Stat. 1054 (Spanish-language version equally valid); *Percheman*, 7 Pet., at 88–89 (looking to Spanish version of a treaty to clear up ambiguity in English version). Compare *Todok* v. *Union State Bank of Harvard*, 281 U. S. 449, 453 (1930) (treating a treaty provision as self-executing even though it *expressly* stated what the majority says the word "undertakes" *implicitly* provides: that "'[t]he United States . . . shall be at liberty to make respecting this matter, such laws as they think proper'").

And even if I agreed with JUSTICE STEVENS that the language is perfectly ambiguous (which I do not), I could not agree that "the best reading . . . is . . . one that contemplates future action by the political branches." *Ante*, at 3. The consequence of such a reading is to place the fate of an international promise made by the United States in the hands of a single State. See *ante*, at 4–6. And that is precisely the situation that the Framers sought to prevent by enacting the Supremacy Clause. See 3 Story 696 (purpose of Supremacy Clause "was probably to obviate" the "difficulty" of system where treaties were "dependent upon the good will of the states for their execution"); see also *Ware*, 3 Dall., at 277–278 (opinion of Iredell, J.).

I also recognize, as the majority emphasizes (*ante*, at 13–14), that the U. N. Charter says that "[i]f any party to a case fails to perform the obligations incumbent upon it under a judgment rendered by the [ICJ], the other party may have recourse to the Security Council." Art. 94(2), 59 Stat. 1051. And when the Senate ratified the charter, it took comfort in the fact that the United States has a veto in the Security Council. See 92 Cong. Rec. 10694–10695 (1946) (statements of Sens. Pepper and Connally).

But what has that to do with the matter? To begin with, the Senate would have been contemplating politically significant ICJ decisions, not, *e.g.*, the bread-and-butter commercial and other matters that are the typical subjects of self-executing treaty provisions. And in any event, both the Senate debate and U. N. Charter provision discuss and describe what happens (or does not happen) when a nation decides *not* to carry out an ICJ decision. See Charter of the United Nations for the Maintenance of International Peace and Security: Hearing before the Senate Committee on Foreign Relations, 79th Cong., 1st Sess., 286 (1945) (statement of Leo

Pasvolsky, Special Assistant to the Secretary of State for International Organization and Security Affairs) ("[W]hen the Court has rendered a judgment and one of the parties refuses to accept it, then the dispute becomes political rather than legal"). The debates refer to remedies for a breach of our promise to carry out an ICJ decision. The Senate understood, for example, that Congress (unlike legislatures in other nations that do not permit domestic legislation to trump treaty obligations, Hollis 47–49) can block through legislation self-executing, as well as non-self-executing determinations. The debates nowhere refer to the method we use for affirmatively carrying out an ICJ obligation that no political branch has decided to dishonor, still less to a decision that the President (without congressional dissent) seeks to enforce. For that reason, these aspects of the ratification debates are here beside the point. See *infra*, at 23–24.

The upshot is that treaty language says that an ICJ decision is legally binding, but it leaves the implementation of that binding legal obligation to the domestic law of each signatory nation. In this Nation, the Supremacy Clause, as long and consistently interpreted, indicates that ICJ decisions rendered pursuant to provisions for binding adjudication must be domestically legally binding and enforceable in domestic courts *at least sometimes*. And for purposes of this argument, that conclusion is all that I need. The remainder of the discussion will explain why, if ICJ judgments *sometimes* bind domestic courts, then they have that effect here.

Second, the Optional Protocol here applies to a dispute about the meaning of a Vienna Convention provision that is itself self-executing and judicially enforceable. The Convention provision is about an individual's "rights," namely, his right upon being arrested to be informed of his separate right to contact his nation's consul. See Art. 36(1)(b), 21 U. S. T., at 101. The provision language is precise. The dispute arises at the intersection of an individual right with ordinary rules of criminal procedure; it consequently concerns the kind of matter with which judges are familiar. The provisions contain judicially enforceable standards. See Art. 36(2), *ibid.* (providing for exercise of rights "in conformity with the laws and regulations" of the arresting nation provided that the "laws and regulations . . . enable full effect to be given to the purposes for which the rights accorded under this Article are intended"). And the judgment itself requires a further hearing of a sort that is typically judicial. See *infra*, at 25–26.

This Court has found similar treaty provisions selfexecuting. See, *e.g.*, *Rauscher*, 119 U. S., at 410–411, 429–430 (violation of extradition treaty could be raised as defense in criminal trial); *Johnson* v. *Browne*, 205 U. S. 309, 317–322 (1907) (extradition treaty required grant of writ of habeas corpus); *Wildenhus's Case*, 120 U. S., at 11, 17–18 (treaty defined scope of state jurisdiction in a criminal case). It is consequently not surprising that, when Congress ratified the Convention, the State Department reported that the "Convention is considered entirely selfexecutive and does not require any implementing or complementing legislation." S. Exec. Rep. No. 91–9, p. 5 (1969); see also *id.*, at 18 ("To the extent that there are conflicts with Federal legislation or State laws the Vienna Convention, after ratification, would govern"). And the Executive Branch has said in this Court that other, indistinguishable Vienna Convention provisions are selfexecuting. See Brief for United States as *Amicus Curiae* in *Sanchez-Llamas* v. *Oregon*, O. T. 2005, Nos. 05–51 and 04–10566, p. 14, n. 2; cf. *ante*, at 10, n. 4 (majority leaves question open).

Third, logic suggests that a treaty provision providing for "final" and "binding" judgments that "settl[e]" treatybased disputes is self-executing insofar as the judgment in question concerns the meaning of an underlying treaty provision that is itself self-executing. Imagine that two parties to a contract agree to binding arbitration about whether a contract provision's word "grain" includes rye. They would expect that, if the arbitrator decides that the word "grain" does include rye, the arbitrator will then simply read the relevant provision as if it said "grain including rye." They would also expect the arbitrator to issue a binding award that embodies whatever relief would be appropriate under that circumstance. Why treat differently the parties' agreement to binding ICJ determination about, *e.g.*, the proper interpretation of the Vienna Convention clauses containing the rights here at issue? Why not simply read the relevant Vienna Convention provisions as if (between the parties and in respect to the 51 individuals at issue) they contain words that encapsulate the ICJ's decision? See Art. 59, 59 Stat. 1062 (ICJ decision has "binding force . . . between the parties and in respect of [the] particular case"). Why would the ICJ judgment not bind in precisely the same way those words would bind if they appeared in the relevant Vienna Convention provisions—just as the ICJ says, for purposes of this case, that they do?

To put the same point differently: What sense would it make (1) to make a self-executing promise and (2) to promise to accept as final an ICJ judgment interpreting that self-executing promise, yet (3) to insist that the judgment itself is not self-executing (*i.e.*, that Congress must enact specific legislation to enforce it)?

I am not aware of any satisfactory answer to these questions. It is no answer to point to the fact that in *Sanchez-Llamas* v. *Oregon*, 548 U. S. 331 (2006), this Court interpreted the relevant Convention provisions differently from the ICJ in *Avena*. This Court's *SanchezLlamas* interpretation binds our courts with respect to individuals whose rights were not espoused by a state party in *Avena*. Moreover, as the Court itself recognizes, see *ante*, at 1–2, and as the President recognizes, see President's Memorandum, the question here is the very different question of applying the ICJ's *Avena* judgment to the very parties whose interests Mexico and the United States espoused in the ICJ *Avena* proceeding. It is in respect to these individuals that the United States has promised the ICJ decision will have binding force. Art. 59, 59 Stat. 1062. See 1 Restatement (Second) of Conflict of Laws §98 (1969); 2 Restatement (Third) of Foreign Relations §481 (1986); 1 Restatement (Second) of Judgments §17 (1980) (all calling for recognition of judgment rendered after fair hearing in a contested proceeding before a court with adjudicatory authority over the case). See also 1 Restatement (Second) of Conflict of Laws §106 ("A judgment will be recognized and enforced in other states even though an error of fact or law was made in the proceedings before judgment . . ."); *id.*, §106, Comment *a* ("Th[is] rule is . . . applicable to judgments rendered in foreign nations . . ."); Reese, The Status in This Country of Judgments Rendered Abroad, 50 Colum. L. Rev. 783, 789 (1950) ("[Foreign] judgments will not be denied effect merely because the original court made an error either of fact or of law").

Contrary to the majority's suggestion, see *ante*, at 15– 16, that binding force does not disappear by virtue of the fact that Mexico, rather than Medellín himself, presented his claims to the ICJ. Mexico brought the *Avena* case in part in "the exercise of its right of diplomatic protection of its nationals," *e.g.*, 2004 I. C. J., at 21, ¶¶13(1), (3), including Medellín, see *id.*, at 25, ¶16. Such derivative claims are a well-established feature of international law, and the United States has several times asserted them on behalf of its own citizens. See 2 Restatement (Third) of Foreign Relations, *supra*, §713, Comments *a, b*, at 217; *Case Concerning Elettronic Sicula S. p. A. (U. S. v. Italy)*, 1989 I. C. J. 15, 20 (Judgment of July 20); *Case Concerning United States Diplomatic and Consular Staff in Tehran (U. S. v. Iran)*, 1979 I. C. J. 7, 8 (Judgment of Dec. 15); *Case Concerning Rights of Nationals of the United States of America in Morocco (Fr. v. U. S.)*, 1952 I. C. J. 176, 180– 181 (Judgment of Aug. 27). They are treated in relevant respects as the claims of the represented individuals themselves. See 2 Restatement (Third) of Foreign Relations, *supra*, §713, Comments *a, b*. In particular, they can give rise to remedies, tailored to the individual, that bind the Nation against whom the claims are brought (here, the United States). See *ibid.*; see also, *e.g.*, *Frelinghuysen* v. *Key*, 110 U. S. 63, 71–72 (1884).

Nor does recognition of the ICJ judgment as binding with respect to the individuals whose claims were espoused by Mexico in any way derogate from the Court's holding in *Sanchez-Llamas, supra*. See *ante*, at 16, n. 8. This case does not implicate the general interpretive question answered in *Sanchez-Llamas*: whether the Vienna Convention displaces state procedural rules. We are instead confronted with the discrete question of Texas' obligation to comply with a binding judgment issued by a tribunal with undisputed jurisdiction to adjudicate the rights of the individuals named therein. "It is inherent in international adjudication that an international tribunal may reject one country's legal position in favor of another's—and the United States explicitly accepted this possibility when it ratified the Optional Protocol." Brief for United States as *Amicus Curiae* 22.

Fourth, the majority's very different approach has seriously negative practical implications. The United States has entered into at least 70 treaties that contain provisions for ICJ dispute settlement similar to the Protocol before us. Many of these treaties contain provisions simi lar to those this Court has previously found selfexecuting—provisions that involve, for example, property rights, contract and commercial rights, trademarks, civil liability for personal injury, rights of foreign diplomats, taxation, domestic-court jurisdiction, and so forth. Compare Appendix A, *infra*, with Appendix B, *infra*. If the Optional Protocol here, taken together with the U. N. Charter and its annexed ICJ Statute, is insufficient to warrant enforcement of the ICJ judgment before us, it is difficult to see how one could reach a different conclusion in any of these other instances. And the consequence is to undermine longstanding efforts in those treaties to create an effective international system for interpreting and applying many, often commercial, self-executing treaty provisions. I thus doubt that the majority is right when it says, "We do not suggest that treaties can never afford binding domestic effect to international tribunal judgments." *Ante*, at 23–24. In respect to the 70 treaties that currently refer disputes to the ICJ's binding adjudicatory authority, some multilateral, some bilateral, that is just what the majority has done.

Nor can the majority look to congressional legislation for a quick fix. Congress is unlikely to authorize automatic judicial enforceability of *all* ICJ judgments, for that could include some politically sensitive judgments and others better suited for enforcement by other branches: for example, those touching upon military hostilities, naval activity, handling of nuclear material, and so forth. Nor is Congress likely to have the time available, let alone the will, to legislate judgment-by-judgment enforcement of, say, the ICJ's (or other international tribunals') resolution of non-politically-sensitive commercial disputes. And as this Court's prior case law has avoided laying down brightline rules but instead has adopted a more complex approach, it seems unlikely that Congress will find it easy to develop legislative bright lines that pick out those provisions (addressed to the Judicial Branch) where selfexecution seems warranted. But, of course, it is not necessary for Congress to do so—at least not if one believes that this Court's Supremacy Clause cases *already* embody criteria likely to work reasonably well. It is those criteria that I would apply here.

Fifth, other factors, related to the particular judgment here at issue, make that judgment well suited to direct judicial enforcement. The specific issue before the ICJ concerned "'review and reconsideration'" of the "possible   prejudice" caused in each of the 51 affected cases by an arresting State's failure to provide the defendant with rights guaranteed by the Vienna Convention. *Avena*, 2004 I. C. J., at 65, ¶138. This review will call for an understanding of how criminal procedure works, including whether, and how, a notification failure may work prejudice. *Id.*, at 56–57. As the ICJ itself recognized, "it is the judicial process that is suited to this task." *Id.*, at 66, ¶140. Courts frequently work with criminal procedure and related prejudice. Legislatures do not. Judicial standards are readily available for working in this technical area. Legislative standards are not readily available. Judges typically determine such matters, deciding, for example, whether further hearings are necessary, after reviewing a record in an individual case. Congress does not normally legislate in respect to individual cases. Indeed, to repeat what I said above, what kind of special legislation does the majority believe Congress ought to consider?

Sixth, to find the United States' treaty obligations selfexecuting as applied to the ICJ judgment (and consequently to find that judgment enforceable) does not threaten constitutional conflict with other branches; it does not require us to engage in nonjudicial activity; and it does not require us to create a new cause of action. The only question before us concerns the application of the ICJ judgment as binding law applicable to the parties in a particular criminal proceeding that Texas law creates independently of the treaty. I repeat that the question before us does not involve the creation of a private right of action (and the majority's reliance on authority regarding such a circumstance is misplaced, see *ante*, at 9, n. 3). *Seventh*, neither the President nor Congress has expressed concern about direct judicial enforcement of the ICJ decision. To the contrary, the President favors enforcement of this judgment. Thus, insofar as foreign policy impact, the interrelation of treaty provisions, or any other matter within the President's special treaty, military, and foreign affairs responsibilities might prove relevant, such factors *favor*, rather than militate against, enforcement of the judgment before us. See, *e.g.*, *Jama* v. *Immigration and Customs Enforcement*, 543 U. S. 335, 348 (2005) (noting Court's "customary policy of deference to the President in matters of foreign affairs").

For these seven reasons, I would find that the United States' treaty obligation to comply with the ICJ judgment in *Avena* is enforceable in court in this case without further congressional action beyond Senate ratification of the relevant treaties. The majority reaches a different conclusion because it looks for the wrong thing (explicit textual expression about self-execution) using the wrong standard (clarity) in the wrong place (the treaty language). Hunting for what the text cannot contain, it takes a wrong turn. It threatens to deprive individuals, including businesses, property owners, testamentary beneficiaries, consular officials, and others, of the workable dispute resolution procedures that many treaties, including commercially oriented treaties, provide. In a world where commerce, trade, and travel have become ever more international, that is a step in the wrong direction.

Were the Court for a moment to shift the direction of its legal gaze, looking instead to the Supremacy Clause and to the extensive case law interpreting that Clause as applied to treaties, I believe it would reach a better supported, more felicitous conclusion. That approach, well embedded in Court case law, leads to the conclusion that the ICJ judgment before us is judicially enforceable without further legislative action.

A determination that the ICJ judgment is enforceable does not quite end the matter, for the judgment itself requires us to make one further decision. It directs the United States to provide further judicial review of the 51 cases of Mexican nationals "by means of its own choosing." *Avena*, 2004 I. C. J., at 72, ¶153(9). As I have explained, I believe the judgment addresses itself to the Judicial Branch. This Court consequently must "choose" the means. And rather than, say, conducting the further review in this Court, or requiring Medellín to seek the review in another federal court, I believe that the proper forum for review would be the Texas-court proceedings that would follow a remand of this case.

Beyond the fact that a remand would be the normal course upon reversing a lower court judgment, there are additional reasons why further state-court review would be particularly appropriate here. The crime took place in Texas, and the prosecution at issue is a Texas prosecution. The President has specifically endorsed further Texas court review. See President's Memorandum. The ICJ judgment requires further hearings as to whether the police failure to inform Medellín of his Vienna Convention rights prejudiced Medellín, even if such hearings would not otherwise be available under Texas' procedural default rules. While Texas has already considered that matter, it did not consider fully, for example, whether appointed counsel's coterminous 6-month suspension from the practice of the law "caused actual prejudice to the defendant"— prejudice that would not have existed had Medellín known he could contact his consul and thereby find a different lawyer. *Id.,* at 60, ¶121.

Finally, Texas law authorizes a criminal defendant to seek postjudgment review. See Tex. Code Crim. Proc. Ann., Art. 11.071, §5(a)(1) (Vernon Supp. 2006). And Texas law provides for further review where American law provides a "legal basis" that was previously "unavailable." See *Ex parte Medellín*, 223 S. W. 3d 315, 352 (Tex. Crim. App. 2006). Thus, I would send this case back to the Texas courts, which must then apply the *Avena* judgment as binding law. See U. S. Const., Art. VI, cl. 2; see also, *e.g.*, *Dominguez* v. *State*, 90 Tex. Crim. 92, 99, 234 S. W. 79, 83 (1921) (recognizing that treaties are "part of the supreme law of the land" and that "it is the duty of the courts of the state to take cognizance of, construe and give effect" to them (internal quotation marks omitted)).

Because the majority concludes that the Nation's international legal obligation to enforce the ICJ's decision is not automatically a domestic legal obligation, it must then determine whether the President has the constitutional authority to enforce it. And the majority finds that he does not. See Part III, *ante*.

In my view, that second conclusion has broader implications than the majority suggests. The President here seeks to implement treaty provisions in which the United States agrees that the ICJ judgment is binding with respect to the *Avena* parties. Consequently, his actions draw upon his constitutional authority in the area of foreign affairs. In this case, his exercise of that power falls within that middle range of Presidential authority where Congress has neither specifically authorized nor specifically forbidden the Presidential action in question. See *Youngstown Sheet & Tube Co.* v. *Sawyer,* 343 U. S. 579, 637 (1952) (Jackson, J., concurring). At the same time, if the President were to have the authority he asserts here, it would require setting aside a state procedural law.

It is difficult to believe that in the exercise of his Article II powers pursuant to a ratified treaty, the President can *never* take action that would result in setting aside state law. Cf. *United States* v. *Pink*, 315 U. S. 203, 233 (1942) ("No State can rewrite our foreign policy to conform to its own domestic policies"). Suppose that the President believes it necessary that he implement a treaty provision requiring a prisoner exchange involving someone in state custody in order to avoid a proven military threat. Cf. *Ware*, 3 Dall., at 205. Or suppose he believes it necessary to secure a foreign consul's treaty-based rights to move freely or to contact an arrested foreign national. Cf. Vienna Convention, Art. 34, 21 U. S. T., at 98. Does the Constitution require the President in each and every such instance to obtain a special statute authorizing his action? On the other hand, the Constitution must impose significant restrictions upon the President's ability, by invoking Article II treaty-implementation authority, to circumvent ordinary legislative processes and to pre-empt state law as he does so.

Previously this Court has said little about this question. It has held that the President has a fair amount of authority to make and to implement executive agreements, at least in respect to international claims settlement, and that this authority can require contrary state law to be set aside. See, *e.g.*, *Pink, supra,* at 223, 230–231, 233–234; *United States* v. *Belmont*, 301 U. S. 324, 326–327 (1937). It has made clear that principles of foreign sovereign immunity trump state law and that the Executive, operating without explicit legislative authority, can assert those principles in state court. See *Ex parte Peru*, 318 U. S. 578, 588 (1943). It has also made clear that the Executive has inherent power to bring a lawsuit "to carry out treaty obligations." *Sanitary Dist. of Chicago* v. *United States*, 266 U. S. 405, 425, 426 (1925). But it has reserved judgment as to "the scope of the President's power to preempt state law pursuant to authority delegated by . . . a ratified treaty"—a fact that helps to explain the majority's inability to find support in precedent for its own conclusions. *Barclays Bank PLC* v. *Franchise Tax Bd. of Cal.*, 512 U. S.

298, 329 (1994).

Given the Court's comparative lack of expertise in foreign affairs; given the importance of the Nation's foreign relations; given the difficulty of finding the proper constitutional balance among state and federal, executive and legislative, powers in such matters; and given the likely future importance of this Court's efforts to do so, I would very much hesitate before concluding that the Constitution implicitly sets forth broad prohibitions (or permissions) in this area. Cf. *ante*, at 27–28, n. 13 (stating that the Court's holding is "limited" by the facts that (1) this treaty is non-self-executing and (2) the judgment of an international tribunal is involved).

I would thus be content to leave the matter in the constitutional shade from which it has emerged. Given my view of this case, I need not answer the question. And I shall not try to do so. That silence, however, cannot be taken as agreement with the majority's Part III conclusion.

The majority's two holdings taken together produce practical anomalies. They unnecessarily complicate the President's foreign affairs task insofar as, for example, they increase the likelihood of Security Council *Avena* enforcement proceedings, of worsening relations with our neighbor Mexico, of precipitating actions by other nations putting at risk American citizens who have the misfortune to be arrested while traveling abroad, or of diminishing our Nation's reputation abroad as a result of our failure to follow the "rule of law" principles that we preach. The holdings also encumber Congress with a task (postratification legislation) that, in respect to many decisions of international tribunals, it may not want and which it may find difficult to execute. See *supra*, at 23–24 (discussing the problems with case-by-case legislation). At the same time, insofar as today's holdings make it more difficult to enforce the judgments of international tribunals, including technical non-politically-controversial judgments, those holdings weaken that rule of law for which our Constitution stands. Compare Hughes Defends Foreign Policies in Plea for Lodge, N. Y. Times, Oct. 31, 1922, p. 1, col. 1, p. 4, col. 1 (then-Secretary of State Charles Evans Hughes stating that "we favor, and always have favored, an international court of justice for the determination according to judicial standards of justiciable international disputes"); Mr. Root Discusses International Problems, N. Y. Times, July 9, 1916, section 6, book review p. 276 (former Secretary of State and U. S. Senator Elihu Root stating that " 'a court of international justice with a general obligation to submit all justiciable questions to its jurisdiction and to abide by its judgment is a primary requisite to any real restraint of law'"); Mills, The Obligation of the United States Toward the World Court, 114 Annals of the American Academy of Political and Social Science 128 (1924) (Congressman Ogden Mills describing the efforts of thenSecretary of State John Hay, and others, to establish a World Court, and the support therefor).

These institutional considerations make it difficult to reconcile the majority's holdings with the workable Constitution that the Founders envisaged. They reinforce the importance, in practice and in principle, of asking Chief Justice Marshall's question: Does a treaty provision address the "Judicial" Branch rather than the "Political

Branches" of Government. See *Foster*, 2 Pet., at 314. And they show the wisdom of the well-established precedent that indicates that the answer to the question here is "yes." See Parts I and II, *supra*.

<u>APPENDIXES TO OPINION OF BREYER, J.</u>

Examples of Supreme Court decisions considering a treaty provision to be self-executing. Parentheticals indicate the subject matter; an asterisk indicates that the Court applied the provision to invalidate a contrary state or territorial law or policy.

1.*Olympic Airways* v. *Husain*, 540 U. S. 644, 649, 657 (2004) (air carrier liability)

2.*El Al Israel Airlines, Ltd.* v. *Tsui Yuan Tseng*, 525 U. S. 155, 161–163, 176 (1999) (same)

3. *Zicherman* v. *Korean Air Lines Co.*, 516 U. S. 217, 221, 231 (1996) (same)

4. Société Nationale Industrielle Aérospatiale *v.* United States Dist. Court for Southern Dist. of Iowa, *482 U. S. 522, 524, 533 (1987) (international discovery rules)*

5.*Sumitomo Shoji America, Inc.* v. *Avagliano*,

457 U. S. 176, 181, 189–190 (1982) (employment

practices)

6.Trans World Airlines, Inc. *v.* Franklin Mint Corp., 466 U. S. 243, 245, 252 (1984) (air carrier liability)

7.*Kolovrat* v. *Oregon*, 366 U. S. 187, 191, n. 6, 198 (1961) (property rights and inheritance)

8. *Clark* v. *Allen*, 331 U. S. 503, 507–508, 517–518 (1947) (same)

9.*Bacardi Corp. of America* v. *Domenech*, 311 U. S. 150, 160, and n. 9, 161 (1940) (trademark)*

10. .... *Todok* v. *Union* (1930) (property rights and inheritance)

11. *Nielsen* v. *Johnson*, 279 U. S. 47, 50, 58 (1929) (taxation)

12.*Jordan* v. *Tashiro*, 278 U. S. 123, 126–127, n. 1, 128–129 (1928) (trade and commerce)

.... Appendix A to opinion of B   , J.

13. *Asakura* v. *Seattle*, 265 U. S. 332, 340, 343–344 (1924) (same)

14. *Maiorano* v. *Baltimore & Ohio R. Co.*, 213 U. S. 268, 273–274 (1909) (travel, trade, access to courts)

15. *Johnson* v. *Browne*, 205 U. S. 309, 317–322 (1907) (extradition)

16.*Geofroy* v. *Riggs*, 133 U. S. 258, 267–268, 273 (1890) (inheritance)

17. *Wildenhus's Case*, 120 U. S. 1, 11, 17–18 (1887) (criminal jurisdiction)

18. *United States* v. *Rauscher*, 119 U. S. 407, 410– 411, 429–430 (1886) (extradition)

19. *Hauenstein* v. *Lynham*, 100 U. S. 483, 485–486, 490–491 (1880) (property rights and inheritance)

20. .... *American Ins. Co.* v. *356 Bales of Cotton*, 1 Pet. 511, 542 (1828) (property)

21. *United States* v. *Percheman*, 7 Pet. 51, 88–89 (1833) (land ownership)

22. *United States* v. *Arredondo*, 6 Pet. 691, 697, 749 (1832) (same)

23. *Orr* v. *Hodgson*, 4 Wheat. 453, 462–465 (1819)

(sam *State Bank of Harvard*, 281 U. S. 449, 453,   455 e)

24. *Chirac* v. *Lessee of Chirac*, 2 Wheat. 259, 270–271, 274, 275 (1817) (land ownership and inheritance)

25. *Martin* v. *Hunter's Lessee*, 1 Wheat. 304, 356–357 (1816) (land ownership)

26. *Hannay* v. *Eve*, 3 Cranch 242, 248 (1806) (monetary debts)

27. *Hopkirk* v. *Bell*, 3 Cranch 454, 457–458 (1806) (same)

28. *Ware* v. *Hylton*, 3 Dall. 199, 203–204, 285 (1796) (same)

29. *Georgia* v. *Brailsford*, 3 Dall. 1, 4 (1794) (same)

....

B

United States treaties in force containing provisions for the submission of treaty-based disputes to the International Court of Justice. Parentheticals indicate subject matters that can be the subject of ICJ adjudication that are of the sort that this Court has found self-executing.

Economic Cooperation Agreements

Economic Aid Agreement Between the United States of America and Spain, Sept. 26, 1953, [1953] 4 U. S. T. 1903, 1920–1921, T. I. A. S. No.

2851 (property and contract)

Agreement for Economic Assistance Between the Government of the United States of America and the Government of Israel Pursuant to the General Agreement for Technical Cooperation, May 9,

1952, [1952] 3 U. S. T. 4174, 4177, T. I. A. S. No. 2561 (same)

Economic Cooperation Agreement Between the United States of America and Portugal, 62 Stat. 2861–2862 (1948) (same)

Economic Cooperation Agreement Between the United States of America and the United Kingdom, 62 Stat. 2604 (1948) (same)

Economic Cooperation Agreement Between the United States of America and the Republic of Turkey, 62 Stat. 2572 (1948) (same)

Economic Cooperation Agreement Between the United States of America and Sweden, 62 Stat. 2557 (1948) (same)

Economic Cooperation Agreement Between the United States of America and Norway, 62 Stat. 2531 (1948) (same)

Economic Cooperation Agreement Between the Governments of the United States of America and the Kingdom of the Netherlands, 62 Stat. 2500

 (1948) (same)

Economic Cooperation Agreement Between the United States of America and the Grand Duchy of Luxembourg, 62 Stat. 2468 (1948) (same)

Economic Cooperation Agreement Between the United States of America and Italy, 62 Stat. 2440 (1948) (same)

Economic Cooperation Agreement Between the United States of America and Iceland, 62 Stat. 2390 (1948) (same)

Economic Cooperation Agreement Between the United States of America and Greece, 62 Stat. 2344 (1948) (same)

Economic Cooperation Agreement Between the United States of America and France, 62 Stat. 2232, 2233 (1948) (same)

Economic Cooperation Agreement Between the United States of America and Denmark, 62 Stat. 2214 (1948) (same)

Economic Cooperation Agreement Between the United States of America and the Kingdom of Belgium, 62 Stat. 2190 (1948) (same)

Economic Cooperation Agreement Between the United States of America and Austria, 62 Stat. 2144 (1948) (same)

<u>Bilateral Consular Conventions</u>

Consular Convention Between the United States of America and the Kingdom of Belgium, Sept. 2, 1969, [1974] 25 U. S. T. 41, 47–49, 56–57, 60–61, 75, T. I. A. S. No. 7775 (domestic court jurisdiction and authority over consular officers, taxation of consular officers, consular notification)

Consular Convention Between the United States of America and the Republic of Korea, Jan. 8, 1963, [1963] 14 U. S. T. 1637, 1641, 1644–1648,

T. I.A. S. No. 5469 (same)

<u>Friendship, Commerce, and Navigation Treaties</u>

Treaty of Amity and Economic Relations Between the United States of America and the Togolese Republic, Feb. 8, 1966, [1967] 18 U. S. T. 1, 3–4,

10, T. I. A. S. No. 6193 (contracts and property)

Treaty of Friendship, Establishment and Navigation Between the United States of America and The Kingdom of Belgium, Feb. 21, 1961, [1963] 14 U. S. T. 1284, 1290–1291, 1307, T. I. A. S. No.

5432 (same)

Treaty of Friendship, Establishment and Navigation between the United States of America and the Grand Duchy of Luxembourg, Feb. 23, 1962, [1963] 14 U. S. T. 251, 254–255, 262, T. I. A. S. No. 5306 (consular notification; contracts and property)

Treaty of Friendship, Commerce and Navigation between the United States of America and the Kingdom of Denmark, Oct. 1, 1951, [1961] 12 U. S. T. 908, 912–913, 935, T. I. A. S. No. 4797 (contracts and property)

Treaty of Friendship and Commerce Between the United States of America and Pakistan, Nov. 12, 1959, [1961] 12 U. S. T. 110, 113, 123, T. I. A. S. No. 4863 (same)

Convention of Establishment Between the United States of America and France, Nov. 25, 1959,

[1960] 11 U. S. T. 2398, 2401–2403, 2417,

T. I. A. S. No. 4625 (same)

Treaty of Friendship, Commerce and Navigation Between the United States of America and the Republic of Korea, Nov. 28, 1956, [1957] 8 U. S. T.

2217, 2221–2222, 2233, T. I. A. S. No. 3947 (same)

Treaty of Friendship, Commerce and Navigation between the United States of America and the Kingdom of the Netherlands, Mar. 27, 1956, [1957] 8 U. S. T. 2043, 2047–2050, 2082–2083, T. I. A. S. No. 3942 (freedom to travel, consular notification, contracts and property)

Treaty of Amity, Economic Relations, and Consular Rights Between the United States of America and Iran, Aug. 15, 1955, [1957] 8 U. S. T. 899, 903, 907, 913, T. I. A. S. No. 3853 (property and freedom of commerce)

Treaty of Friendship, Commerce and Navigation Between the United States of America and the Federal Republic of Germany, Oct. 29, 1954, [1956] 7 U. S. T. 1839, 1844–1846, 1867,

T. I. A. S. No. 3593 (property and contract)

reaty of Friendship, Commerce and Navigation Between the United States of America and Greece, Aug. 3, 1951, [1954] 5 U. S. T. 1829, 1841–1847, 1913–1915, T. I. A. S. No. 3057 (same)

Treaty of Friendship, Commerce and Navigation Between the United States of America and Israel, Aug. 23, 1951, [1954] 5 U. S. T 550, 555–556, 575, T. I. A. S. No. 2948 (same)

Treaty of Amity and Economic Relations Between the United States of America and Ethiopia, Sept. 7, 1951, [1953] 4 U. S. T. 2134, 2141, 2145, 2147, T. I. A. S. No. 2864 (property and freedom of commerce)

Treaty of Friendship, Commerce and Navigation Between the United States of America and Japan, Apr. 2, 1953, [1953] 4 U. S. T. 2063, 2067–2069, 2080, T. I. A. S. No. 2863 (property and contract)

Treaty of Friendship, Commerce and Navigation between the United States of America and Ireland, Jan. 21, 1950, [1950] 1 U. S. T. 785, 792–

794, 801, T. I. A. S. No. 2155 (same)

Treaty of Friendship, Commerce and Navigation between the United States of America and the Italian Republic, 63 Stat. 2262, 2284, 2294 (1948)

(property and freedom of commerce)

<u>Multilateral Conventions</u>

Patent Cooperation Treaty, June 19, 1970, [1976– 77] 28 U. S. T. 7645, 7652–7676, 7708, T. I. A. S. No. 8733 (patents)

Universal Copyright Convention, July 24, 1971, [1974] 25 U. S. T. 1341, 1345, 1366, T. I. A. S. No. 7868 (copyright)

Vienna Convention on Diplomatic Relations and Optional Protocol Concerning the Compulsory Settlement of Disputes, Apr. 18, 1961, [1972] 23 U. S. T. 3227, 3240–3243, 3375, T. I. A. S. No. 7502 (rights of diplomats in foreign nations)

Paris Convention for the Protection of Industrial Property, July 14, 1967, [1970] 21 U. S. T. 1583, 1631–1639, 1665–1666, T. I. A. S. No. 6923 (patents)

Convention on the Privileges and Immunities of the United Nations, Feb. 13, 1946, [1970] 21 U. S. T. 1418, 1426–1428, 1430–1432, 1438–1440,

T. I. A. S. No. 6900 (rights of U. N. diplomats and officials)

Convention on Offences and Certain Other Acts Committed on Board Aircraft, Sept. 14, 1963,

....[1969]   20   U. S. T.
....2941,   2943–2947,
....2952,

T. I. A. S. No. 6768 (airlines' treatment of passengers)

Agreement for Facilitating the International Circulation of Visual and Auditory Materials of an Educational, Scientific and Cultural Character, July 15, 1949, [1966] 17 U. S. T. 1578, 1581, 1586, T. I. A. S. No. 6116 (customs duties on importation of films and recordings)

Universal Copyright Convention, Sept. 6, 1952, [1955] 6 U. S. T. 2731, 2733–2739, 2743, T. I.A.S. No. 3324 (copyright)

Treaty of Peace with Japan, Sept. 8, 1951, [1952] 3 U. S. T. 3169, 3181–3183, 3188, T. I. A. S. No. 2490 (property)

THE PRISON LITIGATION REFORM ACT

The Court is required to screen complaints brought by prisoners seeking relief against a governmental entity or an officer or an employee of a governmental entity. *28 U.S.C. § 1915A(a)*. The Court must dismiss a complaint or portion thereof if a plaintiff has raised claims that are legally frivolous or malicious, that fail to state a claim upon which relief may be granted, or that seek monetary relief from a defendant who is immune from such relief. *28 U.S.C. § 1915A(b)(1)-(2)*.

A pleading must contain a "short and plain statement of the claim *showing* that the pleader is entitled to relief." *Fed. R. Civ. P. 8(a)(2)* (emphasis added). While Rule 8 does not demand detailed factual allegations, "it demands more than an unadorned, the-defendant-unlawfully-harmed-me accusation." *Ashcroft v. Iqbal, 556 U.S. 662, 678, 129 S. Ct. 1937, 173 L. Ed. 2d 868 (2009)*. "Threadbare recitals of the elements of a cause of action, supported by mere conclusory statements, do not suffice." *Id.* "Pro se plaintiffs proceeding [in forma pauperis] must . . . be given an opportunity to amend their complaint [prior to dismissal of the case] unless it is absolutely clear that the deficiencies of the complaint could not be cured by amendment." *Franklin v. Murphy, 745 F.2d 1221, 1228 n. 9 (9th Cir. 1984)*. The United States Court of Appeals for the Ninth Circuit has instructed, courts must "continue to construe *pro se* filings liberally." *Hebbe v. Pliler, 627 F.3d 338, 342 (9th Cir. 2010)*. A "complaint [filed by a *pro se* prisoner] 'must be held to less stringent standards than formal pleadings drafted by lawyers.'" Id. (quoting *Erickson v. Pardus, 551 U.S. 89, 94, 127 S. Ct. 2197, 167 L. Ed. 2d 1081 (2007) (per curiam)*).

Although *pro se* pleadings are liberally construed, *Haines v. Kerner, 404 U.S. 519, 520-21, 92 S. Ct. 594, 30 L. Ed. 2d 652 (1972)*, conclusory and vague allegations will not support a cause of action. *Ivey v. Board of Regents of the University of Alaska, 673 F.2d 266, 268 (9th Cir. 1982)*. Further, a liberal interpretation of a civil rights complaint may not supply essential elements of the claim that were not initially pled. Id.

"[A] complaint must contain sufficient factual matter, accepted as true, to 'state a claim to relief that is plausible on its face.'" *Id.* (quoting *Bell Atlantic Corp. v. Twombly, 550 U.S. 544, 570, 127 S. Ct. 1955, 167 L. Ed. 2d 929 (2007)*). A claim is plausible "when the plaintiff pleads factual content that allows the court to draw the reasonable inference that the defendant is liable for the misconduct alleged." *Id.* "Determining whether a complaint states a plausible claim for relief [is] . . . a context-specific task that requires the reviewing court to draw on its judicial experience and common sense." *Id. at 679*. Thus, although a plaintiff's specific factual allegations may be consistent with a constitutional claim, a court must assess whether there are other "more likely explanations" for a defendant's conduct. *Id. at 681*.

The Prison Litigation Reform Act (PLRA) requires an inmate to exhaust prison grievance procedures before filing suit in federal court. *See 42 U.S.C. § 1997e(a)*; *Jones v. Bock, 549 U.S. 199, 202, 127 S. Ct. 910, 166 L. Ed. 2d 798 (2007)*; *Jones v. Norris, 310 F.3d 610, 612 (8th Cir. 2002)*. Exhaustion under PLRA is mandatory. *Jones, 549 U.S. at 211*. "[T]o properly exhaust administrative remedies, prisoners must 'complete the administrative review process in accordance with the applicable procedural rules,' rules that are defined not by the PLRA, but by the prison grievance process itself." *Id., 549 U.S. at 218* (quoting *Woodford v. Ngo, 548 U.S. 81, 88, 126 S. Ct. 2378, 165 L. Ed. 2d 368 (2006)*). Compliance with a prison's grievance procedures is, therefore, all that is required by the PLRA to properly exhaust. *Id.* Thus, the question of whether an inmate has properly exhausted administrative remedies will depend on the specifics of that particular prison's grievance policy. *See Id.* The prisoner must complete the administrative review process in accordance with the applicable rules. *See Woodford v. Ngo, 548 U.S. 81, 92, 126 S. Ct. 2378, 165 L. Ed. 2d 368 (2006)*. Exhaustion is required for all suits about prison life, *Porter v. Nussle, 534 U.S. 516, 523, 122 S. Ct. 983, 152 L. Ed. 2d 12 (2002)*, regardless of the type of relief offered through the administrative process, *Booth v. Churner, 532 U.S. 731, 741, 121 S. Ct. 1819, 149 L. Ed. 2d 958 (2001)*. The defendant bears the initial burden to show that there was an available administrative remedy and that the prisoner did not exhaust it. *Albino v. Baca, 747 F.3d 1162, 1169, 1172 (9th Cir. 2014)*;

The defendant bears the ultimate burden of proving failure to exhaust. See Brown v. Valoff, 422 F.3d 926, 936 (9th Cir. 2005). If the defendant initially shows that (1) an available administrative remedy existed and (2) the prisoner failed to exhaust that remedy, then the burden of production shifts to the plaintiff to bring forth evidence "showing that there is something in his particular case that made the existing and generally available administrative remedies effectively unavailable to him." Albino, 747 F.3d at 1172. Confusing or contradictory information given to a prisoner is relevant to the question "of whether relief was, as a practical matter, 'available.'" Brown, 422 F.3d at 937. Administrative remedies will be deemed unavailable and exhaustion excused if the inmate had no way of knowing the prison's grievance procedure, if the prison improperly processed an inmate's grievance, if prison officials misinformed an inmate regarding grievance procedures, if the inmate "did not have access to the necessary grievance forms within the prison's time limits for filing the grievance," or if prison staff took any other similar actions that interfered with an inmate's efforts to exhaust. Albino, 747 F.3d at 1173. If a prisoner has failed to exhaust available administrative remedies, the appropriate remedy is dismissal without prejudice. Wyatt v. Terhune, 315 F.3d 1108, 1120 (9th Cir. 2003), overruled in part on other grounds by Albino, 747 F.3d 1162.

"[A] [§ 1983] suit against a state official in his or her official capacity is not a suit against the official but rather is a suit against the official's office," i.e., against the State. Will v. Mich. Dept. of State Police, 491 U.S. 58, 71, 109 S. Ct. 2304, 105 L. Ed. 2d 45 (1989). The State is not a "person" amenable to suit under § 1983. Id. The state and its agencies are immune from suit pursuant to the Eleventh Amendment. Quern v. Jordan, 440 U.S. 332, 340-45, 99 S. Ct. 1139, 59 L. Ed. 2d 358 (1979); see Lawson v. Shelby Cnty., Tenn., 211 F.3d 331, 335 (6th Cir. 2000) ("[T]he [Eleventh] Amendment prohibits suits against a 'state' in federal court whether for injunctive, declaratory or monetary relief."). The only exceptions to a state's immunity are (1) if the state has consented to suit or (2) if Congress has properly abrogated a state's immunity. S & M Brands, Inc. v. Cooper, 527 F.3d 500, 507 (6th Cir. 2008). See Berndt v. Tennessee, 796 F.2d 879, 881 (6th Cir. 1986) (noting that Tennessee has not waived immunity to suits under § 1983); Hafer v. Melo, 502 U.S. 21, 25, 112 S. Ct. 358, 116 L. Ed. 2d 301 (1991) (reaffirming that Congress did not abrogate states' immunity when it passed § 1983). The only other exception is when the Ex parte Young exception applies. See S&M Brands, 527 F.3d at 507. Under this exception, "a federal court can issue prospective injunctive and declaratory relief compelling a state official to comply with federal law." Id. (quoting Will, 491 U.S. at 71 & n.10).

Qualified immunity protects officials who acted in an objectively reasonable manner and shields a government official from liability when his or her conduct does not violate "clearly established statutory or constitutional rights of which a reasonable person would have known." Harlow v. Fitzgerald, 457 U.S. 800, 818, 102 S. Ct. 2727, 73 L. Ed. 2d 396 (1982). Qualified immunity is a question of law, not a question of fact. McClendon v. Story County Sheriff's Office, 403 F.3d 510, 515 (8th Cir. 2005). Thus, issues concerning qualified immunity are appropriately resolved on summary judgment. See Mitchell v. Forsyth, 472 U.S. 511, 526, 105 S. Ct. 2806, 86 L. Ed. 2d 411 (1985) (the privilege is "an immunity from suit rather than a mere defense to liability; and like an absolute immunity, it is effectively lost if a case is erroneously permitted to go to trial.").

To determine whether defendants are entitled to qualified immunity, courts generally consider two questions: (1) whether the facts alleged or shown, construed in the light most favorable to the plaintiff, establish a violation of a constitutional or statutory right; and (2) whether that right was so clearly established that a reasonable official would have known that his or her actions were unlawful. Pearson v. Callahan, 555 U.S. 223, 232, 129 S. Ct. 808, 172 L. Ed. 2d 565 (2009); see also Saucier v. Katz, 533 U.S. 194, 201, 121 S. Ct. 2151, 150 L. Ed. 2d 272 (2001). Defendants are entitled to qualified immunity only if no reasonable fact finder could answer both questions in the affirmative. Nelson v. Correctional Medical Services, 583 F.3d 522, 528 (8th Cir. 2009). Deference to the expertise of prison officials in matters of prison security is not absolute. Cutter v. Wilkinson, 544 U.S. 709, 725 n. 13, 125 S. Ct. 2113, 161 L. Ed. 2d 1020 (2005); United States v. Williams, 791 F.2d 1383 (9th Cir. 1986).

Standard for Injunctive Relief - A request for injunctive relief requires that a plaintiff make a showing of "real or immediate threat" of injury. Hodgers-Durgin v. De La Vina, 199 F.3d 1037, 1042 (9th Cir. 1999) (quoting O'Shea v. Littleton, 414 U.S. 488, 502, 94 S. Ct. 669, 38 L. Ed. 2d 674 (1974)). Plaintiff is entitled to preliminary injunctive relief only if he/she shows either: "(1) a likelihood of success on the merits and the possibility of irreparable injury; or (2) the existence of serious questions going to the merits and the balance of hardships tipping in [the movant's] favor." MAI Sys. Corp. v. Peak Computer, Inc., 991 F.2d 511, 516-517 (9th Cir. 1993) (quoting Diamontiney v. Borg, 918 F.2d 793, 795 (9th Cir. 1990)). Under either formulation of the test, the movant must demonstrate a significant threat of irreparable injury. AGCC v. Coalition for Economic Equity, 950 F.2d 1401, 1410 (9th Cir. 1991).

Further, in unusual circumstances where the preliminary injunction relates to the inmate's access to the district court, the district court need not consider the merits of the underlying complaint in considering whether to grant a preliminary injunction. Diamontiney v. Borg, 918 F.2d 793, 796 (9th Cir. 1990).

Preliminary Relief Different From Ultimate Relief - The purpose of preliminary injunctive relief is to preserve the status quo or to prevent irreparable injury pending the resolution of the underlying claim on the merits. Therefore, the party seeking preliminary injunctive relief "must necessarily establish a relationship between the injury claimed in the motion and the conduct asserted in the complaint." Devose v. Herrington, 42 F.3d 470, 471 (8th Cir. 1994) (Eighth Amendment claim cannot provide basis for preliminary injunction against alleged acts in retaliation for filing claim). Thus, Plaintiff must ordinarily seek injunctive relief related to the merits of his underlying claim. "A district court should not issue an injunction when the injunction in question is not of the same character, and deals with a matter lying wholly outside the issues in the suit." Kaimowitz v. Orlando, Fla., 122 F.3d 41, 43 (11th Cir. 1997).

To state a claim under § 1983 against a private entity performing a traditional public function, such as providing medical care in a prison, a plaintiff must allege facts to support that his constitutional rights were violated as a result of a policy, decision, or custom promulgated or endorsed by the private entity. See Tsao v. Desert Palace, Inc., 698 F.3d 1128, 1138-39 (9th Cir. 2012); Buckner v. Toro, 116 F.3d 450, 452 (11th Cir. 1997). Because there is no respondeat superior liability under § 1983, a defendant's position as the employer of someone who allegedly violated a plaintiff's constitutional rights. , "[A] plaintiff must allege facts, not simply conclusions, that show that an individual was personally involved in the deprivation of his civil rights." Barren v. Harrington, 152 F.3d 1193, 1194 (9th Cir. 1998). For an individual to be liable in his official capacity, a plaintiff must allege that the official acted as a result of a policy, practice, or custom. See Cortez v. County of Los Angeles, 294 F.3d 1186, 1188 (9th Cir. 2001). Further, there is no respondeat superior liability under § 1983, so a defendant's position as the supervisor of someone who allegedly violated a plaintiff's constitutional rights does not make him liable. Monell v. Dep't of Soc. Servs., 436 U.S. 658, 691, 98 S. Ct. 2018, 56 L. Ed. 2d 611 (1978); Taylor v. List, 880 F.2d 1040, 1045 (9th Cir. 1989). A supervisor in his individual capacity "is only liable for constitutional violations of his subordinates if the supervisor participated in or directed the violations, or knew of the violations and failed to act to prevent them." Taylor, 880 F.2d at 1045. To state a claim for failure to train, a plaintiff must allege facts to support that the alleged failure amounted to deliberate indifference. Canell v. Lightner, 143 F.3d 1210, 1213 (9th Cir. 1998). A plaintiff must allege facts to support that not only was particular training inadequate, but also that such inadequacy was the result of "a 'deliberate' or 'conscious' choice" on the part of the defendant. Id. at 1213-14; see Clement v. Gomez, 298 F.3d 898, 905 (9th Cir. 2002) (a plaintiff must allege facts to support that "in light of the duties assigned to specific officers or employees, the need for more or different training is [so] obvious, and the inadequacy so likely to result in violations of constitutional rights, that the policy[]makers . . . can reasonably be said to have been deliberately indifferent to the need." (quoting City of Canton v. Harris, 489 U.S. 378, 390, 109 S. Ct. 1197, 103 L. Ed. 2d 412 (1989))).

JAMES JACKSON ELLSWORTH, PLAINTIFF, VS. CORIZON HEALTH, INC.,[1] ET AL., DEFENDANTS. *2012 U.S. DIST. LEXIS 53276 (AZ. APRIL 16, 2012)*

(SEE ALSO DISCUSSION UNDER ACCESS TO COURTS)

II. Plaintiff's Motion for Summary Judgment re: Exhaustion of Remedies

Plaintiff asserts that he is entitled to summary judgment on Defendants' affirmative defense that Plaintiff failed to exhaust his available administrative remedies. He argues that he was excused from the exhaustion requirement under the plain terms of Arizona Department of Corrections (ADC) Department Order 802.01, § 1.8, which Plaintiff asserts exempts emergency complaints from the formal grievance procedure. Plaintiff further asserts that, even though he was not required to exhaust administrative remedies, he did exhaust his administrative remedies by following the ADC's grievance procedure.

Defendants respond that "Plaintiff's conclusory statements citing to D.O. 802 are not enough to prove that his specific medical complaints constituted an 'emergency condition' within the meaning of D.O. 802" and that Plaintiff has failed to present evidence demonstrating that his prostate cancer presented an emergency medical condition under D.O. 802. Defendants further assert that D.O. 802.01, §1.8 does not obviate an inmate's obligation to exhaust the ADC's grievance and appeals procedures in the event of an emergency, but "simply allows an inmate to bring an emergency to the attention of staff, by any available means, rather than to rely on the written grievance procedure to alert staff to an emergency." (Doc. 137 at 6.)

Defendants next assert that the Grievance Appeal Response signed by Director Ryan on February 28, 2014 does not show that Plaintiff exhausted his administrative remedies because "Plaintiff does not provide any documents that were submitted by him as part of the grievance process related to the Grievance Appeal Response signed by Director Ryan on February 28, 2014, or any additional documents related to the other grievances submitted by Plaintiff." (Doc. 140 at 5.)

B. Exhaustion

Under the Prison Litigation Reform Act, a prisoner must exhaust "available" administrative remedies before filing an action in federal court. *See 42 U.S.C. § 1997e(a); Vaden v. Summerhill, 449 F.3d 1047, 1050 (9th Cir. 2006); Brown v. Valoff, 422 F.3d 926, 934-35 (9th Cir. 2005).* The prisoner must complete the administrative review process in accordance with the applicable rules. *See Woodford v. Ngo, 548 U.S. 81, 92, 126 S. Ct. 2378, 165 L. Ed. 2d 368 (2006).* Exhaustion is required for all suits about prison life, *Porter v. Nussle, 534 U.S. 516, 523, 122 S. Ct. 983, 152 L. Ed. 2d 12 (2002)*, regardless of the type of relief offered through the administrative process, *Booth v. Churner, 532 U.S. 731, 741, 121 S. Ct. 1819, 149 L. Ed. 2d 958 (2001).*

The defendant bears the initial burden to show that there was an available administrative remedy and that the prisoner did not exhaust it. *Albino v. Baca, 747 F.3d 1162, 1169, 1172 (9th Cir. 2014); see Brown, 422 F.3d at 936-37* (a defendant must demonstrate that applicable relief remained available in the grievance process). Once that showing is made, the burden shifts to the prisoner, who must either demonstrate that he, in fact, exhausted administrative remedies or "come forward with evidence showing that there is something in his particular case that made the existing and generally available administrative remedies effectively unavailable to him." *Albino, 747 F.3d at 1172.* The ultimate burden, however, rests with the defendant. *Id.* Summary judgment is appropriate if the undisputed evidence, viewed in the light most favorable to the prisoner, shows a failure to exhaust. *Id. at 1166, 1168; see Fed. R. Civ. P. 56(a).*

If summary judgment is denied, disputed factual questions relevant to exhaustion should be decided by the judge; a plaintiff is not entitled to a jury trial on the issue of exhaustion. *Albino, 747 F.3d at 1170-71.* But if a court finds that the prisoner exhausted administrative remedies, that administrative remedies were not available, or that the failure to exhaust administrative remedies should be excused, the case proceeds to the merits. *Id. at 1171.*

C. Facts regarding Exhaustion

ADC Department Order 802.06 outlines the formal inmate medical grievance process. (Doc. 113-2 at 5.) An inmate may appeal a response to a formal inmate medical grievance to the Director. (*Id.* at 6.) The decision of the Director for medical grievance appeals is final and constitutes exhaustion of all remedies for inmate medical grievances within ADC. (*Id.* at 7.) Section 802.01 entitled "General Information" provides, in part, that "[i]nmates are not required to use the formal Inmate Grievance Procedures to submit a verbal or written emergency complaint." (*Id.* at 3.) An emergency is defined as "a condition which, if processed through the normal grievance time frames, would subject the inmate to substantial risk of medical harm, personal injury or cause other serious and irreparable harm." (*Id.*) The Department Order further provides that "[a]ny emergency complaint received by staff shall be immediately evaluated through the chain of command to determine whether it is an emergency as defined in 1.8.1 of this section and requires immediate response outside of the Inmate Grievance Procedure time frames."

D. Discussion

Plaintiff argues that he was excused from the exhaustion requirement under the plain terms of ADC Department Order 802.01, § 1.8, which provides that "[i]nmates are not required to use the formal Inmate Grievance Procedures to submit a verbal or written emergency complaint." The emergency complaint procedure, however, is not a model of clarity. Section 1.8 clearly states that inmates are not required to use the formal grievance process in the case of an emergency,[4] but provides no further information as to exhaustion of remedies in the case of an emergency. The consequences of this ambiguity are on display in this case.

4   The Court is unconvinced by Defendants' argument that an inmate must still follow the formal grievance process even after submitting an emergency complaint. It is Defendants who are able to define the grievance process and how administrative remedies are exhausted and, thus, any ambiguity in their policy should be construed in favor of Plaintiff. *See Woodford, 548 U.S. at 90* (proper exhaustion requires using all steps that the agency holds out, and doing so properly).

Plaintiff provides a "consultation request" signed by Dr. Kessler, which states that Plaintiff told him that it was important to establish care with a urologist for treatment of his prostate cancer. (Doc. 25-9 at 1.) He argues that this evidence shows he orally pursued treatment for his prostate cancer and, therefore, was exempt from the formal administrative grievance process. Defendants argue that Plaintiff has not shown that his condition constituted an emergency within the meaning of Section 1.8.1, which provides that an emergency is "a condition which, if processed through the normal grievance time frames, would subject the inmate to substantial risk of medical harm, personal injury or cause other serious and irreparable harm." The Department Order, however, does not state who decides which conditions are "medical emergencies" or what happens when, after evaluation, a complaint is deemed to not constitute an emergency.

Despite the substantial ambiguity in the emergency complaint grievance process, Plaintiff is entitled to summary judgment on Defendants' exhaustion of administrative remedies affirmative defense because the uncontroverted evidence shows that he exhausted his claims to the Director's level. Plaintiff provides a January 13, 2014 response from Director Ryan responding to Plaintiff's request for "immediate and thorough treatment for [his] cancer or immediate release to get treatment by a competent doctor due to the life threatening nature of [his] cancer." (Doc. 114-2 at 1-2.) Defendants state that Plaintiff has failed to show that he exhausted his claims in this action because he did not provide any of the grievance documents that led to Director Ryan's final decision with his Motion for Summary Judgment. But Defendants point to nothing in their policy requiring Plaintiff to name every defendant or explicitly set forth his legal claims in his grievances. *Morton v. Hall, 599 F.3d 942, 946 (9th Cir. 2010)* (The level of detail in an administrative grievance necessary to properly exhaust a claim is determined by the prison's applicable grievance procedures, but "when a prison's grievance procedures are silent or incomplete as to factual specificity, a grievance suffices if it alerts the prison to the nature of the wrong for which redress is sought."). Plaintiff provides evidence that he exhausted his claims related to the fact that he was not being provided immediate and thorough treatment for his cancer. Defendants have not met their burden of demonstrating that Plaintiff did not exhaust his claims, and cannot shift the burden to Plaintiff by claiming that Plaintiff has not produced enough evidence to demonstrate that he did exhaust. *See Albino, 747 F.3d at 1172* (the ultimate burden of proof as to exhaustion remains with the defendant). Plaintiff has provided unrebutted evidence that he exhausted his administrative remedies, and thus, the Court finds that Plaintiff is entitled to summary judgment on the exhaustion defense.

ALDRICK JOSEPH LAPORTE, PLAINTIFF, VS. CORIZON HEALTH, INC., ET AL., DEFENDANTS. CIVIL ACTION NO. 14-CV-12231 UNITED STATES DISTRICT COURT FOR THE EASTERN DISTRICT OF MICHIGAN, SOUTHERN DIVISION

A. Plaintiff's Factual Allegations

Plaintiff alleges that in December of 2001, before he was incarcerated, he was in an automobile accident, which resulted in torn ligaments and a severed perineal nerve. (Docket no. 1 ¶9.) In February of 2002, his doctor told him that he could "expect pain forever due to the nerve damage in his leg" and that he could control the pain with medication and by wearing proper "braces, shoes, etc." (*Id.* ¶10.)

Plaintiff was incarcerated in October of 2003, and in January of 2004, he hyperextended his leg and fell. He was then transferred to another prison, where he fell again, in April or May of 2004. At that time, the prison doctor determined that Plaintiff should be seen by a specialist, but the Regional Management Office (RMO) denied the request. Plaintiff did have an MRI taken of his knee, which revealed a "chronically torn" ACL. Plaintiff claims that he was told by the prison doctor that CMS (which Plaintiff contends is not Corizon) "did not want to pay for ACL surgery;" thus, he was given pain medication. Plaintiff claims that his leg continued giving out. (*Id.* ¶11.)

Plaintiff alleges that over the next seven years, he was given various pain medications through the Pain Management Committee (PMC), with varying levels of success; he notes that he continued to fall due to his ACL injury and that he broke his pinky finger trying to prevent one of the falls. (*Id.* ¶12.) Ultimately, Plaintiff began taking Ultram, which "displayed some success" in alleviating his pain but did not help with his falling. (*Id.*) In 2011, Plaintiff tried to get a refill of his Ultram, but Dr. Borgerding denied the refill and ordered Plaintiff to return to the PMC for evaluation. (*Id.* ¶13.) The PMC changed Plaintiff's medication, which Plaintiff alleges caused him additional pain. (*Id.*)

In 2012, Plaintiff was transferred to another prison, at which time he requested a knee sleeve and new shoes. Plaintiff alleges that from that time through the time he filed his Complaint, several physical therapists ordered braces and shoes, but each time, Dr. Borgerding denied the request. (*Id.* ¶¶ 14-19.) One Physical Therapist even provided Plaintiff with a brace found in the back room of the clinic, but the brace was not fitted properly, so it "ate the skin off plaintiff's leg." (*Id.* ¶16.) Plaintiff alleges that he now suffers from "holes in his leg, severe pain/burns from brace rubbing and deformity." (*Id.* ¶17.)

Plaintiff claims that Defendants Corizon and Borgerding are liable for violating his *Eighth Amendment* rights "in refusing to medical care for a condition that is serious and ongoing;" that Defendant Corison showed "deliberate indifference resulting from somewhere between mere negligence (carelessness) and actual malice (intent to cause harm)" because it "plac[ed] the craven for profits above providing needed medical care;" that Defendant Borgerding "evidences his deliberate indifference and recklessness, and his actions falls (sic) somewhere between mere negligence and actual malice" because of his "outright denials of treatment;" that Defendants Corizon and Borgerding "disregarded the excessive risk to Plaintiff's health, safety, and wellbeing;" that all the Defendants violated the *Eighth Amendment* when they failed to provide adequate care; and that Defendants Corizon and Borgerding committed "the tort of negligence under the law of Michigan." (*Id.* ¶¶ 21-26.)

C. Analysis

Through its Motion for Judgment on the Pleadings, Defendant asserts that (1) Plaintiff has failed to exhaust his administrative remedies; (2) Plaintiff's claims related to medical care prior to June 5, 2011, are barred by the applicable statute of limitations; and (3) Plaintiff's Complaint fails to state a claim. (Docket no. 21.) As noted, Plaintiff has not filed a Response.

1. Exhaustion of Administrative Remedies

Defendant first argues that Plaintiff has failed to properly exhaust his administrative remedies. The Prison Litigation Reform Act (PLRA) of 1995 requires that a prisoner exhaust all administrative remedies before filing a *Section 1983* action. Specifically, the statute provides, "no action shall be brought with respect to prison conditions under *section 1983* . . . , or any other Federal law, by a prisoner confined in any jail, prison or other correctional facility until such administrative remedies as are available are exhausted." *42 U.S.C. § 1997e(a)*. But "while the preferred practice is for inmates to complete the grievance process prior to the filing of an action and to attach to their complaint documentation of that fact, 'because the exhaustion requirement is not jurisdictional, district   courts have some discretion in determining compliance with the statute.'" *Curry v. Scott, 249 F.3d 493, 502 (6th Cir. 2001)*(citations omitted). Notably, the Sixth Circuit "requires an inmate to make 'affirmative efforts to comply with the administrative procedures,' and analyzes whether those 'efforts to exhaust were sufficient under the circumstances.'" *Risher v. Lappin, 639 F.3d 236, 240 (6th Cir. 2011)* (citing *Napier v. Laurel Cnty., Ky., 636 F.3d 218, 224 (6th Cir. 2011)*(internal quotation marks and citation omitted)).

The MDOC Policy Directive regarding prisoner grievances requires a prisoner to file a Step I grievance within five days of attempting to resolve the grievable issue with prison staff. MDOC Policy Directive 03.02.130(V). The prisoner must then proceed through Steps II and III of the grievance process and receive a Step III response to complete the process. *See Muttscheler v. Martin, No. 12-1221, 2013 U.S. Dist. LEXIS 99025, 2013 WL 3730095, at *3-5 (W.D. Mich. July 15, 2013).*

As part of its Motion, Defendant has provided the Court with Plaintiff's Step III Grievance Record going back to May of 2009. (Docket no. 21-2.) In that time, Plaintiff has filed seven grievances; Defendant argues that only four of those grievances related to Plaintiff's medical care, and none of those grievances exhausts Plaintiff's claims against Defendant. (Docket no. 21 at 13, 20-23.) The undersigned agrees. February 5, 2014, Plaintiff alleged that Defendant Borgerding (in his position as RMO) denied his request for medical shoes, even though the shoes were prescribed by one of the doctors at the prison. (*See* docket no. 21-2 at 7.) In grievance no. URF-13-05-1474-24b, filed by Plaintiff on May 13, 2013, Plaintiff requested a prison transfer. (*See id.* at 14.) In grievance no. LMF-11-08-1792-12d1, filed by Plaintiff on August 19, 2011, Plaintiff alleged that Defendant Borgerding's decision to send Plaintiff to the PMC on July 26, 2011, was inappropriate. (*See id.* at 20.) In grievance no. LMF-11-08-1728-12d3, filed by Plaintiff on August 12, 2011, Plaintiff alleged that the PMC's decision to take him off his medication was unethical. (*See id.* at 26.) And in grievance no. LMF-11-02-0325-12e4, filed by Plaintiff on February 2, 2011, Plaintiff alleged in general that the "MDOC PHS" improperly denied him athletic shoes. (*See id.* at 34.)

"The point of the PLRA exhaustion requirement is to allow prison officials 'a fair opportunity' to address grievances on the merits, to correct prison errors that can and should be corrected and to create an administrative record for those disputes that eventually end up in court." *Reed-Bey v. Pramstaller, 603 F. 3d 322, 324 (6th Cir. 2010)* (citation omitted). Thus, compliance with the PLRA requires that prisoners file a grievance against the person(s) they ultimately seek to sue. *Curry v. Scott, 249 F.3d 493, 505 (6th Cir. 2001).* In the first four of the above-referenced grievances, although Plaintiff does mention Defendant Borgerding and the PMC, Plaintiff makes no mention of Defendant Corizon. And as Defendant contends, although Plaintiff does mention "PHS" in the grievance he filed in February of 2011, the allegations against Corizon in his Complaint do not relate to Corizon's failure to provide proper shoes. (*See* docket no. 1.) Moreover, according to grievance records, Plaintiff ultimately received tennis shoes. (Docket no. 21-2 at 31.) Therefore, Plaintiff has not exhausted his administrative remedies with regard to Defendant Corizon, and his claims should be dismissed.

EARL FARMER, PLAINTIFF, V. C.L. "BUTCH" OTTER; RANDY BLADES; MS. WAMBLE-FISHER; CATHY STEFFEN; CORIZON MEDICAL SERVICES; IDAHO STATE DEPARTMENT OF CORRECTION; AND IDAHO STATE BOARD OF CORRECTION, DEFENDANTS. CASE NO. 1:14-CV-00345-BLW UNITED STATES DISTRICT COURT FOR THE DISTRICT OF IDAHO

BACKGROUND

1. Introduction

Plaintiff Earl Farmer is a prisoner in the custody of the Idaho Department of Correction (IDOC), currently incarcerated at Idaho State Correctional Institution (ISCI). On August 21, 2014, Farmer filed his Complaint against several defendants, including Corizon, LLC (misnamed Corizon Medical Services), Shell Wamble-Fisher, and Randy Blades, alleging that Defendants failed to protect him from physical and sexual assault by other inmates and were deliberately indifferent to his mental health. *Compl.*, Dkt. 3. Farmer asserted civil rights claims under § 1983, as well as unidentified state law claims.

On November 5, 2014, the Court issued an Initial Review Order dismissing several defendants and all but one claim: an *Eight Amendment* cruel and unusual punishment claim for deliberate indifference to Farmer's mental health care needs against Defendants Blades, Wamble-Fisher, and Corizon. *Initial Review Order*, Dkt. 7. The Court summarized Farmer's only remaining claim as follows:

> Plaintiff asserts that IDOC policy allows only 6 mental health counseling sessions, regardless of the individual prisoner's mental health needs. He also alleges that he requested more sessions from Defendants Blade and Wamble-Fisher, as well as from individual medical providers employed by Corizon, Inc., the private entity that provides medical treatment to the inmates; however, he was not allowed any more than the 6 sessions provided by policy.

Id. at 9.

SPECIFICALLY, FARMER ALLEGES THAT DEFENDANTS WERE DELIBERATELY INDIFFERENT TO HIS MENTAL HEALTH WHEN IT DID NOT FOLLOW THE STANDARDS AS PROVIDED FOR IN CORIZON'S CONTRACT WITH THE IDOC. *COMPL.*, P. 6, DKT. 3. HE ALLEGES THAT HE REQUESTED TO HAVE MENTAL HEALTH COUNSELING, BUT HIS REQUEST WAS REFUSED DUE TO BUDGETARY CONCERNS. *ID.* FARMER FURTHER ALLEGES THAT DEFENDANTS DID NOT PROVIDE HIM NEEDED MENTAL HEALTH CARE BECAUSE IT ONLY HAS ONE PSYCHOLOGIST AND NO PSYCHIATRIST ON STAFF. *ID.* AT 6-7. IN ADDITION, FARMER ALLEGES THAT HIS MENTAL HEALTH ISSUES HAVE NOT BEEN PROPERLY DIAGNOSED BY A COMPETENT LICENSED MENTAL HEALTH PROFESSIONAL, AND THAT HE HAS NOT BEEN PLACED ON A MENTAL HEALTH PROGRAM OR PATHWAY THAT FITS HIS NEEDS. *ID.* AT 7. BECAUSE, HE RECEIVED INADEQUATE MEDICAL CARE, FARMER CLAIMS HE WAS PLACED IN A LIVING ENVIRONMENT WHERE HE WAS PHYSICALLY ATTACKED BY ANOTHER INMATE IN JANUARY 2014. *ID.*

Defendant Corizon and Defendants Blades and Wamble-Fisher have filed separate motions for summary judgment. Corizon argues that Farmer's Complaint should be dismissed because he failed to exhaust administrative remedies within the prison system for the allegations in this Complaint. Blades and Wamble-Fisher argue the merits of the claim--that Farmer was and is being provided appropriate mental health services.

ANALYSIS

1. CORIZON'S MOTION FOR SUMMARY JUDGMENT FOR FAILURE TO EXHAUST

A. *EXHAUSTION REQUIREMENTS*

The defendant bears the ultimate burden of proving failure to exhaust. *See Brown v. Valoff, 422 F.3d 926, 936 (9th Cir. 2005)*. If the defendant initially shows that (1) an available administrative remedy existed and (2) the prisoner failed to exhaust that remedy, then the burden of production shifts to the plaintiff to bring forth evidence "showing that there is something in his particular case that made the existing and generally available administrative remedies effectively unavailable to him." *Albino, 747 F.3d at 1172*. Confusing or contradictory information given to a prisoner is relevant to the question "of whether relief was, as a practical matter, 'available.'" *Brown, 422 F.3d at 937*. Administrative remedies will be deemed unavailable and exhaustion excused if the inmate had no way of knowing the prison's grievance procedure, if the prison improperly processed an inmate's grievance, if prison officials misinformed an inmate regarding grievance procedures, if the inmate "did not have access to the necessary grievance forms within the prison's time limits for filing the grievance," or if prison staff took any other similar actions that interfered with an inmate's efforts to exhaust. *Albino, 747 F.3d at 1173*.

If a prisoner has failed to exhaust available administrative remedies, the appropriate remedy is dismissal without prejudice. *Wyatt v. Terhune, 315 F.3d 1108, 1120 (9th Cir. 2003)*, overruled in part on other grounds by *Albino, 747 F.3d 1162*.

B. *GRIEVANCE PROCEDURE*

Idaho has adopted a grievance procedure for inmates in its custody. *Whittington Aff.* ÷ 3, Dkt. 18-3. The IDOC grievance procedure consists of a three-step process: (1) the inmate seeks an informal resolution of the matter by completing an Offender Concern Form; (2) the inmate completes a Grievance Form if informal resolution cannot be accomplished; and (3) the inmate appeals any unfavorable response to the grievance. *Id.* ÷ ÷ 5-8. Once all three steps are completed, the offender grievance process is exhausted. *Id.* ÷ 9.

As an inmate incarcerated by the Idaho Department of Corrections, the Offender Grievance Process has been available to Famer. *Id.* ÷ 4; *Grievance and Informal Resolution Procedure for Offenders*, Dkt. 18-4. Farmer fully exhausted two grievances by completing all three steps: Grievance II 130001139 and Grievance II 140001240. *Whitting Aff.* ÷ 11. Grievance II 130001139 concerned the Prison Rape Elimination Act. *Id.* ÷ 13. In Grievance II 140001240, Farmer complained on November 17, 2014, after this suit was filed, that the IDOC and Corizon refused to provide him a parole plan for mental health aftercare (after his release) due to cost. *Id.* ÷ 14. In particular, he wanted the IDOC and Corizon to provide him mental health assistance after his release. *Id.* Farmer also filed a third grievance, which he apparently did not fully complete: Grievance II 130001073. In this last Grievance, Farmer requested counseling or therapy from an outside specialist, but that grievance   did not allege that he was denied adequate mental health care due to cost. *Id.* ÷ 12. Farmer concedes that he received six additional counseling sessions as a result of the grievance. *Id.*; *Compl.* at 15, Dkt. 3.

Corizon now moves for summary judgment on the grounds that Farmer has failed to exhaust his administrative remedies because none of the grievances Farmer submitted raised the issues contained in the Complaint.

C. *FARMER'S FAILURE TO EXHAUST ADMINISTRATIVE REMEDIES*

The record demonstrates that Farmer did not exhaust his administrative remedies through the grievance process any of the allegation raised in his Complaint. In his Complaint, Farmer alleges that Corizon was deliberately indifferent to his mental health when it did not follow the standards as provided for in Corizon's contract with the IDOC. *Compl.*, p. 6, Dkt. 3. He alleges that he requested to have mental health counseling, but his request was refused due to budgetary concerns. *Id.* Farmer further alleges that Corizon does not provide him needed mental health care because it only has one psychologist and no psychiatrist on staff. *Id.* at 6-7. In addition, Farmer alleges that his mental health issues have not been properly diagnosed by a competent licensed mental health professional, and that he has not been placed on a mental health program or pathway that fits his needs. *Id.* at 7. Because he allegedly received inadequate medical care, Farmer claims, he was placed in a living environment where he was physically attacked by another inmate in January 2014. *Id.*

Yet, Farmer never filed a grievance alleging that: (1) Corizon did not follow the mental health standards as provided for in its contract with the IDOC; (2) his mental health care was inadequate due to staffing; (3) his mental health issues have not been properly diagnosed by a competent mental health professional; (4) he has not been placed on a mental health program or pathway that fits his needs; and (5) due to inadequate mental health care, he was placed in a living environment where he was physically assaulted by another inmate in January 2014. *Whittington Aff.* ÷ 15. Because Farmer did not raise any of these specific issues contained in his Complaint in a grievance, the claims in his Complaint are unexhausted and must be dismissed. *Woodford, 548 U.S. at 85.*

Farmer, however, argues that (1) Grievance II-130001073 includes the issues in the Complaint; (2) Grievance II-140001240 is "a continuation" of   Grievance II-130001073; (3) Defendant Shell Wamble-Fisher did not allow his Concern Forms or Grievances to be processed between January 2013 and late 2014; and (4) Prison Rape Elimination Act ("PREA") claims do not need to be addressed through the grievance process. *Pl.'s Resp.*, Dkt. 21. The Court disagrees with each of these arguments and will address each in turn.

First, Grievance II-130001073, filed September 9, 2013, does not address the issues raised in the Complaint. Rather, with this grievance, Farmer requested counseling from an outside specialist. This grievance was granted at the Level II response, and Farmer received six outside counseling sessions. But Farmer's contends in his Complaint that he was denied counseling sessions beyond the six sessions provided in response to this Grievance. In other words, this Grievance 1240 did not raise the same issues as those raised in the Complaint..

SECOND, GRIEVANCE 1240 IS NOT A CONTINUATION OF GRIEVANCE II-130001073, AS FARMER CONTENDS. IN GRIEVANCE 1073, FARMER COMPLAINED THAT THE IDOC AND CORIZON REFUSED TO PROVIDE HIM A PLAN FOR MENTAL HEALTH CARE *AFTER* HIS RELEASE FROM PRISON BECAUSE OF COST. WHETHER ADDITIONAL CARE SHOULD HAVE BEEN PROVIDED *WHILE* FARMER REMAINED IN PRISON, WHICH IS WHAT FARMER CONTENDS IN HIS COMPLAINT, IS AN ENTIRELY DIFFERENT ISSUE FROM WHETHER FARMER SHOULD

RECEIVE CARE *AFTER* HIS RELEASE, WHILE HE IS ON PAROLE. MOREOVER, THE IDAHO GRIEVANCE POLICY REQUIRES THAT EACH GRIEVANCE ADDRESS ONLY A SINGLE ISSUE AND THERE CANNOT BE "CONTINUING" GRIEVANCES. *GRIEVANCE AND INFORMAL RESOLUTION PROCEDURE FOR OFFENDERS*, P. 9, DKT. 18.

However, even if Grievance 1073 did arguably encompass the allegations in Farmer's Complaint, it was not filed until after the Complaint was filed, and therefore Farmer did not exhaust his administrative remedies prior to initiating this action. *See 42 U.S.C.* ˜ 1997e(a); *see also Hall v. Reinke*, No. 1:13-cv-118-REB, 2014 U.S. Dist. LEXIS 136372, 2014 WL 4793955, at *6 (D. Idaho Sept. 25, 2014) (unpublished) ("A claim may be exhausted prior to filing suit or during suit, *so long as exhaustion was completed before the first time the prisoner sought to include the claim in the suit.*") (emphasis added). If Corizon did not know about the specific problem, they could not attempt to remedy it.

Third, there is no evidence that Wamble-Fisher denied Farmer access to the grievance process. The only evidence Farmer provides is a series of documents that appear to come from an unrelated whistleblower case; Farmer argues that these documents demonstrate Wamble-Fisher's lack of credibility and propensity to alter documents. But these documents do nothing to show that Wamble-Fisher somehow impeded *Farmer's* access to the grievance process. Indeed, the fact that Farmer filed five concern forms and grievances in 2013, and two more in 2014 belies his allegations that Wamble-Fisher prevented him from filing a grievance during this same time frame. Farmer does not explain how he filed these five concern forms or grievance but failed to file a single grievance raising the same concerns raised in his Complaint.

However, even assuming that Farmer's allegations were true, it would not matter because Farmer did not have to go through Wamble-Fisher to file a grievance. The Idaho Grievance Policy makes clear that if a staff member does not respond to an Offender Concern Form within seven days, the inmate can elect to submit another Offender Concern Form to another staff member or use the grievance process. *Grievance and Informal Resolution Procedure for Offenders*, p. 3. Dkt. 18. So, if Wamble-Fisher ignored or impeded Farmer's concern forms or delayed the grievance process as Farmer alleges, he could have simply bypassed that step and filed a grievance in a lockbox that is provided for all inmates to use for confidential offender/grievance/appeal forms. *Id.*, p. 6.

Finally, several problems exist with Farmer's argument that his claim qualifies as a "PREA" claim and thus does not need to be exhausted. Congress enacted the PREA to address the problem of rape in prison by creating national standards to prevent, detect, and respond to prison rape. *See, e.g. Hatcher v. Harrington*, No. 14-00554 JMS/KSC, 2015 U.S. Dist. LEXIS 13799, 2015 WL 474313, at *4 (D. Haw. Feb. 5, 2015). Neither Farmer's deliberate indifference claim at issue here nor any of the grievances he filed in 2013 and 2014 raise concerns about sexual abuse or prison rape (which he contends occurred in 1997); instead, his claims and grievances involve issues with access to mental health counseling. Thus, it is not clear that Farmer's claim would qualify as a PLRA. Indeed, it is questionable that PREA even creates a private cause of action that can be brought by an individual plaintiff. *Hatcher v. Harrington*, No. 14-00554 JMS/KSC, 2015 U.S. Dist. LEXIS 13799, 2015 WL 474313, at *5 (D. Haw. Feb. 5, 2015) (listing cases) ("Nothing in the PREA explicitly or implicitly suggests that Congress intended to create a private right of action for inmates to sue prison officials for noncompliance with the Act."). Finally, many courts have held that the PREA's reporting requirements do not supersede the PLRA's exhaustion requirements. *See, e.g., Omaro v. Annucci*, 68 F. Supp. 3d 359, 2014 WL 6068573, at *4 (W.D.N.Y. 2014) ("Nothing in the text or legislative history of the PREA suggests that it was intended to abrogate the PLRA's exhaustion requirement."); *Lamb v. Franke*, No. 2:12-cv-367-MO, 2013 U.S. Dist. LEXIS 22708, 2013 WL 638836, at *2 (D.Or. Feb. 14, 2013) (unpublished) ("The PREA does not impose an alternative remedial scheme, nor does it supersede PLRA's exhaustion requirement.").

In sum, Farmer was required to exhaust his administrative remedies before filing suit but failed to so. Accordingly, the Court will grant Corizon's motion for summary judgment.

JASON KEEL, PLAINTIFF, VS. CORIZON MEDICAL SERVICES, ET AL., DEFENDANTS. CAUSE NO. 3:14-CV-1492 UNITED STATES DISTRICT COURT FOR THE NORTHERN DISTRICT OF INDIANA, SOUTH BEND DIVISION

BACKGROUND

Jason Keel, a former inmate at the Miami Correctional Facility ("Miami"), brought this action on May 2, 2014, pursuant to *42 U.S.C. § 1983*. (DE #1.) The Court screened the complaint pursuant to *28 U.S.C. § 1915A*, and granted him leave to proceed on a claim that Dr. Mitcheff, the regional medical director for Corizon Medical Services[1], refused to treat Keel's hand problems in March 2014. (DE #6.) And, because Keel alleged that he is still receiving inadequate medical care with respect to his hand, he was also granted leave to proceed on a claim for injunctive relief against Dr. Mitcheff, pertaining to his current medical needs. (*Id.*)

1   A private company which provides medical care at Indiana   Department of Correction facilities.

In his motion for summary judgment, Dr. Mitcheff argues that Keel has failed to exhaust his available administrative remedies prior to filing suit as required by the Prisoner Litigation Reform Act ("PLRA") and, therefore, these claims must be dismissed. Keel was provided with a "Notice of Summary Judgment Motion" as required by *N.D. Ind. L.R. 56-1* and a copy of both *Federal Rule of Civil Procedure 56* and *Local Rule 56-1*. (DE #36.) That notice clearly informed him that unless he disputed the facts presented by the defendant, the court could accept those facts as true. *Fed. R. Civ. P. 56(e)* ("If a party . . . fails to properly address another party's assertion of fact . . . the court may . . . consider the fact undisputed for purposes of the motion."). It also told him that unless he submitted evidence creating a factual dispute, he could lose this case. *Fed. R. Civ. P. 56(a)* ("The court shall grant summary judgment if the movant shows that there is no genuine dispute as to any material fact and the movant is entitled to judgment as a matter of law."). Keel has filed his response (DE #46) and Defendant filed a reply (DE #47). The motion is therefore fully briefed and ripe for adjudication.

Facts

At all relevant times, and pursuant to Indiana Department of Correction ("IDOC") policy, Miami has an Offender Grievance Process under which an inmate can grieve a broad range of issues related to their conditions of confinement. (DE #34-1, Ex. A ¶ 7; Ex. B.) All inmates are made aware of the grievance process during orientation and a copy of the process is available in the law library. (Ex. A ¶ 7; Ex. B.) The process begins with the inmate attempting to resolve the matter informally with staff. (Ex. A ¶ 9.) If the issue cannot be resolved informally, the inmate must file a formal grievance within 10 days of the underlying incident. (*Id.* ¶ 9; Ex. B.) If the grievance is not resolved to the inmate's satisfaction, he must file an appeal within 10 working days of the grievance response. (*Id.* ¶ 8; Ex. B.) The grievance manager reviews the appeal and submits a response. (*Id.* ¶ 7; Ex. B.) An inmate has not fully exhausted the Offender Grievance Process until he completes all three steps of the process and receives a response from the Department's Offender Grievance Manager. (*Id.* ¶ 10; Ex. B.) Moreover, exhausting the grievance procedure requires timely pursuing each step of the informal and formal process. (*Id.*)

On October 21, 2013, Keel filed Grievance No. 79052, complaining about the medical care he received from Dr. Kream, Dr. Loveridge and Nurse Shalala. (DE #46 at 11.) He fully exhausted that grievance on December 18, 2013. (*Id.* at 6.) According to the grievance records kept and maintained at Miami, Keel has initiated   three (3) grievances in 2014 that have been fully exhausted: Grievance Numbers 81396, 81760 and 82172 (Ex. A, ¶ 11; Ex. C.) In Grievance No. 81396, Keel complained about prison staff losing his property in conjunction with a move to the infirmary. (Ex. A ¶ 12; Ex. C.) This grievance was not fully exhausted until May 22, 2014. (*Id.*) In Grievance No. 81760, he complained about his medical care, including being in continuous pain and not being able to exercise. (*Id.*) Notably, this grievance complained about Dr. Mandaret, not Dr. Mitcheff. It was not fully exhausted until June 3, 2014. (*Id.*) In Grievance No. 82172, he complained about not being able to obtain information from the state medical licensing board. (*Id.*) This grievance was not fully exhausted until May 29, 2014. (*Id.*)

Pursuant to the Prison Litigation Reform Act ("PLRA"), prisoners are prohibited from bringing an action in federal court with respect to prison conditions "until such administrative remedies as are available are exhausted." *42 U.S.C. § 1997e(a)*. An inmate must exhaust before bringing his lawsuit, and efforts to exhaust while the case is pending do not satisfy *42 U.S.C. § 1997e(a)*. *Ford v. Johnson, 362 F.3d 395, 398 (7th Cir. 2004)* ("exhaustion must precede litigation"); *Perez v. Wisconsin Department of Corrections, 182 F.3d 532, 535 (7th Cir. 1999)* (compliance with *42 U.S.C. § 1997e(a)* is a "precondition to suit"). For exhaustion purposes, an inmate is deemed to have "brought" the action on the date when his complaint is tendered for mailing. *Ford, 362 F.3d at 400.*

The failure to exhaust is an affirmative defense on which the defendant bears the burden of proof. *See Jones v. Bock, 549 U.S. 199, 216, 127 S. Ct. 910, 166 L. Ed. 2d 798 (2007); Dole v. Chandler, 438 F.3d 804, 809 (7th Cir. 2006).* The U.S. Court of Appeals for the Seventh Circuit has taken a "strict compliance approach to exhaustion." *Dole, 438 F.3d at 809.* Thus, "[t]o exhaust remedies, a prisoner must file complaints and appeals in the place, and at the time, the prison's administrative rules require." *Pozo v. McCaughtry, 286 F.3d 1022, 1025 (7th Cir. 2002).* "[A] prisoner who does not properly take each step within the administrative process has failed to exhaust state remedies." *Id. at 1024.*

Here, Dr. Mitcheff argues that Keel did not properly exhaust his administrative remedies before filing suit. As outlined above, the record reflects that Keel exhausted three grievances in 2014 and none were related to Mr. Mitcheff's March 2014 treatment of his hand.

Keel nevertheless maintains that he exhausted his administrative remedies by pointing to a grievance he filed on October 21, 2013. (DE #46 at 6.) However, that grievance was filed four months before Dr. Mitcheff allegedly denied him medical treatment for his hand. In addition, that October 2013 grievance did not relate to Dr. Mitcheff's treatment of Keel's hand. Thus, the October 2013 grievance is insufficient to demonstrate that Keel exhausted his administrative remedies for his claims against Dr. Mitcheff in this case. Therefore, the undisputed facts show that Keel did not exhaust his administrative remedies regarding his claims that Dr. Mitcheff denied him medical treatment for his hand in March 2014 and beyond.

WILLIAM R. TUBBS, PLAINTIFF V. CORIZON, INC.; ET AL., DEFENDANTS 5:13CV00377-BSM-JJV UNITED STATES DISTRICT COURT FOR THE EASTERN DISTRICT OF ARKANSAS, PINE BLUFF DIVISION

(SEE ALSO DISCUSSION UNDER MEDICAL CARE)

I. INTRODUCTION

William R. Tubbs ("Plaintiff") is an inmate of the Arkansas Department of Correction ("ADC") and he alleges the named Defendants[1] exhibited deliberate indifference toward his serious medical needs. (Doc. No. 52.) Pending before the Court is Defendants' Motion for Summary Judgment. (Doc. No. 167.) Plaintiff has not responded to this Motion and the time for doing so has passed.

1   Only Defendants Estella Bland, Corizon, LLC, Annette Esaw, Laura Morgan, Amanda Pevey, and Sherie Rice remain. All other Defendants have been dismissed. (Doc. No. 174.)

III. ANALYSIS

Plaintiff alleges Defendants violated his rights by (1) denying him a cane; (2) failing to refer him to a provider in January 2013; and (3) not giving him appropriate doses of pain medication for back pain. (Doc. No. 52 at 7-9.) Defendants argue (1) Plaintiff failed to exhaust his administrative remedies against Defendants Morgan, Pevey, and Corizon, LLC; (2) he only exhausted claims related to a July 23, 2013, encounter against Defendant Bland; and (3) the record establishes that none of the named Defendants were deliberately indifferent to Plaintiff's medical needs. For the reasons below, I conclude Defendants are entitled to summary judgment.

A. Exhaustion of Administrative Remedies

The Prison Litigation Reform Act (PLRA) requires an inmate to exhaust prison grievance procedures before filing suit in federal court. *See 42 U.S.C. § 1997e(a); Jones v. Bock, 549 U.S. 199, 202, 127 S. Ct. 910, 166 L. Ed. 2d 798 (2007); Jones v. Norris, 310 F.3d 610, 612 (8th Cir. 2002).* Exhaustion under the PLRA is mandatory. *Jones, 549 U.S. at 211.* "[T]o properly exhaust administrative remedies, prisoners must 'complete the administrative review process in accordance with the applicable procedural rules,' rules that are defined not by the PLRA, but by the prison grievance process itself." *Id., 549 U.S. at 218 (quoting Woodford v. Ngo, 548 U.S. 81, 88, 126 S. Ct. 2378, 165 L. Ed. 2d 368 (2006)).* Compliance with a prison's grievance procedures is, therefore, all that is required by the PLRA to properly exhaust. *Id.* Thus, the question of whether an inmate has properly exhausted administrative remedies will depend on the specifics of that particular prison's grievance policy. *See Id.* Plaintiff's claims are governed by Administrative Directive 12-16. (Doc. No. 169-1 at 3.) An inmate who believes he has been wronged is first required to file an informal resolution. (*Id.* at 7-10.) If the inmate is unsatisfied with the outcome of the informal resolution, he may proceed to the formal grievance procedure which entitles him to a response, first from the appropriate medical personnel, and then, if desired, from the ADC Deputy Director. (*Id.* at 10-14.) Inmates must be specific as to their issues and any personnel involved. (*Id.* at 7.)

The record shows Plaintiff exhausted eight grievances[2] during the time period relevant to this suit. (Doc. No. 169-1 at 2.) Defendants state none of these grievances properly exhausted any claims against Defendants Morgan, Pevey, or Corizon, LLC. I agree. Neither Morgan nor Corizon, LLC is explicitly referenced in the eight grievances. Plaintiff only names "Pevey" in grievance CU-13-2065. (*Id.* at 45.) Defendants state this is not a reference to Defendant Pevey, who is a nurse, but rather an ADC Garment Factory Supervisor of the same name. (Doc. No. 169 at 4 n.1.) A review of CU-13-2065 supports their assertion. Plaintiff states he sought permission from Glover and "Pevey", his garment factory supervisors, "not to come back to P.M. work do (sic) to my pain." (Doc. No. 169-1 at 45.)

2   These grievances are numbered: CU-13-00237, CU-13-00568, CU-13-00637, CU-13-01058, CU-13-01226, CU-13-01514, CU-13-02064, and CU-13-02065. (Doc. No. 169-1 at 2.)

With respect to Defendant Bland, only grievance CU-13-2064 exhausts relevant claims against her. (*Id.* at 41.) These claims relate to a July 23, 2013, encounter where Plaintiff complained of severe pain but was allegedly not given sufficient pain medication. (*Id.*) Defendant Bland was also referenced in CU-13-01226, but no actual claim was stated against her. (*Id.* at 35.) Rather, this grievance stated Defendant Esaw had not provided Plaintiff with a cane which Bland had previously authorized. (*Id.*)

Based on the foregoing, I recommend Defendants Morgan, Pevey, and Corizon, LLC be dismissed for Plaintiff's failure to exhaust administrative remedies. Additionally, any claims against Defendant Bland which do not arise from the July 23, 2013, encounter should also be dismissed on this basis.

HAROLD DAVEY CASSELL ADC # 073885, PLAINTIFF V. CORRECT CARE SOLUTIONS, LLC AND CORIZON, INC., DEFENDANTS 5:14CV00403-DPM-JJV UNITED STATES DISTRICT COURT FOR THE EASTERN DISTRICT OF ARKANSAS, PINE BLUFF DIVISION

(SEE ALSO DISCUSSION UNDER MEDICAL CARE)

I. INTRODUCTION

Harold Davey Cassell ("Plaintiff") is an inmate of the Arkansas Department of Correction ("ADC"). He alleges that Corizon, LLC[1] and Correct Care Solutions, LLC ("Defendants") have exhibited deliberate indifference to his serious medical needs. (Doc. No. 1.) Specifically, Plaintiff suffers from Hepatitis-C and contends that Defendants failed to treat his condition with the drugs Victrelis and Incivek when both were approved by the Food and Drug Administration in 2011. (*Id.* at ¶¶ 12-15.) He claims Defendants were also deliberately indifferent when they failed to administer the drugs Olysio and Savaldi, which were approved in 2013. (*Id.* at ¶¶ 23-26.) Defendants have now motioned for summary judgment (Doc. No. 27) and Plaintiff has responded (Doc. No. 32).

1   This Defendant is currently listed as "Corizon, Inc" on the docket. The Clerk shall alter the listing to reflect the appropriate name.

III. ANALYSIS

Defendants raise three arguments in support of their Motion for Summary Judgment. First, they argue that Plaintiff failed to exhaust his administrative remedies against Defendant Correct Care Solutions prior to filing this suit. Second, they contend that Defendants, both of whom are corporations, cannot be held liable for the alleged misconduct of their employees pursuant to a theory of *respondeat superior*. Finally, Defendants argue that Plaintiff has now been provided with Havaroni, one of the newest drug treatments for Hepatitis-C, and that he suffered no injury as a result of any delay in treatment. For the reasons stated hereafter, I conclude that Defendants' Motion should be granted.

A. Exhaustion of Administrative Remedies

The Prison Litigation Reform Act (PLRA) requires an inmate to exhaust prison grievance procedures before filing suit in federal court. *See 42 U.S.C. § 1997e(a); Jones v. Bock, 549 U.S. 199, 202, 127 S. Ct. 910, 166 L. Ed. 2d 798 (2007); Jones v. Norris, 310 F.3d 610, 612 (8th Cir. 2002).* Exhaustion under the PLRA is mandatory. *Jones, 549 U.S. at 211.* "[T]o properly exhaust administrative remedies, prisoners must 'complete the administrative review process in accordance with the applicable procedural rules,' rules that are defined not by the PLRA, but by the prison grievance process itself." *Id., 549 U.S. at 218* (quoting *Woodford v. Ngo, 548 U.S. 81, 88, 126 S. Ct. 2378, 165 L. Ed. 2d 368 (2006)).* Compliance with a prison's grievance procedures is, therefore, all that is required by the PLRA to properly exhaust. *Id.* Thus, the question as to whether an inmate has properly exhausted administrative remedies will depend on the specifics of that particular prison's grievance policy. *See Id.*

Here, Plaintiff's claims are governed by Administrative Directives 12-16 and 14-16. The relevant procedures for medical grievances are consistent across both directives, which require an inmate who believes he has been wronged to file an informal resolution. (Doc. No. 28-2 at 5-6.) If the inmate is unsatisfied with the outcome of the informal resolution, he may proceed to the formal grievance procedure which entitles him to a response, first from the Health Service Administrator, and then, if desired, from an ADC Deputy, Chief Deputy, or Assistant Director. (*Id.* at 8-11.) Inmates must be specific as to their issues and any personnel involved. (*Id.* at 5-6.)

Defendants state that Correct Care Solutions did not begin their contract with the ADC until January 1, 2014. (Doc. No. 29 at 9.) Plaintiff does not appear to dispute this assertion. From January 1, 2014, until this suit was filed on October 30, 2014, Plaintiff filed thirteen medical grievances.[2] (Doc. No. 28-4 at 1-2.) After review of these grievances, I conclude Plaintiff failed to properly exhaust the claims which he now brings against Correct Care Solutions. Notably, none of the grievances makes any reference to Victrelis, Incivek, Olysio, or Savaldi, the drugs which Plaintiff now alleges should have been administered to him. Instead, the grievances raise various issues which are not relevant to this case: (1) CU-14-00162 complained of anal bleeding, possibly related to hemorrhoids, and alleged that the medication prescribed for this ailment had been ineffective; (2) CU-14-00255 complained that non-party Lasonya Griswold found no need for a medical follow-up despite a diagnostic result indicating that Plaintiff's platelet levels had dropped; (3) CU-14-00477, CU-14-00536, and CU-14-00803 each complain about non-party Laura Morgan's failure to adhere to ADC grievance policy; (4) CU-14-00804 complains that Plaintiff was not afforded an opportunity to discuss the results of a colonoscopy with medical staff; (5) CU-14-00805 and CU-14-00850 allege that Correct Care Solutions and unit medical staff denied him a follow-up with an outside specialist to discuss various medications which that specialist had prescribed; (6) CU-14-00932 and CU-14-01045 allege that non-party Dana Peyton was untruthful in her responses to Plaintiff's earlier grievances; (7) CU-14-01514 asks for the results of a blood test; and (8) CU-14-01515 complains that he has not received boots which medical staff indicated would be prescribed for him. (Doc. No. 28-3 at 4-45.)

2   The affidavit of Medical Grievance Coordinator Shelly Byers notes, however, that only twelve of these grievances were actually exhausted. (Doc. No. 28-4 at 1.) She states that Plaintiff failed to fully appeal grievance CU-14-01567. (*Id.*)

For his part, Plaintiff argues that some of the medical conditions raised in the grievances, most notably the anal bleeding, are "extraheptic manifestations" and therefore related to Plaintiff's Hepatitis-C. (Doc. No. 32-3 ¶¶ 2-3, 7-8.) Accepting this argument as true, Plaintiff still failed to raise the issues which underlie this case, namely whether Correct Care Solutions was deliberately indifferent in failing to prescribe certain drugs to combat his Hepatitis-C. Plaintiff also contends that those grievances which raise issues of inadequate procedure are indicative of an effort by Correct Care Solutions to "cause external impediment" and "deny prisoners due process to the grievance procedure." (*Id.* ¶¶ 5-6.) These arguments are unsupported by any substantive evidence. Moreover, even if prison staff failed to respond adequately or truthfully to Plaintiff's grievances, there is no indication that anyone prevented Plaintiff from grieving and exhausting the claims he raises in this suit. Finally, Plaintiff states that he apprised Correct Care Solutions of his situation by way of a letter sent by his counsel to the Regional Director. (Doc. No. 32-3 at 36.) This communication was not part of the official grievance procedure, however, and cannot substitute for a properly exhausted grievance.

Based on the foregoing, I recommend that Defendant Correct Care Solutions be dismissed for failure to exhaust administrative remedies.

DWAYNE R. STEPHENSON, PLAINTIFF, VS. CORIZON MEDICAL SERVICES, DR. YOUNG, NP POULSON, ET AL., DEFENDANTS. CASE NO. 1:14-CV-00460-BLW UNITED STATES DISTRICT COURT FOR THE DISTRICT OF IDAHO

DEFENDANTS' MOTION FOR SUMMARY JUDGMENT: EXHAUSTION OF ADMINISTRATIVE REMEDIES

In the pending Motion for Summary Judgment, the Corizon Defendants argue that Plaintiff failed to exhaust his administrative remedies completely before filing his lawsuit, mandating dismissal without prejudice. For the reasons that follow, the Court agrees.

1. Plaintiff's Allegations and Undisputed Material Facts

Plaintiff filed his Complaint on October 28, 2014. He contends that, after undergoing a neck surgery in October 2013, something in his neck "snapped," and thereafter he suffered continuous pain. He asserts that the medical providers at the prison--Defendants Dr. Murray Young and Nurse Practitioner William Poulson, who work for Corizon, LLC --have refused to give him proper diagnoses and treatments after that date.

In March 2014, Plaintiff signed forms giving permission for inmate representatives in an ongoing class action lawsuit to discuss his medical issues with Idaho Department of Correction (IDOC) Medical Services Administrator Rona Siegert and others at status meetings where the monitoring of the provision of medical services is discussed among IDOC officials, Corizon officials, inmates, lawyers, and other interested representatives. The permission form states:

I understand that this form is not a substitute for a . . . grievance form. . . . I am also still required to follow the concern/grievance process if I want to grieve this issue.

(Plaintiff's Exhibit, Dkt. 17-2, p. 1.)

On October 6, 2014, Plaintiff filed a grievance on the same medical issues, which was denied. On November 5, 2014, he filed an appeal, but his appeal form was returned because the handwriting was partially illegible, and he resubmitted it. The response was returned to Plaintiff on November 12, 2014. However, Plaintiff filed his Complaint in this matter on October 28, 2014, before the appeal was completed.

3. IDOC Grievance Process

The IDOC has a simple grievance process, consisting of three stages. First, an inmate with a concern must seek resolution of the problem by filling out an offender concern form, addressed to a staff person capable of resolving the issue. If the issue cannot be resolved through the use of a concern form, the inmate must then file a grievance form. The grievance is then resolved by a Level 1 Initial Response, which is reviewed by a Level 2 Reviewing Authority Response, and then returned to the inmate. If the grievance did not resolve the issue satisfactorily, the inmate must file an appeal, which is reviewed and decided by a Level 3 Appellate Authority Response. When all three of these steps--concern form, grievance form, and grievance appeal--are completed, the administrative grievance process is exhausted. (Affidavit of Jill Whittington, Dkt. 13-3.) The procedure requires that the grievance and appeal forms be handwritten legibly; if they are not, they are returned to the inmate with instructions to make the writing legible. (IDOC Grievance Procedures, Dkt. 13-4, p. 10.)

4. Discussion and Conclusion

The law is clear that (1) the particular prison grievance procedures must be followed as specified in the prison's written policies; and (2) a claim cannot be included in a civil rights complaint unless it was exhausted before the time it is first included in the lawsuit. Here, Plaintiff attempted to informally resolve his problem by taking it to the class action medical monitoring meeting. However, nowhere does Plaintiff point to any procedures that state that this method is an acceptable alternative to filing a prison grievance, or to any official statement by a prison administrator letting him know that he had satisfied the grievance procedures in an alternative manner and had the green light to file a lawsuit without using the established grievance procedures. The form itself contradicts his argument.

The fact that completion of the grievance process was delayed because Plaintiff submitted a partially illegible appeal was his own fault, and he was simply required to rewrite it and resubmit it, which he did. A legible appeal is a reasonable requirement, because prison officials cannot know of the problem if they cannot read the grievance appeal. However, after resubmitting the grievance appeal in a legible form, Plaintiff then was required to wait for a response from his grievance appeal before filing his lawsuit, which he did not do.

One of the reasons prisoners must follow the internal grievance system is to allow prison officials to fix problems internally, without the need for filing a costly, time-consuming lawsuit. Another reason is to provide them with legal notice, so that a lawsuit can be filed if officials do not fix the problem at the grievance or appeal stage. Yet another reason is to aid prisoners in the rehabilitative process--they are in prison for failing to follow society's rules, and the sooner they understand the importance of rules and learn how to follow them with exactness, the better able they are to function within the prison society and, if released, within the society at large. The bottom line is that "before" means before.

The undisputed material facts show Plaintiff did not follow the rules of administrative exhaustion. The United States Supreme Court has clarified that exactness in following the administrative exhaustion rules is required. No adequate excuse for failing to follow the rules is evident from the record. The Court rejects Plaintiff's argument that he did not first present his claim in his lawsuit at the time he first presented the lawsuit for filing--simply because his lawsuit was "conditionally" filed by the Clerk of Court. It is not the category in which the Clerk accepted and filed the lawsuit that is at issue, but the fact that Plaintiff presented it for filing at that time.

Therefore, this case must be dismissed without prejudice. However, because Plaintiff is still within the statute of limitations period on his more current lack-of-care claims, he may re-file his lawsuit immediately, based upon any completed grievances, and so Defendants' procedural victory may be short-lived.

ROBERT SCHILLEMAN, PLAINTIFF, V. CORIZON HEALTH INCORPORATED, ET AL., DEFENDANTS. NO. CV 14-01825-PHX-DLR (BSB) UNITED STATES DISTRICT COURT FOR THE DISTRICT OF ARIZONA

II. Plaintiff's Motion for Summary Judgment re: Exhaustion of Remedies

Plaintiff asserts that he is entitled to summary judgment on Defendants' affirmative defense that Plaintiff failed to exhaust his available administrative remedies. He argues that he was excused from the exhaustion requirement under the plain terms of Arizona Department of Corrections (ADC) Department Order 802.01, § 1.8, which Plaintiff asserts exempts emergency complaints from the formal grievance procedure. Plaintiff further asserts that, even though he was not required to exhaust administrative remedies, he did exhaust his administrative remedies by following the ADC's grievance procedure.

Defendants respond that "Plaintiff's conclusory statements citing to D.O. 802 are not enough to prove that his specific medical complaints constituted an 'emergency condition' within the meaning of D.O. 802" and that Plaintiff has failed to present evidence demonstrating that his prostate cancer presented an emergency medical condition under D.O. 802. Defendants further assert that D.O. 802.01, §1.8 does not obviate an inmate's obligation to exhaust the ADC's grievance and appeals procedures in the event of an emergency, but "simply allows an inmate to bring an emergency to the attention of staff, by any available means, rather than to rely on the written grievance procedure to alert staff to an emergency." (Doc. 137 at 6.)

Defendants next assert that the Grievance Appeal Response signed by Director Ryan on February 28, 2014 does not show that Plaintiff exhausted his administrative remedies because "Plaintiff does not provide any documents that were submitted by him as part of the grievance process related to the Grievance Appeal Response signed by Director Ryan on February 28, 2014, or any additional documents related to the other grievances submitted by Plaintiff." (Doc. 140 at 5.)

B. Exhaustion

Under the Prison Litigation Reform Act, a prisoner must exhaust "available" administrative remedies before filing an action in federal court. See 42 U.S.C. § 1997e(a); Vaden v. Summerhill, 449 F.3d 1047, 1050 (9th Cir. 2006); Brown v. Valoff, 422 F.3d 926, 934-35 (9th Cir. 2005). The prisoner must complete the administrative review process in accordance with the applicable rules. See Woodford v. Ngo, 548 U.S. 81, 92, 126 S. Ct. 2378, 165 L. Ed. 2d 368 (2006). Exhaustion is required for all suits about prison life, Porter v. Nussle, 534 U.S. 516, 523, 122 S. Ct. 983, 152 L. Ed. 2d 12 (2002), regardless of the type of relief offered through the administrative process, Booth v. Churner, 532 U.S. 731, 741, 121 S. Ct. 1819, 149 L. Ed. 2d 958 (2001).

The defendant bears the initial burden to show that there was an available administrative remedy and that the prisoner did not exhaust it. Albino v. Baca, 747 F.3d 1162, 1169, 1172 (9th Cir. 2014); see Brown, 422 F.3d at 936-37 (a defendant must demonstrate that applicable relief remained available in the grievance process). Once that showing is made, the burden shifts to the prisoner, who must either demonstrate that he, in fact, exhausted administrative remedies or "come forward with evidence showing that there is something in his particular case that made the existing and generally available administrative remedies effectively unavailable to him." Albino, 747 F.3d at 1172. The ultimate burden, however, rests with the defendant. Id. Summary judgment is appropriate if the undisputed evidence, viewed in the light most favorable to the prisoner, shows a failure to exhaust. Id. at 1166, 1168; see Fed. R. Civ. P. 56(a).

If summary judgment is denied, disputed factual questions relevant to exhaustion should be decided by the judge; a plaintiff is not entitled to a jury trial on the issue of exhaustion. Albino, 747 F.3d at 1170-71. But if a court finds that the prisoner exhausted administrative remedies, that administrative remedies were not available, or that the failure to exhaust administrative remedies should be excused, the case proceeds to the merits. Id. at 1171.

C. Facts regarding Exhaustion

ADC Department Order 802.06 outlines the formal inmate medical grievance process. (Doc. 113-2 at 5.) An inmate may appeal a response to a formal inmate medical grievance to the Director. (Id. at 6.) The decision of the Director for medical grievance appeals is final and constitutes exhaustion of all remedies for inmate medical grievances within ADC. (Id. at 7.) Section 802.01 entitled "General Information" provides, in part, that "[i]nmates are not required to use the formal Inmate Grievance Procedures to submit a verbal or written emergency complaint." (Id. at 3.) An emergency is defined as "a condition which, if processed through the normal grievance time frames, would subject the inmate to substantial risk of medical harm, personal injury or cause other serious and irreparable harm." (Id.) The Department Order further provides that "[a]ny emergency complaint received by staff shall be immediately evaluated through the chain of command to determine whether it is an emergency as defined in 1.8.1 of this section and requires immediate response outside of the Inmate Grievance Procedure time frames."

D. Discussion

Plaintiff argues that he was excused from the exhaustion requirement under the plain terms of ADC Department Order 802.01, § 1.8, which provides that "[i]nmates are not required to use the formal Inmate Grievance Procedures to submit a verbal or written emergency complaint." The emergency complaint procedure, however, is not a model of clarity. Section 1.8 clearly states that inmates are not required to use the formal grievance process in the case of an emergency,4 but provides no further information as to exhaustion of remedies in the case of an emergency. The consequences of this ambiguity are on display in this case.

4 The Court is unconvinced by Defendants' argument that an inmate must still follow the formal grievance process even after submitting an emergency complaint. It is Defendants who are able to define the grievance process and how administrative remedies are exhausted and, thus, any ambiguity in their policy should be construed in favor of Plaintiff. See Woodford, 548 U.S. at 90 (proper exhaustion requires using all steps that the agency holds out, and doing so properly).

Plaintiff provides a "consultation request" signed by Dr. Kessler, which states that Plaintiff told him that it was important to establish care with a urologist for treatment of his prostate cancer. (Doc. 25-9 at 1.) He argues that this evidence shows he orally pursued treatment for his prostate cancer and, therefore, was exempt from the formal administrative grievance process. Defendants argue that Plaintiff has not shown that his condition constituted an emergency within the meaning of Section 1.8.1, which provides that an emergency is "a condition which, if processed through the normal grievance time frames, would subject the inmate to substantial risk of medical harm, personal injury or cause other serious and irreparable harm." The Department Order, however, does not state who decides which conditions are "medical emergencies" or what happens when, after evaluation, a complaint is deemed to not constitute an emergency.

Despite the substantial ambiguity in the emergency complaint grievance process, Plaintiff is entitled to summary judgment on Defendants' exhaustion of administrative remedies affirmative defense because the uncontroverted evidence shows that he exhausted his claims to the Director's level. Plaintiff provides a January 13, 2014 response from Director Ryan responding to Plaintiff's request for "immediate and thorough treatment for [his] cancer or immediate release to get treatment by a competent doctor due to the life threatening nature of [his] cancer." (Doc. 114-2 at 1-2.) Defendants state that Plaintiff has failed to show that he exhausted his claims in this action because he did not provide any of the grievance documents that led to Director Ryan's final decision with his Motion for Summary Judgment. But Defendants point to nothing in their policy requiring Plaintiff to name every defendant or explicitly set forth his legal claims in his grievances. Morton v. Hall, 599 F.3d 942, 946 (9th Cir. 2010) (The level of detail in an administrative grievance necessary to properly exhaust a claim is determined by the prison's applicable grievance procedures, but "when a prison's grievance procedures are silent or incomplete as to factual specificity, a grievance suffices if it alerts the prison to the nature of the wrong for which redress is sought."). Plaintiff provides evidence that he exhausted his claims related to the fact that he was not being provided immediate and thorough treatment for his cancer. Defendants have not met their burden of demonstrating that Plaintiff did not exhaust his claims, and cannot shift the burden to Plaintiff by claiming that Plaintiff has not produced enough evidence to demonstrate that he did exhaust. See Albino, 747 F.3d at 1172 (the ultimate burden of proof as to exhaustion remains with the defendant). Plaintiff has provided unrebutted evidence that he exhausted his administrative remedies, and thus, the Court finds that Plaintiff is entitled to summary judgment on the exhaustion defense.

CARL RUPERT SMITH, #137 787, PLAINTIFF, V. CORIZON HEALTH SERVICES, ET AL., DEFENDANTS. CIVIL ACTION NO. 2:15-CV-20-MHT UNITED STATES DISTRICT COURT FOR THE MIDDLE DISTRICT OF ALABAMA, NORTHERN DIVISION

This *42 U.S.C. § 1983* action involves a dispute over the of medical care and treatment afforded Plaintiff, an inmate incarcerated at the Staton Correctional Facility in Elmore, Alabama. Plaintiff names as defendants Corizon, LLC, Darryl Ellis, Michele Sagers-Copeland, and Domineek Guice. Plaintiff seeks damages and injunctive relief for the alleged violation of his constitutional rights. *Doc. No. 1.*

Defendants filed an answer, special report, and supporting evidentiary materials addressing Plaintiff's claims for relief. In these documents, Defendants argue this case is due to be dismissed because prior to filing this cause of action Plaintiff failed to properly exhaust an administrative remedy available to him through the prison system's medical care provider, Corizon, Inc., prior to initiation of this case. *Doc. No. 13,* at 12-15. Defendants base their exhaustion defense on Plaintiff's failure to submit any medical grievances regarding the claims presented. *Id., Sagers-Copeland Affidavit.* In addition, Defendants maintain, and the evidentiary materials, including Plaintiff's medical records, indicate that Plaintiff received appropriate medical treatment during the time relevant to the matters alleged in the instant complaint. *See Doc. No. 13, Ellis, Sagers-Copeland, & Guice Affidavits & Exh. A.* On April 13, 2015, the court provided Plaintiff an opportunity to file a response to Defendants' report in which he was advised to "specifically address Defendants' argument that he [] failed to exhaust his available administrative remedies as required by *42 U.S.C.* ~ 1997e(a) of the Prison Litigation Reform Act ('PLRA')." *Doc. No. 17* at 1 (footnote omitted). On May 5, 2015, the court granted Plaintiff's request for additional time to file his response. *Doc. No. 19.* Plaintiff has filed no response within the time allowed by the court.

"[A]n exhaustion defense . . . is not ordinarily the proper subject for a summary judgment [motion]; instead, it should be raised in a motion to dismiss, or be treated as such if raised in a motion for summary judgment." *Bryant v. Rich*, 530 F.3d 1368, 1374-75 (11th Cir. 2008) (internal quotations omitted); *Trias v. Fla. Dep't of Corr.*, 587 F. App'x 531, 534 (11th Cir. 2014) (District court properly construed defendant's "motion for summary judgment as a motion to dismiss for failure to exhaust administrative remedies"). Therefore, the court will treat Defendants' report as a motion to dismiss.

I. STANDARD OF REVIEW

In addressing the requirements of *42 U.S.C. § 1997e* regarding exhaustion, the Eleventh Circuit has recognized that "[t]he plain language of th[is] statute makes exhaustion a precondition to filing an action in federal court." *Higginbottom v. Carter*, 223 F.3d 1259, 1261 (11th Cir. 2000) (per curiam) (quoting *Freeman v. Francis*, 196 F.3d 641, 643-44 (6th Cir. 1999)). This means that "until such administrative remedies as are available are exhausted," a prisoner is precluded from filing suit in federal court. *See id.* (affirming dismissal of prisoner's civil rights suit for failure to satisfy the mandatory exhaustion requirements of the PLRA); *Harris v. Garner*, 190 F.3d 1279, 1286 (11th Cir. 1999) ("reaffirm[ing] that *section 1997e(a)* imposes a mandatory requirement on prisoners seeking judicial relief to exhaust their administrative remedies" before filing suit in federal court), *modified on other grounds*, 216 F.3d 970 (11th Cir. 2000) (en banc); *Miller v. Tanner*, 196 F.3d 1190, 1193 (11th Cir. 1999) (holding that under the PLRA's amendments to ~ 1997e(a), "[a]n inmate incarcerated in a state prison . . . must first comply with the grievance procedures established by the state department of corrections before filing a federal lawsuit under *section 1983*"); *Harper v. Jenkin*, 179 F.3d 1311, 1312 (11th Cir. 1999) (per curiam) (affirming dismissal of prisoner's civil suit for failure to satisfy the mandatory exhaustion requirements of ~ 1997e(a)); *Alexander v. Hawk*, 159 F.3d 1321, 1328 (11th Cir. 1998) (affirming dismissal of prisoner's *Bivens* action under ~ 1997e(a) for failure to exhaust administrative remedies prior to filing suit in federal court).

Leal v. Ga. Dep't of Corr., 254 F.3d 1276, 1279 (11th Cir. 2001). The court has, therefore, determined that "the question of exhaustion under the PLRA [is] a 'threshold matter' that [federal courts must] address before considering the merits of the case. *Chandler v. Crosby*, 379 F.3d 1278, 1286 (11th Cir. 2004). Because exhaustion is mandated by the statute, [a court has] no discretion to waive this requirement. *Alexander v. Hawk*, 159 F.3d 1321, 1325-26 (11th Cir. 1998)." *Myles v. Miami-Dade Cnty. Corr. and Rehab. Dep't*, 476 F. App'x 364, 366 (11th Cir. 2012). The court will "resolve this issue first." *Id.*

When deciding whether a prisoner has exhausted his remedies, the court should first consider the plaintiff's and the defendants' versions of the facts, and if they conflict, take the plaintiff's version of the facts as true. "If in that light, the defendant is entitled to have the complaint dismissed for failure to exhaust administrative remedies, it must be dismissed." *Turner v. Burnside*, 541 F.3d 1077, 1082 (11th Cir.2008) (citing *Bryant*, 530 F.3d at 1373-74). If the complaint is not subject to dismissal at this step, then the court should make "specific findings in order to resolve the disputed factual issues related to exhaustion." *Id.* (citing *Bryant*, 530 F.3d at 1373-74, 1376).

Myles, 476 F. App'x at 366. A district court

may resolve disputed factual issues where necessary to the disposition of a motion to dismiss for failure to exhaust [without a hearing]. *See [Turner, 541 F.3d at 1082]*. The judge properly may consider facts outside of the pleadings to resolve a factual dispute as to exhaustion where doing so does not decide the merits, and the parties have a sufficient opportunity to develop the record. *Bryant, 530 F.3d at 1376*.

Trias, 587 F. App'x at 535.

Upon review of the complaint, Defendants' special report, and the evidentiary materials filed in support thereof, the court concludes that Defendants' motion to dismiss is due to be granted.

II. DISCUSSION

Plaintiff challenges the adequacy of medical care received at the Staton Correctional Facility for a heart condition. *Doc. No. 1*. In response to the complaint, Defendants deny that they provided Plaintiff with constitutionally inadequate medical care and argue this case is subject to dismissal because Plaintiff failed to exhaust the administrative remedy provided by the institutional medical care provider prior to filing this complaint as required by the Prison Litigation Reform Act, *42 U.S.C. § 1997e(a). Doc. No. 13, Sagers-Copeland Affidavit, Exh. A.* As explained, federal law directs this court to treat Defendants' response as a motion to dismiss for failure to exhaust an administrative remedy and allows the court to look beyond the pleadings to relevant evidentiary materials in deciding the issue of proper exhaustion. *Bryant, 530 F.3d at 1375.*

The Prison Litigation Reform Act compels exhaustion of available administrative remedies before a prisoner can seek relief in federal court on a ˜ 1983 complaint. Specifically, *42 U.S.C.* ˜ *1997e(a)* states that "[n]o action shall be brought with respect to prison conditions under *section 1983* of this title, or any other Federal law, by a prisoner confined in any jail, prison, or other correctional facility until such administrative remedies as are available are exhausted." "Congress has provided in ˜ *1997e(a)* that an inmate must exhaust irrespective of the forms of relief sought and offered through administrative remedies." *Booth v. Churner, 532 U.S. 731, 741 n.6, 121 S. Ct. 1819, 149 L. Ed. 2d 958 (2001).* "[T]he PLRA's exhaustion requirement applies to all inmate suits about prison life, whether they involve general circumstances or particular episodes, and whether they allege excessive force or some other wrong." *Porter v. Nussle, 534 U.S. 516, 532, 122 S. Ct. 983, 152 L. Ed. 2d 12 (2002).* Exhaustion of all available administrative remedies is a precondition to litigation and a federal court cannot waive the exhaustion requirement. *Booth, 532 U.S. at 741; Alexander, 159 F.3d at 1325; Woodford v. Ngo, 548 U.S. 81, 126 S. Ct. 2378, 165 L. Ed. 2d 368 (2006).* Moreover, "the PLRA exhaustion requirement requires proper exhaustion." *Id. at 93.*

Proper exhaustion demands compliance with an agency's deadlines and other critical procedural rules [as a precondition to filing suit in federal court] because no adjudicative system can function effectively without imposing some orderly structure on the courts of its proceedings . . . . Construing ˜ *1997e(a)* to require proper exhaustion . . . fits with the general scheme of the PLRA, whereas [a contrary] interpretation [allowing an inmate to bring suit in federal court once administrative remedies are no longer available] would turn that provision into a largely useless appendage.

Id. at 90-91, 93. The Supreme Court reasoned that because proper exhaustion of administrative remedies is necessary an inmate cannot "satisfy the Prison Litigation Reform Act's exhaustion requirement . . . by filing an untimely or otherwise procedurally defective administrative grievance or appeal[,]" or by effectively bypassing the administrative process simply by waiting until the grievance procedure is no longer available to her. *Id. at 83-84; Bryant, 530 F3d at 1378* (quoting *Johnson v. Meadows, 418 F3d 1152, 1158 (11th Cir. 2005)* ("To exhaust administrative remedies in accordance with the PLRA, prisoners must 'properly take each step within the administrative process.'"); *Johnson, 418 F.3d at 1157* (inmate who files an untimely grievance or spurns the administrative process until it is no longer available fails to satisfy the exhaustion requirement of the PLRA); *Higginbottom, 223 F.3d at 1261* (inmate's belief that administrative procedures are futile or needless does not excuse the exhaustion requirement). "The only facts pertinent to determining whether a prisoner has satisfied the PLRA's exhaustion requirement are those that existed when he filed his original complaint." *Smith v. Terry, 491 F. App'x 81, 83 (11th Cir. 2012)* (per curiam).

The record is undisputed that the health care provider for the Alabama Department of Corrections provides a grievance procedure for inmate complaints related to the provision of medical treatment. *Doc. No. 13, Sagers-Copeland Affidavit.* Defendants submitted evidence which reflects that when inmates are processed into the custody of the Alabama Department of Corrections they are informed of the process and procedure for obtaining medical care and medication and are also educated about the availability of the medical grievance process whereby they may voice complaints regarding any medical treatment sought or received during their incarceration. *Id.* Inmate grievance forms are available to inmates at Staton to submit a grievance related to the provision of health care, inmate grievances are answered within approximately ten days of receipt of the grievance, and the inmate grievance form provides information about how an inmate may appeal the response he receives to his initial inmate grievance. *Id.* A written response to a formal grievance appeal is provided in approximately ten days of receipt. *Id.* Inmates are provided with a copy of the completed grievance and/or grievance appeal containing the health service administrator's response. *Id.* Defendants state Plaintiff has submitted no medical grievances or medical grievance appeals of any kind nor did he ever request any assistance in notifying the Staton medical staff of any complaints, concerns or grievances he possessed relative to the medical care he has received at Staton. *Id.; Exh. A.*

The court granted Plaintiff an opportunity to respond to the exhaustion defense raised by Defendants in their motion to dismiss but he did not do so. *Doc. No. 17.* The court, therefore, finds that a grievance system is available at Staton for Plaintiff's claims, but he failed to exhaust the administrative remedy available to him. Plaintiff does not dispute his failure to submit any grievances related to the provision of his medical care at Staton, and the unrefuted record before the court demonstrates he failed to properly exhaust an administrative remedy available to him at Staton regarding his allegation of inadequate medical care prior to seeking federal relief, a precondition to proceeding in this court on his claims. Any grievances filed after initiation of this federal cause of action have no bearing on Plaintiff's proper exhaustion of the administrative remedy provided by the facility's medical provider. *Terry, 491 F. App'x at 83.*

Accordingly, Defendants' motion seeking dismissal for Plaintiff's failure to exhaust available administrative remedies should be granted, and such dismissal should be without prejudice. *See Ngo, 548 U.S. at 87-94; Bryant, 530 F.3d at 1374-1375* (dismissal for failure to exhaust an administrative remedy when the remedy remains available is not an adjudication of the merits and is without prejudice); *Woodford, 548 U.S. at 87-94.*

JAMES COLEN #604910, PLAINTIFF, V. CORIZON MEDICAL SERVICES, ET AL., DEFENDANTS. CIVIL ACTION NO.: 14-12948 UNITED STATES DISTRICT COURT FOR THE EASTERN DISTRICT OF MICHIGAN, SOUTHERN DIVISION

I. BACKGROUND

Colen's claims stem from medical care related to an injury he sustained in 2010, when he allegedly broke his foot playing basketball. When he was first evaluated by defendant Rogers, he was diagnosed with a sprain and given an ace bandage. [R. 13, PgID 82]. Over the next two and a half years, he continually kited various medical providers for assistance for increasing pain in his foot, swelling, and new pain in his knee, but he was told that his pain was either a sprain or simply arthritis and he was given minimal care. X-rays taken much later revealed knee deterioration requiring replacement, arthritis, and an old foot fracture that had not healed properly. [*Id.,* PgID 83-92]. Colen had knee replacement surgery in 2014, but continued to experience foot pain that remained untreated. [*Id.* 93-94].

Colen's amended complaint alleges that the MDOC Defendants' conduct violated his *Eighth* and *Fourteenth Amendment* rights, and constituted intentional infliction of emotional distress and gross negligence. [R. 13]. The MDOC Defendants now move for summary judgment, alleging that Colen failed to properly exhaust his administrative remedies. This Court disagrees.

III. ANALYSIS

Colen filed five arguably relevant grievances between April and October 2013, but the Court will address only one because it is dispositive. In grievance ARF-13-09-2586-12d1, Colen addressed the entire medical history that gave rise to his amended complaint, stating, "I am continually being denied medical treatment for the injury sustained on my foot where I have broken bones and torn ligaments which have worsened over the last two years." [*Id.,* PgID 323]. He emphasized, "I have tried unsuccessfully to resolve my condition with the Health care staff, and the Adrian Administration. Nothing is being done to correct my foot, knee and leg, and I am in excruciating pain." [*Id.*]. He alleged that "Health Care and the Adrian Staff are being deliberately indifferent by purposefully ignoring my request [to see a specialist and receive injections] and ailment." [*Id.*]. MDOC resolved this grievance on its merits. [*Id.,* PgID 320-22]. In fact, MDOC informed Colen on January 31, 2014, that its denial of this Step III grievance represented an exhaustion of his administrative remedies. [*Id.,* PgID 320].

Nonetheless, the MDOC defendants now argue that grievance ARF-13-09-2586-12d1 was not properly exhausted because Colen did not specify the names of those involved, in violation of MDOC policy. [R. 40, PgID

297]. But, that argument was rejected by the Sixth Circuit in *Reed-Bey v. Pramstaller, 603 F.3d 322, 324-25 (6th Cir. 2010)*, because the state failed to follow its own procedural rule requiring the prisoner to name those involved, and instead decided the otherwise defaulted claims on the merits. "When prison officials decline to enforce their own procedural requirements and opt to consider <u>otherwise-defaulted claims on the merits, so as a</u> general rule will we." *Id. at 325*.

Since MDOC decided grievance ARF-13-09-2586-12d1 on its merits, in disregard for the requirement that he name all those involved, this Court should decide the merits of his claims, too.

DAVID WILSON (ADC#138042), PLAINTIFF V. DON NELSON, CORIZON LLC, JAMES PRATT, JOHN HAROLD AND JIM MCLEAN, DEFENDANTS CIVIL NO. 6:13-CV-06036 UNITED STATES DISTRICT COURT FOR THE WESTERN DISTRICT OF ARKANSAS, HOT SPRINGS DIVISION

(SEE DISCUSSION UNDER MEDICAL CARE)

I. BACKGROUND

During the time at issue here Plaintiff was incarcerated in the Arkansas Department of Corrections Diagnostic Unit in Pine Bluff ("Diagnostic Unit") and the Ouachita River Unit in Malvern, Arkansas ("ORU"). Plaintiff filed his Complaint in the Eastern District of Arkansas on March 29, 2013. ECF. No. 2. His Complaint was transferred to this District on April 15, 2013 after the ADC was dismissed as a Defendant. ECF. No. 3.

In his Complaint, Plaintiff named Don Nelson (ADC Head of Construction), Corizon, James Pratt (Corizon employee), John Harold (ADC Construction Supervisor), and Jim McLean (ADC Construction Supervisor). ECF No. 1. On October 29, 2013, the Court ordered service on the Medical Defendants in care of the law firm Humphries and Lewis, and the ADC Defendants in care of the Arkansas Board of Correction. ECF No. 9. Humphries and Lewis accepted service on behalf of Corizon, Inc. but declined to accept service for James Pratt, as he had been terminated from Corizon on August 22, 2013. ECF No. 11. Subsequently,   the Court ordered James Pratt to be served at the address provided by Humphries and Lewis. ECF No. 24. Humphries, Odum, and Eubanks[1] subsequently filed a Notice of Appearance on behalf of both Corizon and James Pratt. ECF No. 22, 38.

1   It appears that this is the same law firm, as the address of PO Box 20670, White Hall, AR is used consistently despite the changes in named partners.

In his Complaint, Plaintiff alleges his *Eighth Amendment* right to be free from cruel and unusual punishment were violated in relation to back, arm, hip, and knee injuries he suffered when he fell through a prison barracks ceiling while doing electrical work on his ADC job assignment.

III. DISCUSSION

Plaintiff argues the ADC Defendants failed to properly train and supervise him, resulting in his fall and injuries. He argues the Medical Defendants repeatedly delayed or denied medical care after he was injured.

The ADC Defendants argue Summary Judgment should be granted as to Plaintiff's claims against them because he failed to file a grievance against them, his claim is based on the theory of respondeat superior, and his claims are barred by both qualified and sovereign immunity. ECF No. 61. The Medical Defendants argue Summary Judgment should be granted as to Plaintiff's claims against them because Plaintiff did not exhaust his claims against Corizon, James Pratt had no direct involvement or authority in the medical consultation process, and his claim fails as a matter of law because he was treated for those conditions deemed medically necessary. ECF Nos. 91, 92.

A. Plaintiff Failed to Exhaust His Administrative Remedies Against The ADC Defendants

The Prison Litigation Reform Act ("PLRA"), mandates exhaustion of available administrative remedies before and inmate files suit. *Section 1997e(a)* of the PLRA provides: "[n]o action shall be brought with respect to prison conditions under *section 1983* of this title, or any other Federal law, by a prisoner confined in any jail, prison, or other correctional facility until such administrative remedies as are available are exhausted." *42 U.S. C. § 1997e(a)*.

In *Jones v. Bock, 549 U.S. 199, 127 S. Ct. 910, 166 L. Ed. 2d 798 (2007)*, the Supreme Court concluded that "exhaustion [as required by the PLRA] is not *per se* inadequate simply because an individual later sued was not named in the grievances." *Id. at 219*. "[T]o properly exhaust administrative remedies prisoners must complete the administrative review process in accordance with the applicable procedural rules." *Id. at 218* (internal quotation marks and citation omitted). The

Court stated that the "level of detail necessary in a grievance to comply with the grievance procedures will vary from system to system and claim to claim, but it is the prison's requirements, and not the PLRA, that define the boundaries of proper exhaustion." *Id.*

In this case, Plaintiff admits that he never filed a grievance against the ADC Defendants. He argues that he did not do so because the Administrative Directive 09-01, section III G, 4 states that job assignments are non-grievable. ECF No. 90-10.

This section does state that a number of matters are not grievable:

1. Parole;

2. Release;

3. Transfer;

4. Job assignments unless in conflict with medical restrictions;

5. Disiplinaries;

6. Anticipated Events (i.e. events or activities which may or may not occur in the future);

7. Matters beyond the control of the Department of Correction, including issues controlled by State or Federal law or regulation.

AD 12-16.III.G. Items that are grievable include:

1. A policy applicable within his or her unit/center of assignment that personally affects the inmate;

2. A condition in the facility that personally affects the inmate;

3. An action involving an inmate(s) of his or her facility that personally affects the inmate;

4. An action of an employee(s), contractor(s), or volunteer(s) at his or her facility that personally affects the inmate;

5. An incident occurring within his her facility that personally affects the inmate.

AD 12-16.III.B. Reading these two provisions together, it is clear from the plain language of this policy that an inmate is prevented from grieving exactly what work assignment he or she may receive, unless the assignment conflicts with medical restrictions. It does not prevent an inmate from grieving an injury that he or she believes was the result of a faulty policy, action, condition, or incident simply because it occurred during a work assignment.

Nor does Plaintiff's subjective belief that he could not grieve the incident excuse his failure to exhaust his Administrative remedies against these Defendants. The Eighth Circuit has repeatedly held that a court is not permitted "to consider an inmate's merely subjective beliefs, logical or otherwise, in determining whether administrative procedures are "available.'" *Lyon v. Vande Krol, 305 F.3d 806, 809 (8th Cir. 2002)*(citing *Chelette v. Harris, 229 F.3d 684, 688 (8th Cir.2000), cert. denied, 531 U.S. 1156, 121 S. Ct. 1106, 148 L. Ed. 2d 977 (2001))*.

Because Plaintiff did not exhaust his Administrative remedies against the ADC Defendants his claim against them is barred by *Section 1997e(a)* of the PLRA.

B. Plaintiff Failed to Exhaust His Administrative Remedies Against Corizon

Corizon argues Plaintiff failed to exhaust his administrative remedies against them because he did not explicitly name the company in his grievances and that, despite delays, Plaintiff ultimately received all medically necessary treatment. Because Plaintiff failed to name Corizon in the grievances exhausted before he filed his complaint, he failed to exhaust his Administrative remedies against the company.

The Eighth Circuit has held "the PLRA's exhaustion requirement is satisfied if prison officials decide a procedurally flawed grievance on the merits." *Hammett v. Cofield, 681 F.3d 945, 947 (8th Cir. 2012)*. In *Hammett*, Plaintiff's grievance appeals were untimely, but otherwise complete. Therefore, the Court reasoned that the policies underlying the exhaustion requirement were met when the institution waived the procedural timing requirements and instead decided the claims on the merits. *Id.* Specifically, the Court noted that the benefits of exhaustion: are fully realized when an inmate pursues the prison grievance process to its final stage and receives an adverse decision on the merits, even if the decision-maker could have declined to reach the merits because of one or more procedural deficiencies. A complete administrative record exists, and a reviewing court will have the benefit of the agency's institutional perspective. This rule also takes into account the likelihood that prison officials will benefit if given discretion to decide, for reasons such as fairness or inmate morale or the need to resolve a recurring issue, that ruling on the merits is better for the institution and an inmate who has attempted to exhaust available prison remedies.

Id. at 947-48.

Failure to name a party is more than a "mere procedural flaw" when it prevents the agency from fully addressing the merits of the grievance and thereby defeats the purpose of the exhaustion requirement. *Burns v. Eaton, 752 F. 3d 1136, 1141 (8th Cir.2014).* In *Burns,* the Plaintiff failed to name an officer in a grievance about an incident, and his amended complaint about that incident later added facts not in the original incident grievance against that second officer. *Id.* Although the prison had decided the greivance on the merits, the Court of Appeals held that the failure to name the second officer rendered it "completely unexhausted" against that second officer because although the officers were both involved in the incident, "they had different responsibilities and took different actions." *Id.* "Thus, this was not a case where prison officials declined to enforce their own procedural requirements and opted to consider otherwise-defaulted claims on the merits. *Id.* (internal quotations omitted)(quoting *Reed-Bey v. Pramstaller, 603 F.3d 322, 325 (6th Cir.2010)).* "Rather, the amended complaint against [the second officer] asserted a new greivance . . . completely unexhausted." *Id. at 1141-42.* (internal quotations omitted.). Therefore, the policy concerns underlying the exhaustion requirement were not met.

Several later unpublished Eighth Circuit cases by different panels, while not binding on this Court, appear at first glance to be split over whether failure to name is always more than a "mere procedural flaw." *See Morrow v. Kelley, 2013 U.S. Dist. LEXIS 173437, 2013 WL 6500616 (E.D. Ark Dec. 11, 2013)* for discussion of these cases. However: overwhelming recent precedent has harmonized these Eighth Circuit opinions by focusing on whether - despite the procedural flaw- prison officials reached and decided the merits of the specific claims asserted against each defendant. To make that determination, the Court must look beyond the prisoner's grievances and examine the issues that the prison officials reviewed and decided during the administrative appeal process. This approach is consistent with the *Hammett* opinion and the purposes of the PLRA's exhaustion requirement.

Colten v. Hobbs, 2014 U.S. Dist. LEXIS 42090, 2014 WL 1309069 (E.D. Ark. Mar. 28, 2014)(internal quotations omitted)(quoting *Morrow, 2013 U.S. Dist. LEXIS 173437, 2013 WL 6500616 (E.D.Ark. Dec. 11, 2013)* and citing *Jones v. Bond, 2013 U.S. Dist. LEXIS 171490, 2013 WL 6332681 (E.D.Ark. Dec. 5, 2013); Hooper v. Kelley, 2013 U.S. Dist. LEXIS 155522, 2013 WL 5881613 (E.D.Ark. Oct. 30, 2013); Scott v. Burl, 2013 U.S. Dist. LEXIS 183431, 2013 WL 5522404 (E.D.Ark. Oct. 1, 2013); Wallace v. Warner, 2013 U.S. Dist. LEXIS 140668, 2013 WL 5531280 (E.D.Ark. Sept. 30, 2013)).* Using this approach, "the Courts have consistently dismissed named defendants who were not otherwise identified in exhausted grievances, either by their names, descriptions of their positions, or the conduct which led to the complaint at issues. *Leggett v. Corizon, Inc., 2014 U.S. Dist. LEXIS 147916, 2014 WL 5325170 (E.D. Ark. Oct. 17, 2014).*

In this case, the record shows Plaintiff completed the grievance process for three grievances prior to filing his complaint. ECF. Nos. 69-1, 70-1-56.)These are OR-12-1350. OR-12-1408, and OR-12-1580. ECF Nos. 69-7, ECF 70-1-56.

OR-12-1350 was filed on October 10, 2012. ECF No. 70-57. It concerned the delay in getting a post-MRI followup on his hip, and named Mr. Pratt. It did not name Corizon. Therefore it will be discussed below in the section for Mr. Pratt.

OR-12-1408 was filed on October 25, 2102. ECF No. 70-60. It concerned the fact that another inmate's medical information was in his medical jacket. He wanted to be able to review his own medical information and was concerned about other inmates seeing his information. It did not name Corizon or any specific personnel. The response on October 19, 2012 apologized for the misfiling, and instructed Plaintiff to file a new request to review his records.

OR-12-1580 was filed on December 18, 2012. ECF 70-1-61. This grievance stated "I have repeatedly not been seen and/or received the needed medical treatment in a timely manner since I fell on Construction and broke my right hip, hurt my right knee, and fractured my right elbow on 4-7-10." *Id.* The first response to this greivance was dated January 15, 2013, the day before he saw orthopedic surgeon Dr. Crowell on January 16 for his MRI followup and was informed that he needed a hip replacement. This grievance was found to be without merit. Specifically, it stated that "you have been seen for this issue in sick call and by a provider. You currently are scheduled to see an orthopedic provider on 1/16/2013. Your grievance is without merit." *Id.* Plaintiff appealed on January 17, 2013. He repeats that he has not been seen and/or received treatment in a timely manner for his injuries, provided several time delay examples, and that Dr. Crowell told him that his hip now needs to be replaced - "hopefully in a timely manner." It did not name Corizon or any specific personnel. On March 11, 2013, his appeal was found to be without merit, noting that he had received a hip replacement on February 22, 2013.

The appeal notice also states "you must be specific as to the substance of the issue, including the date, the staff involved, place, and witnesses. . . .You did not grieve a specific incident or provide dates within the time frame allowed by policy." *Id.* at 63.

Because Plaintiff did not name Corizon in these grievances, and further did not provide sufficient detail as required by policy, he failed to exhaust his Administrative remedies as to Corizon. Although the grievances did proceed through the greivance appeals process, the failure to name and to provide sufficient detail on the grievances prevented the agency from fully addressing the merits of the grievance, thereby defeating the purpose of the exhaustion requirement.

<u>C. Plaintiff Fully Exhausted His Claim Against James Pratt</u>

Plaintiff did name James Pratt in OR--12-1350, filed on October 12, 2012. In this greivance he stated that:

I received an MRI of my right hip on 7-25-12 and I was told that I should be seen within two weeks . On 8-7-12 I was seen at sick call and was told that they would check on this matter. On 8-20-2012 I sent Mr. Pratt a request to check on this matter. On 9-4-12 I sent Mr. Pratt another request on this matter. I was seen at sick call on 9-18-12 and was told that they would check on this matter. I would like to know when I will be seen by Dr. Crowell to discuss the results of the MRI that was taken of my right hip.

ECF No. 70-57.

On November 2, 2012, Mr. Pratt signed a health services response which stated:

Ms. McGrath did review your MRI results and has submitted a consult to Dr. Crowell. There was not enough information present to approve the consult. The request was returned to Ms. McGrath. Ms. McGrath met with you on 10/25/12 and prescribed medications to address any problems your knee may be causing you. Your greivance is with merit but resolved. If you have any other problems with your knee drop a sick call request so the nurses can get you back to see Ms. McGrath.

ECF No. 70-58.

On November 6, 2012 Plaintiff appealed the response stating:

I disagree with this decision because I have not been seen by Dr. Crowell for a consult to discuss the results of the MRI that was taken on 7-27-12 on my right hip as the greivance states. I do not understand why being seen by Ms. Graft [sic] and being prescribed medications to address my pain I have with my knee stops me from being seen by Dr. Crowell to discuss the results of the MRI on my right Hip that Dr. Crowell ordered and I received on 7-27-12.

ECF No. 70-58.

On December 28, 2012 this appeal was found to be "with merit" "due to the delays." ECF No. 70-59.

Thus, it is clear that Plaintiff fully exhausted his Administrative remedies against Mr. Pratt for this grievance.

SHAWN HODGES, PLAINTIFF, V. CORIZON, CORIZON OF MICHIGAN, PRISON HEALTH SERVICES, INC., HARRIET A. SQUIER, M.D., ASTER BERHANE, M.D., JOSHUA A. BUSKIRK, P.A., DANIEL A. HEYNS, AND GEORGE PRAMSTALLER, DEFENDANTS. CIVIL ACTION NO. 14-11837 UNITED STATES DISTRICT COURT FOR THE EASTERN DISTRICT OF MICHIGAN, SOUTHERN DIVISION

2. The Corizon Defendants Have Not Met Their Burden on Exhaustion

Next, the Corizon Defendants argue that, with respect to his claims against Dr. Squier, Dr. Berhane, and P.A. Buskirk, Hodges failed to properly exhaust his administrative remedies, as required by the Prison Litigation Reform Act ("PLRA"), 42 U.S.C. §1997e(a). (Id. at 14-18).

a. The Applicable Law and Grievance Procedure

Under the PLRA, a prisoner may not bring an action, "under [§1983] or any other Federal law," to challenge his conditions of confinement until all available administrative remedies have been exhausted. 42 U.S.C. §1997e(a); Woodford v. Ngo, 548 U.S. 81, 85, 126 S. Ct. 2378, 165 L. Ed. 2d 368 (2006) . This "exhaustion" requirement serves two main purposes: it promotes efficiency by encouraging the resolution of claims at the agency level before litigation is commenced, and it protects administrative authority by allowing the agency an opportunity to correct its own mistakes before being haled into federal court. See Woodford, 548 U.S. at 89. The Supreme Court has held that this "exhaustion requirement requires proper exhaustion." Id. at 93. Proper exhaustion requires "compliance with an agency's deadlines and other critical procedural rules." Id. at 90. Failure to exhaust is an affirmative defense that must be raised by a defendant, and on which the defendant bears the burden of proof. See Jones v. Bock, 549 U.S. 199, 216, 127 S. Ct. 910, 166 L. Ed. 2d 798 (2007); Vandiver v. Corr. Med. Servs., Inc., 326 F. App'x 885, 888 (6th Cir. 2009).

In determining whether a plaintiff has properly exhausted his claim, the only relevant rules "are defined not by the PLRA, but by the prison grievance process itself." Jones, 549 U.S. at 200. In Michigan's correctional facilities, prisoner grievances are governed by MDOC Policy Directive 03.02.130 ("Prisoner/Parolee Grievances"). (Doc. #14-2). A state prisoner must first complete the process outlined in the Policy - including pursuing a grievance through "all three steps of the grievance process" - before he can file a lawsuit challenging the alleged unlawful conduct. (Id. at ¶B). If the prisoner cannot resolve his dispute with the staff member involved, he has five business days to file a Step I grievance. (Id. at ¶¶P, V). "Information provided [in the Step I grievance] is to be limited to the facts involving the issue being grieved (i.e., who, what, when, where, why, how). Dates, times, places, and names of all those involved in the issue being grieved are to be included." (Id. at ¶R). If the prisoner is dissatisfied with the Step I response, he may submit a Grievance Appeal to the Step II Grievance Coordinator within ten business days after receipt of the Step I response, or if no timely response is received, within ten business days of the date the response was due. (Id. at ¶BB). If the grievant is dissatisfied with, or does not receive, a Step II response, he has ten business days within which to file a final appeal at Step III. (Id. at ¶FF). Again, an inmate may only pursue a claim in court if he has complied with his obligations at each of these three steps. (Id. at ¶B).

b. The Key Grievances Filed by Hodges

After thoroughly reviewing the documents attached to Hodges' complaint, as well as those submitted by the Corizon Defendants as attachments to their reply brief, it is apparent that Hodges filed numerous grievances between the time he injured his right wrist (in November 2010) and the filing of his complaint in this case (in May 2014). With respect to Dr. Squier, Dr. Berhane, and P.A. Buskirk, the Corizon Defendants focus on three grievances - Grievance Nos. SRF-2011-11-1630-12D1 (the "SRF Grievance"), JCF-2012-01-0127-28G (the "JCF Grievance"), and LMF-2012-02-0450-28E (the "LMF Grievance") - and argue that none of these grievances was properly exhausted. (Doc. #14 at 16). Thus, in order to determine whether Hodges' claims against Dr. Squier, Dr. Berhane, and P.A. Buskirk are properly exhausted, a thorough examination of these grievances is required.[5]

5   In his response brief, Hodges also mentions Grievance No. JCF-2013-09-1592-12E2. (Doc. #22 at 13). In this grievance, Hodges asserted that his Special Accommodation Notices - pertaining to a bottom bunk, extra bedding, etc. - were expiring and "JCF Medical staff" and Corizon were not "promptly making sure" he did not suffer. (Doc. #24-5 at 26). Because the incidents described in this grievance are not at issue in this lawsuit, however, the fact that Hodges pursued this grievance to Step III does not serve to exhaust any of the claims in his complaint.

(1) The Grievances Highlighted by the Corizon Defendants

(a) The SRF Grievance

In the SRF Grievance, dated November 10, 2011, Hodges makes numerous allegations about the medical care he did and did not receive related to his wrist. While it is true that most of his complaints in that grievance seem to relate to the alleged failure to treat his broken wrist in late 2010, rather than the failure to provide radiation treatment for his tumor in late 2011, importantly, the grievance does specifically challenge the delayed radiation for the tumor in his hand. (Doc. #1-5 at 2-3). Hodges, after specifically referencing that "in August 2011 the Doctor told me that I had a Tumor in my hand and in September of 2011, the Doctor told me that I had [a malignant form of cancer]," stated, "I am now at a very critical stage in which I need medical attention A.S.A.P. ..." (Id.) (emphasis added). Indeed, the grievance respondent summarized Hodges' Step I grievance as follows (in pertinent part): "I had an MRI & CT Scan & surgery in August & I was told I had a tumor in my hand. The doctor told me I had cancer cells. Because PA Buskirk denied me urgent medical treatment & I waited 5 months, I am now at a critical stage." (Doc. #24-5 at 97).

In responding to this Step I grievance, RN Alton reviewed Hodges' electronic medical record and summarized the care he was provided at SRF between November 2010 and September 2011 (when he was transferred to Alger Correctional Facility ("LMF")). (Id. at 97-98). RN Alton concluded that there "was no evidence of denied medical treatment" and denied the SRF Grievance at Step I. (Id.). In his Step II appeal, Hodges reiterated that he was challenging P.A. Buskirk's alleged refusal to act on Dr. Haverbush's "recommendation for radiation after surgery in my hand as right now had (PVNS) with malign[ant] giant cell tumor and cancer." (Doc. #1-5 at 7). Hodges further clarified, "all this time since surgery I am [being denied] radiation at SRF by Buskirk, P.A. ...." (Id.). In RN Lamb's Step II response, however, Hodges was advised that there was no evidence that he was denied urgent treatment following his wrist injury. (Doc. #24-5 at 94). With respect to Hodges' allegation that P.A. Buskirk was denying him radiation, the grievance response indicated, "New issues[6] raised at Step II Appeal will not be addressed in this response." (Id.). Hodges subsequently filed a Step III appeal, which was denied, this time on the basis that: (a) Hodges originally grieved P.A. Buskirk's failure to respond to his letters - as opposed to his failure to provide medical treatment - and Buskirk was not required by policy to do so; and (b) the grievance was untimely, as it was dated November 10, 2011 but referred in "the body of his grievance [to] issues from November 2010," and Hodges had not "provided reasoning for the substantial delays."[7] (Doc. #24-5 at 92).

6   As discussed in the preceding paragraph, Hodges' complaint about being denied the recommended radiation treatment was not a "new issue" presented for the first time at Step II of the grievance process.

7   There is an inherent inconsistency in these two bases for denying the grievance: if Hodges actually was grieving P.A. Buskirk's failure to respond to his letters, as the Step III grievance response concluded, then he was not challenging "issues from November 2010."

In their motion, the Corizon Defendants argue that the SRF Grievance was not properly exhausted because it was rejected on procedural grounds as untimely. (Doc. #14 at 16). The applicable Policy Directive provides that a "Step I grievance must be filed within five business days after the grievant attempted to resolve the issue with appropriate staff." (Doc. #14-2 at ¶P). However, under the MDOC's own grievance policy, although a grievance "may be rejected" if "filed in an untimely manner," it "shall not be rejected if there is a valid reason for the delay, e.g., transfer." (Id. at ¶G(3) (emphasis added)). Here, the SRF Grievance was deemed untimely because Hodges had purportedly not "provided reasoning for the substantial delays." (Doc. #24-5 at 92). There are several problems with this conclusion, however.

First, looking only at the face of Hodges' grievance, it is not at all clear that this grievance was untimely, as Hodges grieved in part P.A. Buskirk's failure to respond to a letter dated November 7, 2011 (just three days before the date of the grievance). (Doc. #1-4 at 67). It also addressed the denial of the radiation treatment which had been recommended only a few months prior to Hodges' submission of the grievance. Moreover, the fact that the SRF Grievance was not rejected at Steps I or II of the grievance process further calls into question the Corizon Defendants' timeliness argument (as does the fact that the "MDOC Prisoner Step III Grievance Report" attached to the Corizon Defendants' reply brief indicates that this grievance was "Denied" at Step III, not "Rejected"). (Doc. #24-5 at 7).

But, even assuming that the SRF Grievance was untimely, the Step III contention that Hodges failed to "provide reasoning" for any delay in its filing is inaccurate. Indeed, Hodges explained in the grievance that he had undergone surgery and been diagnosed with PVNS, and it was apparent from the MDOC records that he had been transferred between facilities more than once in the intervening time period. Both of these facts could have provided a valid explanation for any delay in filing the SRF Grievance, had they been considered. See, e.g., Boling v. Corr. Med. Servs.., 2007 U.S. Dist. LEXIS 80479, 2007 WL 3203133, at *5 (E.D. Mich. Oct. 31, 2007) (hospital stay and medical condition were valid reasons for delay in filing grievance); Coleman v. Gullet, 2013 U.S. Dist. LEXIS 81885, 2013 WL 2634581, at *11 (E.D. Mich. June 10, 2013) (plaintiff's transfer was conceivably a valid reason for the delay in appealing a grievance).[8]

8   Additionally, the SRF Grievance was addressed - to some extent, at least - on the merits at Steps I, II, and III. Courts have held that, under certain circumstances, procedural objections to timeliness can be waived where a grievance is addressed on the merits. See, e.g., Christian v. Michigan Dep't of Corr. - Health Servs., 2013 U.S. Dist. LEXIS 136311, 2013 WL 5348832, at *5 (Sept. 24, 2013) ("[W]hen the prison elects to address a grievance on the merits rather than invoke a procedural bar to the grievance, the prisoner has exhausted his claim.") (quoting Allen v. Shawney, 2013 U.S. Dist. LEXIS 80822, 2013 WL 2480658, at *4 (E.D. Mich. June 20, 2013)); Flentall v. Lange, 2011 U.S. Dist. LEXIS 27695, 2011 WL 1045443, at *4 (W.D. Mich. Jan. 31, 2011).

In sum, resolving all reasonable inferences in Hodges' favor, as must be done at the motion to dismiss stage, the Corizon Defendants fail to satisfy their burden of proof on this affirmative defense, and the Court cannot conclude that Hodges failed to exhaust the SRF Grievance against P.A. Buskirk.

(b) The JCF Grievance

On or about October 25, 2011, Hodges was transferred from LMF to the G. Robert Cotton Correctional Facility ("JCF") in Jackson, Michigan. (Doc. #1 at ¶¶126-27). Once there, Hodges filed the JCF Grievance on January 13, 2012, specifically asserting that, while he was incarcerated at LMF, Dr. Berhane "was denying/delaying requests for an off-site referral with an orthopedic specialist, acting alone or in concert with others." (Doc. #1-4 at 1). He also asserted that P.A. Buskirk delayed treating him following his November 2010 injury. (Id.). And, he alleged that "Dr. Berhaney (and the others) simply threw their hands up in the air, without trying to help me get further treatment [for] my wrist or the cancer." (Id.). The JCF grievance was rejected at Step I on January 17, 2012, because "JCF lacks jurisdiction over medical treatment at LMF." (Id. at 2). Hodges was further advised: "You may re-submit your complaint and send it to the Grievance Coordinator at LMF using ID Mail. However; JCF takes medical issues/complaints very seriously. Because of this, a copy of your complaint has been forwarded to the JCF HUM for review." (Id.). Although there is no clear evidence that Hodges resubmitted this grievance to LMF, there is at least some indication - based on a letter Hodges sent to the "JCF Mail Room, JCF Grievance Coordinator and ECF/DWH Mail Room" - that he attempted to do so. (Doc. #1-5 at 158). That letter provides as follows:

On January 27, 2012, I was admitted at the University of Michigan Hospital for a lung biopsy. I stayed there for roughly a day to day and a half and was then transported to [Duane Waters Health Center ("DWH")]. I was admitted to DWH until February 8, 2012, when I was discharged back to JCF.

During this period of time, I am certain a piece of interdepartmental (I.D.) mail was returned to my housing unit in error. As I was not in the housing unit, but had been admitted at the U of M, the mail was dropped back in the B Unit mail box. To this date, that white envelope, addressed to the grievance coordinator at Alger, has not found its way back to me.

If any mail was temporarily held during my transition from JCF to U of M, from U of M to DWH, then DWH to JCF, please forward it to me now. I am most grateful for your attention in this matter. (Id.). The Court has located no response to this letter in the record, nor does it appear that the JCF Grievance was pursued to Step II or Step III (and it is not listed on the "MDOC Prisoner Step III Grievance Report"). (Doc. #24-5 at 3-7).

In their motion, the Corizon Defendants argue that the JCF Grievance was properly rejected - and, thus, was not exhausted - because Hodges "submitted [it] to JCF staff, who lacked jurisdiction over grievances pertaining to SRF and LMF." (Doc. #14 at 16). Although this fact might be correct, it is not dispositive under the circumstances. From the contents of Hodges' letter quoted above, it appears to the Court that Hodges attempted to send this grievance to LMF and that, for some unexplained reason, it was neither accepted nor returned to him for further action. That Hodges apparently was in and out of two different hospitals during the relevant time period - during which time he learned that his cancer had metastasized to his lungs - certainly might explain some of the confusion surrounding re-submission of this grievance and, indeed, could have provided a "valid reason" for any delay in filing the grievance with LMF. Where the MDOC's own grievance policy provides that a grievance shall not be rejected if there is a valid reason for the delay (Doc. #14-2 at ¶G(3)), the Court cannot conclude that Hodges failed to exhaust the JCF Grievance against Dr. Berhane.

(c) The LMF Grievance

It appears that after Hodges learned that LMF had not received the JCF Grievance, he submitted the LMF Grievance. (Doc. #1-4 at 2). The LMF Grievance largely tracked the prior JCF Grievance. In the LMF Grievance, dated February 18, 2012, Hodges again asserted that, while he was incarcerated at LMF, Dr. Berhane delayed and/or denied "requests for off-site referral with an orthopedic specialist, acting alone or in concert with others." (Doc. #1-3 at 15). As with the JCF Grievance, Hodges also alleged that, "Dr. Berhane (and the others) simply threw their hands up in the air, without trying to help me get further treatment for my hand/wrist or the cancer therein." (Id.). The LMF Grievance was rejected as untimely at Step I, however, and Hodges was advised that the grievance investigation reveals that "you have exceeded your time limits in filing a grievance on issue(s) that concern you, and at the same time provided no reasonable circumstance beyond your control that would have prevented you from filing this grievance in a timely fashion." (Id. at 10; Doc. #24-5 at 90). Hodges submitted a Step II appeal, explaining that he had been taking medication for his wrist pain, which produced side effects (including drowsiness, difficulty focusing, etc.). (Doc. #1-3 at 6). He further indicated that he had only recently learned who was (at least partially) responsible for denying his requests for referral to a radiation oncologist and then had been hospitalized for a period of time. (Id. at 6-7). Hodges' appeal was denied at Step II because (1) investigation revealed that Hodges was "provided continuous medical care while at [LMF]" and there was "no evidence of deliberate indifference" to a serious medical need, and (2) the grievance was untimely.[9] (Id. at 21). Hodges appealed to Step III, again arguing that he should be "granted considerable leeway in pursuing medically related appeals," given the medication he was taking, the pain he was experiencing, and the other difficulties his condition presented. (Id. at 23). The grievance was denied at Step III. (Id. at 13).

9 As to the untimeliness rejection, the Step II response indicates that Hodges'"Step II Appeal was due to the Grievance Coordinator on 3/26/12; however it was not received until 4/2/12." (Doc. #1-3 at 21). Pursuant to applicable MDOC policy, however, "Grievances and grievance appeals at all steps shall be considered filed on the date sent by the grievant." (Doc. #14-2 at 5, ¶S). Here, Hodges' Step II appeal is dated March 21, 2012, and he indicates this appeal was mailed prior to the due date (March 26, 2012). The fact that Hodges was housed at JCF at the time his appeal was mailed to LMF may explain why it was not received at that facility until April 2, 2012. Thus, the evidence before the Court shows that Hodges' Step II appeal was timely filed pursuant to MDOC policy and should not have been rejected on timeliness grounds.

The Corizon Defendants argue that the LMF Grievance was properly rejected as untimely and, thus, was not properly exhausted. Again, however, the MDOC's own grievance policy provides that a grievance "shall not be rejected if there is a valid reason for the delay, e.g., transfer." (Doc. #14-2 at ¶G(3)). In this case, it does not appear that any consideration was given as to whether there was a valid reason for Hodges' delay in filing the grievance; rather, the Step I grievance response indicates only that Hodges "provided no reasonable circumstance beyond [his] control that would have prevented [him] from filing this grievance in a timely fashion." (Doc. #1-3 at 10).

In appealing this untimeliness rejection, however, Hodges provided multiple explanations for the delay in filing this grievance. For example, he mentioned his ongoing medical treatment and medication, which he indicated caused drowsiness and "prohibit[ed] focus." (Id. at 6). He also indicated that he had been delayed in obtaining the names of the staff to be included in the grievance. (Id.). Moreover, it bears keeping in mind that Hodges first filed a nearly-identical grievance at JCF in January 2012; this grievance was rejected because JCF "lack[ed] jurisdiction over medical treatment at LMF." (Doc. #1-4 at 2). It appears that Hodges then immediately attempted to send this grievance to LMF, as instructed, but for reasons outside his control - he was hospitalized for nearly two weeks after a lung biopsy - and other reasons not entirely clear, the grievance was not immediately sent to LMF. Thus, there is at least a question of fact as to whether this grievance was properly rejected at Step I as untimely, and, consequently, the Court cannot conclude that Hodges failed to exhaust the LMF Grievance against Dr. Berhane.

(d) Exhaustion as to Dr. Squier

In summary, a genuine issue of material fact exists as to whether Hodges properly exhausted the SRF Grievance, the JCF Grievance, and the LMF Grievance. These grievances name only P.A. Buskirk and Dr. Berhane, however, and the Corizon Defendants argue that Hodges' failure to specifically name Dr. Squier in these grievances bars his claims against her. (Doc. #14 at 17).

It is true that proper exhaustion of administrative remedies means "using all steps that the agency holds out, and doing so properly." Woodford, 548 U.S. at 90. And, the applicable MDOC Policy Directive provides that grievances must include "[d]ates, times, places, and names of all those involved in the issue being grieved." (Doc. #14-2 at ¶R). The Sixth Circuit, however, has cautioned courts against being too technical when deciding whether a prisoner's grievance has been properly exhausted. See LaFountain v. Martin, 334 Fed. Appx. 738, 2009 WL 1546376, at *2 (6th Cir. 2009) ("It is sufficient for a court to find that a prisoner's [grievance] gave prison officials fair notice of the alleged mistreatment or misconduct that forms the basis of the constitutional or statutory claim made against a defendant in a prisoner's complaint."). Notably, then, "[a]lthough the [MDOC] policy requires a grievance to include specific names, those requirements are relaxed when the purpose of the grievance has been achieved." Hall v. Raja, 2010 U.S. Dist. LEXIS 77651, 2010 WL 3070141, at *3 (E.D. Mich. Aug. 2, 2010). In other words, "The exhaustion requirement was not designed as a web to ensnare unsophisticated prisoners in procedural technicalities, but rather to prevent inmates from using the federal courts as their first forum to resolve grievances." Hall v. Raja, 2009 U.S. Dist. LEXIS 126333, 2009 WL 6315346, at *5 (E.D. Mich. Aug. 28, 2009) (emphasis in original).

As set forth above, in both the JCF Grievance and the LMF Grievance, Hodges alleged that Dr. Berhane, "acting alone or in concert with others," denied his requests for off-site referral to an orthopedic specialist as well as treatment for his cancer. (Docs. #1-3 at 15, 1-4 at 1). Neither of these grievances was rejected for lack of specificity, nor was Hodges asked to identify who the "others" were. Moreover, the Step II response to the LMF Grievance specifically indicated that: "Investigation into this matter has revealed you were provided continuous medical care while at this facility. There is no evidence of deliberate indifference to your health care needs as you have claimed." (Doc. #1-3 at 21). Presumably, then, Hodges' medical record and/or history were reviewed - which would have revealed Dr. Squier's decision to monitor Hodges, rather than send him to a radiation oncologist.

On the present record, then, the Court cannot say that Hodges failed to comply with the "spirit and purpose of the administrative exhaustion rules" with respect to Dr. Squier. Hall, 2010 U.S. Dist. LEXIS 77651, 2010 WL 3070141, at *3. There is no indication that Dr. Squier ever provided direct patient care to Hodges; thus, it is certainly reasonable to infer that, at the time he filed these grievances, he had no way of knowing that she was the individual who he now alleges was making the ultimate decision not to refer him to a radiation oncologist. For these reasons, despite the fact that neither the JCF Grievance nor the LMF grievance specifically named Dr. Squier, the Court finds that, on the current record, a reasonable jury could find that these grievances gave Dr. Squier fair notice of the claims against her. See, e.g., Stevenson v. Mich. Dep't of Corr., 2008 U.S. Dist. LEXIS 16459, 2008 WL 623783, at * (W.D. Mich. Mar. 4, 2008) (grievance naming specific individuals and "all those equally involved" was substantially similar to the facts alleged in Plaintiff's complaint and, thus, "gave Defendants sufficient notice to address and resolve the claim that Plaintiff brings against them in his complaint"); Contor v. Caruso, 2008 U.S. Dist. LEXIS 24937, 2008 WL 878665, at *3 (W.D. Mich. Mar. 28, 2008) (noting that "prisoners may not be able to learn the names of all persons involved in a situation given prisoners' limited access to information" and concluding that grievance sufficiently put prison officials on notice); Austin v. Corr. Med. Servs., 2008 U.S. Dist. LEXIS 77008, 2008 WL 4426342, at *5 (W.D. Mich. Sept. 26, 2008) (grievance naming "the Medical Service Department here at M.C.F." was sufficient to exhaust claims against the named defendants).

For all of these reasons, the Court finds that the Corizon Defendants' motion to dismiss based on exhaustion grounds should be denied, and Hodges should be permitted to proceed with his Eighth Amendment denial-of-medical-care claims against Dr. Squier, Dr. Berhane, and P.A. Buskirk.

JAMES MERRION, PLAINTIFF VS. CORIZON HEALTH, INC., ET AL., DEFENDANTS. CIVIL ACTION NO. 1:13-CV-1757 UNITED STATES DISTRICT COURT FOR THE MIDDLE DISTRICT OF PENNSYLVANIA

(SEE DISCUSSION UNDER MEDICAL CARE)

C. The Prison Litigation Reform Act ("PLRA") Does Not Apply

Defendants argue that they are entitled to summary judgment because Plaintiff is subject to the PLRA, and was required to exhaust his administrative remedies prior to filing suit. According to Plaintiff, because he was not incarcerated when he filed suit, the PLRA does not apply to him. Pursuant to the plain language of the statute, as well as controlling case law from the Third Circuit Court of Appeals, we must agree with Plaintiff.

The PLRA states that "[n]o action shall be brought with respect to prison conditions . . . by a prisoner confined in any jail, prison, or other correctional facility until such administrative remedies as are available are exhausted." 42 U.S.C. § 1997e(a) (emphasis added). In Ahmed v. Dragovich, 297 F.3d 201 (3d Cir. 2002), the Third Circuit explicitly held that the PLRA does not apply to former prisoners who file suit after their release. Id. at 210. "Any other view would be inconsistent with the spirit of the PLRA, which was designed to deter frivolous litigations by idle prisoners." Id. (emphasis added). The Third Circuit noted that every court of appeals to have considered this issue has arrived at the same conclusion. Id. at 210 n.10 (collecting cases). Defendants' contention that Plaintiff should be considered a prisoner because he was subject to electronic monitoring is unavailing. A "prisoner" is defined in the statute as "any person incarcerated or detained in any facility who is accused of, convicted of, sentenced for, or adjudicated delinquent for, violations of criminal laws or the terms and conditions of parole . . . ." 28 U.S.C. § 1915(h) (emphasis added). Because Plaintiff was not "incarcerated or detained in any facility" when he filed suit, he is not bound by the PLRA's exhaustion requirement. See Kerr v. Puckett, 138 F.3d 321, 323 (7th Cir. 1998) (finding PLRA not applicable to lawsuit filed by inmate after he was released on parole).

LAWRENCE MARTIN ADC # 106491, PLAINTIFF V. CORIZON CORRECTIONAL MEDICAL SERVICES; ET AL., DEFENDANTS 5:13CV00364-KGB-JJV UNITED STATES DISTRICT COURT FOR THE EASTERN DISTRICT OF ARKANSAS, PINE BLUFF DIVISION

(SEE ALSO ARGUMENT UNDER MEDICAL CARE)

B. ADC Defendants

1. Administrative Exhaustion

The Prison Litigation Reform Act (PLRA) requires an inmate to exhaust prison grievance procedures before filing suit in federal court. See 42 U.S.C. § 1997e(a); Jones v. Bock, 549 U.S. 199, 202, 127 S. Ct. 910, 166 L. Ed. 2d 798 (2007); Jones v. Norris, 310 F.3d 610, 612 (8th Cir. 2002). Exhaustion under the PLRA is mandatory. Jones, 549 U.S. at 211. "[T]o properly exhaust administrative remedies, prisoners must 'complete the administrative review process in accordance with the applicable procedural rules,' rules that are defined not by the PLRA, but by the prison grievance process itself." Id., 549 U.S. at 218 (quoting Woodford v. Ngo, 548 U.S. 81, 88, 126 S. Ct. 2378, 165 L. Ed. 2d 368 (2006)). Compliance with a prison's grievance procedures is, therefore, all that is required by the PLRA to properly exhaust. Id. Thus, the question as to whether an inmate has properly exhausted administrative remedies will depend on the specifics of that particular prison's grievance policy. See Id.

ADC Directive 12-16 governs exhaustion of Plaintiff's claims. (Doc. No. 181-3.) The directive requires inmates to submit an informal resolution, a formal grievance, and an appeal to the Assistant and/or Deputy Director level in order to fully exhaust a claim. (Doc. No. 181-4 ÷ 5.) According to the affidavit of Barbara Williams, ADC Inmate Grievance Supervisor, Plaintiff exhausted four grievances -- CU-13-01340, CU-13-01435, CU-13-01608, and CU-13-02109 -- which are relevant to the claims underlying this action. (Id. ÷ 8.) She states that none of these grievances identified Defendants Selvey, Warner, Brown, or Puckett and, therefore, no claims against them were exhausted. (Id.) The Court agrees.

Directive 12-16 clearly states a requirement that inmates must be specific as to the personnel involved in any grieved incident. (Doc. No. 181-3 at 5.) The Court has reviewed the grievances in question and confirmed that these four Defendants are not specifically named or otherwise referenced therein. (Doc. Nos. 181-5 - 181-8.) Plaintiff has not offered any argument to the contrary. Accordingly, the Court recommends that Defendants

Selvey, Warner, Brown, and Puckett be dismissed without prejudice due to Plaintiff's failure to exhaust administrative remedies against them. See Barbee v. Correctional Medical Services, 394 Fed. Appx. 337, 338 (2010) ("Once the court determined that the claims were unexhausted, it was required to dismiss them without prejudice.").

2. Qualified Immunity[5]

5   In their brief, ADC Defendants raise a separate argument that the weight of evidence does not support a violation of Plaintiff's Eighth Amendment rights. Analysis of that argument overlaps with a discussion of qualified immunity, and the Court elects to evaluate immunity first because "Qualified immunity is immunity from suit rather than a mere defense to liability, and therefore, immunity issues should be resolved at the earliest possible stage of the litigation." Saucier v. Katz, 533 U.S. 194, 201, 121 S. Ct. 2151, 150 L. Ed. 2d 272 (2001).

Qualified immunity protects officials who acted in   an objectively reasonable manner and shields a government official from liability when his or her conduct does not violate "clearly established statutory or constitutional rights of which a reasonable person would have known." Harlow v. Fitzgerald, 457 U.S. 800, 818, 102 S. Ct. 2727, 73 L. Ed. 2d 396 (1982). Qualified immunity is a question of law, not a question of fact. McClendon v. Story County Sheriff's Office, 403 F.3d 510, 515 (8th Cir. 2005). Thus, issues concerning qualified immunity are appropriately resolved on summary judgment. See Mitchell v. Forsyth, 472 U.S. 511, 526, 105 S. Ct. 2806, 86 L. Ed. 2d 411 (1985) (the privilege is "an immunity from suit rather than a mere defense to liability; and like an absolute immunity, it is effectively lost if a case is erroneously permitted to go to trial.").

To determine whether defendants are entitled to qualified immunity, courts generally consider two questions: (1) whether the facts alleged or shown, construed in the light most favorable to the plaintiff, establish a violation of a constitutional or statutory right; and (2) whether that right was so clearly established that a reasonable official would have known that his or her actions were unlawful. Pearson v. Callahan, 555 U.S. 223, 232, 129 S. Ct. 808, 172 L. Ed. 2d 565 (2009); see also Saucier v. Katz, 533 U.S. 194, 201, 121 S. Ct. 2151, 150 L. Ed. 2d 272 (2001).[6] Defendants are entitled to qualified immunity only if no reasonable fact finder could answer both questions in the affirmative. Nelson v. Correctional Medical Services, 583 F.3d 522, 528 (8th Cir. 2009).

6   Courts are "permitted to exercise their sound discretion in deciding which   of the two prongs of the qualified immunity analysis should be addressed first in light of the circumstances in the particular case at hand." Nelson v. Correctional Medical Services, 583 F.3d 522, 528 (8th Cir. 2009) (quoting Pearson v. Callahan, 555 U.S. at 236).

After reviewing the record, the Court finds that the facts shown, construed in a light most favorable to Plaintiff, do not establish a violation of his rights. ADC Defendants state that Plaintiff received his medical classification based on determinations made by licensed medical personnel. (Doc. No. 181-13   ÷ 7.) In turn, his job assignment was based on the restrictions, or lack thereof, specified by his medical classification. (Id.) The Court is convinced that the overwhelming weight of evidence indicates that "inside lawn duty" did not exceed Plaintiff's physical abilities, as determined by medical staff. The record indicates that Plaintiff's work day was not particularly strenuous or long. Defendant Swygart avers that Plaintiff was primarily assigned to pick up trash, none of which exceeded his nineteen-pound lifting restriction. (Id.   ÷ 10-11.) He was not made to work more than his four-hour restriction, and he was provided frequent breaks for water and rest. (Doc. Nos. 183-13   ÷ 10-12, 183-14.)

Even assuming, for the sake argument, that Plaintiff's medical classification was made erroneously, ADC Defendants would still not be liable. It is established that, where a defendant lacks medical expertise, they cannot be held liable for the diagnostic decisions of medical staff. See Camberos v. Branstad, 73 F.3d 174, 176 (8th Cir. 1995). Plaintiff's medical classification fits squarely within the category of a "diagnostic decision" and there is no evidence indicating that any ADC Defendant had the medical expertise to reach a different conclusion. As such, they were completely justified in relying on the determinations of the medical staff.

Based on the foregoing, the Court finds that Defendants Jones, Lay, May, Swygart, and Wood are entitled to qualified immunity and Plaintiff's claims against them should be dismissed.

3. Official Capacity Claims

Lastly, any official capacity claims for damages against the ADC Defendants should also be dismissed. These claims are akin to claims against the state itself. See Kentucky v. Graham, 473 U.S. 159, 166, 105 S. Ct. 3099, 87 L. Ed. 2d 114 (1985). It necessarily follows that these official capacity damage claims are barred by the Eleventh Amendment. Will v. Mich. Dep't of State Police, 491 U.S. 58, 70-71, 109 S. Ct. 2304, 105 L. Ed. 2d 45 (1989).

KENNETH R. HARRISON, #160623, PLAINTIFF, V. CORIZON MEDICAL SERVICES, DEFENDANT. CIVIL ACTION NO. 2:14-CV-1251-MHT UNITED STATES DISTRICT COURT FOR THE MIDDLE DISTRICT OF ALABAMA, EASTERN DIVISION

I. INTRODUCTION

In this *42 U.S.C. § 1983* action, Kenneth R. Harrison ("Harrison"), a former state inmate, challenges the medical treatment provided to him for an atrial septal defect ("ASD"), congenital heart condition, during his incarceration in the Alabama prison system. *Complaint - Doc. No. 1* at 3.[1] Specifically, Harrison contends that after his appointment with a free-world cardiologist in April of 2014 the defendant acted with deliberate indifference to his heart condition. Harrison names Corizon Medical Services as the sole defendant in this cause of action. He seeks monetary damages for the alleged violation of his constitutional rights. *Id.* at 4.

1 Harrison was released from state custody on February 1, 2015.

The defendant filed a special report and supporting evidentiary materials addressing Harrison's claims for relief. In these documents, the defendant adamantly denies that it acted with deliberate indifference to Harrison's heart condition. The defendant further asserts that the complaint is due to be dismissed because prior to filing this cause of action Harrison failed to properly exhaust an administrative remedy available to him during his incarceration in the Alabama prison system. *Defendant's Special Report - Doc. No. 6* at 6-7. The defendant bases its exhaustion defense on Harrison's failure to file a grievance in accordance with the grievance procedure provided by Corizon regarding the claims raised in the instant complaint. *Id.* at 7.

"[A]n exhaustion defense . . . is not ordinarily the proper subject for a summary judgment; instead it should be raised in a motion to dismiss, or be treated as such if raised in a motion for summary judgment." *Bryant v. Rich, 530 F.3d 1368, 1374-75 (11th Cir. 2008)* (internal quotations omitted); *Trias v. Fla. Dep't of Corr., 587 F. App'x 531, 534 (11th Cir. 2014)* (holding that the district court properly construed defendant's "motion for summary judgment as a motion to dismiss for failure to exhaust administrative remedies"). The court will therefore treat the defendant's report as a motion to dismiss. *Bryant, 530 F.3d at 1375; Order of February 12, 2015 - Doc. No. 9* (advising Harrison that the defendant's report will be treated as a dispositive motion and explaining the manner in which to respond to such a motion).

II. STANDARD OF REVIEW

The Eleventh Circuit has determined that the question of exhaustion under the PLRA [is] a "threshold matter" that [federal courts must] address before considering the merits of the case. *Chandler v. Crosby, 379 F.3d 1278, 1286 (11th Cir. 2004)*. Because exhaustion is mandated by the statute, [a court has] no discretion to waive this requirement. *Alexander v. Hawk, 159 F.3d 1321, 1325-26 (11th Cir. 1998).Myles v. Miami-Dade Cnty. Corr. and Rehab. Dep't, 476 F. App'x 364, 366 (11th Cir. 2012)*. Based on the foregoing, the court will "resolve this issue first." *Id.*

When deciding whether a prisoner has exhausted his remedies, the court should first consider the plaintiff's and the defendants' versions of the facts, and if they conflict, take the plaintiff's version of the facts as true. "If in that light, the defendant is entitled to have the complaint dismissed for failure to exhaust administrative remedies, it must be dismissed." *Turner v. Burnside, 541 F.3d 1077, 1082 (11th Cir. 2008)* (citing *Bryant, 530 F.3d at 1373-74*). If the complaint is not subject to dismissal at this step, then the court should make "specific findings in order to resolve the disputed factual issues related to exhaustion." *Id.* (citing *Bryant, 530 F.3d at 1373-74, 1376*). *Myles, 476 F. App'x at 366*.

Consequently, a district court may resolve disputed factual issues where necessary to the disposition of a motion to dismiss for failure to exhaust [without a hearing]. *See* [*Turner, 541 F.3d at 1082*]. The judge properly may consider facts outside of the pleadings [i.e., evidentiary materials submitted in support of the special report] to resolve a factual dispute as to exhaustion where doing so does not decide the merits, and the parties have a sufficient opportunity to develop the record. *Bryant, 530 F.3d at 1376. Trias, 587 F. App'x at 535.*

Upon review of the undisputed facts of this case as evidenced by the evidentiary materials filed by the defendant, the court concludes that the defendant's motion to dismiss is due to be granted.

III. DISCUSSION

Harrison challenges the constitutionality of medical treatment he received for a heart condition. In response to the complaint, the defendant denies Harrison's allegations and further argues that this case is subject to dismissal because Harrison failed to properly exhaust the available administrative remedy prior to filing this complaint as required by the Prison Litigation Reform Act, *42 U.S.C. § 1997e(a)*.

The Prison Litigation Reform Act compels exhaustion of available administrative remedies before a prisoner can seek relief in federal court on a *§ 1983* complaint. Specifically, *42 U.S.C. § 1997e(a)* states that "[n]o action shall be brought with respect to prison conditions under *section 1983* of this title, or any other Federal law, by a prisoner confined in any jail, prison, or other correctional facility until such administrative remedies as are available are exhausted." "Congress has provided in *§ 1997e(a)* that an inmate must exhaust irrespective of the forms of relief sought and offered through administrative remedies." *Booth v. Churner, 532 U.S. 731, 741 n.6, 121 S. Ct. 1819, 149 L. Ed. 2d 958 (2001).* "[T]he PLRA's exhaustion requirement applies to all inmate suits about prison life, whether they involve general circumstances or particular episodes, and whether they allege excessive force or some other wrong." *Porter v. Nussle, 534 U.S. 516, 532, 122 S. Ct. 983, 152 L. Ed. 2d 12 (2002).* Exhaustion of all available administrative remedies is a precondition to litigation and a federal court cannot waive the exhaustion requirement. *Booth, 532 U.S. at 741; Alexander v. Hawk, 159 F.3d 1321, 1325 (11th Cir. 1998); Woodford v. Ngo, 548 U.S. 81, 126 S. Ct. 2378, 165 L. Ed. 2d 368 (2006).* Moreover, "the PLRA exhaustion requirement requires *proper exhaustion*." *Woodford, 548 U.S. at 93* (emphasis added).

Proper exhaustion demands compliance with an agency's deadlines and other critical procedural rules [as a precondition to filing a civil action in federal court] because no adjudicative system can function effectively without imposing some orderly structure on the courts of its proceedings. . . . Construing *§ 1997e(a)* to require proper exhaustion . . . fits with the general scheme of the PLRA, whereas [a contrary] interpretation [allowing an inmate to bring suit in federal court once administrative remedies are no longer available] would turn that provision into a largely useless appendage.

548 U.S. at 90-91, 93. The Court reasoned that because proper exhaustion of administrative remedies is necessary an inmate cannot "satisfy the Prison Litigation Reform Act's exhaustion requirement . . . by filing an untimely or otherwise procedurally defective administrative grievance or appeal[,]" or by effectively bypassing the administrative process simply by waiting until the grievance procedure is no longer available to him. *548 U.S. at 83-84; Johnson v. Meadows, 418 F.3d 1152, 1157 (11th Cir. 2005)* (inmate who files an untimely grievance or simply spurns the administrative process until it is no longer available fails to satisfy the exhaustion requirement of the PLRA). "*The only facts pertinent to determining whether a prisoner has satisfied the PLRA's exhaustion requirement are those that existed when he filed his original complaint.*" *Smith v. Terry, 491 F. App'x 81, 83 (11th Cir. 2012)* (per curiam) (emphasis added).

The record in this case is undisputed that the defendant provides a grievance procedure for inmate complaints related to the provision of medical treatment. The defendant explains the procedure and relevant facts as follows:

. . . The initial orientation process with the ADOC correctional system includes educating inmates as to the availability of the grievance process. The existence of this grievance procedure is well-known among the prison population, as indicated by the fact that the medical staff at Ventress receives inmate requests and/or inmate grievances on a daily basis. The physicians, nurse practitioners, nurses and other medical personnel at Staton [and other facilities] attempt to resolve all inmate concerns prior to an "inmate grievance" being submitted.

The grievance process is initiated when an inmate submits a Medical Grievance form to the HSA through the institutional mail system. After reviewing the Medical Grievance, the HSA [or her designee] then provides a written response [to the grievance] within approximately ten (10) days of receipt of the Inmate Grievance. The written response to a Medical Grievance is included on the bottom portion of the same form containing an inmate's Medical Grievance. Below the portion of the form designated for the "Response," the following notation appears:

IF YOU WISH TO APPEAL THIS REVIEW YOU MAY REQUEST A GRIEVANCE APPEAL FORM FROM THE HEALTH SERVICES ADMINISTRATOR. RETURN THE COMPLETED FORM TO THE ATTENTION OF THE HEALTH SERVICE ADMINISTRATOR. YOU MAY PLACE THE FORM IN THE SICK CALL REQUEST BOX OR GIVE IT TO THE SEGREGATION SICK CALL NURSE ON ROUNDS.

As stated in the Medical Grievance forms, the second step of the grievance process involves the submission of a formal Medical Grievance Appeal, at which time the inmate may be brought in for one-on-one communication with the medical staff, HSA and/or the Director of Nursing. A written response to a formal Medical Grievance Appeal is provided within approximately ten (10) days of receipt. Medical Grievance and Medical Grievance Appeal forms are available from the Health Care Unit and the correctional shift commander office at [each facility]. Inmates are instructed to place completed Medical Grievance and Medical Grievance Appeal forms in the sick call boxes located [in the facility]. The HSA reviews the grievances daily, provides a written response within approximately ten (10) days at the bottom of the form and returns a copy of the completed forms to the inmate. The HSA encourages inmates who have complaints about the medical care they have sought or received at [the facility] to utilize this grievance process. Mr. Harrison did not submit any Medical Grievances or Medical Grievance Appeal [regarding the treatment provided for his heart condition] during the course of his incarceration at Staton.

Defendant's Exhibit 1 (Aff. of Darryl Ellis, Director of Nursing for Staton) - Doc. No. 6-1 at 5-6; Defendant's Exhibit 6 (Aff. of Loris Baugh, Health Services   Administrator at Kilby) - Doc. No. 6-6 at 2 ("The grievance process at [the relevant correctional facilities] is identical and I am the individual typically responsible for overseeing and responding to grievances at Kilby. During his incarceration at Kilby, Mr. Harrison did not submit any grievance of any kind.").

Upon review of the arguments set forth by the defendant, the court entered an order which provided Harrison an opportunity to file a response to these arguments in which he was advised to "specifically address the defendant's assertion[] that . . . [h]is claims are due to be dismissed because he failed to exhaust his available administrative remedies as required by *42 U.S.C. § 1997e(a)* of the Prison Litigation Reform Act ('PLRA')" prior to filing this federal civil action. *Order of February 12, 2015 - Doc. No. 9* at 1. The time allowed Harrison to file his response expired on February 26, 2015. *Id.* at 2. As of the present date, Harrison has filed no response to this order.

The evidentiary materials filed by the defendant demonstrate that Harrison failed to file the requisite grievance prior to initiation of this federal civil action. Harrison does not dispute his failure to exhaust the administrative remedy available to him in the prison system prior to filing this case. In addition, there is nothing before the court which justifies Harrison's failure to exhaust the grievance procedure provided by Corizon. It is likewise clear that the administrative remedy provided by the defendant is no longer available to Harrison due to his release from prison. Under these circumstances, dismissal with prejudice is appropriate. *Bryant, 530 F.3d at 1375 n.1; Johnson, 418 F.3d at 1157; Marsh v. Jones, 53 F.3d 707, 710 (5th Cir. 1995)* ("Without the prospect of a dismissal with prejudice, a prisoner could evade the exhaustion requirement by filing no administrative grievance or by intentionally filing an untimely one, thereby foreclosing administrative remedies and gaining access to a federal forum without exhausting administrative remedies."); *Berry v. Kerik, 366 F.3d 85, 88 (2d Cir. 2004)* (footnotes omitted) (inmate's "federal lawsuits . . . properly dismissed with prejudice" where previously available administrative remedies had become unavailable). Consequently, the court concludes that this case is subject to dismissal with prejudice as   Harrison failed to properly exhaust an administrative remedy available to him during his prior term of incarceration which is a precondition to proceeding in this court on his complaint.

NORMAN GRAY, # 108144, PLAINTIFF, V. CORIZON HEALTH SERVICES, ET AL., DEFENDANTS. CASE NO. 1:14-CV-947 UNITED STATES DISTRICT COURT FOR THE WESTERN DISTRICT OF MICHIGAN, SOUTHERN DIVISION

This is a civil rights action brought by a state prisoner under *42 U.S.C. § 1983*. Plaintiff filed this lawsuit on September 15, 2014, regarding conditions of his confinement at the Muskegon Correctional Facility (MCF). The defendants are Corizon Health Services (Corizon) and Dr. William D. Nelson. Plaintiff alleges that defendants violated his rights under the *Eighth Amendment's Cruel and Unusual Punishments Clause*.[1]

1   Plaintiff's complaint refers to defendant Corizon as "Corizon Health Services, Inc." His pleading also contains passing references to the *First* and *Fourteenth Amendments*. The *Eighth Amendment's Cruel and Unusual Punishments Clause* applies to the states through the *Fourteenth Amendment's Due Process Clause. See Graham v. Florida, 560 U.S. 48, 53, 130 S. Ct. 2011, 176 L. Ed. 2d 825 (2010)*. Plaintiff has not alleged any facts supporting a claim under the *Fourteenth Amendment's Equal Protection Clause* or the *First Amendment*.

Dr. Nelson

Plaintiff alleges that in December 2013 and January 2014, Dr. Nelson found that plaintiff had a suspected case of tuberculosis and ordered that he be transported to Muskegon Mercy Hospital spread of tuberculosis. (Compl. at Page ID 3). According to plaintiff, hospital tests revealed that he did not have tuberculosis, but did have a possible fungal infection in his lungs. Plaintiff was sent back to prison with prescription medication for the suspected fungal infection. When follow-up x-rays suggested that plaintiff's lung problem was getting worse, plaintiff was transported back to the hospital for a CT scan and a lung biopsy. In July 2014, Mercy Hospital Staff informed plaintiff of the diagnosis of lung cancer. (*Id.*).

Corizon

Plaintiff alleges that Corizon is Dr. Nelson's employer and a conclusion that the medical care that plaintiff received was delayed, inadequate, and inconsistent. (*Id.* at Page ID 4-5). Plaintiff seeks an award of damages. (*Id.* at Page ID 6).

The matter is now before the court on defendants' motion for summary judgment based on the affirmative defense provided by *42 U.S.C. § 1997e(a)*. For the reasons set forth herein, I recommend that defendants' motion for summary judgment (docket # 11) be granted and that all plaintiff's claims against defendants be dismissed without prejudice.

Proposed Findings of Fact

The following facts are beyond genuine issue. Plaintiff filed this lawsuit on September 15, 2014, while he was an inmate at the Muskegon Correctional Facility (MCF). The defendants are Dr. William D. Nelson and Corizon Health Services, Inc. (Corizon).

Plaintiff concedes that he did not exhaust any claim against defendants through the MDOC's grievance process before he filed this lawsuit. (Plf. Brief at 2-3, docket # 19, Page ID 68-69).

Discussion

Defendants have raised the affirmative defense that plaintiff did not properly exhaust his administrative remedies against them as required by *42 U.S.C. § 1997e(a)*. Plaintiff argues that he should be excused from the exhaustion requirement "because of a serious illness, see medical records." (Plf. Brief at 3, Page ID 69). Plaintiff did not submit any medical evidence in support of his argument. Thus, there is no evidence before the court that plaintiff's medical condition prevented him from utilizing the MDOC's grievance process. Exhaustion is mandatory. *Woodford, 548 U.S. at 85*. "[N]o unexhausted claim may be considered." *Jones v. Bock, 549 U.S. at 220*. Plaintiff did not properly exhaust any claim against defendants before he filed this lawsuit. I find that defendants have carried their burden on the affirmative defense and are entitled to dismissal of all of plaintiff's claims.

TELLY ROYSTER, PLAINTIFF V. CORIZON, ET AL., DEFENDANTS CIVIL NO. 3:CV-13-1449 UNITED STATES DISTRICT COURT FOR THE MIDDLE DISTRICT OF PENNSYLVANIA

I. Introduction

Plaintiff, Telly Royster, filed this civil rights action pursuant to 42 U.S.C. § 1983. He is currently confined at the Greene State Correctional Institution (SCI-Greene), in Waynesburg, Pennsylvania. He names 31 defendants who are either employed by the Pennsylvania Department of Corrections (DOC) at SCI-Camp Hill, in Camp Hill, Pennsylvania, or by Corizon, the contract medical care providers at SCI-Camp Hill, Mr. Royster's former place of confinement. Mr. Royster claims defendants violated his Eighth Amendment rights by delaying his receipt of his migraine medication. He also claims some of the defendants retaliated against him by rewriting his migraine script after he complained about the delay. (Doc. 1-1, Comp.)

Presently before the court is Mr. Royster's Second Motion to Compel. (Doc. 72.) Mr. Royster seeks to compel the defendants to produce the name of all inmates (and their current locations) that were housed with him in the same area of SCI-Camp Hill's Special Management Unit (SMU). He also seeks the defendants to produce copies of his medical and grievance records requested in discovery free of charge. Finally, Mr. Royster claims "Defendants are refusing to cooperate in any manner to plaintiff's discovery request". (Doc. 73, ECF p. 1.) Defendants urge the court to deny the motion based on Mr. Royster's failure to specify which of their discovery responses he finds lacking, why he should be entitled to free copies of discovery documents, or any facts to support his conclusory allegation that they are intentionally thwarting his discovery efforts. (Doc. 74.) In his reply brief, Mr. Royster claims to be "dissatisfied with every response and objection made by defendants" to his discovery requests. (Doc. 77.) However, Mr. Royster has not supplied a copy of defendants' responses. (Id.) Additionally, he interjects that he should be permitted to correspond with any inmates housed at SCI-Camp Hill, not just the ones housed in the same housing unit, because conferring with them may "lead to admissible evidence". (Doc. 77.)

II. Standard of Review

Fed. R. Civ. P. 37(a) allows a party to file a motion to compel discovery where the opposing party fails to respond adequately to document request propounded pursuant to Fed. R. Civ. P. 34. Fed. R. Civ. P. 37(a)(3)(B)(iv). Pursuant to Fed. R. Civ. P. 26(b)(1), a party "may obtain discovery regarding any nonprivileged matter that is relevant to any party's claim or defense." Fed. R. Civ. P. 26(b)(1). Relevant information sought in discovery need not be admissible at trial, as long as it "appears reasonably calculated to lead to the discovery of admissible evidence. (Id.) Relevance is generally "construed broadly to encompass any matter that bears on, or that reasonably could lead to other matter that could bear on, any issue that is or may be in the case." Oppenheimer Fund, Inc. v. Sanders, 437 U.S. 340, 351, 98 S.Ct. 2380, 2389, 57 L.Ed.2d 253 (1978). The moving party bears the initial burden of showing that the requested discovery is relevant. Morrison v. Phila. Hous. Auth., 203 F.R.D. 195, 196 (E.D.Pa. 2001).

While generally liberal, permissible discovery is not without limitations, it "should not serve as a fishing expedition." Provine v. Ambulatory Health Services, Inc., No. 13-334, 2014 U.S. Dist. LEXIS 702, 2014 WL 47771, *2 (M.D. Pa. Jan. 6, 2014). It is well established that the scope and conduct of discovery are within the sound discretion of the trial court. In re Cendant Corp. Sec. Litig., 343 F.3d 658, 661-62 (3d Cir. 2003). "Rulings regarding the proper scope of discovery, and the extent to which discovery may be compelled, are matters consigned to the Court's discretion and judgment." McConnell v. Canadian Pacific Realty Co., 280 F.R.D. 188, 192 (M.D. Pa. 2011). A court's decision regarding the conduct of discovery will be disturbed only upon a showing of an abuse of discretion. Ohntrup v. Makina Ve Kimya Endustrisi Kurumu, 760 F.3d 290, 296 (3d Cir. 2014).

III. Discussion

A. SCI-Camp Hill's SMU D-Pod Housing Logs for March 2012[1]

1 "Identify each inmate housed on D-pod of the SMU in March of 2012. Produce the document(s) used to answer this interrogatory." (Doc. 73, ECF p. 2).

In his Complaint, Mr. Royster claims that between March 2011 and April 2012 he was regularly denied migraine medication. In his motion to compel he argues that defendants have objected to his prior requests to correspond with inmates who were not housed in the same housing area. He claims that defendants refused to produce   documents indicating who those inmates were. (Doc. 73.) Without addressing the merits of Mr. Royster's allegations, defendants argue that "Plaintiff has failed to identify a discovery request which sought" the identification of these inmates, suggesting they never received a request for production of documents asking for the logbook. However, attached to Mr. Royster's brief in support of his Motion to Compel is a document entitled "Interrogatories and Production of Documents on Sgt. Flinn." (Doc. 73, ECF p. 2.) The document is dated October 18, 2014. (Id.) If this is a properly served discovery request, Mr. Royster must supply the court with proof of proper service of this request, defendants' response to his discovery request, and advise the court why the response is inadequate or otherwise improper. Without this information the court cannot accurately assess Mr. Royster's motion to compel. Mr. Royster's motion to compel the production of SCI-Camp Hill's SMU D-Pod housing log for March 2012 is denied without prejudice.

B. Defendants are not Required to Produce Gratis Discovery.

Mr. Royster seeks defendants to provide him with free copies of his medical and grievance records he requested   via discovery. Although Mr. Royster proceeds in forma pauperis, there "is no provision in the [in forma pauperis] statute for the payment by the government of the costs of deposition transcripts, or any other litigation expenses, and no other statute authorizes courts to commit federal monies for payment of the necessary expenses in a civil suit brought by an indigent litigant." Tabron v. Grace, 6 F.3d 147, 159 (3d Cir. 1993). Thus, with respect to discovery documents, defendants have the obligation to produce them for Mr. Royster's inspection. To the extent he seeks copies of these documents, he should consult prison policies which will allow him, provided he follows the policy guidelines, to go into debt for the purpose of making photocopies of legal documents. Accordingly, Mr. Royster's motion to compel defendants to provide him with free copies of his medical and grievance records is denied.

C. Defendants Non-Compliance with Discovery.

Fed. R. Civ. P. 37(b) permits a court to impose sanctions for a party's noncompliance with discovery obligations. Mr. Royster's allegations that defendants "are refusing to cooperate in any manner" with his discovery requests is not persuasive. Mr. Royster has failed to carry his burden to demonstrate that the defendants have either failed to respond to his discovery requests or have failed to produce documents responsive to a document request. In fact, Mr. Royster has failed to point to any specific discovery request that defendants have failed to answer. While "dissatisfied" with defendants' responses, he is not guaranteed satisfying discovery responses, he is guaranteed complete answers or objections to his properly served interrogatories or documents requests. To date Mr. Royster has not demonstrated any dilatory or obstructive behavior by defendants in responding to properly served discovery requests. Therefore, Mr. Royster's allegations of defendants' non-cooperation with discovery, standing alone, cannot support the imposition of sanctions.

DENIAL OF MEANINGFUL ACCESS TO COURTS

Courts require litigants provide citations to authority that support their positions. Even though appointed counsel clearly fail to provide adequate representation, prison systems, to deny litigants the opportunity to present their claims, refuse to provide them with access to cases law and use paralegals, not authorized to assist them in presenting arguments and case law, violating the right to equal opportunity. These decisions reflect violations of the right to equal access to the courts.

STATE OF ARIZONA, Appellee, v. HECTOR E. APARICIO VASQUEZ, Appellant. 2015 Ariz. App. Unpub. LEXIS 1484 (December 8, 2015)

FACTS AND PROCEDURAL BACKGROUND

In June 2013, Vasquez backed a truck out of a parking space and ran into the victim's car. The victim testified that Vasquez--who got out of the driver's side of the truck--smelled of alcohol, was stumbling, and appeared to be drunk.

Phoenix Police officers who arrived at the scene noticed that Vasquez's eyes were bloodshot and watery, and that his breath smelled moderately of alcohol. Vasquez acknowledged hitting the other car, and he told an officer that he drank a few beers before driving and that his license was suspended. A Motor Vehicle Division report confirmed that Vasquez's license was suspended at the time.

About one and a half hours after the collision, a police phlebotomist drew two samples of Vasquez's blood. Testing showed a blood alcohol concentration ("BAC") of 0.098.

The State charged Vasquez with two class 4 felony counts of aggravated DUI: (1) driving while impaired to the slightest degree with a suspended license, see Ariz. Rev. Stat. ("A.R.S.") §§ 28-1381(A)(1),-1383(A)(1), and (2) driving with a BAC of at least 0.08 with a suspended license, see A.R.S. §§ 28-1381(A)(2),-1383(A)(1). After a five-day trial, a jury found Vasquez guilty as charged.

After a subsequent trial to determine whether Vasquez had prior convictions, the superior court found that Vasquez had one historical prior felony conviction: a conviction of aggravated DUI in 1995. See A.R.S. § 13-105(22)(a)(iv). The court sentenced Vasquez as a category two repetitive offender to concurrent, presumptive terms of 4.5 years, with credit for 405 days of presentence incarceration. Vasquez timely appealed.

We have reviewed the record for reversible error, see Leon, 104 Ariz. at 300, and we find none. Vasquez was present and represented by counsel at all stages of the proceedings against him. The record reflects that the superior court afforded Vasquez all his constitutional and statutory rights, and that the proceedings were conducted in accordance with the Arizona Rules of Criminal Procedure. The court conducted appropriate pretrial hearings, and the evidence presented at trial supported the jury's verdicts. Vasquez's sentences fall within the range prescribed by law, with proper credit given for presentence incarceration.

After the filing of this decision, defense counsel's obligations pertaining to Vasquez's representation in this appeal will end after informing Vasquez of the outcome of this appeal and his future options, unless counsel's review reveals an issue appropriate for submission to the Arizona Supreme Court by petition for review. See State v. Shattuck, 140 Ariz. 582, 584-85, 684 P.2d 154 (1984). Vasquez shall have 30 days from the date of this decision to proceed, if he desires, with a pro se motion for reconsideration or petition for review.

STATE OF ARIZONA, Appellee, v. MARK RYAN GERI, Appellant. 2015 Ariz. App. Unpub. LEXIS 1483 (December 8, 2015)

FACTS AND PROCEDURAL HISTORY

We view the facts in the light most favorable to sustaining the trial court's judgment and resolve all reasonable inferences against Geri. State v. Fontes, 195 Ariz. 229, 230 ¶ 2, 986 P.2d 897, 898 (App. 1998).

At dawn one morning in February 2013, an apartment security guard saw two men on the roof of a neighboring strip mall. Although he could not see the facial features of either person, the guard noted that one man--later identified as Geri--wore a lighter colored jacket and the other wore a darker colored jacket. The man in the dark jacket descended from the roof and received a duffle bag from Geri. After lowering the bag, Geri also descended and both men took off on bicycles. The security guard called 911 to report what he had witnessed.

Within one minute of receiving the call, police officers in the area observed two men matching the security guard's description exit the strip mall's rear parking lot. The officers stopped the men and had them sit on the curb where Geri and the other man, who was still carrying the duffle bag, identified themselves. Inside the duffle bag the officers discovered a copper pipe, folded and broken in several spots.

Another team of officers climbed onto the roof where the security guard saw Geri. There, the officers found that the copper drainage pipes on several air conditioning units had been broken off and that the remaining pipes had "broke, jagged" edges that were shiny, indicating that the break had occurred recently. The officers later noted that the weathering on the roof's pipes matched that of the pipes found in the duffle bag and that the two pipes were the same size. The State subsequently charged Geri with one count of third degree burglary.

Before the jury trial, the State requested a hearing pursuant to Arizona Rule of Evidence 609, which provides that the State may impeach a testifying defendant with his prior convictions if the probative value of those convictions outweighs their prejudicial effect. The State alleged that Geri had four prior felony convictions. The trial court did not conduct the hearing, but because Geri elected to not testify, defense counsel did not raise any objection to that. The State also alleged other aggravating circumstances, including the taking of property, the presence of an accomplice, the expectation of the receipt of pecuniary gain, and victim financial harm.

After the State rested its case-in-chief at the trial, defense counsel moved for an Arizona Rule of Criminal Procedure 20 judgment of acquittal, but the trial court denied the motion. Then, before closing arguments, Geri moved to remove his counsel, arguing that counsel "did not do his job" because counsel failed to ask the witnesses any of the pages of questions that Geri gave him to ask. The trial court denied Geri's motion. After deliberating, the jurors convicted Geri of third degree burglary. The jurors also found that the State had proved the aggravating factors of expectation of the receipt of anything of pecuniary value and the presence of an accomplice.

At the subsequent sentencing hearing conducted in compliance with Arizona Rule of Criminal Procedure 26, Geri admitted to having four prior felony convictions, which the trial court accepted. The trial court then sentenced Geri to eight years' imprisonment with 147 days' presentence incarceration credit. Geri timely appealed.

DISCUSSION

We review Geri's conviction and sentence for fundamental error. See State v. Gendron, 168 Ariz. 153, 155, 812 P.2d 626, 628 (1991).

Counsel for Geri has advised this Court that after a diligent search of the entire record, he has found no arguable question of law. We have read and considered counsel's brief and fully reviewed the record for reversible error. See Leon, 104 Ariz. at 300, 451 P.2d at 881. We find none. All of the proceedings were conducted in compliance with the Arizona Rules of Criminal Procedure. So far as the record reveals, Geri was represented by counsel at all stages of the proceedings, and the sentence imposed was within the statutory limits. We note that although Geri effectively claimed ineffective assistance of counsel at trial, we do not address that issue on direct appeal. State v. Spreitz, 202 Ariz. 1, 3 ¶ 9, 39 P.3d 525, 527 (2002). Such claims can only be addressed in a post-conviction proceeding pursuant to Arizona Rule of Criminal Procedure 32. See State ex rel. Thomas v. Rayes, 214 Ariz. 411, 415 ¶ 20, 153 P.3d 1040, 1044 (2007). We decline to order briefing, and we affirm Geri's conviction and sentence.

Upon the filing of this decision, defense counsel shall inform Geri of the status of his appeal and of his future options. Defense counsel has no further obligations unless, upon review, counsel finds an issue appropriate for submission to the Arizona Supreme Court by petition for review. See State v. Shattuck, 140 Ariz. 582, 584-85, 684 P.2d 154, 156-57 (1984). Geri shall have 30 days from the date of this decision to proceed, if he desires, with a pro per motion for reconsideration or a petition for review.

JON HOUSER, PLAINTIFF, VS. CORIZON, SCOTT LOSSMANN, GARTH GULICK, CATHERINE WHINNERY, GLEN BABICH, AND MARK SPELICH, DEFENDANTS. Case No. 1:13-cv-00006-EJL UNITED STATES DISTRICT COURT FOR THE DISTRICT OF IDAHO

BACKGROUND

Plaintiff filed this action on January 4, 2013 alleging that Defendants were deliberately indifferent in responding to his medical needs. The Court reviewed the Complaint pursuant to 28 U.S.C. §§ 1915 and 1915A and allowed Plaintiff to proceed on his Eighth Amendment claims against Defendants. Initial Review Order (Dkt. 4). The Court then considered whether to dismiss some claims for failure to exhaust administrative remedies. The Court allowed Plaintiff to proceed on Counts 1, 2, 3, 4, 6, 8 and 9 of his Complaint and dismissed without prejudice Counts 5 and 7. Order (Dkt. 43).

Plaintiff now has the assistance of counsel and seeks to file an Amended Complaint. Plaintiff's counsel filed a three-paragraph memorandum to support the requested amendments, arguing only that an amended complaint will "streamline the case, clarify the allegations and causes of action, . . . and allow for a more orderly litigation of this matter." (Dkt. 49, p. 2). Defendant Mark Spelich does not object to the amendments. (Dkt. 50). However, Defendants Glen Babich, M.D., Corizon, LLC, Scott Lossmann, M.D., Catherine Whinnery, M.D., and Garth Gulick, M.D. (collectively the "Medical Provider Defendants"), oppose several of the proposed amendments. (Dkt. 51). Unfortunately, Plaintiff's counsel did not respond to the Medical Provider Defendants' opposition or substantive arguments. For the reasons set forth below, the Court will grant in part, and deny in part, Plaintiff's Motion.

B. Discussion

1. Proposed Claims and Allegations Reiterating Dismissed Claims Should be Excluded from the Proposed Amended Complaint.

Count 5 of the original Complaint alleged deliberate indifference in Defendants Gulick and Lossman "rushing [Plaintiff] into surgery for his (L) knee before having him seen by a Mental Health provider." Dkt. 1, p. 17. Count 7 of the original Complaint alleged deliberate indifference in Defendants Gulick, Lossmann, and Spelich failing to remove Plaintiff from Hepatitis C treatment after the first MRSA outbreak. Dkt. 1, p. 17.

Paragraphs 77 and 79 of the proposed Amended Complaint repeat the same claims made in Counts 5 and 7, which the Court dismissed for failure to exhaust.[1] (Dkt. 43). Accordingly, amending the Complaint to reiterate these dismissed claims would be futile. Additionally, to the extent paragraphs 62 and 64 of the proposed Amended Complaint include factual allegations that relate solely to claims made in paragraphs 77 and 79 (recycled from dismissed Counts 5 and 7 of the original Complaint), those allegations also should be excluded from any Amended Complaint.

1   Plaintiff conceded that Count 5 was unexhausted, Order (Dkt. 43, p. 10), and the Court found Plaintiff failed to exhaust Count 7. Order (Dkt. 43, pp. 14-15). Even though both counts were dismissed without prejudice, Order (Dkt. 43, p. 16), Plaintiff has not argued that he would be able to demonstrate exhaustion if he were allowed to amend his Complaint to include the dismissed counts. Thus, on the record before the Court, nothing has changed to prompt the Court to reconsider its earlier ruling that Counts 5 and 7--containing claims that are repeated in paragraphs 77 and 79 of the proposed Amended Complaint--should be dismissed.

2. Plaintiff May Not Amend His Complaint to Add or Continue State Law Medical Malpractice Claims That Did Not go Through the Required Prelitigation Review.

Plaintiff's attempt to allege malpractice claims against Dr. Lossmann, Dr. Whinnery, and Dr. Babich in the proposed Amended Complaint is futile because he did not undergo the required prelitigation review, and Plaintiff has not provided any argument that such review is not required. See Idaho Code § 6-1001 (requiring prelitigation consideration of personal injury and wrongful death claims and stating those proceedings are "compulsory as a condition precedent to litigation"). For the same reasons, his claims against Dr. Gulick are limited to the actual issue that underwent prelitigation review-- Dr. Gulick's alleged failure to fully inform Plaintiff of the consequences of three surgeries performed between April and May of 2011. Burke Aff., Ex. A (Dkt. 52). In short, Plaintiff's Amended Complaint should include only medical malpractice claims that went through prelitigation review, a prerequisite imposed by Idaho law.

3. The Amended Complaint May Include a Negligent Training and Supervision Claim Against Corizon.

The Medical Provider Defendants argue that Plaintiff's third cause of action against Corizon--for negligent retention, training and supervision--fails to state a claim because Plaintiff has not identified by name any employee whose specific conduct is at issue. However, the Idaho caselaw relied upon by Defendants to support this argument deal with the requirements for establishing a genuine issue of material fact at the summary judgment and/or trial stages of proceedings. In this case, Plaintiff has not had the assistance of counsel in obtaining discovery and crafting the case. Hence, the issue presented is whether the Complaint may be amended with the assistance of counsel now that it has passed the initial review stage. At this point in the proceedings, the Court finds amendment to include the third cause of action against Corizon is not futile, and the Court will apply its discretion and the liberal amendment policy of Rule 15 to allow the proposed amendment in this regard.[2]

2   This does not, of course, mean that Plaintiff is excused from ultimately proving his claim on the merits, or that his third cause of action will survive a motion to dismiss or motion for summary judgment. Those questions are for another day.

MICHAEL L. ARNOLD, PLAINTIFF, VS. CORIZON, INC., ET AL., DEFENDANTS. CASE NO. 1:15-CV-62 SNLJ UNITED STATES DISTRICT COURT FOR THE EASTERN DISTRICT OF MISSOURI, SOUTHEASTERN DIVISION

Plaintiff requests counsel because he says he has no knowledge of the law or how to litigate a claim and because he is not permitted to seek help from other inmates. Plaintiff says he lost his last case before this court, No. 1:13-cv-121 SNLJ, because he was not appointed an attorney. That case, however, was dismissed for failure to exhaust administrative remedies. Plaintiff claims he has since exhausted his administrative remedies, and the present case is a refiling of the same claims at issue in 1:13cv121.

The appointment of counsel for an indigent *pro se* plaintiff lies within the discretion of the Court. Indigent civil litigants do not have a constitutional or statutory right to appointed counsel. *Stevens v. Redwing, 146 F.3d. 538, 546 (8th Cir. 1998); Edgington v. Mo. Dept. of Corrections, 52 F.3d. 777, 780 (8th Cir. 1995); Rayes v. Johnson, 969 F.2d. 700, 702 (8th Cir. 1992).* The standard for appointment of counsel in a civil case involves the weighing of several factors which include the factual complexity of a matter, the complexity of legal issues, the existence of conflicting testimony, the ability of the indigent to investigate the facts, and the ability of the indigent to present his claim. *See McCall v. Benson, 114 F.3d 754 (8th Cir. 1997); Stevens, 146 F.3d. at 546; Edgington, 52 F.3d. at 780; Nachtigall v. Class, 48 F.3d 1076, 1081-82 (8th Cir. 1995); Johnson v. Williams, 788 F.2d. 1319, 1322-1323 (8th Cir. 1986).*

In this matter, the Court finds that appointment of counsel is not mandated at this time. The plaintiff appears able to litigate this matter. This action appears to involve straightforward questions of fact rather than complex questions of law, and plaintiff appears able to clearly present and investigate his claim. The Court will continue to monitor the progress of this case, and if it appears to this Court that the need arises for counsel to be appointed, the Court will do so.

WAYNE DOUGLAS MERKLEY, PLAINTIFF - APPELLANT, V. STATE OF IDAHO; CORIZON HEALTH SERVICES INCORPORATED, DEFENDANTS - APPELLEES. 2015 U.S. APP. LEXIS 17000 (SEPTEMBER 25, 2015)

Idaho state prisoner Wayne Douglas Merkley appeals pro se from the district court's order denying his motion for leave to proceed in forma pauperis ("IFP") in his *42 U.S.C. § 1983* action alleging various constitutional claims and claims under the Americans with Disabilities Act. We have jurisdiction under *28 U.S.C. § 1291*. We review for an abuse of discretion. *Escobedo v. Applebees, 787 F.3d 1226, 1234 (9th Cir. 2015).* We reverse and remand.

The district court denied Merkley's motion to proceed IFP because it concluded that Merkley did not make a sufficient showing of indigency. However, there was inadequate support in the record to conclude that Merkley had access to sufficient funds to pay the court costs and his basic needs. *See id. at 1234* (explaining that a district court abuses its discretion when it "rules on an issue without giving a party an opportunity to explain, or without adequate support on the record"). The record shows that Merkley received approximately $130.00 per month, but does not show how much his monthly expenses were and what items he purchased at the prison's commissary. Accordingly, we reverse the judgment and remand for further proceedings.

JAMES JACKSON ELLSWORTH, PLAINTIFF, VS. CORIZON HEALTH, INC.,[1] ET AL., DEFENDANTS. 2012 U.S. DIST. LEXIS 53276 (AZ. APRIL 16, 2012)

1   This is the accurate name of the defendant formerly knows as Prison Health Services, Inc., as more fully explained in this court's recent order. See Ord. (Doc. 66) at 1-2.

Background

Plaintiff is an inmate housed at the Mohave County Jail ("the Jail"), alleging a violation of his *Eighth Amendment* right to be free from cruel and unusual punishment. More specifically, plaintiff alleges that he was denied certain medical treatment relating to his diagnosis of multiple sclerosis, allegedly because the Jail's protocol did not allow it. See Co. (Doc. 1) at 3, ¶ 3.

By order entered February 23, 2012, the Magistrate Judge denied four motions by plaintiff. On March 16, 2012, plaintiff filed a motion for "review" of that Order, directed to three of those four motions. See Mot. (Doc. 65). In particular, plaintiff is challenging the Magistrate Judge's denial of his motions to: (1) compel compliance with a subpoena directed to a non-party entity (Doc. 43); (2) extend the time for completion of discovery (Doc. 48); and (3) "'join' parties[2] to this matter[.]" Ord. (Doc. 56) at 1:24.

2   As explained in Ellsworth v. Prison Health Services, CV-11-8070, actually, plaintiff was seeking to add non-parties to this action. See Ord. (Doc. 66) at 2, n.2.

Additionally, plaintiff seeks review of the Magistrate Judge's order, filed March 7, 2012, denying plaintiff's motions to compel compliance with subpoenas *duces tecum* directed to three other non-party entities (Docs. 41; 44; and 45). See Ord. (Doc. 63) at 4:4-10. On April 3, 2012, plaintiff filed a separate motion seeking "[r]eview" of that order. Mot. (Doc. 67) at 1:9.

Discussion

With one exception, all of the rulings to which plaintiff objects directly pertain to discovery. Hence, those rulings are non-dispositive matters within the meaning of *Fed.R.Civ.P. 72(a)*. See *Gabriel Techs. Corp. v. Qualcomm Inc., 2012 U.S. Dist. LEXIS 33417, 2012 WL 849167, at *2 (S.D.Cal. Mar. 13, 2012)* (citing *Maisonville v. F2 Am., Inc., 902 F.2d 746, 748 (9th Cir. 1990)*) ("Discovery orders are ordinarily considered non-dispositive because they do not have the effect of dismissing a cause of action.") Plaintiff's challenge to the denial of his motion to "join parties" also is non-dispositive as it is not among the eight types of motions explicitly excluded from determination by *28 U.S.C. § 636(b)(1)(A)*. Nor is that motion "analogous to a motion listed in th[at] [excepted] category[.]" See *United States v. Rivera-Guerrero, 377 F.3d 1064, 1067 (9th Cir. 2004)* (citation omitted) (emphasis omitted). Thus, plaintiff's joinder motion "falls within the non-dispositive group of matters which a magistrate may determine." See *id. at 1068* (citation omitted). Given the non-dispositive status of the motions which plaintiff Ellsworth is challenging, *Rule 72(a)* and *28 U.S.C. § 636(b)(1)(A)* provide the governing legal standards.

Timeliness

Pursuant to *Rule 72(a) of the Federal Rules of Civil Procedure*, "[a] party may serve and file objections to [a] [nondispositive pretrial order of a magistrate judge] within 14 days after being served with a copy[]" of that order. *Fed.R.Civ.P. 72(a)*. "The district judge in the case *must* consider *timely* objections and modify or set aside any part of the order that is clearly erroneous or is contrary to law." Id. (emphasis added); see also *28 U.S.C. § 636(b)(1)(A)* ("A judge of the court may reconsider any pretrial matter under this subparagraph (A) where it has been shown that the magistrate judge's order is clearly erroneous or contrary to law.") However, "[a] party may not assign as error a defect in the order not timely objected to." *Fed.R.Civ.P. 72(a)*.

In the present case, the court construes plaintiff's motions for "review," as objections to the Magistrate Judge's rulings on nondispositive matters, as *Rule 72(a)* allows. Plaintiff's objections were not timely filed, however. As just stated, objections pursuant to that Rule must be filed and served within 14 days after being served with a copy of a magistrate judge's order. On March 26, 2012, plaintiff filed his objections to the February 23, 2012 order. Computing the time for service in accordance with *Rule 6*, plaintiff had until March 12, 2012 in which to file his objections.[3] Plaintiff did not meet that filing deadline though.

3   In accordance with *Fed.R.Civ.P. 6(a)(1)(A)*, February 23, 2012, the entry date of the order, is excluded from computing plaintiff's time to file objections. Beginning to count on February 24, 2012, and adding three days for service pursuant to *Fed.R.Civ.P. 6(d)*, means that the 14 day time frame ended on March 11, 2012. Because March 11, 2012, was a Sunday, that time frame is extended until Monday, March 12, 2012. See *Fed.R.Civ.P. 6(a)(1)(C)*.

Plaintiff also did not meet the filing deadline with respect to the Magistrate Judge's March 7, 2012 order. Computing the time for service in accordance with *Rule 6*, plaintiff had until March 26, 2012 in which to file his objections to that order.[4] Yet, plaintiff did not file his objections until April 3, 2010. Untimeliness alone is a sufficient basis for denying both of plaintiff's motions for "review." See *Matthewson v. Ryan, 2012 U.S. Dist. LEXIS 20848, 2012 WL 510318, at *2 (D.Ariz. Feb. 16, 2012)* (citing, inter alia, *Simpson v. Lear Astronics Corp., 77 F.3d 1170, 1174 (9th Cir.1996)*) ("The absence of a timely objection precludes later assignment of error in this court or in any higher court of the non-dispositive rulings of a magistrate judge.")

4   In accordance with *Fed.R.Civ.P. 6(a)(1)(A)*, March 7,, 2012, the entry date of the order, is excluded from computing plaintiff's time to file objections. Beginning to count on March 8, 2012, and adding three days for service pursuant to

Fed.R.Civ.P. 6(d), means that the 14 day time frame ended on March 24, 2012. Because March 24, 2012, was a Saturday, that time frame is extended until Monday, March 26, 2012. See *Fed.R.Civ.P. 6(a)(1)(C)*. **State agents consistently insist procedures not provided for be utilized. In Robert Schilleman, Plaintiff, v. Corizon Health Incorporated, et al., Defendants. *2015 U.S. Dist. LEXIS 161675 (*December 2, 2015) the court states in part:**

In a March 26, 2015 Order, the Court found that Plaintiff stated the following claims in his First Amended Complaint: (1) *Eighth Amendment* claims against Corizon in Counts One and Three; (2) an *Eighth Amendment* claim against Ryan in Count One; (3) *Eighth Amendment* claims against Defendants Hegmann, Mulhorn, Medical Director, Medical Providers, Montano, Facility Health Administrators, and Fansler in Count Two; and (4) state law negligence claims against Defendants Hegmann, Mulhorn, Medical Director, Medical Providers, Montano, Facility Health Administrators, and Fansler in Count Three. (Doc. 23.) The Court noted that because unnamed Medical Director, Medical Providers, and Facility Health Administrators could not be served, Plaintiff should seek to amend his complaint to add the proper names of those Defendants when they were discovered. (*Id.* at 15.)

Plaintiff seeks leave to add claims against Patrick Arnold, Duc Vo, Winfred Williams, Cynthia Ripsin, Kent Ainslie, "Facility Health Administrators, ASPC-Eyman," "Corizon's Clinical Coordinator assigned to the ASPC-Eyman (Cook Unit)," and "Corizon's Regional Medical Director responsible for the ASPC-Eyman (Cook Unit)."

A. Legal Standard

Although the decision to grant or deny a motion to amend is within the discretion of the district court, "*Rule 15(a)* [of the Federal Rules of Civil Procedure] declares that leave to amend 'shall be freely given when justice so requires'; this mandate is to be heeded." *Foman v. Davis, 371 U.S. 178, 182, 83 S. Ct. 227, 9 L. Ed. 2d 222 (1962).* "In exercising its discretion[,] . . . 'a court must be guided by the underlying purpose of Rule 15--to facilitate decision on the merits rather than on the pleadings or technicalities . . . . Thus, 'Rule 15's policy of favoring amendments to pleadings should be applied with extreme liberality.'" *Eldridge v. Block, 832 F.2d 1132, 1135 (9th Cir.1987)* (citations omitted). Motions to amend should be granted unless the district court determines that there has been a showing of: (1) undue delay; (2) bad faith or dilatory motives on the part of the movant; (3) repeated failure to cure deficiencies by previous amendments; (4) undue prejudice to the opposing party; or (5) futility of the proposed amendment. *Foman, 371 U.S. at 182.* "Generally, this determination should be performed with all inferences in favor of granting the motion." *Griggs v. Pace Am. Grp., Inc., 170 F.3d 877, 880 (9th Cir. 1999).* Significantly, "[t]he party opposing amendment bears the burden of showing prejudice," futility, or one of the other permissible reasons for denying a motion to amend. *DCD Programs Ltd. v. Leighton, 833 F.2d 183, 187 (9th Cir. 1987); see Richardson v. United States, 841 F.2d 993, 999 (9th Cir. 1988)* (stating that leave to amend should be freely given unless the opposing party makes "an affirmative showing of either prejudice or bad faith").

Here, there is no evidence of undue delay, bad faith, repeated failure to cure, or undue prejudice. Defendants assert that allowing Plaintiff leave to amend to add additional allegations against additional Defendants would be futile because Plaintiff fails to state a claim upon which relief can be granted against those Defendants. Accordingly, the Court will examine whether Plaintiff states claims upon which relief may be granted in his Second Amended Complaint.

B. Futility

1. Count One

Plaintiff continues to assert *Eighth Amendment* claims against Defendants Corizon and Ryan in Count One. Consistent with the Court's findings in its March 26, 2015 Order, Plaintiff states an *Eighth Amendment* claim against Defendants Corizon and Ryan in Count One of his Second Amended Complaint.

. . . .

2. Count Two

In Count Two, Plaintiff seeks to add an *Eighth Amendment* claim based on deliberate indifference to serious medical needs against Defendants Kent Ainslie, Unknown FHAs, Unknown Clinical Coordinators, the Corizon Regional Medical Director, Patrick Arnold, Duc Vo, Winfred Williams, and Cynthia Ripsin. Having reviewed Plaintiff's allegations in Count Two, the Court finds that Plaintiff states an *Eighth Amendment* claim against Defendants Kent Ainslie, Unknown FHAs, Unknown Clinical Coordinators, the Corizon Regional Medical Director, and Patrick Arnold, Duc Vo, Winfred Williams, and Cynthia Ripsin in Count Two. The Court will therefore allow Plaintiff to amend his complaint to add his *Eighth Amendment* claims in Count Two against Defendants Kent Ainslie, Patrick Arnold, Duc Vo, Winfred Williams, and Cynthia Ripsin. However, to the extent Plaintiff seeks to add Corizon's Clinical Coordinator, Unknown Facility Health Administrators, and Corizon's Regional

Medical Director, he must seek to amend his claims against those Defendants when he discovers their proper names for the same reasons set forth in the Court's March 26, 2015 Order.

Additionally, Plaintiff reasserts *Eighth Amendment* claims against Defendants Hegmann, Mulhorn, and Montano in Count Two. Consistent with the Court's findings in its March 26, 2015 Order, Plaintiff states an *Eighth Amendment* claim against Defendants Hegmann, Mulhorn, and Montano in Count Two of his Second Amended Complaint.

Finally, after Plaintiff filed his proposed Second Amended Complaint, which included claims against Fansler, the parties stipulated to the dismissal of Fansler from this action (Doc. 142). Accordingly, the Court will deny Plaintiff's Motion to Amend as moot to the extent he asserts claims against Fansler in his Second Amended Complaint.

3. Count Three

Plaintiff asserts a state law negligence claim against all Defendants in Count Three. Having reviewed Plaintiff's allegations in Count Three, the Court finds that Plaintiff states state law negligence claims against all Defendants in Count Three. The Court will therefore allow Plaintiff to amend his complaint to add his state law negligence claims in Count Three against Defendants Corizon, Ryan, Montano, Hegmann, Mulhorn, Arnold, Vo, Williams, Ripsin, and Ainslie. However, to the extent Plaintiff seeks to add Corizon's Clinical Coordinator, Unknown Facility Health Administrators, and Corizon's Regional Medical Director, he must seek to amend his claims against those Defendants when he discovers their proper names for the same reasons set forth in the Court's March 26, 2015 Order.

The Court will therefore direct the Clerk of the Court to file Plaintiff's Second Amended Complaint currently lodged at Doc. 130-2. The Court will further direct the Clerk of the Court to dismiss Defendants Fansler, Corizon's Clinical Coordinator, Unknown Facility Health Administrators, and Corizon's Regional Medical Director from the Third Amended Complaint and this action without prejudice.

LEONARD DEWITT, PLAINTIFF-APPELLANT, V. CORIZON, INC., ET AL., DEFENDANTS-APPELLEES. NO. 13-2930 UNITED STATES COURT OF APPEALS FOR THE SEVENTH CIRCUIT

I. BACKGROUND

Because the district court decided this case on a motion for summary judgment, we recite the facts in the light most favorable to the nonmoving party, Dewitt. *See Greeno v. Daley*, 414 F.3d 645, 652 (7th Cir. 2005). Dewitt's eye problems began in 2007 during his first incarceration at the Wabash Correctional Facility, which is a part of the Indiana Department of Corrections ("IDOC"). The IDOC contracts with Appellee Corizon, Inc. to provide medical care to Indiana prisoners. Dewitt submitted the first of many Requests for Healthcare to Corizon stating something was very wrong with his bloodshot left eye and his vision was "like looking through a dirty piece of plastic." Corizon's eye doctor diagnosed him with astigmatism and presbyopia (old-age nearsightedness causing slightly blurry vision), and prescribed eyeglasses.

Three months later, Dewitt submitted another Request for Healthcare after being transferred to a local work-release facility. IDOC medical staff contacted the Plainfield Correctional Facility to set up an appointment for him since the work-release facility did not have any specialists on staff. But Appellee Patty Wirth said that no appointment would be available for three months, so IDOC medical staff sent Dewitt to a prison physician who noted no obvious abnormalities in his left eye.

In May 2008, Dewitt was released on parole. A doctor determined that Dewitt had a form of glaucoma in his left eye and he was advised in late 2008 to undergo laser-eye surgery to prevent any future attacks. He underwent a surgical procedure on his right eye in early 2009 to remove part of the iris to decrease eye pressure. His left eye continued to have higher than normal intra-ocular pressure.

Dewitt was again incarcerated in 2009, this time at the Putnamville Correctional Facility, where he filed another Request for Healthcare, noting exceptional irritation in his left eye. He was referred to Wishard Hospital where an ophthalmologist prescribed medicated eye drops in order to decrease the pressure. The ophthalmologist told Dewitt if they did not work, he might need to have the eye or portions of it removed. The drops did not work, and, believing he had no real alternative, Dewitt submitted another Request for Healthcare in November to have his left eye removed.

Dewitt received treatment both inside and outside the facility over the next several months, and filed another Request for Healthcare to have his eye removed in February 2011. Corizon's regional medical director, Appellee Dr. Michael Mitcheff, viewed removal as an extreme last resort and suggested a more conservative approach, including medicated eye drops and pain medication. Dewitt was prescribed medication, including a 90-day prescription for Vicodin by defendant Dr. Naveen Rajoli, ultimately received a glaucoma evaluation at the Midwest Eye Institute and eye removal was recommended. In May 2012, he underwent surgery to remove part of his left eye's ciliary body.

Dewitt filed suit under *42 U.S.C. ~ 1983* against Corizon, Wirth, and Mitcheff, asserting that they were deliberately indifferent to his glaucoma condition. He also sued Dr. James Stewart and Dr. Rajoli, but Stewart was dismissed from the suit and Dewitt does not mention Rajoli in his brief. In April 2012, Dewitt moved for assistance of counsel, stating his vision problems combined with his tenth-grade education made it difficult for him to conduct discovery and litigate his case. The district court denied his request, finding that Dewitt's claims were not overly complex or meritorious, that Dewitt was familiar with his claims and able to present them, and he was "within the spectrum of most indigent parties." Six months later, Dewitt moved again for assistance of counsel, repeating his earlier statements. He also complained that Appellees had abused discovery rules and delayed their responses. The court denied this request using the same language as the first denial and without addressing the alleged discovery abuses.

After Appellees moved for summary judgment, Dewitt filed a "reply" to Appellees' reply in support of summary judgment, and a request under *Federal Rule of Civil Procedure 56(f)* (now *Rule 56(d)*) for further discovery. He again begged the court to recruit counsel so he could conduct discovery. The district court did not address Dewitt's *Rule 56(d)* motion, but granted Appellees' motion for summary judgment, in part, because Dewitt failed to show Corizon had any "official policy or custom" to delay medical treatment and because Dr. Mitcheff exercised reasoned professional judgment. Dewitt now appeals.

II. ANALYSIS

Though Dewitt argues the merits of the summary judgment order, we do not reach that issue because we hold that Dewitt should have had an attorney throughout the litigation. There is no right to recruitment of counsel in federal civil litigation, but a district court has discretion to recruit counsel under *28 U.S.C. § 1915(e)(1)*. See *Henderson v. Ghosh, 755 F.3d 559, No. 13-2035, 2014 U.S. App. LEXIS 11816, 2014 WL 2757473, at *4 (7th Cir. June 18, 2014)* (per curiam). If an indigent plaintiff has made a reasonable attempt to obtain counsel and then files a motion for recruitment of counsel, the district court should ask "whether the difficulty of the case--factually and legally--exceeds the particular plaintiff's capacity as a layperson to coherently present it to the judge or jury himself." *Pruitt v. Mote, 503 F.3d 647, 655 (7th Cir. 2007)* (en banc). We acknowledge this is a "difficult decision" since "[a]lmost everyone would benefit from having a lawyer, but there are too many indigent litigants and too few lawyers willing and able to volunteer for these cases." *Olson v. Morgan, 750 F.3d 708, 711 (7th Cir. 2014)*. So we review the denial of the recruitment of counsel for an abuse of discretion and will re-verse only if the plaintiff was prejudiced by the denial--*e.g.*, if there is a reasonable likelihood that the recruitment of counsel would have made a difference in the outcome of the litigation. *See Santiago v. Walls, 599 F.3d 749, 765 (7th Cir. 2010)*. In so deciding, our case law is clear that a plaintiff can be prejudiced by the lack of counsel pretrial just as easily as during the briefing or trial itself. *See id. at 765* (noting prejudice when plaintiff "was incapable of engaging in any investigation[] or locating and presenting key witnesses or evidence" (quoting *Pruitt, 503 F.3d at 659*)); *see also Henderson, 2014 U.S. App. LEXIS 11816, 2014 WL 2757473 at *7* (finding prejudice where plaintiff "was incapable of obtaining the witnesses and evidence he needed to prevail on his claims"); *Bracey v. Grondin, 712 F.3d 1012, 1017 (7th Cir. 2013)* ("Complexities anticipated (or arising) during discovery can justify a court's decision to recruit counsel").

The first question, then, is whether the district court abused its discretion in denying the motions for recruitment of counsel. In his first motion, Dewitt requested the recruitment of counsel because of his **tenth-**grade education, the fact that he was incarcerated and unable to investigate and discover relevant facts. He also pointed out that he was "now totally blind in his left eye and the vision in his right eye is impaired." He discussed the medical complexity of his case, his reliance on "jailhouse lawyers," and his inability "to comprehend with any legal understanding, the discovery rules and the Defendants [sic] motions." The court denied the motion and stated that "the claims by the plaintiff are not of sufficient complexity or merit as to surpass the plaintiff's ability to properly develop and present them," and that "the plaintiff is within the spectrum of 'most indigent parties' because he has and will have a meaningful opportunity to present his claim, he has demonstrated familiarity with his claims and the ability to present them." The court stated that it had considered the complexity of the case and Dewitt's ability to litigate the case--without delving into any of Dewitt's personal characteristics or the specifics of the case--before denying the motion.

The court abused its discretion by failing to explain its reasoning and failing to address all the relevant arguments Dewitt raised. For example, the court characterized Dewitt as fitting within the spectrum of most pro se litigants and said it had considered his personal characteristics, but it did not identify those characteristics. However, the court did not address the challenges that Dewitt, as a blind and indigent prisoner with a tenth-grade education and no legal experience, faced in being able to investigate crucial facts and depose witnesses, doctors, and other allegedly resistant prison personnel. *See Pruitt, 503 F.3d at 655* (noting the court "should review any information submitted in support of the request for counsel, as well as the pleadings, communications from, and any contact with the plaintiff"); *see also Navejar v. Iyiola, 718 F.3d 692, 696 (7th Cir. 2013)* (noting judge should have considered plaintiff's "limited education, mental illness, language difficulties, and lack of access to fellow prisoners or other resources for assistance after his transfer from Stateville"). Moreover, the court's statement that Dewitt "has demonstrated familiarity with his claims and the ability to present them" does not demonstrate that the district court specifically examined Dewitt's personal ability to litigate the case, versus the ability of the "jailhouse lawyer" who Dewitt said in his motion was helping him. The analysis should be of the *plaintiff's* ability to litigate *his own* claims, and the "fact that an inmate receives assistance from a fellow prisoner should not factor into the decision whether to recruit counsel." *Henderson, 2014 U.S. App. LEXIS 11816, 2014 WL 2757473 at *5.*

Nor did the court explain why the claims were not of "sufficient complexity" to merit recruitment of counsel. In fact, the case presents complicated medical matters, involves varying recommended courses of treatment by numerous physicians, and required discovery into what constitutes reasonable care for medical professionals. Though not every deliberate indifference case is so complex and beyond the individual plaintiff's capacity as to warrant the recruitment of counsel, this one was. *See Henderson, 2014 U.S. App. LEXIS 11816, 2014 WL 2757473 at **6-7* (noting case required recruitment of counsel because it "involves complex medical terms and concepts," requires proof of the "defendants' state of mind" and proof of doctor's knowledge of a substantial risk of harm and disregard of that risk). *But see, e.g., Olson, 750 F.3d at 711-12* (holding no abuse of discretion in denying recruitment of counsel motion for medical indifference case when disputed issue was whether defendant knew of plaintiff's physical condition); *Romanelli v. Suliene, 615 F.3d 847, 854 (7th Cir. 2010)* (finding no abuse of discretion in denying motion in medical indifference case when neither side contested that plaintiff was ill). We are aware that the appointment of counsel in civil cases can pose challenges for judges, who ask lawyers to volunteer their time to take these assignments, and the attorneys who are asked by the judges and who ultimately take the assignments. As a way to combat those issues, we again highlight the work done by the Pro Bono Program for the United States District Court for the Northern District of Illinois Trial Bar, which mandates that members of the Trial Bar serve as an appointed attorney in pro se civil or appellate matters. *See N.D. Ill. L.R. 83.35; N.D. Ill. L.R. 83.11(g). See also Henderson, 2014 U.S. App. LEXIS 11816, 2014 WL 2757473 at *3 n.1; Synergy Assocs. v. Sun Biotechnologies, Inc., 350 F.3d 681, 684 (7th Cir. 2003).* While other districts in this circuit have similar procedures, *see C.D. Ill. L.R. 83.5(J), N.D. Ind. L.R. 83-7, S.D. Ind. 4-6, 83-7,* the mandatory nature of the Northern District of Illinois's program ensures that judges are not put in the position of repeatedly asking the same counsel to take on appointments, and attorneys are not put in the position of being asked time and again to take cases by the judges in front of whom they appear on a regular basis.

In Dewitt's second motion to recruit counsel, Dewitt made basically the same arguments while adding that "Defendants are intentionally abusing the discovery rules, they have delayed their responses to the Plaintiff's interrogatories so as to gain an upper hand with the closing of the deadlines the Court has imposed, and [are] now claiming that they have no obligation to answer further interrogatories." The court denied Dewitt's motion without addressing this new argument. Though the district court need not address every point raised in recruitment motions, it must address those that bear directly on whether "the difficulty of the case--factually and legally--exceeds the particular plaintiff's capacity as a layperson to coherently present it to the judge or jury himself." *Pruitt, 503 F.3d at 655.* That includes whether Dewitt was capable of putting a stop to alleged discovery abuses. *See, e.g., Henderson, 2014 U.S. App. LEXIS 11816, 2014 WL 2757473 at *6* (finding court erred by not considering substantive issue, namely appellant's personal capabilities, that was raised in recruitment motion).

Moreover, in his *Federal Rule of Civil Procedure 56(f)* (now *56(d)*) "reply" to Appellees' reply in support of summary judgment, Dewitt requested more time for discovery as well as the recruitment of counsel to aid him in conducting such discovery. Although this was not a separate formal motion requesting counsel, the court should have addressed it. *See McNeil v. United States, 508 U.S. 106, 113, 113 S. Ct. 1980, 124 L. Ed. 2d 21 (1993)* ("[W]e have insisted that the pleadings prepared by prisoners who do not have access to counsel be liberally construed"); *Santiago, 599 F.3d at 765* (noting "the magistrate judge's methodological lapse in failing to give full consideration to each factor constitutes an abuse of discretion"); *Pruitt, 503 F.3d at 658.*

Finding that the district court abused its discretion does not end our inquiry. We must now determine whether Dewitt was prejudiced. Based on the reasons the court gave in granting the motion for summary judgment, we find Dewitt was. For example, the district court determined that Dr. Mitcheff exercised "reasoned professional judgment" inconsistent with deliberate indifference. But could a lawyer have helped Dewitt present sufficient facts to create a genuine issue about why the doctor declined to follow a specialist's recommendations or advised a continuation of ineffective treatments that prolonged his pain? We think there is a reasonable likelihood counsel could have aided here and made a difference in the outcome. *See Greeno, 414 F.3d at 658* (holding case was "legally more complicated than a typical failure-to-treat claim because it require[d] an assessment of the adequacy of the treatment that [plaintiff] did receive, a question that will likely require expert testimony"); *Ortiz v. Webster, 655 F.3d 731, 735 (7th Cir. 2011)* (analyzing complexities of deliberate indifference claims).

Counsel also could have assisted Dewitt in addressing his concerns about the alleged discovery violations. Dewitt filed a motion to compel, to which Appellees responded that they had replied to all outstanding discovery. The court found the issue moot based on Appellees' response and denied the motion. Yet, two months later, Dewitt stated in his second motion for recruitment of counsel that Appellees were not complying with all discovery requests. That was still a problem when Dewitt filed his *Rule 56(f)* request for more time to conduct discovery. We do not make any determinations on the merits of Dewitt's allegations relating to discovery abuses, but find that had Dewitt had counsel to navigate through discovery, there is a reasonable likelihood that he could have better advocated his position and changed the outcome of the litigation. *See Santiago, 599 F.3d at 765-66* (noting Appellant's "later attempts to conduct relevant discovery were not successful" and "[t]he treatment afforded him by the defendants was not, it is safe to say, the same treatment that would have been afforded a member of the bar").

Finally, we observe the district court disregarded Dewitt's request under *Federal Rule of Civil Procedure 56(f)* seeking more time to conduct discovery before the court ruled on Appellees' motion for summary judgment. While a district court has broad discretion to deny such motions, *see Kalis v. Colgate-Palmolive Co., 231 F.3d 1049, 1056 (7th Cir. 2000)*, it is improper to decide summary judgment without first ruling on a pending 56(f) motion. *Doe v. Abington Friends School, 480 F.3d 252, 257 (3d Cir. 2007).*

IVES T. ARTIS, PLAINTIFF, VS. BYUNGHAK JIN, MEDICAL DIRECTOR (INDIVIAUL COMPASITY); CORIZON HEALTH, FORMERLY PRISON HEALTHCARE SERVICES (OFFICIAL COMPASITY), DEFENDANTS. Civil Action No. 13-1226 UNITED STATES DISTRICT COURT FOR THE WESTERN DISTRICT OF PENNSYLVANIA

A. FACTUAL AND PROCEDURAL BACKGROUND

Plaintiff's Complaint (ECF No. 4) and Amended Complaint (ECF No. 59)(supplementing allegations contained in original Complaint) allege that in July 2010, Plaintiff sustained an injury to his left ankle, which was followed by a three-year course of inadequate medical treatment, while incarcerated at SCI-Greene. Plaintiff alleges that the treatment received was based upon economic nonmedical factors and resulted in three years of pain and the exacerbation of his condition.

In particular, Plaintiff alleges that his medical treatment included physical therapy beginning in November 2010; outside shoes for comfort in January 2011; high dosages of acetaminophen for a year; at least four sets of x-rays from July 12, 2010, through April 24, 2012, (in lieu of his request for an MRI); an eight-month course of Vicodin from February 2012 through October 2012; and, on April 16, 2012, an MRI which revealed arthritic changes, mild swelling,   small fracture fragments and apparent ligament tears in his left ankle. (ECF No. 4, pp. 5-6). Plaintiff alleges that he was then prescribed air cushioned shoes, two ankle braces and pain medication, but these treatments were revoked for three months while he was housed in the Restrictive Housing Unit ("RHU"), causing him to suffer in pain.[1] Plaintiff alleges that these prescribed aids were returned to him on January 3, 2013, upon his release from the RHU, and that he was provided a walker for mobility due to his deteriorating condition three weeks later. Plaintiff alleges that the walker was defective, causing him to fall, but a new walker was not provided. Defendant Park allegedly ordered a wheelchair for Plaintiff, but this order was rescinded by Dr. Jin as not necessary.

1   Attached to Plaintiff's Complaint are copies of several grievances filed in accordance with the Pennsylvania Department of Corrections' administrative review process (ECF No. 1-2). The grievances indicated that Plaintiff's medication was "adjusted" after he was caught selling his Vicodin and that his air cushioned shoes and braces were removed while he was housed in the RHU for security reasons and as not medically   necessary while restricted to his cell for 23 hours per day. (ECF No. 1-2, pp. 25, 28).

Plaintiff alleges that he was then seen and treated by an orthopedic specialist at Allegheny General Hospital, who conducted a second MRI, and confirmed that the injuries to his left ankle persisted despite a course of conservative treatment, and that his right ankle also suffered from osteoarthritis. (ECF No. 4, pp. 6-7).

Plaintiff alleges that he underwent surgery on his left ankle in June 2013, but only after the Pennsylvania Department of Corrections changed corporate medical providers. After surgery, Plaintiff alleges Dr. Jin continued to delay or deny treatment during his recovery, by waiting 6 days to provide a blood thinner to prevent a blood clot (Plaintiff does not allege he suffered a blood clot) and by forcing him to use crutches to support his left ankle, when his right ankle suffered from arthritis.

Thereafter, Plaintiff filed a Motion for Injunction, seeking a transfer to a different facility so that he could be treated by a new doctor. (ECF No. 6). Plaintiff's Motion was denied as not meeting the heightened standard required for a preliminary injunction. (ECF No. 8). Plaintiff filed a second Motion for a Preliminary Injunction and Motion for Temporary Restraining Order on August 6, 2014, again seeking a transfer to a different facility. (ECF No. 39). In resolving the Motion, this Court ordered the production of certain of Plaintiff's medical records to determine whether Plaintiff was receiving any required treatment for his ankle post-surgery (ECF No. 43).. The records establish that while Plaintiff continued to complain of pain and request authorization to wear air cushioned shoes instead of prison issued boots, it was determined that there was no medical need for special accommodations because he had an "old, healed injury," and "[p]ain is expected." (ECF No. 50-1). The records also reveal that Plaintiff is non-compliant with psychiatric medication, and that for ongoing pain, he was provided with knee high compression stockings. It was determined that his ankle injury appeared "fully recovered." (ECF No. 50-1, p. 6). The records reveal Plaintiff insisted that he required surgery on his right ankle, but there are no indications in his records from any medical provider, including his treating orthopedist at Allegheny General Hospital, to support this request. Id. at p. 8.

In resolving the Motion for a Preliminary Injunction, it was determined that Plaintiff had been moved to a new facility, and therefore the requested injunctive relief was denied as moot. See, No. 13-1226, (W.D. Pa. September 11, 2014).

Defendants, through their Motions to Dismiss, contend that the allegations contained in Plaintiff's Complaint and the evidence of record produced in conjunction with the Motion for Preliminary Injunction, establish that Plaintiff was provided consistent but conservative medical treatment for his ankle injury and, accordingly, there is no evidence of deliberate indifference to his condition. Defendants also argue that Plaintiff has failed to exhaust available administrative remedies and thus his claim is barred pursuant to the Prison Litigation Reform Act ("PLRA"), *42 U.S.C. § 1997e(a)*.

1. Defendants Jim and Park

Plaintiff alleges that Defendants Jin and Park violated his *Eighth Amendment* right to be free from "cruel and unusual punishment" because Defendants were "deliberately indifferent" to his serious medical needs. In particular, Plaintiff alleges Defendants failed to properly investigate his foot pain by failing to conducting additional tests, including an MRI, and failing to promptly schedule appropriate surgical treatment, in the face of his continued pain and evident decline in mobility.

In this case, the Court assumes that Plaintiff's ankle pain constituted a serious medical need. However, the records attached to his Complaint as well as to his brief in opposition to the Motion to Dismiss establish that the treatment provided prior to surgery was consistent with a conservative treatment plan, and that several different treatment options were attempted including physical therapy, medication, and supportive braces, crutches and a walker. When surgery was provided, Plaintiff's medical records indicate that surgery was not the only treatment option available to provide relief, and that more conservative options such as those already implemented would be appropriate.[2] (ECF No. 73-1, p.3). Under these circumstances, it is apparent that the record in this case shows only a difference over opinion over the course of proper medical treatment, rather than a complete denial of medical care. In such situations, the United States Court of Appeals for the Third Circuit has held that courts should not second guess medical judgments to constitutionalize claims which sound in state tort law. *U. S. ex rel. Walker v. Fayette Cnty., Pa., 599 F.2d 573, 575 n.2 (3d Cir. 1979)*(citing *Westlake v. Lucas, 537 F.2d 857, 860 n. 5 (6th Cir. 1976)*). Thus, because Plaintiff has failed to allege facts evidencing deliberate indifference giving rise to a constitutional claim under *Section 1983*, it is recommended that the Motion to Dismiss filed on behalf of Defendants Park and Jin be granted.[3]

2   Plaintiff has provided a copy of his medical records from the date of his admission to Allegheny General Hospital for left ankle surgery. The "Indications for Procedure" note that "[t]reatment options were discussed with the patient including both nonoperative and operative treatment options. The patient had attempted conservative measures in the past and had failed." (ECF No, 73-1, p.3).

3   In his brief in opposition to the Motion to Dismiss, Plaintiff references the Universal Declaration of Human Rights as a basis for his claims against Defendants. However, Plaintiff cannot sustain such claims because the Universal Declaration of Human Rights is a non-binding declaration that provides no private rights of action. *Sosa v. Alvarez--Machain, 542 U.S. 692, 734, 124 S. Ct. 2739, 159 L. Ed. 2d 718 (2004)* (explaining that Universal Declaration is simply a statement of principles and not a treaty or international agreement that would impose legal obligations.).

2. Defendant Corizon Health

Defendant Corizon Health is identified in Plaintiff's Complaint as providing medical staff to Pennsylvania correctional institutions "through an independent contract." ECF No. 4, p. 7. Plaintiff alleges that Corizon "employed and conducted regulations and ta[c]tics to save money." Id. For § 1983 purposes, Corizon Health "cannot be held responsible for the acts of its employees under a theory of respondeat superior or vicarious liability." Natale v. Camden County Corrections Facility, 318 F.3d 575, 584 (3d Cir. 2003). However, the United States Court of Appeals for the Third Circuit has held that a contracted health care provider, such as Corizon Health, could be held liable if the plaintiff shows that there was a relevant policy or custom, and that the policy or custom caused the constitutional violation plaintiff alleges. Specifically, there are three situations where acts of a government employee may be deemed to be the result of a policy or custom of the governmental entity for whom the employee works, thereby rendering the entity liable under § 1983. The first is where "the appropriate officer or entity promulgates a generally applicable statement of policy and the subsequent act complained of is simply an implementation of that policy." The second occurs where "no rule has been announced as policy but federal law has been violated by an act of the policymaker itself." Finally, a policy or custom may also exist where "the policymaker has failed to act affirmatively at all, [though] the need to take some action to control the agents of the government 'is so obvious, and the inadequacy of existing practice so likely to result in the violation of constitutional rights, that the policymaker can reasonably be said to have been deliberately indifferent to the need.'" Id. at 584 (footnote and citations omitted). The same standard applies to claims against a private corporation that is functioning as a "state actor." See Weigher v. Prison Health Services, 402 F. App'x 668, 669-70 (3d Cir.2010).

Here, Plaintiff has not alleged facts giving rise to a constitutional violation or suggesting that any decision to refuse or delay medical treatment to Plaintiff was the result of an actionable policy, practice, or custom of Corizon Health. Rather, Plaintiff broadly speculates that the course of treatment was the result of an unspecified policy to "save money," but fails to allege any supportive facts sufficient to "nudge [his] claims ... across the line from conceivable to plausible." Iqbal, 556 U.S. at 680-81. Accordingly, it is recommended that the Motion to Dismiss filed on behalf of Corizon Health be granted.

3. Futility

If a civil rights complaint is subject to Rule 12(b)(6) dismissal, a district court must permit a curative amendment unless such an amendment would be inequitable or futile. Fletcher--Harlee Corp. v. Pote Concrete Contractors, Inc., 482 F.3d 247, 251 (3d Cir. 2007). In this case, Plaintiff's allegations, coupled with the medical records he has provided to the Court in conjunction with his Complaint and brief in opposition to the Motions to Dismiss, unequivocally demonstrate that Plaintiff has received care consistently, but he disagrees with the propriety and adequacy of the care received. Because Plaintiff cannot sustain a § 1983 claim under these circumstances, leave to amend would be futile. Accordingly, it is recommended that Plaintiff's Complaint and Amended Complaint be dismissed with prejudice.

AMILCAR GABRIEL, PLAINTIFF-APPELLANT, VS. JIM HAMLIN, BOB DOERR, ALLEN WISELY, BRIAN RUIZ, M.D. AND WEXFORD HEALTH SOURCES, INC., DEFENDANTS -Appellees. No. 06-3636 UNITED STATES COURT OF APPEALS FOR THE SEVENTH CIRCUIT

STATEMENT OF THE CASE

This lawsuit involves actions under 42 U.S.C.§l983 for knowing exposure of the plaintiff prisoner to dangerous work conditions, and denial of medical care. Plaintiff suffered burns when he was working in the kitchen at Big Muddy River Correctional Center, and his leg went into a kettle of scalding water when he fell, causing serious burns. Plaintiff claimed that he was knowingly exposed to dangerous work conditions, and that he was denied proper medical care for his burns, infections and pain.

The case was first set for trial to commence on July 12, 2005, and was rescheduled by the court to August 23, 2005. (Doc.57) On July 18, 2005 the defendants filed a motion to continue trial, (Doc.68), which the court granted and reset the trial for Tuesday through Thursday of the weeks of September 19 and 26, 2005. (Doc. 69) On September 12, 2005 the district court, on its own motion, rescheduled the trial from Tuesday through Thursday the weeks of September 19 and September 26, 2005 to Monday through Friday of the week of September 19, 2005. (Doc.77)

On September 14, 2005 plaintiff filed his first and only motion to continue trial, setting forth that the plaintiff's expert was not able to testify the week of September 19, 2005, and in the alternative for voluntary dismissal without prejudice. (Doc.81) On September 15, 2005 the court denied plaintiff's motion to continue trial, denied the motion for voluntary dismissal without prejudice, and dismissed the actions with prejudice for want of prosecution. (Doc.85; Short. Appendix)

On September 27, 2005 plaintiff filed a timely Rule 60(b) motion to reconsider the dismissal, (Doc.87), which was denied on September 5, 2006. (Doc.92) Plaintiff appeals the dismissal with prejudice, the denial of the motion to continue trial or voluntary dismissal without prejudice, and the denial of his Rule 60(b) motion.

STATEMENT OF FACTS

Allegations of the Complaint

The amended complaint alleged that on December 4, 2000 the plaintiff was a resident at Big Muddy River Correctional Center, and was employed in the prison kitchen. (Doc.16, Amended Complaint, Count I, Par.10) Defendants, Jim Hamlin and Bob Doerr, were employed as food service supervisors in the kitchen. (Id., pars. 11-12)

Jim Hamlin assigned Mr. Gabriel to the job of cleaning the exhaust system in the kitchen on a weekly basis. (Id., Count I, par.11) In order to clean the exhaust system, it was necessary to reach portions over an area where there were two (2) large pots of scalding hot water, by leaning over them or standing over them.

Count I alleged that Jim Hamlin and Bob Doerr knew that the plaintiff would have to reach over the pots of scalding hot water to clean the exhaust system, but did not provide any ladder or other means of safe access to the area, and observed the plaintiff on many occasions cleaning the exhaust system by standing over the pots. (Id., pars.14-15)

Count I further alleged that, fearing for his safety, Mr. Gabriel began to empty the pots of scalding hot water before cleaning the exhaust system, and then refilling them after completing the work. (Id., par.17) Jim Hamlin and Bob Doerr disregarded the substantial risk to the plaintiff's safety, ordered him not to empty the pots of scalding hot water again, and forced him to risk serious injury when he cleaned the exhaust system. (Doc.16, Count I, pars.19-20)

The defendant, Brian Ruiz, M.D. was employed by Wexford Health Sources and performed medical services under their contract with the Illinois Department of Corrections as a physician at Big Muddy River Correctional Center. (Doc.16, Count II, par.11) Allen Wisely was the health care administrator. (Id. par.12)

On December 4, 2000 the plaintiff, Amilcar Gabriel, sustained second and third degree burns to his right leg when he fell while cleaning the exhaust hood and his leg went into a pot of scalding hot water. He was taken to the health care unit, where he became a patient of Dr. Ruiz. (Id., pars. 13-14)

Count II further alleged that it was the duty of the defendants, Allen Wisely, Brian Ruiz, M.D. and Wexford Health Sources, under 730 ILCS 5/3-7-2(d) to provide necessary medical care and treatment to Mr. Gabriel. (Doc.16, Count II, par.16)

Dr. Ruiz treated Mr. Gabriel's burns at the prison, and refused to send him to an outside hospital. Although he knew that the plaintiff had sustained serious burns to his leg, Dr. Ruiz only wrapped the wounds and sent plaintiff back to his housing unit the next day. (Id., par.19) Mr. Gabriel could barely walk and was in severe pain. (Id., par.20). He asked Dr. Ruiz for a wheelchair because of his difficulty walking and the severe pain, but Dr. Ruiz denied the plaintiff's request for a wheelchair. (Id., pars. 21-22)

During a period from December 4, 2000 through August, 2001, the plaintiff was under the care of Dr. Ruiz and sought treatment for his burns, infections and severe pain from Dr. Ruiz. (Id. par.15) Count II further alleged that the defendants disregarded the plaintiff's serious medical need, and refused to send plaintiff to an emergency room to provide necessary medical care to the plaintiff for his serious burns and pain. (Id., par.17)

Dr. Ruiz refused to provide the plaintiff with effective pain medication, and gave him only regular over-the-counter motrin and aspirin tablets on December 4 and December 5, 2000. (Id. par.18)

On December 18, 2000 the plaintiff was returned to the health care unit because the burns had not begun to heal well, and complications and infection had begun. (Doc.16, Count II, par. 24) Plaintiff asked Dr. Ruiz to send him to an outside specialist, but Dr. Ruiz denied plaintiff's request for care by an outside specialist. (Id., pars. 25-26) Mr. Gabriel asked Dr. Ruiz for strong pain medication for his severe pain, and Dr. Ruiz denied the plaintiff's request. (Id., par. 27)

Plaintiff remained in the health care infirmary until February 16, 2001, a total of fifty-eight (58) days, during which time the only pain medication Dr. Ruiz ordered was over-the-counter Ibuprofen until December 28, 2000 and over-the-counter Motrin until February 2, 2001. (Doc.16, Count II, par.28) Dr. Ruiz discontinued pain medication and refused to authorize any pain medication for the plaintiff between February 2 and March 5, 2001, and he received no medication for his pain after March, 2001 other than two doses of Motrin in July, 2001. (Id., pars. 33-34)

Allen Wisely, as acting health care unit administrator, investigated the plaintiff's complaints, knew of the plaintiff's severe burns, knew that the burns had become infected and that plaintiff was in great pain, but did nothing to obtain medical care for the plaintiff's pain, a consultation with a specialist or other assistance. (Id., pars. 31-32)

Plaintiff's terrible pain and suffering was not addressed until Dr. Ruiz left Big Muddy River Correctional Center, and other physicians, including Dr. Garcia, took over his care in September or October, 2001. (Id., par.37)

Proceedings Below

The plaintiff filed a pro se complaint under 42 U.S.C.§l983, alleging violation of his civil rights by the defendants in requiring him to work in conditions which presented a substantial risk of serious bodily injury and by the denial of prompt necessary medical care for his injuries and pain. (Doc.1) On September 16, 2002, after leave was given for Barbara J. Clinite to file her appearance for the plaintiff, plaintiff filed an amended complaint. (Doc.16)

Discovery was extended by order entered on March 26, 2004, in part because the depositions of defendant, Dr. Ruiz, and Dr. Garcia had not been taken. Dr. Garcia was the subsequent treating physician at the correctional center, had left the state of Illinois, and was difficult to locate and depose.

On August 4, 2004 the defendants filed a motion to bar plaintiff's expert witnesses, (Doc.45), and plaintiff filed a response, arguing that the deposition of Dr. Garcia had not been taken, and was necessary for his expert to finalize opinions. (Doc.50) The court entered an order barring plaintiff's experts. (Doc.69) Magistrate Judge Frazier based the order barring plaintiff's experts on the fact that plaintiff had not provided the expert's report.

Plaintiff filed a motion on August 26, 2004 seeking to reopen discovery and for leave to disclose his expert's report after the deposition of Dr. Garcia. (Doc.52) The motion set forth that the failure to provide a report from the expert was due to the fact that Dr. Garcia had not given his deposition. The motion sought time to depose Dr. Garcia, time for plaintiff's expert to review the deposition, and time to provide his expert's report.

In the motion to reopen discovery, Par.8, plaintiff stated that he had served unsigned Supplemental Answers to Interrogatories disclosing his expert, but without a report, on May 25, 2004, and provided signed answers two weeks later. (Doc. 52, Ex.B) Plaintiff identified Richard Lewan, M.D. as his expert. The court entered an order on August 31, 2004 granting plaintiff's motion, and stated that "Plaintiff's expert shall review this deposition and provide his report on or before November 19, 2004." (Doc.53; Short Appendix)

Plaintiff complied with the court's order and served his Rule 26 Expert Opinion Witness Disclosure with Dr. Lewan's preliminary draft report on the defendants on October 25, 2004, within the time ordered. After reviewing the deposition of Dr. Garcia, Dr. Lewan had no changes in his opinions and, therefore, the preliminary draft was allowed to stand as his report in the case.

In his Rule 26 Expert Opinion Witness Disclosure plaintiff set forth the following regarding Dr. Lewan's opinion testimony:

"SUBJECT MATTER: discussion of the medical notes and reports in DOC records, including nurses' notes; discussion of Plaintiff's burns, infections and treatment given; explanations of medical terms; discussion of materials reviewed; discussion of pain behavior, discussion of pain medications used and not used, but available; discussion of Plaintiff's pain at various times; and other matters set forth in his preliminary report attached hereto.

OPINIONS/CONCLUSIONS: It is Dr. Lewan's opinion that 800 mg. Tylenol or Motrin was totally inadequate treatment for the Plaintiff's pain - so wholly inadequate as to be cruel. As a result Plaintiff suffered intense unnecessary pain and suffering. Notes in the medical chart, and the nature of the condition under treatment, showed that the Plaintiff's pain was genuine, and his pain behaviors showed that his complaints were genuine. The refusal to provide effective pain treatment showed deliberate indifference to Mr. Gabriel's well-being. See also preliminary report attached hereto."

Dr. Lewan's report also criticized the defendants for not referring Mr. Gabriel to a specialist for treatment of infection and pain.

None of the Defendants requested a deposition of Dr. Lewan. On August 12, 2004 the parties filed the final pretrial order. (Doc. 49) On February 14, 2005, a pretrial conference was held, at which the court informed counsel that trial would be conducted on Tuesday through Thursday of each week, starting July 12, 2005 and being completed the following week. (Doc.57)

On October 29, 2004 the deposition of Dr. Garcia was taken and was available for presentation at trial. On March 16, 2005 the plaintiff's trial testimony was taken by video deposition. Plaintiff's counsel contacted Dr. Lewan, and arranged for him to testify during the July trial dates.

On June 24, 2005 the district judge changed the starting trial date from July 12 to August 23, 2005. (Doc. 62) Counsel for plaintiff contacted Dr. Lewan and arranged for his testimony at the August trial. On July 18, 2005 the defendants Hamlin and Doerr filed a motion to continue trial, (Doc.68), which the court granted and reset the trial to start September 20, 2005. (Doc.69)

Counsel for plaintiff contacted Dr. Lewan to arrange his testimony for September 27, 2005 and scheduled witnesses based on the trial being conducted Tuesday through Thursday of the weeks of September 19 and 26, 2005.

On September 12, 2005 the district court, on its own motion, rescheduled the trial from Tuesday through Thursday the weeks of September 19 and 26, 2005 to Monday through Friday of the week of September 19, 2005. (Doc.77) Counsel for plaintiff immediately contacted Dr. Lewan and was informed that he could not testify or give a deposition the week of September 19, 2005, but was available September 27, 2005. (Doc.81)

On September 14, 2005 plaintiff filed his first and only motion to continue trial, setting forth that his expert was not able to testify the week of September 19, 2005, and in the alternative for voluntary dismissal without prejudice. (Doc.81) In the motion plaintiff stated that Dr. Lewan is the only live witness, other than the defendants, plaintiff would present at trial, set forth the opinions shown in the opinion witness disclosure, and discussed the importance of his testimony. (Doc.81)

On September 15, 2005 the court denied plaintiff's motion to continue trial, denied the alternative motion for voluntary dismissal without prejudice, and dismissed the actions with prejudice for want of prosecution. (Doc. 85; Short.Append) The order stated that the plaintiff's motion to continue trial was based upon the unavailability of Dr. Lewan, and that plaintiff's expert witnesses had been barred by an order entered by Magistrate Judge Frazier.

Plaintiff then filed a timely Rule 60(b) motion for reconsideration, pointing out the later order granting leave to reopen discovery and disclose the expert's report. (Doc. 87) The court denied the motion for reconsideration, because plaintiff had not taken Dr. Lewan's deposition for use at trial. (Doc.92)

SUMMARY OF ARGUMENT

The plaintiff respectfully submits that the district judge erred in dismissing his actions with prejudice for want of prosecution, because plaintiff had diligently prepared his case for trial, and confirmed his expert's availability to testify during the July, August and the original September trial dates. The court's action in changing the trial dates only one week before trial meant that the trial would not continue into the second week as originally scheduled, when Dr. Lewan planned to testify.

A dismissal for want of prosecution is a harsh sanction and should be used sparingly, only in extreme situations where there is a clear record of delay or conduct which is contumacious. *Grun v. Pneumo Abex, Corp., 163 F.3d 411, 425* (7th Cir.1998)

In the instant case, other than the unavailability of Dr. Lewan, plaintiff was prepared for trial, and there was no record of a course of delay which would call for a sanction of dismissal with prejudice.

The plaintiff further respectfully submits that the district court abused its discretion in denying the plaintiff's motion to continue trial. It was the first and only motion by plaintiff to continue trial, after the court had continued it from July to August because of a conflict in the court's schedule, and after a defense motion to continue trial had been granted.

The plaintiff's motion was necessary because the trial judge changed the dates only a week before trial, and instead of rescheduling the trial to a later date, scheduled it to take place in one week, instead of the two weeks original ordered. As a result, plaintiff's expert would not have been able to testify.

While a district court has inherent power to manage its docket and schedule trials, the court must balance the need to control its docket with the rights of litigants. *Arthur Pierson Co., Inc. v. Provini Veal Corp., 887 F.2d 837, 839* (7th Cir.1989)

Plaintiff respectfully submits that the denial of his motion to continue the trial was an abuse of discretion, because there were reasonable grounds for the motion.

In addition, the plaintiff combined with the motion to continue trial an alternative motion for voluntary dismissal without prejudice.

As a general rule, a defendant must demonstrate plain legal prejudice in order to prevent a voluntary dismissal of a claim. *Quad/Graphics, Inc. v. Fass, 724 F.2d 1230, 1233* (7th Cir. 1983); *Tyco Laboratories, Inc., v. Koppers Co., Inc., 627 F.2d 54,56* (7th Cir.1980) Plaintiff legal prejudice requires more than the prospect of another lawsuit. *Stern v. Barnett, 452 F.2d 211,213 (7th Cir.1971)*

Plaintiff respectfully submits that the denial of the motion for voluntary dismissal without prejudice was an abuse of discretion, because there was no plain legal prejudice to be suffered by the defendants, and the prejudice suffered by the plaintiff from the denial of the motion was substantial.

FEDERAL RULE OF CIVIL PROCEDURE 41

"(a) Voluntary Dismissal: Effect Thereof.

(1) *By Plaintiff, by Stipulation.* Subject to the provisions of Rule 23(e), of Rule 66, and of any statute of the United States, an action may be dismissed by the plaintiff without order of court (i) by filing a notice of dismissal at any time before service by the adverse party of an answer or of a motion for summary judgment, whichever first occurs, or (ii) by filing a stipulation of dismissal signed by all parties who have appeared in the action. Unless otherwise stated in the notice of dismissal or stipulation, the dismissal is without   prejudice, except that a notice of dismissal operates as an adjudication upon the merits when filed by a plaintiff who has once dismissed in any court of the United States or of any state an action based on or including the same claim.

(2) *By Order of Court.* Except as provided in paragraph (1) of this subdivision of this rule, an action shall not be dismissed at the plaintiff's instances save upon order of the court and upon such terms and conditions as the court deems proper. If a counterclaim has been pleaded by a defendant prior to the service upon the defendant of the plaintiff's motion to dismiss, the action shall not be dismissed against the defendant's objection unless the counter-claim can remain pending for independent adjudication by the court. Unless otherwise specified in the order, a dismissal under this paragraph is without prejudice.

(b) Involuntary Dismissal: Effect Thereof.

For failure of the plaintiff to prosecute or to comply with these rules or any order of court, a defendant may move for dismissal of an action or of any claim against the defendant. Unless the court in its order for dismissal otherwise specifies, a dismissal under this subdivision and any dismissal not provided for in this rule, other than a dismissal for lack of jurisdiction, for improper venue, or for failure to join a party under Rule 19, operates as an adjudication upon the merits.

(c) Dismissal of Counterclaim, Cross-Claim, or Third Party Claim.

The provisions of this rule apply to the dismissal of any counterclaim, cross-claim, or third-party claim. A voluntary dismissal by the claimant alone pursuant to paragraph (1) of subdivision (a) of this rule shall be made before a responsive pleading is served or, if there is none, before the introduction of evidence at the trial or hearing.

(d) Costs of Previously-Dismissed Action.

If a plaintiff who has once dismissed an action in any court commences an action based upon or including the same claim against the same defendant, the court may make such order for the payment of costs of the action previously dismissed as it may deem proper and may stay the proceedings in the action until the plaintiff has complied with the order."

ARGUMENT

I. STANDARD OF REVIEW

In reviewing a dismissal for want of prosecution the issue is whether the trial court abused its discretion. *Grun v. Pneumo Abex Corp., 163 F.3d 411, 424* (7th Cir.1999)

A dismissal for want of prosecution will be reversed only if it was a mistake, or if the judge did not consider factors essential to the exercise of sound discretion. *Sharif v. Wellness International Network, 376 F.3d 720, 725 (7th Cir.2004)*

Also, in reviewing the denial of a motion to continue trial, the reviewing court applies an abuse of discretion standard. *Brooks v. United States, 64 F.3d 251, 256* (7th Cir.1995) Matters of trial management are for the district judge, and the court of appeals intervenes only when it appears that the trial judge acted unreasonably. *Mraovic v. Elgin, Joliet & Eastern Ry.Co., 897 F.2d 268, 270-71* (7th Cir.1990)

In reviewing the decision whether to grant or deny a motion for voluntary dismissal without prejudice, the court of appeals will not reverse the denial of the motion, absent an abuse of discretion. *United States v. Outboard Marine Corp., 789 F.2d 497, 502* (7th Cir.1986); *Kovalic v. DEC Intern, Inc., 855 F.2d 471, 473* (7th Cir.1988)

II. THE DISTRICT COURT SHOULD NOT HAVE DISMISSED THE ACTIONS WITH PREJUDICE FOR WANT OF PROSECUTION

This appeal presents a situation in which a trial judge dismissed plaintiff's actions with prejudice for want of prosecution, because plaintiff was unable to proceed to trial without the testimony of his expert, Dr. Lewan. The dismissal order does not mention any other delay, failure to appear or failure to comply with court deadlines and orders.

Initially, the trial judge denied plaintiff's motion to continue trial or for voluntary dismissal without prejudice under a mistaken impression that plaintiff's experts were barred from testifying. (Doc.85; Short Append) After the plaintiff filed his motion for reconsideration, pointing out the later order reopening discovery and granting leave for plaintiff to disclose his expert's report, the trial judge denied the motion for reconsideration based upon the fact that plaintiff had not taken a deposition of Dr. Lewan for use at trial. (Doc.92, Short Append)

Plaintiff respectfully submits that the trial judge erred in dismissing his actions with prejudice for want of prosecution, because plaintiff had diligently prepared his case for trial, and there was no record of delay or contumacious conduct by the plaintiff.

A dismissal for want of prosecution is a harsh sanction and should be used sparingly, only in extreme situations where there is a clear record of delay or conduct which is contumacious. *Grun v. Pneumo Abex, Corp., 163 F.3d 411, 425* (7th Cir.1998)

In *Sharif v. Wellness International Network, 376 F.3d 720, 725 (7th Cir.2004),* the Court reversed a dismissal for want of prosecution, where counsel had actively participated in the case, and there was no record that counsel needlessly delayed the case.

In reversing a dismissal with prejudice for want of prosecution in *GCIU Employer Retirement Fund v. Chicago Tribune Co., 8 F.3d 1195* (7th Cir.l993), based upon the plaintiff's failure to promptly seek entry of judgment after an appeal was dismissed for lack of a final judgment, the Court held that the dismissal was an abuse of discretion. Although twenty-two (22) months had passed while the parties negotiated, the Court found that the plaintiff's conduct was not contumacious and:

"...the Fund did not fail to respond adequately to discovery requests, did not repeatedly miss deadlines, and did not engage in 'a continuing pattern of delay, non-cooperation and disobedience,' ... and did not display a 'distinct lack of prosecutorial intent dat[ing] back to the inception of the case[,]' as in *Daniels, 887 F.2d at 786;* and it did not disregard pre-trial orders, did not request numerous continuances, did not fail to file pre-trial orders, and did not 'flagrant[ly] abuse judicial time and resources..." *(8 F.3d at 1199-1200)*

Plaintiff respectfully submits that the same is true in the instant case. Counsel for plaintiff had diligently prepared his case for trial, taking a deposition of Dr. Garcia, subsequent treating physician, for trial, and the video deposition of Mr. Gabriel for trial, serving request to admit facts, (Doc.61), and timely filing the pre-trial order. After his case was set for trial to start on July 12, 2005, plaintiff notified his expert, filed petition for writs of *habeas corpus* for inmate witnesses to testify by video conference at trial, (Doc.60), sent subpoenae to other witnesses and filed a motion in limine (Doc.58).

Plaintiff had confirmed his expert's availability to testify during the July, August and the original September trial dates. The court's action in changing the trial dates only one week before trial meant that the trial would not continue into the second week as originally scheduled, when Dr. Lewan planned to testify.

Plaintiff respectfully submits that dismissing the case with prejudice for want of prosecution was too harsh a sanction, based only on the fact that plaintiff had not taken a deposition of Dr. Lewan earlier to have it available just in case the court changed the trial dates to a time when Dr. Lewan could not appear to testify. Plaintiff's expert had cooperated and arranged to testify each time the trial was continued to a *later* date.

Taking a deposition of Dr. Lewan would have been expensive, involving travel to Wisconsin and the doctor's fee for preparation and giving the deposition. While the expense would have been reasonable if plaintiff was having difficulty in arranging Dr. Lewan's appearance when he was contacted for the July, August and original September trial dates, each time he was given sufficient notice Dr. Lewan agreed to arrange his schedule so that he could testify in open court.

In addition, Dr. Lewan's live testimony was of great importance, as he was the primary witness on liability and damages, and the only live in court witness plaintiff was going to call, other than the defendants. Using a deposition of Dr. Lewan would have left plaintiff with no live in court witnesses, and the advantage to the defendants in countering with numerous live witnesses would have been unfair to the plaintiff.

Dr. Lewan's testimony was needed to present to the jury a discussion of the medical notes and his opinions. Without Dr. Lewan's testimony and opinion that the lack of care and pain treatment was so wholly inadequate as to be cruel, and his opinions and discussion of notes reflecting deliberate indifference, plaintiff's cause of action likely would not have survived a motion for directed verdict at the close of plaintiff's case.

Plaintiff respectfully submits that it was through no fault of the plaintiff that Dr. Lewan could not testify at trial the week of September 19, 2005, but rather the result of circumstances which required the court to change the trial dates with extremely short notice.

It is well established that district courts have inherent authority to dismiss a case *sua sponte* for a plaintiff's failure to prosecute. *GCIU Employer Retirement Fund v. Chicago Tribune, 8 F.3d 1195, 1199* (7th Cir.l993) However, the authority is not unfettered. (Id.) The district court must balance the competing interests of keeping a manageable docket against deciding cases on their merits. (*Id. at 1199*)

Under the circumstances, plaintiff respectfully submits that the trial judge acted unreasonably in punishing the plaintiff for not having taken a deposition of Dr. Lewan. Other than the unavailability of Dr. Lewan, plaintiff was prepared for trial, and there was no record of a course of delay which would call for a sanction of dismissal with prejudice.

Therefore, plaintiff's respectfully submits that it was error to dismiss the actions with prejudice for want of prosecution.

III. IT WAS AN ABUSE OF DISCRETION TO DENY THE MOTION TO CONTINUE TRIAL

The plaintiff further respectfully submits that it was an abuse of discretion for the district court to deny the plaintiff's motion to continue the trial. Plaintiff diligently prosecuted his case, prepared for trial and confirmed his expert's availability for trial in July, 2005, August, 2005 and the week of September 26, 2005.

On June 24, 2005 when the court continued the trial to August 23, 2005, (Doc.62), plaintiff's counsel contacted Dr. Lewan and arranged for his testimony at the August trial. However, defendants Jim Hamlin and Bob Doerr filed a motion to continue the trial. (Doc.68) Although plaintiff was inconvenienced, he did not file objections. The court continued the trial to September 20, 2005. (Doc.69)

Counsel for plaintiff contacted Dr. Lewan in August to arrange for his in court testimony on September 27, 2005.

On September 8, 2005 counsel for plaintiff received a phone message, telephoned Judge Stiehl's clerk and was told that the judge wanted to change the trial dates to start September 19, 2005 and finish in that one week. Counsel stated that her expert was not available that week and she was asked to check on taking a deposition for trial. Counsel immediately phoned Dr. Lewan and was told that he had no openings the week of September 19, 2005 for either trial or deposition and was "totally booked". (Doc.81)

On September 12, 2005 the court e-mailed notice to the parties that trial was rescheduled to begin September 19, 2005. (Doc. 77)

Plaintiff respectfully submits that when the trial judge found that there was a problem having the trial continue into the week of September 26, 2005, it would have been reasonable to continue the trial to a later date. However, by changing the trial dates one week before trial to Monday through Friday of the week of September 19, 2005, the trial judge did not provide sufficient time for the plaintiff's expert to reschedule his testimony.

Because Dr. Lewan was the plaintiff's retained opinion witness whose testimony was essential to establishing deliberate indifference to plaintiff's serious medical need, and because he was the only witness, other than the defendants, who was going to appear in open court to testify for plaintiff, it was very important for plaintiff to be able to present his testimony live in open court.

Had it not been for the last minute change in trial dates, plaintiff would have proceeded to trial, and would have been able to present Dr. Lewan's live testimony in open court. Therefore, plaintiff respectfully submits that Dr. Lewan's unavailability on short notice to testify the week of September 19, 2005 was a reasonable and compelling basis for a continuance of the trial.

A district court has substantial inherent power to control and manage its docket and schedule trials. *Arthur Pierson & Co., Inc. v. Provini Veal Corp.*, 887 F.2d 837, 839 (7th Cir.1989) However, in exercising its power, the court is required to "strike a balance between the needs for judicial efficiency and the rights of litigants." *Arthur Pierson & Co., Inc. v. Provini Veal Corp.*, 887 F.2d at 839; *In re Strandell*, 838 F.2d 884, 886 (7th Cir.1987)

In the instant case, the plaintiff respectfully submits that the district court did not balance the interests of the plaintiff with the court's need to manage its docket. The court gave little, if any, consideration to the fact that the plaintiff had adjusted to prior continuances by the court on its own motion, and on the defendants' motion to continue trial, and one week prior to the original September trial dates was fully prepared to proceed as originally scheduled. The delay from the first trial date in July, 2005 was not due in any part to conduct or motion by the plaintiff, and had it not been for the last minute change in the September trial dates, plaintiff would have had no need to request a continuance.

In the case at bar, the defendants would have suffered no legal prejudice had the motion been granted. The defendants had been planning on the trial taking place during two weeks, into the week of September 26, 2005, and presenting their case the second week. Therefore, when the court moved the dates to the one week of September 19, 2005, the defendants had to change their plans anyway.

Plaintiff respectfully submits that he submitted reasonable grounds for the motion, and that the trial judge acted unreasonably in denying the plaintiff's motion to continue trial, because plaintiff had not previously sought a continuance or unreasonably delayed the case, the defendants would not have been prejudiced, and the court could have continued the trial to a later date to avoid the conflict in the court's schedule.

For the above reasons, plaintiff submits that the denial of the motion to continue trial was an abuse of discretion.

IV. IT WAS AN ABUSE OF DISCRETION TO DENY THE PLAINTIFF'S MOTION FOR VOLUNTARY DISMISSAL

The plaintiff combined with the motion to continue trial an alternative motion under Fed.R.Civ.Pro. 41(a) for voluntary dismissal without prejudice. (Doc.81) Plaintiff respectfully submits that the district court abused its discretion in denying the alternative motion for voluntary dismissal without prejudice.

Rule 41(a) provides that after a defendant has filed an answer or motion for summary judgment, the plaintiff may voluntarily dismiss the action without prejudice, by order of court and upon such terms and conditions as the court deems proper. *Marlow v. Winston & Strawn, 19 F.3d 300, 303* (7th Cir.1994)

In the instant case, plaintiff sought a voluntary dismissal without prejudice only if the court denied his motion to continue trial. A continuance would have enabled all parties to proceed to trial at a later date, and avoid the need for a second lawsuit. Plaintiff had no real choice if the continuance were not granted, because he could not proceed to trial without the testimony of Dr. Lewan.

Plaintiff respectfully submits that, because the motion to continue trial was denied, the court should have allowed the voluntary dismissal without prejudice, rather than dismiss the action with prejudice for want of prosecution. While all parties would have been inconvenienced by another lawsuit, any prejudice to the defendants would have been small compared to the prejudice to plaintiff by the dismissal with prejudice.

As a general rule, a defendant must demonstrate plain legal prejudice in order to prevent a voluntary dismissal of a claim. *Quad/Graphics, Inc. v. Fass, 724 F.2d 1230, 1233* (7th Cir. 1983); *Tyco Laboratories, Inc., v. Koppers Co., Inc., 627 F.2d 54, 56* (7th Cir. 1980); *Kovalic v. DEC International, Inc., 855 F.2d 471, 474* (7th Cir. 1988)

In exercising its discretion, a district court should follow the principle that voluntary dismissal should be allowed unless the defendant will suffer some plain legal prejudice other than the prospect of another lawsuit. *Stern v. Barnett, 452 F.2d 211, 213* (7th Cir. 1971); *Tyco Laboratories, Inc. v. Koppers Co., Inc., 627 F.2d 54, 56* (7th Cir.1980)

The Court has, in the past, discussed certain factors to be considered in determining whether a defendant would suffer plain legal prejudice if an action is voluntarily dismissed without prejudice. They include:

"...the defendants's effort and expense of preparation for trial, excessive delay and lack of diligence on the part of the plaintiff in prosecuting the action, insufficient explanation for the need to take a dismissal, and the fact that a motion for summary judgment has been filed by the defendant." (*Pace v. Southern Express Co., 409 F.2d 331, 334* (7th Cir.1969).)

The factors to be considered are a guide to the exercise of discretion by the court, not a mandate. *Kovalic v. DEC Intern, Inc., 855 F.2d 471, 474* (7th Cir.1988)

In the case at bar, the defendants did not demonstrate any plain legal prejudice which they would have suffered if the action were voluntarily dismissed without prejudice. There was no evidence of excessive delay and lack of diligence by plaintiff, and plaintiff submitted a reasonable explanation for the need to take a voluntary dismissal without prejudice. There was no pending motion for summary judgment.

The other factor set forth in *Pace v. Southern Express Co., 409 F.2d 331, 334* (7th Cir.1969), is the defendants' effort and expense of preparing for trial, which alone would not constitute plain legal prejudice, since the prospect of another lawsuit is not enough. *Stern v. Barnett, 452 F.2d 211, 213* (7th Cir. 1971) In a second lawsuit much of the expense and time spent preparing for trial in the first one would be useful and beneficial.

The fact that discovery had been completed would not mean that the defendant would suffer plain legal prejudice. In *Tyco Laboratories, Inc. v. Koppers Co., Inc., 627 F.2d 54, 56* (7th Cir.1980), the Court rejected the argument that the fact that discovery had been done meant that the defendant would suffer plain legal prejudice.

Furthermore, in the instant case, the prejudice, if any, to the defendants could have been minimized by the fact that discovery they have taken in this action could have been used in a refiled action, and most of their time invested in the defense would still have been useful.

In addition, Rule 41(d) provides that if the case is refiled, the court may make an order for payment of costs of the action previously dismissed as may be deemed proper. Generally, the terms and conditions of a voluntary dismissal without prejudice include reasonable expenses and fees for work which would not be beneficial to or used in a refiled case. *Cauley v. Wilson, 754 F.2d 769, 772* (7th Cir. 1985)

In *Marlow v. Winston & Strawn, 19 F.3d 300* (7th Cir. 1994), as in the case at bar, the plaintiff filed a motion for voluntary dismissal without prejudice, and the court dismissed the case with prejudice. In reversing, the court of appeals emphasized that Rule 41(a) preserves a plaintiff's right to take a voluntary nonsuit and start over so long as the defendant is not harmed. *(19 F.3d at 303;* See also, *McCall-Bey v. Franzen, 777 F.2d 1178, 1184* (7th Cir. 1985)

Plaintiff respectfully submits that the district court abused its discretion in denying the plaintiff's motion for voluntary dismissal without prejudice and dismissing the case with prejudice.

KENNETH F. LEONARD, PLAINTIFF/APPELLANT, V. FLORIDA DEPARTMENT OF CORRECTIONS, WEXFORD HEALTH SOURCES, INC., DAVID HARRIS, G. SOMODEVILLA, A. PIPIN, J.L. GREEN, AND G.J. SMITH, DEFENDANTS /Appellees. 06-11223-FF UNITED STATES COURT OF APPEALS FOR THE ELEVENTH CIRCUIT

B. Statement of Facts.

At the time of filing his Complaint and "Emergency" Motion for Temporary Restraining Order and/or Preliminary Injunction, Mr. Leonard was incarcerated at the Dade Correctional Institution. In both pleadings, as well as in the Complaint previously filed against Defendant John Holmes, a correctional officer at Dade Correctional Institution, Mr. Leonard claims that the Appellees failed to provide him with special shoes in violation of his Eighth Amendment constitutional rights.

Indeed, in the first Exhibit attached to his "Emergency" Motion for Temporary Restraining Order and/or Preliminary Injunction, the Inmate Grievance of July 18, 2005 (Dkt. 6), Mr. Leonard refers to special passes for Brogans. Brogans are state-issued boots. The response to the above-mentioned Inmate Grievance indicates that "Plaintiff states that Plaintiff had already received a pair of Brogans." The second Exhibit attached to Plaintiff's "Emergency" Motion for Temporary Restraining Order and/or Preliminary Injunction (Dkt. 6) refers to the fact that Plaintiff received Bobos. Again, said Exhibit does not indicate that Mr. Leonard cannot have Brogans; it reflects that if the Bobos shoes are the incorrect size, he may exchange them on Thursdays. The remainder of Plaintiff's Complaint, and his "Emergency" Motion for Temporary Restraining Order and/or Preliminary Injunction, appear to be directed to allegations of all inmates as a class at Dade Correctional Institution, which is improper absent class certification. The aforementioned Exhibits demonstrate that Mr. Leonard could access sick call regarding orthopedic shoes, that he was already in possession of Brogan shoes, and that if the Bobos shoes were too small, they would be replaced.

Since the filing of the pleadings at issue, Mr. Leonard has been transferred and is now incarcerated at Avon Park Correctional Institution.

C. Standard of Review

In addition to the standard of review set forth in Appellant's Initial Brief, Appellees submit that the standard of review is abuse of discretion for the District Court's denial of Plaintiff's "Emergency" Motion for Temporary Restraining Order and/or Preliminary Injunction. *See, Swatch Watch, F.A. v. Taxor, Inc., 785 F.2d 956 (11th Cir. 1986).*

SUMMARY OF THE ARGUMENT

The District Court appropriately denied Plaintiff's "Emergency" Motion for Temporary Restraining Order and/or Preliminary Injunction because the Plaintiff did not fulfill the prerequisites necessary for the issuance of a preliminary injunction, and the Plaintiff's claims did not rise to the level of an emergency. Moreover, denial of the "Emergency" Motion for Temporary Restraining Order and/or Preliminary Injunction was appropriate as Mr. Leonard alleges simply that he was deprived of adequate footwear, but does not allege facts indicative of an Eighth Amendment violation.

The District Court appropriately dismissed Plaintiff's claims for failure to state a claim upon which relief may be granted as Plaintiff's claims do not rise to the level of a violation of an Eighth Amendment constitutional right pursuant to *42 U.S.C. § 1983.* Additionally, dismissal of Plaintiff's Complaint was appropriate as Plaintiff improperly brought forth multiple causes of action on the same claim.

ARGUMENT AND CITATION OF AUTHORITY

A. The District Court Was Correct in Denying Plaintiff's "Emergency" Motion for Temporary Restraining Order and/or Preliminary Injunction.

1. The Allegations in the "Emergency" Motion for Temporary Restraining Order and/or Preliminary Injunction are Insufficient to Rise to the Level of "Emergency" and Mr. Leonard's Claims Do Not Establish the Prerequisite Elements Needed for the Issuance of a Permanent Injunction or Temporary Restraining Order.

It is axiomatic that the prerequisites for the issuance of a preliminary injunction are: (1) the inadequacy of a remedy at law; (2) the likelihood of irreparable injury if not issued; and (3) the probability of success in the action by the party seeking relief. *Aoude v. Mobil Oil Corp., 862 F.2d 890, 892 (1st Cir. 1988).* Mr. Leonard filed two separate Complaints and therefore, clearly has not established the inadequacy of a remedy at law.

Moreover, it is essential that the facts upon which Mr. Leonard bases his right to relief must be essentially undisputed or appear with such substantial clarity that the Court can weigh and determine the probability of success. *Bass v. Holberman, 295 F. Supp. 358, 361 (D.C. N.Y. 1968).* In order to grant injunctive relief, the relief requested must also be a presently existing actual threat. To this point, it is noted as follows:

The dramatic and drastic power of injunctive force may be unleashed only against conditions generating a presently existing actual threat; it may not be used simply to eliminate the possibility of a remote future injury, or a future invasion of rights, by those rights protected by statute or by the common law.

Holiday Inns of America, Inc. v. B&B Corporation, 409 F.2d 614, 618 (C.A. Vir. 1969). Further, it has long been established that an injunction will not be issued merely to allay the fears and apprehensions or to soothe the anxieties of individuals which may well exist without substantial reasons and may be absolutely groundless. *U.S. v. Dogan, 206 F. Supp. 446, 446 (D.C. Miss. 1962).* Here, Mr. Leonard has neither established a likelihood of success nor has he established irreparable injury. The evidence Mr. Leonard relied upon at the District Court level was two exhibits attached to his "Emergency" Motion for Temporary Restraining Order and/or Preliminary Injunction. Contrarily, however, both exhibits showed that: (i) Mr. Leonard could access sick call regarding orthopedic shoes, (ii) he was already in possession of Brogan shoes, and (iii) if the Bobos shoes were too small, they would be replaced. Accordingly, these allegations clearly do not demonstrate the likelihood of success or irreparable harm. For these reasons alone, Plaintiff's "Emergency" Motion for Temporary Restraining Order and/or Preliminary Injunction should have been denied.

2. Mr. Leonard Has Not Demonstrated a Deprivation of Constitutional Rights.

The Courts have carved out an exception to the requirement of irreparable injury in the prerequisites enumerated above for the issuance of a preliminary injunction where the alleged deprivation of constitutional rights is involved. In the case at bar, however, Mr. Leonard cannot establish that he has suffered a constitutional violation. In order to support a claim of an Eighth Amendment violation, a plaintiff must demonstrate acts or omissions sufficiently harmful to evidence deliberate indifference to serious medical needs. *Olsen v. Stotts, 9 F.2d 1475, 1476-77 (10th Cir. 1993)*. Mr. Leonard simply alleges that he has been deprived of adequate footwear. It cannot reasonably be disputed that this allegation is not indicative of a serious medical need giving rise to an Eighth Amendment violation.

<u>B. The District Court Was Correct in Dismissing Plaintiff's Complaint.</u>

1. Plaintiff Has Failed to State a Claim Upon Which Relief May Be Granted.

The allegations in Plaintiff's Complaint were brought pursuant to *42 U.S.C. § 1983* and Plaintiff argued that Defendants/Appellees failed to provide him with special shoes. In order to state an Eighth Amendment violation, Plaintiff must show acts or omissions sufficiently harmful to evidence deliberate indifference to serious needs. *Olsen v. Stotts, supra.* Appellant's claims relate solely to the inadequacy of footwear. In considering claims brought pursuant to Section 1983 regarding footwear, courts have indeed determined that such claims do not demonstrate "deliberate indifference" to an inmate's "serious medical needs." For example, in a case involving an inmate's claim that being forced to work in hard soled boots exacerbated an ankle injury, the Fifth Circuit Court of Appeals, in affirming the District Court's dismissal of the inmate's claim as frivolous, found that the inmate's claim does not involve a medical problem that is serious nor does it involve deliberate indifference. *Banuelos v. McFarland, 42 F.3d 232 (5th Cir. 1995).* Moreover, the Seventh Circuit Court of Appeals, in upholding the District Court's finding that preliminary injunction was not warranted, found that "reasonable measures" had been taken by the prison and that a prisoner was not entitled to the medical treatment of his choice relating to a claim of deliberate indifference to his serious medical needs by the prison's refusal to prescribe the inmate footwear for lumps and ulcers on his feet. *Hall-Bey v. Ridley-Turner, 154 Fed. Appx. 493 (7th Cir. 2005).* In the case at bar, even if all allegations together are taken as true, these claims do not rise to the level of a violation of an Eighth Amendment constitutional right.

2. An Individual's Claims May Not Be Split and All Grounds Upon Which a Single Claim is Based Must be Asserted and Included in One Action.

Plaintiff filed one Complaint in April 2005 against Defendant John Holmes, a correctional officer at Dade Correctional Institution. Subsequently, Plaintiff filed a second Complaint on July 25, 2005, alleging the same claims against Defendants/Appellees herein. Thereafter, on August 15, 2005, Plaintiff filed the "Emergency" Motion for Temporary Restraining Order and/or Preliminary Injunction with the same exact allegations as set forth in the previously-filed two Complaints.

Plaintiff improperly brought forth two actions on the same claim - and both cases are before the United States District Court for the Southern District of Florida. Under controlling law, it is improper for Plaintiff to split his causes of action. In fact, it has been held that all parts of a single claim or cause of action should be advanced in one single claim. *McConnell v. Travelers Indemnity Company, 346 F.2d 219 (5th Cir. 1965).* Here, Mr. Leonard failed to do so. Accordingly, Plaintiff's Complaint was appropriately dismissed by the District Court.

<u>James E. Skinner, Plaintiff, vs. Charles L. Ryan, et al., Defendants. No. CV-12-1729-PHX-SMM (LOA) UNITED STATES DISTRICT COURT FOR THE DISTRICT OF ARIZONA*2014 U.S. Dist. LEXIS 91711 (July 7, 2014)*</u>

<u>I. Background</u>

Plaintiff, a maximum security inmate housed in maximum security units of maximum security prison complexes within the Arizona Department of Corrections, filed a First Amended Complaint on October 2, 2012. (Docs. 8; 141 at 1) Plaintiff raised two grounds for relief against seventeen separate defendants. In Count I, Plaintiff alleged he is being deprived of basic necessities in violation of the *Eighth Amendment*, including inadequate plumbing in his cell, unsanitary conditions in his cell and other areas, and the failure to provide cleaning supplies to address the unsanitary conditions. Plaintiff claims that, for nine months, he was housed in a cell in which the base of the toilet leaked every time it was used, which caused flooding, and he was not provided adequate supplies to address the problem. He further claims that when he was eventually moved to a different cell in a different housing unit, the walls of the cell appeared to have blood and dried feces on them. He claims that, during the several months he was there, he repeatedly requested supplies to clean his cell but received adequate supplies on only one occasion. Plaintiff also claims that outdoor recreation cages and an outer stairwell were covered with cat waste and pigeon droppings. He claims these contaminants were then tracked back into his cell. Plaintiff claims he informed Defendants of these issues but they failed to take any action to resolve the problems.

In Count II, Plaintiff alleged that prison officials retaliated against him in violation of the *First Amendment* for filing a previous federal civil rights lawsuit. The District Judge screened the First Amended Complaint in accordance with *28 U.S.C. § 1915A(a)* on February 19, 2013. (Doc. 9) The District Judge dismissed Count II for failure to state a claim, along with three defendants, but ordered fourteen defendants to answer the allegations in Count I.[1] (Doc. 9 at 15) Plaintiff seeks unspecified compensatory and punitive damages, along with declaratory and injunctive relief. (Doc. 8 at 20)

1   Thirteen defendants have answered. The fourteenth, Rita Duarte, was dismissed without prejudice, on March 13, 2014, for failure to serve pursuant to *Fed.R.Civ.P. 4(m)*. (Doc. 134)

II. Motion to Compel

In the February 6, 2014 Motion to Compel, Plaintiff identifies thirty-three interrogatories to which he claims Defendants failed to adequately respond. (Doc. 113) He asks the Court to order more complete responses. Defendants argue in the response that their responses are sufficient and any objections asserted are proper.

A. Legal Standards for Discovery

Federal Rule of Civil Procedure 26(b)(1) provides that "[p]arties may obtain discovery regarding any nonprivileged matter that is relevant to any party's claim or defense . . . Relevant information need not be admissible at the trial if the discovery appears reasonably calculated to lead to the discovery of admissible evidence. All discovery is subject to the limitations imposed by *Rule 26(b)(2)(C)*." *Fed.R.Civ.P. 26(b)(1)*. These limitations reflect that, in addition to being relevant, discovery must also be proportional to the issues and needs of the case. *Kaiser v. BMW of North America, LLC, 2013 U.S. Dist. LEXIS 63855, 2013 WL 1856578, at *3 (N.D. Cal. May 2, 2013)* (citing *Fed.R.Civ.P. 26(b)(2)(C)*). *Rule 26(b)(2)(C)* provides:

 On motion or on its own, the court must limit the frequency or extent of discovery otherwise allowed by these rules or by local rules if it determines that:

(i) the discovery sought is unreasonably cumulative or duplicative, or can be obtained from some other source that is more convenient, less burdensome, or less expensive;

(ii) the party seeking discovery has had ample opportunity to obtain the information by discovery in the action; or

(iii) the burden or expense of the proposed discovery outweighs its likely benefit, considering the needs of the case, the amount in controversy, the parties' resources, the importance of the issues at stake in the action, and the importance of the discovery in resolving the issues.

Thus, the court must "strike[ ] the proper balance between permitting relevant discovery and limiting the scope and burdens of the discovery to what is proportional to the case." *Kaiser, 2013 U.S. Dist. LEXIS 63855, 2013 WL at *3*. Moreover, "[b]road discretion is vested in the trial court to permit or deny discovery, and its decision to deny discovery will not be disturbed except upon the clearest showing that denial of discovery results in actual and substantial prejudice to the complaining litigant." *Hallett v. Morgan, 296 F.3d 732, 751 (9th Cir. 2002)* (citing *Goehring v. Brophy, 94 F.3d 1294, 1305 (9th Cir. 1996)*).

B. Application

1. Defendant Heet

Plaintiff first challenges two interrogatory responses from Defendant Assistant Deputy Warden Heet. The Court finds Defendant Heet's responses are sufficient. In response to Plaintiff's question, Heet identifies the procedure by which an inmate can request a mop from the floor officer. Plaintiff's motion complains that Heet failed to identify "all documents specifically referenc[ing the] mopping of cells" is without merit in light of the vagueness of the request. (Doc. 114-2 at 2) Likewise, Heet sufficiently responded that documentation of cell cleaning was completed on pod sheets and correctional service journals. The Court will not compel further responses from Defendant Heet.

2. Defendant Barrios

Next, Plaintiff challenges Defendant Deputy Warden Barrios's responses to certain interrogatories. Defendant Barrios sufficiently responded to interrogatories four and five. Regarding Plaintiff's request for mopping procedures, Barrios referenced housing unit post orders, which specify expectations for cell cleaning. Regarding Plaintiff's extremely broad request to identify any and all documents pertaining to sanitation at Plaintiff's housing unit, Barrios identified correctional service journals, and the information contained therein. He also referred to individual inmate detention records, which document inmate receipt of cleaning supplies. The Court will not compel additional responses.

With regard to interrogatories 12 and 13, Barrios properly responded to the questions, which pertained to the steps taken to ensure compliance with cell cleaning procedures. The Court will not order further responses to those questions, nor to interrogatory 22, which again deals with oversight.

3. Defendant Hetmer

Next, Plaintiff challenges Defendant Hetmer's responses to interrogatories 16, 17 and 24. The Court finds that Hetmer's response to the questions about mopping and cleaning procedures at Central Unit to be sufficient. He explains there is a cell cleaning schedule that is overseen by sergeants on each shift and cell block tours are done to ensure compliance with cell cleaning. He also states that Plaintiff was scheduled to receive cleaning supplies on Thursdays during the day shift. Likewise, Hetmer's identification of five separate work orders between August and December 2011 pertaining to the toilet in Plaintiff's cell was a proper response to Plaintiff's question. The Court will not compel any additional responses from Defendant Hetmer.

4. Defendant Kane

Plaintiff next challenges Defendant Kane's responses to interrogatories 16, 21 and 22. The Court finds Kane, the Central Unit Assistant Deputy Warden, properly responded to Plaintiff's question concerning compliance with sanitation procedures. Kane addressed how cleaning schedules were posted on bulletin boards and how walk-throughs are performed to observe conditions and operations. Regarding who was responsible for reviewing cell inspection records, Kane referred Plaintiff to a policy, presumably one that explains the cell inspection review policy. Plaintiff does not assert otherwise. Finally, Kane properly referred Plaintiff to records previously disclosed to Plaintiff pursuant to a request for production when asked to identify all cell inspection records. The Court finds no basis to compel additional responses from Defendant Kane.

5. Defendant Ryan

Plaintiff next challenges Defendant Ryan's responses to interrogatories 10, 13, 15, 16, 17, 19 and 23. Director Ryan's response to Plaintiff's question regarding the potential for, or incidents of, a MRSA ("methicillin-resistant staphylococcus aureus") infection was sufficient. Defendant Ryan, the Director of the Arizona Department of Corrections, said he knows it has occurred, the potential exists, but he is not familiar with specific conditions that may increase or diminish the risk. Regarding Plaintiff's four questions pertaining to cleaning supplies and cell cleaning schedules, Director Ryan properly explained that the day-to-day operations of the Arizona prisons, including cell cleaning issues, are delegated to the wardens and he has little knowledge of those issues. In response to another interrogatory regarding a specific grievance response, Director Ryan referred Plaintiff to the response, explaining that it speaks for itself. Lastly, in response to another extremely overbroad question in which Plaintiff asks Director Ryan to identify specific documents, Director Ryan responds that he does not have sufficient personal knowledge to respond because the documents pertain to the day-to-day operation of the prisons which is delegated to the wardens. The Court finds no basis to compel additional responses from Defendant Ryan.

6. Defendant Fizer

Lastly, Plaintiff challenges Defendant Deputy Warden Fizer's responses to interrogatories 4, 5, 7, 8, 9-14, and 16. In the first and second questions, Plaintiff asked Fizer to explain any and all priorities and funding issues that Fizer referenced in a response to Plaintiff regarding a request to repair or replace his toilet. He also asked about the cost of repairing and replacing a toilet. In addition to objecting, Fizer responded that there are a multitude of demands on prison budgets that Plaintiff does need not know about, including that the replacement of a toilet in Plaintiff's housing unit costs more than $4,000 each. While this seems to be an incredibly high figure, it is Fizer's response and may be properly used at trial for impeachment if it is not accurate. Without more evidence, it is not the province of the trial court to determine the credibility of an adverse party's answers to discovery requests at the discovery stage provided such answers are complete and responsive to the discovery request. Fizer's response is sufficient for now.

"Complete and accurate responses to discovery are required for the proper functioning of our system of justice. . . [and] parties have a duty to provide true, explicit, responsive, complete and candid answers to discovery[.]" *Wagner v. Dryvit Systems, Inc., 208 F.R.D. 606, 609-610 (D. Neb. 2001)* (citations omitted). "Providing false or incomplete discovery responses violates the Federal Rules of Civil Procedure and subjects the offending party and its counsel to sanctions." *Id. at 610.* One of the primary "purpose[s] of discovery is to make a trial 'less a game of blind man's bluff and more a fair contest with the basic issues and facts disclosed to the fullest practicable extent possible'. . . ." *Equal Rights Center v. Post Properties, Inc., 246 F.R.D. 29, 32 (D.D.C. 2007)* (citations omitted). Moreover, *Rule 26(e)(2), Fed.R.Civ.P.,* mandates that a party "[i]s under a duty seasonably to amend a prior response to an interrogatory . . . if the party learns that the response is in some material respect . . . incorrect and if the additional or corrective information has not otherwise been made known to the other parties during the discovery process or in writing." If there is intentional bad faith in answering discovery requests, sanctions may be appropriate as "[l]itigation is not a game. It is the time-honored method of seeking the truth, finding the truth, and doing justice." *Haeger v. Goodyear Tire & Rubber Co., 906 F.Supp.2d 938, 940 (D. Ariz. 2012).*

Plaintiff also asked whether the Central Unit was "adequately funded" during the relevant time frame and if not, whether Fizer notified others. Fizer's response referring to his previous response in which he said he did not believe the Central Unit had a funding problem. Additionally, in response to Plaintiff's question regarding whether the Central Unit tracked work orders, Fizer's responded "yes," and directed Plaintiff to work orders produced pursuant to a request of production. Fizer's responses are sufficient.

In response to Plaintiff's question about the number of times a work order was submitted on the toilet in Plaintiff's cell from ninety days before Plaintiff arrived in the cell to when it was repaired or replace, Fizer objected, stating it would require speculation on his part. He further stated that as the deputy warden, he did not keep track of such things. The Court will not compel Fizer to respond further to something about which he does not have specific knowledge.

Regarding Plaintiff's question about the identities of any inmates housed in the cell after it was "initially realized" that the toilet needed to be repaired, Fizer properly objects on vagueness grounds. Also, Fizer correctly explains that as a maximum security inmate, Plaintiff is not entitled to the "name(s) and number(s)" of any inmates housed in the cell, as his question requests, for legitimate security and appropriate penological reasons. Courts are required to consider the competing interests of the parties in deciding discovery requests and defer to the expertise of prison officials in matters of prison security. *Cutter v. Wilkinson, 544 U.S. 709, 725 n. 13, 125 S. Ct. 2113, 161 L. Ed. 2d 1020 (2005); United States v. Williams, 791 F.2d 1383 (9th Cir. 1986).*

Plaintiff also asked about Central Unit's procedures for mopping the cells. In response, Fizer explains the cell cleaning process at Central Unit, including the existence of a cleaning schedule, distribution of supplies, and oversight to ensure compliance. Fizer's response is sufficient. Similarly, Fizer's response that he does not have first-hand knowledge of what specific cleaning supplies are available for inmate use, is also sufficient. Plaintiff apparently does not believe Fizer is providing a truthful response, but the Court has no basis to conclude Fizer is not being truthful.

With regard to Plaintiff's overly broad request in Interrogatory No. 13 for "any and all ADC documents you were aware of that in any way relates to cell sanitation to include policies, procedures, protocols, post orders, logs, correctional standards, directives, audit reports, Arizona and Federal law, schedules, individual inmate detention records, budget records, supplies purchasing records, [and] supplies inventory records," the Court will order no further response. Plaintiff's request is disproportional to the issues in this case. The same is true with regard to Plaintiff's request for an equally-long laundry list of documents pertaining to sanitation of the outside areas of the Central Unit. Fizer will not be directed to respond to these two requests in Interrogatories No. 13 and 14.

Finally, Plaintiff is dissatisfied with Fizer's response to his request to explain the circumstances that led to Plaintiff's removal from the "Max Phase Program." Fizer stated he has no personal knowledge pertaining to the information requested. Fizer claims that "[a]part from the problems with [Plaintiff's] discovery (i.e. compound lines of inquiry, asking for production of documents in an interrogatory, and failing to identify the 'relevant time frame'), [Plaintiff] is simply upset that Fizer either does not remember or lacks the personal knowledge [Plaintiff] believes he should remember or know." (Doc. 141 at 8) The Court has no basis or evidence to conclude Fizer is not being truthful and will not order a further response. The Court, therefore, finds no basis to compel additional responses from Defendant Fizer.

IMMUNITY TO PUBLIC OFFICIALS AND PUBLIC ENTITIES

WILLIAM CHAPMAN MACH, PLAINTIFF/APPELLANT, V. STATE OF ARIZONA; ARIZONA DEPARTMENT OF CORRECTIONS; CORIZON, INC.; WEXFORD HEALTH SOURCES, INC., DEFENDANTS /Appellees. *2015 Ariz. App. Unpub. LEXIS 636* (May 14, 2015)

FACTS AND PROCEDURAL HISTORY

While an ADOC inmate, Mach sued the State, ADOC, Ryan, and Wexford for negligence, breach of contract, *Eighth Amendment* violations, and claims arising under *42 U.S.C. § 1983*. The claims were based on Appellees' alleged failure to properly treat Mach's knee, which had been diagnosed with "arthritic changes." Mach subsequently filed an amended complaint ("First Amended Complaint") that added Corizon as a defendant.

Appellees removed the case to federal district court pursuant to *28 U.S.C. § 1441(a)*. The district court dismissed the First Amended Complaint but granted Mach leave to file an amended complaint, which he did ("Second Amended Complaint"). The Second Amended Complaint omitted Ryan as a defendant and did not carry forward the *Eighth Amendment* or *§ 1983* claims. Because the Second Amended Complaint included only state-law claims, the district court remanded the case to the superior court.

The State moved to dismiss the Second Amended Complaint under *Arizona Rule of Civil Procedure 12(b)(6)* for failure to state a claim upon which relief could be granted, and Wexford joined in that motion. Corizon filed a separate motion to dismiss under *Rule 12(b)(6)*. After ruling that the Second Amended Complaint was the operative pleading, the superior court granted the State's motion to dismiss. It also granted Corizon's motion to dismiss the breach of contract count, but gave Mach until May 30, 2014 to file a statutorily compliant physician's affidavit regarding the negligence claim against Corizon. After Mach failed to do so, the court dismissed the case in its entirety.

The Second Amended Complaint did not include Ryan as a defendant. Therefore, the superior court correctly ruled that Mach could not proceed against Ryan.

III. Negligence Claim

Count one of the Second Amended Complaint alleged negligence against the State, Wexford, and Corizon for "denying reasonable medical care to [Mach's] right knee." The superior court dismissed the negligence claim against the State because it was barred by *A.R.S § 31-201.01(L)*, which prevents incarcerated felons from seeking damages for injury by the State or its agencies "unless the complaint alleges specific facts from which the court may conclude that the plaintiff suffered serious physical injury or the claim is authorized by a federal statute." "Serious physical injury" is defined as "an impairment of physical condition that creates a substantial risk of death or that causes serious disfigurement, prolonged impairment of health or prolonged loss or impairment of the function of any bodily organ." *A.R.S. § 31-201.01(N)(2)*.

Mach argues "[a] fair reading of the pleadings will disclose allegations of a serious knee condition . . . which caused [him] unceasing severe pain and prolonged impairment of function." He also suggests his complaint established "a claim authorized by federal statute." However, Mach's argument relies primarily on the First Amended Complaint, which is not the operative pleading. The Second Amended Complaint does not allege facts necessary to satisfy the requirements of *A.R.S. § 31-201.01(L)*. It includes only conclusory statements, such as "the injury is a medical condition which [Appellees] were required by law to treat, but which they negligently failed to treat." Furthermore, Mach expressly identified the negligence claim in the Second Amended Complaint as a "state claim," not one arising under federal law. Under these circumstances, the superior court properly dismissed the negligence claim against the State.

In its motion to dismiss, Corizon argued count one was a medical negligence claim because Mach was contending "his medical care providers [were] not providing the requisite care for his medical conditions." Accordingly, Corizon argued, Mach was required to comply with *A.R.S. § 12-2603* by providing a preliminary expert affidavit. In response, Mach filed an affidavit from Brian Leslie Finkel. Appellees objected that Finkel's affidavit was insufficient because it did not establish Finkel was licensed to practice medicine in Arizona. The superior court agreed and ordered Mach to provide an affidavit in compliance with statutory requirements. When Mach failed to do so, the court dismissed his complaint.

Mach argues he did not assert a claim governed by *A.R.S. § 12-2603*. He further contends his "claim in tort" alleged all of the requisite elements. Once again, though, his argument is based on information not included in the Second Amended Complaint. The negligence count of the Second Amended Complaint contains only conclusory statements. Nonetheless, the superior court did not dismiss the claim outright, gave Mach "the benefit of all inferences" which his complaint could reasonably support, and gave Mach an opportunity to present a competent physician's affidavit. *See Gatecliff v. Great Republic Life Ins. Co., 154 Ariz. 502, 508, 744 P.2d 29, 35 (App. 1987)* (court gives plaintiffs benefit of all inferences when considering *Rule 12(b)(6)* motions). Mach failed to comply, and the court properly dismissed the negligence claim against Corizon and Wexford.

JENNIFER JONES, PLAINTIFF, V. CORIZON, LLC, ET AL., DEFENDANTS. Case No. 4:15 CV 346 RWS UNITED STATES DISTRICT COURT FOR THE EASTERN DISTRICT OF MISSOURI, EASTERN DIVISION

PLAINTIFF JENNIFER JONES' SON (DECEDENT JONES) WAS ARRESTED ON OUTSTANDING WARRANTS AND INCARCERATED AT THE ST. LOUIS CITY JUSTICE CENTER. FIVE DAYS AFTER HIS ARREST, DECEDENT JONES DIED IN HIS CELL FROM A STAPH INFECTION. MS. JONES FILED THIS LAW SUIT AGAINST SEVERAL CORRECTIONS OFFICERS AND MEDICAL STAFF MEMBERS EMPLOYED AT THE JUSTICE CENTER ASSERTING CLAIMS FOR DENIAL OF MEDICAL CARE AND WRONGFUL DEATH. DEFENDANT DALE GLASS IS THE COMMISSIONER OF THE CITY OF ST. LOUIS DIVISION OF CORRECTIONS. MS. JONES' COMPLAINT ALLEGES THAT GLASS WAS DELIBERATELY INDIFFERENT TO DECEDENT JONES' MEDICAL NEEDS IN VIOLATION OF THE FOURTEENTH AMENDMENT THROUGH A 42 U.S.C. § 1983 CLAIM AND ALSO ASSERTS A CLAIM AGAINST GLASS FOR WRONGFUL DEATH. GLASS HAS BEEN SUED IN HIS INDIVIDUAL CAPACITY.

Glass also moves to dismiss Ms. Jones' state law wrongful death claim based on official immunity. Official immunity shields public officers and state officials from civil liability for injuries arising out of their discretionary acts, functions, or omissions performed in the exercise of their official duties. Harris v. Munoz, 43 S.W.3d 384, 387 (Mo. Ct. App. 2001). The wrongful death claim in this case alleges that Defendants failed to provide adequate health care to Decedent Jones. The complaint does not allege any specific ministerial duty which Glass failed to perform in connection with Decedent Jones' death. Glass's official duties as the Commissioner of Corrections such as the general supervision of employees, supervisory conduct, and policy making are all discretionary acts covered by the official immunity doctrine. Nguyen v. Grain Valley R-5 School Dist., 353 S.W.3d 725, 733 (Mo. Ct. App. 2011). As a result, I will grant Glass's motion to dismiss the wrongful death claim.

TIMOTHY A BAXTER, PLAINTIFF, VS. CORIZON HEALTH INC., ET AL., DEFENDANTS. No. 1:14-cv-1347-JDT-egb UNITED STATES DISTRICT COURT FOR THE WESTERN DISTRICT OF TENNESSEE, EASTERN DIVISION

(SEE ALSO DISCUSSION UNDER MEDICAL CARE)

I. THE COMPLAINT

Baxter states that he has a medical history of chronic, severe joint pain, back pain, and sepsis in the upper jaw area which has caused extreme weight loss and headaches that Defendants have refused to treat through deliberate indifference, failure to have policies for medical treatment, and a failure to hire and train appropriate staff. (Comp. at 12, ECF No. 1.) Baxter alleges that the corrections and medical staff at NWCX were aware of his medical problems. (*Id.*) In 2012, Baxter received steroid injections to his elbow and shoulder to manage his joint pain; however, these treatments have stopped. (*Id.*) The staff discontinued any pain management care after October 2013, causing Baxter to lose sleep and suffer further pain. (*Id.*) Since October 2013, Baxter has over twenty-seven requests for treatment for which he received ibuprofen, but not an opportunity for a rheumatologist or orthopedic specialist to evaluate his pain. (*Id.*) Baxter alleges that he "has developed sepsis in his upper jaw, an area that reoccurs on a monthly basis which," he concludes has resulted in the loss of 50 pounds. The only treatment Defendants have offered Baxter was physical therapy; however, due to a conflict he was unable to go and no further appointments have been scheduled. On December 11, 2014 Baxter states he was called to the clinic for his three month chronic care visit. (*Id.*) He was seen by Defendant Collins who stated said she would keep an eye on his weight, but offered no tests or evaluations. (*Id.*) Baxter states that he has only received palliative treatment for his serious medical conditions. (*Id.*)

Baxter has suffered severe physical and emotional injury. (*Id.* at 16.) He seeks punitive and compensatory damages. (*Id.*) At the time of filing his complaint, Baxter also filed a Motion for Preliminary Injunctive Relief requesting the court enjoin Defendant Corizon Health, Keldie, and Schofield from applying a custom or practice that has prevented him from receiving adequate medical care.

1. Claims against Defendants in their Official Capacity and State of Tennessee

Baxter sues all Defendants in their official capacity. "[A] suit against a state official in his or her official capacity is not a suit against the official but rather is a suit against the official's office. As such, it is no different from a suit against the State itself." *Will v. Mich. Dep't of State Police, 491 U.S. 58, 71, 109 S. Ct. 2304, 105 L. Ed. 2d 45 (1989)* (citation omitted). Baxter's claim against Defendants Schofield, Posey, Thrasher, Hodge, Lewis, Steward, Poole, and Tirey in their official capacities is brought against the State of Tennessee, which is a named Defendant. Baxter's claim against Defendants Keldie, Pinney, Collins and Phillips in their official capacities is brought against Corizon Health or Corizon, which are named Defendants.

The *Eleventh Amendment to the United States Constitution* provides that "[t]he Judicial power of the United States shall not be construed to extend to any suit in law or equity, commenced or prosecuted against one of the United States by Citizens of another State, or by Citizens or Subjects of any Foreign State." *U.S. Const. amend. XI.* The *Eleventh Amendment* has been construed to prohibit citizens from suing their own states in federal court. *Welch v. Tex. Dep't of Highways & Pub. Transp., 483 U.S. 468, 472, 107 S. Ct. 2941, 97 L. Ed. 2d 389 (1987); Pennhurst State Sch. & Hosp. v. Halderman, 465 U.S. 89, 100, 104 S. Ct. 900, 79 L. Ed. 2d 67 (1984); Employees of Dep't of Pub. Health & Welfare v. Mo. Dep't of Pub. Health & Welfare, 411 U.S. 279, 280, 93 S. Ct. 1614, 36 L. Ed. 2d 251 (1973); see also Va. Office for Protection & Advocacy v. Stewart, 563 U.S. 247, 131 S. Ct. 1632, 1638, 179 L. Ed. 2d 675 (2011)* ("A State may waive its sovereign immunity at its pleasure, and in some circumstances Congress may abrogate it by appropriate legislation. But absent waiver or valid abrogation, federal courts may not entertain a private person's suit against a State.") (citations omitted). By its terms, the *Eleventh Amendment* bars all suits, regardless of the relief sought. *Pennhurst, 465 U.S. at 100-01.* Tennessee has not waived its sovereign immunity. *Tenn. Stat. Ann.* ~ 20-13-102(a). Moreover, a state is not a person within the meaning of *42 U.S.C.* ~ *1983. Lapides v. Bd. of Regents of the Univ. Sys. of Ga.,* 535 U.S. 613, 617, 122 S. Ct. 1640, 152 L. Ed. 2d 806 (2002); *Will,* 491 U.S. at 71.

JOHNNY L. MCGOWAN, JR., PLAINTIFF, V. CORIZON MEDICAL, LT. KEVIN GUNN, DR. CLEMENT BARNARD, AND DARREL THOMAS, DEFENDANTS. No. 3:14-cv-0578 UNITED STATES DISTRICT COURT FOR THE MIDDLE DISTRICT OF TENNESSEE, NASHVILLE DIVISION

(SEE ALSO DISCUSSION UNDER MEDICAL CARE)

1. The Official-Capacity Claims

Based on the record before him, the magistrate judge found, and this court agrees, that, insofar as the plaintiff brings suit against the Transportation Defendants in their official capacity, they are immune from such liability. These defendants are TDOC employees. "[A] [§ 1983] suit against a state official in his or her official capacity is not a suit against the official but rather is a suit against the official's office," i.e., against the State. Will v. Mich. Dept. of State Police, 491 U.S. 58, 71, 109 S. Ct. 2304, 105 L. Ed. 2d 45 (1989). Because the Transportation Defendants were employees of TDOC, which is a department of the State of Tennessee, they stand in the shoes of the State of Tennessee. The State of Tennessee is not a "person" amenable to suit under § 1983. Id. Moreover, the state of Tennessee and its agencies are immune from suit pursuant to the Eleventh Amendment. Quern v. Jordan, 440 U.S. 332, 340-45, 99 S. Ct. 1139, 59 L. Ed. 2d 358 (1979); see Lawson v. Shelby Cnty., Tenn., 211 F.3d 331, 335 (6th Cir. 2000) ("[T]he [Eleventh] Amendment prohibits suits against a 'state' in federal court whether for injunctive, declaratory or monetary relief."). The only exceptions to a state's immunity are (1) if the state has consented to suit or (2) if Congress has properly abrogated a state's immunity. S & M Brands, Inc. v. Cooper, 527 F.3d 500, 507 (6th Cir. 2008). Neither of these exceptions applies to § 1983 suits against the state of Tennessee. See Berndt v. Tennessee, 796 F.2d 879, 881 (6th Cir. 1986) (noting that Tennessee has not waived immunity to suits under § 1983); Hafer v. Melo, 502 U.S. 21, 25, 112 S. Ct. 358, 116 L. Ed. 2d 301 (1991) (reaffirming that Congress did not abrogate states' immunity when it passed § 1983).

The only other exception is when the Ex parte Young exception applies. See S&M Brands, 527 F.3d at 507. Under this exception, "a federal court can issue prospective injunctive and declaratory relief compelling a state official to comply with federal law." Id. (quoting Will, 491 U.S. at 71 & n.10). It is apparently this exception the plaintiff seeks to invoke in his objection to the recommendation that his official-capacity claims be dismissed on immunity grounds. His objection is unfounded, because, although he seeks equitable relief in the form of the "immediate termination" of defendants' jobs and revocation of their pensions (see Complaint, ECF No. 1, at 15), this is not the type of prospective injunctive relief permitted by the Ex part Young exception. See S&M Brands, 527 F.3d at 507. The events of which the plaintiff complains took place between March and May 2013, and the plaintiff does not allege an ongoing deprivation of his rights by TDOC transportation officials. He is not entitled to prospective injunctive relief. Consequently, he cannot sustain his official-capacity claims against the Transportation Defendants.

CHRISTINA BOBBIN, IN HER CAPACITY AS PLENARY GUARDIAN OF CARLO DANIEL LAUDADIO, AN INCAPACITATED ADULT, PLAINTIFF, V. CORIZON HEALTH, INC., NATALIA SAUNDERS, H.S.A., JANICE STEPNOSKI, L.C.S.W., WALTER CARL MORRIS, RN, NOEL DOMINGUEZ, M.D., ANDREW PAUL SAFRON, III, D.O., SVOBODA MARIA HOLT, LMHC, JANET JOAN MEMOLI, RN, MIKE SCOTT, IN HIS OFFICIAL CAPACITY AS LEE COUNTY SHERIFF, PAUL A. PAVESE, SERGEANT, AND RODNEY K. PAYNE, DEPUTY, INDIVIDUALLY, DEFENDANTS. CASE NO: 2:14-CV-158-FTM-29MRM UNITED STATES DISTRICT COURT FOR THE MIDDLE DISTRICT OF FLORIDA, FORT MYERS DIVISION

THE PERTINENT, UNDISPUTED FACTS ARE AS FOLLOWS: ON OCTOBER 14, 2011, CARLO DANIEL LAUDADIO (LAUDADIO) WAS ARRESTED FOR A VIOLATION OF PROBATION AND BOOKED INTO THE LEE COUNTY JAIL. (DOC. #50, ¶ 37; DOC. #57, P. 2; DOC. #62, P. 7.) ON OCTOBER 19, 2011, WHILE IN CUSTODY, LAUDADIO HANGED HIMSELF WITH HIS JUMPSUIT. (DOC. #50, ¶ 58.) AS A RESULT OF THE INCIDENT, LAUDADIO'S BRAIN WAS DEPRIVED OF OXYGEN FOR A SUFFICIENT TIME TO RESULT IN ANOXIC BRAIN INJURY, WHICH HAS RENDERED HIM WHOLLY DEPENDENT UPON THE CARE OF OTHERS. (ID. ¶ 59.)

On March 26, 2012, plaintiff Christina Bobbin (plaintiff), Laudadio's biological sister, was appointed plenary guardian of the person and property of Laudadio and obtained a Court Order authorizing her to file a lawsuit on his behalf. (Doc. #50-1; Doc. #50-2.) On August 5, 2013, Plaintiff served defendant Corizon with a Notice of Intent to Initiate Litigation for Medical Malpractice. (Doc. #56-1.) On August 1, 2013, Plaintiff filed a Petition for 90-Day Extension. (Doc. #62-1, ¶ 4.) Plaintiff served Dominguez with a Notice of Intent to Initiate Litigation for Medical Malpractice on June 23, 2014. (Doc. #62-1; Doc. #56-2, p. 2.)

III.

Count V asserts a claim for medical negligence against Dominguez. Dominguez asserts that he is entitled to summary judgment on Count V because plaintiff failed to comply with the presuit notice requirement of a medical malpractice claim within the statute of limitations period. Plaintiff seeks summary judgment in her favor on this same issue.

Florida Statute § 766.106 - part of the Comprehensive Medical Malpractice Reform Act of 1985 - identifies medical negligence or medical malpractice claims as those "arising out of the rendering of, or the failure to render, medical care or services." Fla. Stat. § 766.106(1)(a), (2015). A claimant must comply with certain procedural requirements prior to initiating a lawsuit, including providing the defendant with a notice of intent to sue and conducting presuit screening. Id. at §§ 766.106(2) and 766.203(2). "No suit may be filed for a period of 90 days after notice is mailed to any prospective defendant." Id. at § 766.106(3)(a). These requirements are conditions precedent to maintaining a suit for medical malpractice. Univ. of Miami v. Wilson, 948 So. 2d 774, 776 (Fla. 3d DCA 2006). A complaint alleging medical malpractice is properly dismissed if these provisions are not satisfied. Goldfarb v. Urciuoli, 858 So. 2d 397, 398-99 (Fla. 1st DCA 2003).

A plaintiff is typically afforded leave to amend, however, if the statutory period for initiating suit has not "run before the plaintiff attempts to fulfill the presuit notice or screening requirements." Southern Neurological Assocs., P.A. v. Fine, 591 So. 2d 252, 255 (Fla. 4th DCA 1991). Thus, if Plaintiff's suit is one for malpractice rather than ordinary negligence and if the medical defendants are "health care providers" plaintiff's suit should be dismissed with leave to file a new complaint after complying with the statutory prerequisites to bringing suit.

The Court acknowledges plaintiff's June 20, 2014, presuit notice to Dominguez occurred after litigation had already begun in violation of the presuit requirements of Fla. Stat. ˜ 766.106(2). However, plaintiffs are entitled to cure this type of defect provided that the two-year limitation period has not run. Smith ex rel Ashley v. Brevard Cnty., Fla., No. 6:06-CV-715-ORL-31JGG, 2006 U.S. Dist. LEXIS 57210, 2006 WL 2355583, at *8 (M.D. Fla. Aug. 14, 2006). Therefore, the Court must determine when plaintiff's two year limitation period expired.

1. Statute of Limitations

Plaintiff asserts that the statute of limitations did not begin to run until she was named guardian on March 26, 2012. Plaintiff further asserts that she is entitled to a ninety (90) day extension for the statutory Petition for 90-day Extension that was filed on August 1, 2013 (Doc. #35-1, p. 34), and another ninety (90) day extension for the service of the Notice of Intent served on Corizon on August 5, 2013. Thus, plaintiff alleges the statute of limitations did not run until after September 22, 2014. Accordingly, plaintiff contends that the June 23, 2014 notice of intent served on Dominguez was timely.

In his Reply, Dominguez asserts that November 11, 2011, is the proper start of the limitations period because that is when plaintiff's counsel took action to inquire into the potential liability of this case. (Doc. #67, p. 3.) Dominguez contends that even if plaintiff is granted the ninety (90) days for presuit period and an additional ninety (90) days for the purchased extension, the statute of limitations ran on May 10, 2014, and thus, the notice served on Dominguez on June 23, 2014, was untimely.

"An action for medical malpractice shall be commenced within 2 years from the time the incident giving rise to the action occurred or within 2 years from the time the incident is discovered, or should have been discovered with the exercise of due diligence . . . ." ˜ 95.11(4)(b), Fla. Stat. (2010). In Tanner v. Hartog, 618 So. 2d 177 (Fla. 1993), the Florida Supreme Court held that, to trigger this statute, the plaintiff must have both knowledge of the injury and "knowledge that there is a reasonable possibility that the injury was caused by medical malpractice." Id. at 181 (footnote omitted). Such knowledge may not be imputed, however, to an adult who has no ability to be consciously aware of such injury. Arthur v. Unicare Health

FACILITIES, INC., 602 SO.2D 596 (FLA. 2D DCA 1992). THUS, WHERE THE VICTIM WAS BLIND, DEAF, AND SENILE, HE COULD NOT "DISCOVER" THE ACTION, AND NOTICE COULD NOT BE IMPUTED TO HIM TO COMMENCE THE RUNNING OF THE STATUTE OF LIMITATIONS. ID.

Where the victim of the malpractice is an adult, knowledge of another cannot be imputed to him unless that person has a legal duty, such as a guardian's duty, to protect the ward's interest. In *Thomas v. Lopez, 982 So. 2d 64, 68 (Fla. 5th DCA 2008),* the court held that, even if the victim's mother knew of malpractice, her knowledge could not be imputed to her unconscious adult daughter prior to the mother's appointment as plenary guardian, because the mother had no duty to pursue medical malpractice until her appointment. Likewise, the court in *Barrier v. JFK Med. Ctr. Ltd. P'ship, No. 4D13-3041, So. 3d , 2015 Fla. App. LEXIS 9264, 2015 WL 3759641, at *5 (Fla. 4th DCA, June 17, 2015),* found that the knowledge the emergency temporary guardian had about the possibility of medical malpractice should not be imputed to the ward to commence the running of the statute of limitations. Rather, "knowledge may be imputed from the date a permanent plenary guardian is appointed." Id.

It is undisputed the Laudadio has been an incapacitated adult since the October 19, 2011 incident. Plaintiff was appointed plenary guardian on March 26, 2012. The Court finds that the statute of limitations did not begin to run until that time. Therefore, the statute of limitations would have expired on March 26, 2014. However, the Plaintiff was provided two ninety (90) day extensions which are not contested by Dominguez. Thus, the statute of limitations period did not expire until September 22, 2014. Dominguez was served a notice of intent on June 23, 2014. The Court finds that this is within the statute of limitations period.[1] Accordingly, the plaintiff cured the presuit defect before the statute of limitations had expired.

[1] BECAUSE THE COURT FINDS PLAINTIFF'S JUNE 23, 2014, NOTICE OF INTENT WAS TIMELY, THE COURT FINDS NO NEED TO DETERMINE WHETHER PLAINTIFF'S NOTICE OF INTENT SENT TO CORIZON ON AUGUST 5, 2013, WAS IMPUTED TO DOMINGUEZ.

2. PRESUIT NOTICE

DESPITE THE TIMELY PRESUIT NOTICE TO DOMINGUEZ, THE PLAINTIFF'S JUNE 23, 2014 NOTICE OF INTENT WAS STILL FILED AFTER LITIGATION HAD ALREADY BEEN INITIATED IN VIOLATION OF *FLA. STAT. § 766.106(2).* THEREFORE, THE COURT MUST NOW DETERMINE WHETHER PLAINTIFF HAS CURED THIS DEFECT.

The remedy for failure to comply with the statutory prerequisites to bringing suit is dismissal with leave to amend. *Southern Neurological Assocs., P.A. v. Fine, 591 So. 2d at 255.* This Court dismissed plaintiff First Amended Complaint on October 29, 2014. (Doc. #49.) Plaintiff filed a Second Amended Complaint on November 12, 2014.[2] (Doc. #50.) Consequently, at the time of filing the Second Amended Complaint, plaintiff had complied with the statutory presuit notice requirement by serving Dominguez with a notice of intent on June 23, 2014. Therefore, the Court finds that plaintiff has satisfied the presuit notice requirements of *Fla. Stat.* ˜ *766.106(2).*

[2] WHERE A COMPLAINT AND PRESUIT NOTICE ARE SERVED WITHIN THE APPLICABLE STATUTE OF LIMITATIONS, "THE PLAINTIFF MAY SUBSEQUENTLY (EVEN AFTER EXPIRATION OF THE STATUTORY PERIOD) FILE AN AMENDED COMPLAINT ASSERTING COMPLIANCE WITH THE PRESUIT SCREENING PROCESS. *STEBILLA V. MUSSALLEM, 595 SO. 2D 136, 139 (FLA. 5TH DCA 1992).*

GLENDA S. SIMMONS, AS GUARDIAN AND CONSERVATOR OF BRYAN O'NEIL SIMMONS, CALVIN C. SIMMONS, AS GUARDIAN AND CONSERVATOR OF BRYAN O'NEIL SIMMONS, BRYAN O'NEIL SIMMONS, AND TIFFANY SIMMONS, PLAINTIFFS, V. CORIZON HEALTH, INC., CORIZON, LLC, B.J. BARNES, IN HIS OFFICIAL CAPACITY AS SHERIFF OF GUILFORD COUNTY, NORTH CAROLINA, GUILFORD COUNTY, AND THE LOCAL GOVERNMENT EXCESS LIABILITY FUND, INC., DEFENDANTS. 1:14cv730 UNITED STATES DISTRICT COURT FOR THE MIDDLE DISTRICT OF NORTH CAROLINA

(SEE ALSO ISCUSSION UNDER MEDICAL CARE)

3. *Section 1983* Claim Against Sheriff Barnes in His Official Capacity

Guilford Defendants next contend that the ˜ *1983* claim against Sheriff Barnes in his official capacity fails to state a claim for relief. Plaintiffs respond that their amended complaint pleads sufficient facts to avoid *Rule 12(b)(6)* dismissal.

Plaintiffs have sued Sheriff Barnes only in his official capacity. (Doc. 20 at 30.) "[A] suit against a sheriff in his official capacity constitutes a suit against a local governmental entity, i.e., a sheriff's office." *Parker v. Burris, No. 1:13CV488, 2015 U.S. Dist. LEXIS 41433, 2015 WL 1474909, at *6 (M.D.N.C. Mar. 31, 2015),* report and recommendation adopted, *No. 1:13CV488, 2015 U.S. Dist. LEXIS 60308, 2015 WL 2169148 (M.D.N.C. May 8, 2015)*; see also *Gantt v. Whitaker, 203 F. Supp. 2d 503, 508 (M.D.N.C. 2002)*. Here, both parties devote almost their entire briefing to argue about Sheriff Barnes' personal involvement in, and his supervisory liability arising from, Plaintiffs' allegations. (See Doc. 29 at 14-16; Doc. 33 at 13-15; Doc. 34 at 5-7.) However, "when supervisory liability is imposed, it is imposed against the supervisory official *in his individual capacity* for his own culpable action or inaction in the training, supervision, or control of his subordinates." *Clay v. Conlee, 815 F.2d 1164, 1170 (8th Cir. 1987)* (emphasis added); see also *Shelley v. Cnty. of Kershaw, No. CA 3:11-3477-CMC, 2013 U.S. Dist. LEXIS 101914, 2013 WL 3816708, at *4 n.6 (D.S.C. July 22, 2013)* (holding that, because the sheriff was not sued in his individual capacity, "no claim under ~ 1983 for supervisory liability has been properly asserted against [the sheriff] in this court"). Insofar as Sheriff Barnes is sued only in his official capacity, supervisory liability may not be imposed upon him.

In order to state a claim against Sheriff Barnes in his official capacity, Plaintiffs "must allege that the alleged constitutional violations resulted from an official policy or custom of the Sheriff's office." *Evans v. Guilford Cnty. Det. Ctr., No. 1:13CV499, 2014 U.S. Dist. LEXIS 129221, 2014 WL 4641150, at *3 (M.D.N.C. Sept. 16, 2014)*; *Lytle v. Doyle, 326 F.3d 463, 471 (4th Cir. 2003)* ("[N]ot every deprivation of a constitutional right will lead to municipal liability. Only in cases where the municipality causes the deprivation 'through an official policy or custom' will liability attach." (quoting *Carter, 164 F.3d at 218*)).

Guilford Defendants' only argument related to Plaintiffs' official capacity claim against Sheriff Barnes is that "it must be dismissed as Monell precludes liability predicated on vicarious liability or *respondeat superior*." (Doc. 29 at 14.) This argument overlooks that ~ 1983 imposes liability based on an official capacity claim, such as here, if an "action pursuant to official municipal policy of some nature caused a constitutional tort." *Monell v. Dep't of Soc. Servs., 436 U.S. 658, 691-95, 98 S. Ct. 2018, 56 L. Ed. 2d 611 (1978)*. Guilford Defendants make no argument that Plaintiffs' amended complaint fails to allege facts of an official policy causing the claimed *Eighth Amendment* violation. In the absence of their having raised this argument, the court will not do so.

Guilford Defendants' motion to dismiss Plaintiffs' ~ 1983 claim against Sheriff Barnes, in his official capacity, will therefore be denied.

4. State Law Claims Against Guilford Defendants

Finally, Guilford Defendants argue that Plaintiffs' State law claims should be dismissed as barred by State sovereign or governmental immunity. Under State sovereign immunity, sheriffs are immune from suit absent a waiver of immunity. See *Phillips v. Gray, 163 N.C. App. 52, 592 S.E.2d 229, 232 (N.C. Ct. App. 2004)* ("The doctrine of sovereign immunity bars actions against public officials sued in their official capacities. Sheriffs and deputy sheriffs are considered public officials for purposes of sovereign immunity." (citation omitted)). "Substantially the same immunity is given to a county and its agencies, absent a waiver, under the rubric of 'governmental immunity.'" *Russ v. Causey, 732 F. Supp. 2d 589, 610 (E.D.N.C. 2010)* (quoting *Craig ex rel. Craig v. New Hanover Cnty. Bd. of Educ., 363 N.C. 334, 678 S.E.2d 351, 353 n.3 (N.C. 2009)*), aff'd in part, *468 F. App'x 267 (4th Cir. 2012)*. Plaintiffs contend that immunity has been waived as to both Sheriff Barnes and the County.

Unlike the analysis above, "[a] motion to dismiss based on sovereign immunity is a jurisdictional issue." *M Series Rebuild, LLC v. Town of Mount Pleasant, Inc., 222 N.C. App. 59, 730 S.E.2d 254, 257 (N.C. Ct. App. 2012)*. Guilford Defendants' motion raises an immunity defense based on a lack of personal jurisdiction under *Federal Rule of Civil Procedure 12(b)(2)*, citing *Green v. Kearney, 203 N.C. App. 260, 690 S.E.2d 755 (N.C. Ct. App. 2010)*. In Green, the North Carolina Court of Appeals concluded, "[T]he general rule is that sovereign immunity presents a question of personal jurisdiction, not subject matter jurisdiction." *Id. at 760*; see also *Meherrin Indian Tribe v. Lewis, 197 N.C. App. 380, 677 S.E.2d 203, 207 (N.C. Ct. App. 2009)* ("[A]n appeal of a motion to dismiss based on sovereign immunity presents a question of personal jurisdiction rather than subject matter jurisdiction." (quoting *Data Gen. Corp. v. Cty. of Durham, 143 N.C. App. 97, 545 S.E.2d 243, 245-46 (N.C. Ct. App. 2001)*) (internal quotation marks omitted)). Thus, the court will consider Guilford Defendants' motion to dismiss under *Rule 12(b)(2)*.[5]

5   The North Carolina Supreme Court has yet to decide whether dismissal based on State sovereign or governmental immunity is a matter of personal or subject-matter jurisdiction. North Carolina courts continue to hold that "whether sovereign immunity is grounded in a lack of subject matter jurisdiction or personal jurisdiction is unsettled in North Carolina." *M Series Rebuild, 730 S.E.2d at 257*; see also *Atl. Coast Conference v. Univ. of Md., 751 S.E.2d 612, 617 (N.C. Ct. App. 2013)*. Whether to assess the State sovereign immunity defense under *Rule 12(b)(1)* or *12(b)(2)*, however, appears to be immaterial here. See *AGI Assocs., LLC v. Profile Aviation Ctr., Inc., No. 5:13CV61-RLV, 2013 U.S. Dist. LEXIS 118808, 2013 WL 4482933, at *3 (W.D.N.C. Aug. 21, 2013)* (noting that the court could conduct jurisdictional analysis of State sovereign immunity under *Rule 12(b)(1)* or *Rule 12(b)(2)*), aff'd sub nom. *AGI Assocs., LLC v. City of Hickory, N.C., 773 F.3d 576 (4th Cir. 2014); Collum v. Charlotte-Mecklenburg Bd. of Educ., No. 3:07CV534-RJC-DSC, 2010 U.S. Dist. LEXIS 15824, 2010 WL 702462, at *6 (W.D.N.C. Feb. 23, 2010)* (assessing State sovereign and governmental immunity under both *Rule 12(b)(1)* and *Rule 12(b)(2)*); *Pettiford, 556 F. Supp. 2d at 524 n.8* ("[T]he distinction appears to have no impact on the method of review."). Notably, Plaintiffs do not object to assessing Guilford Defendants' motion under *Rule 12(b)(2)*.

Plaintiffs bear the burden of establishing personal jurisdiction by a preponderance of the evidence. See *Universal Leather, LLC v. Koro AR, S.A., 773 F.3d 553, 558 (4th Cir. 2014); Carefirst of Md., Inc. v. Carefirst Pregnancy Ctrs., Inc., 334 F.3d 390, 396 (4th Cir. 2003); Combs v. Bakker, 886 F.2d 673, 676 (4th Cir. 1989)*. "When, however, as here, a district court decides a pretrial personal jurisdiction motion without conducting an evidentiary hearing, the plaintiff need only make a prima facie showing of personal jurisdiction." *Carefirst, 334 F.3d at 396*. The court may consider supporting affidavits when determining whether a plaintiff has made a prima facie showing of personal jurisdiction. See *Universal Leather, 773 F.3d at 558*. "In deciding whether the plaintiff has proved a prima facie case of personal jurisdiction, the district court must draw all reasonable inferences arising from the proof, and resolve all factual disputes, in the plaintiff's favor." *Mylan Labs., Inc. v. Akzo, N.V., 2 F.3d 56, 60 (4th Cir. 1993)*; see also *Carefirst, 334 F.3d at 396*. If the existence of jurisdiction turns on disputed factual questions, the court may resolve the challenge on the basis of an evidentiary hearing or, when a prima facie demonstration of personal jurisdiction has been made, it can proceed "as if it has personal jurisdiction over th[e] matter, although factual determinations to the contrary may be made at trial." *Pinpoint IT Servs., L.L.C. v. Atlas IT Exp. Corp., 812 F. Supp. 2d 710, 717 (E.D. Va. 2011)* (citing 2 James Wm. Moore et al., Moore's Federal Practice ÷ 12.31 (3d ed. 2011)). Nevertheless, either at trial or at a pretrial evidentiary hearing, the plaintiff must eventually prove the existence of personal jurisdiction by a preponderance of the evidence. *New Wellington Fin. Corp. v. Flagship Resort Dev. Corp., 416 F.3d 290, 294 n.5 (4th Cir. 2005)*.

As to Sheriff Barnes, North Carolina law permits suits against "a sheriff and the surety on his official bond for acts of negligence in the performance of official duties."[6] *Myers v. Bryant, 188 N.C. App. 585, 655 S.E.2d 882, 885 (N.C. Ct. App. 2008)* (citing *N.C. Gen. Stat. ˜ 58-76-5*). North Carolina law requires that all sheriffs purchase a bond not exceeding $25,000. *N.C. Gen. Stat. ˜ 162-8*. Under North Carolina law, a sheriff waives State sovereign immunity by purchasing that bond. *N.C. Gen. Stat.   ˜ 58-76-5*.

6   North Carolina law also waives immunity of a sheriff by the purchase of liability insurance under *N.C. Gen. Stat. ˜ 153A-435*. See *Russ, 732 F. Supp. 2d at 610; Myers, 655 S.E.2d at 885* (holding that county's purchase of liability insurance can waive sheriff's immunity beyond $25,000 bond). Plaintiffs, however, make no allegation or contention that the County's participation in the LGELF further waives Sheriff Barnes' immunity. See *Russ, 732 F. Supp. 2d at 611* ("Any effective waiver of immunity through the insurance policy would have to be in addition to and separate from the waiver of the bond."). Guilford Defendants have also submitted the affidavit of Randall R. Zimmerman, President of the LGELF, who states that Guilford County's "Fund B" is "separate and distinct" from Sheriff Barnes' bond. (Doc. 30   ÷ 10.) Zimmerman further states, "In his capacity as Sheriff of Guilford County, Sheriff B.J. Barnes is not a principal under any other surety bonds nor is he a member of any Local Government Risk Pool nor is he insured under any General Liability Insurance Policy or Law Enforcement Liability Insurance Policy." (Id. ÷ 11.)

Here, Sheriff Barnes allegedly purchased a $25,000 bond, as required by *N.C. Gen. Stat.   ˜ 162-8*. (Doc. 20 ÷ ÷ 33; Doc. 30 at 7.) Plaintiffs sued both Sheriff Barnes and the surety on his official bond, LGELF, for negligence and loss of consortium stemming from that negligence. (Doc. 20 ÷ ÷ 33, 141, 153-58; Doc. 30 at 7.) Under North Carolina law, therefore, the amended complaint states sufficient allegations that State sovereign immunity is waived as to Sheriff Barnes to this extent. See *Myers, 655 S.E.2d at 885*; *Smith v. Phillips, 117 N.C. App. 378, 451 S.E.2d 309, 313 (N.C. Ct. App. 1994)*; see also *Russ, 732 F. Supp. 2d at 610*.

Recognizing this potential conclusion, Guilford Defendants ask the court to limit Plaintiffs' claims to the amount of Sheriff Barnes' bond -- $25,000. (Doc. 29 at 20; Doc. 30.) They argue that such a limitation is consistent with *N.C. Gen. Stat.* ˜ 153A-435(a). See *N.C. Gen. Stat.* ˜ 58-76-5. Plaintiffs offer no response to Guilford Defendants' proposed limitation.

North Carolina courts have held that purchase of a bond by a sheriff, as required under *N.C. Gen. Stat.* ˜ 162-8, waives State sovereign immunity but "only to the extent of the amount of the bond." *White v. Cochran, 748 S.E.2d 334, 339 (N.C. Ct. App. 2013)*; see also *Hill v. Medford, 357 N.C. 650, 588 S.E.2d 467 (N.C. 2003)* (per curiam) (adopting dissent in *158 N.C. App. 618, 582 S.E.2d 325 (N.C. Ct. App. 2003)*, which stated, "As a public official, if sued in his or her official capacity, a sheriff is protected against tort actions by governmental immunity unless the sheriff purchases a bond pursuant to G.S. ˜ 58-76-5, and then, can only be liable on tort claims to the extent of the amount of that bond"); *Summey v. Barker, 142 N.C. App. 688, 544 S.E.2d 262, 264 (N.C. Ct. App. 2001)* (holding that, "to the extent of the bond required" by a different North Carolina law, a public officer's immunity did not bar plaintiff's claim). Federal courts interpreting North Carolina law have reached the same conclusion. See *Oliver v. Harper, No. 5:09-CT-3027-H, 2011 U.S. Dist. LEXIS 29499, 2011 WL 1104134, at *10 (E.D.N.C. Mar. 22, 2011)* ("[T]he defendants' purchase of a $25,000.00 bond does waive immunity for damages but only up to the amount of the bond."); *Russ, 732 F. Supp. 2d at 610*.

Because Sheriff Barnes allegedly purchased a $25,000 bond as required by *N.C. Gen. Stat.* ˜ 162-8 (Doc. 20 ÷ 33; Doc. 30) and Plaintiffs have not presented (nor has this court found) any reason to reach a contrary conclusion, the court will limit Plaintiffs' State law claims against the Sheriff (Counts III and V) to the $25,000 amount of the bond.

As for the County, Plaintiffs first argue that *N.C. Gen. Stat.* ˜ 153A-225 waives the County's governmental immunity. In support of this argument, Plaintiffs cite *Beckles-Palomares v. Logan, 202 N.C. App. 235, 688 S.E.2d 758 (N.C. Ct. App. 2010)*, for the proposition that "if a governmental unit is under a statutory obligation to perform an act, then it may not claim governmental immunity when it fails in that duty." (Doc. 33 at 18.) This is a misreading of that decision. In Beckles-Palomares, the North Carolina Court of Appeals applied established law that *N.C. Gen. Stat.* ˜ 160A-296 waives the governmental immunity doctrine. *202 N.C. App. at 242-43*. In doing so, the court applied "the safe streets exception," which states that maintenance of municipality streets and sidewalks is a proprietary, not governmental, function unprotected by governmental immunity. See *Sisk v. City of Greensboro, 183 N.C. App. 657, 645 S.E.2d 176, 179 (N.C. Ct. App. 2007)*. Plaintiffs fail to explain how that case demonstrates that a different statute -- *N.C. Gen. Stat.* ˜ 153A-225 -- establishes a waiver of governmental immunity. See *Meyer v. Walls, 347 N.C. 97, 489 S.E.2d 880, 884 (N.C. 1997)* (stating, in reference to waiver of governmental immunity, "[w]aiver of sovereign immunity may not be lightly inferred" (quoting *Guthrie v. N.C. State Ports Auth., 307 N.C. 522, 299 S.E.2d 618, 627 (N.C. 1983)*)). Plaintiffs' waiver argument as to ˜ 153A-225 is thus unpersuasive.

Plaintiffs also argue that the County waived its immunity by purchasing liability insurance pursuant to *N.C. Gen. Stat.* ˜ 153A-435(a). Under ˜ 153A-435(a), a county may "purchase liability insurance, which includes participating in a local government risk pool, for negligence caused by an act or omission of the county or any of its officers, agents, or employees when performing government functions." *Myers, 655 S.E.2d at 885*. Purchase of insurance pursuant to ˜ 153A-435(a) "waives the county's governmental immunity, to the extent of insurance coverage." ˜ 153A-435(a). In their amended complaint, Plaintiffs allege that the County "may be insureds under a liability insurance policy or participation [sic] in a Risk Pool." (Doc. 20 ÷ 34.)

Guilford Defendants acknowledge that the County has participated in the LGELF since 2001, but they claim that this participation does not constitute a waiver of immunity under ˜ 153A-435(a). (Doc. 29 at 19; Doc. 30 ÷

5.) In support of their defense, Guilford Defendants filed the affidavit of Randall R. Zimmerman, President of the LGELF. (Doc. 30.) According to Zimmerman, the County is self-insured up to $100,000. (Id.   ÷ 4.) The LGELF pays claims against the County between $100,000 and $5,000,000, but the County is obligated to repay the LGELF in the entirety. (Id.)

Based on the County's evidence, which is uncontested, the LGELF does not waive the County's immunity. The   LGELF fails to meet the statutory requirements of a local government risk pool because (1) two LGELF members, the Guilford County Board of Education and Guilford Technical Community College, are not local governments, see *N.C. Gen. Stat.* ˜ ˜ *58-23-1, 58-23-5(a)*; (Doc. 30   ÷ 7(a)); (2) no notice was given to the Commissioner of Insurance that the participating entities "intend[ed] to organize and operate [a] risk pool[]" under North Carolina law, as required by *N.C. Gen. Stat.* ˜ *58-23-5(e)*, (Doc. 30   ÷ 7(b)); and (3) the LGELF does not contain a provision for a system or program of loss control, see *N.C. Gen. Stat.* ˜ *58-23-15(1)*; (Doc. 30   ÷ 7(c)). See *Pettiford, 556 F. Supp. 2d at 525* (finding similar failures to meet the statutory requirements of a local government risk pool); *Lyles v. City of Charlotte, 344 N.C. 676, 477 S.E.2d 150, 153 (N.C. 1996)* (same); *Dobrowolska ex rel. Dobrowolska v. Wall, 138 N.C. App. 1, 530 S.E.2d 590, 595-96 (N.C. Ct. App. 2000)* (same). The LGELF also does not constitute a local government risk pool because the County must repay the entire amount for claims between $100,000 and $5 million.[7] *N.C. Gen. Stat.* ˜ *153A-435(a)*; see also *Pettiford, 556 F. Supp. 2d at 525* (applying similar statutory provision applicable to North Carolina cities); *White, 748 S.E.2d at 340* (holding that immunity is waived under ˜ *153A-435(a)* only to the extent that a county is indemnified). Finally, the County's Board of Commissioners did not adopt a resolution deeming "the creation of [the LGELF] to be the same as the purchase of insurance," which would have also waived its governmental immunity. *N.C. Gen. Stat.* ˜ *153A-435(a)*; (Doc. 30   ÷ 8).

7   The LGELF fails to meet several other statutory requirements. In particular, it (1) does not make any accounting reports available to the Commissioner of Insurance, *N.C. Gen. Stat.*   ˜ *58-23-26*, (Doc. 30   ÷ 7(d)); and (2) has no authority or mechanism to assess members of the pool to satisfy any financial deficiencies, *N.C. Gen. Stat.* ˜ *58-23-30(b)*; (Doc. 30   ÷ 7(e)).

Plaintiffs argue finally that they should be able to conduct "at least minimal discovery" to investigate the County's involvement in the risk pool. (Doc. 33 at 20.) But to do so, in light of the County's affidavit, would deprive the County of the very immunity to which it is entitled. In the absence of some reason to question the County's affidavit, Plaintiffs' request for jurisdictional discovery is denied. See *Carefirst of Md., Inc. v. Carefirst Pregnancy Ctrs., Inc., 334 F.3d 390, 402 (4th Cir. 2003)* ("When a plaintiff offers only speculation or conclusory assertions . . ., a court is within its discretion in denying jurisdictional discovery."); *Base Metal Trading, Ltd. v. OJSC "Novokuznetsky Aluminum Factory", 283 F.3d 208, 216 n.3 (4th Cir. 2002)* (upholding district court's denial of jurisdictional discovery where "the plaintiff simply wants to conduct a fishing expedition in the hopes of discovering some basis of jurisdiction").

Guilford Defendants' motion to dismiss the amended   complaint's State law claims against the County (Counts III and V) will therefore be granted.

EDWARD E. STEWART, III, PLAINTIFF, V. MICHAEL WENEROWICZ, DENNIS BRUMFIELD, MICHAEL DOYLE, JOHN HOFER, KEITH VANCLIFF, ROBERT GRUBER, CORIZON HEALTH, INC., RICHARD STEFANIK, M.D., MICHAEL HERBIK, D.O., RAYMOND MARCHAK, P.A., AND SUSAN BERRIER, R.N., DEFENDANTS. CIVIL ACTION NO. 12-4046 UNITED STATES DISTRICT COURT FOR THE EASTERN DISTRICT OF PENNSYLVANIA

(SEE ALSO DISCUSSION UNDER MEDICAL CARE)

c) Qualified Immunity

Commonwealth defendants next contend that, to the extent that the Court concludes that plaintiff has adequately alleged his Eighth Amendment claims against defendants Wenerowicz, Doyle, Brumfield, Hofer, Vancliff, and Gruber, defendants are entitled to qualified immunity. Commonwealth defendants argue that, as the "Third Circuit has not specifically dealt with the issue of seatbelts in state vehicles" "there is no way that Commonwealth defendants would have been aware that their actions were unlawful" and thus defendants are entitled to qualified immunity. (Cmmw. Defs.' Mot. to Dismiss 15-16.) The Court rejects this argument.

The qualified immunity analysis involves two steps: "(1) whether the plaintiff alleged sufficient facts to establish the violation of a constitutional right, and (2) whether the right was 'clearly established' at the time of the defendant's actions." Estate of Lagano v. Bergen Cnty. Prosecutor's Office, 769 F.3d 850, 858 (3d Cir. 2014) (quoting Pearson v. Callahan, 555 U.S. 223, 232, 129 S. Ct. 808, 172 L. Ed. 2d 565 (2009)). "The doctrine of qualified immunity protects government officials 'from liability for civil damages insofar as their conduct does not violate clearly established statutory or constitutional rights of which a reasonable person would have known.'" Pearson, 555 U.S. at 231 (quoting Harlow v. Fitzgerald, 457 U.S. 800, 818, 102 S. Ct. 2727, 73 L. Ed. 2d 396 (1982)). The Third Circuit has held that "qualified immunity will be upheld on a 12(b)(6) motion only when the immunity is established on the face of the complaint." Leveto v. Lapina, 258 F.3d 156, 161 (3d Cir. 2001) (internal quotations and citations omitted).

As discussed supra, plaintiff has adequately plead his Eighth Amendment claims against the moving Commonwealth defendants. Thus, the Court turns to the second prong of the qualified immunity analysis -- whether the right at issue was "clearly established" at the time plaintiff was injured while being transported to SCI-Graterford, on June 9, 2011.

For a right to be "clearly established," "[t]he contours of the right must be sufficiently clear that a reasonable official would understand that what he is doing violates that right." Anderson v. Creighton, 483 U.S. 635, 640, 107 S. Ct. 3034, 97 L. Ed. 2d 523 (1987). However, to find that a right is clearly established, there need not be "'a previous precedent directly in point.'" Acierno v. Cloutier, 40 F.3d 597, 620 (3d Cir. 1994) (quoting Good v. Dauphin County Soc. Servs. for Children & Youth, 891 F.2d 1087, 1092 (3d Cir. 1989)). "'[R]elatively strict factual identity' between applicable precedent and the case at issue" is not required. Stoneking v. Bradford Area Sch. Dist., 882 F.2d 720, 726 (3d Cir. 1989) (quoting People of Three Mile Island v. Nuclear Regulatory Comm., 747 F.2d 139, 144 (3d Cir. 1984)).

The Third Circuit recently examined what precedential authority is required to satisfy the second prong of the qualified immunity analysis. In Estate of Lagano, the Third Circuit explained that a plaintiff need not point to a binding decision recognizing a well-established right's application to the specific context at issue to overcome a qualified immunity defense. 769 F.3d at 859. Instead, "[t]he ultimate question is whether an officer had 'fair warning' that his conduct deprived the plaintiff of a constitutional right." Kingsmill v. Szewczak, No. 15-2386, 2015 U.S. Dist. LEXIS 100115, 2015 WL 4621456, at *9 (E.D. Pa. July 30, 2015) (citing Schneyder v. Smith, 653 F.3d 313, 329 (3d Cir. 2011)). In some cases the unconstitutionality of outrageous conduct will be obvious, but "even as to action less than an outrage, officials can still be on notice that their conduct violates established law in novel factual circumstances." Gaymon v. Borough of Collingdale, No. 14-5454, 2015 U.S. Dist. LEXIS 93014, 2015 WL 4389585, at *4 (E.D. Pa. July 17, 2015) (quoting Hope v. Pelzer, 536 U.S. 730, 741, 122 S. Ct. 2508, 153 L. Ed. 2d 666 (2002)). When no case law addresses the specific facts at issue, "a general constitutional rule already identified in the decisional law may apply with obvious clarity to the specific conduct in issue." Id. (quoting Hope, 536 U.S. at 741).

The fact that the Third Circuit has not issued a binding decision addressing officials' deliberate indifference to an inmate's health and safety while transporting the inmate in a prison vehicle is not dispositive of whether the Eighth Amendment right alleged by plaintiff is clearly established law. The Court must instead focus its inquiry on "whether 'it would be clear to a reasonable [official] that the alleged [conduct] was unlawful under the circumstances." Estate of Lagano, 769 F.3d at 859 (quoting Saucier, 533 U.S. at 202 (2001)). The Court concludes that it would have been clear to a reasonable prison official that the conduct plead by plaintiff with respect to his transportation in the prison van, and defendants' policies or lack of policies which lead to the dangerous transportation, were unlawful under the Eighth Amendment at the time of the alleged violations.

It has long been established that prison officials have an affirmative duty to "take reasonable measures to guarantee the safety of inmates," Farmer, 511 U.S. at 832, and when officers act with deliberate indifference in exposing an inmate to a substantial risk of serious harm, this conduct violates the Eighth Amendment, id. at 828;

see, e.g., Atkinson v. Taylor, 316 F.3d 257, 266-67 (3d Cir. 2003) (determining that plaintiff alleged a violation of the Eighth Amendment where prison officials were deliberately indifferent to plaintiff's exposure to second hand smoke, leading to chronic health problems); Bistrian, 696 F.3d at 368-69 (concluding that plaintiff alleged a violation of the Eighth Amendment where prison officials placed plaintiff in locked recreation yard with other inmates who were aware that he had acted as an informant against them).

In light of this well-established principle, the Court concludes that any reasonable officer would have known that he had a duty under the Eighth Amendment not to place an inmate at substantial risk of serious injury by driving recklessly and erratically, or by failing to intervene to stop such driving, particularly when inmates were not secured with safety restraints, were shackled and unable to protect themselves in the event of a sudden turn or accident, and were pleading with the officers to stop driving in such a manner. The substantial risk of serious harm to inmates from reckless and erratic driving, as alleged by plaintiff in this case, is obvious, and no reasonable officer would think that driving in this way could constitute lawful behavior. Because of the obviousness of the danger, and because the right to safe and humane conditions of confinement is clearly established, "the concomitant constitutional violation was apparent notwithstanding the fact that the very action in question had not previously been held to be unlawful" by the Third Circuit. Sterling v. Borough of Minersville, 232 F.3d 190, 198 (3d Cir. 2000) (adopting similar reasoning in concluding that defendant who allegedly violated plaintiff's right to privacy by disclosing information about plaintiff's sexuality was not entitled to qualified immunity).

The Court also notes that, prior to the alleged incident on June 9, 2011, a court in the Western District of Pennsylvania determined in a case similar to the present that a plaintiff stated an Eighth Amendment claim where the driver of a prison transport van drove recklessly and consciously ignored plaintiff's pleas for him to stop doing so, resulting in serious injury to plaintiff. Otero, 2010 U.S. Dist. LEXIS 102160, 2010 WL 3883444 at *11. Although not binding precedent, the Otero decision further supports the conclusion that the conduct of defendants Hofer, Gruber, and Vancliff, as alleged by plaintiff, was "sufficiently outrageous that a reasonable officer would have known that [their conduct] could violate" plaintiff's constitutional rights. Kingsmill, 2015 U.S. Dist. LEXIS 100115, 2015 WL 4621456 at *9.

With respect to defendants Wenerowicz, Doyle, and Brumfield, the law was clear at the time of the alleged transport incident that failing to adopt or enforce policies to protect prisoners, in deliberate indifference to a known and substantial risk of serious harm to them, amounts to a violation of the Eighth Amendment. See, e.g., A.M. ex rel. J.M.K. v. Luzerne Cnty. Juvenile Dep't Ctr., 372 F.3d 572, 586 (3d Cir. 2004). Thus, the Court concludes that no reasonable official would have believed that their failure to enforce an established policy requiring safety restraints in prison transport vehicles, coupled with their failure to adopt policies against reckless and erratic driving, was lawful where defendant-officials were also aware that their deficient policies created an unreasonable risk of serious harm to inmates.

In sum, the Court determines that plaintiff has alleged sufficient facts to establish a violation of his Eighth Amendment rights by defendants Hofer, Vancliff, Gruber, Wenerowiz, Doyle, and Brumfield, and that the rights at issue were clearly established at the time of defendants' actions. As a consequence, these defendants are not entitled to qualified immunity at this stage of the proceedings. The denial is without prejudice to Commonwealth defendants' right to reassert this defense after completion of discovery, if warranted by the facts and applicable law. See Dix v. City of Philadelphia, No. 15-532, 2015 U.S. Dist. LEXIS 101457, 2015 WL 4624248, at *6 (E.D. Pa. Aug. 3, 2015) (DuBois, J.) (rejecting qualified immunity defense at the motion to dismiss stage but permitting Commonwealth defendants to raise the defense after completion of discovery).

JANET MOSELY, ET AL., PLAINTIFFS, V. STATE OF MISSOURI; CORIZON, INC.; IAN WALLACE; TRAVIS WILHITE; AND DONNA SPAVEN, DEFENDANTS Case No. 1:15CV00052 AGF UNITED STATES DISTRICT COURT FOR THE EASTERN DISTRICT OF MISSOURI, SOUTHEASTERN DIVISION

BACKGROUND

The five-count complaint alleges that Wallace, with knowledge of the decedent's medical issues, including insulin-dependent diabetes, ordered the decedent placed in a restraint chair after the decedent inflicted harm on himself.

Spaven conducted an assessment of the decedent after he was placed in the restraint chair, checking that the restraints were in the proper place, but failed to review his medical records. Wilhite, the shift supervisor at the time, ordered that the decedent remain in the restraint chair for six hours, despite being told that the decedent was experiencing medical problems. A few minutes after being released from the restraint chair, the decedent died.

Count I of the complaint is brought under § 1983 against the State and Corizon for deliberate indifference to the substantial risk of serious harm to the decedent when kept in the restraint chair for six hours, in light of his known medical condition, in violation of his *Eighth Amendment* and *Fourteenth Amendment* rights. The complaint alleges that "this violation was committed as a result of the policies and customs of the State of Missouri and the [SECC]." (Doc. No. 1 at 2.) Count II is also brought under § 1983 on the same theory, but is against the individual Defendants. Counts III is a state law claim for wrongful death against all Defendants. Counts IV and V are against the State and Corizon for negligent hiring (Count IV) and negligent supervision (Count V) of the individual Defendants. Each count seeks actual and punitive damages.

The moving Defendants argue that the § 1983 claims against them are barred by the *Eleventh Amendment*, and that the state claims against them are barred by sovereign immunity pursuant to *Missouri Revised Statutes § 537.600*. Plaintiffs concede that the § 1983 claims against the State, and all claims against Wallace and Wilhite in their official capacity, are subject to dismissal. Plaintiffs, however, take issue with the State's reliance on sovereign immunity with respect to the Missouri tort claims against it. Plaintiffs argue that the State may have purchased liability insurance for tort claims   such as those asserted in Counts III, IV, and V, and if the State did so, its sovereign immunity would be waived to the maximum amount of such insurance, pursuant to *Missouri Revised Statutes § 537.610*, which provides that the state may purchase liability insurance for tort claims made against the state, and that "[s]overeign immunity for the state of Missouri . . . is waived only to the maximum amount of and only for the purposes covered by such policy of insurance . . . ." Plaintiffs seek leave to amend the complaint to plead facts that would establish such a waiver. The moving Defendants have not filed a reply.

DISCUSSION

A complaint must set out a "short and plain statement of [a plaintiff's] claim showing that the pleader is entitled to relief." *Fed. R. Civ. P. 8(a)(2)*. "To survive a motion to dismiss, a complaint must contain sufficient factual matter, accepted as true, to 'state a claim to relief that is plausible on its face.'" *Ashcroft v. Iqbal, 556 U.S. 662, 678, 129 S. Ct. 1937, 173 L. Ed. 2d 868 (2009)* (quoting *Bell Atl. Corp. v. Twombly, 550 U.S. 544, 570, 127 S. Ct. 1955, 167 L. Ed. 2d 929 (2007)*).

As Plaintiffs acknowledge, "neither a State nor its officials acting in their official capacity are 'persons' under § 1983." *See Smith v. Depriest, No. 414-CV-2106-NAB, 2015 U.S. Dist. LEXIS 9034, 2015 WL 362687, at *4 (E.D. Mo. Jan. 27, 2015)* (quoting *Will v. Mich. Dep't of State Police, 491 U.S. 58, 71, 109 S. Ct. 2304, 105 L. Ed. 2d 45 (1989)*). Plaintiffs also do not challenge the dismissal of their state law claims for damages against Wallace and Wilhite in their official capacity. Accordingly, the Court will grant the present motion with respect to Plaintiffs' § 1983 claims, and their state law claims against Wallace and Wilhite in their official capacity. As Plaintiffs urge, the state law claims against Wallace and Wilhite in their individual capacity remain viable.

With respect to Plaintiffs' state tort claims against the State, plaintiffs seeking to establish that the State of Missouri's sovereign immunity from tort liability was waived under § 537.610 by the State's purchase of liability insurance, "'must plead with specificity facts demonstrating'" that their claims fall within this exception to sovereign immunity because finding the State "'liable for torts is the exception to the general rule of sovereign immunity.'" *White v. Jackson, No. 4:14CV1490 HEA, 2015 U.S. Dist. LEXIS 31731, 2015 WL 1189963, at *6 (E.D. Mo. Mar. 16, 2015)* (quoting *Gregg v. City of Kansas City, 272 S.W.3d 353, 359-60 (Mo. Ct. App. 2008)*). The Court notes that the State would not waive its sovereign immunity by maintaining an insurance policy where that policy includes a provision stating that the policy is not meant to constitute a waiver of sovereign immunity. *See id.* (citing *Brooks v. City of Sugar Creek, 340 S.W.3d 201, 208 (Mo. App. Ct. 2011)*).

The Court will grant Plaintiffs' request for an opportunity to amend their complaint to plead facts sufficient to withstand the State's assertion of sovereign immunity with respect to the state law tort claims against it. Any such amendment must, of course, comply with *Federal Rule of Civil Procedure 11(b)(3)*'s mandate that factual contentions have evidentiary support or, if specifically so identified, will likely have evidentiary support after a reasonable opportunity for investigation or discovery.

ERIK SCOTT MALONEY, PLAINTIFF, VS. CHARLES L. RYAN, ET AL., DEFENDANTS. No. CV 13-0314-PHX-RCB (BSB) UNITED STATES DISTRICT COURT FOR THE DISTRICT OF ARIZONA 2014 U.S. Dist. LEXIS 39360 (March 25, 2014)

I. Background

In Count One of his Second Amended Complaint (SAC), Plaintiff alleges a violation of his *First Amendment* right to the free exercise of his religion. He contends that Defendants inhibited the exercise of his religion when they created, implemented, or enforced a regulation that inhibited his sincerely held religious beliefs by not accommodating his meal requirements during Ramadan. Plaintiff asserts that Defendants knowingly set the time for breakfast for Muslims during Ramadan for a time *after* the religiously mandated time for fasting had begun and that the policy forced him to either forgo breakfast during Ramadan or violate the tenets of his religion.

In Count Two, Plaintiff alleges that he has been subjected to an *Eighth Amendment* violation and denied due process and equal protection because Defendants knowingly provided him with a nutritionally inadequate diet during Ramadan. Plaintiff contends that in prior years during Ramadan, Muslims were provided a portion and a half of breakfast pre-dawn and a portion and a half of dinner, so that they received the same amount of food as general population inmates. Plaintiff asserts that in 2012, Defendants deliberately set the time for breakfast for Muslims during Ramadan at a time when they knew the Muslims would be prohibited from eating. In addition, for three days, Defendant Mason instructed kitchen staff to withhold a lunch sack at dinner. As a result, Plaintiff received only one of three meals on these days and suffered abdominal pain, headaches, severe exhaustion, weight loss, and mental and emotional distress.

In Count Three, Plaintiff alleges a violation of RLUIPA, arguing that he sought to engage in Sahur, an obligatory Islamic exercise during Ramadan in which Muslims prepare to fast each day before dawn by eating breakfast, drinking water, and praising and glorifying God. Plaintiff contends that the exercise of his religion was substantially burdened and he was prohibited from practicing Sahur because Defendants implemented a breakfast policy for Muslim inmates that provided breakfast after dawn.

In its screening of the original complaint, the Court determined that Plaintiff stated *First Amendment* and RLUIPA claims against Defendants Ryan and Linderman in Counts One and Three and stated deliberate indifference and equal protection claims against Defendants Ryan, Linderman, and Mason in Count Two. (Doc. 5.) As the Court noted in its Order of July 23, 2013, the first three counts in the SAC, all pertaining to Ramadan, are virtually identical to the first three counts in the original complaint. (Doc. 23 at 4.)

Defendants now move under *Federal Rule of Civil Procedure 12(c)* to dismiss Counts One and Three of Plaintiff's SAC on grounds of qualified immunity, arguing that there is no "clearly established constitutional right" for Muslim inmates to eat meals during Ramadan prior to 5:00 a.m., that no damages are available for RLUIPA claims, and that the Court has already determined that the injunctive relief is moot. (Doc. 35.)

II. Motion for Judgment on the Pleadings

A. Legal Standards

1. *Rule 12(c)*

Under *Federal Rule of Civil Procedure 12(c)*, a party may move for judgment on the pleadings "[a]fter the pleadings are closed--but early enough not to delay trial." The purpose of a *Rule 12(c)* motion is "to dispose of cases where the material facts are not in dispute and a judgment on the merits can be rendered by looking to the substance of the pleadings and any judicially noticed facts." *Herbert Abstract Co. v. Touchstone Props., Ltd., 914 F.2d 74, 76 (5th Cir. 1990)* (per curiam).

When brought by a defendant, a *Rule 12(c)* motion for judgment on the pleadings is a "means to challenge the sufficiency of the complaint after an answer has been filed." *New.Net, Inc. v. Lavasoft, 356 F. Supp.2d 1090, 1115 (C.D. Cal. 2004).* It is thus similar to a motion to dismiss. *Id.* Indeed, the standard for deciding a *Rule 12(c)* motion is the same as that applied to a *Rule 12(b)* motion to dismiss. *McGlinchy v. Shell Chem. Co., 845 F.2d 802, 810 (9th Cir. 1988).*

2. Qualified Immunity

A defendant in a *§ 1983* action is entitled to qualified immunity from damages for civil liability if his conduct does not violate clearly established federal statutory or constitutional rights of which a reasonable person would have known. *Harlow v. Fitzgerald, 457 U.S. 800, 818, 102 S. Ct. 2727, 73 L. Ed. 2d 396 (1982).* The qualified immunity analysis formerly required the court to make two distinct inquires, the "constitutional inquiry" and the "qualified immunity inquiry." *See Estate of Ford v. Ramirez-Palmer, 301 F.3d 1043, 1049 (9th Cir. 2002).* The "constitutional inquiry" asks whether, when taken in the light most favorable to the non-moving party, the facts alleged show that the official's conduct violated a constitutional right. *Saucier v. Katz, 533 U.S. 194, 201, 121 S. Ct. 2151, 150 L. Ed. 2d 272 (2001).* The "qualified immunity inquiry" asks if the right was clearly established at the relevant time. *Id. at 201-02.*

In *Pearson v. Callahan*, the Supreme Court held that the two-prong procedure established in *Saucier* is not an inflexible requirement; judges should be permitted to exercise their discretion in deciding which of the two prongs should be addressed first in light of the particular case. *555 U.S. 223, 242, 129 S. Ct. 808, 172 L. Ed. 2d 565 (2009).* That is, a court need not first determine if there was a constitutional violation before determining if a defendant is entitled to qualified immunity.

The qualified immunity inquiry "must be undertaken in light of the specific context of the case, not as a broad general proposition." *Saucier, 533 U.S. at 201.* The plaintiff has the burden to show that the right was clearly established at the time of the alleged violation. *Sorrels v. McKee, 290 F.3d 965, 969 (9th Cir. 2002); Romero v. Kitsap County, 931 F.2d 624, 627 (9th Cir. 1991).* For qualified immunity purposes, "the contours of the right must be sufficiently clear that at the time the allegedly unlawful act is [under]taken, a reasonable official would understand that what he is doing violates that right;" and "in the light of pre-existing law the unlawfulness must be apparent." *Mendoza v. Block, 27 F.3d 1357, 1361 (9th Cir. 1994)* (quotations omitted). Therefore, regardless of whether the constitutional violation occurred, the officer should prevail if the right asserted by the plaintiff was not "clearly established" or the officer could have reasonably believed that his particular conduct was lawful. *Romero, 931 F.2d at 627.*

B. Discussion

1. Qualified Immunity

Defendants contend that this action concerns a dispute over the breakfast feeding time of incarcerated inmates, who belong to the Islamic faith, during the Holy Month of Ramadan in the year 2012. There is no dispute that Ramadan is a Holy Month in the Islamic faith and that it requires fasting on a daily basis throughout its duration. But Defendants dispute that prison officials can be sued for monetary damages under the *First Amendment* and RLUIPA simply because they served breakfast at 5:00 a.m. rather than the astronomically-calculated time mandated by Plaintiff's interpretation of the Qur'an. (Doc. 35 at 1.)

Defendants ask the Court to take judicial notice of three facts: (1) in 2012 Ramadan began on July 20; (2) sunrise in Florence, Arizona--where Plaintiff alleges he was housed--was at 5:31 a.m. on July 20, 2012; and (3) the language of the Qur'an instructs observant Muslims during Ramadan to "eat and drink until the white thread of dawn becomes distinct to you from the black thread. Then complete the fast until the sunset" or variations of that language. (Doc. 35 at 3-6, citing *Fed. R. Evid. 201; Outdoor Media Grp., Inc. v. City of Beaumont, 506 F.3d 895, 899-900 (9th Cir. 2007).*) As to the last point, Defendants argue that the Qur'an speaks to the distinction between the dark of night and the light of day and is not more specific than that. (Doc. 35 at 6.)

Defendants maintain that given these facts, there is no caselaw that would have put them on notice that serving breakfast to Muslim inmates prior to sunrise between 5:00 a.m. and 5:30 a.m. would violate an inmate's constitutional rights. (*Id.* at 8-9.)

Plaintiff responds that Defendant misstate the nature of his claim; he asserts that the SAC alleges that "he was denied his liberties . . . by putting in place and/or enforcing a regulation which prohibits Plaintiff's sincerely held beliefs by not accommodating meal requirements during Muslim Holy month of Ramadan." (Doc. 39 at 2; ref. Doc. 17.) He claims that his SAC alleges nothing about the 5:00 am time in the first five lines. (Doc. 39 at 2.)

The Court rejects Plaintiff's argument; plainly the gist of the claims in Counts One and Three relate to the breakfast feeding time, which according to Plaintiff's SAC was set at 5:00 am rather than a pre-dawn time. (Doc. 17 at 3.) As to Counts One and Three, the feeding time was the alleged failure to accommodate Plaintiff's sincerely held belief.

Plaintiff also claims that his rights were clearly established at the time in question. (Doc. 39 at 5, citing *Washington v. Garcia, 977 F.Supp. 1067 (S.D. Cal. Sept. 10, 1997); Makin v. Colo. Dep't Corrs., 183 F.3d 1205, 1209-10 (10th Cir. 1999); Lovelace v. Lee, 472 F.3d 174, 196-99 (4th Cir. 2006).*) Plaintiff also asserts that he wrote to the "top officials" at his unit about the proper feeding times and they said they spoke with Linderman, so Linderman was aware that inmates were complaining that the 5:00 am feeding time was too late.[2] (Doc. 39 at 7.)

2 This fact is outside the pleadings.

First, the issue for these Counts is whether it was clearly established that during Ramadan Muslims must eat breakfast before dawn rather than before sunrise; a general duty to satisfy an inmate's religious dietary requirements defines the right in question too broadly. *See Dunn v. Castro, 621 F.3d 1196, 1200 (9th Cir. 2010).* Second, the Court is not persuaded that the cited authority demonstrates that there was such a clearly established right. In *Garcia*, the issue was denial of a special diet during Ramadan and denial of Suhoor meals to an inmate in administrative segregation. *977 F. Supp. at 1072.* The court found that eating a special meal is not an essential practice during Ramadan but that fasting and prayer during daylight hours is such a practice. *Id. at 1072.* The court held that prison officials had failed to show that offering the inmate the alternative of saving food served during the day for consumption during non-daylight hours passed the test under *Turner v. Safley. Garcia, 977 F. Supp. at 1073-74*, citing *Turner, 482 U.S. 78, 107 S. Ct. 2254, 96 L. Ed. 2d 64.* The court did not address whether during Ramadan Muslims must eat breakfast before dawn rather than before sunrise.

The issue in *Makin* was similar; the plaintiff was in segregation and unable to eat his meals when delivered. *183 F.3d at 1208-09.* Although the policy for other Muslim inmates noted that Muslims must fast from two hours prior to sunrise until after sunset during Ramadan, the issue decided by the court was unrelated to the required time for breakfast. *Id.* In *Lovelace*, the court addressed whether an inmate's rights were violated when he was unable to participate in Ramadan after he was falsely accused of violating a prison rule. *472 F.3d at 195-199.* The court did not determine the required time for breakfast during Ramadan.

This Court recently determined in a similar case that Linderman and Ryan were entitled to qualified immunity on this issue. *Bomar v. Linderman, et al.*, CV-13-0253-PHX-ROS (LOA) (Doc. 30). And even assuming that Plaintiff wrote to prison officials about the issue of feeding time, that is not legal authority. The Court finds that there was no legal authority that would have put Defendants on notice that providing the morning meal before sunrise, rather than before dawn, would violate inmates' constitutional rights.

www.ingramcontent.com/pod-product-compliance
Lightning Source LLC
Chambersburg PA
CBHW051750200326
41597CB00025B/4497

* 9 7 8 1 9 4 7 1 7 0 1 0 0 *